S0-DTB-180

FRENCH MUSIC SINCE BERLIOZ

Massenet at the piano: illustration from *Le Théâtre*, 1899

French Music Since Berlioz

Edited by
RICHARD LANGHAM SMITH and CAROLINE POTTER

ASHGATE

Published by
Ashgate Publishing Limited
Gower House
Croft Road
Aldershot
Hants GU11 3HR
England

Ashgate Publishing Company
Suite 420
101 Cherry Street
Burlington, VT 05401-4405
USA

Ashgate website: http://www.ashgate.com

British Library Cataloguing in Publication Data
French music since Berlioz
1. Music – France – 20th century – History and criticism
2. Music – France – 19th century – History and criticism
I. Smith, Richard Langham II. Potter, Caroline
780.9'44'0904

Library of Congress Cataloging-in-Publication Data
French music since Berlioz / edited by Richard Langham Smith and Caroline Potter.
p. cm.
Includes bibliographical references.
ISBN 0–7546–0282–6 (alk. paper)
1. Music–France–19th century–History and criticism. 2. Music–France–20th century–History and criticism. I. Smith, Richard Langham. II. Potter, Caroline.

ML270.4.F74 2003
780'.944—dc22

2003065058

ISBN 0-7546-0282-6

Typeset by Express Typesetters Ltd, Farnham, Surrey.
Printed in Great Britain by MPG Books Ltd, Bodmin, Cornwall.

Contents

List of Plates

List of Figures and Tables

Figures

Tables

List of Music Examples

List of Contributors

Thomas Cooper is an Associate Lecturer with the Open University. He trained as a pianist at the Royal College of Music and took his Ph.D. at Liverpool University. He has contributed to the revised *New Grove* and is currently working on a book investigating nineteenth-century French musical exoticism and concepts of empire.

Déirdre Donnellon studied for an M.Phil. on 'Debussy in the Political and Social Context of his Time' at the University of Liverpool before going on to complete a Ph.D. on the late nineteenth- and early twentieth-century Parisian critical press and the reception of the music of Debussy and Satie. She has contributed to *The Cambridge Companion to Debussy* (CUP, 2003).

Roy Howat's interest in French music led to the groundbreaking book *Debussy in Proportion* (CUP, 1983) and to his involvement in the *Œuvres completes de Claude Debussy*; he has also edited Urtexts of music by Chabrier and Fauré. He tours internationally as concert pianist, has held university positions in various countries, and has recorded numerous CDs. From 2000 until 2003, he was AHRB Research Fellow at the Royal College of Music in London.

Timothy Jones holds an academic post at the Royal Northern College of Music in Manchester. He has written on analytical aspects of instrumental music from the late eighteenth and nineteenth centuries and is the author of *Beethoven, the 'Moonlight' and Other Sonatas* (CUP, 1999). He is currently working on a history of the symphonic poem in nineteenth-century France.

Deborah Mawer is Senior Lecturer in Music at Lancaster University, where she specializes in French music (*c*.1889–1939). She is author of *Darius Milhaud* (Ashgate, 1997) and editor of *The Cambridge Companion to Ravel* (CUP, 2000); from 1996 to 2000 she served as Vice-President of the Society for Music Analysis. She also writes on issues in music education.

Peter O'Hagan is Reader in Music at Roehampton University, where he lectures on contemporary music. He is also a pianist, and has commissioned several works from British composers as well as giving numerous recitals of the contemporary repertoire in the UK, Europe and the USA. His principal area of academic research is the music of Pierre Boulez, and as well as publishing articles on Boulez's music, he has recently performed unpublished material from the Third Sonata with the composer's permission.

Robert Orledge is Emeritus Professor at the University of Liverpool where he worked from 1971–2004. He has published books on Fauré, Debussy, Koechlin and Satie, and has recently edited, completed and orchestrated Debussy's Poe opera *The Fall of the House of Usher*.

Caroline Potter is Senior Lecturer in Music at Kingston University. She is the author of *Henri Dutilleux* (Ashgate, 1997) and several articles and book chapters on twentieth-century French music, and is currently writing a book on Nadia and Lili Boulanger, also for Ashgate.

James Ross conducts orchestras and operas worldwide, including a large repertoire of nineteenth- and twentieth-century French music. His doctorate from Oxford University, 'Crisis and Transformation: French Opera, Politics and the Press, 1897–1903' won the Sir Donald Tovey Prize in 1998. He is a frequent guest speaker and has contributed to *English Historical Review*, *Opera* and *Music and Letters*, where his article on d'Indy's opera *Fervaal* appeared in May 2003.

Nigel Simeone is Professor of Music at the University of Sheffield. His research is primarily on French music and on Janáček. Books include *Paris – A Musical Gazetteer* (Yale UP, 2000); *Olivier Messiaen: A Bibliographical Catalogue* (Schneider, 1997) and *Janáček's Works* (with John Tyrrell and Alena Nemcova, OUP, 1997). He has recently published, with Peter Hill, a new book on *Messiaen* (Yale University Press, 2005) for which the authors have been given unprecedented access to Messiaen's diaries and private papers.

Richard Langham Smith has written extensively on French music of the nineteenth and twentieth centuries. He has translated and edited the complete criticism of Debussy and is co-author of the Cambridge Opera Guide to the same composer's *Pelléas et Mélisande*. His completion of Debussy's 'other' opera *Rodrigue et Chimène* was published in the *Œuvres Complètes de Claude Debussy* in 2003 and used as a basis for the first performance in Lyon in 1993. He has held positions at Lancaster, City and Exeter Universities, and is currently Arnold Kettle distinguished scholar in Music at The Open University. He is currently preparing a new edition of *Carmen* for Peters Edition.

Preface and Acknowledgements

Any book must have its *raison d'être*, not least a book with blanket coverage of quite a large area of music in some way definably 'French'. There are a few gaps at the side where, it was decided, the sheets would have to be ruffled and the blanket tucked in, somehow to make the centre warmer. Most important is that it has not addressed popular music, jazz, film music or indeed ballet music as a genre in itself. For Piaf, Chevalier, Richard Anthony or Serge Gainsbourg in context the reader must look elsewhere (even if a couple of these turn up in a chapter): this is essentially a book centred on classical music and its dissemination.

There was a feeling, in the initial discussion between the publishers and ourselves, that a sequel to Martin Cooper's *French Music from the Death of Berlioz to the Death of Fauré* was somehow due. It was a nice idea but it soon proved problematic. First of all, let it be said, he wrote so well, with that confident and perceptive overview that those real writers of the period had. We still get his writings down from the shelves, as we do those of Calvocoressi, Lockspeiser, Myers, Demuth and Aprahamian and all the rest of the English critics of their generation with their overviews. But by present standards, their lack of footnotes and analysis, and failure to engage with some of the wider issues now *de rigueur*, has motivated the present volume in its desire to reassess the repertoire.

Positivist musicology has played its part since their overarching and brilliantly-written approaches. Facts, you might say, replaced eloquently articulated unsubstantiated ideas: precision replaced vague impressionism. On one side, writing about music has become more precise analytically: a couple of chords shared between pieces no longer constitutes an 'influence'; deeper structures and processes have to be uncovered. On the other, politics, gender issues and a more critical view of borrowings from 'other' cultures – among other issues – have provoked interesting new approaches to the discussion of music, not least French music.

Moreover, there is a received idea that French music had a peculiarly close relationship with the other arts, that composers were often inspired by visual art and were more likely to give their works picturesque titles than their contemporaries from other countries. This book suggests that this is by no means always true, and if anything the present authors tend to focus on the social and political context of music rather than on the nebulous notion that French music somehow has a privileged relationship with the visual and the literary.

In reconsidering French music our idea was to draw upon the insights of scholars we knew and trusted, and who we believed to have perspectives on the repertoire which together would break new ground. So unlike Cooper, Hodéir, Landormy or Laloy (to name a few) the book follows in the train of Rohozinski, the compiler of the first major twentieth-century multi-author book: a weighty tome which is surely the first proof that French music is best covered by an *éventail de producteurs*.[1] His '50 years of French music' was a masterpiece of its time. Adorned with otherwise irretrievable pictures, and with the insight of contemporaries, a fresh approach to each chapter and commentary on what seem to be minor items, it prepares the ground for future commentators who might want to refocus the lens and fisheye different pieces or composers.

So the book, in the editors' view, emerges as a mosaic. Its focus, somehow, is this elusive concept of 'French Music' so often enhanced by composers born outside France; French music would be very different without the contributions of Offenbach and Meyerbeer, or Xenakis and Ohana. It is hoped that the various specialized views will somehow throw light on their own centre. Furthermore, where the books of the mid-twentieth century somehow *presented* a view of French music, the present authors hope to *suggest* one and open up avenues for fresh approaches. There was a sense in many of the English writers of the middle to later twentieth century that they were 'telling us how it was', their audience was the educated layman, who is perhaps not as frequently encountered as he was.

Books like that no longer exist. Now we have academics writing for academics, and also for their students: a crucial difference. After all, the student population is enormously larger today than it was in the 1950s: has writing for students perhaps replaced writing for the enlightened amateur? It is also hoped that the present book will be taken down by some of those involved in the trade – performers, producers, presenters, compilers and critics – among others. Hopefully some will still read books such as this for interest, and for the enthusiasm which is a quality shared by every single one of its contributors. This, without question, is the overarching quality which has made this compilation worthwhile.

Our book is written by British scholars and is aimed at an English-speaking audience. It assumes no knowledge of French historical or cultural events, so these are explained where relevant. All quotations appear in the text in English translation (usually by the author of the chapter concerned), though the original French is provided in footnotes. While familiarity with some basic musical concepts (tonality, serialism, the octatonic mode) is assumed, more obscure concepts are explained.

Déirdre Donnellon's chapter outlines some of the most important issues and debates in French music of the nineteenth and twentieth centuries, providing context for the book as a whole and introducing key figures and important institutions. Tim Jones investigates nineteenth-century French chamber music and symphonies, assessing the French contribution to these most Germanic of genres. Thomas Cooper and Richard Langham Smith draw out the themes of opera and spectacle in the nineteenth and twentieth centuries respectively. Cooper, in particular, explores the important related issues of exoticism and 'otherness' which are taken up by several other authors. James Ross's chapter penetrates the nineteenth-century salon: a place where high society mingled with the most gifted artists of the time and where composers often found sympathetic patrons (or more accurately, given that most of these important commissioners were women, matrons). Nigel Simeone introduces the unique importance of the most musically significant churches in Paris and the contribution their organists made to music of their time.

Roy Howat views the transition from the nineteenth into the twentieth century as a period of modernization and concentrates on four significant figures: Fauré and Chabrier, and then the towering figures of Debussy and Ravel. Besides focusing on the harmonic languages of these composers, Howat opens up a debate on performance practice in French music. Robert Orledge, in his chapter on Satie and Les Six, draws attention to the vital role of the media in the promotion of French music and reassesses this group of composers united by friendship but essentially disparate, even though Jean Cocteau attempted to promote them as a group inspired by Satie. Deborah Mawer's chapter on music in the 1930s introduces the composers associated with La Jeune France and focuses on the importance of the mechanistic aesthetic. Caroline Potter writes on Parisian musical life during the Second World War and on key works composed in this period, when the impact of the socio-political scene on French music was particularly pronounced. Drawing on manuscript material and other original sources, Peter O'Hagan assesses the immense contribution of Pierre Boulez to the contemporary musical scene, and Caroline Potter outlines some of the most representative trends in French music since 1945.

At the end of each chapter is a list of suggested additional reading, which is biased towards English-language works and current translations of key French texts, though some important French sources have been included. No attempt has been made to provide a comprehensive bibliography of the subject, not least because this would be a substantial book in its own right.

The editors are indebted to their contributors not only for their contributions but also for other qualities brought to the book – above all their enthusiasm and not least their patience. Many have also had considerable input through a chance comment, a desperate phone call or an e-mail, causing improvements and adjustments other than in their own chapters. Ideas for illustrations have also been largely provided by the contributors. We are also very grateful to Rachel Lynch, Heidi May and Barbara Pretty of Ashgate Publishing, for nurturing this project during its long gestation period.

Richard Langham Smith and Caroline Potter
December 2005

Reference

1 L. Rohozinski (ed.): *Cinquante ans de musique française (1874–1925)* (Paris, 1926).

List of Abbreviations

CDMC	Centre de documentation de la musique contemporaine
GRM	Groupe de Recherches Musicales
IRCAM	Institut de Recherche et Coordination Acoustique/Musique
MQ	*Music Quarterly*
RGM	*Revue et gazette musicale de Paris*
RM	*La Revue musicale*
RTLMF	Réunion de Théâtres Lyriques Municipaux de France
SACEM	Société d'Auteurs, Compositeurs et Éditeurs de Musique
SMI	Société musicale indépendante
SN	Société nationale de musique

Chapter 1

French Music Since Berlioz: Issues and Debates

Déirdre Donnellon

The death of Hector Berlioz in 1869 marked a significant turning point in the history of French music. This was not a reflection on the unfortunate Berlioz himself, but a symptom of a reaction against the domination of French musical life by foreign composers. At the time, the prevailing public taste was for the German Romanticism of Beethoven, Mendelssohn and Schumann, and the more flamboyant styles of Liszt and Chopin. Ironically, despite his romantic credentials, Berlioz enjoyed no such popularity in France during his own lifetime. Meanwhile, much to his chagrin, the Parisian stage was virtually monopolised by repeat performances of operas that had first seen the light of day in the 1830s and 1840s, and the public's love of spectacle ensured the ongoing popularity of flamboyant productions of historical subjects in the grand opera style. The jaded repertoire of the Opéra consisted largely of Rossini's *Guillaume Tell* (1829), Donizetti's *Lucia di Lammermoor* (1835) and *La favorite* (1840) and Meyerbeer's *L'Africaine* (1865) and *L'étoile du nord* (1854). The only French composers to have achieved comparable success were Daniel-François Auber (*La muette de Portici*, 1828) and Jacques Halévy (*La Juive*, 1835), while composers such as Adolphe Adam, Ferdinand Hérold and Adrien Boieldieu had to content themselves with more modest successes at the Opéra-Comique. Young native talent was given little encouragement, apart from those composers lucky enough to be produced by the Théâtre-Lyrique. This venue saw the premiere of Gounod's *Faust* in 1859 (and numerous other operas by him), as well as Ernest Reyer's *La statue* (1861), Bizet's *Les pêcheurs de perles* (1863) and the first part of Berlioz's *Les Troyens à Carthage* (1863). However, before the 1870s, with the possible exception of Gounod, French operatic composers were largely unsuccessful in their bid for public favour.

Meanwhile, in the concert halls, foreign composers also reigned supreme. In fact, the music of Beethoven, Mozart, Mendelssohn, Haydn and Weber accounted for half of all music performed in public concerts in Paris in the years immediately prior to 1870.[1] This apparent inability of French composers to make their mark in the concert halls was partly due to the commonly held belief in France that dramatic music was the true measure of a composer's talent. This belief was encouraged by the importance placed on dramatic music in the curriculum of the Paris Conservatoire, and the relative neglect of such skills as counterpoint and fugal writing.[2] Students were generally limited to the study of classical

1 See Jeffrey Cooper: *The Rise of Instrumental Music and Concert Series in Paris, 1828–1871* (Ann Arbor, 1983), 108–10.

2 The most coveted prize at the Conservatoire, for which candidates were required to submit a

models, with an overemphasis on dramatic works at the expense of the more intimate charms of chamber music. The neglect of instrumental writing was further exacerbated by the relative lack of public concert societies before 1870. Established concert societies (such as the Société des concerts du Conservatoire which was founded in 1828) catered mostly for a very select audience with conservative tastes. Although Jules Pasdeloup introduced music to a wider audience with his Concerts populaires (which began life as the Société des jeunes artistes du Conservatoire in 1851), this laudable aim was dampened somewhat by his preference for the German classical repertoire.[3]

The Franco-Prussian war ended the dissolute reign of Napoleon III and heralded the birth of the Third Republic. Following their humiliating defeat, anti-German feelings ran very high among the French. Shock at the ease with which France had been defeated inspired a revival of national pride. There was a growing realization among French musicians that national talent had been neglected in favour of what were now felt to be the over-indulgent excesses of the German romantic style. This had an inevitable impact on the popularity of German music.[4] In particular, Wagner was virtually boycotted during the 1870s, although this was partly due to the composer's misguided public taunting of the defeated French.[5] This same climate also brought with it a decline in the popularity of foreign opera. Before the war, the success of Gounod's *Faust* (1859), *Mireille* (1864) and *Roméo et Juliette* (1867) had already marked a change from the spectacle of grand opera in favour of greater emphasis on sentimental characterization and emotional intensity.

This more intimate approach is an important feature of Bizet's *Carmen* (1875) but Bizet's use of what was regarded as scandalous subject matter meant relative failure for the opera. Massenet had rather more success with audiences, although he, too, dealt with affairs of the heart. However, his gift for musical portraiture ensured him a string of successes, including *Le roi de Lahore* (1877), *Manon* (1884), *Le Cid* (1885), *Thaïs* (1894), *Cendrillon* (1899) and *Grisélidis* (1901). Mindful of the public mood in the aftermath of war, when the Opéra-Comique reopened its doors in 1872, the new season began with works by three French composers: Saint-Saëns's *La princesse jaune* (1872), Bizet's *Djamileh* (1872) and Émile Paladilhe's *Le passant* (1872). Before the turn of the century, Chabrier and Lalo would also benefit from this revival of native opera, as would Vincent

---

cantata, was the annual Prix de Rome. Debussy won the prize with *L'enfant prodigue* in 1884, but the competition was also notable for those composers who failed to win it (including Saint-Saëns and Ravel).

3 The staples of the programmes of the Concerts populaires were Beethoven, Mendelssohn and Schumann. However, Pasdeloup certainly brought music to a wider audience. The venue for the Concerts populaires, the Cirque d'hiver, had a capacity of 4000 (compared to the more modest setting for the Concerts du Conservatoire) and, whereas the admission prices for Berlioz's Société Philharmonique in 1850 had ranged from 2 to 6 francs (i.e. the equivalent of a day's wages for a worker), entrance fees at the Concert populaires in 1861 ranged from 75 centimes to 5 francs. (See Danièle Pistone: 'Réflexions sur l'évolution du public musical parisien', *Romantisme*, 38 (1982), 19–23.)

4 The Société des concerts du Conservatoire went so far as to strike Wagner from its repertoire, having previously performed extracts of both *Tannhäuser* and *Lohengrin*.

5 See Richard Wagner: 'An das deutsche Heer von Paris' and 'Eine Kapitulation', *Gesammelte Schriften und Dichtungen* (Leipzig, 1897), 1–41. The composer's remarks were undoubtedly a symptom of his bitterness towards the French following the resounding failure of *Tannhäuser* in Paris in 1861.

d'Indy, Alfred Bruneau, Reynaldo Hahn and André Messager. In particular, Bruneau produced his own brand of naturalist opera in collaboration with Émile Zola on no fewer than nine occasions, the most successful being *Le rêve* (1891), *L'attaque du moulin* (1893) and *L'ouragan* (1901). A further experiment in this direction was made by Gustave Charpentier, and his *Louise* (1900) was a resounding success. However, this success was not so much due to the popularity of realist opera as to Charpentier's rather sentimental approach, and it was not to be repeated. Bruneau's efforts in the genre also failed to find enduring popular support, and this is also reflected in the failure of Italian verismo opera composers to make their mark in Paris. Late nineteenth-century French opera could not have been said to form a cohesive style but its very diversity was a measure of the more healthy state of French opera in the thirty years since the Franco-Prussian war, while Massenet's appointment as professor of composition at the Conservatoire between 1878 and 1896 ensured the continuation of this trend among the younger generation of composers.

It was with the aim of providing a platform for homegrown talent that the Société nationale was founded by Saint-Saëns and the singer Romain Bussine in 1871. Bearing the motto *Ars gallica*, the new society was originally conceived with the aim of devoting all of its resources to the performance of new French music.[6] The new society was hugely successful and became a showcase for young talent. Between 1871 and 1918 it gave a total of 415 concerts and its members included many of the most prominent French musicians of the day, including Massenet, César Franck, Gabriel Fauré, Vincent d'Indy and Claude Debussy. However, financial limitations meant the new society was unable to present many orchestral concerts. As a result, chamber music experienced a revival as composers, eager to have their music performed, wrote music requiring smaller forces. Chamber music societies also flourished during this era, including the Nouvelle société de musique de chambre and Paul Taffanel's Société de musique de chambre pour instruments à vent, in addition to which the numerous quartets and trios resident in Paris also held their own concert series.[7] Meanwhile, the more populist concert societies also began to pay greater attention to French orchestral music. The first concert of Pasdeloup's 1871 season included Massenet's *Les scènes hongroises* (1865) and he also included performances of Lalo, Bizet, Saint-Saëns and Gounod in his concerts. The conservative audiences of the Société des concerts du Conservatoire were also introduced to works by Gounod, Franck, Saint-Saëns, Dubois, Massenet and Lenepveu in the 1871–72 season and, when Édouard Colonne gave his first Concert national in 1873, the inaugural programme included Massenet's *Marie Magdeleine* (1872) and Franck's *Rédemption* (1871). The Concerts Lamoureux (formed in 1881) became the main rival of the Concerts Colonne, but in the early twentieth century both faced increasing competition from the Concerts Sechiari, Concerts Rouge and Société Philharmonique de Paris. Although many of these societies had unashamedly populist programmes, they all contributed to the number

---

6 In 1886 Vincent d'Indy introduced a motion to allow foreign music to be performed at the Société nationale. This led to Saint-Saëns's resignation from the presidency in favour of César Franck.

7 A more extensive list can be found in Serge Gut and Danièle Pistone: *La musique de chambre en France de 1870 à 1918* (Paris, 1978).

of performances of native music in the French capital, as did the more avant-garde Société musicale indépendante, founded in 1910 as a rival to the Société nationale.[8]

Pride in French talent was also fostered by the Expositions Universelles that took place in Paris in 1867, 1878, 1889 and 1900. A government report on the 1878 event recorded a total of 108 official concerts, of which sixty-five featured French music. For the 1889 Exposition, five concerts were presented at the Trocadéro, showcasing exclusively French music, and featuring leading contemporary French composers. In addition, leading French organists gave a total of fifteen recitals while various chamber music societies also presented French music.[9] Concerts of contemporary French music were used as a means of showing to the world (and particularly the Germans) that French musicians were as innovative and as advanced as their foreign counterparts. In this climate, French musical talent thrived to a degree that the previous generation, much as they might have wished for it, could not have foreseen.

However, despite this resurgent pride in French music, performances of German music were still the mainstay of Parisian concert life.[10] Meanwhile, Wagner's fall from grace proved short-lived. This was partly due to the composer's death in 1883 (thereby removing the issue of his overbearing personality), but also due to the curiosity aroused by reports of the successful Bayreuth premieres of *Der Ring des Nibelungen* (1876) and *Parsifal* (1882). Younger composers, for whom the 1870–71 war was only a childhood memory, were particularly excited by Wagner. Although Pasdeloup's performance of a brief extract from *Rienzi* (1842) was the only orchestral performance of Wagner's music in 1871, by 1885 he was honoured with twenty-nine performances of orchestral extracts from the operas, and by 1895 this figure had reached thirty-five. Concert performances proved the main form of transmission of Wagner's music during these years, although productions of *Tannhäuser* (1845), *Lohengrin* (1850), *Die Walküre* (1856), *Die Meistersinger von Nürnberg* (1868), *Der fliegende Holländer* (1843) and *Tristan und Isolde* (1859) also took place in Paris before the turn of the century.[11]

In fact, despite its apparent incompatibility with the concurrent reawakening of interest in French music, *Wagnérisme* was a dominant issue in the musical life of the French capital before the Great War. Many of the most fervent French Wagnerites (such as the younger Saint-Saëns and Vincent d'Indy) were also those most actively involved in the promotion of French music. This seeming contradiction gives an indication of the extent to which Wagner's music fascinated French composers. He was both their greatest source of inspiration and the greatest single impediment to their finding a distinctively French musical language. Composers such as Chabrier, Saint-Saëns, Chausson, d'Indy, Duparc, de Bréville, Dukas, Massenet, Debussy, Charpentier and Dubois all made the pilgrimage

8 The original committee included Fauré, Ravel, Florent Schmitt, Jean Huré and Charles Koechlin and their aim was to perform the music of composers otherwise neglected by the SN.

9 More information about the music at the Expositions Universelles can be found in Elaine Brody: 'Music at the Great Expositions', *Paris – The Musical Kaleidoscope 1870–1925* (London, 1988).

10 For an account of the disillusionment of critics obliged to review repeated performances of Beethoven, see Christian Goubault: *La critique musicale dans la presse française de 1870 à 1914* (Paris, 1984), 318.

11 For full details of performances of Wagner's music in Paris during these years see Danièle Pistone: 'Wagner et Paris', *Revue internationale de musique française*, 1 (Feb. 1980), 7–84.

to Bayreuth and they all, to some degree, came under his influence.[12] His potent harmonies, rich orchestration and the semi-mystical atmosphere induced by the mythological subject matter of his operas proved too seductive to resist. However, there were some who were more covert in their relations with Wagner. In his articles Debussy deplored Wagner's detrimental influence on French music, but he himself struggled to resist that influence. As Robin Holloway has noted, '[Debussy's] hostility to Wagner is ... entirely verbal; musically he remained a follower of Wagner, though in devious manner, for the rest of his life.'[13] And, despite their varying degrees of submission, when questioned by the *Mercure de France* in 1903, those composers interviewed concluded that Wagner's influence had waned, although they disagreed about the extent and nature of that influence.[14]

This last issue was complicated by extra-musical considerations. Wagner's music was undoubtedly attractive to musicians, but French Wagnérisme was not only their affair. Many French Wagnérites, such as Catulle Mendès, Édouard Dujardin and Villiers de l'Isle-Adam, came from the French literary world, and the fanaticism with which they defended their idol was frequently inspired by the intensity and vividness of his music, which, to some extent, achieved the emotive and expressive qualities which they were often struggling to find in their own art. Wagner had found an early advocate in Baudelaire, who also sought to evoke a similar intensity of feeling in his poetry. The decadent movement, associated with Baudelaire, was indicative of a desire among poets and writers to create a language that could express and suggest feelings, as opposed to the external, objective realities depicted by their predecessors. This retreat to a rarefied inner world of sensation found a parallel in the all-encompassing world of Wagner's operas.

However, there were also negative aspects to French decadence, such as an unhealthy obsession with the self, an introspection, and an indifference to the modern world that did not bode well for the progress of French music. Wagner drew more muted admiration from symbolists such as Paul Verlaine and Stéphane Mallarmé. For them, the sound, or the music, of their poetry was seen as paramount and, as in decadent art, there was a desire to express in poetry certain ideas and sensations for which language is inadequate. They aimed to touch all the senses by gradual suggestion, and inherent in this aesthetic was a belief in the musicality of poetry. This idealization of the potential power of music inevitably drew symbolists towards the Wagner experience, but the reality is that very few of them had any understanding of music. Their reliance on Wagner to provide a musical illustration of their ideal was at odds with the bold leitmotifs he employed. The Wagnerian leitmotif was far more akin to the bold statement of, as opposed to an evocative allusion to, a symbolic representation. This gulf between symbolist ideal and Wagnerian reality is best revealed by the views of the contributors to the short-lived *Revue wagnérienne* (1885–88). The contributions of writers as diverse as Huysmans, Verlaine, Mallarmé and Mendès failed to form any cohesive aesthetic link between Wagner's music and symbolist

12 One need look no further than Chabrier's *Gwendoline* (1886), Reyer's *Sigurd* (1883) and d'Indy's *Fervaal* (1897) for evidence of Wagnerian influence, while no less a critic than Claude Debussy detected Wagnerisms in a whole range of music including Albert Savard's *Le roi Lear*, Bruneau's *L'ouragan*, Massenet's *Grisélidis* and Alfred Bachelet's *L'amour des ondines*. (Claude Debussy: *Monsieur Croche et autres écrits,* ed. François Lesure (Paris, 1987)).

13 Robin Holloway: *Debussy and Wagner* (London, 1979), 17.

14 See Jacques Morland: 'Enquête sur l'influence allemand – Musique', *Mercure de France*, 157 (Jan. 1903), 89–110.

PRIX : 10 C.

L'ANTI-WAGNER

PRIX : 10

PROTESTATION CONTRE LA REPRÉSENTATION ALLEMANDE DE L'EDEN-THÉATRE

A NOS LECTEURS

Mardi prochain 26 avril 1887, *M. Lamoureux*, momentanément directeur de l'*Eden-Théâtre*, offrira à la population parisienne, la première du *Lohengrin* de RICHARD WAGNER.

Ce monsieur fort peu français, qui sans doute a oublié nos désastres de 1870, se défend de ce manque de patriotisme en disant que l'ART N'A PAS DE PATRIE.

Sans être chauvin, on peut faire remarquer à M. Lamoureux, qu'il a fort mal choisi son moment pour célébrer la gloire et la musique du musicien anti-français.

RICHARD WAGNER, personne ne l'a oublié, est l'individu qui au moment de nos désastres, nous a insulté dans une brochure restée célèbre.

Cet individu à mœurs infâmes a également publié un poème dont nous donnons plus bas quelques vers.

Nous laissons la plume à d'autres plus autorisés que nous, et nous nous faisons un devoir de reproduire l'article de *M. Mermeix*, rédacteur à la *France*, un de ceux qui n'ont pas oublié!

M. Grandmougin, le poète Franc-Comtois, avait publié l'année dernière, l'article ci-dessous.

M. Carvalho avait compris et dès lors s'était abstenu; il a fallu que *M. Lamoureux* évoqua encore, le spectre insulteur du mangeur de choucroute allemand.

L'Editeur.

M. LAMOUREUX offrant à Wagner l'or français provenant des représentations faites à l'Eden-Théâ

Plate 1.1 ***L'anti-Wagner*: illustrated pamphlet of April 1887 depicting Wagner as a sorcerer, standing on a plinth on which an alleged quotation of his is written: 'The French people are a race of monkeys'. The conductor Lamoureux is depicted as a satyr offering Wagner French money gained from the performances of his operas at the Eden-Théâtre. The depiction of Wagner's music as a cacophony was several times portrayed by his detractors in terms of the beating of kitchen utensils.**

Plate 1.1 (translation)

The editorial reads: Next Tuesday, 26 April 1887, M. Lamoureux, currently director of the Eden theatre, will offer the Parisian public the premiere of Wagner's *Lohengrin*. This gentleman, who could hardly be less French, and who without doubt has forgotten the disasters of 1870, defends his lack of patriotism by claiming that art has no homelands.

Without being chauvinist, M. Lamoureux would do well to remind himself that he has chosen a most inopportune moment to celebrate the glory and music of this anti-French musician. Richard Wagner, nobody has forgotten, is the very individual who in a brochure which has remained famous insulted us at the peak of our troubled times. This same individual with the lowest of morals has also published a poem, some verses from which are quoted below. We pass the pen to others better equipped than ourselves and feel it our duty to reprint the article of M. Mermeix, editor of *La France*, one of those who hasn't forgotten.

M. Grandmougin, the poet of the Franche-comté published the article beneath. M. Carvalho understood and up to now has abstained. But M. Lamoureux has had to conjure up once again the insulting spectre of he who dines on German sauerkraut.

* * *

literature. Meanwhile, French composers were increasingly dubious about the benefits of following Wagner's lead and it was a combination of this, the confusion among French Wagnérites and a resurgence of French national pride that led to the gradual demise of French *Wagnérisme*.[15]

The debt to both the literary and musical strands of French Wagnérisme can be detected in Debussy's *Pelléas et Mélisande* (1902), despite the composer's earnest attempts to shake off the 'ghost of old Klingsor' during the composition of his opera.[16] Yet, despite certain musical similarities to Wagner, the interior quality of the score and its elusiveness, was far closer to the symbolists' ideal than anything their idol had produced. Debussy skilfully transformed Maeterlinck's drama, which abounds in symbolic imagery, into a musical setting. However, despite this achievement, the score's interior quality and elusiveness meant that it did not spawn the series of imitations feared by its detractors.[17]

15 Wagner's popularity among concert audiences endured well beyond that of composers and literary Wagnérites. Right up to the eve of the First World War he was by far the most frequently performed composer in Parisian concerts, and even after 1918 he quickly regained this position, as witnessed by an account published by the music critic Adolphe Jullien in *Le journal des débats* of 6 Jan. 1924. (In the previous season Wagner's music had been performed 334 times as opposed to the thirty performances achieved by Dukas, d'Indy and Ravel).

16 See Claude Debussy, letter to Ernest Chausson dated 2 Oct. 1893, cited in *Claude Debussy – Correspondance 1884–1918*, ed. François Lesure (Paris, 1993), 87–8. The degree of influence of Wagner on Debussy's opera was a subject of much debate among contemporary critics. However, many agreed with Alfred Bruneau that the opera 'pushes Richard Wagner's patented imitators and their bastard productions into the grave' ('elle pousse au tombeau les imitateurs patentés de Richard Wagner et leurs bâtardes productions'. Alfred Bruneau: 'La musique dramatique', *La Grande revue* (1 July 1902), 219).

17 The conservative critic Camille Bellaigue famously wrote of *Pelléas*: 'Such an art is evil and unhealthy … it strives towards the diminution and the ruin of our being. It contains the seeds, not of life and of progress, but of decadence and death.' ('Un tel art est malsain et malfaisant … elle tend à la diminution et à la ruine de notre être. Elle contient des germes non pas de vie

However, Debussy's growing recognition as a composer, which was greatly enhanced by the success of his opera, was of concern to those who saw him as an advocate of symbolism/impressionism in music. The common ground between the discreet allusions of the symbolists and the aim of the impressionist painters to depict, rather than to represent, their subject matter, caused a certain amount of confusion among contemporaries.[18] Although most critics preferred to trace similarities with the symbolists in Debussy's music, analogies with both symbolism and impressionism were drawn upon to help them to describe the vague, dream-like quality of Debussy's music. References to the paintings of Monet and Whistler were frequently crossed with references to the poetry of Mallarmé and other symbolist poets. However, on balance, Debussy's association with contemporary literary circles, his preference for setting symbolist poetry, his musical interpretation of Mallarmé's *Prélude à l'Après-midi d'un faune* (1892–94), as well as his own symbolist texts for the *Proses lyriques* (1892–93) and *Nuits blanches* (1899–1902), made contemporaries more inclined to point out his literary affiliations.

Debussy's association with literary symbolists inevitably affected public and critical perceptions of his work, and so the crimes of 'vagueness', 'malaise' and 'decadence' of which the symbolist poets were accused were also applied to his music. Debussysme in music was seen as an 'interiorization' of feelings, an ability to 'express the inexpressible' that many of the younger generation admired, but which met with resistance from the older generation. This resistance was further strengthened by the perceived revolutionary nature of Debussy's aesthetic. This revolutionary image was enhanced by his association with *La Revue blanche* (Debussy served as a music critic from April to December 1901), whose editor and other contributors enjoyed shocking their peers by indulging in a brief, but fashionable, fling with anarchism.[19] The journal was also notable for adopting a pro-Dreyfus stance during the Dreyfus Affair. Debussy's bohemian lifestyle and preference for such non-conformist company firmly associated him with a modern desire for change. However, Debussy's musical innovations attracted relatively little attention before the successful premiere of *Pelléas et Mélisande* in 1902. Up to that time, the composer's works were not often performed, and his reputation was mostly based on hearsay. With the appearance of *Pelléas et Mélisande*, Debussy suddenly became the centre of attention. In particular, as younger composers began to imitate his music, it created a good deal of unease regarding the future direction of French music. For his contemporaries, Debussysme implied a rejection of the recent musical past and a revolutionary desire to abandon the inherited forms and rules governing musical tradition. While this aspect of his music appealed to supporters and fellow composers who were, themselves, trying to forge a new style independent of Wagnerian influence, it unsettled those who felt there was still a lot to be learned from the recent past. Debussy's most vociferous opponents came from the older generation, such as Saint-Saëns, whose own career showed a tendency to

---

et de progrès, mais de décadence et de mort.' Camille Bellaigue: 'Revue musicale', *Revue des deux mondes* (15 May 1902), 455).

18 Stefan Jarocinski has clearly demonstrated the confusion that arose between the two terms in the field of Debussy studies after the composer's death. (For further details, see chapter 3 of Stefan Jarocinski: *Debussy: Impressionism and Symbolism*, trans. Rollo Myers (London, 1981).

19 See Richard D. Sonn: *Anarchism and Cultural Politics in Fin-de-siècle France* (Lincoln, Nebr., 1989).

consolidate traditional forms rather than forge new paths.[20]

Aside from the rather vague accusations of decadence and self-indulgent 'interiorization', the aspect of Debussy's style which caused the greatest unease was his harmonic innovations. However, Debussy's creation of new orchestral sonorities and his use of whole-tone and pentatonic harmonies were, in part, inspired by music he had heard at the Exposition Universelle in 1889. In particular, he was entranced by the musical colouring of the Javanese gamelan and these varied encounters, as well as the adoption of some of the modal harmonies favoured by the Russian national school, were all incorporated into his 'revolutionary' music. Debussy's orchestral recreation of exotic sounds, and his interest in fashionable orientalism (which also extended to a fascination with precious *objets d'art*), was not unique to French composers. In 1844 Félicien David had composed his symphonic ode *Le désert*, and further evidence of the long-standing fascination of the French with all things oriental can be found in operas such as Saint-Saëns's own *La princesse jaune* (1872), Georges Bizet's *Djamileh* (1872), André Messager's *Mme Chrysanthème* (1892) and Florent Schmitt's *La tragédie de Salomé* (1907), while orientalism in orchestral music can be traced in works such as Saint-Saëns's *Suite algérienne* (1879) and *Mélodies persanes* (1870), and Ravel's *Shéhérazade* (1898).

Orientalism also exploded spectacularly into the public arena with Diaghilev's Ballets Russes. Their seasonal presence in Paris, besides introducing the French to the colourful music of Stravinsky, also coincided with the appearance of more oriental music such as d'Indy's *Istar* (1912), Dukas's *La péri* (1912) and Ravel's *Ma mère l'oye* (1912). This fashion for all things oriental opened up a world of new orchestral sonorities which was less homogenous than those provided by recent Austro-German tradition and provides one of the characteristics of French music of this period. Debussy merely took this one step further, and experimented with timbre and harmonies to create a musical language unique to himself and ahead of his time. His harmonic innovations broke down the traditional relationships of chords, thereby focusing greater attention on the sound of the individual chord. This dismantling of traditional chord progressions also led to the use of parallel chords and rhythmic cells to provide a sense of movement, and this, in turn, led to a freer approach to the overall structure of the individual piece of music. The fascination these innovations held for young composers produced a rush of poor-quality imitations which lacked the accompanying artistry that characterized the original. Debussysme soon fell foul of contemporary audiences, and Debussy was seen as a disruptive influence on the young; one which prevented them finding a personal musical voice. In this climate, despite his repeated denials of such a role, Debussy gained a reputation as the head of the revolutionary school of Debussysme, which challenged orthodoxies and defied tradition.

The defenders of this tradition came in the form of the recently established Schola Cantorum. The Schola Cantorum was founded in 1894 with the aim of training young composers in the areas of counterpoint, analysis and music history that were otherwise marginalized at the Conservatoire. Vincent d'Indy had been involved from the start and in 1900 became director of the Schola. In the aftermath of *Pelléas*, Debussy was posited by critics as the alternative, and even as the antithesis, to the teachings of Vincent d'Indy. As

20 Saint-Saëns's hostility towards Debussy's music was reciprocated. Debussy was particularly scathing of Saint-Saëns's dramatic works, such as *Les barbares* (1901) and *Parysatis* (1902). See Debussy: *Monsieur Croche*, 57–8, 122–5.

the head (albeit unwilling) of a new school of composition Debussy was declared the 'revolutionary' to d'Indy's 'reactionary', the composer of 'vertical' to d'Indy's 'horizontal' music, of 'musique sensorielle' to d'Indy's 'musique cérébrale', and the exponent of Conservatoire (as opposed to Schola) training, thus introducing an element of musical politics into what was otherwise a purely musical debate. Debussy's revolutionary image, his association with symbolist circles and his artistic independence were at odds with the Catholic, militarist and traditionalist attitudes of the aristocratic d'Indy. Since its inception, the Schola Cantorum was seen as a rival to the Conservatoire but now, as Debussy's influence grew, the divide expanded to encompass a battle between two schools (or 'chapels') of composition: Debussysme and d'Indysme. In December 1902, William Morland made the following distinction between the two composers: 'The composer of *Fervaal* remains the defender of construction and counterpoint, the author of *Pelléas et Mélisande* remains the defender of the magic of harmony and the rapture or the astonishment of the ear.'[21] However, it was not so much a musical debate as a polemic. Debussy was the revolutionary head of the unhealthy school of Debussysme; d'Indy the pioneering figure behind the traditional Schola Cantorum. It was not so much their own music that was at stake as the extent to which they might influence the future. This 'mauvais magicien',[22] as Pierre Lalo called him, was the alternative to the adherence to traditional forms that d'Indy taught.[23]

However, the differences between the two men were nowhere near as clear-cut as would at first appear. Debussy's personal artistic development, driven by his horror of repeating himself musically, soon left his Debussyste imitators behind. His continued search for an independent musical voice led him to produce works such as *La mer* (1905) and the orchestral *Images* (1910–13) which are notable for their directness and new-found amplitude of line. This tendency is also evident in his settings of sixteenth-century French verse, such as the *Trois chansons de Charles d'Orléans* (1909) and the *Trois ballades de Villon* (1911) which, of necessity, called for a more simple and spare musical language than his earlier settings of symbolist texts.[24] This use of ancient sources was coupled with Debussy's growing conviction of the need to simplify music and rid it of the excesses of nineteenth-century romanticism in order to develop a distinctively French style. In his articles he made clear that the source of inspiration for this was to be early French music, and in particular the music of Rameau and Couperin. Meanwhile, in his role as director of

21 'L'auteur de *Fervaal* reste le défenseur de la construction et du jeu des lignes, celui de *Pelléas et Mélisande*, le défenseur de la magie de l'harmonie et du ravissement ou de l'étonnement de l'oreille.' William Morland: 'La Musique', *L'ermitage* (Dec. 1902), 472.

22 The music critic Pierre Lalo wrote that 'in truth, in the world of sound, Mr. Claude Debussy is something of a magician. But he is a bad magician ... Ordinary musicians, in imitating him, are on the road to ruin. May they beware of the prince of darkness, of his pomps and of his works' ('En vérité, dans le monde des sons, M. Claude Debussy est quelque chose comme un magicien. Mais c'est un mauvais magicien ... Les musiciens ordinaires, en l'imitant, vont à leur perte. Qu'ils se défient du prince des ténèbres, de ses pompes et de ses œuvres'). Pierre Lalo: 'La Musique', *Le temps* (28 Aug. 1900), 3.

23 The ins and outs of this rather protracted debate have been detailed by Christian Goubault in his article 'Les Chapelles musicales françaises ou La Querelle des "Gros-Boutiens" et des "Petits-Boutiens"', *Revue internationale de musique française*, 2 (June 1981), 99–112.

24 However, Debussy's continued fondness for the symbolists led him to compose his *Trois poèmes de Stéphane Mallarmé* in 1913.

the Schola Cantorum, d'Indy was active in promoting the revival of the ancient operatic tradition by way of performances of the works of Rameau, Gluck and Monteverdi.[25] In addition to this, the demanding curriculum at the Schola required pupils to have a thorough understanding of the instrumental writing of Beethoven, Wagner and César Franck. A combination of all these elements, as well as knowledge of church music and French folk songs, was d'Indy's recipe for the renewal of a truly French music.[26] While Debussy's own path drew him away from the German instrumental style, he shared d'Indy's enthusiasm for early opera and church music. Their turn to the past as a source of inspiration was part of a growing revival of interest in early music.

This early music revival had begun with the introduction, in 1871, of music history classes at the Conservatoire. As musicians became more interested in the music of the distant past, music history classes were also introduced at the Schola Cantorum and the Sorbonne. During the late nineteenth century and the early years of the twentieth century many of these early musicology enthusiasts published studies of hitherto neglected early music, such as Jules Échorcheville's *De Lulli à Rameau, 1690–1730* and Henri Quittard's *Les Couperins*. Meanwhile, performances of early music were most actively promoted by the Schola Cantorum. Aside from d'Indy's staging of ancient opera, one of the co-founders, Charles Bordes, had been performing ancient church music with his Chanteurs de Saint-Gervais since 1892. At the Schola he taught Gregorian plainchant and Palestrina-style counterpoint, while his co-founder, Alexandre Guilmant, provided the necessary background in church organ music and other early keyboard music. While a large number of early music concerts took place under the aegis of the Schola Cantorum, these were complemented by the concerts of music societies such as Henri Casadesus's Société des instruments anciens (1901–39), and later by those of the keyboard player Wanda Landowska, who worked tirelessly promoting and performing early keyboard music. Even more notable was the enthusiasm with which French musicians devoted their time to the preparation of new editions of ancient French music. These included joint collaborations such as *Les clavecinistes français*, which was edited by Louis Diémer, Saint-Saëns, d'Indy, Dukas, Guilmant and Georges Marty and, even more impressively, the preparation of the *Œuvres complètes* of Rameau, which were undertaken by an even larger group of French musicians under the direction of Charles Malherbe (until his death in 1911) and Saint-Saëns.[27]

In the increasingly chauvinistic climate of pre-war France, the inspiration of the past played a key role in discussions regarding the development of a distinctively French

---

25 In his role as music critic for *Gil Blas*, Debussy gave an enthusiastic account of the performance of Rameau's *Castor et Pollux* at the Schola Cantorum (See Claude Debussy: 'Gil Blas' (2 Feb. 1903), in Debussy: *Monsieur Croche*, 89–93).

26 D'Indy also maintained a special love of Wagner, and throughout his career he insisted that advances in French music were an 'unquestionable progress, due, I must repeat, to Wagnerian influence, without any manifestation of servile imitation but, on the contrary, accentuated by the force and vitality of the French *esprit*' ('incontestable progrès, dû, il faut le répéter, à l'influence wagnérienne sans présenter aucune servile imitation, mais accusant au contraire la force et la vitalité de l'esprit français'). Vincent d'Indy: *Richard Wagner et son influence sur l'art musical français* (Paris, 1930), 65.

27 Work on the edition was not completed until 1920, by which time such illustrious names as d'Indy, Dukas, Guilmant, Reynaldo Hahn, Georges Marty, Auguste Chapuis, Henri Busser and Debussy had all contributed to the editorial work.

musical style. However, the nationalist fervour ignited by the Great War played into the hands of the traditionalists, for whom the war was seen as a manifestation of the underlying tensions between the classical Latin world of France and that of the German barbarians. The war became a necessary source of purification and renewal, and was the inevitable result of the decadence of French – and implicitly Parisian – life prior to the war. The war was seen as central to the rejuvenation of French music for, as Léon Daudet wrote in its early stage, 'One of the most beautiful privileges of arms is the restoration of values of all kinds, and especially intellectual [ones], that were previously neglected or renounced'.[28] During the war these values manifested themselves primarily in the attempted exclusion of foreign, or at least non-Latin, music from Parisian concert life. A Ligue nationale pour la défense de la musique française was formed in 1916 with an unashamedly isolationist agenda. Yet when one looks at the members of this league, there is little evidence of a shared musical aesthetic, beyond their advanced years and a certain conservatism.[29] On the other hand, those composers who, before the war, had been applauded for their originality had, in the eyes of the younger generation, begun to repeat themselves and reached an impasse in their creative output. In the case of Debussy, despite his later efforts at composing pure music such as the three wartime sonatas and the two books of *Études* (1915), for many he remained the creator of musical symbolism. Similarly, Ravel's orchestral style placed him firmly with the pre-war generation, particularly as his first post-war composition was the richly orchestrated and overtly romantic *La valse* (composed 1919–20, but not performed until 1928). Meanwhile, the toast of the immediate pre-war years, Igor Stravinsky, whose ballets *Firebird* (1910), *Petrushka* (1912) and *The Rite of Spring* (1913) were greeted with uproar when premiered by the Ballets Russes, had introduced a wild, savage music that was far removed from the simplicity and terseness of what was vaguely identified as the French national style.

However, in an atmosphere in which the pre-war excesses of decadent symbolism were rejected as symptoms of a *fin-de-siècle* malaise, change was inevitable. The *esprit nouveau* in French music was provocatively launched with the Ballets Russes's premiere of Erik Satie's *Parade* on 18 May 1917. The outrageous costumes designed by the 'Kubist' Picasso and the freshness and light-heartedness of the score were (predictably) condemned for their frivolity in the face of the everyday hardships of war, and the production was seen as a deliberate act of aggression against traditional patriotic values. However, the 'fairground' and 'ragtime' quality to the music was welcomed by the younger generation of musicians present. As Poulenc later recalled, 'Satie's music, so simple, so raw, so naïvely intricate, like a painting by the Douanier Rousseau shocked everybody by its breeziness ... For the first time – it has happened often enough since, God knows, – the music hall was invading Art with a capital A.'[30] It was this approval of *Parade* by the young that marked Satie's path over the following years. Confronted with the incomprehension of his own generation, he led the young in their quest for novelty and renewal after the perceived impasse of the pre-war years. Cocteau later claimed: '[the

28 Léon Daudet: *Hors du joug allemand*, cited in Kenneth Silver: *Esprit de Corps – The Art of the Parisian Avant Garde and the First World War, 1914–1925* (London, 1989), 27.

29 The committee members included Saint-Saëns, Théodore Dubois, Vincent d'Indy, Gustave Charpentier and Xavier Leroux.

30 Cited in Francis Steegmuller: *Cocteau – A Biography* (London, 1992), 185.

score] opened a door to young musicians who were a little tired of nice impressionist polyphony.'[31]

Parade marked a turning point in the career of Satie who, until the war, had primarily been viewed as a composer of humorous but insignificant piano pieces such as the *Véritables préludes flasques* (1913) and the *Embryons desséchés* (1913). In contrast, *Parade* became known as the departure point for *l'esprit nouveau* and established Satie's importance in the post-war musical scene. *Parade* won him the admiration of a younger generation of artists, writers and composers, who felt he had made a decisive break with the past. This was confirmed by the controversial stance adopted by Jean Cocteau in *Le coq et l'arlequin* (1918), in which he boldly proposed Satie as an alternative to both Stravinsky and Debussy, the main reason being the simplicity of Satie's music: 'The opposition put forward by Erik Satie consists of a return to simplicity. Moreover, that is the only possible kind of opposition in an age of extreme refinement.'[32] Cocteau also posited the validity of the circus, fairground, music hall and ragtime as forms of art. This aspect of *Parade* became a key feature in the early works of young composers who flocked to Satie in the 1920s. Les Six, who consisted of Darius Milhaud, Francis Poulenc, Georges Auric, Germaine Tailleferre, Louis Durey and Arthur Honegger, were never more than a loose association of composers, alike only in their determination to re-energize French music. The circus/fairground aspect of Satie's *Parade* featured highly in some of their early works, such as Milhaud's *Le Bœuf sur le toit* (1920) and *Les mariés de la Tour Eiffel* (1921), a Cocteau ballet with a score by five members of Les Six. A parallel to the primitivist movement in the fine arts is also evident in their adoption of jazz influences, particularly rhythmic influences, as evident in such works as Poulenc's *Rapsodie nègre* (1917) and *Cocardes* (1919), and Milhaud's *La création du monde* (1923).

However, Satie's *Socrate* (1920) provided a different interpretation of *l'esprit nouveau* and marked the point at which his path began to diverge from that of Les Six. Prior to *Socrate*, Satie's simplicity and *esprit nouveau* were couched in the language of the music hall found in *Parade* and the *Trois petites pièces montées* (1920). The stark simplicity of *Socrate*, its sincerity and emotional quality, were at odds with the rather tongue-in-cheek tone of the *esprit nouveau* to date. *Socrate* was in a very different style and, with the simultaneous appearance of both *Socrate* and the *Nocturnes* (1919), Satie's role as mascot of Les Six became tenuous. Also, they were all very young when they first came under public scrutiny, and as their individual styles began to develop, it was increasingly hard to find any connection between the fresh melodies and rhythmic vitality of Poulenc, the tightly constructed but lyrical style of Milhaud, and the often complex polyphonic structures of Honegger. However, despite their short-lived existence as a group, the music of Les Six was a definitive break with the past. Their irreverence toward tradition, and what Madeleine Milhaud later referred to as that 'manifestation of ... impertinence' which characterized the heady days of the 1920s, were a clear departure from the serious tone of pre-war musical aesthetics.[33] Their fusion of high art with the more popular genres of jazz, music hall and cabaret was a deliberate challenge to the status quo, a determined effort to

31 'Il [the score] ouvrira une porte aux jeunes musiciens un peu fatigués de la belle polyphonie impressionniste.' Jean Cocteau: 'La collaboration de "Parade"', *Nord-Sud: Revue littéraire* (June/July 1917), 31.

32 Ibid., 314.

33 See Roger Nichols: *Conversations with Madeleine Milhaud* (London, 1996), 21.

demythologize the role of the composer and the supposed superiority of 'serious' music. The whimsicality and levity of their brand of neoclassicism found parallels with Tristan Tzara's Dadaism, and the surrealism of André Breton, both of which they had direct contact with. However, the very lightness of French neoclassicism also caused a dearth of 'serious' music between the wars, as was evident from the lack of native operatic productions. With the exception of Fauré's *Pénélope* (1919), Ravel's *Les enfants et les sortilèges* (1926), Roussel's *Padmâvatî* (1923) and *Aenéas* (1938), and Milhaud's *Maximilien* (1932), most new productions were not operatic. These years were especially fruitful in terms of dance music, particularly with the seasonal presence of both Sergei Diaghilev's Ballets Russes (Poulenc's *Les biches* (1924), Auric's *Les fâcheux* (1924) and *Les matelots* (1925), and Milhaud's *Le train bleu* (1924)) and of Rolf de Maré's rival Ballets suédois (*Les mariés de la tour Eiffel* (1921), Milhaud's *L'homme et son désir* (1921) and *La création du monde* (1923), Tailleferre's *Le marchand d'oiseaux* (1923) and Honegger's *Skating Rink* (1922)).

Moreover, the presence of both Stravinsky and Prokofiev in Paris during the inter-war years ensured that the French capital had the honour of premiering such important works as Stravinsky's *Mavra* (1922), *Renard* (1922) and *Les noces* (1923) and Prokofiev's *Le chout* (1921) and *Le pas d'acier* (1927). In view of all this activity, Paris became the centre of the neoclassical movement during the inter-war years and beyond. The symphonic concerts of Koussevitzsky, Poulet, Delgrange and Siohan and the ORTF, alongside those of the more established Lamoureux, Colonne and Pasdeloup, all included neoclassical works alongside more traditional fare, while Walter Straram's concerts of 'musique moderne internationale', Pierre-Octave Ferroud's Le Triton and Jean Wiéner's concerts also gave neoclassical pieces pride of place alongside other contemporary music. Performances of modern chamber music also flourished, thanks to the concert series held by *La Revue musicale*, while a steady influx of international soloists also ensured the wider dissemination of contemporary music.

This greater receptiveness towards contemporary music was an inevitable backlash against the isolationism and chauvinism of 1914–18, during which time young French composers had difficulty in gaining access to new foreign music. Les Six, and others of their generation, felt no need to adopt a protectionist attitude towards their music. If anything, they welcomed outside influences. Their curiosity had been aroused by what little of Schoenberg's music they had heard performed in Paris before the war, and the growing reputation of Schoenberg and his two pupils Berg and Webern led them to study their scores with great interest.

But, before 1921, public feeling was such that none of the music of these modern Austro-Germans was performed in Paris.[34] In December 1921 a performance of Schoenberg's *Pierrot lunaire* (1912), conducted by Milhaud at the Concerts Wiéner, created interest in expressionist works and the successful performance was followed by a further two in January 1922.[35] However, despite several performances of their works

---

34 This attitude towards Austro-German music was also evident in the paucity of performances of the music of Brahms, Mahler, Wolf and Reger during the inter-war years. On the other hand, although Richard Strauss's symphonic poems were performed, they were mostly greeted with indifference or open hostility.

35 However, the mood of the times dictated that the text was translated into French for, as Milhaud explained, 'a part of our public still found the German language hateful to hear'. Darius

including a gala performance at the Concerts Colonne on 8 December 1927, the music of the Second Viennese School did not achieve any lasting success in inter-war Paris. This was partly due to the essential difference between the intensity of the expressionist ethos and the comparative levity of French neoclassicism. As Auric explained in 1924, '*Pierrot lunaire* ... is decadent romanticism ... Harmful and disturbing music which one had to know, and which is odious to me because it shatters all that I love, and poses its nervous assertions in opposition to the light-hearted genius of Igor Stravinsky.'[36] In this sense, the two musical cultures had never been so far apart. Both were at the farthest poles of their respective traditions. Nor did Schoenberg's early serialist music meet with greater openness; as Armand Machabey explained, the general consensus among the French musical community was that Schoenberg's serialist music was what 'some describe as barbaric, others as scientific, and yet others as charlatan: [but] truth to tell, is that of a intellectual'.[37] The French did not warm to either the seralism of Schoenberg or Webern. On the other hand, the lyrical and dramatic qualities of Berg's music brought him moderate success. In particular, the three fragments from *Wozzeck* (1924) which were performed by Pierre Monteux's Orchestre symphonique de Paris on 29 March 1931 met with a warm response, and his expressive atonality found much greater favour with the French than the strict serialism of his friends.[38]

However, the studied lightness of French neoclassicism was not to the taste of all French composers, and the reaction took shape in 1936 in the form of La Jeune France, which consisted of Olivier Messiaen, Daniel-Lesur, Yves Baudrier and André Jolivet. La Jeune France were not so much united by a common aesthetic as by a desire to counter the perceived levity of contemporary French music and to present their own musical works to the public. Their activities were interrupted by the outbreak of war, but Messiaen had already made a name for himself thanks both to performances of works such as *Les Offrandes oubliées* (1931) and *Le Tombeau resplendissant* (1932) and to his activities as a teacher at the École normale de musique and the Schola Cantorum. During the occupation, after a period as a prisoner of war, Messiaen became professor of harmony at the Conservatoire. Concert life was seriously affected by the Occupation (one of the most notable productions being *Ariadne auf Naxos* (1912) at the Opéra-Comique in 1943), but music teaching was relatively unaffected. Messiaen's reputation as a teacher of international renown began to grow during these years; among his wartime pupils he could boast Pierre Boulez, Jean-Louis Martinet, Maurice Le Roux and Yvonne Loriod. Messiaen himself had been a pupil of Dukas at the Conservatoire, and was strongly influenced by the pre-war generation. In particular, the important role played by rhythm in his music finds a precedent in the rhythmic styles of Debussy and Stravinsky. This is particularly true of his piano pieces such as the *Visions de l'Amen* (1943) and the *Vingt regards sur l'enfant*

Milhaud, *Musical Quarterly* (Oct. 1944), 382.

36 '*Pierrot lunaire*, c'est le romantisme décadent ... Musique néfaste et inquiétante qu'il fallait connaître, et qui m'est odieuse parce qu'elle bouleverse tout ce que j'aime et oppose son affirmation crispée à l'allègre génie d'Igor Stravinsky.' Georges Auric: *Les nouvelles littéraires* (26 Apr. 1924), 7.

37 'cette musique que les uns qualifent de barbare, les autres de scientifique, les troisièmes de charlatanesque; à la vérité, c'est celle d'un cérébral'. Armand Machabey: *Le ménestrel* (6 June 1930), 258–9.

38 However, it was not until 1974 that *Wozzeck* was performed in full at the Paris Opéra.

Jésus (1944). Debussy's influence is also evident in Messiaen's explorations of timbre (such as in the later *Chronochromie* (1960)), and his preoccupations with the tone colours in music finds direct lineage with Debussy's isolation of the individual chord . To a certain extent, Messiaen's debt to Debussy's musical language can be viewed as a refutation of the rejection of Debussy by Les Six and their milieu, just as the activities of La Jeune France in the 1930s can be seen as a direct challenge to the continued domination of contemporary French music by members of Les Six.

Meanwhile, in the post-war years Milhaud had divided his time between America and Paris, working both as a teacher and as a composer of dramatic and pure music, Honegger turned towards large-scale symphonic and chamber works as opposed to the more flamboyant works of his years of association with Les Six (such as *Pastorale d'été* (1921) and *Pacific 231* (1924)). Similarly, Poulenc's mischievous neoclassicism, although it was still present in his songs and works such as *Les mamelles de Tirésias* (1947), was replaced by a simpler, lyrical style in such works as *Les dialogues des Carmélites* (1957) and the large number of sacred choral works which followed his return to the Catholic faith in 1935. Auric became noted primarily for his film scores and dramatic music, and was also particularly active in Parisian musical life (as president of SACEM and later as director of the Opéra and the Opéra-Comique). Indeed, after the initial euphoria of the 1920s, the members of Les Six were prepared to acknowledge that their pretended rejection of Debussy and the immediate past had been a deliberately provocative stance on their part. Milhaud acknowledged in an interview in 1958 that theirs was not so much a rejection of Debussy as a rejection of his Debussyste imitators: 'You might be surprised that, while fighting Impressionism, I always kept this deep love for the music of Debussy. As a matter of fact the quality of Debussy is different ... Everything, as I have told you already, came from his heart; and his human qualities are always in his music.'[39] This humanity was also a key component of Messiaen's musical aesthetic and, if Milhaud is to be believed, also figured highly in the aesthetic of Les Six, although it was initially sidelined by the comic and light-hearted associations of their earlier work.

Messiaen's activities as a teacher ensured his influence on the next generation of French composers. However, the strongest personality to emerge from this generation was undoubtedly Pierre Boulez, whose explorations as a composer ultimately took him along a different path from that of his teacher. While early works such as the *Trois psalmodies* (1945) reveal Messiaen's influence, Boulez was already becoming preoccupied with the possibilities of atonality. When the opportunity presented itself, he took lessons in dodecaphonic composition from René Leibowitz, the results of which were his First Piano Sonata (1946), the *Sonatine* (1946), and *Le visage nuptial* (1946).[40] Boulez first came to public attention with the Second Piano Sonata, which was performed by Yvonne Loriod at the Darmstadt Festival in 1952. His experiments in rhythmic serialization also found a parallel in similar experiments by Messiaen (such as in his *Mode de valeurs et d'intensités* (1949)), but Boulez's application of total serialism (where serial techniques are applied not just to the pitch, but also to the timbre, duration and intensity of each sound), moved

39 Darius Milhaud: 'Reminiscences of Debussy and Ravel', *Essays on Music – An Anthology from 'The Listener'*, ed. Felix Aprahamian (London, 1967), 81–2.

40 A pupil of Schoenberg, René Leibowitz was instrumental in the promotion of serialism in France through his book, *Schönberg et son école* (Paris, 1947) and the lessons he gave to young French composers.

Plate 1.2 *Siegfried* at Cauterets in the Pyrenees. By the early twentieth century, political antipathy to Germany had to some extent been forgotten. The fashion for outdoor productions of opera extended to Wagner.

beyond Messiaen's concept. Boulez's *Structures I* (1952) illustrates his application of the technique with which Stockhausen and Nono also experimented.

However, the obvious problems arising from total serialism in live performance make this work incredibly difficult to perform. To overcome this, Boulez began his first studio compositions at Pierre Schaeffer's RTF studio for *musique concrète* in 1951, the results of which were his *Études*. *Musique concrète* (as opposed to 'abstract' music composed through notation and performance), and the pioneering work of Schaeffer and Pierre

Henry, again brought French music to the cutting edge of contemporary music. The Club d'essai, which was formed in 1948, was renamed the Groupe de recherche de musique concrète in 1951, and its early pioneers included, besides Schaeffer and Henry, Edgard Varèse and Iannis Xenakis. The 1950s in Paris were also marked by the formation of Boulez's Domaine musical concerts, whose eclectic programmes ranged from old masters to contemporary works via twentieth-century classics. The Domaine musical concerts corrected the imbalance of works being performed in Paris and revitalized concert life in the French capital. Their very eclecticism was symptomatic of the international flavour of modern French music. Boulez himself has been in demand as a teacher on both sides of the Atlantic and he made several appearances at the Darmstadt Festival (his book *Boulez on Music Today* (1963) was based on a series of lectures he gave there).

Moreover, his peers, such as Henri Dutilleux and Maurice Ohana, also betray a wide range of influences in their music. Given his Conservatoire training, it is not surprising that Dutilleux's earlier compositions show the combined influences of Debussy and Ravel. He also shared their interest in the qualities of the individual sound moment, as shown by his experiments with seating arrangements in his Second Symphony, 'Le double' (1955–59). However, Dutilleux's originality lies in his refusal to limit himself within musical conventions. Ohana's multicultural background ensured a wide range of influences from an early age, but his foundation of the Zodiaque group in 1947, whose aim was the rejection of established tradition in favour of artistic freedom, is symptomatic of his desire for independence from musical schools of thought. Ultimately, the issue of a French music, which was of such importance to French musicians before the First World War, has given way to a more international flavour which is a reflection of the richness and diversity of contemporary French musical life.

Suggested Further Reading

Elaine Brody: *Paris – The Musical Kaleidoscope 1870–1925* (London: Robson, 1988).

Jeffrey Cooper: *The Rise of Instrumental Music and Concert Series in Paris, 1828–1871* (Ann Arbor: UMI Research Press, 1983).

Martin Cooper: *French Music: From the Death of Berlioz to the Death of Fauré* (London: Oxford University Press, 1951).

Claude Debussy: *Monsieur Croche et autres écrits,* ed. François Lesure (Paris: Gallimard, 1987); English edn ed. and trans. Richard Langham Smith as *Debussy on Music* (London: Secker & Warburg, 1977).

Michel Fleury: *L'impressionnisme et la musique* (Paris: Fayard, 1996).

Serge Gut and Danièle Pistone: *La musique de chambre en France de 1870 à 1918* (Paris: Champion, 1978).

James Harding: *The Ox on the Roof: Scenes from Musical Life in Paris in the Twenties* (London: Macdonald, 1972).

Robin Holloway: *Debussy and Wagner* (London: Eulenberg, 1979).

Stefan Jarocinski: *Debussy: Impressionism and Symbolism*, trans. Rollo Myers (London: Eulenberg, 1981).

Roger Nichols: *Conversations with Madeleine Milhaud* (London: Faber, 1996).

Roger Shattuck: *The Banquet Years* (London: Faber, 1955; rev. edn New York: Vintage, 1968).

Kenneth E. Silver: *Esprit de Corps – The Art of the Parisian Avant Garde and the First World War, 1914–1925* (London: Princeton University Press, 1989).

Richard D. Sonn: *Anarchism and Cultural Politics in Fin-de-siècle France* (Lincoln: University of Nebraska Press, 1989).

Chapter 2

Nineteenth-Century Spectacle

Thomas Cooper

Introduction

At the time of Berlioz's death, spectacular performances of all kinds had been familiar to the French for many years. This was particularly apparent in the by now venerable genre of grand opera, which had reached its apogee in the 1830s with works such as Giacomo Meyerbeer's *Robert le diable* (1831) and *Les Huguenots* (1836). 'Grand opera' refers to a style in which both the subject matter and treatment tended to be on a large scale. One of the main formal differences between it and other types of opera was the use of sung recitative rather than spoken dialogue between numbers. The subject matter was frequently historical, and typically dealt with the conflict between public and private concerns. Some of the roots of this important genre lay in the past. French opera had always been associated with spectacular effects, and this reached new heights following the Revolution of 1789 with works such as Gasparo Spontini's *Fernand Cortez* (1809), an immediate predecessor of grand opera. The Revolution had also established a tradition of massive open-air concerts, many of which included choral items. Such spectacles continued into the later nineteenth century, particularly after 1871 as the newly established Third Republic attempted to bolster its authority by cautious reference to the trappings of a revolutionary past.[1] Another principal genre of opera inherited from the eighteenth century was *opéra-comique*, where the subject matter and treatment tended to be on a more domestic scale. While frequently comic, as the title of the genre implies, these operas also touched on more serious or sentimental issues, but mostly dealt with the mundane concerns of a less rarified strata of society than the kings and princesses of grand opera. The 'lower' forms of opera tended to be distinguished by the use of spoken dialogue, but were otherwise equally reliant on the concept of the 'number', whether solo, duet, ensemble or choral.

By the latter part of the century, the world prominence previously enjoyed by Paris in the field of ballet had passed to Russia with the departure of Marius Petipa in 1847. However, ballets continued to be a staple of performances in France, and were frequently as spectacular as any opera. The appearance of ballet sections within operas was regarded as inevitable: they served to diversify the spectacle. In addition, the musical spectacles presented by the Expositions of the period had a significant impact. These exhibitions of

1 See E. Hobsbawm: 'Mass-Producing Traditions: Europe, 1870–1914', in E. Hobsbawm and T. Ranger (eds): *The Invention of Tradition* (Cambridge, 1992) for the example of Bastille Day during the period. Concerning some of the concerts, see J. Fulcher: 'The Concert as Political Propaganda in France and the Control of "Performative Context"', *MQ*, 82/1 (1998), 55–7.

the artistic and industrial products of France and its empire occurred with increasing regularity in Paris from 1867 and in other major cities, such as Lyon, where an Exposition Universelle was held in 1872. Best known of these was the Paris Exposition of 1889, where, among other exhibits, the presentation of music theatre, ostensibly from Annam (under French control since 1883), had a significant impact on Debussy.

The composition of a successful opera continued to be seen as the most sure way of achieving musical fame and fortune in the years following Berlioz's death, just as it had in his youth. The number of operas produced by French composers during this period was colossal. Many of them were only of fleeting interest, even at the time, and most have sunk into obscurity since. The attention given in the past to major works such as Debussy's *Pelléas et Mélisande* (1902), Bizet's *Carmen* (1875) and Berlioz's *Les Troyens* (first partial performance 1863) has tended to overshadow the works surrounding them and distract attention from their context. In recent years this trend has been somewhat reversed, and interest has reawakened in formerly less-regarded composers of the period such as Massenet, Ambroise Thomas, Saint-Saëns, Alfred Bruneau and Vincent d'Indy.

While commercial success was undoubtedly one motivating factor in the production of opera, both for composers and management, various other influences were naturally also apparent. The form which operas took in the later nineteenth century was often dependent, at least to some extent, on previously successful works. Opera was largely understood by predominantly conservative audiences and critics to consist of clearly articulated and preferably tuneful airs, ensembles and choruses. Publishers added to the pressure on composers to produce detachable numbers, which could be easily extracted from the resulting *opéra à numéros*. Any opportunity for the inclusion of dances was avidly grasped, particularly in grand opera. Tableaux were an important feature. Stage and lighting effects, sets and costumes, were generally extremely lavish, particularly in Paris, where the Opéra had led the way in their development for many years.

Foreign opera was also well represented. Italian opera had a long tradition of support in France. In Paris, the Théâtre-Italien presented a range of operas mostly consisting of well-established favourites by Verdi, Donizetti and Bellini. Even the conservative Paris Opéra eventually put on operas such as Verdi's *Aida* (1880), *Rigoletto* (1885) and *Otello* (1894). The Opéra-Comique presented Verdi's *Falstaff* shortly after its Italian premiere in 1893 and also promoted operas such as Mascagni's *Cavalleria rusticana*. The passionate realism of works such as the latter opera had a significant impact on French composers such as Bruneau and even wrung a response from the more pragmatic Massenet. While Russian opera was not known to French audiences until the twentieth century, German opera was commonly presented throughout the period. Weber and Mozart were frequently performed, and there was a particular fondness for *Der Freischütz*. The failure of Wagner's *Tannhäuser* in Paris in 1861, partly due to his refusal to supply the expected second-act ballet, illustrates some of the potential pitfalls of a foreign composer working in a conservative atmosphere (it also presents a telling contrast to Verdi's readiness to adapt his operas for the Parisian stage). The omission galled the aristocratic Jockey Club, admirers of the dancers rather than of opera, who engineered the riotous heckling that accompanied the opera's three performances. However, through the production of *Tristan und Isolde* (Munich, 1865) in particular, Wagner unleashed a wave of influence so profound that French composers were forced to respond. The musical world of Paris increasingly split into pro- and anti-Wagner camps.

Nevertheless, the impact of Wagner on French opera was not as clear-cut as might be expected. To begin with, it did not cause the complete change in national style that had resulted from some earlier influences, such as that of Italian opera in the seventeenth century. Composers formerly seen as completely Wagnerian in their operas, such as Chausson, Chabrier and Ernest Reyer, were not in fact slavish imitators. At the same time, some composers who had little sympathy with Wagner's ethic (such as, in later years, Debussy) revealed his influence by drawing on Celtic, Germanic or Nordic folk-tale and mythology for their librettos, for example.

The impact of Wagner was further complicated by France's crushing military defeat by Prussia in 1870, which brought about the collapse of the Second Empire. The wave of nationalism which resulted was nothing new in French history, but it acquired an ever more far-reaching influence as the nineteenth century progressed. The criticism of the period is full of references to 'the French school' of music, and new works of all kinds were eagerly scanned for evidence of 'French' qualities, usually characterized as those of clarity and concision. In an article written in 1893 entitled 'Le drame lyrique', the novelist and journalist Émile Zola invoked 'the sharp clarity characteristic of the spirit of our race' when arguing for an abandonment of 'the current fashion of northern mythologies' in French opera.[2] The critic Paul Bernard, writing in 1872, used the same notion to criticize one *opéra-comique*, grumbling that 'almost all our young musicians covet a kiss from modern Germany's muse' (again meaning Wagner, an unlikely influence in this instance).[3] Reviews of Massenet's *opéra-comique Don César de Bazan* the same year approved of the work, partly because it was seen as 'free of such pernicious elements'.[4] An increasingly anti-semitic slant became evident, in France as throughout Europe, one of its high water marks being the Dreyfus Affair of the 1890s. The most notable French composer actively involved in such propaganda was Vincent d'Indy, whose attacks on Jewish composers were broadened to include also those who belonged to what he identified as the 'école judaïque' (by which he meant what he perceived as decadent and Italianate).[5]

A corollary of the rise of nationalism was a further surge of interest in the exotic and in French historical themes among opera composers. Again, neither was new: exoticism had been apparent in French music since at least the seventeenth century, and historical themes had been richly mined since the eighteenth century. One example of the latter, frequently performed throughout the period, was Meyerbeer's *Les Huguenots*. As French culture of the later nineteenth century became more focused on self-definition in the wake of the catastrophic defeat by Germany, so there was also an increasing concern to delineate others. This was most noticeable, perhaps, in the colonies, which by the end of the century were extensive. Here, the racial theories of the time could be put into practice, despite the often violent resistance of the indigenous populations. In works of art, also, exoticism

---

2 Quoted in S. Huebner: 'Naturalism and supernaturalism in Alfred Bruneau's *Le Rêve*', *Cambridge Opera Journal*, 11/1 (1999), 82.

3 Quoted in K. Ellis: *Music Criticism in nineteenth-century France* (Cambridge, 1995), 216.

4 Ibid., 217.

5 From d'Indy's *Cours de composition musicale* (Paris, 1920). Quoted in J. Fulcher: 'Vincent d'Indy's "Drame anti-Juif" and its meaning in Paris, 1920', *Cambridge Opera Journal*, 2/3 (1990), 302.

became increasingly popular. While the characterizations of exotic peoples in these works were almost invariably of the most superficial kind, they differed from previous renditions in being increasingly concerned to identify what were seen as the essential natures of races. In this, the creators of exotic works increasingly drew (albeit unconsciously at times) on such quasi-scientific ideas as those of the French propagandists Ernest Renan, a philologist and Hebrew scholar, and the populist philosopher Joseph-Arthur de Gobineau, who later contributed to Nazi ideology. These writers, especially the latter in his *Essai sur l'inégalité des races humaines* (1853–55), expressed both what Tzvetan Todorov has called 'the ordinary anonymous racialist ideology of the period'[6] and marked the emergence of a new kind of racism based on pseudo-scientific theory. In his *Histoire générale et système comparé des langues sémitiques* (1855), Renan expressed the idea that the races (which he identified by the immediately visible signs of skin colour and facial features) have different rather than common origins. According to Renan, they thus have innate and inevitable characteristics, which in turn lead each to a 'natural' sphere of activity with the Aryans firmly in charge at the apex of the pyramid of races. Many musicians were subscribers to these views. Wagner's interest in Gobineau is well documented; the two met several times, and Wagner read Gobineau's *Essai*, quoting from it in his own *Heldentum und Christentum* (*Heroism and Christianity*) (1881). Other subjects for opera included the age-old theme of magic or fairy-tale, familiar to French audiences from at least the time of Lully. At the opposite extreme, mainly dating from nearer the end of the nineteenth century, lie the operas which take a 'realist' approach (*Carmen* might be cited as an early example).

The institutions which promoted French operas and ballets of the period were many and varied, and lay at the heart of French musical life. In addition to the dozen or so theatres in the capital, many provinces boasted an opera house whose productions vied with those of the metropolis. Such theatres were seen as monuments of national or regional pride, and were strongly subsidized even at times of national crisis. Following the devastating fire of 1873 in which the Salle Le Péletier, the old home of the Opéra, was destroyed, the infant Third Republic voted more than 6 million francs for the re-establishment of the institution in the almost completed Palais Garnier (opened 1875).[7] However, the policies of the Opéra were so conservative that only a very few new works by French composers were given a hearing there during the rest of the nineteenth century. Many operas of the period were first performed in regional theatres or outside France altogether, often at the Théâtre de la Monnaie in Brussels. Other Parisian theatres, most notably the Opéra-Comique, were much more adventurous, although, then as now, operas which were old favourites with the mainly conservative audiences were always a useful standby for theatre managements who needed a financial boost. The now little-known figure Henri Maréchal (1842–1924), a former *Prix de Rome* winner, wrote an opéra-comique *Les amoureux de Catherine*, produced in 1876, which is an example of such a hit. It was endlessly revived for this purpose during the period and was still being performed in the 1920s.[8]

---

6 T. Todorov: *Of Human Diversity*, trans. C. Porter (Cambridge, Mass, 1993), 106.

7 Reported in the *RGM*, 25 Jan. 1874, 25.

8 Others included Boieldieu's *La dame blanche* (1825) and Grétry's even older *Richard Cœur-de-lion* (1784).

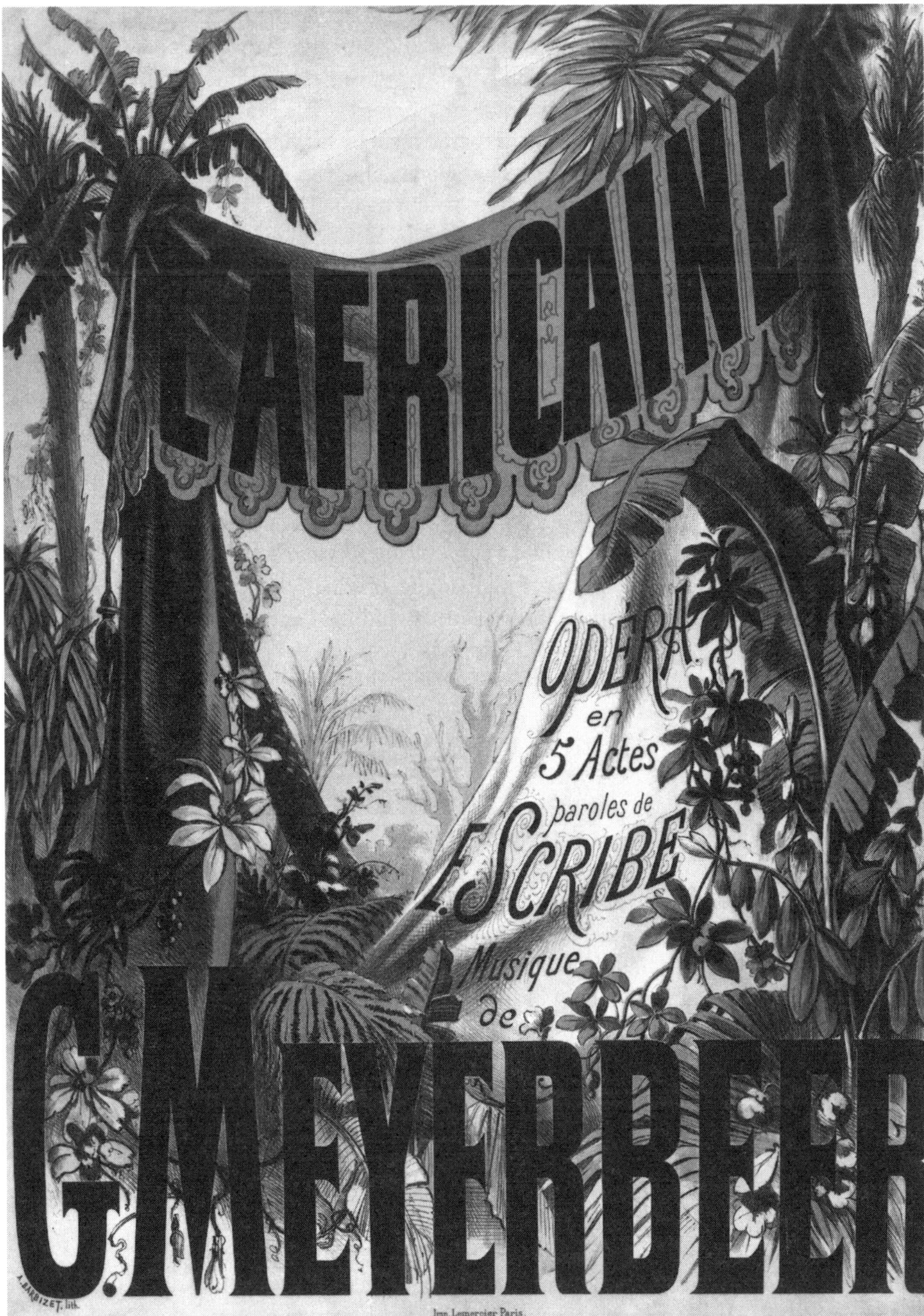

Plate 2.1 Poster for Meyerbeer's *L'Africaine* (1865), one of many nineteenth-century operas with an oriental setting.

The works that emanated from these institutions are frequently of a somewhat nebulous character. The old-established distinctions between both the form and content of grand opera and *opéra-comique* were increasingly blurred during the period, though periodically there was official pressure to maintain them. For example, the Opéra-Comique was exhorted to boost spoken dialogue in its performances at the time of Bizet's *Carmen*. Indeed, this may be a reason why the opera includes much spoken dialogue in the original version. The common method of opera composition resulted in extensive adaptation in the light of performance conditions, both during the rehearsal period and after the first performance (*Carmen* is an example of a score radically revised during the lengthy preparations for the premiere). Thus the printed score (often produced to coincide with the premiere) cannot always be taken as an indication of the actual performance. Likewise, the material that made up performances was not always within the composer's control. Performers, publishers and theatre management could influence the placement, form, existence or continuance of particular numbers, according to their needs. Thus opera can be seen as a flexible and contingent genre, lending itself to very different critical approaches from those involving more 'finished' composition. Critical readings even of works previously considered to be monumental in the extreme, such as grand operas, may be considerably adapted in the light of such considerations. An example of this is the practice of adapting successful works with dialogue, originally given at venues such as the Opéra-Comique, for production at the Opéra by adding recitatives. As in the case of *Carmen*, 'recitatived' by Ernest Guiraud after Bizet's death, the pace, characterization and even the plot could be significantly affected by such adaptations.

Prelude: *L'Africaine*

One of the most successful operas of the late nineteenth century illustrates this underlying precept: that opera must be considered as a spectacle, not simply a score. The grand opera by Meyerbeer, *L'Africaine*, was played repeatedly at the Opéra from its premiere in 1865 until into the twentieth century. It clocked up more than 400 performances there during that time, roughly twice as many as Verdi's *Aida* during much the same period (*Aida* was first produced in 1871 at the opening of the Cairo opera house, and was shortly afterwards presented in Paris). Moreover, *L'Africaine* was hugely successful elsewhere, both in the provinces and worldwide. By 1871 it had appeared in France in Angoulême, Lyon, Metz and Poitiers, and had also been given in Italy, Spain, Germany, Britain, Belgium and the United States. By 1876 it had conquered opera houses in Besançon, Marseille and Toulouse, and had been exported to Russia, Egypt, Portugal, Austria-Hungary and South America. *L'Africaine* was a staple of programmes everywhere, including opera houses in the colonies (it was performed in Algiers, for example, in 1870).[9]

The work is in some ways typical of the grand operas of the nineteenth century, not least because its roots can be traced back to a date much earlier than that of its first performance.[10] Partly set on board a ship, which is wrecked in a storm, the plot concerns

9 See *RGM*, 1870, 1871 and 1876.

10 Meyerbeer had begun work on the opera in 1838. It was prepared for production after his death by F. J. Fétis.

the expeditions of the Portuguese explorer and imperialist Vasco da Gama. The last two acts are set on an unnamed African island, giving the opportunity for much exotic spectacle including dances, ceremonies and the eventual suicide of the African heroine by inhalation of the poisonous fumes of a native tree. The enormously costly sets and costumes needed for its production probably accounted in part for the opera's demise (for example, the creation of the requisite movements of the ship gave great trouble, even at the well-resourced Paris Opéra).

Example 2.1 Giacomo Meyerbeer, *L'Africaine*, opening of Act IV

Musically, the opera departs somewhat from Meyerbeer's earlier style. It consists of a kaleidoscopic pattern of numbers which are frequently short. Acts II, IV and V have rather restrained endings instead of the customary grand set-pieces. The exoticism of the score is somewhat muted, with limited use of the percussion so often associated with this style. Instead, Meyerbeer exploits darker wind timbres in music associated with the Africans, much of which shows his customary skill at writing music suggestive of action (Example 2.1). It is likely that Meyerbeer's Italianate lyricism (exemplified in Vasco's expression of wonder at the beauties of the 'unknown land' in Act IV, no. 15, 'Pays merveilleux') and the opera's overall conservatism, combined with its glorification of the imperial theme, account for its success. A reason for the opera's eventual decline may lie in its being perceived as somewhat overweight, a quality increasingly found in nineteenth-century grand opera. Meyerbeer's operas also fell victim to the increasingly hysterical nationalism and anti-semitism of the period (the composer was both German and Jewish, and was singled out for special opprobrium, for example by d'Indy). Wagner also covertly attacked the older composer in his essay *Das Judentum in der Musik* (*Jews in Music*) (1850, reprinted 1869).

The 1870s

Delibes's ballet *Coppélia*, based on one of the short stories of the nineteenth-century writer E. T. A. Hoffmann, was premiered at the Opéra in 1870. This was his first success, and has become a classic thanks to its energetic, colourful and melodically distinctive score. Ballet, perhaps even more than opera, frequently relied on costume and sets to create effects, the music often being relegated to providing a suitably neutral background to the dance movements. The most distinguished dance music of the nineteenth century had often appeared in operas such as Daniel Auber's *La muette de Portici* (1828), where the tarantella of Act III set new standards in providing colour and liveliness that matched the dance.[11] The score of *Coppélia* equals that of the best opera dances, and Delibes's work in this area had enormous influence on composers such as Tchaikovsky. *Coppélia* has also been held to have marked the halt in the decline of French ballet which had been noticeable since the death in 1863 of the dancer Emma Livry, the successor to Marie Taglioni. Delibes showed a concern to establish character through musical means which had been largely absent in previous ballet scores. For example, the distinctive rhythm of the double-dotted motif applied in canon which heralds the entry of both the mechanical doll Coppélia and her sinister master Coppélius in Act I (Example 2.2) becomes more relaxed as she becomes more natural in Act II. Delibes's success in the genre was sealed by the production in 1876 of his second masterpiece, *Sylvia*, which further developed the application of motif to character.

Example 2.2 Léo Delibes, *Coppélia*, Coppélia's motive, Act I

A composer of the period whose ballets have not held the stage is Ernest Guiraud. His one-act ballet *Le Kobold* (Opéra-Comique, 1870) was closed by the outbreak of the Franco-Prussian war. Another, enticingly entitled *Gretna-Green*, was performed at the Opéra in 1874, though this also appears not to have made a lasting mark. Guiraud frequently had a poor response to his operas, though his *opéra-comique Piccolino* (Opéra-Comique, 1876) had some success. He is now best known for his role as Debussy's teacher and for his completion of other composers' works. He had been due to complete Delibes's *Kassya* (Opéra-Comique, 1893), but instead this was orchestrated by Massenet following Guiraud's death. Ironically, Guiraud's last opera, *Frédégonde* (Opéra, 1895) was completed after his death by Saint-Saëns and Dukas. Even this accolade did not ensure its success.

Much of the appeal of Bizet's *Djamileh* (Opéra-Comique, 1872), like *L'Africaine*, lay in its exotic location. However, while the former opera involved a huge cast, with a plot that spans continents, the latter takes place within the narrow confines of a classic exotic setting, the harem. There was a long history of the representation of harems in French opera as well as in art and literature. The appeal to European male fantasies concerning the domination of women is clear in *Djamileh*, as in many similar works; another blatant example in the exotic genre is formed by the servant-courtesans of Massenet's *Hérodiade* (1881). *Djamileh* is based on a variant of the *Scheherazade* story, in which the eponymous heroine pleads for the continued love of her owner, Haroun, with eventual success. In this version, however, she faces only rejection rather than execution as a result of his fickleness. Although the libretto lacks the element of action which Bizet was so adept at depicting, the music looks forward in significant ways, not least in the use of themes

11 Ballet scores of similar distinction of this period include Hérold's *La fille mal gardée* (1828) and Adam's *Giselle* (1841).

associated with character, and the modest use of through-composition in some numbers. These factors, along with Bizet's characteristically daring harmony at moments of particular emotional tension, probably contributed to the work's failure. The critic Moreno accused Bizet of an 'absence of tonality'.[12] The kind of music which elicited such comment is shown in Example 2.3, which accompanies Djamileh's dance, *L'almée*. Bizet, like Meyerbeer in *L'Africaine*, here makes use of low wind timbres (in this case the cor anglais). The melody mixes major and minor modes, and its sinuous shape and syncopated bass pedal points are key indicators of exoticism. Théodore Dubois (1837–1924), later better known for his compositional treatises, had more success with his *opéra-comique La guzla de l'émir*, produced at the Théâtre de l'Athénée in the following year, though the music was much less colourful and was written as a string of set-pieces.

Example 2.3 Georges Bizet, *Djamileh*, Introduction to No. 7

Another exotic work produced at the Opéra-Comique in 1872 was Saint-Saëns's early work *La princesse jaune*, also a one-act *opéra-comique*, this time with a Japanese subject. The plot underlines the essentially fictive nature of orientalism by making the Japanese element entirely a figment of the hero's imagination. Significantly, in view of the customary attitudes of the time to non-Europeans, the Japanese *princesse* of the title turns out to be merely a figurine, and the hero comes to his senses and returns to his true (European) love. The pentatonic scale is used extensively to create the Japanese

12 In *Le ménestrel*. Quoted in W. Dean: *Bizet* (London, 1975), 98.

Example 2.4 Camille Saint-Saëns, *La princesse jaune*, offstage chorus

atmosphere: as the hero experiences his hallucinatory vision of Japan, for example, he is accompanied by an offstage chorus singing a unison pentatonic melody to Japanese words. A further exotic effect here is the somewhat original idea of an accompaniment of offstage bells sounding throughout the chorus, a timbre which looks forward to Debussy and Ravel (Example 2.4). A now lesser-known example of a similarly exotic *opéra-comique* is Charles Lecocq's *Les cent vierges*, also given in Paris in 1872, although it had been premiered two months previously in Brussels. Lecocq (1832–1918), though now little known, rivalled Offenbach in popularity in the 1870s as a composer of comic operas. Several of his works were performed in England, where, along with those of Offenbach, they influenced Arthur Sullivan. *Les cent vierges* speedily became one of the most successful comic operas of the period, with hundreds of performances worldwide. The mildly risqué plot concerns a boat-load of women sent to assist in populating an English colony on a tropical isle; mistakenly detained on board as the ship leaves are two (French) bourgeois wives, the comedy being provided by the anguished pursuit of their husbands.

Carmen (Opéra-Comique, 1875), based (at the suggestion of the composer) on the novel by Prosper Mérimée (first published in 1845 but later revised with an extra chapter on gypsies), eventually became one of the most popular operas ever produced, but ironically is hardly ever heard in the version first intended by Bizet. The still frequently performed recitatives, added by Guiraud after Bizet's death, remove a great deal of the pacing and character of the original and erase many pertinent details in the dialogue.

Contemporary criticism focused on the content, which was seen as being alien to the 'sweet and moral tradition' of the *opéra-comique* genre, and the music, which was held to be confusing and, in the case of Carmen and Escamillo, vulgar.[13] The unrepentant nature of Carmen accounts for the former reaction, though for at least one critic the ending (which includes her onstage murder) was considered 'grand', rather than the challenge to convention which it undoubtedly was.[14] A comment from the same critic that the score was 'perhaps a little diffuse' probably refers to the through-composed element, developed from *Djamileh*, noticeable in the extended duets of Acts I, II and IV, though it may also refer to the mixture of styles, ranging from oriental pastiche to Gounod-like arias. It is significant that at the premiere 'numbers' such as the Toreador's song of Act II were applauded.

Carmen may also be seen as an exotic opera. Despite the popular view of the work, the opera is not 'authentically Spanish' in any sense. Bizet made use of some Spanish devices, but he consciously avoided direct quotation. The exotic fingerprints used in the opera, such as scales with flattened second, characteristic rhythms, drones instead of moving harmony and instruments associated with 'local colour' such as tambour de basque and castanets, had already appeared in works dating back to Grétry's *La caravane du Caire* of 1783. Melodic concision and unification of themes are further developed in the opera, the intensely concentrated nature of which is perfectly suited to their use. The use of a cell of intervals of the perfect fourth and its subdivisions, the second and third, occurs frequently, and is adapted to very different musical and emotional effects (Example 2.5). Its most memorable manifestation is as the motif associated with Fate, death and Carmen herself, which appears throughout the opera. Its simplicity ensures that it always has a powerful impact, nowhere more so than at its stunning reiterations at the end of the work. Less intense music, indebted to Bizet's mentor Gounod, appears where it is suited to character, for example in Micaëla's 'Je dis que rien' of Act III. The orchestration of the score had enormous influence on a wide range of composers, from Tchaikovsky and Chabrier to Strauss. The opera was not revived in Paris until 1883, when it began to establish itself in France, but by 1876 it had appeared in Vienna, London and Brussels and its success elsewhere was assured.

In addition to its memorable tunefulness, its vivid use of local colour, and its success in bringing characters to life, which must account for its popularity with audiences, the opera also provides an extremely fertile field for recent criticism of various kinds. Susan McClary, for example, has presented a feminist reading of the opera which has raised the hackles of those who prefer to focus specifically on the music, or who see the opera as purely a psychologically realistic study of human nature. While some aspects of McClary's reading now appear over-simplified in their polarizations of class and gender, she does draw attention to the political and cultural context of the opera, especially with regard to its attitude to women. The opera can be read as mirroring the patriarchal misogyny of the society of which it is a product, and which it can also be seen to challenge. As McClary has pointed out, the removal of the novel's distancing device of the narrator allows Carmen to appear to speak for herself, emphasizing her dissenting voice and her effect on the dominant male world around her.[15] The opera undermines bourgeois constructions of love,

13 Paul Bernard, writing in the *RGM*, 7 Mar. 1875, 73.

14 Ibid., 74. The quote which follows is from the same page.

15 See S. McClary: *Georges Bizet: Carmen* (Cambridge, 1992), 20–21.

Example 2.5 Georges Bizet, *Carmen*, motives

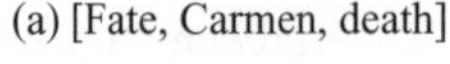

Act I

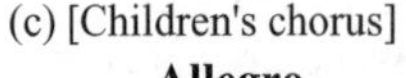

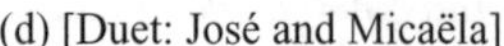

Act II

(e) [Entry of Escamillo]

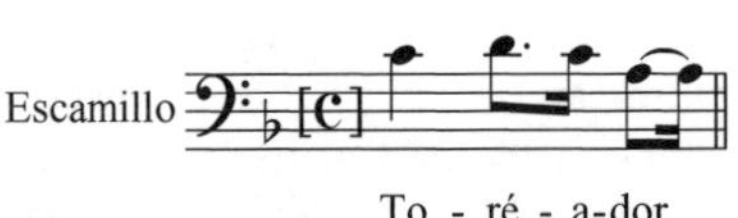

(f) [Carmen's dance-song]

showing desire contained by conventional society through violent suppression (José's murder of Carmen, which will lead to his own death) or sublimation (Micaëla's self-sacrifice).

Three now little-known composers had operas produced in 1876, one being Victorin de Joncières (1839–1903), whose opera *Dmitri* appeared at the Gaîté. While the composer was known as one of Wagner's disciples, the opera, in common with most French productions of its period, owes more to French and Italian influences. Although it was praised by critics, the work was not a success; Joncières followed it with *La reine Berthe*, which managed only five performances at the Opéra in 1878. Another was Auguste Mermet (1810–89), whose opera *Jeanne d'Arc* appeared at the Opéra. More obviously modelled on earlier French grand opera, the failure of Mermet's work is taken to indicate the end of Meyerbeer's dominance of the French stage although, as we have seen, Meyerbeer's works themselves continued to be widely performed into the twentieth century. A third was Victor Massé (1822–84), whose opera *Paul et Virginie* appeared at the Opéra National Lyrique. The opera is derived from the once enormously popular novel by Bernardin de Saint-Pierre, published in 1787, which is set in Mauritius and deals with the perennial French theme of the 'noble savage'. It had little success; a later opera, *Une nuit de Cléopâtre* (Opéra-Comique, 1885), was also speedily forgotten. Like many of the now lesser-known French composers of the period, Massé was more successful in a lighter vein.

Another operatic casualty was Gounod, whose later operas, *Cinq Mars* (from the novel by de Vigny, Opéra-Comique, 1887), *Polyeucte* (Paris Opéra, 1878) and especially *Le tribut de Zamora* (Paris Opéra, 1881) were all greeted with less than enthusiasm. Criticisms of the last contained veiled hints that the composer should give up operatic composition, advice which he appears to have taken as he produced no more before his death in 1893. However, Gounod himself was still regarded as a leading composer, and his two most successful operas, *Faust* (Théâtre Lyrique, 1859) and *Roméo et Juliette* (Théâtre Lyrique, 1867), continued to hold the stage and to provide a benchmark against which new compositions were judged. Gounod's melodic gift had always been valued, though partisans of Meyerbeer tended to regard his dramatic passages as more effective. Supporters, on the other hand, argued that Gounod's contribution had been to show how French opera could be freed from foreign influences. In this regard it is strange to reflect that, at its first performance, Gounod's grand opera *La reine de Saba* (Paris Opéra, 1862) was seen as Wagnerian, such was the paranoia following the performances of *Tannhäuser* the previous year.

Among other operas produced in 1877 were Massenet's grand opera *Le roi de Lahore* at the Paris Opéra, Chabrier's *L'étoile* at the Théâtre des Bouffes-Parisiens, and Saint-Saëns's *Samson et Dalila* at Weimar. All three composers have undergone some long-overdue reassessment in recent years. Massenet in particular was the major French opera composer of the last quarter of the nineteenth century, with a sustained record of success: several of his works still hold the stage. One of the reasons for this, his frequently astute assessment of his audience's tastes, was also one of the causes of his lack of favour after his death. However, few of his successes came easily, many of his best works only gaining acceptance gradually. Chabrier, now rightly seen as a force in his own right rather than merely a quirky forerunner of Debussy, showed in his operas a wealth of original and striking musical ideas, though fewer of his works are still staged. Saint-Saëns's operatic works are surprisingly large in number, given that only *Samson et Dalila* is now widely known. While showing himself perhaps to be less adaptable to changing tastes and less skilled in theatrical craft than Massenet, and less original than Chabrier in his staged works, Saint-Saëns's operas are by no means an insignificant part of his output.

Contemporary criticism of *Le roi de Lahore* was very positive, hailing the 'young and sympathetic composer'[16] (though this was not Massenet's first performed work – the *opéras-comiques La grand'tante* and *Don César de Bazan* had appeared at the Opéra-comique in 1867 and 1872 respectively). Significantly, and typically for an opera of this kind, critics especially praised the sets, costumes and dances. Massenet's dance music was a particularly successful part of his otherwise somewhat uneven output, thanks to his command of lyrical melody, energetic rhythm and colourful orchestration.[17] The plot of *Le roi de Lahore* resembles several earlier exotic works, in particular Auber's *Le dieu et la bayadère* (1830), and follows a long tradition of French interest in the exotic potential of India. The music is clearly influenced by Gounod in the melodic passages, and by Meyerbeer in the more bombastic choruses. The combination evidently pleased one critic, who exclaimed that 'in France, we love audacity'.[18] The irony of this remark is increased

16 *RGM*, 29 Apr. 1877, 132.

17 Massenet makes notable use of the saxophone in *Le roi de Lahore, Hérodiade* and *Werther*.

18 Paul Bernard, *RGM*, 6 May 1877, 137.

by the fact that it was penned by the same critic who had found *Carmen* too diffuse a few years earlier. Despite its success, a change of management at the Opéra led to the opera's withdrawal in 1880.

Chabrier's *L'étoile* followed from his uncompleted previous essays in the farcical genre, *Fisch-Ton-Kan* and *Vaucochard et fils 1er*, which date from the Second Empire period. Like these works, *L'étoile* follows the tradition of much *opéra-bouffe* in ridiculing those in power and, like them, it had some of its libretto written by the poet Paul Verlaine, a friend of the composer. Musical parody – in this case of Offenbach and Donizetti – was a staple of this style, and something of which Chabrier was a master. His immaculate sense of timing, evident in many of his works, made him particularly suited to *opéra-bouffe*. The critic H. Lavoix was impressed by this first completed opera, writing positively about Chabrier's future. Nevertheless, Lavoix noted, 'the phrase is often too contorted, and the scenes badly cut', an illustration of the difficulties facing innovative composers during the period.[19]

Saint-Saëns's *Samson et Dalila* is one of the many works whose production in France was delayed by the obstructive attitudes of the Paris Opéra (a mark of the conservative nature of the management was that the opera was not performed there until 1892). Like many operas of the period, the work used a mixture of styles. Some early criticism noted the composer's debt to Wagner, comparing the duet between Samson and Delilah with that in Act II of *Tristan*, although remarking that it is 'less long, but very developed'.[20] The use of 'typical motives' was noted, though one critic was relieved to find that the influence did not extend to the imitation of Wagner's melody, rhythm or orchestration.[21] The set-pieces in the score had their expected success, with 'Mon cœur s'ouvre à ta voix' marked down early as 'a capital episode'.[22] Saint-Saëns's more original use of baroque pastiche was not commented upon, though it plays a large part in the music for the chorus of Israelites who sing several fugati in Handelian style. Earlier Western traditions are drawn upon for the music of the Israelite elders, who have a chant-like melody in Act I, scene v. This is contrasted with the markedly exotic music given to the Philistines, which is particularly noticeable in Act III. In addition to the modal melody, low winds, drone basses and repeated rhythms already noted in similar situations in Bizet's *Djamileh*, Saint-Saëns uses a variety of percussion to add to the exotic effect: glockenspiel, wood and metal castanets, and crotales. Ralph P. Locke has noted how the music given to these groups reinforces the notion that the noble, God-fearing and ultimately victorious Hebrews stand in for the West in the opera, while the decadent and eventually conquered Philistines represent the Orient[23] (a similar apportionment of musical characteristics is meted out to the Trojans and the Nubians in Berlioz's *Les Troyens*). In this regard both operas reflect typical concerns of the exotic: to reinforce the superiority of the West, in part by reducing the musical characteristics recognized as 'Oriental' to a number of handy signifiers which interrelate, creating a widely-understood representation of an inferior 'other' which can be easily evoked.

---

19 *RGM*, 2 Dec. 1877, 378.
20 *RGM*, 9 Dec. 1877, 388.
21 Ibid.
22 Ibid.
23 See R. P. Locke: 'Constructing the oriental "other": Saint-Saëns's *Samson et Dalila*', *Cambridge Opera Journal*, 3/3 (1991), 266.

The year 1879 saw the production in Lyon of Saint-Saëns's next opera, *Étienne Marcel*. It tells of popular unrest in fourteenth-century Paris. An increasing emphasis on the construction and reinforcement of national identity is evident in the opera, perhaps because the composer was concerned to have an opportunity to deal with a subject drawn from French history. It testifies further to Saint-Saëns's interest in music of the past, including pastiches of period dances in the *divertissement*.

The 1880s

Offenbach's last work, the *opéra-comique Les contes d'Hoffmann*, was produced at the Opéra-Comique in 1881, the year after the composer's death. As in the case of Meyerbeer's *L'Africaine*, the opera has definitely not been bequeathed to us as the composer left it. Guiraud added the orchestration, the recitatives and some numbers in Acts IV and V. The opera is of notable scope, being much more ambitious than Offenbach's normal fare. It also has an unusual structure, consisting, in Acts II–IV, of three variations on the basic theme outlined in Act I, namely the poet's struggle between the ideal and the real. The more maudlin elements, such as the ending where a drunk Hoffmann is left alone with only his art to console him, are offset by the rhythmic vitality of the score and the dramatic quality of the music for Act III in particular. Contemporary critics were struck by the range of this act, seeing it as an addition to the composer's style.[24]

The trio in Act III, where the portrait of the heroine Antonia's dead mother comes to life while the sinister Dr Miracle plays furiously on the violin, gains some of its intensity through three repetitions of the main melody, each time a step higher. The final version takes Antonia up to a top C, the 'note Eiffel' that kills her, while Dr Miracle gloats over her imminent demise. The structures used in individual numbers are the more customary and conservative self-enclosed solos, ensembles and choruses, rather than through-composed. Nevertheless, they are mostly in ABA' form. The notion of varied repeat is thus apparent in the music as well as the plot. Georges Hüe (1858–1948), who had studied the organ with Franck, had his *opéra-comique Les pantins* ('The Jumping Jacks') produced at the Opéra-Comique the same year to great acclaim.

Massenet's *Hérodiade* was produced in Brussels in 1881 (despite his earlier success with *Le roi de Lahore*, *Hérodiade* had been rejected by the Paris Opéra the previous year). In this work Massenet had the benefit of a good libretto (adapted from Flaubert) which suited his talent for what d'Indy disapprovingly described as 'l'érotisme discret et quasi-religieux' (though d'Indy was ignoring the traditional link between eroticism and religion dating back at least to the sexually-charged songs of Hildegard of Bingen). The libretto included grand opera elements of turmoil in public affairs to match that in the private lives of the characters. The resulting portentousness, noted in the choruses of *Le roi de Lahore*, was here countered by the love interest and religious element. Massenet used certain themes associated with characters or situations, though typically for the composer these tend to be flexibly applied. An example is the telling melodic parallel between Salomé's celebrated paean to the Baptist, 'Il est doux, il est bon', and Hérod's outburst of frustrated

24 See A. Jacobshagen (ed.): *Jacques Offenbach: 'Les contes d'Hoffmann'. Dossier de presse parisienne* (1881) no. vii in *Critiques de l'opéra français du XIXème siècle* (Heilbronn, 1995).

Example 2.6 Jules Massenet, *Hérodiade*, melodic parallels

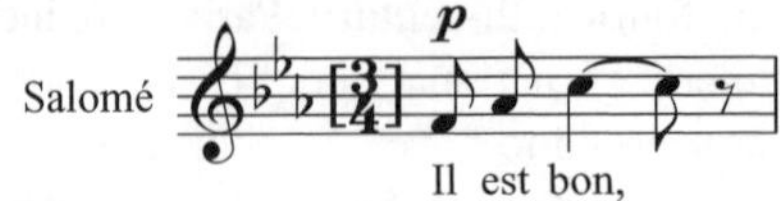

desire for her later in Act I (Example 2.6). These and the similar melodic shapes elsewhere in these arias serve to link the feelings of the characters in subtle ways, suggesting by musical means that Salomé's passion for the Baptist has as much of a destructive potential as Hérod's for her. Much of the harmonic and melodic style derives from earlier composers, most notably Gounod. This undoubtedly contributed to Massenet's success in the conservative atmosphere of the period.

Lalo's ballet *Namouna* was produced at the Opéra in 1882, as compensation by the management for the refusal by the institution of his opera *Le roi d'Ys* in 1879. Adapted from an exotic poem by de Musset, the ballet depicts the rivalry of two brothers for the love of the slave-girl of the title. The music reveals Lalo's command of rhythm in particular, along with a certain melodic angularity which often makes the mood more savage than is customary in French exotic music. The use of low wind timbres, the mixture of major and minor modes, and the employment of drones and persistent rhythms (often as cross-rhythms), may reveal the influence of Bizet's *Djamileh*. Typically for an exotic work, Lalo employed styles from various locations, for example by using the habanera rhythm. The large orchestra includes notably active parts for percussion and timpani, which occasionally play melodically. Unison writing is another exotic fingerprint. The tendency of ballet as a whole to be episodic is notable, and probably accounts in part for its success as it conforms so readily with the French tastes of the time in this respect.

The year 1883 saw the production of Delibes's *Lakmé* at the Opéra-Comique and of Saint-Saëns's grand opera *Henry VIII* at the Opéra. *Lakmé* speedily became one of the most successful exotic operas, with hundreds of performances in France and elsewhere. This can be attributed partly to the setting and plot, both of which had proved their efficacy in earlier works in the genre. The music, while showing the influence of earlier composers, represents the variety of European and oriental elements to great effect in the most popular numbers. The use of the supertonic major chord in Lakmé's prayer to the Gods from Act I is a typical means of creating the modal feel particularly associated with its Indian setting, while the accompaniment illustrates the increasing use of the harp as a vehicle for exotic atmosphere (Example 2.7). The melodic contours, rhythms, accompaniment and layout are, however, strongly reminiscent of Leïla's invocation to Brahma in Act I of Bizet's *Les pêcheurs de perles* (1863).

Many aspects of the opera nevertheless show a new approach to the exotic. Unlike *Les pêcheurs de perles* or *Le roi de Lahore*, *Lakmé* involves both Europeans and Indians in a colonial setting, and depicts an interracial love match. As a result of the power relation

Example 2.7 Léo Delibes, *Lakmé*, Lakmé's entry in Act I

between the rulers and ruled, the threat of miscegeny is here more of an issue than in previous works where it may be a possibility, such as *L'Africaine* or even Spontini's *Fernand Cortez*. Attitudes to interracial relationships were changing during the period, with the apparently liberal attitudes generated by the Enlightenment being replaced by those which emphasized irreconcilable differences between rigidly defined races. *Lakmé* is based on Pierre Loti's *Rarahu* (1880), a novel which encapsulates this new approach to race in its tale of a naval officer who settles down with, then abandons, a Tahitian woman, in his search for new impressions in a life blighted by cynicism. Apart from shifting the locale to India and giving the character of the cynic to the hero's friend Frédéric, the opera softens the tale by making the heroine sacrifice herself when she realizes her English lover Gerald can never be hers (in a scene reminiscent of that in Act II of *Carmen*, his attention is drawn by the sound of an offstage military band when he should be attending to her attractions). The similarity between the concepts of race in Loti, *Lakmé* and the doctrines of Renan and Gobineau mentioned earlier are striking. The return of the hero to his approved racial sphere, both in terms of his affections and his duty, is firmly enforced.

Parallel to the developing interest in the exotic throughout the period lay an increased fascination with European historical themes. Saint-Saëns's *Henry VIII*, commissioned by the Opéra, and first given in 1883, originally consisted of four acts and six tableaux. In the 1889 revival it was pared down to three acts, on the instruction of the opera management.

Such demands were frequently made. Saint-Saëns refused to make the cuts demanded of him, so the entire third act was cut instead. *Henry VIII* became the composer's next most popular opera after *Samson et Dalila*. His use of some folk melodies in Act II (such as 'The Miller of Dee') to provide exotic colouring parallels his custom in earlier works (we should remember that, for the French, even England was exotic, which perhaps also explains the English colonial setting in *Lakmé*). The composer's use of a contemporary theme – which he found in a manuscript in the Buckingham Palace library – is a further illustration of his interest not only in music of the past, but also in 'authenticity' (in the sense of returning to 'pure' origins). Saint-Saëns describes how he removed 'thickets of pointless ornamentation' from the melody, thereby revealing its essential nature. In this 'purified' form, he records that it 'supplied ... the framework of the opera'.[25] The idea that a melody could be purified in this way, and that it could in this form act as a stable basis for a larger structure, parallels the search for the essential underlying nature of the French in the culture of the period.

The composer and critic Ernest Reyer (1823–1909) was a friend of both Berlioz and the poet Théophile Gautier, who had supplied the texts for some of his earlier works on oriental themes. His *Sigurd* (Brussels, 1884), however, has frequently been cited as a work thoroughly suffused with the spirit of Wagner. This is true as regards the plot, which resembles that of *Götterdämmerung* (Bayreuth, 1876) and is drawn from the same Germanic myths, though it seems certain that when Reyer was composing the work in the 1860s he was not aware of this planned addition to the *Ring* cycle. Moreover, certain characteristics long associated with French narrative, such as an emphasis on chivalry, prevent it being a straightforward copy. There are links between earlier opera plots and that of *Sigurd*, such as the final ascent of Sigurd and Brunehild to paradise, which finds a parallel in *Le roi de Lahore*. Nevertheless such a source for opera was new to French sensibilities, and its elevated tone repudiates comparisons with Massenet's work. Hints of Wagner appear in the use of through-composition, with little reference to the tradition of the self-contained number. Melodically, the use of repeated motifs also recalls Wagner, especially when these are used to comment ironically on the action. An example is the motif associated with Sigurd's rescue of Brunehild, which reappears when Gunther, having deceived both of them, claims her hand (Example 2.8).

Example 2.8 Ernest Reyer, *Sigurd*, motives

Massenet's *Manon* (Opéra-Comique, 1884), despite being in five acts, moves away from the grand-opera style of his previous two operas towards the often more sentimental world of *opéra-comique*. It became his most popular work, surviving its temporary exclusion

25 Quoted in J. Harding: *Saint-Saëns and his circle* (London, 1965), 162.

from the Opéra-Comique in 1886. Based on the famous novel by Antoine-François Prévost (1731) detailing the stormy relationship between the young, idealistic Chevalier des Grieux and his equally young but worldly lover Manon Lescaut, the opera gave Massenet another opportunity to write a part for an overtly erotic female character. The music draws on eighteenth-century style for local colour. The composer was proud of his use of a recurrent motif in the work, which he considered helped to render the characters distinctly. However, his use of repeated motifs at the end of the opera is more a referral back to earlier highlights than a genuine symphonic technique. A cautious link with the procedures of Wagner was also reflected in the opera's overall through-composed nature, the composer's flexible treatment of recitative being one of the most striking features of the score. However, Massenet was frequently an expert judge of how much his audiences could take in the way of innovation, and his allegiance to the set-piece format remained clear. His success in presenting a sensual element associated with his female characters is particularly noticeable in Act III, scene ii, where Manon rekindles des Grieux's passion for her as he is about to enter holy orders with the suggestive music of 'N'est-ce plus ma main'. Here, Manon flaunts her sexual attraction with decorative melodic lines, chromatically-altered variants of the simpler figure with which she opened the number, and the coquettish grace note as she speaks her name, while the harmony reflects her suppleness through the use of second-inversion chords and added sevenths. Des Grieux responds initially with a chant-like single note over firm root-position harmony, but as his resolve evaporates the harmony inverts and he is drawn into the downward melodic shape of some of Manon's earlier utterances (Example 2.9).

Le Cid, produced the following year at the Opéra, marked a return by Massenet to his former territory, grand opera. The scenes of ceremony, centred on a cathedral, make use of effects such as bells and organ, a technique which had also been used by Saint-Saëns in similar circumstances in his *Étienne Marcel* (1879). The ballet music from the customary Act II *divertissement* is commonly regarded as the most successful section of the opera, and is still frequently performed.

Of the operas appearing in 1886, Chabrier's *Gwendoline*, first given at the Théâtre de la Monnaie in Brussels, is now the best known and most significant. At the time, however, the now little-known Émile Paladilhe (1844–1926), lover of the celebrated singer Célestine Galli-Marié (who had created the role of Carmen in 1875), had far more success with his opera *Patrie!* (Paris Opéra), probably in part because it was strongly influenced by Gounod and Meyerbeer. The opera, which was Paladilhe's first success, was performed frequently at the Opéra and elsewhere until 1918.

The influence of Wagner on Chabrier's *Gwendoline* is more apparent than real, but has been frequently commented upon, often as a stick with which to beat the composer. Certain influences closely associated with Wagner are apparent, such as the use of leitmotifs and chromatic harmony, but these lie alongside more general ones increasingly used by many French composers not associated with Wagner, such as through-composition and librettos based on myths. The duet for the Danish hero, Harald, and the Saxon heroine, Gwendoline, is reminiscent of the love duet in *Tristan und Isolde*, which Chabrier had heard at Munich in 1880 (Example 2.10). A number of motifs are used throughout, transformed and combined in Wagnerian style. However, the score is more suggestive and eclectic than a mere Wagnerian imitation, and is full of effects, sonorities and harmonies which influenced many French composers, among them Debussy and Ravel. Examples are

Example 2.9 Jules Massenet, *Manon*, Act III, 2nd tableau – Le parloir du séminaire de St Sulpice

the harmonic excursion before the return of the simple folk melody sung by Gwendoline in the spinning scene, and the whole-tone scale in the trumpets in the final battle scene, which looks forward to Debussy in particular (Example 2.11).

The following year Chabrier's last completed opera, *Le roi malgré lui*, was produced at the Opéra-Comique. It has parallels with *L'étoile*, such as the *opéra-bouffe* atmosphere of fun and satire, aimed at both the ruling elite and other composers (Meyerbeer, Berlioz and Offenbach in particular). Satie was particularly impressed by the opera. On the other hand, Chabrier's uncompleted opera, *Briséïs*, the first act of which was performed at the Opéra in 1899, has more of a Wagnerian theme and manner. Both scores illustrate Chabrier's incomparable richness of invention in melody, harmony and orchestration.

Alfred Bruneau's *Kérim* (Château d'eau) also appeared in 1887. This exotic opera was the composer's first success but, like his later works, it has not held the stage. Bruneau is now best known for his lengthy collaboration with Émile Zola on a number of operatic adaptations of the latter's novels, for some of which Zola himself supplied the librettos.

Example 2.10 Emmanuel Chabrier, *Gwendoline*, Act II, love duet

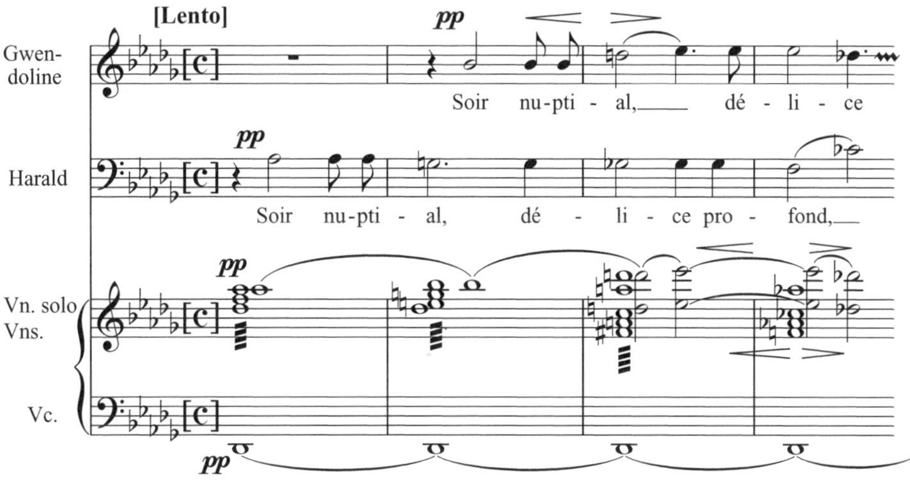

Example 2.11 Emmanuel Chabrier, *Gwendoline*, final battle scene

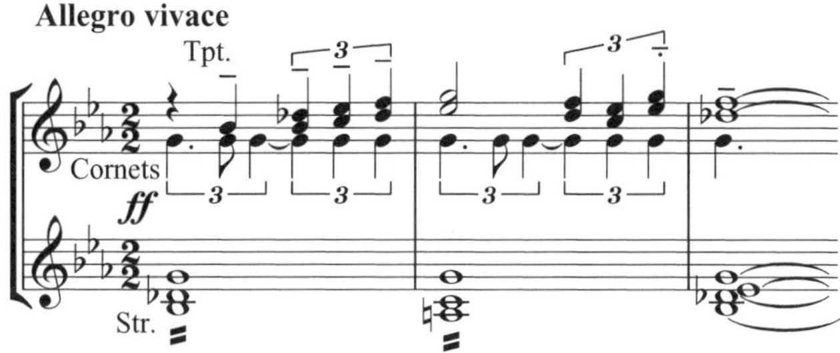

The early success of some of these works was partly due to their adherence to the musical and thematic preoccupations of the moment; as tastes changed, so Bruneau's operas fell out of favour. Later, Bruneau suffered for his passionate support for Zola's political views during the Dreyfus controversy, as a result of which public opinion turned against him. *Kérim* shows both the grand-opera influence of Gounod and that of Bruneau's teacher, Massenet, and makes use of typically colourful orchestration. An early sign of Bruneau's later concern with naturalism appears in his use of folk melodies, in this context oriental. Unusually, Bruneau derived the harmonies accompanying these from the melodies themselves. This ran counter to the practice frequently followed by composers such as Félicien David and Saint-Saëns, who tended either to add Western harmonies to their exotic material or avoid the problem by using drone basses. David (1810–76), once hailed as a great composer by Berlioz for his most famous exotic work *Le désert* (1844) but less regarded since his death, is now increasingly recognized as a significant figure in the development of musical orientalism. He was one of the first to use 'authentic' (or at least, authentic-sounding) melodies in his exotic works. His oriental opera *Lalla-Roukh* (1862) was extremely influential, not least in its expansion of exotic effects in the use of percussion and orchestral colour.

Lalo's *Le roi d'Ys* (1888, Opéra-Comique) had been revised by the composer in 1886 following its refusal by the Opéra (mentioned earlier) and the Opéra National Lyrique (1878). The plot concerns the unrequited love of the heroine Margared, her betrayal of her father's semi-mythical kingdom to the enemy (an inundation by the sea is prevented by supernatural intervention), and her eventual suicide through remorse. Margared is one of the less-usual mezzo heroines in the repertoire. The opera had some success, though it became embroiled in the increasingly hostile attitude of critics and others to the perceived influence of Wagner. Lalo's indebtedness is mainly apparent in the orchestration of the opera, and he avoids the use of thematic development. The French influence is shown above all in the inclusion of a set-piece Breton wedding complete with folk songs (which had been sung to the composer by his Breton wife, for whom the role of Margared was intended). Lalo's last stage works (a pantomime, *Néron*, Hippodrome, 1891, and *La jacquerie*, of which only one act was completed) were unsuccessful.

Massenet's *Esclarmonde* (1889, Opéra-Comique), a magic, exotic opera with a truly ancient plot concerning a sorceress's pursuit of the French hero Roland, lends itself to some of the grandiose effects familiar from several of Massenet's earlier works. The heroine is given spectacular coloratura passages, in the manner of many opera villains such as the Queen of the Night. The use of vocalise, associated here with Esclarmonde, is common in exotic works, and acts as a reminder of 'otherness'. In this trope, the Westerner is depicted as a rational, articulate being, while his inferior opposite has animal instincts and lacks speech.

The Exposition Universelle of 1889 illustrates the political nature of much spectacle and its potential to misrepresent its subject in support of a particular argument. This Exposition was marked by many spectacular events, in particular the exotic exhibits which were popular at successive exhibitions. The music accompanying these had a major impact on French composers. Such exhibits frequently drew on imperial themes and were ideologically inspired, rather than accurate depictions of native life.[26] In common with many others, the exhibits noted by Debussy at the 1889 exposition were subtly manipulated in order to present a particular view of their subjects. The Annamite theatre productions, for example, were based on traditional legends but had been much condensed for Western consumption. The performers in fact came from Cochin-China (present-day South Vietnam) and adopted the identity of Annamites for the purposes of the Exhibition.[27]

The 1890s

Reyer's five-act grand opera *Salammbô* (1890, Théâtre de la Monnaie, Brussels) is based on Flaubert's novel and was planned, like *Sigurd*, in the 1860s. Flaubert had originally wanted Verdi to write the opera, but asked Reyer to do so after Verdi declined. The opera was a success, cementing Reyer's position as one of France's major opera composers. Lucien Solvay wrote that the opera was 'worthy in all respects of the composer of *Sigurd*' and 'a success for all concerned', but deliberated on the question of whether or not it was

26 See E. Hobsbawm: *The Age of Empire 1875–1914* (London, 1995), 80.

27 For details of the theatre performances, see A. Devriès: 'Les musiques d'extrême-orient à l'Exposition universelle de 1889', *Cahiers Debussy, Nouvelle série* No 1 (1977), 25–37.

Wagnerian, deciding (obviously with relief) that on balance it was not.[28] As in Reyer's earlier works, the influence of Berlioz can be felt in the opera. Like the section of *Les Troyens* which had been performed in 1863, the opera is set in Carthage. Despite the periodic appearance of spectral voices, the tale has a classic, unsentimental theme of betrayal redeemed by self-sacrifice. Of monumental size, dense complexity and extravagant spectacle, the opera concerns a rebellion against their Carthaginian masters by a huge chorus of mercenaries. The refusal of payment after their latest victory prompts their leader, Matho, to steal the sacred veil of the Goddess Tanit from its shrine, where Tanit is served by the priestess Salammbô. She vows to win it back but wavers when she falls for Matho. A surprise attack by the Carthaginians led by Salammbô's father, Hamilcar, leads to the slaughter of the mercenaries. Ordered to take Matho's life, Salammbô instead takes her own. Matho joins her in death, thus fulfilling the prophecy that 'all who touch the sacred veil must die'.[29] The large orchestra is frequently used in a varied and imaginative way, for example at the beginning of Act II where the horns are joined by strings and harps playing light ascending scales, while bassoons and double bass play drones, in an atmospheric evocation of night. Reyer makes use of two principal motifs, one a descending melodic minor scale which sets the sombre tone at the opening and reappears at moments connected with the veil. The opera, while falling into recognisable sections, has a strongly continuous momentum. Reyer frequently varies the phrase length, and uses a wide range of percussion instruments including the tam-tam which announces Salammbô's appearance in Act II. A typically colourful touch is the onstage band of piccolos, clarinet, brass, tambourine, triangle and cymbal which accompanies the entry of the Carthaginian paymaster Giscon in Act I.

Saint-Saëns's *Ascanio* was also produced in 1890, at the Opéra. It was another of the composer's operas to be based on French history. Though it concerns an episode in the life of the sculptor Benvenuto Cellini, it is set in Paris. The story is similar to that of Berlioz's work (Paris Opéra, 1838, where it was set in Italy), but *Ascanio* avoided direct comparisons by leaving out the scene of the casting of the statue. The opera was not well received. Like *Henry VIII*, it contains a *divertissement* (here set at Fontainebleau) which draws for one of the dances upon a contemporary theme, taken from the French cleric and author Thoinot Arbeau's famous dance manual *Orchésographie* (1588). Here Saint-Saëns's search for pure origins finds its natural sphere in a French source.

Bruneau's *Le rêve* (Opéra-Comique, 1891) shows the continued influence of Massenet, not least in the treatment of the source for the work. The scientific novel of the same title (*The Dream*) by Zola, offered to Bruneau by the author shortly after they met in 1888 (the work was published the same year), which (typically for the time) had explored the effects of environment on a girl of dissolute inheritance, was transformed into a quasi-erotic religious fable, in which form it had great success. Bruneau makes use of the cathedral setting to portray realistically the sound of organ, bells and choir as Saint-Saëns and Massenet had done in *Étienne Marcel* and *Le Cid*, thus pointing the way to his future development. However, Steven Huebner has shown how the religious music is also frequently used in a more mythical manner as a way of revealing and exploring the heroine

28 See *Le ménestrel*, 16 Feb. 1890, 49–51.

29 E. Reyer: *Salammbô* (Paris, 1892), 697.

Angélique's state of mind as she falls for the hero Félicien, particularly through that staple of French opera, the offstage chorus.[30]

Notwithstanding the more supernatural elements of the opera, Bruneau broke new ground by presenting characters on stage in modern-day dress, a feature he was to take further in *Messidor*. As had been the case in the reception of Reyer's *Salammbô*, the question of the extent of Wagner's influence preoccupied contemporary criticism of the work. This was a particularly pertinent query, since 1891 was the year of the serious riots aroused by the performances of *Lohengrin* at the Paris Opéra, the first Wagner opera to be staged there for thirty years. Arthur Pougin expressed several of the negative attitudes of the time concerning Wagner, noting that Bruneau 'presses to their most extreme limit the purest Wagnerian traditions', though he also regrets that the composer has not, in compensation for this, adopted Wagner's 'incomparable orchestration'. He illustrates the longevity of the French taste for the set-piece format by remarking sadly 'that one looks in vain … for the shadow or appearance of a *morceau*'.[31] Oddly, Pougin does not mention the modernist harmony which characterizes the score, such as the use of parallel augmented chords.

Also in 1891, Massenet's grand opera *Le mage* failed at the Opéra, and another opera project, *Amadis*, was also abandoned, marking a temporary crisis in the composer's career. His next opera, *Werther*, although it had been completed by 1887, appeared at the Vienna Hofoper only in 1892, having been turned down by the Opéra-Comique in 1887, and again shelved in 1889 in favour of *Esclarmonde*. *Werther*'s success in Vienna, which followed on the heels of *Manon* at the same venue, led to its adoption by the Opéra-Comique in 1893, but its popularity became sustained only after 1903. The opera is based on Goethe's epistolary novel *Die Leiden des jungen Werthers* (1774). Despite the similarity of period of the opera to that of *Manon*, Massenet avoided the repetition of devices. He responded more powerfully to the tone of the libretto, avoiding pastiche and creating a darker emotional atmosphere through, for example, the emphasis on lower wind and brass in the orchestra. He also wrote the heroine, Charlotte, as a mezzo role. The opera avoids the grand effects associated with many of his other works, and trims the chorus down to only six children's voices. His use of recurring motives develops more subtlety in the opera, though the structure is reminiscent of *Manon* as it remains faithful to the set-piece format, albeit with Massenet's by now familiarly flexible recitative. A feature in the unfolding of the tragedy is the juxtaposition of dramatically contrasting elements, for example the voices of children celebrating Christmas at the moment when Charlotte laments Werther's suicide in Act IV (Example 2.12).

The year 1891 also saw the production of an exotic opera with a less-usual Russian subject, *Thamara* (Paris Opéra), by Louis Bourgault-Ducoudray (1840–1910), better known as an influential professor of music history at the Conservatoire. The opera was apparently admired by Debussy, and was successful enough to be revived in a revised version in 1907. Bourgault-Ducoudray followed it in 1892 with *Anne de Bretagne* (Nantes), which included folk elements.

---

30 See S. Huebner: 'Naturalism and supernaturalism in Alfred Bruneau's *Le Rêve*', *Cambridge Opera Journal*, 11/1 (1999), 77–101.

31 In *Le ménestrel*, 21 June 1891, 195. The original French of the first quote reads: 'pousse à leur point le plus extrême les plus pures traditions wagnériennes'.

Example 2.12 Jules Massenet, *Werther*, children's voices, Act IV

Bruneau's *L'attaque du moulin* (Opéra-Comique, 1893) and *Messidor* (Opéra, 1897) mark the composer's move into 'realism'. Both are based on novels by Zola. The earlier opera is the more 'realistic' of the two, and has a particularly violent plot, recounting an episode in the Franco-Prussian war. This gave the composer the opportunity to include realistic military effects such as bugle calls. *Messidor* is notable for the inclusion of symbolist elements, all the more telling as Zola himself supplied the libretto for the opera. Bruneau and Zola were further linked during this period by their vociferous support for the revolutionary ideals of the Republic which were seen to be endangered by the Dreyfus Affair, and for which the composer eventually became the official musical spokesman. Bruneau's avowed intention in the operas was to create a third way for French opera between what he saw as the opportunistic Wagnerian pastiche of works such as d'Indy's *Fervaal* and the gross brutality of the Italian *verismo* school (Mascagni's *Cavalleria rusticana* had been premiered in Paris at the Opéra-Comique in 1892).[32] However, this did

32 For more on this argument, see Huebner: 'Naturalism and supernaturalism', especially 81–2.

not mean the rejection of Wagner, but rather the adaptation of his ideas to what Bruneau saw as the 'essential national qualities of French art'.[33]

André Messager is now best known as the musical director of the Opéra-Comique at the time of the premiere of Debussy's *Pélleas et Mélisande*. In the 1880s and 1890s he had some success as a composer of ballets and *opéras-comiques* such as *Les deux pigeons* (1886) and *La Basoche* (Opéra-Comique, 1890). His most successful work was the brilliant *opérette Les p'tites Michu* (Théâtre des Bouffes-Parisiens, 1897). (The previous two titles do not easily translate, though *The Low-Brow* might capture the pejorative aspect of the first.) His larger-scale works were less successful. One of these, *Madame Chrysanthème* (Théâtre de la Renaissance, 1893), was based on a novel of the same title by Pierre Loti (later also used as the source for Puccini's *Madame Butterfly* (Milan, 1904)). Like Loti's earlier purportedly autobiographical novel *Rarahu*, *Madame Chrysanthème* describes Loti's visit to a foreign country, his relationship with a native woman, and his abandonment of her on his return to his native land. In the novel, Loti treats Chrysanthème with amused contempt, referring to her constantly as either an animal, toy or doll. His only moment of self-doubt is as he leaves, when he notices that Chrysanthème is contentedly humming a tune, concerned only to make sure that the coins with which he has paid her are genuine. In Messager's opera, there is a hint that she will die after her abandonment, like Lakmé.

Nevertheless, the opera retains the attitude to the Japanese which marks the novel. The go-between and procurer of women for European men is seen as the principal source of comedy. Even his name, Monsieur Kangourou, is intentionally ridiculous, and reinforces the equation of the Japanese with animals. The characterization centres on Kangourou's hybrid nature, drawing attention to the way in which he operates between two cultures (by speaking pidgin French and dressing in imitation of Westerners, for example). The roots of the comedy lie in the attitude that there cannot be any genuine point of contact between the races. Nations are viewed not as parts of a wider human family but as separate species.

Furthermore, racial intermingling is deplored as it leads to a reduction in the exotic charm of the unfamiliar. The opera makes this clear from the opening, which is set on board the French naval vessel in which the hero, Pierre, is travelling to Japan. In addition to depicting the slow rolling movement of the ship, the chromatic opening chords, heard over a pedal note, also establish the dream-like character of the hero's destination. The influence of Bizet and Delibes is plain here, also possibly the early music of Debussy (Example 2.13). Further examples of the influence of Delibes can be seen in the music for Monsieur Kangourou, whose hectic pace of delivery and frequent changes of time-signature mirror the style of comic numbers in the composer's earlier *Le roi l'a dit* (Opéra-Comique, 1873) and *Jean de Nivelle* (Opéra-Comique, 1880).

However, there are some more complex areas in Messager's opera which reveal further differences from *Madame Butterfly*. In *Madame Chrysanthème* the market scene of Act I and the festival scene of Act III display characteristics of frenetic energy and kaleidoscopic change of mood which undermine the often complacent tone of the Europeans. This contrasts strongly with the mainly internal world of *Madame Butterfly*, where the Japanese are seen to be less in control of events. The alternation of acts set in

33 Quoted ibid., 82.

Example 2.13 André Messager, *Madame Chrysanthème*, Prélude

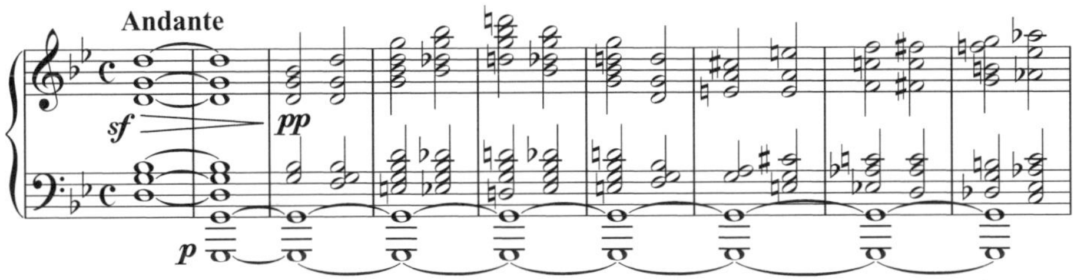

public and private spaces in Messager's work adds another dimension to the experience of Japan related by the opera, forcibly reminding the listener of the existence of a teeming world which is ultimately beyond the control of Europeans. Here the opera transcends its origins in the novel, which is principally concerned with the narrow sphere bounded by Chrysanthème's garden fence, within which the European hero reigns supreme. Further, the inability of European males to have full control over the inner life of the subject country (represented in the opera by Pierre's doubts over Chrysanthème's fidelity) could be seen to cast doubt over their continued domination over its external features. There is a significant contrast between Pierre's inability to comprehend and master Chrysanthème and Pinkerton's complete dominance and possession of Butterfly. While superficially more sympathetic to the plight of colonized peoples than Messager's work, Puccini's opera is revealed by this contrast to be less potentially subversive in its treatment of the Japanese.

Benjamin Godard's *opéra-comique La vivandière* was completed by Paul Vidal (1863–1931), a friend of Debussy and pupil of Massenet, who was a conductor at the Paris Opéra (he directed the first performance of Chabrier's *Gwendoline*), and was performed in the Théâtre de la Monnaie in Brussels, 1893. It was as much of a success as his grand operas had been failures. After its Paris premiere in 1895, the work had more than eighty performances before 1900. Vidal's own three-act *fantaisie-lyrique Éros*, produced at the Théâtre des Bouffes-Parisiens in 1892, was one of his most successful operas.

It is often forgotten that César Franck composed operas as well as being an organist. His *Hulda* (Monte Carlo, 1894) was premiered after his death, and was his first opera to be performed (another large-scale opera, *Ghisèle*, had been orchestrated by several of his students including d'Indy and Chausson, and was performed at Monte Carlo in 1896). *Hulda* exists in two versions, a number of cuts having been introduced in the second version in an attempt to make the opera more dramatic. The story, set in Norway, concerns the tangled emotions of the heroine of the title, whose lover is killed by an enemy from a rival clan. She falls for the victor, but connives at his murder after she finds him in the arms of her rival, Swanhilde. Filled with despair, she leaps into the sea.

As a result of the cuts, the end of the opera lost one of its finest moments when a chorus of spectral voices, accompanied by four saxophones, beckons Hulda to her watery fate. The influence of Wagner is clear, both in the writing for brass and also in the love duets (the plot allows for two) which are strongly reminiscent of *Tristan und Isolde* (Example 2.14). Franck's seriousness of expression and characteristic chromatic harmony is also clear in his writing. In the second version, Act IV included self-contained ballets in the traditional grand opera manner.

Example 2.14 César Franck, *Hulda*, Act IV

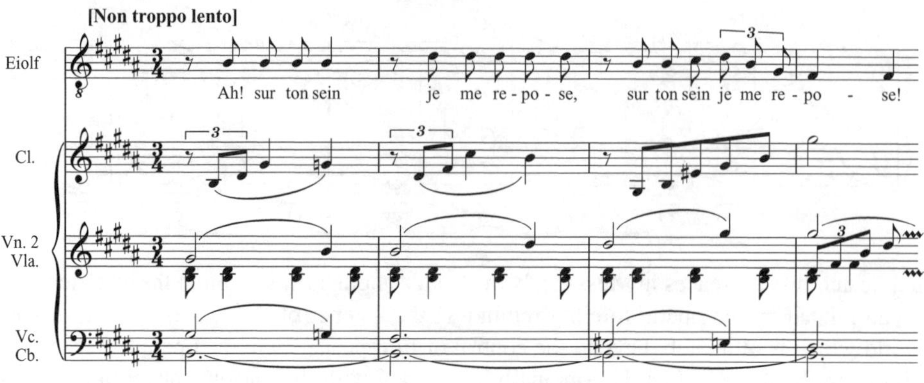

Massenet's *Thaïs* (Paris Opéra, 1894) marked his return to a more familiar scenario, style, scale and mood after the intensity of *Werther*. The opera is based on a searingly anti-clerical text by Anatole France (published as a novel in 1890), though much of the social criticism is lost in the translation onto the stage. The opera tells of a courtesan (Thaïs) who discovers religion and dies in the odour of sanctity. Her story is paralleled by that of an anchorite (Athanaël) whose admission of his physical yearnings leads to his loss of faith. It intersects with the themes of sex, death and religion which run through Massenet's music from the time of his oratorio *Marie-Magdeleine* (1873). The production, which was adapted for performance at the Opéra at a late stage, drew on the resources of spectacle associated with *Le roi de Lahore*. As in the case of the earlier opera, the costumes were particularly celebrated. These features tend to make the spectacle more important than any social comment. The music that Massenet composed for the ballet in Act II and the Oasis scene in Act III in a revision of 1897 underline the exotic content, and also show how little oriental representation had changed in fifty years. The music that evokes the desert in the latter scene is reminiscent of similar moments in Félicien David's *Le désert*, while some of the ballet music recalls, in a milder version, that of Bizet's *Djamileh* (Example 2.15). The reliance on set-pieces is notable in the opera, the most famous being the richly ornamental and wide-ranging 'Méditation' that illustrates Thaïs's conversion. Like many of Massenet's works, the opera became securely popular only several years after its first performance.

Massenet's second première of 1894, *La Navarraise* (Covent Garden), was an earthy exercise in *vérisme*. The composer attempted with some success to exploit the popularity of the style epitomized by *Cavalleria rusticana*, and drew on the emphasis on violence in this opera as well as on its concise dimensions. The melodramatic plot of *La Navarraise* describes a very unlikely scenario, set in the Spanish Carlist wars in 1874, which involves the heroine in the murder of a rebel leader to gain the money to marry her loyalist lover. The lover imagines she has betrayed him, and the story ends with his death and her descent into madness. The realist mode employed by Massenet relies on the military background for the majority of its effects.

Later works by Massenet included *Sapho* (Opéra-Comique, 1897), a 'sung play' which is also in realist style, and *Cendrillon* (Opéra-Comique, 1899) in which the fairy-tale

Example 2.15 Jules Massenet, *Thaïs*, Act II ballet

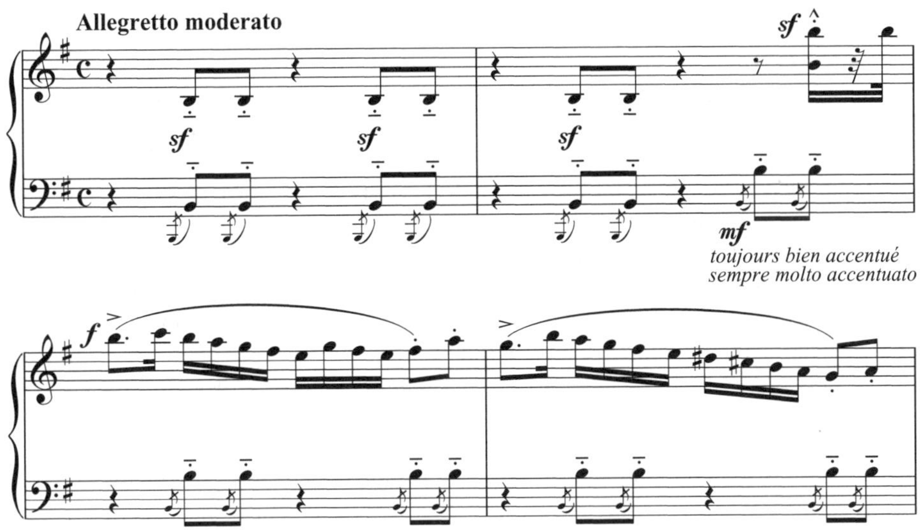

element is captured in glittering music owing a debt to Mendelssohn, for example in the staccato chordal horn writing when the Fairy Godmother warns Cinderella that she must return at midnight in Act I. Humorous touches are supplied by the treatment of the Ugly Sisters, whose fond hopes that they will make a beautiful appearance at the ball are commented on sardonically by the accompaniment of solo timpani. The large and imaginatively varied orchestra includes an array of percussion instruments, both wood and metal; its use greatly extends the normal range of effects in a work of this kind. For example, a harmonium accompanies the offstage chorus of spirits in Act III, and a dance that follows is exquisitely scored for harmonium, celesta, harps, chimes, flutes and oboes. Not surprisingly, the opera is still performed.

Augusta Holmès (1847–1903) is worthy of note as one of the few female composers of the period to have her operas produced. The prevailing notions of the time concerning women also led contemporaries to remark on her gender, particularly as she was an extremely attractive woman, beloved by composers from Saint-Saëns (whose offer of marriage she refused) to Vincent d'Indy and her teacher César Franck. Her four-act opera *La montagne noire* (Paris Opéra), set in Montenegro and dealing with its seventeenth-century struggle for independence from Turkey, is one of several operas by now lesser-known composers to appear in 1895. It was not a success, but some critics were too gallant to say so. One, writing in *L'illustration*, commended the work's 'charm, grace and tenderness', significantly adding 'in a word, all the instinctive gifts of the female'.[34] The expressive music for Yamina, a Turkish dancer who provides the hero with the requisite conflict between his affections and his patriotism, was particularly commended. Arthur Pougin also dwelt on the composer's personal attractions, but summoned up enough distance from his subject to criticize the dramatic writing, which was seen as 'simply noisy', with the music swamped by the over-importance of the

34 *L'illustration*, 16 Feb. 1895, 139.

orchestra.[35] Criticisms such as these were commonly aimed at those who, like Holmès, were known to be supporters of Wagner though, like that of most other French devotees, the music is not by any means a complete imitation.

D'Indy's *Fervaal* (Théâtre de la Monnaie, Brussels, 1897) was immediately received as evoking Wagner's name. This was almost inevitable for the period, particularly in view of d'Indy's well-known veneration for the master which had been apparent since their first meeting in 1873. Like Holmès, d'Indy followed Wagner in writing his own libretto. The plot, which has a strong racial element and concerns the triumph of Christianity over paganism, has parallels with *Parsifal* (Bayreuth, 1882), while the hero's struggles with the Saracen heroine Ghuilen are reminiscent of those between faith and seduction in *Tannhäuser* (Dresden, 1845). D'Indy made use of the symphonic technique of employing different tonal centres to distinguish sections of the work. Another symphonic feature is the treatment of motifs, one of which is finally transfigured at the end of the opera and marked in the score as the 'theme of love' (Example 2.16). Nevertheless, d'Indy was far from attempting the opportunistic Wagnerian pastiche of which Bruneau unfairly accused him.[36] Despite their opposing views on the Dreyfus Affair, the Republic and the history of French music (which both rewrote to suit their political arguments), d'Indy and Bruneau equally saw in Wagner's ideas a means to find a form of opera that would articulate national aspirations.

Example 2.16 Vincent d'Indy, *Fervaal*

'Theme of Love'

Accompaniment: rushing contrary motion scales in harps, arpeggios in clarinets. Trills in flute, oboe and horns

Reynaldo Hahn (1874–1947), born in Venezuela but brought up in France, had a critical success with his first opera, *L'île du rêve* (Opéra-Comique, 1897), which shows its debt to Massenet, who was Hahn's teacher. It is significant as another French opera to be based on a novel by the doyen of exotic writers of the period, Pierre Loti. The source is *Rarahu*, here retaining its original locale. One change is that Loti himself appears as a character, cutting a much more sympathetic figure on stage than he did in the book (this was, perhaps, not unconnected with the fact that Loti was one of the librettists). The dreamy nature of Tahiti, the island of the title, is conveyed through the use of slow tempi and harmonic excursion, often to the subdominant. A Tahitian song is used as local colour (Example 2.17). Common features of exotic works which are also noticeable here include the equation made between the natives and their flora – the heroine, Mahénu, is compared specifically by the island princess to a plant – and the depiction of the exotic country almost entirely in terms of its women. The only Tahitian male to appear is the aged

35 *Le ménestrel*, 10 Feb. 1895, 43.

36 In Bruneau's *Musiques d'hier et de demain*, quoted in Huebner: 'Naturalism and supernaturalism', 81.

Example 2.17 Reynaldo Hahn, *L'île du rêve*, use of Tahitian song

Chœur lointain et chantant fort.
À l'aise, mais pas trop lent. (Avec une certaine langueur)
Ti hi u - ra té - ié I - te va - i to - é to - é

stepfather of the heroine; while a male chorus sing the native song, they sing offstage. This concentration on the exotic female has the effect of eroticizing the relationship between the colonizer and the colonized. As Tsvetan Todorov remarks, 'the visitor loves the foreign country as the man loves the woman, and vice versa'.[37] This equation is consistently made throughout the history of exotic representation, and acts powerfully as a metaphor for colonial rule.

Conclusion

The taste of the French public for spectacle was as strong at the end of the century as it had been at the time of Berlioz's death. The display of sets and costumes reflected the opulent wealth of the era, as can be seen by the lavish productions of operas such as *Thaïs*. The work also illustrates how ballet was still routinely considered an indispensable part of opera, as well as an entertainment on its own account. The opportunity for the variety of spectacle presented by opera made it still the dominant genre for composers and audiences, and the one in which composers still hoped to excel.

The expectations of operas had changed somewhat over the period, with a certain level of through-composition and the use of motif tolerated by audiences. However, the set-piece was still the most popular format, as *Thaïs* again shows. Many of the successes of the last years of the century were comic operas or farces. While most of these have now vanished from the repertoire, they testify to the enduring popularity of light music, in particular dance-inspired music of all kinds.

The influence of Wagner remained strong in turn-of-the-century opera, although it was about to receive some serious shocks. Composers tended to use Wagner's ideas as an model of how they might achieve a national style of their own along similar lines. D'Indy and Bruneau both took this view, even though they were on different sides of a serious political divide. The composers of lighter works were naturally more able to ignore the influence of Wagner, as they had a lengthy and specifically French tradition of their own on which to draw. The composer who was able to bend Wagner's procedures most to his will was, perhaps, Massenet. While he tended to focus on certain issues, Massenet ranged widely through different styles and genres, and he was the only major French composer of the period to have serious successes with both lighter as well as more weighty works.

Nationalism remained a dominant force in the cultural life of France. The disturbances surrounding the performances of Wagner's operas in the capital declined somewhat after their peak in 1891 (in the provinces they did not present problems), and by the end of the

37 See Todorov: *Of Human Diversity*, 314.

Plate 2.2 Meyrianne Heglon as Myrtale and Jeanne Marcy as Crobyle in the premiere of Massenet's *Thaïs* with Albert Alvarez as Nicias.

century most had been premiered there. Nevertheless, the influence of Wagner was still contentious; the right-wing group Action Française condemned d'Indy's adherence to Wagner, though it approved all his other views.[38] The search for purity of origins in the operas of Saint-Saëns among others forms a powerful metaphor for the focus on racial purity of the period. The concentration on folk elements, noticeable in many operas and ballets of the period, also reflects nationalist concerns. The virulence of anti-semitism at the end of the century is illustrated by the decline in popularity of Bruneau's operas, due to his support for Dreyfus.

The example of Massenet's *Thaïs* illustrates the enduring popularity of the exotic in French opera of the period, although this needs to be placed alongside the many and varied subjects of other operas, such as those based on historical themes. As with the influence of Wagner, the nature of exoticism in music was to change as composers moved away from the application of external devices long associated with it, such as percussion instruments and modal scales, towards a more profound engagement with native musical material. As we have seen, the way forward had already been explored somewhat by Bruneau in his radical approach to the harmonization of oriental melodies in *Kérim*, and further exploration of potentially explosive issues such the relationship between pitch and duration was to follow shortly in instrumental music such as Debussy's *Pagodes*. However, the emphasis on spectacle in nineteenth-century opera in general did not lend itself to subtleties of approach with regard to the exotic or, indeed, to anything else. As in the example of *Thaïs*, the method that most successfully evoked the exotic for audiences at the turn of the century was often the most obvious.

The institutions of the French theatre ended the century with more distinction than they had possessed in 1869. Even the Paris Opéra was beginning to open up to a slightly wider repertoire of modern works, particularly with the 1897 premiere of Bruneau's *Messidor*. The Opéra-Comique remained the driving force in modern opera in the capital, with an extraordinarily long record of distinguished premieres of a great variety of works. The appointment to the directorship of Albert Carré in 1898 ushered in an even more daring phase of experiment, as was to be seen shortly thereafter. Provincial theatres had often led the way in approaching works which caused contention in the capital, as we have seen; the list of Wagner premieres in France, while often taking place in the 1890s, reveals how much ahead of Paris such opera houses as those of Nice, Rouen and Lille could be.

The nature of opera itself had changed by the end of the century. Landmark works such as *Carmen* had already expanded the boundaries of the possible in *opéra-comique*, and by 1900 the old distinctions between subject matter of the various operatic genres were mainly redundant. The grand opera genre perhaps resisted change more than any of the others, as the example of *Thaïs* again shows. The development of a greater emphasis on continuity in musical styles had also contributed to the merging of genres. Recitative was no longer a distinguishing mark of *opéra*, and spoken dialogue was more rarely heard. Massenet had perhaps done more than any other composer to promote this flexibility, with *Werther* in particular standing out as prophetic of a new style of setting the French language.

---

38 See Fulcher: 'Vincent d'Indy's "Drame anti-Juif"', 299.

Suggested Further Reading

D. Charlton: 'Romanticism (1830–1890)', in G. Abraham (ed.): The *New Oxford History of Music* (Oxford: Oxford University Press, 1990), Vol. IX.

—: *The Cambridge Companion to Grand Opera* (Cambridge: Cambridge University Press, 2003).

W. Dean: *Bizet* (London: Dent, 1975).

A. Devriès, A.: 'Les musiques d'extrême-orient à l'Exposition universelle de 1889', *Cahiers Debussy, Nouvelle série* No. 1 (1977).

K. Ellis: *Music Criticism in nineteenth-century France* (Cambridge: Cambridge University Press, 1995).

J. Fulcher: 'Vincent d'Indy's "Drame anti-Juif" and its meaning in Paris, 1920', *Cambridge Opera Journal*, 2/3 (1990), 295–319.

—: 'The Concert as Political Propaganda in France and the Control of "Performative Context"', *MQ*, 82/1 (1998), 41–67.

—: *French cultural politics and music: from the Dreyfus Affair to the First World War* (New York and Oxford: Oxford University Press, 1999).

J. Harding: *Saint-Saëns and his circle* (London: Dent, 1965).

E. Hobsbawm: 'Mass-Producing Traditions: Europe, 1870-1914', in E. Hobsbawm and T. Ranger (eds.): *The Invention of Tradition* (Cambridge: Cambridge University Press, 1992).

—: *The Age of Empire 1875–1914* (London: Abacus, 1995).

S. Huebner: 'Naturalism and supernaturalism in Alfred Bruneau's *Le Rêve*', *Cambridge Opera Journal*, 11/1 (1999), 77–101.

—: *French opera at the fin-de-siècle: Wagnerism, nationalism and style* (New York and Oxford: Oxford University Press, 1999).

D. Irvine: *Massenet: a chronicle of his life and times* (Portland, Ore.: Amadeus Press, 1994).

A. Jacobshagen (ed.): *Jacques Offenbach: 'Les contes d'Hoffmann'. Dossier de presse parisienne (1881)* no. vii in *Critiques de l'opéra français du XIXème siècle* (Heilbronn: Lucie Galland, 1995).

H. Lacombe, *Les voies de l'opéra français au XIXe siècle* (Paris: Fayard, 1997).

R. Langham Smith (trans. and ed.): *Debussy on Music* (London: Secker & Warburg, 1977).

R. P. Locke: 'Constructing the oriental "other": Saint-Saëns's *Samson et Dalila*', *Cambridge Opera Journal*, 3/3 (1991), 261–302.

S. McClary: *Georges Bizet: Carmen* (Cambridge Opera Handbook) (Cambridge: Cambridge University Press, 1992).

B. Olivier: *J. Massenet: itinéraires pour un théâtre musical* (Arles: Actes Sud, 1996).

S. Studd: *Saint-Saëns: a critical biography* (London: Cygnus Arts, 1999).

A. Thomson: *Vincent d'Indy and his world* (Oxford: Clarendon Press, 1997).

T. Todorov: *Of Human Diversity*, trans. C. Porter (Cambridge, Mass: Harvard University Press, 1993).

N. Wild and D. Charlton: *Théâtre de l'Opéra-Comique de Paris, Repertoire 1762–1972* (Sprimont (Belgium), Mardaga, 2005).

Chapter 3

Nineteenth-Century Orchestral and Chamber Music

Timothy Jones

A culture of high-minded and ambitious instrumental music developed in Paris during the last three decades of the nineteenth century. At its heart was a repertoire of new French music whose best pieces were of European, not just local, significance. Many leading composers initially looked to models from the German canon (especially the orchestral and chamber music of Beethoven, Mendelssohn, Schumann, Liszt, and Wagner), and sought to assimilate their stylistic traits without losing the essentially French qualities of their own music. Towards the end of the century alternative sources of influence began to make an impact. The burgeoning historicism of European musical culture was reflected locally in a deepening interest in old French music; this in turn led some French composers to rethink the expressive vocabularies of their music, in particular the contrast between the austere harmonic language of much old music and the intense chromaticism that many of them had developed in the 1870s. Exotic sources also exerted a strong attraction: the rhythmic and timbral characteristics of Spanish folk music, the orchestral techniques of Russian and Eastern European composers, and the alien sounds of music from the Far East all suggested fruitful alternatives to Germanic influences. The many cross-currents that affected French instrumental music during this period sparked long-running debates in the French musical press. Two issues excited particular controversy: the pro-German tendencies of many French modernists; and the aesthetic legitimacy of programme music.

This chapter focuses primarily on the earlier phase of this history. It explores some of the ways in which the repertoire remained distinctively French, despite the strong Germanic influences that were initially felt in the 1870s and 1880s; it investigates some of the technical resources used by French composers during this period; it reviews the critical debates that surrounded instrumental music, and it evaluates the achievements and historical significance of the repertoire.

It has long been considered a historical truism that 1871 was a watershed in the history of French music. Fifty years later Fauré confessed that 'before 1870 I would never have dreamt of composing a sonata or a quartet. At that period there was no chance of a composer getting a hearing with works like that.'[1] And writing of the period before the Franco-Prussian war, Duparc complained: 'Young composers had no means of becoming known, not only to the general public, but even to a more limited public ... The only French artists who counted were Boieldieu, Auber, Hérold, Victor Massé, Adolphe Adam,

1 Interview in the *Petit parisien*, 28 Apr. 1922.

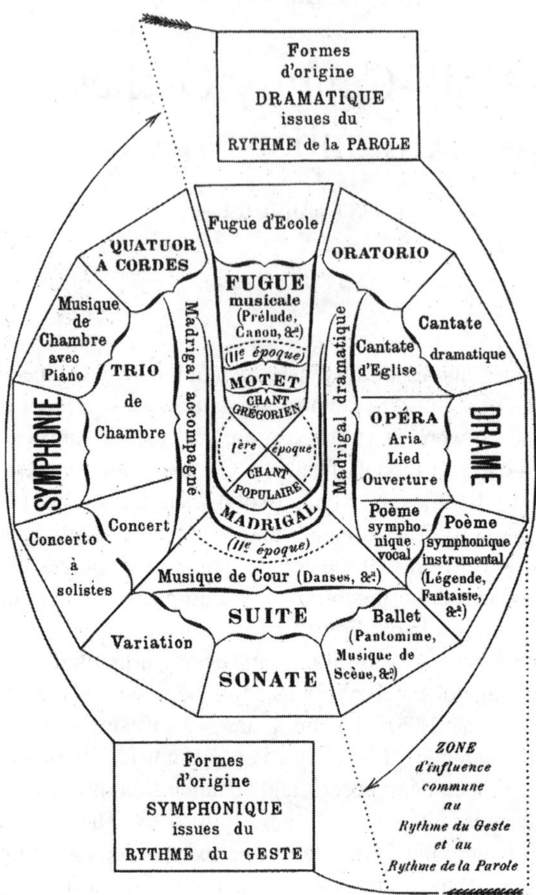

Plate 3.1 Classification of musical forms from d'Indy's *Cours de composition.*

In his *Cours de composition* (3rd edition, 1909, p. 13) d'Indy described this diagram as '[*une*] *sorte d'arbre généalogique*' [a type of family tree], intending the figure to be read both diachronically and synchronically.

Its diachronic aspect is embodied in the three concentric circles that represent the epochs governing d'Indy's historical account of musical genres: the central core contains the main genres before 1600; in the next circle are subsequent genres that flourished mostly in the seventeenth and early eighteenth centuries (though the presence in this section of opera, fugue, and the vocal symphonic poem obfuscates the periodic aspect of d'Indy's scheme). The outer circle takes the development one stage further to show the contemporary (late-nineteenth-century) state of play.

Read synchronically, the diagram represents an opposition between symphonic forms (genres ultimately based on the gestural rhythm of dance) and dramatic forms (based on textual rhythm ['*rythme de la parole*']). At one level this opposition seems relatively unproblematic: the dramatic forms are rooted in the more concrete aspects of musical representation associated with word setting, story-telling and enactment, while the symphonic forms are characterized by the purity of their freedom from the word. However, d'Indy's account of the origins of this bifurcation leads to seemingly paradoxical generic groupings. For example, since he believed that medieval popular song ('*chant populaire*') had emerged from dance music, d'Indy perceived the symphony, concerto and concerted chamber music to have arisen from an intermediate texted genre: the seventeenth-century '*madrigal accompagné*'. Conversely, he categorized fugue as a dramatic genre because it owed so much to technical processes developed in sixteenth-century polyphony. The liminal characteristics of the symphonic poem are signalled by its position in a 'zone of common gestural and textual influence', though it is noteworthy that d'Indy places it next to music drama and well away from the 'pure' symphonic genres.

The size of typeface used in the diagram's outer circle gives a clear sense of generic hierarchy. With his Wagnerian credentials, d'Indy inevitably placed the symphony and music drama at the pinnacle of their respective families, followed by the sonata, string quartet and oratorio. Given the wealth of first-rate French chamber music with piano in the late nineteenth century, it might seem surprising that d'Indy gave the quartet precedence over chamber music with piano; but this reflects his reverence for Beethoven and Franck, as well as his own compositional interests.

Maillart ... As for a French symphonic art, there wasn't one, nor was one possible'.[2] After 1871, the climate became more favourable for composers of serious instrumental music. As Serge Gut and Danièle Pistone have argued, the austere national mood after the defeat at Sedan in 1870 and the straitened economic circumstances that followed in the wake of the Prussian victory were to the advantage of chamber music.[3] In a mood of national introspection, and calls for political and cultural renewal, the highbrow mediums of chamber and symphonic music had a good chance of flourishing. In an atmosphere of patriotic fervour young French composers at last had more opportunities to secure performances of their instrumental works.

The new repertoire did not emerge from a musical vacuum. Although the artistic climate in Paris was not favourable to new French instrumental music before the 1870s, there was nonetheless a rich culture of orchestral and chamber music societies during the middle of the century. The Quatuor Dancla's thirty-two-year career stretched from 1838 to 1870; between 1848 and 1870 many new chamber music societies and quartets were founded, including the Société Alard-Franchomme (1848), the Société des derniers quatuors de Beethoven (1851), the Quatuor Armingaud (1856), the Quatuor Lamoureux (1860), and the Société de Musique Jacoby-Vuillaume (1864). In addition to that permanent fixture, the Société des concerts du conservatoire, there were several orchestral societies: the Société Sainte-Cécile, founded by François Seghers, lasted for five years (1849–54); the Concerts des jeunes auteurs was active in the late 1850s and early 1860s; and Jules Pasdeloup founded the Concerts populaires de musique classique in 1861. The repertoire of these organizations was primarily based on the Viennese classics, but it was not simply a musical museum culture. They also performed chamber and orchestral music by leading nineteenth-century German musicians, including quartets by Mendelssohn and Schumann, and orchestral music by Liszt and Wagner. The difficulty that young French composers faced in breaking into this magic circle did not result from a resistance to new music *per se*, but from the prevailing attitude that instrumental music was the province of German genius, and lyric drama the sole province of French.

After the war the number of societies devoted to instrumental music continued to increase, and there was a growing sympathy for home-grown repertoire. Two champions of new French music founded orchestras in Paris: Édouard Colonne established the Concert national in 1873, and Charles Lamoureux began his Concerts Lamoureux in 1881. New chamber music organizations included the Quatuor Sainte-Cécile (1875), the first all-female ensemble in Paris; the Société des instruments à vent (1879); the Société de musique française d'Édouard Nadoud (1880); and the Concerts modernes de Godard (1884).

The organization that most changed attitudes towards new instrumental music was undoubtedly the Société nationale de musique, founded in February 1871 by Saint-Saëns, Franck, Fauré, Duparc, Massenet, Guiraud, Taffanel, Dubois, Garcin, and Bussine. In the patriotic atmosphere of 1871, the society took the nationalist motto *Ars gallica*. Its aim was simply to privilege French music at the expense of the German repertoire that dominated other organizations. To this end, membership was restricted to French citizens,

2 Henri Duparc: 'Souvenirs de la Société Nationale', *La Revue musicale*, 8/12 (1 Dec. 1912), 2.

3 Serge Gut and Danièle Pistone: *La musique de chambre en France de 1870 à 1918* (Paris, 1978), 44.

and only French music was programmed. The first concert was given at the Maison Pleyel on 17 November 1871, followed by fifteen concerts in 1872, and from eight to twelve concerts a year thereafter. Economic considerations meant that the first two seasons consisted solely of chamber music, but from 1873 an annual subvention from the Ministère des beaux-arts allowed the Society to mount orchestral concerts as well. In the early years these were conducted by Édouard Colonne, though some composers directed premieres of their own works. The first orchestral concert took place at the Théâtre de l'Odéon, but in later seasons they were given at other venues, including the Salle Herz, the Salle Érard, the Cirque d'hiver, the Châtelet, and the Salle Pleyel. These concerts were well supported – the society grew from its initial fifty members in 1871 to a high of 358 in 1887 – but they were never popular in the true sense of the word: tickets were limited to members of the society and their guests, and they were not available to the general public.

Between 1871 and 1909 the Society gave the world or French premieres of 52 string quartets, 48 sonatas for piano and string instrument, 47 piano trios, and 17 piano quartets. Among the symphonic poems premiered were d'Indy's *Le camp de Wallenstein* (1880), Messager's *Loreley* (1883), Bruneau's *La belle au bois dormant* (1887), Franck's *Le chasseur maudit* (1883), Chausson's *Viviane* (1885), Debussy's *Prélude à l'après-midi d'un faune* (1894), and Dukas's *L'apprenti sorcier* (1897). A few significant works were premiered elsewhere: Saint-Saëns's Third Symphony by the Royal Philharmonic Society in London, Franck's Symphony by the Concerts du conservatoire, and Chabrier's *España* at the Lamoureux concerts.[4]

As Michael Strasser has argued, the Society's patriotic agenda was perfectly compatible with the interest many of its leading members took in the latest developments in German music.[5] There had long been a current of French opinion that contrasted the seriousness of German culture favourably with the cultural superficiality of the Second Empire. Even in the face of Prussian militarism, and after the defeat of 1870, many French intellectuals maintained their admiration for the enemy: had the defeat not demonstrated France's current weakness and shown how she could learn from her neighbour? In music, too, there was a natural tendency for composers interested in instrumental music to look to the example of the German classics as a means of renewing their own culture. Saint-Saëns wrote in overtly Darwinist terms about the need for French music to evolve in competition with the German canon: 'France needs a robust musical school, capable of trading blow for blow with foreign schools. Try as we may to ridicule Darwin's theories, the struggle for survival continues none the less, and the weak won't stop being eaten by the strong. Let us be strong or we will inevitably be devoured.'[6] Not everyone held the view that French music should look towards the German example to survive. Voices were raised in

4 The list of major instrumental works promoted by the Society is impressive, but it represents quite a small proportion of the Society's repertoire. Chamber music for strings (with or without piano) accounted for only 12%, and symphonic music 15%; as much as 41% of the programmes consisted of works for wind ensemble, organ, harp, and harmonium; see Michel Duchesneau: *L'avant-garde musicale à Paris de 1871 à 1939* (Paris, 1997), 15–33.

5 Michael Strasser, 'The Société nationale and its Adversaries: The Musical Politics of *L'Invasion germanique* in the 1870s', *Nineteenth-Century Music*, 24 (2001), 225–51.

6 Camille Saint-Saëns, 'A propos de Bayreuth', *L'Estafette*, 5 Sept. 1876; 'il faut à la France une école de musique robuste, capable de traiter de puissance à puissance avec les écoles étrangères.

warning against a musical 'invasion germanique' before the war, and after 1870 conservative critical opinion hardened against what was perceived to be the pernicious influence of Wagner and his followers.[7] There were several attempts to found alternative societies for the promotion of new French instrumental music during the 1870s, suggesting that not all French composers shared the pro-German tastes of Franck and his followers.[8] And this plurality also lies behind the factionalism that split the Société nationale itself in the mid- 1880s, when the issue of introducing foreign repertoire into the society's programmes merely crystallized a growing lack of sympathy between Saint-Saëns and the more strident pro-Germanism of Franck's followers.

It is, therefore, misleading to view the society's activities in narrowly nationalist terms. The historical significance of the Société nationale ultimately lies neither in the French nationalism of its initial aims, nor in the receptivity of its leading members to the musical style of the 'new German' school, but in its successful attempt to build and sustain a culture of indigenous, serious instrumental music in France.

What was meant by 'serious', as opposed to trivial, instrumental music? In a general sense it was related to the most highly valued genres in the canon: the sonata and its related genres such as the piano trio and quartet, the string quartet, and the symphony. 'Serious' music was expected to make exacting demands of executants and listeners, and to strive for high originality. But in nineteenth-century France there was also a more concrete concept of the aesthetic and technical basis of serious music. This idea was first articulated in the 1820s, but its ramifications were still felt in the decades after 1870.

In Volume 2 of his *Traité de haute composition musicale* (Paris, 1824), Anton Reicha described a contemporary decline in the musical tastes of the public. The reign of the charlatan had begun, and true art was neglected in favour of the instant gratification afforded by popular trivia. At the very moment when instrumental music had reached a peak of perfection in the works of the Viennese classical composers, its popularity had sown the seeds of its own destruction. For, with mass popularity, instrumental music had become a commodity and therefore subject to the vagaries of fashion:

> Unfortunately our ears gradually get used to bad music as well as good ... Composers who depend on public support sacrifice the interest of art to the desire to please the multitude. Moreover, the majority of musical compositions are nothing but fashionable goods which have only an ephemeral existence. It is again for this reason that the genres of music have become confused. The same approach – that of pleasing the public by whatever means – and the desire to charm everyone's ears, is now the norm of musical creation.[9]

On a beau tourner en ridicule les théories de Darwin, la lutte pour l'existence n'en continue pas moins son œuvre, les faibles ne cessent pas pour cela d'être dévorés par les forts. Soyons forts, ou nous serons infailliblement dévorés.'

7 For a detailed discussion of the anti-German position promoted by Léon Escudier and his circle, see Strasser: 'The Société nationale', 242–8.

8 For example, the foundation of *L'Harmonie française* in July 1872 by a group consisting largely of Conservatoire professors who were unsympathetic to the tastes of the leaders of the Société nationale.

9 Anton Reicha: *Traité de haute composition musicale* (Paris, 1824), 328; 'Malheureusement les oreilles s'habituent peu à peu à la mauvaise musique comme à la bonne ... Les compositeurs qui dépendent du publique, sacrifient l'intérêt de l'art au désir de plaire à la multitude. Aussi la plupart des productions musicales ne sont-elles que des marchandises de mode, qui n'ont qu'une existence éphémère. C'est par cette raison encore que tous LES GENRES de musique se

Reicha was pessimistic about an immediate remedy for this problem. The public wanted to be entertained by novelties, but the resources of what Reicha called *haute composition* were not sufficiently entertaining for the multitude, so they were abandoned by fashionable (and commercially successful) composers. Against the backdrop of this vicious circle, it was clear that the production of new masterpieces would be extremely rare. To create such a work a musician must not only have uncommon genius and a deep understanding of the art, but also a strong character, able to brave the brickbats of hostile critics and an uncomprehending public, and impervious to the attractions of material success.

For Reicha the art of *haute composition* is principally about the creation and development of individual musical ideas. In the *Traité* he gives seven basic methods of motivic development:

- by the transposition of phrases
- by progression (sequential development)
- by imitation that can sometimes become a canon
- by dialogue with two or three phrases
- by adding a countersubject in double counterpoint
- by varying the distribution and design of accompanying parts
- by changing the order of ideas or phrases.

In general he advises variety, but warns that the means of development must suit the nature of the musical ideas:

> ABRIDGE long ideas, LENGTHEN short ideas, MODULATE deftly and often, if possible ACCOMPANY ONE IDEA WITH ANOTHER, RUN an idea through the different parts: all these are in the spirit of development, provided they produce a good effect. True development is ultimately some combination or other of musical ideas. If you change the ideas you must change the development, otherwise modifying the resources or the means indicated above (which are always the same) by new combinations.[10]

Within this framework Reicha locates the masterpiece at the sublime end of the creative spectrum: it must be vast, with extraordinary combinations, and new, big ideas; it should be neither heard nor appreciated by the multitude, since it will be too far above their level of appreciation.[11]

As a diagnosis of musical culture, Reicha's discussion was as relevant in the 1860s as it had been in the 1820s.[12] Not only do the aims of the Société nationale amount to an

confondent; le même esprit, celui de satisfaire tout le monde, n'importe par quels moyens, et de FLATTER, n'importe quelles oreilles, préside à toutes les productions musicales.'

10 Ibid., 262. The capitalization is Reicha's: 'ABREGER les idées longues, ALLONGER les idées courtes, MODULER adroitement et souvent, ACCOMPAGNER UNE IDÉE PAR L'AUTRE (quand cela se peut), PROMENER une idée dans les différentes parties, tout cela est du ressort du développement, pourvu que l'on produise de l'effet. Enfin, le véritable développement est une combinaison quelconque des idées musicales. En changeant les idées, il faut changer le développement, en modifant autrement les ressources ou les moyens ci-dessus indiqués (qui sont toujours les mêmes) par de nouvelles combinaisons.'

11 Ibid., 328, footnote.

12 For instance, an anonymous critic wrote in *La France musicale*, 24/12 (18 Mar. 1860), 'At this

attempt to create an elite culture of *haute composition*, but the instrumental music of composers associated with the Société nationale is technically and aesthetically indebted to Reicha's concepts of *haute composition* and the musical masterpiece. The ideal that serious instrumental music should be about strong musical ideas developed in complex and imaginative ways in works of ample proportions was absolutely central to the progressive aesthetic climate of the 1870s. In particular, the close attention paid by these composers to techniques of motivic transformation, the combinatorial treatment of themes, and cyclic organization are remarkably close to Reicha's detailed precepts.

Writing in the 1820s, Reicha advised that the music of Haydn and Mozart was the best model for *haute composition*. For conservative critics and composers in the 1870s the Viennese classics were still the paragon of pure instrumental music, and they believed that inherently French musical characteristics could best be perpetuated by an adherence to classicism. But for many progressive French composers the best models of *haute composition* were by the modern German composers who had consolidated the canon: Beethoven, Schubert, Mendelssohn, Schumann, and – above all – Liszt and Wagner. They held the view that it was imperative to engage with the new styles of music emerging from Germany if French instrumental music was to be of any significance. It was, perhaps, not so much a question of imitating the Germans to become more French, as of assimilating at a deeper level their harmonic, textural and expressive vocabularies.

Inevitably, though, debates about the competing claims of conservatism and modernism became bound up with nationalist sentiment, and feelings ran high. The level of mutual intolerance was especially rancorous in the immediate aftermath of the war against Prussia, when the concept of a musical *invasion germanique* carried particular force. For example, Armande de Montgarde, writing in 1872, contrasted the authentic Frenchness of classical values with a revolutionary strand in French musical life which he associated with the supporters and imitators of Wagner. He argued that while conservative musicians respected 'the immutable laws of art' and were wise and honest, the revolutionaries revelled in music that was 'obscure', 'abstract', 'algebraic', 'either incomprehensible or grotesque': 'for them, music must either be an enigma or a grimace; a trigonometric formula or the prank of a hooligan'.[13] Carefully exonerating Wagner himself from any blame, Montgarde was scathing about French Wagnerians for whom there was no other music than Wagner's, comparing them to flies around an open wound.

Although its striking imagery is unusual, the basis on which Montgarde articulated the perceived contrasts between French and German musical ideals was common enough in more measured critical discourse at that time. Values identified as typically French included clarity of expression, form and technique; emphasis on melody; elegance, refinement and wit; lightness of texture; expressive decorum; and a classic sense of genre.[14] Modern German music, on the other hand, was usually characterized by an

---

time a composer of instrumental music must make a double sacrifice, the sacrifice of his popularity and the sacrifice of his fortune'.

13 Armande de Montgarde: 'Les Deux Courants', *L'art musicale*, 11/8 (22 Feb. 1872), 57–9.

14 These qualities are cited with remarkable consistency over a long period of time. In his survey of chamber music in vol. 2 of L. Rohozinsky (ed.): *Cinquante ans de la musique française: de 1874 à 1925* (Paris, 1926), Pierre Hermant asked: 'Faudrait-il croire ... qu'il y aurait une conception particulière, française, de l'art musical, s'opposant à celle des Allemands, par conséquence des qualités propres de notre race? L'élégance, le raffinement, l'esprit, l'ironie ou

obscurity (of expression, form and technique) essentially related to 'excessive' chromaticism; dense motivic work (*motivische Arbeit*) and 'difficult' counterpoint ('algébraique'); textural heaviness; lack of decorum in its emphasis on expressive extremes; and the mixing of different generic traits.

Yet for progressive French composers the contrast was not so clear-cut, and in their most successful instrumental music the leading figures accommodated the best of both traditions. While the chromatic harmony, motivic transformation and instrumental colour of this repertoire certainly owed something to German models, French composers used them in ways that are found in no German music from the period.

The assimilation of German models, together with the aesthetics and techniques of *haute composition*, is especially clear in the chamber music of composers associated with the Société nationale. Although these composers had highly individual musical languages, there was nevertheless a remarkable unanimity in the values underpinning the repertoire during the 1870s and 1880s: the interdependence of motivic working and texture; the development of chromatically- or modally-inflected harmony as an alternative to classical diatonicism; and a concern for formal coherence, especially the unifying impulse of cyclicism.

In the sonatas and quartets for piano and strings that dominated the French repertoire in the 1870s, composers tended to blur functional distinctions between melody and accompaniment. Inner voices and bass lines were conceived contrapuntally and staked their claim to melodic significance by sharing motivic cells with the treble. This approach is evident in the marvellously flexible relationship between texture and motive that characterizes the broad opening paragraph of Fauré's Piano Quartet no. 1 in C minor op. 15 (1876). As the brackets in Example 3.1 show, even the chordal accompaniment of the first phrase participates in the motivic discourse, outlining pitch patterns that creep into the strings in bars 6 and 7. Following an exchange of ideas between the strings and piano in bars 8 and 9, it is not clear who has the leading voice in bars 10 to 13: the registers of the first violin and piano treble are intertwined, and they share rhythmic and chromatic pitch cells. The piano's treble only emerges as the principal voice in bar 14, where its climactic gesture (reaching g^3) caps the earlier apex of the string phrase (b flat^2 in bar 12). This exchange of roles is underpinned by one of Fauré's typically bold bass lines. There are numerous moments of passing harmonic astringency between the successive diminished sevenths supported by the ascending chromatic bass and the descending string octaves in bars 12 and 13. But the overall effect is softened by the firmly diatonic cadential basis of the whole paragraph (Example 3.2). For all its technical finesse, motivic density and harmonic daring, this passage has the effect of a spontaneous outpouring of melody. Perhaps this is the technical basis for the quality that Saint-Saëns had in mind when he wrote of Fauré's Violin Sonata no. 1 op. 15, 'Over it and around it hovers a charm which persuades the mass of ordinary listeners to accept the most violent novelties as being entirely natural'.[15]

– aussi bien – l'équilibre, la raison ne peuvent nous faire dénier cependant par ailleurs le mouvement, la passion et l'enthousiasme': 68 ('Can we believe that there is a particularly French conception of music, as opposed to the German, springing from the distinctive qualities of our race? Elegance, refinement, wit, irony, or – equally – balance; moreover, reason cannot deny dynamism, passion, and enthusiasm').

15 Saint-Saëns: Review of Fauré's Violin Sonata, *Journal de musique*, 7 Apr. 1877.

Example 3.1 Gabriel Fauré, Piano Quartet in C minor op. 15, I, bars 1–18

continued

Example 3.1 *concluded*

Example 3.2 Gabriel Fauré, Piano Quartet op. 15, bars 1–18

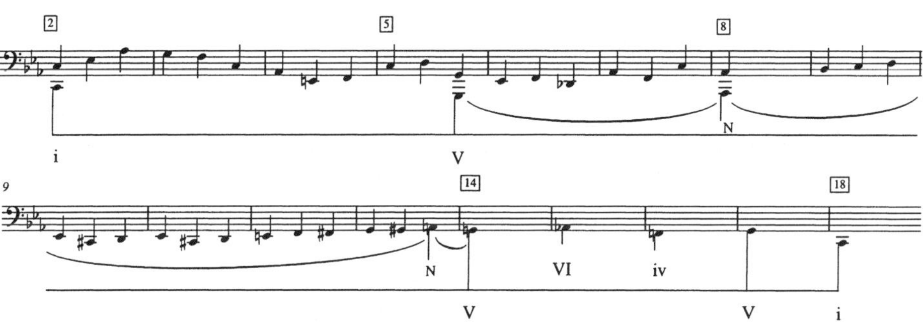

The type of textural motivic working shown in Example 3.1 also links the different themes in the first movement of Fauré's Quartet. Its second subject (bar 38 onwards) embodies a much more classically oriented dialogue style between the four instruments, in which short ideas overlap in various contrapuntal and textural variations. However, the strongest connection between the first and second subjects is their common motivic substance: the complete lower neighbour-note progression, together with the rising third and its inversion (see Example 3.3a). Such surreptitious binding processes also stretch onwards into the Scherzo. The outer sections of this movement are organized into three-bar hypermeasures. If Fauré's metronome marks are taken, one hypermeasure of the Scherzo is metrically almost identical to one bar of the first movement.[16] In addition to this strong underlying continuity, the skittish opening theme of the Scherzo plays with two pitch cells from the opening of the first movement (Example 3.3b).

The *motivische Arbeit* described briefly above is, of course, quite different from the cyclic treatment of themes found in so many French instrumental works of the period. If the Germanic type of motivic development involved complex transformational processes that were sometimes not casually audible, then cyclic organization was concerned with reinterpreting relatively fixed musical ideas by placing them in new contexts. It was therefore fundamentally important that themes should be easy to recognize when they returned. In this respect cyclicism must be understood as springing from the French aesthetic of clarity and audibility, rather than from the *algébraique* quality that conservative critics perceived in German-influenced music.

Unmotivated thematic returns are unlikely to forge any sort of meaningful unity between movements, and cyclic procedures are most convincing when they are most deeply embedded in other aspects of musical organization, whether long-term structural trajectories or expressive designs. French composers tackled this issue in several different ways in their chamber music. Thematic return is intimately bound up with classical tonal processes in Saint-Saëns's Violin Sonata no. 1 in D minor op. 75 (1885). In this work the traditional four movements of the nineteenth-century sonata are conflated into two movements. The first is a composite of sonata allegro and slow movement, though the sonata allegro is radically deformed: instead of comprising the usual exposition, development and recapitulation, its sonata-style exposition is followed by two large-scale

16 In the *Allegro molto moderato* one bar equals 3 × ♩ = 84; in the Scherzo one hypermeasure equals 3 × 𝅗𝅥. = 80.

Example 3.3 Gabriel Fauré, Piano Quartet in C minor, motivic connections

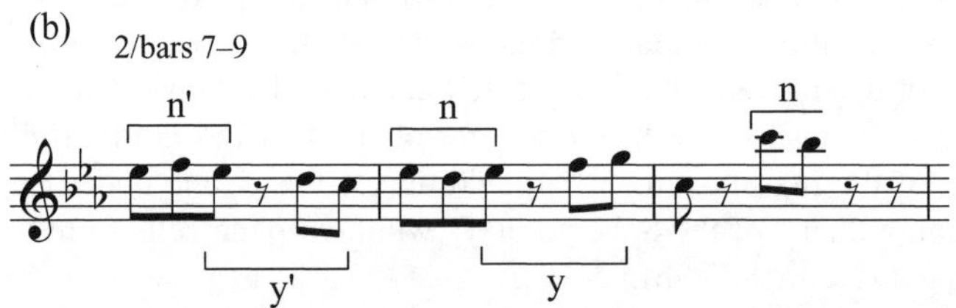

variations. In each section the opening theme is in the tonic (D minor) but the second subject occurs in different tonal areas: F major in the exposition, G major in the second section, and (incomplete) in E flat major in the third. On its last appearance the second subject liquidates into the following *Adagio*, which is also in E flat. In this way the opening *Allegro agitato* fails to achieve tonal closure. In particular, the structural dissonance of the second subject appearing in three non-tonic keys is not resolved. The second movement of the Sonata conflates a Scherzo in G minor and a *moto perpetuo* in the D major. The reappearance of the *Allegro agitato*'s second subject in the final section is motivated less by processes of motivic integration than by its long sought-for resolution in the tonic.

An expressive narrative seems to have motivated Fauré's single overt use of cyclicism in his chamber music. In his Piano Quartet in G minor op. 45 (1885–86), the Scherzo is not constructed in the conventional ternary form (scherzo–trio–scherzo) but instead incorporates two episodes that recapture and transform the main ideas of the first movement. These inhabit a technical half-world: they are neither obvious returns of those earlier themes nor thorough-going developments of their motives. Expressively too they seem to inhabit shadowlands: like Adorno's concept of Wagnerian Phantasmagoria, the colour of the music is distorted (solo lines are turned into the uncanny sound of string unisons, strong tuttis become muted *pianissimo*), and the themes are detached from their original context; therefore they appear to be heard at a distance. The effect is unsettlingly enigmatic and might be more puzzling still were it not for the subtle resonance with a letter that Fauré wrote to his wife on 11 September 1906:

> The slow movement of my second Quartet is one of the few places where I realize that, without really meaning to, I recalled a distant peal of bells we used to hear in the evening ... at Montgauzy . . . Their sound gives rise to a vague dream, which, like all vague dreams, cannot be translated into words. Isn't it often the case that some external thing plunges us into thoughts that are so imprecise that they are not really thoughts at all, though the mind certainly finds pleasure in them. Perhaps it's a longing for something beyond what actually exists, which is very much the domain of music.[17]

Viewed in this light, it is all too tempting to interpret the Scherzo's nightmarish cyclic episodes as part of a larger pattern of dreamscapes in the G minor Quartet, in which the transcendent tranquillity of the third movement arises (evidently unconsciously) in counterpoise to the dark memories of the work's opening themes.[18]

Some of the most compelling cyclic strategies, however, are those that tie thematic returns to combinatorial counterpoint so that the climax of a work reveals latent relationships between different themes. Franck was particularly adept at such contrapuntal displays, and in his most successful chamber music he yoked them to *motivische Arbeit* and powerful long-term linear processes. The first movement of his Piano Quintet (1878–79) is a highly developed sonata form, containing a large number of short themes that lend themselves to different contrapuntal combinations. As the movement unfolds, so Franck seems to try out different combinations of ideas, but none seems to achieve a final, fully worked-out form. The implications of this unfinished business are realized in the last two movements with a particularly complex interplay of chromatic voice-leading, motivic transformation, and thematic recall. In order to explain how this works, some technical discussion is necessary.

Example 3.4 shows a transitional form of the first movement's second subject. Two of the ingredients for Franck's long-term strategy are present here: the melodic patterns highlight a pitch motive that underpins most of the movement's other themes, $\hat{5} - \flat\hat{6} - \hat{5}$; and the supporting harmonic progression typically uses chromatic shifts to move through an ascending cycle of minor thirds (C♯ – E – G). Another ingredient, shown in Example 3.5a, occurs towards the end of the *Molto moderato quasi lento* introduction, where a descending cycle of minor thirds (E♭ – C – A) leads to climactic antagonism between A minor and D flat major chords. As Example 3.5b demonstrates, the A minor triad is related both to D flat and the tonic F minor by incremental chromatic shifts; both

17 Gabriel Fauré: *Lettres intimes (1885–1924),* ed. P. Fauré-Fremiet (Paris, 1951), 132; 'Ce n'est guère que dans l'andante du second *Quatuor* que je me souviens avoir traduit, et presque involontairement, le souvenir bien lointain d'une sonnerie de cloches ... le soir, à Montgauzy ... sur ce bourdonnement s'élève une vague rêverie qui, comme toutes les vagues rêveries, serait *littérairement* intraduisible. Seulement, n'est-il pas fréquent qu'un fait extérieur nous engourdisse ainsi dans un genre de pensées si imprécises qu'en réalité elles ne sont pas des pensées, et qu'elles sont cependant quelque chose où on se complaît? Désir de choses inexistantes, peut-être; et c'est bien là le domaine de la musique.

18 For a discussion of other cyclic aspects of this quartet, see Robert Orledge: *Gabriel Fauré* (London, 1979), 99–104; and Jean-Michel Nectoux: *Gabriel Fauré: a Musical Life*, trans. R. Nichols (Cambridge, 1991), 91–4.

Example 3.4 César Franck, Piano Quintet, I, bars 90–98

Example 3.5 César Franck, Piano Quintet, I, bars 26–37

(a)

continued

Example 3.5 *concluded*

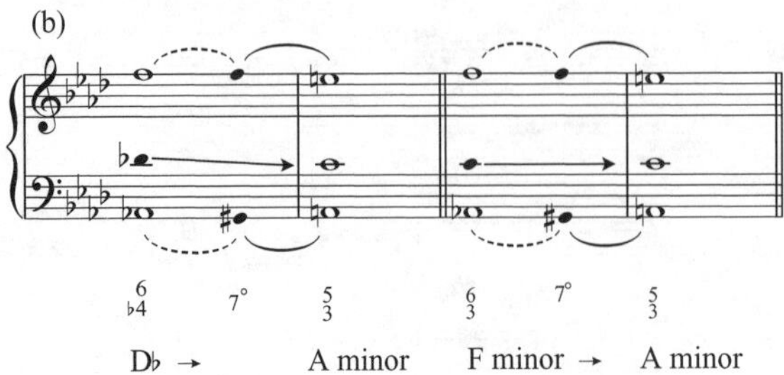

relationships play on the enharmonic ambiguity of A flat (the mediant of F minor) and G sharp (the leading tone of A minor).[19]

All three ideas come into play again in the barcarolle-like second movement. The relationship between F minor and A minor, hinted at in the first movement, is actualized in the harmonic progression between the first and second movements, and in the delicate tonal instability of the opening theme of the *Lento*. A countersubject added in the lower strings at bar 20 clarifies the relationship between the harmony's chromatic transformations and the $\hat{5}$ – $\flat\hat{6}$– $\hat{5}$ motive (bracketed as 'X' in Example 3.6) though it remains subservient to the violin cantilena floating above. In the sonata-form finale these three elements achieve even more stable forms. Its key of F major verticalizes the relationship between F and A (though continual jostling between A natural and A flat gives the music a bittersweet tinge that persists almost to the end). The $\hat{5}$ – $\flat\hat{6}$– $\hat{5}$ motive dominates the first subject, and the Lento's countersubject returns as the second subject. This newfound stability unleashes centripetal forces that whip together disparate strands of the first two movements into a delirious waltz-like coda.

The expressive intensity and unremittingly febrile chromaticism of Franck's Quintet was not to everybody's taste. Liszt is reported to have found it inappropriately dramatic for chamber music.[20] And Debussy complained that the music was in a continual paroxysm.[21] Its overtly dramatic tone prompted more than one critic to speculate that it must embody a secret programme, and several went so far as to claim that the work was a sublimation of Franck's alleged (unrequited) infatuation with his pupil Augusta Holmès.[22] There seems to have been no biographical basis for the assertion, but perhaps the real significance of this critical reception is that the Quintet was perceived to be pushing at the boundaries of pure instrumental music.

The 1880s saw a widening of the chamber music repertoire: on the one hand the favoured piano-based genres of the sonata, quartet and quintet were occasionally enlarged by the addition of extra instruments and, on the other, composers began to turn their attention to chamber music for strings alone. Two significant works from this period expand the traditional ensemble of piano and strings with original, if eccentric, results.

---

19 For a comprehensive theoretical discussion of third progressions and chromaticism in nineteenth-century harmonic practice see David Kopp: *Chromatic Transformations in Nineteenth-Century Music* (Cambridge, 2002).

20 Pierre de Bréville, cited in Joël-Marie Fauquet: *César Franck* (Paris, 1999), 524.

21 Maurice Emmanuel: César Franck: *Étude critique* (Paris, 1930), 147.

22 See, for example, Léon Vallas: *La véritable histoire de César Franck, 1822–1890* (Paris, 1955).

Example 3.6 César Franck, Piano Quintet, II, bars 20–28

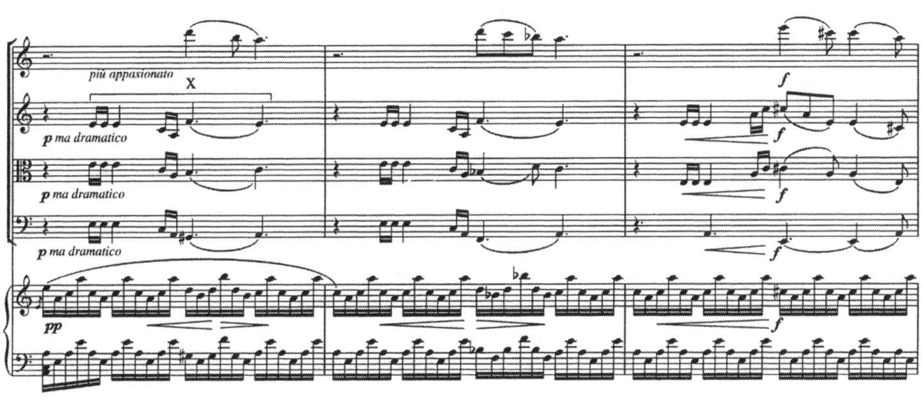

Saint-Saëns's Septet op. 65 (1880) for string quartet, double bass, trumpet and piano anticipates neoclassicism, in that it ironizes baroque styles and forms within a contemporary cyclic framework.[23] The tone is set by the fantasy-like *Préambule* in which improvisatory piano flourishes jostle with fugal sections and brief snatches of cantabile melody, producing the sort of mixed-style prelude at which Bach excelled (for example, the E flat major Prelude from Book 1 of *Das wohltemperirte Clavier*). None of these musical ideas is developed in a post-classical sense during the first movement, but they inform the themes of the later movements: a minuet, a moderately paced *Intermède*, and a *Gavotte et final*. The last movement is a rondo, whose peroration is a combinatorial apotheosis of themes from the *Préambule* and motives from the gavotte. As a closing gambit, this subscribes to the motivic preoccupations of *haute composition*, and the sudden reassertion of contemporary values is underlined by its gestural similarity to the end of Schumann's Piano Quintet. But the effect is curiously deracinated in the Septet: the earlier movements generate insufficient dramatic momentum to motivate such a climax. In textural terms, too, the Septet is at odds with much late nineteenth-century chamber music. Saint-Saëns largely treats his forces as three blocks – piano, strings and trumpet – and apart from some imitative writing in the first and last movements the string lines have little individuality.

Chausson's *Concert* op. 21 (1889–92) for piano, violin and string quartet exploits the textural possibilities of its expanded ensemble with much greater subtlety. Its implicit combination of several traditional textural types – string quartet, piano quintet, piano and violin duet – plays an important role in the shaping of the music: although the piece is not a concerto in the conventional sense, Chausson makes great play with the concertante effects that can arise from these different permutations. Sometimes he maintains a sharp distinction between the quartet and the 'solo' instruments, as, for example, in the quartet-dominated *Calme* at the start of the first movement, and the violin/piano *Animé* that follows it. But in most of the work he mixes the different combinations to produce an exceptionally wide range of colours, from forceful tuttis to the most delicate of effects (Example 3.7).

Although French composers of serious instrumental music found it difficult to secure performances of their works in the middle decades of the nineteenth century, there was a continuous tradition of quartet composition in France.[24] Winners of the Prix de Rome were obliged to compose a quartet during their time at the Villa Medici, and professional quartets occasionally programmed French music alongside the classical canon. The quartets of mid-century composers such as Dancla, David and Gouvy have a melodic charm, but they lack the intellectual rigour of the Viennese classical masterpieces, and in the new aesthetic climate of the 1870s they failed to make a mark on the repertoire. Early concert programmes of the Société nationale included performances of the more polyphonically conceived quartets of Lalo (1856, rev. 1884) and Alexis de Castillon (1860s), but most composers of the front rank shied away from the string quartet for more than a decade. This may have been due partly to the fact that the leading composers of

23 Saint-Saëns's use of consciously archaic styles was anticipated by Alexis de Castillon's *Pièces dans le style ancien* which Saint-Saëns performed at the SN concert on 10 Mar. 1877.

24 Joël-Marie Fauquet: 'Le Quatuor à cordes en France avant 1870: de la partition à la pratique', in Bernard Crozier (ed.): *Le Quatuor à cordes en France de 1750 à nos jours* (Paris, 1995), 97–117.

chamber music in the 1870s were all primarily keyboard players, so it was perhaps natural that they cultivated genres that included the piano. But equally inhibitive was the genre's paramount reputation and the collective weight of the German canon; Beethoven's achievements alone were enough to give pause for thought. Creative anxiety of this sort emerges in d'Indy's dictum that 'the string quartet must be a work of maturity, if it is to have any real significance ... Even among musicians of genius there is no example of a really *good* string quartet which dates from a youthful period.'[25]

This situation changed with the performance of quartets by Sylvio Lazzari (1857–1944) and Franck at Société nationale concerts in the years around 1890. Lazzari's String Quartet in A minor op. 17 met with little public success at its premiere in 1888, but it set a new trend in quartet composition which led to the production of several masterpieces in the following fifteen years. Its serious ambitions and allegiance to German romantic models are signalled at the outset with an unmistakable reference to Beethoven's E minor 'Razumovsky' Quartet op. 59 no. 2. Like Beethoven's middle-period quartets, Lazzari's work has a tough linear integrity, motivic economy, and its louder passages come close to breaking away from the traditional intimacy of quartet textures to the more public rhetoric of orchestral music. The first movement is a tautly argued sonata form with a novel twist. Towards the end of the development section the conversational give and take liquidates into a recitative-like passage for the first violin. With a change of tempo and metre, there follows a new lyrical theme in the style of a sarabande; this unfolds at a leisurely pace over twenty-six bars before the original *molto agitato* reasserts itself, quickly driving towards a regular recapitulation.

The function of the interrupted development section becomes clearer at the start of the second movement, when the sarabande theme returns as the movement's main idea. Schubert, rather than Beethoven, seems to be the presiding spirit in this Andante. In a manner that echoes the slow movements of Schubert's late G major Quartet D. 885 and String Quintet D. 960, the middle section of this ternary form distorts motives from the calm opening theme into nightmarish parodies. It modulates widely (and sometimes wildly), before winding down to a reprise of the sarabande theme.

The cyclic element in Lazzari's design comes to the fore again in the finale, a rondo *alla zingarese* with a new theme as its refrain. Its connections with the first movement are set up in the episodes, which increasingly integrate motives from the *molto agitato* as the movement progresses. This process culminates in a combinatorial presentation of the finale's rondo theme with the opening theme of the first movement. Once again, German models for this strategy spring to mind: the transformation processes in the final variations of Beethoven's Sonata in E op. 109, for example, or those in the last movement of Brahms's String Quartet in B flat op. 67.

Franck's great String Quartet of 1889–90 also makes explicit references to canonic German repertoire. Its second movement Scherzo is an overt homage to Mendelssohn's gossamer style in *A Midsummer Night's Dream*; and at the start of the finale, themes from the earlier movements are reprised and rejected in direct imitation of Beethoven's Ninth Symphony. While imitation like this could wreck the work of a less-experienced or weaker composer, the sheer quality of Franck's musical invention and the strength of his musical *persona* overcome these dangers, and the lingering effect of the quartet as a whole is one

25 Vincent d'Indy: *César Franck*, trans. R. Newmarch (London, 1909), 182.

Example 3.7 Ernest Chausson, *Concert* op. 21, II, bars 57–62

of high originality. This is largely due to the unprecedented rich sonorities that Franck conjures from the quartet, giving the whole work a strikingly individual sound world. Texture is, of course, a notoriously slippery concept, and any attempt to analyse the secret of Franck's success here is unlikely to capture its essence. Two examples, however, may give some indication of the underlying principles. The first is taken from the Scherzo's second subject (Example 3.8a), and the second from the central section of the *Larghetto* third movement (Example 3.8b). Although these two extracts have contrasting expressive characters and different timbres (the instruments are muted in the Scherzo), their textural clarity and richness rest on common premises. Each instrument has its own rhythmic profile that contrasts sharply with the others (the second violin and viola pairing at the start of Example 3.8b function as a composite voice within a three-part texture); and each has its own clearly defined registral space. Franck often achieves this by keeping the first violin and cello in extreme registers, but more impressive are those passages where he maintains the effect within narrower overall limits. Even the densest contrapuntal textures attain a luminosity that often escaped other composers' quartet writing during this period (and which also escaped Franck himself in parts of his Symphony).

Like Lazzari, Franck deforms classical sonata form in the first movement of his quartet. In his celebrated analysis, d'Indy interpreted this movement as a composite of lied form and sonata form (see Figure 3.1).[26]

This reading gives a convincing account of the movement's broad formal outlines, but it presents a false distinction in style and tone between the lied and sonata sections. D'Indy emphasizes a contrast between the stasis of the lied and the dynamism of the sonata which is, in reality, difficult to perceive. Similarly, he plays down the motivic and gestural links between the different sections, and the immense care with which Franck constructs the transitions between the two types. In sketches for the Quartet, Franck referred obliquely to Beethoven's Quartet op. 127, whose first movement also involves ideas presented in different tempos. And, like Beethoven, he was surely aiming to integrate the material of this movement, rather than emphasizing the dissociation of disparate ideas. A similar process of integration occurs in the finale where, for once, the cyclic process is coloured by wit. Its initial Beethovenian gestures rejecting themes from the second and third movements turn out to be ironic when the movement culminates in a combinatorial fusion of the two rejected ideas.

The powerful rhetoric and compelling cyclical organization of Franck's Quartet held the imagination of many younger French composers in the 1890s, and inspired a series of ambitious cyclical works from his pupils, including d'Indy (two quartets, in 1890 and 1897 respectively), Guy Ropartz (1894), and Chausson (whose quartet was incomplete at his death in 1899). Even the quartets by Debussy (1893) and Ravel (1903) do not entirely escape the influence of Franck's masterpiece.

On 12 June 1870 the *Revue et gazette musicale* published an essay 'On the modern symphony and its future'. Its author, Ives Kéramzer, argued that the musical autonomy of the classical symphony, expressing the indeterminate, had become enfeebled because it was resistant to the advances achieved by modern dramatic music in determinate expression. In contrast, the modern symphony (which he associated with Berlioz and

26 D'Indy: *César Franck*, 182–97.

Liszt) had a 'narrative character': its form and development of musical ideas could enact a plot, and 'translate events'. Kéramzer believed that this new concept had advantages over the old. Conventional structures and expressive devices would no longer cramp the symphony, but radical new forms, styles, and orchestral colours would spring from the individual action-types imagined by the composer:

> Nothing is more stimulating for the imagination of the composer than this struggle against a programme fixed in advance, for which it is necessary, at all costs, to find musical expression. Nothing is more fecund, nothing more likely to extend the horizons of the art, when the musician is very gifted, than that the novelty of his conception obliges him to seek a translation of it in the novelty of his dramatic effects.[27]

Kéramzer's essay is remarkable for trenchantly articulating an arch-modernist position in a journal which usually aired more conservative aesthetic views in the early 1870s. His prescience was, perhaps, less remarkable. Progressive French composers certainly

Example 3.8(a) César Franck, String Quartet, II, bars 67–78

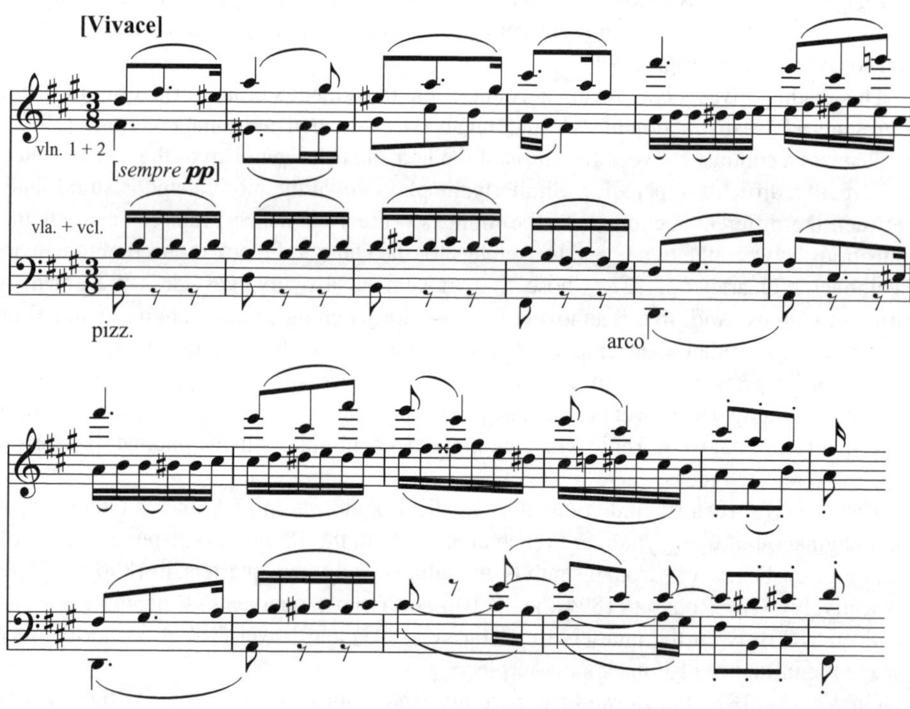

27 Ives Kéramzer: 'De la symphonie moderne et de son avenir', *RGM*, 37/24 (12 June 1870), 185–6; 'Rien de plus stimulant pour l'invention du compositeur que cette lutte contre un programme fixé d'avance, dont il lui faut, à tout prix, trouver l'expression musicale; rien de plus fécond, rien de plus propre à étendre l'horizon de l'art, quand le musicien est bien doué et que la nouveauté de sa conception l'oblige d'en chercher la traduction dans la nouveauté de ses effets dramatiques' (p. 186).

Example 3.8(b) César Franck, String Quartet, III, bars 93–101

developed his dramatic concept of instrumental music in the 1870s and 1880s, but they confined programmatic elements to character pieces and symphonic poems, rather than applying them to the symphony.

No doubt the reasons for the sudden flourishing of the symphonic poem in France were various and complex. While it represented progressive trends in contemporaneous German

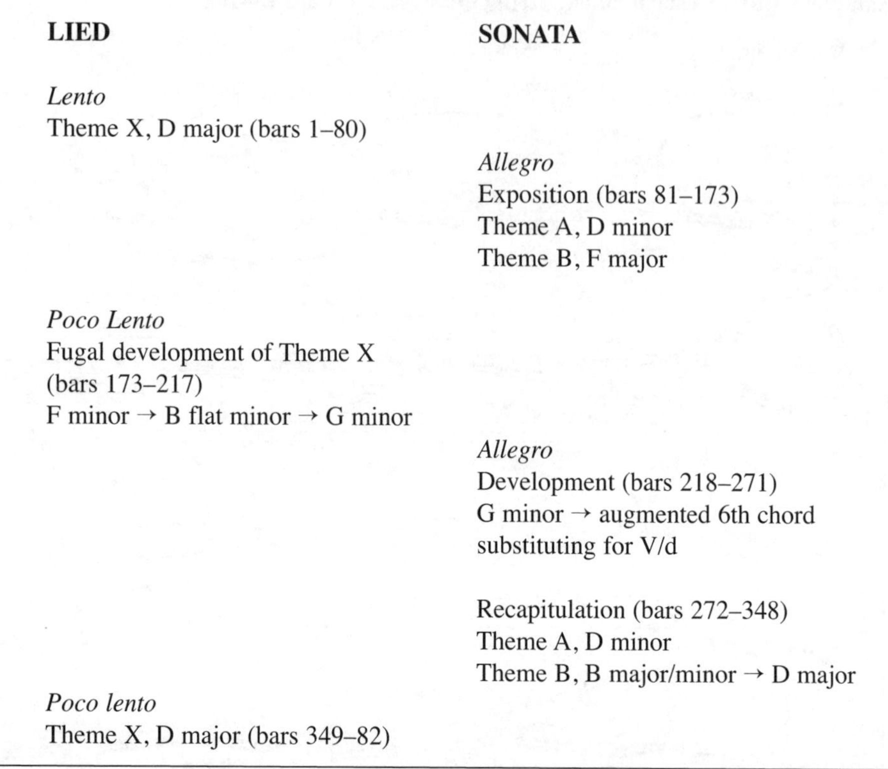

LIED
SONATA
Lento
Theme X, D major (bars 1–80)
Allegro
Exposition (bars 81–173)
Theme A, D minor
Theme B, F major
Poco Lento
Fugal development of Theme X
(bars 173–217)
F minor → B flat minor → G minor
Allegro
Development (bars 218–271)
G minor → augmented 6th chord
substituting for V/d
Recapitulation (bars 272–348)
Theme A, D minor
Theme B, B major/minor → D major
Poco lento
Theme X, D major (bars 349–82)

Figure 3.1 Form of Franck's String Quartet, first movement

orchestral music, the symphonic poem did not carry the same weight of tradition as the symphony. It therefore presented a relatively blank slate on which composers could inscribe a new type of French orchestral music. With its emphasis on dramatic incident, instrumental colour, and non-standard forms, the symphonic poem provided composers with the opportunity to draw on the rich orchestral style associated with French stage music. And, not least, the discipline of working to the demands of a literary or dramatic programme undoubtedly had the paradoxical effect of freeing the imaginations of composers, in the ways anticipated by Kéramzer.[28]

With the sudden popularity of the symphonic poem in Paris, long-running debates about autonomy and materialism in music flared up once more in the French musical press. The arguments pressed on both sides were enmeshed in complex ways with the parallel controversies about the influence of German music and modernism. But in essence the French debate had many points of contact with contemporaneous aesthetic discourses in Germany. Materialists like Kéramzer subscribed to the position of Franz

28 Saint-Saëns, for example, declared that 'for the artist, programme music is only a pretext to try new paths; new effects require new techniques', Saint-Saëns: *Harmonie et mélodie* (Paris, 1885), 161. (La musique à programme n'est pour l'artiste qu'un prétexe à tenter des voies nouvelles.)

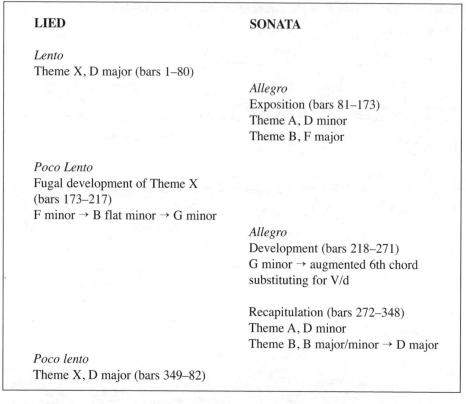

Brendel, who held that by moving from indeterminate expression to the determinate characterization of programmatic content, instrumental music had progressed from sentiment to spirit.[29] Accordingly, the non-musical dimension is an essential part of the work, whose meaning arises from the interaction of the programme and the sound of the music.

The opposing absolutist argument was most clearly articulated by Eduard Hanslick, who argued that musical form is the spiritual essence of music; programmes are 'extra-musical' accretions to instrumental music and are therefore aesthetically irrelevant. Hanslick's ideas became easily accessible in France after his seminal essay 'Vom Musikalisch-Schönen' appeared in translation as 'Du beau dans la musique' in 1877.[30] His perspective was the starting point for almost all conservative critiques of programmatic music in France, criticism which held that the proper subject for instrumental music was music itself. For example, Charles Bannelier, writing about Saint-Saëns's earliest symphonic poem *Le rouet d'Omphale* in December 1875, distinguished between the work's praiseworthy musical logic and the aesthetic irrelevance of its programme.[31]

Some commentators whose outlook was otherwise essentially conservative nevertheless allowed some pragmatism when it came to programme music. In his *Élements d'esthétique musicale* (1884), Antoine-François Marmontel wrote that 'we do not believe that plastic and realistic effects applied to music are the ideal goal of great art; but when they are used discretely and appropriately by talented composers, they give orchestral works, programmatic symphonies and orchestral suites a new appeal, a variety of effects, and a musical fluency whose characteristic charm must be recognised and admired'.[32] But for critics with a strong sense of generic decorum the proper domain of representative music was staged musical drama, and the autonomy of symphonic music should not be compromised by mixing its nature with other genres. The anonymous reviewer of d'Indy's *La forêt enchantée* in the *Revue et gazette musicale* equivocally praised the work's content while damning its genre: 'This poetic, powerful and colourful work, although a little dense in its second half, reveals a musician of the first order, whom we advise only to abandon the bastard genre of the programme symphony in order to throw himself resolutely into musical drama, which seems to us to be his true path.'[33]

---

29 C. Dahlhaus: *The Idea of Absolute Music*, trans R. Lustig (London, 1989); chapter 5, 'The Musically Absolute and Programme Music'.

30 E. Hanslick: *Du beau dans la musique: Essai de réforme de l'esthétique musicale … traduit de l'allemand sur la cinquième édition par Charles Bannelier* (Paris, 1877); Bannelier's translation was also serialized in the *RGM* between 11 Mar. and 15 July 1877.

31 *RGM*, 26 Dec. 1875, 415.

32 Antoine-François Marmontel: *Elements d'esthétique musicale* (Paris, 1884), 229–30; 'Les effets plastiques et réalistes appliqués à la musique ne sont pas, croyons-nous, le but idéal du grand art; mais employés avec discretion, avec habilité, par des compositeurs de talent, ils donnent aux œuvres orchestrales, aux symphonies à la programme, aux suites d'orchestre, un attrait nouveau, une variété d'effets, un coloris musical dont il faut reconnaître et admirer le charme caractéristique'. Such arguments relating to the propriety and discretion of the representational element in programme music can be traced back to Berlioz's essay 'De l'imitation musicale', *RGM*, 4 (1837), 9–11 and 15–17.

33 *RGM*, 12 May 1878, 149; 'Cette œuvre poétique, puissante et colorée, quoique un peu trop touffue dans sa seconde moitié, révèle un musicien de premier ordre, à qui nous conseillerons seulement d'abandonner le genre bâtard des symphonies à programme, pour se lancer résolument dans le grand drame musical, qui nous paraît être sa véritable voie'. Katharine Ellis

Even among those who fundamentally supported programme music, there was a distinction between the acceptability of indirect representation (the type of arbitrary connection between a musical symbol and the phenomenon it represents, as in Wagnerian leitmotives) and the more problematic direct imitation of the material world (such as birdsong, cowbells, thunder, and so forth). The most stinging criticism that could be aimed at a symphonic poem was that the prosaic nature of a programme or the direct imitation of natural phenomena trivialized the musically poetic and logical aspect of the work or, worse still, that without its programme the music lacked coherence altogether. The satirical deflation of a programme's pretensions was likely to be effective against composers who were striving hard to create a culture of *haute composition*. In this context Bonnerot's anecdote about the wag who heard in Saint-Saëns's *Phaëton* 'the noise of a hack coming down from Montmartre' rather than the galloping of fiery steeds from Mount Olympus is especially telling.[34]

Saint-Saëns himself was happy to describe in purely musical terms Liszt's concept of the symphonic poem, the ideal that formed the technical foundation of his own works:

> The symphonic poem, in the form which Liszt gave it, is usually a series of different sections which depend on each other and derive from the initial idea, sections connecting and forming a single movement. The construction of the musical poem understood in this way can be varied *ad infinitum*. In order to obtain the greatest possible variety, Liszt most often chose a musical phrase which he transformed by means of rhythmic devices in order to express the most dissimilar sentiments.[35]

Furthermore, in a letter to Durand of 6 March 1899, responding to a performance of Dukas's *L'apprenti sorcier*, he spelled out what he regarded as the aesthetic limits of the symphonic poem:

> I am delighted that Dukas has composed a fine piece and that it has been successful. But in principle I do not favour pieces which *tell a story*. In the *Danse macabre* there are the terrors and ironies of death; in *Le rouet d'Omphale*, seduction; in *Phaëton*, pride; in *La jeunesse d'Hercule*, the struggle between heroism and sensual pleasure. I cannot see what there is in *L'apprenti sorcier* or in Rimsky-Korsakov's *Sadko*. If there is no sentiment to express, I do not see what purpose music serves unless it is pure music, limited to the cultivation of form and the expression of an aesthetic idea.[36]

---

attributes the review to Bannelier; Katharine Ellis: *Music Criticism in Nineteenth-Century France* (Cambridge, 1995), 177.

34 Quoted in Michael Fallon: 'The Symphonies and Symphonic Poems of Camille Saint-Saëns' (unpublished diss., Yale University, 1973), 254.

35 Saint-Saëns, *Harmonie et Mélodie*, 163–4; 'Le poème symphonique, dans la forme que Liszt lui a donnée, est d'ordinaire un ensemble de mouvements différents dépendant les uns des autres et découlant d'une idée première, qui s'enchaînent et forment un seul morceau. Le plan de poème musical ainsi compris peut varier à l'infini. Pour obtenir une grande variété possible, Liszt choisit le plus souvent une phrase musicale qu'il transforme au moyen des artifices du rythme de façon à lui faire servir à l'expression des sentiments le plus dissembables.'

36 'Enchanté que Dukas ait fait un joli morceau et qu'il ait eu du succès. Mais en principe je ne suis pas pour les morceaux qui *racontent une histoire*. Sous le *Danse macabre*, il y a les terreurs et les ironies de la mort; sous *Le rouet d'Omphale*, la séduction; sous *Phaëton*, l'orgueil; sous la *jeunesse d'Hercule*, la lutte contre l'héroïsme et la volupté. Je ne voir pas ce qu'il peut y avoir sous *L'apprenti sorcier* et sous *Sadko* de Rimsky-Korsakoff. Et là où il n'y a pas un sentiment à exprimer, je ne vois pas ce que vient faire la musique à moins que ce ne soit de la musique pure, borne au culte de la forme et à l'expression d'un caractère esthétique.'

But in what sense does *L'apprenti sorcier* tell the story of Goethe's *Der Zauberlehrling*? In her study of Dukas's symphonic poem, Carolyn Abbate rejects as 'trite and unprofitable' conventional narrative readings that simplistically map literary moments onto musical moments.[37] Despite the similarities in dramatic shape between Dukas's music and Goethe's poem, she argues that it is absurdly reductive to interpret the symphonic poem as a string of leitmotives that mirror the events of the story. At many points the piece functions as absolute music, engaging in purely musical processes. We can speak of *L'apprenti sorcier* as narrative in the sense that it is a succession of gestures, but in this respect it is no different from any other piece of music, programmatic or absolute. In a more specific sense narrative is diegetic: it is distanced from the actual events of the story by a detached, selecting storyteller. But music is mimetic. It does not have a past tense: it can enact dramatic events but it cannot report them. Even works that 'seem to interpret or examine themselves through widely spaced and altered repetitions of musical matter' cannot entirely escape their constant presentness.[38] However, Abbate sees in *L'apprenti sorcier* a unique instance of a narrating voice coming to the fore in music. She takes the work's ten-bar epilogue to lie outside the enacted drama of the sorcerer's apprentice, and interprets its radical change of style as a metaphor for the narrative formula where inverted commas encapsulate reported speech – " he said.

While it could be argued, then, that *L'apprenti sorcier* is the only piece of its type actually to 'narrate', many French symphonic poems from this period draw on the dramatic potential of narrative plots. German ballads were especially popular literary sources: narrative poems by G. A. Bürger form the basis of Duparc's *Lénore* (1875) and Franck's *Le chasseur maudit* (1882); Uhland's poetry lies behind d'Indy's *La forêt enchantée* (1878), and Schiller is the source of his *Wallenstein* trilogy. Others drew on Arthurian legend (such as Chausson's *Viviane* of 1882) or the rich repertoire of *contes de fées* (for instance, Bruneau's *La belle au bois dormant* of 1884). All these works enact in more or less detail the dramatic incidents of their literary plots, using the full resources of the post-Wagnerian orchestra, and sometimes building unconventional additive musical forms. But they also draw on absolute musical archetypes and intertextual references to stage music. In *Le chasseur maudit* Franck symbolizes the supernatural galloping of the unrepentant huntsman in absolutist terms with an extended *moto perpetuo*, but he also alludes to earlier programmatic representations of this idea (Berlioz's 'Wild ride' from *Faust* and Liszt's *Mazeppa*) and comes dangerously close to quoting the beginning of Act III of Wagner's *Die Walküre*. Similarly, Saint-Saëns's *Danse macabre* (1874) contains a particularly unintegrated mixture of direct imitation, intertextual references, and formalist musical development. On the one hand the harp strikes midnight, the oboe crows, and the xylophone performs a skeletal dance; on the other, the theme that seems to symbolize Death's violin is treated to fugal development, and the diabolic tritone with which Death announces the dance motivates sophisticated modulatory patterns that in themselves have no symbolic significance. The range of intertextual reference is extremely wide in *Danse macabre*: from Saint-Saëns's earlier vocal setting of Cazalis's poem, through Lizst's 'Mephisto' Waltzes and the 'Ronde du Sabbat' of Berlioz's *Symphonie fantastique*, to the

37 Carolyn Abbate: *Unsung Voices: Opera and Musical Narrative in the Nineteenth Century* (Princeton, 1991); chapter 2, 'What the Sorcerer Said', 30–60).

38 Ibid., 55.

traditional symbolic power of the descending chromatic tetrachord and the chant of the Dies Irae. Intertextual emphasis overrides the relationship between the music and the poem in one fundamental respect: Cazalis described the dance of the dead as a sarabande, not the energetic waltz with which Saint-Saëns depicts it.

The use of a dramatic narrative could take on powerful conceptual or idealistic overtones. Franck was doubtless drawn to the moral aspect of *Le chasseur maudit*. And in *Irlande* (1882–85) and *Pologne* (1883) Augusta Holmès gave the symphonic poem an overtly political tone. *Irlande* reflects both current anti-British sentiment and Holmès's own Irish descent in its nationalist programme. The legend, written by Holmès herself, contrasts the proud independence of the early Celtic kingdoms with the country's current 'slavery' under British imperialism. The people are exhorted to rise against their yoke in the hope of regaining their feedom: 'Chante, ô peuple misérable, ton vieux chant triomphal: car les héros de l'antique Irlande sortent des tombeaux séculaires pour la déliverance de leurs enfants' (Sing, O miserable people, your old triumphant song: for the heros of Ancient Ireland are coming out of their age-old tombs to save their children!). Holmès's music has specific points of contact with this scheme, and draws heavily on local ethnic colour. It begins with an unaccompanied lament on the clarinet; this is interrupted by a furious reel in the Dorian mode which is developed into a type of arrested sonata form. The lament returns, this time played by the cor anglais, an instrument perhaps suggested by *Tristan*'s 'irisch Kind'? The call to revolution appears from nowhere with a *fortissimo* drum roll, and the expected victory is symbolized by a triumphal march in C major, overlaid with swirling motives from the earlier reel.

In contrast to these narrative-inspired pieces, other symphonic poems were more concerned with a play of abstract ideas extracted from their literary sources. In the letter quoted above, Saint-Saëns drew attention to the emblematic basis of *Le rouet d'Omphale* (1872), *Phaëton* (1873) and *La jeunesse d'Hercule* (1876). The emphasis on concepts, rather than dramatic incidents, is reflected in both the form and style of these pieces. Although they include Lisztian thematic transformations, all three works have less varied expressive and gestural ranges than narrative symphonic poems, and they conform more closely to conventional absolute musical forms such as sonata form, rondo and ternary form. While their initial musical ideas might be materially inspired – the spinning figures that recall Schubert's 'Gretchen am Spinnrade' in *Le rouet d'Omphale*, and galloping dactyls in *Phaëton* – their musical development is more consistently abstract. This 'solid state' approach to programmatic music is also found in Franck's *Les éolides* (1875–76), a delicate scherzo representing the classical winds of Leconte de Lisle's poem, and *Les djinns* (1883–84), in which the diabolic conflict of Hugo's poem is symbolized by the concertante relationship between the piano and orchestra. D'Indy used broad formal outlines to symbolize the slow striptease of the eponymous character in *Istar* (1896) by writing a reversed series of variations in which the musical materials become increasingly simple until the 'naked' theme appears at the end.

A solid state approach also characterizes the many programmatic pieces that evoke time and place. Holidaying in southern Spain in 1882, Emmanuel Chabrier wrote to friends back home about his intoxicating encounters with Andalusian dancing and songs:

> Those eyes, those flowers in their lovely hair, those shawls around their waists, those feet that go on tapping their ever-changing rhythms, those quivering arms running down their supple bodies,

> and the wavy movements of their hands, those sparkling smiles and that marvellous Sevillian bum that goes on turning and turning while the rest of the body doesn't seem to move at all! ... The cries of the women excite the dancers, and when they get to the end of their dance they become literally mad with passion ... They have a marvellous trick of clapping a syncopated 3/4 while the guitarist goes on with a rhythm of his own, as if nothing were happening. Some of them clap the first beat of every bar *forte*, but each girl has a rhythm of her own, and the result is most curious. I'm noting it all down – but what a job!

From Grenada he reported to Edouard Moullé that:

> If you saw [the dancers] wiggling their bums, swaying their hips and writhing their bodies you wouldn't want to be off in a hurry. At Malaga things got so hot that I had to take my wife away ... I can't write to you about it, but it's not to be forgotten and I'll tell you about it. Needless to say, I've copied down loads of tunes; the tango, a kind of dance in which a woman moves her bum like the pitching of a ship, is the only one in duple time; all the others are in 3/4 (Seville) or 3/8 (Malaga and Cadiz).[39]

Among the 'loads of tunes' that Chabrier jotted down at this time were ideas that with minimal adjustment he was able to incorporate into *España*. Naturally, rhythmic aspects of the music held most fascination for him, especially the way in which short rhythmic patterns could be permutated into large chains to generate incredible momentum. This principle is incorporated into *España* at many different levels, from the syncopated permutations of tiny cells in its opening theme, through to the reversal of the phrases in the fourth theme, the reordering of themes in the reprise, and even the sly dig at combinatorial cyclic form in the epilogue. The emphasis on rhythm affects other domains. Although Chabrier writes for a large orchestra, he uses it with delicacy and finesse, favouring bright, unmixed instrumental colours for individual contrapuntal lines. (Relative to the 'fat' Wagnerian sound cultivated by many progressive composers in their programmatic music, the textures here could be said, oddly enough, to lack bottom.) And in contrast to the prevalent chromatic language of the symphonic poem, *España*'s harmonies are refreshingly simple, confined almost completely to I and V in F major in its outer sections.

39 Chabrier letters trans. Edward Lockspeiser: *The Literary Clef* (London, 1958). 'Ces yeux, ces fleurs dans d'admirables chevelures, ces châles noués à la taille, ces pieds qui frappent un rythme varié à l'infini, ces bras qui courent frissonnants le long d'un corps toujours en mouvement, ces ondulations de la main, ces sourires éclatants, et cet admirable derrière sévillan qui se tourne en tous sens alors que le reste du corps semble immobile [...] Les cris des femmes excitent la danseuse qui, sur la fin de son pas, devient littéralement folle de son corps. [...] elles battent avec un instinct merveilleux le 3/4 *à contre-temps*: pendant que la guitare suit pacifiquement son rythme. [...] Comme d'autres battant le temps fort de chaque mesure – chacun battant un peu à sa fantaisie, c'est un amalgame de rythmes des plus curieux, - Du reste, je note tout cela, – mais quel métier, mes enfants! (to MM. Enoch et Costallat, Seville, 21 Oct. 1882). 'Si tu les voyais tortiller du derrière, se déhancher, se contorsionner, je crois que tu ne demanderais pas à t'en aller! A Malaga, la chose devint tellement forte que j'ai dû sortir mon épouse de là-dedans: [...]. Ça ne s'écrit pas, mais ça se retient et je te le raconterai. Je n'ai besoin de te dire que j'ai noté une masse de choses; le tango, une manière de danse où la femme imite avec son derrière le langage du navire est la seule à 2 temps; tout le reste; tout, est à 3/4 (Séville) ou à 3/8 (Malaga et Cadix)' (to Edouard Moullé, Granada, 4 Nov. 1882). From *Emmanuel Chabrier: Correspondence*, ed. Delage and Durif (Paris, 1994), 166–7 and 172.

Like other similarly characteristic pieces, such as Massenet's *Scènes hongroises, dramatiques* and *pittoresques* (all from the 1870s) and Charpentier's *Impressions d'Italie* (1891), *España* has an impressionistic rather than symbolic basis. It would be a mistake to dismiss them as mere musical postcards. Their evocation of exotic local colour and indigenous music offered a strong alternative to the Wagnerian stranglehold that increasingly gripped narrative programme music in the 1880s. In terms of colour and harmonic language, they anticipate most clearly the orchestral music of the banquet years.

The mid-nineteenth-century 'symphonic crisis' identified by Carl Dahlhaus was a European phenomenon.[40] In Germany no pure symphonic masterpieces appeared between Schumann's 'Rhenish' (1850) and Brahms's First (1877); and in France, too, no absolute symphonies of high originality were produced between the 1840s and the 1880s. Looking back from the turn of the century, Julien Tiersot recalled that 'In France the symphony was considered a school exercise ... It appeared that a well-written symphony was the supreme test of talent among young composers who graduated [from the Conservatoire]... But without a doubt, in the eyes of the judges the symphony had neither great importance nor elevated artistic significance.'[41] This is not to say that the symphony was neglected altogether; but, as Émile Vuillermoz pointed out, French composers had few opportunities to get their symphonies performed, despite the increasing number of orchestral societies in the 1850s and 1860s. In forty years, the Société des Concerts played only six symphonies by living composers: Onslow, Scipion Rousselat, Schneitzhoeffer, Félicien David, Henri Reber, and Louise Farrenc.[42] Gounod's two well-crafted symphonies (no. 1 in D, 1853; no. 2 in E flat, 1856) achieved some success in Paris; and Saint-Saëns's early symphonies were given performances in Paris and Bordeaux.[43] However, none of these works had the power to maintain a grip on the repertoire.

It is quite understandable that for economic and practical reasons the culture of *haute composition* fostered by the Société nationale in the 1870s focused initially on chamber music. Even in the orchestral concerts that the Society sponsored from 1873 onwards, new symphonies were very thin on the ground. Saint-Saëns twenty-year-old Symphony no. 2 was performed at the SN in February 1874. Fauré's Symphony in F, later to be withdrawn, appeared on the programme a few months later. Extracts from d'Indy's *Symphonie chevaleresque* were given at several concerts in the 1875 and 1876 seasons. But other composers preferred to signal the symphonic aspirations of their music more obliquely, as

40 Carl Dahlhaus: *Nineteenth-Century Music*, trans. J. B. Robinson (Berkeley, 1989).

41 Julien Tiersot: 'La symphonie en France': *Sammelbände der Internationalen Musikgesellschaft*, 3 (July 1902), 393; 'Il est si vrai que la symphonie était considérée en France comme un travail d'école ... Une symphonie bien écrite était, semble-t-il, l'épreuve suprême du talent des jeunes compositeurs couronnés par l'Académie ... mais elle n'avait sans doute pas aux yeux des juges beaucoup plus d'importance ni une plus haute signification artistique.'

42 Emile Vuillermoz: 'La Symphonie', in *Cinquante ans de la musique française: de 1874 à 1925* (Paris, 1926), vol. I, 325. Bizet's Symphony in C never saw the light of day in its orchestral version; see H. Shanet: 'Bizet's Suppressed Symphony' *MQ*, 44 (1958), 431–47.

43 Saint-Saëns's Symphony in E flat, op. 2 was premiered by the Société Sainte-Cécile under François Seghers on 18 Dec. 1853; his 'Urbs Roma' Symphony had its Paris premiere on 15 Feb. 1857 (Jules Pasdeloup and the Société de Jeunes Auteurs) and its Bordeaux premiere on 10 June 1857; and his cyclic A minor Symphony was first performed by Pasdeloup and the Société de Jeunes Auteurs on 25 Mar. 1860.

in Théodore Dubois's *Fragments symphoniques* (performed at the Society's first orchestral concert on 4 May 1873) and de Castillon's *Esquisses symphoniques* (13 May 1877).

Why did the front-rank French composers avoid tackling the symphony in the 1870s? Doubtless they preferred to experiment with abstract musical concerns – thematic transformation and cyclical form – in the more intimate (and elite) medium of chamber music, without the additional problems of handling a large orchestra. They seem to have found it more conducive to explore the colouristic possibilities of the Wagnerian orchestra, with all its theatrical and dramatic associations, when their imagination was fired by a programme. Perhaps most important of all, the symphony, like the string quartet, generated an enormous anxiety of influence: the weight of the canon, and especially Beethoven's long shadow, had a hugely inhibitive effect. For in a culture of serious instrumental music, the symphony had to be the ultimate genre.

So when French composers returned to the genre in the late 1880s, closely following the symphonic renaissance in Germany, central Europe and Russia, they faced some severe artistic tests. At a technical level they had to reconcile abstract motivic and formal processes with the drama-inspired use of the large romantic orchestra that had developed in the symphonic poem. Like all symphonic composers after Beethoven, they had to reconcile two conflicting impulses: on the one hand, the tendency to expressive grandeur and length that Dahlhaus described as the 'monumental style'; and on the other, the need to preserve individuality, which was associated above all with expressive intimacy. Coupled with this, composers had somehow to establish a claim for their music to belong to the symphonic canon; they had to engage with the great repertoire of the past but still emerge triumphantly original.

The two acknowledged French masterpieces from this era attempted to overcome these problems in very different ways. Saint-Saëns's C minor ('Organ') Symphony op. 78 (1886) has all the accoutrements of a successful late romantic work: formal ambition, motivic integrity and an imposing sound world. Yet it has been criticized for its ostentatious display of colour and for a rift between its architecture and the logic of its thematic transformations.[44] Like his D minor Violin Sonata, the symphony conflates the traditional four-movement plan into two composite movements, but the tonal trajectory follows a very traditional route: that of Beethoven's Fifth and Ninth Symphonies from the minor mode to a 'triumphant' major-mode conclusion. In Beethoven's symphonies the achievement of the minor-major succession has an inexorable motivic logic that fully complements the powerful rhetoric of the final breakthrough. It cannot be denied that Saint-Saëns's work has an impeccable motivic logic. His Liszt-like transformation of the first movement's main theme from an initially quiet *agitato* minor-mode idea to the chorale-like C major tutti in the last movement is utterly lucid, and novel in its instrumental effects.[45] A more subtle web of motivic relationships runs concurrently through the Symphony. Example 3.9 shows how the theme of the scherzo is derived from the first movement's theme by permutational processes. By stretching its central intervals, Saint-Saëns then turns the Scherzo theme into the idea which, in obvious reference to Mozart's 'Jupiter' Symphony, he subjects to fugal treatment in the transition between the

44 Dahlhaus: *Nineteenth-Century Music*, 289.

45 In particular, the statement in unison for bowed cellos and plucked double basses at bars 374–80 in the last movement looks ahead twenty-five years to the opening of Stravinsky's *Firebird*.

two parts of the Finale and in the final development section. The Symphony's off-tonic opening (on a first inversion D flat major chord) also has long-term consequences: the *Poco Adagio* section of the first movement is in D flat major, and the key keeps breaking through with some violence in the Scherzo (for example, at bars 34–40 and from bar 55 onwards). But how successfully do these ideas motivate and underpin the breakthrough to C major at bar 386 of the Finale? 'Breakthrough' is perhaps the wrong word to use here: the *forte* organ entry announcing the arrival of C major is a magnificent *coup de théâtre*, but it does not seem like a hard-won victory. Furthermore, if the goal of the animating motivic processes is the choral-like transformation of the main theme, what necessitates the rest of the movement? Its combinatorial processes place it firmly in the *haute composition* tradition. Yet such extravagant contrapuntal display cannot, in the large public framework of a symphony, generate enough musical tension to power the culminating frenzy. Consequently the end seems forced in comparison with the rest of the work. Ultimately, the monumental rhetoric of Saint-Saëns's Symphony is insufficiently supported by its musical processes.

The monumental aspect of Franck's D minor Symphony (1886–88), however, springs almost entirely from its strong connections between thematic development and formal weight. Franck appropriates the type of subtle, allusive motivic development that he had perfected in his chamber music, and the various cyclic thematic returns that characterize the Finale are thoroughly prepared by the dense network of ideas that marks the Symphony from the outset. Example 3.10a shows some of the pitch cells that connect themes in different movements; but even more important here are the rhythmic cells that keep returning from one theme to the next (Example 3.10b). Rhythmic identity also plays a significant role at larger formal levels. Many of the themes are in bar form (AA'B), and this is reflected on a larger scale in the first-movement exposition and at the start of the second movement, where large-scale repetitions of the initial material produce giant bar forms.[46] This emphasis on rhythmic profiles and broad repetition is reminiscent of Bruckner's approach to symphonic form. But while Bruckner generally subsumes expressive details within long-term processes, Franck's ideas display a lyricism that keeps attention focused on the surface of the music. This might explain why Franck's Symphony is barely half as long as most of Bruckner's. In this respect there is a rift in Franck's conception too: the impeccable logic with which the thematic development supports the monumental architecture is compromised by the very expressive qualities of the themes themselves.

Franck's use of the orchestra in his Symphony has been justly criticized. Superb organist that he was, his general principle was to mix raw instrumental sounds; his colour combinations look imaginative on the page, but they often sound like subtly varied shades of brown. (Perhaps, like Schumann's orchestral music, Franck's Symphony would benefit from sympathetic performance on period instruments.) The dramatic power of the orchestra in *Le Chasseur maudit* and the delicacy of *Les Éolides* largely eluded Franck here. The most successful orchestral textures are those that exploit unmixed sounds, such

46 In the first movement the initial D minor section (bars 1–48) is repeated with minor modifications of detail in F minor in bars 49–94; the remaining 84 bars of the exposition follow a normal plan of second subject and cadential material. So the whole exposition can be understood as a bar form.

Example 3.9 Camille Saint-Saëns, Symphony no. 3, motivic development

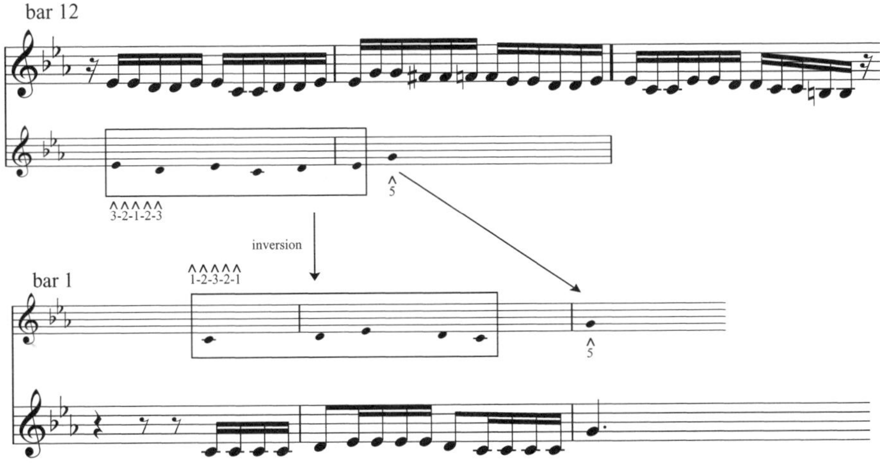

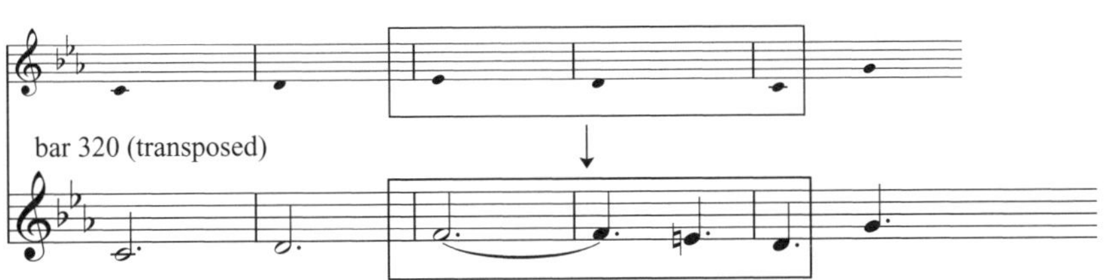

as the cor anglais and viola duet in the opening section of the second movement. Franck tends to over-orchestrate climactic passages, and moments like the start of the finale's recapitulation can all too easily sound hysterical rather than ecstatic.

What all this suggests, of course, is that the two greatest French symphonies from the end of the nineteenth century are deeply problematic works, despite their success at infiltrating the symphonic canon. The means by which both Saint-Saëns and Franck achieved formal cogency and expressive intensity in their chamber music translated inadequately into the public monumentality expected of a late romantic symphony. Younger French symphonists ducked this problem by focusing on other values. Although cyclical principles continued to dominate formal thinking, more emphasis was placed on orchestral colour, both for its own sake and as a structural determinant. Chausson's Symphony in B flat op. 20 (1890–91) has less stylistic coherence and motivic integrity than Franck's Symphony, but it flows better and is orchestrated with much more panache. Dukas's gifts as an orchestrator raised his Symphony in C (1896) to a higher plane than its somewhat derivative materials would otherwise warrant. The piece that kicked most vigorously against Germanic traditions was d'Indy's *Symphonie sur un chant montagnard français* (1886). By basing the work on a folk tune from his native Ardèche region and by

Example 3.10(a) César Franck, Symphony, pitch cells

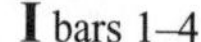

bars 9–10

x

II bars 17–18 y

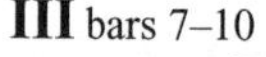

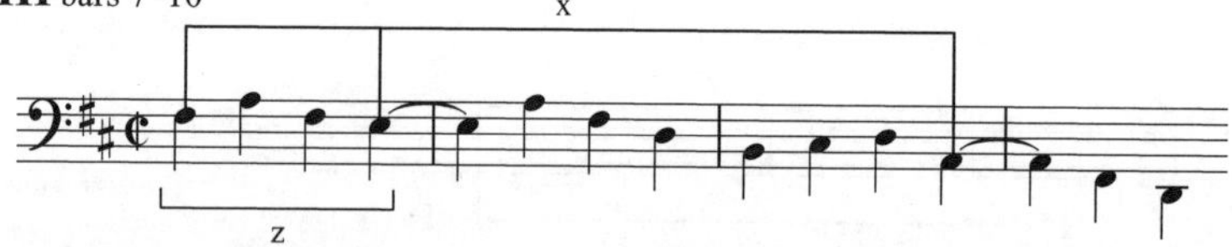

bars 31–2

Example 3.10(b) César Franck, Symphony, rhythmic cells

I bar 13

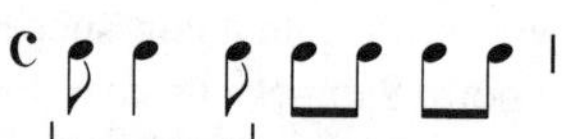

bars 43–4

bars 129–32

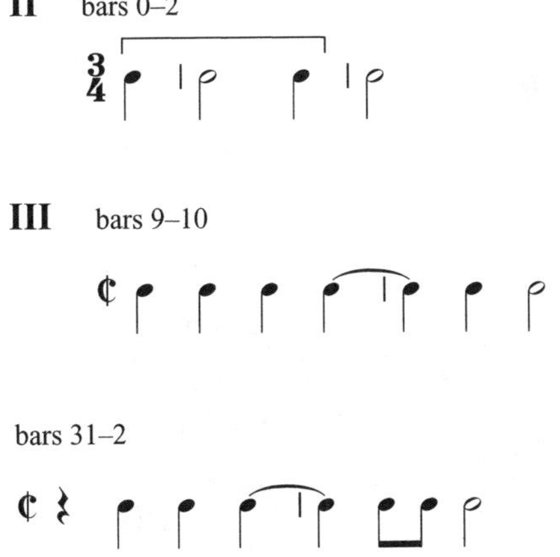

incorporating a prominent solo piano part, d'Indy at a stroke severed connections with the absolutist aesthetics, the consciously high-art ideals, and the profoundly anti-concertante nature of the German symphony.

It could be argued that French composers achieved a more complete success in their concertos and concertante orchestral pieces than in their symphonies. Following the rise of the virtuoso concerto in the 1830s and 1840s, with its total emphasis on the soloist at the expense of any musical interest in the orchestral accompaniment, the reputation of the concerto had taken a serious blow. France, however, had a parallel tradition of symphonic concerto writing in which thematic integration and complex relations between the soloist and orchestra took precedence over 'empty' virtuosity: a tradition that stretched back to Litolff's concertos from the 1850s and beyond.[47] The idea that the soloist should be *primus inter pares*, engaging in a dialogue with the orchestra, was still the defining feature of French repertoire in the closing decades of the century. Since the late classical period the concerto had been a medium in which the grandeur of the symphony could be softened by the intimacy of chamber-like textures in solo sections. As textural contrast was at the heart of the concerto, there was more room to explore the colouristic potential of the orchestra without compromising the integrity of the underlying conception of the genre. In short, the concerto was perhaps better suited to the talents of French composers than was the symphony. Moreover, they were not competing with a strong, modern German canon in their concertos, and the relative lack of an anxiety of influence tells here: French composers seem to inhabit their concertos much more comfortably than their symphonies. However, these works do reflect many of the contemporaneous developments in symphonic and chamber music. Cyclical principles and transformations processes animate Saint-Saëns's Fourth Piano Concerto (op. 44, 1875) and Franck's *Variations symphoniques* (1885); exotic colour permeates Lalo's *Symphonie espagnol* (op. 21, 1873) and Saint-Saëns's Fifth Piano Concerto ('Egyptian' op. 103; 1896); and several concertante works

47 For a detailed account of the classical tendency in this area, see Michael Stegemann: *Camille Saint-Saëns and the French Solo Concerto from 1850 to 1920*, trans. A. C. Sherwin (Aldershot, Ashgate, 1991).

NEUVIÈME ANNÉE — N° 93 JUIN 1910

MUSICA

ABONNEMENTS : France et Belgique : 12 fr. par an ; Étranger : 18 fr. (Changement d'adresse : 0 fr. 50 centimes)
PUBLICATIONS PIERRE LAFITTE ET Cie, 90, Avenue des Champs-Élysées. (Téléph. : 528-64, 528-66, 528-68).
(*Pour la publicité* : Huguet, Minart et Cie 11, boulevard des Italiens. PARIS.)

M. Louis Aubert. M. A.-Z. Mathot. M. André Caplet. M. Charles Kœcklin. M. Emile Vuillermoz. M. Jean Huré.
M. Maurice Ravel. M. Gabriel Fauré. M. Roger-Ducasse.

Plate 3.2 Cover of the large-format glossy musical review *Musica* for June 1910 showing the reading of a new work at the Société Musicale Indépendente.

The caption reads 'Under the chairmanship of the president, Gabriel Fauré, a very important musical gathering is in session, having assumed the title of the 'Société Musicale Indépendente'. The committee is composed of MM Louis Aubert, André Caplet, Roger Ducasse, Florent Schmitt, Jean Huré, Charles Koechlin, Maurice Ravel, Émile Vuillermoz, A-Z Mathot (secretary).

have a programmatic basis, including Franck's *Les Djinns* (1884), and Chausson's *Poème* (op. 25, 1898; 'Le chant de l'amour triomphant' based on a short story by Turgenev).

Discussing the innovations of French orchestral music in the years after 1870, Émile Vuillermoz identified decisive developments in harmonic language and orchestral colour, but played down the French contribution to the evolution of new forms.[48] In terms of stylistic detail, Vuillermoz was undoubtedly right to single out the novelties of these traits and to see them as precursors of twentieth-century orchestral practices. But from a broader historical angle, the real French achievements during this period were the creation and development of a culture of serious instrumental music, together with the assimilation and ultimate transcendence of musical techniques and aesthetic values appropriated from the canon of German instrumental music. The profound change in musical culture whereby instrumental music was placed on a more equal footing with spectacle, even if it did not topple its dominance, was of paramount importance for future developments. And at its best, French chamber music from this period did not merely ape the advances of the new German school, but it far outstripped the achievements of all but its choicest German rivals.

Suggested Further Reading

Carolyn Abbate: *Unsung Voices: Opera and Musical Narrative in the Nineteenth Century* (Princeton: Princeton University Press, 1991).

Michel Chion: *Le poème symphonique et la musique à programme* (Paris: Fayard, 1993).

Carl Dahlhaus: *Nineteenth-Century Music*, trans. J. B. Robinson (Berkeley and Los Angeles: University of California Press, 1989).

Michel Duchesneau: *L'avant-garde musicale à Paris de 1871 à 1939* (Sprimont: Mardaga, 1997).

Katharine Ellis: *Music Criticism in Nineteenth-Century France* (Cambridge: Cambridge University Press, 1995).

Joël-Marie Fauquet: *César Franck* (Paris: Fayard, 1999).

Serge Gut and Danièle Pistone: *La musique de chambre en France de 1870 à 1918* (Paris: Champion, 1978).

Jean-Paul Holstein: 'Le renouveau de la symphonie française, 1870–1900: les œuvres', (unpublished dissertation, Université de Paris IV, 1991).

David Kopp: *Chromatic Transformations in Nineteenth-Century Music* (Cambridge: Cambridge University Press, 2002).

Ralph P. Locke: 'The French Symphony: David, Gounod, and Bizet to Saint-Saëns, Franck, and their followers', in D. Kern Holoman (ed.) *The Nineteenth-Century Symphony* (New York: Schirmer, 1997), 163–94.

Jean-Michel Nectoux: *Gabriel Fauré: a Musical Life*, trans. Roger Nichols (Cambridge: Cambridge University Press, 1991).

Robert Orledge: *Gabriel Fauré* (London: Eulenberg, 2/1983).

Angelus Seipt: *César Francks symphonischer Dichtungen* (Regensburg: Bosse,1981).

Basil Smallman: *The Piano Quartet and Quintet: Style, Structure, and Scoring* (Oxford: Clarendon Press, 1994).

Michael Stegemann: *Camille Saint-Saëns and the French Solo Concerto from 1850 to 1920*, trans. A. C. Sherwin (Aldershot: Ashgate, 1991).

48 Emile Vuillermoz: 'La Symphonie', in L. Rohozinsky (ed.): *Cinquante ans de la musique française* (Paris, 1925), 327.

Chapter 4

Music in the French Salon

James Ross

'Salon music' is a cursed phrase, with implications of the sentimental and the second rate. Commercial 'Hausmusik' – opera arrangements, potpourris and *morceaux* – flourished in France as elsewhere. However, the importance of the salon to the history of music during the Third Republic (1871–1940) comes from a few private Parisian institutions which were fundamental to musical life until the Second World War. These salons connected musicians with the worlds of art and literature, publishing, politics and patronage, and provided an informed and sympathetic ambience for new works. The salon in the first half of the nineteenth century was, according to Dahlhaus, 'on a par with the opera house and the concert hall as a crucial venue for the history of music'.[1] Dahlhaus's chronology could be extended by another century.

Music was pre-eminent in only a minority of salons throughout the institution's history from the early seventeenth century to the middle of the twentieth. Traditionally they were places of refined conversation varying from elegantly accomplished verbal trifling to the intellectually profound. Ladies of the aristocracy and the haute bourgeoisie presided in grand style; music rarely rated as more than a diversion. Influenced especially by Chopin and by Liszt, music became of increasing importance in the salon during the 1830s and 1840s. In the Paris season of 1846, there were 850 recorded salon performances.[2]

When Berlioz died in 1869, the salons were still at the centre of musical life in Paris. Regular and often weekly performances were given during the social season. Hosts included composers such as Offenbach; aristocrats such as Princesse Mathilde Bonaparte, Emperor Napoleon III's cousin; the republican writer and Berlioz supporter Juliette Adam; and singers Pauline Viardot and Marie Trélat. Offenbach's experience demonstrates the role salons played: the composer Friedrich von Flotow arranged for him to play the cello at a soirée held by Comtesse Bertin de Vaux in 1838. The performance, which included music specially composed for the occasion, was so popular that the Comtesse agreed to

1 Carl Dahlhaus: *Nineteenth-Century Music*, trans. J. B. Robinson (Berkeley and Los Angeles, 1989), 147. Dalhaus notes that 'what is referred to nowadays as salon music is almost invariably pseudosalon music'. Meg Freeman Whalen discusses the denigration of 'salon music' to mean 'sentimental, shallow, brilliant-but-not-too-difficult music' in 'A Little Republic filled with Grace: The Nineteenth-Century Music Salon', *Women of Note Quarterly*, 3 (Nov. 1995), 23. I am most grateful to Annegret Fauser, Anthony Freemantle, Jann Pasler and Laura Roman for their advice in the development of this chapter.

2 *Die Theaterzeitung* (16 Apr. 1846), cited in William Weber: *Music and the Middle Class: The Social Structure of Concert Life in London, Paris and Vienna* (London, 1975), 31. See also Jeffrey Cooper: *The Rise of Instrumental Music and Concert Series in Paris, 1828–1871* (Ann Arbor, 1983), 86–9.

sponsor a public concert; further engagements followed.[3] This means of establishing a career would become a serious alternative for young musicians to the traditional paths of the theatre and the church, forming an important influence on the development of French music during the Third Republic.

Offenbach's 'vendredis de Jacques' on the Rue Laffitte, frequented by Bizet, Delibes, Halévy, artists, writers and the great photographer Nadar (Félix Tournachon), were dominated by 'charades, little revues, burlesques and parodies of grand opera' rather than serious chamber music and art song.[4] More serious performances were found at the weekly Séances of the pianist Achille Gouffé, whose private chamber music concerts ran from 1836 to 1874; these were reviewed regularly in *La Revue et gazette musicale de Paris*, a valuable source for the musical life of the Second Empire.

The siege of Paris and the Commune (1870–71) caused short-term but transient chaos in the salon. During the siege, and until the final days of the Commune, concerts flourished. Many salonnières took up charity work to help wounded soldiers; the Comtesse de Flavigny headed a Ladies Ambulance Committee, and concerts were held to raise funds for patriotic causes.[5] The end of the Second Empire did, however, have consequences for salons. Juliette Adam was in the city during the siege; Princesse Mathilde fled to Belgium after popular hostility in Paris towards Napoleon III but returned in June 1871. She revived her salon, which endured until her death in 1904 but without its pre-war influence. What Princesse Mathilde lost, Pauline Viardot gained. She had left France from antipathy for the Second Empire but in 1872 returned from Baden-Baden to 50 rue de Douai. Her 'jeudis', frequented by Fauré, and the writers George Sand, Ivan Turgenev, Flaubert and Renan, were described by Saint-Saëns as 'musical festivals'.[6] However, many music salons of the Second Empire, including the Gouffé Séances, the long-running Sunday matinées in the salons of pianists Sophie Pierson-Bodin and Clara Pfeiffer and the weekly soirées of Adrienne Picard, ended during the 1870s. Offenbach, who had escaped Paris during the war, never revived his salon and lived largely outside the city until his death in 1880. A perception of decline after 1870 allowed the American observer Amelia Mason to claim that 'the old conditions have ceased to exist, and the prestige of the salon is gone'.[7] Her pessimism was unwarranted: a new generation of composers and salonnières emerged in the 1880s and their salons are crucial in the history of French music.

The Republic channelled support for music into subsidies of official institutions such as the Opéra, the Opéra-Comique and the Conservatoire. Public funds for music were otherwise meagre: the Société nationale de musique received a government subvention of only 2000 francs per year in 1893 compared with members' subscriptions of 6250 francs.[8]

3 Freifrau von Flotow: *Friedrich Flotows Leben, von seiner Witwe* (Leipzig, 1892), 67–70.

4 James Harding: *Jacques Offenbach: A Biography* (New York, 1980), 103.

5 Arthur Pougin: 'Tablettes artistiques, 1870–71: Les femmes artistes pendant le siège de Paris', *Le Ménestrel* (29 Oct. 1871), 380–82 and (5 Nov.), 389–90.

6 Roger Valbelle: 'Entretien avec M. Gabriel Fauré', *L'Excelsior* (12 June 1922), 2; Camille Saint-Saëns: *Musical Memories*, trans. E. G. Rich (Boston, 1919), 148. Saint-Saëns's memoirs are an important source for Second Empire salons, including Rossini's.

7 Amelia Gere Mason: *The Women of the French Salons* (New York, 1891), 285.

8 Vincent d'Indy, letter to Pierre de Bréville (29 Oct 1893), *Bibliothèque nationale de France, Département de la Musique: Lettres autographes* vol. 55/1 no. 52/130. The sum of 6250 francs is based on d'Indy's estimate of 250 subscribing members.

Plate 4.1 Pauline Viardot at the console of the Cavaillé-Coll organ in her salon.

As today, most composers earned more from teaching, performing and journalism than from writing music; only high-profile singers and virtuosos earned significant fees. State nonchalance was reflected by the lowly place of music in schools: a law of 1850 put singing at the bottom of a list of options alongside gymnastics, and educational reforms of the 1880s and 1922 were so unsuccessful that a 1941 report could claim that 'musical education has failed to find a place in the school'.[9] Limited state support made salons and private patronage essential to sustain interest in new music and its performance. The orchestral *Concerts populaires de musique classique*, founded by Pasdeloup in 1861, the *Concerts Colonne* (1873) and the *Concerts Lamoureux* (1881) performed contemporary French music, but only within the context of established repertoire. Salons offered an alternative and non-commercial setting for serious performance. They were a haven for the new and the controversial, and were central to French understanding and eventual acceptance of Wagner in the 1880s and 1890s. The memoirs of Arved Poorten, from 1890, show musicians at the heart of salon culture. 'The musician is the soul of the salons. He is almost master of them. ... Welcomed and well received in aristocratic society, he is courted among the haute bourgeoisie, respected and adulated among the middle classes.'[10] More practical considerations also encouraged salon performance: they did not need the permits from the Préfecture de la Police required by public concerts, nor were they liable to the *droit des pauvres* tax that continued into the twentieth century.

---

9 Theodore Zeldin: *France 1848–1945. Intellect, Taste and Anxiety* (Oxford, 1977), 483.

10 'Le musicien est l'âme des salons. Il en est presque le maître. ... Accueilli et bien reçu dans le monde aristocratique, il est courtisé dans la haute bourgeoisie, considéré et adulé dans les classes moyennes.' Aved Poorten: *Testament d'un musicien* (Paris, 1890), 118.

Three general types of salon fostered music in the Third Republic: first, those run by musicians; second, literary salons, and finally the great salons of the aristocracy and haute bourgeoisie. Only a minority of the latter centred on music, but some, such as the salons of Comtesse Greffulhe (Elisabeth de Caraman-Chimay) and the Princesse de Polignac (Winnaretta Singer) are fundamental to the history of French music. The boundary between private salons and semi-public institutions cannot be drawn too clearly. The latter, including the Société nationale de musique (SN; 1871–1939) and its rival the Société musicale indépendante (SMI; 1909–35), were private organizations funded by members' subscriptions. The SN's chamber music evenings at the Salle Pleyel and orchestral concerts at the Salle Érard remained private until 1892; even when its concerts were opened to the public, audiences were small and dominated by connoisseurs which made them little different from salon performances. For the SN's orchestral concerts at the Salle Érard during the 1893–94 season, d'Indy calculated that out of the 494 places, only eighty would be available for sale to the public after the Society's members and the press had received their tickets.[11]

The ambiguity in distinguishing between public and private, and the lack of a single accepted meaning of the term 'salon' is illustrated by the Salon des XX in Brussels. Lasting from 1884 until 1893, and continuing as the Salon de la libre esthétique until the First World War, it was founded by two Belgian lawyers and Wagner enthusiasts, Octave Maus and Edmond Picard. 'Les XX' was primarily a 'salon' in the 'art exhibition' sense: it was avant-garde, linked intimately to French and Belgian Symbolist movements and was where, coincidentally, van Gogh made the only gallery sale in his lifetime.[12] During its annual month-long exhibition, the salon held concerts and lectures. These were integral to the founders' aim of realizing a true *Gesamtkunstwerk* by performing in rooms lined by Impressionist and Symbolist paintings and sculptures. By 1888, Les XX was attracting performers of the calibre of Cortot and Ysaÿe and launching the music of young French and Belgian composers. Its list of first performances is a roll call of the greatest French chamber music of the age; it includes Franck's Violin Sonata (1886), d'Indy's *Poème des montagnes* (1888) and Suite in D (1892); Chausson's *Concert* (1892) and *Poème de l'amour et la mer* (1893); and Lekeu's Violin Sonata (1893). The first Libre Esthétique salon in March 1894 included a Debussy festival where his *Proses lyriques* and String Quartet were performed at a time when the composer was almost unknown beyond musical circles. Subsequent salons included first performances of Duparc's celebrated Baudelaire setting *L'invitation du voyage* in a version with orchestra (1895) and Fauré's *Le don silencieux* (1906). 'Les XX' and the 'Libre Esthétique' showed how art and music could coexist to their common benefit. It influenced Picard's gallery La Maison d'art founded in 1895 which held seven concerts in its first year, and the Belgian Labour Party

---

11 The SN held 411 concerts between 1871 and the outbreak of the First World War. Elaine Brody: *Paris: The Musical Kaleidoscope, 1870–1925* (London, 1988), 17. Members (of whom there were 248 in 1893) received two tickets for each concert; 20 were reserved for the press; d'Indy to Pierre de Bréville (29 Oct. 1893), *Lettres autographes*, vol. 55/1 no. 52, 130. SMI meetings were normally held at the house of composer Maurice Delage. These societies are discussed in Michel Duchesneau: *Le rôle de la Société nationale et de la Société musicale indépendante dans la création musicale à Paris de 1909 à 1935* (Ann Arbor, 1994).

12 The painting was *Red Vineyards at Arles*, exhibited in the 1890 salon and sold to Anna Boch for 400 francs. Jean Clay (ed.): *Impressionism* (London, 1977), 309.

(Parti Ouvrier Belge), whose idealistic notions of the role of the arts in advancement of social equality led it to create a concert-sponsoring 'Section d'art'.[13]

When Maus replaced the Salon des XX with the Libre Esthétique in 1894, one of its first Parisian visitors was the eccentric novelist and occultist Joséphin Péladan. In 1892, Péladan had created the first 'Salon de La Rose†Croix catholique', inspired by hearing *Parsifal* at Bayreuth in 1888. Its ostensible aim was to renew art through mysticism, seeking 'to destroy realism and to bring art closer to Catholic ideas, mysticism, legend, myth, allegory and dreams'.[14] Sâr Péladan's exotic showmanship and talent for hyperbole – he dressed in purple and described himself as 'Maccabaeus of the Beautiful' – can easily obscure the Salon's achievement. Between 1892 and 1897, the Rose†Croix, financed initially by Comte Antoine de La Rochefoucauld, brought together 231 artists including Odilon Redon and the young Georges Rouault in the Galerie Durand-Ruel; it also hosted theatre and concert performances. Péladan engaged Erik Satie and then Louis Benedictus as the Salon's 'official composers'. Satie's 'Rosicrucian' music was important both to the salon and to his own development as a composer. According to Alan Gillmor, it was Satie's 'first stylistically unified body of work'.[15] This included incidental flute and harp music accompanying Péladan's Wagnerian play *Le fils des étoiles*, a *Hymne pour le 'Salut Drapeau'* written for the writer's five-act drama *Le prince de Byzance*, the three *Sonneries de la Rose†Croix* and, after his break with Péladan, a prelude to the Satanist Jules Bois's 'esoteric drama' *La porte héroïque du ciel* (1894), and his *Pages mystiques*. The second of these is the notorious 'Vexations', which Satie asks to be repeated 840 times. Benedictus, the lifelong admirer of Judith Gautier, set her Beethoven-inspired play *La sonate du clair de lune* for the 1894 Salon.

The works of Satie and Benedictus were composed specifically under the 'Rose†Croix' aesthetic, but the Salon also promoted a wide range of ambitious and neglected repertoire. The first Salon in 1892 featured a choral concert including Palestrina's *Pope Marcellus Mass* – at a time when Renaissance polyphony was substantially neglected – and a Wagner concert conducted by Lamoureux which included most of the third act of *Parsifal*, not to be staged complete in Paris until 1914. The Salon also included two concerts organized by d'Indy; the first was in memory of Franck while the second promoted the latter's pupils. There was also a bizarre juxtaposition of Beethoven's two last string quartets with a *Marche antique pour la Rose†Croix* written by 'Bihn Grallon', probably a pseudonym for Satie.[16]

Public concerts in art salons were an important performance platform for composers, but their seasons were short; a month-long exhibition, mounted annually, would allow only half a dozen concerts at most. By definition these would be special events, unable to offer

13 Mary-Anne Stevens (ed.): *Impressionism to Symbolism. The Belgian Avant-Garde, 1880–1900* (London, 1994), 49. Details of musicians involved appear in 'Les XX: Dix années de campagne, un peu de statistique', *L'art moderne* (9 Apr. 1893), 115–17. Concerts continued at the Libre Esthéthique, including in 1904 music by Franck and Debussy to accompany that year's Impressionist retrospective.

14 Harold Osborne (ed.): 'Rosicrucians', *The Oxford Companion to Art* (Oxford, 1970), 1014.

15 Gillmor: *Erik Satie* (London, 1988), 71. See also Philippe Jullian: *Esthètes et magiciens* (Paris, 1969); and Roger Shattuck: *The Banquet Years, The Origins of the Avant-garde in France, 1885 – World War I* (New York, 1968).

16 Gilmor: *Erik Satie*, 78 and 271, n. 12.

a sustained network of patronage and professional exchange. However, salons such as Les XX and the Rose†Croix were part of a larger social nexus. Many had links with the newspapers and journals which cheap printing methods and liberalization of censorship laws allowed to flourish from the 1870s. 'Les XX' and 'La Libre Esthétique' were connected intimately with *L'Art moderne*, the symbolist supporting weekly which Maus had helped found in 1881. Out of the 'Rose†Croix' movement came *Le Cœur*, a short-lived Catholic-occult review edited by Jules Bois, which published parts of Satie's *Messe de pauvres* (1895). Some newspapers and periodicals outside the specialist music press also disseminated composers' works directly. *Le Figaro* celebrated operatic premieres with a 'page musicale', publishing a section of the new work in piano reduction. The nationalist journal *Montjoie*, subtitled 'l'organe de l'impérialisme artistique français', lasted long enough to print extracts of music by Roussel, Satie, Schmitt and Stravinsky during 1913 and 1914.

Like most newspapers and journals, *Montjoie* held regular salons, in its case frequented by Satie and Varèse.[17] Leading newspapers like *Le Gaulois*, *Le Figaro* and *Le Journal* held 'cinq à sept' receptions in the editors' offices. According to the foreign correspondent of *The Times*, these were 'veritable salons in which the Paris élite was to be found'.[18] At these gatherings, which included ambassadors, lawyers, playwrights and politicians, he recorded that 'it is the custom to provide first-class entertainments', although how much music was performed is unclear. However, if not major performance outlets, the 'cinq à septs' were obvious points of exchange for musicians and critics.

The sophisticated interconnection between salons, journals and music is illuminated by the story of French Wagnerism in the 1880s and 1890s. Wagner's insensitive comedy ballad *Eine Kapitulation* (1870) and ode *An das Deutsche Heer von Paris* (1871), combined with his opportunistic willingness to associate himself with German nationalism, helped keep his work off the Paris stage after the notorious Opéra production of *Tannhäuser* in 1861 until the 1890s, except for Lamoureux's riot-threatened *Lohengrin* at the Eden Théâtre in 1887 and Pasdeloup's *Rienzi* at the Théâtre Lyrique in 1869. While public performance of Wagner's music dramas was unacceptable, and even fragments played by Pasdeloup or Lamoureux could meet with angry protests, private gatherings played an essential role in the dissemination of his work in France. Interest in Wagner was stimulated by the inauguration of the Bayreuth Festival in 1876, which became a fashionable summer haunt not only for musicians and writers but also the more artistically minded of the Parisian *gratin* (or *Faubourg*, the other commonly used epithet for the city's social elite). In Paris, fashionable Wagnerism was cultivated in salons which included Judith Gautier's 'Bayreuth de poche', the weekly 'soirées wagnériennes' of publisher Wilhelm Enoch, conductor Charles Lamoureux and critic Victor Wilder between 1880 and 1890, and Petit Bayreuth, all connected closely with the journal *La Revue wagnérienne*, published between 1885 and 1888.

The salon thus acted as a base on which Wagner's ideas and works were introduced into France and was not simply a necessity in the face of public hostility. The private character of the salon suited perfectly the exclusivity and refinement cultivated by many of the early French Wagnerites. Belonging to a hermetic club of Wagnerian initiates appealed

---

17 Jane Fulcher: *French Cultural Politics and Music* (New York, 1999), 204.
18 Sisley Huddleston: *Paris Salons, Cafés, Studios* (New York, 1928), 160.

enormously to such cultivated dandies of the 'belle époque' as Péladan, Villiers de l'Isle-Adam and Robert de Montesquiou, horrified by the rapid development of industrialized popular culture, and epitomized and inspired by the fictional Des Esseintes in Huysmans's novel *A rebours* (1884). Théodor de Wyzéwa, who founded the *Revue wagnérienne*, made no apology for claiming that 'the aesthetic value of a work is always in an inverse ratio to the number of minds capable of understanding it'.[19] This rum blend of aestheticism, erudition and snobbery would serve the musical avant-garde well. Later, in 1902, Debussy would have cause to be grateful for the support of the *gratin*, which played a critical role in establishing *Pelléas et Mélisande* amid widespread critical opposition.

The core of Petit Bayreuth, initially meeting in secret to avoid public protest, was a chamber orchestra of amateurs and professionals. Starting in members' salons, Petit Bayreuth performed sections of Wagner's music dramas arranged by Humperdinck. Its leaders included the magistrate Antoine Lascoux, painter Charles Toché, and salon hosts Marcel Gaupillat and Marguerite Pelouze; performers included the violinist Lascoux; the composers Fauré, d'Indy and Messager; and the pianist Pugno as well as Paul Taffanel, flautist and music director of the Opéra, with Chabrier conducting. This was anything but a socially or artistically homogenous group, and eventually it outgrew its salon origins, with meetings held in the hall of the Société d'encouragement.

Parallel with Petit Bayreuth, Judith Gautier's Bayreuth de poche (the nickname was coined by Wagner) started with six Wagner evenings in March and April 1880. The venue was Nadar's photographic studio, home of the first Impressionist exhibition in 1874. The threat of having to endure the music of Wagner evidently caused Nadar's neighbours on rue d'Anjou-Saint-Honoré considerable consternation: some fled Paris in fear of the cacophonous noise which they expected to be inflicted upon them.[20] Gautier also wrote one of the first detailed French studies of Wagner (*Richard Wagner et son œuvre poétique*, 1882) and organized the first complete French production of *Die Walküre*: performed in 1894 at her Paris house by marionettes. These salons complimented the growing interest in Wagner during the 1880s amongst the concert-going public. Excerpts from the music dramas became standard repertoire at orchestral concerts soon after the composer's death in 1883, although the complete works remained controversial on stage until the 1890s.

Even when the Opéra and Opéra-Comique began to present Wagner regularly, starting with *Lohengrin* in 1891, the lead in mounting the first French performances of *Tristan* (28 October 1899), *Das Rheingold* (concert, 13 January 1901), *Götterdämmerung* (17 May 1902) and *Parsifal* (3 June 1914) was not taken by state institutions. Instead, these premieres were promoted by the Comtesse Greffulhe's Société des grandes auditions musicales, one of the most innovative concert-giving organizations of the age.

Of the composers who participated in Petit Bayreuth, some held their own salons, including Chausson, Chabrier and Holmès. After Chausson's marriage in 1883, he combined contacts with his brother-in-law, the painter Henri Lerolle. The ensuing combination of artists, musicians and writers at Chausson's house on the Boulevard de Courcelles was immense.[21] Together they created one of the most significant centres of

---

19 Clay: *Impressionism*, 29.

20 Joanna Richardson: *Judith Gautier* (London, 1986), 138.

21 Chausson's guests included painters Besnard, Carrière, Degas, Denis, Manet, Redon, Renoir, Rodin and Vuillard; writers Bouchor, Gide, de Heredia, Pierre Lalo, Mallarmé, Mauclair, de

creative exchange in Paris, recorded in paintings by Lerolle and Odilon Redon. Chausson was active in the SN, becoming joint secretary after d'Indy's 'coup' of 1886; he was an enthusiastic if anxious Wagner devotee and a beneficiary of the enlightened concert programming at the Salon des XX. A letter from Lerolle describes a 'little meeting' at Chausson's in 1893 where a reading of the final act of d'Indy's *Fervaal* was the main attraction.

> Yesterday we had our little meeting. Present were d'Indy, the hero of the evening, Poujard, Benoît, Bordes, Debussy, Maurice Denis [and his wife]. … I had asked Debussy to bring *Pelléas* but on arriving told me that he had not brought it because that would amount to too much music. So, after dinner d'Indy went to work. He told us in his most bizarre style the subject of the third act, then he played and sang it for us. … After *Fervaal* we talked, some sincere compliments – then at midnight Denis left. … Benoît wanted to go home with Poujard who preferred to stay and meanwhile Debussy was tinkling on the piano, seemingly thinking of something else – the "Now, come on" – "But I have nothing to play" – I find *Pelléas* in his briefcase – and Debussy becomes enthusiastic, d'Indy turns the pages, and Poujaud looks very much impressed.[22]

Lerolle's account shows how a salon could disseminate new compositions among the musical community. The most important consequence was the possibility of mutual exchange and influence between composers long before either publication or first performance of new works. This was particularly important in opera because years could elapse between a work's completion and a staged production. *Fervaal*, *Pelléas* – apart from its pre-performance amendments – and Chausson's *Le roi Arthus* were all completed in 1895 yet not performed until 1897, 1902 and 1903 respectively.[23] Salon performances could prepare influential theatre-goers and win support before a premiere: the reception of *Pelléas* shows how important this could be for an opera's public success.

Chausson was among the composers gathered in Chabrier's salon at 23 rue Mosnier. Manet, Duparc, Chausson, de Bréville, d'Indy, Messager, Lecocq and Saint-Saëns attended, with Chabrier frequently performing at the piano. The music could be serious or light-hearted, such as Chabrier's quadrille parody of Wagner, *Un souvenir de Munich* for piano duet. Like Chausson, Chabrier's substantial collection of contemporary paintings, which included works by Cézanne, Manet, Monet, Renoir and Sisley, illustrates the breadth of his artistic interests.[24]

The salons of prominent writers tended not to feature musical performance; their importance to musicians came from the literary contacts and inspiration they provided. Chabrier attended the Goncourt brothers' and the Marquise de Ricard's receptions, at 10 Boulevard des Batignolles, the central salon of the Parnassian poets; he and Chausson

---

Régnier, Willy and Colette, and composers Albéniz, Chabrier, Debussy (from 1892 to 1894), Dukas, Fauré, Franck and his pupils, Kœchlin, Messager, Samazeuilh and Satie. Chausson's literary and artistic connections are discussed in Jean Gallois: *Ernest Chausson* (Paris, 1994), 352–9. A Chausson salon concert is described in the unpublished memoirs of politician Henry Cochin, quoted in Gallois, *Chausson*, 583–5.

22 Lerolle to Chausson (19 Oct. 1893). J.-P. Barricelli and Leo Weinstein: *Ernest Chausson: the Composer's Life and Works* (Norman, Okla., 1955), 35–6.

23 *Fervaal*: Théâtre de La Monnaie, Brussels, 12 Mar. 1897; *Pelléas*: Opéra-Comique, 30 Apr. 1902; *Arthus*: La Monnaie, 30 Nov. 1903.

24 Chabrier's art collection auctioned in 1896 is listed in Rollo Myers: *Emmanuel Chabrier* (London, 1969), 149–51.

attended Stéphane Mallarmé's 'mardis' held in his tiny fourth-floor apartment at 80 rue de Rome. Mallarmé's circumstances and provincial background – he worked as an English teacher in a lycée and did not return to Paris until he was almost thirty – did not prevent him from attracting the city's artistic elite to his modest apartment. Its small size precluded music-making; however his salon (not a term he would have used) was a major point of contact between the musical and literary avant-garde. His German wife introduced him to Wagner's works, an interest developed by Catulle Mendès, whose publisher, Alphonse Lemerre, introduced him to the impressionist art critic Philippe Burty. Through Burty he met Degas, Manet, Berthe Morisot and Renoir. Mallarmé's direct poetic stimulus for Debussy's *Prélude à l'après-midi d'un faune* (1892) may be the best-known result, however Mallarmé also inspired a group of musicians called L'École Évolutionniste-Instrumentiste; one of them, the Italian composer Victor Emmanuele Lombardi, anticipated Debussy by attempting to set Mallarmé's *L'après-midi d'un faune* in 1887.[25]

Another integral member of the French Wagnerian coterie that developed in the 1870s and 1880s was Augusta Holmès. A member of the 'Bande à Franck' and mother of five children by Judith Gautier's husband, Catulle Mendès, Holmès was simultaneously an important salonnière in the musical world and a major composer whose *La Montagne noire* was performed at the Opéra in 1895. A description of Holmès's salon shows how these gatherings compelled conservative listeners to hear the new. One evening Saint-Saëns played extracts from *Samson et Dalila*, followed by Holmès playing a transcription of her early symphonic poem *Les filles de Jephté* while 'Gounod had to listen with thoughtful surprise'.[26] Listeners might hear music not normally to their taste or unlikely to be heard in public performance; social decorum and the intimacy of the salons inhibited the articulation of dissent still common in public concerts.

Gounod's 'thoughtful surprise' may have had reasons other than Holmès's innovative music. Her status as a female musician in a profession still dominated by men was an evident source of tension. 'Do not believe … that the artistic career is more accessible to my sex. This is a grave error. The steps are infinitely more difficult, and the good fellowship, which helps so many artists, is in a way shut out from a woman who has the good – or the ill – luck to be born a musician!'[27]

Holmès used the salon to promote her own music and to maintain her professional status. This contrasts strikingly with the career of Cécile Chaminade, once regarded as the

25 Rollo Myers: *Modern French Music, its Evolution and Cultural Background from 1900 to the Present Day* (Oxford, 1971), 75. Mallarmé's guests also included de Banville, Coppée, Dujardin, Gide, de Heredia, Hérold, de Lisle, Louÿs, Manet, Mauclair, Robert de Montesquiou, de Régnier, Rodin, Swinburne, Valéry, Whistler and from circa 1892, Debussy. The influence of Wagner in his work is discussed in Philippe Lacoue-Labarthe: *Musica Ficta, Figures of Wagner*, trans. Felicia McCarren (Stanford, 1994), 41–84.

26 Elaine Leung-Wolf: *Women, Music and the Salon Tradition: Its Cultural and Historical Significance in Parisian Musical Society* (DMA thesis: University of Cincinnati, 1996), 300.

27 Ibid., 302. The role of gender identity in the career of Holmès is discussed in Karen Henson: 'In the House of Disillusion: Augusta Holmès and *La Montagne noire*', *Cambridge Opera Journal*, 9/3 (1997), 233–62. Marie Scheikévitch: *Time Past: Memoirs of Proust and Others*, trans. Françoise Delisle (London, 1936), 64, mentions how 'a society woman whose talent might even surpass that of a professional player' would perform at the Lemaire salon. Issues of female performers and social class are discussed in Nancy Reich: 'Women as Musicians: A Question of Class'; in Ruth Solie (ed.): *Musicology and Difference* (Berkeley and Los Angeles, 1993), 125–46.

defining 'salon composer' of her age.[28] Chaminade's early career conforms to type: private performances at the salon of her parent's Paris residence, 69, rue de Rome, included her *opéra-comique La Sévillane* and regular appearances during the 1880s at SN concerts.[29] However, for personal and commercial reasons, and with the encouragement of the publishing house Enoch, Chaminade's career from the late 1880s diverged sharply from that of Holmès. Chaminade now eschewed the Parisian salons and the SN and instead of substantial orchestral works such the 'symphonie dramatique' *Les Amazones* (1888), concentrated exclusively on short piano pieces and songs. The origins of the celebrated 'Scarf Dance' are instructive. Initially part of her ballet *Callirhoé* (1888), she followed standard commercial practice by extracting a version for piano aimed at the domestic 'parlour' market. In this form, alongside *Automne* (1886) and the mélodie *L'anneau d'argent* (1891), her mass-market fame was established worldwide, especially in the USA, where as many as 200 Chaminade Clubs were established or renamed from existing institutions during the 1890s and 1900s.[30] Ironically, the composer most celebrated for her 'musique du salon' was no salon composer.

The salon thus presents a social paradox. It was an institution that reflected yet also challenged prevailing gender divisions. Men and women could perform as equals in the salon as they could not in the male-run public domain. As a respectable arena for female musicians, the salon both constrained and gave performance opportunities not otherwise available, except for the few who, like Holmès, were willing to challenge accepted norms or, like Chaminade, accepted a distinctly 'feminine' image for commercial branding and composed accordingly. The higher a woman's social status, the less likely she was to perform outside the salon, and often only in her own, even if – like Madame de Saint-Marceaux and the Princesse de Polignac – she was an accomplished musician. Some salonnières were early advocates of female emancipation: Juliette Adam and the Duchesse d'Uzès, President of the Union of Women Painters and Sculptors, were joint founders of an association demanding equal legal rights for women.[31]

Holmès's reference to 'good fellowship' was pointed; all-male music institutions were only gradually extended to women. The Paris Conservatoire had taught women – in separate classes – since its foundation in 1795. It admitted women to its composition class from 1861, but they were not able to compete for the Prix de Rome until 1904, when Hélène Fleury was awarded a 'Deuxième Second Prix' after Fauré's pupil Juliette Toutain was excluded amid controversy in 1903.[32] Success in winning the 'Premier Grand Prix' came only to Lili Boulanger in 1913, but, as Annegret Fauser has shown, the price of

28 Gustave Feran and Jean Mongrédien: Chaminade, Cécile'; in Stanley Sadie (ed.): *The New Grove Dictionary of Music and Musicians*, 4 (London, 1980), 125; Nicolas Slonimsky: *Music Since 1900*, 4th edn (New York, 1971), 1484.

29 The sole performance of *La Sévillane* took place on 23 Feb. 1883, Marcia Citron: *Cécile Chaminade: A Bio-Bibliography* (New York, 1988), but 1882 according to Cécile Tardif: *Portrait de Cécile Chaminade* (Montreal, 1993), 56. Chaminade's music appeared in fourteen out of ninety SN concerts held between Mar. 1880 and Dec. 1888. Ibid., 54.

30 Ibid., 108–10.

31 Anne de Cossé Brissac: *La Comtesse Greffulhe* (Paris, 1991), 97; Cornelia Skinner, 'Some Salons and their Leaders': *Elegant Wits and Grand Horizontals* (Boston, 1962), 86.

32 Annegret Fauser: '*La Guerre en dentelles*: Women and the *Prix de Rome* in French Cultural Politics', *Journal of the American Musicological Society*, 51/1 (1998), 83–129.

victory was to play the socially acceptable role of a *femme fragile* who 'skilfully negotiated the concerns over women's emancipation pervading the cultural politics of pre-war French society'.[33] A carefully devised public image was also fashioned by Princesse Armande de Polignac, Prince Edmond's niece born in 1876. She became both a composer and the first French female conductor of professional orchestras. The full integration of women into professional musical life was to be a long process; orchestras went on resisting long after the end of the First World War; d'Indy's admission of women, including Armande de Polignac, on equal terms with men at the Schola and employment of female professors at the Schola Cantorum was considered radical. The 'messieurs de l'orchestre' at the Opéra, who included many critics and unaccompanied subscribers, only accepted ladies in the front ten rows of the stalls from 1896; even so, this space retained the atmosphere of a gentleman's club for some time.

The disruption caused by Jockey Club members at the Opéra's *Tannhäuser* in 1861 generates no expectation that the all-male aristocratic clubs of Paris could be centres of music. However, like salons, the interest in music shown by the clubs varied enormously. Even the Jockey Club was not universally philistine: its members included the Comte Greffulhe, whose father had been one of the Club's founders, several members of the Montesquiou family (excluding, apparently, Robert de Montesquiou), several Polignacs including Vicomte Armand and Marquis Melchior, and the Rothschilds. After Bizet's widow Geneviève Halévy married the Rothschilds' relation Émile Straus in 1886, Jockey Club members were among the *tout-Paris* who attended her salon.[34] The Cercle des Mirlitons, otherwise known as the Cercle de l'union artistique, founded near the end of the Second Empire, brought together aristocrats with musicians, painters and writers, and helped launch many artists into Parisian high society. Its membership of over 150 reflected this mixture: presided over by Prince Poniatowski, it included Comte d'Osmond and Viscomte Eugène-Melchior de Vogüé, Manet, René de Saint-Marceaux and a music committee including Alexis de Castillion, Chabrier, Delibes, Fauré, Gounod, d'Indy, Massenet, Messager, Prince Edmond de Polignac and Prince Troubetzkoï. Musical activity centred on weekly private performances at its clubhouse at 18 place Vendôme. Regular chamber music recitals, given either by members or by guest professionals, were supplemented by larger-scale productions. In 1872 a lost operetta part-written by Chabrier entitled *Le service obligatoire*, and in 1873 Massenet's early *L'adorable Bolboul* were performed by the members.[35] The substantial number of musicians amongst the Mirlitons was exceptional, however: the entries of prominent musicians in the annual Parisian 'Who's Who' of the Third Republic, *Qui êtes-vous?* shows few listing club membership. It is evident from the 1908 edition of *Qui êtes-vous?* that the Cercle de l'union artistique remained the most popular club, with members including Henri Cain, Henry Malherbe and Édouard Noël, while composers Georges Huë and André Wormser were members of the Cercle artistique et littéraire, although club members appear to have remained a minority amongst musicians. One reason requires little explanation: the Mirlitons' 3000 franc

---

33 Ibid., 127.

34 Skinner: 'Some Salons and Their Leaders', 167.

35 Roger Delage: *Emmanuel Chabrier* (Paris, 1999), 107–11. The other composers of *Le Service* were René de Boisdeffre and Jules Costé, *Le Gaulois* (30 Dec. 1872). Jacques-Émile Blanche discusses the Mirlitons, which later became 'L'Epatant' and moved to the Hôtel Brillat-Savarin in Rue Boissy-d'Anglas, in *La Pêche aux souvenirs* (Paris, 1949), 153–8.

subscription was far beyond the means of most musicians unless independently wealthy or sponsored by a patron.[36]

Interest in music among the salons of the aristocratic *hôtels particuliers* of Paris varied from predominant to marginal. There is little evidence for serious music in the 'spirited and not over-intellectual salon' of the Duchesse d'Uzès, dominated by painters and sculptors, or of Laure de Sade, Comtesse Adéhaume de Chevigné, founder of the Cercle Interallié.[37] The gatherings of Madame Arman de Caillavet, patron and friend of Anatole France, embraced a huge variety of writers and politicians, but they remained centred on literature, not music. The same applied to the literary salons of Madeleine Aubernon, Natalie Barney, Madame Alphonse Daudet (Julia Allard), Comtesse Diane, the Comtesse de Loynes (Jeanne Detourbey), Baronne de Pierrebourg (Marguerite Thomas-Galline) and Baronne Annette de Poilly.[38] Some salonnières, including Princesse Mathilde, featured music among diverse artistic activities; for others, most famously the Comtesse Greffulhe and the Princesse de Polignac, their wealth equalled their sophistication, and support for new music lay at the heart of their salons.

Princesse Mathilde's is illustrative of how a 'salon' in the best-understood sense of the word could operate. The Princess, niece of Napoleon I and separated from her Russian husband Count Anatole Demidoff, whose fortune from the mines of the Urals bolstered her own, held both literary dinners and Sunday evening salons from 1851. She had played no small role in promoting the cause of her cousin, the future Napoleon III, after he returned from exile in 1848. The Princess was nicknamed 'Notre Dame des Arts' by Saint-Beuve; her niece, Princesse Caroline Murat, described her salon as 'a court in itself' which 'had no equal in the nineteenth century for length of ascendancy' and was 'the home and centre of Parisian intellect'.[39] During the Second Empire her sculptor lover Comte Alfred-Emilien de Nieuwerkerke became director of the École des Beaux-Arts through her influence, and her salon became the centre of an informal network of patronage. She manipulated elections to the Académie française and helped Saint-Saëns to avoid military service.[40] According to the violinist Eugène Sauzay, her 'music salon' consisted of four rooms, of which two had pianos, a third was reserved for string chamber music, and the fourth a chamber organ; when serious performances were given, she imposed silence on her guests, something rarely experienced in public concerts. After 1870, the Princess's political influence diminished, her imperial pension stopped and mansion in the rue de Courcelles expropriated, but she maintained her salon in barely less grand surroundings in the rue de Berry. She still attracted composers including Bizet, Gounod and Vicomtesse de Grandval,

36 *Qui êtes-vous?* (Paris, 1908). Other club affiliations included Henry Bauër, Cercle républicain; Alfred Edwards and former Opéra director Pierre Gailhard, Automobile-Club; Comte Henri Greffulhe, Cercle de l'Union; Edmond Missia, Le Caveau; Prince André Poniatowski, Cercle de la rue royale; and Raoul Pugno in the Cercle Volney, described by Blanche as 'fac-similé' of the Mirlitons. Blanche: *La Pêche*, 156.

37 Skinner: *Elegant Wits*, 86 and 64–6.

38 Other prominent figures at Madame de Caillavet's included Barrès, Clemenceau, Jaurès, Loti, Poincaré, Proust, Renan and Maurras. Huddleston: *Paris Salons*, 139.

39 Princesse Caroline Murat: *My Memoirs* (New York, 1910), 70–71.

40 Joanna Richardson: *Princess Mathilde* (New York, 1969), 72–3 and 92; Huddleston: *Paris Salons*, 161; Raymond Rudorff: *The Belle Epoque: Paris in the Nineties* (New York, 1972), 240–41.

and writers such as Coppée, Flaubert, Edmond de Goncourt, Hugo, Renan, Taine and, in the early 1890s, Barrès and the young Proust, in whose *A l'ombre des jeunes filles en fleurs* she appears in person.[41]

While Princesse Mathilde's salon typified the social and patronage functions that salons had performed for decades, a new generation of salonnières came to prominence in the 1870s and 1880s who raised the salon's importance to music still higher. The most important of this generation were Bizet's widow, Geneviève Halévy, Marguerite de Saint-Marceaux, Madeleine Lemaire, the Comtesse Greffulhe, the Princesse de Polignac and the Godebskis. The history of their salons reveals a closely interconnected world fundamental to any insight into late nineteenth- and early twentieth-century French music.

The salon of Geneviève Halévy, daughter of the composer and wife of Bizet, attained a new social level by her second marriage in 1886 to the affluent lawyer Émile Straus. As with Chausson's and Lerolle's pooling of contacts, this marriage brought together Halévy's musical contacts, including Ernest Guiraud (Debussy's teacher and composer of the recitatives for *Carmen*), Reynaldo Hahn and Saint-Saëns, with her husband's politician and financier friends. The result, assisted by the advice and friendship of Princesse Mathilde, was a salon on rue Miromesnil that was 'one of the liveliest and least formal in Paris'.[42] Musicians, writers and politicians mingled also with other salonnières, including Princesse Mathilde, Comtesse Greffulhe and the Princesse de Polignac.

Family background, the posthumous reputation of Bizet and an astute second marriage raised the status of Geneviève Halévy's salon; well-judged marriages provided the social and economic foundation on which a salon's musical activities could flourish. However, the most historically significant salonnières would be that minority who had maintained close relationships with composers far beyond mere fashionable socializing and intimations of cultural refinement; for them the salon would become a demonstration of real commitment to the careers and work of the musicians they supported.

The quintessential 'salon composer' of the Third Republic was not Cécile Chaminade but Gabriel Fauré. This epithet is no disparagement but a fair reflection on much of his music and the social environment for which it was created. His livelihood was gained mainly through performance, teaching, working as the government's provincial music school inspector during the 1890s, as music critic for *Le Figaro* from 1903 and director of the Paris Conservatoire from 1905. Even so, the salon dominated his creative life. His first sustained contact with salon culture was Pauline Viardot's 'Thursdays', to which he was introduced courtesy of Saint-Saëns in 1872. Fifty years later, Fauré was asked to justify the role that salons had played in his career in an interview for the popular illustrated newspaper *L'Excelsior*; he emphasised their importance in supporting a composer who had concentrated on instrumental music rather than making a reputation in the theatre.

41 Brigitte François-Sappey: 'La vie musicale à Paris à travers les *Mémoires* d'Eugène Sauzay', *La Revue de musicologie*, 60/1–2 (1974), 204–10; Richardson: *Princess Mathilde*, 224–5. The salon's gradual decline in the two decades after 1871 is depicted in Goncourt: *Journal*, vol. 10 (Monaco, 1956); and Richardson: *Princess Mathilde*, 269; Barrès's and Proust's attendance, ibid., 295. See also Proust: *A la recherche du temps perdu*, 3 (Paris, 1949), 142–6; his description of the salon was published under the alias of 'Dominique', 'Un Salon historique. Le Salon de S.A.I. la Princesse Mathilde', *Le Figaro* (25 Feb. 1903).

42 Skinner: *Elegant Wits*, 174.

'I was very much involved in making a living. I had some good friends, and when you're an unknown to the musical public at large it's nice to find people who understand you.'[43] Fauré was fortunate that these 'people who understood' were the most prominent salonnières of his time.

After Fauré's engagement to Pauline Viardot's daughter, Marianne, was broken off in 1877, his relationship with the family was unable to maintain its closeness, and the composer turned for support to Marguerite Baugnies, whom he met through her half-brother, the painter Roger Jourdain. Madame Baugnies's first husband Eugène was a painter and her second was the sculptor René de Saint-Marceaux, whom she married in 1892. She held twice-weekly salon receptions at 110 boulevard Malesherbes from the mid-1870s, with a large primarily social Sunday gathering complemented by Friday evening receptions. While the Sundays could involve music in one room and conversation in another, the Fridays were specialist events, with about fifteen guests invited for dinner, followed by musical performance and discussion. Guests included leading French composers and foreign visitors, and the salon was a formative influence on the Princesse de Polignac, who paid tribute to the quality and exclusivity of gatherings in which 'music, books and pictures were discussed … until the night was almost spent':

> One of the most interesting Salons I ever knew in Paris was that of the sculptor, René de St. Marceaux and his wife. They lived in the Boulevard Malesherbes, and every Friday there used to be an informal reception, after an excellent dinner. Nobody who had not exhibited a piece of sculpture or a picture, or who was not a composer, a scientist or an inventor would ever be invited to these gatherings, to which no simple 'mondain' or mere social star was admitted.[44]

Marguerite Baugnies played other important roles in Fauré's life, both artistic and personal. As her guest in Munich during September 1881, Fauré heard *Lohengrin* and *Tristan und Isolde* on stage for the first time; Baugnies would increase the composer's exposure to Wagner further by funding his joint visit with Messager to Bayreuth in 1888, hearing *Die Meistersinger* and *Parsifal*. Her salon was also where Fauré's marriage in 1883 to Marie Frémiet was arranged.[45]

In 1886 Fauré met the poet and socialite Robert de Montesquiou, who became his informal literary adviser, and introduced him to the poetry of Verlaine and Villiers de l'Isle-Adam; Montesquiou also opened doors to the salons of Paris *gratin*, including those of the Comtesse Adhéaume de Chevigné (Laure de Sade), the Princesse Rodolphe de Cystria, the Comtesse de Gauville, the Comtesse Othenin d'Haussonville (Pauline d'Harcourt), the Princesse Potocka and the Comte and Comtesse Henri de Saussine. By 1897, Fauré was in such great demand that he was complaining that 'there's *too much* of my music being played this winter and too many people want me actually to be there, no

43 *L'Excelsior* (12 June 1922).

44 Princesse Edmond de Polignac: 'Memoirs', *Horizon*, 12/68 (Aug. 1945), 126. The salon is also described in playwright and critic Miguel Zamacoïs' memoirs, *Pinceaux et stylos* (Paris, 1948), 201–203. Foreign guests included Puccini, whom Fauré records as having met twice at Saint-Marceaux's; letter to Marie Fauré (27 Oct. 1900): J. Barrie Jones (ed. and trans.): *Gabriel Fauré: A Life in Letters* (London, 1989), 103.

45 The composer George Migot's extraordinary story of Fauré drawing one of three female names out of a hat is recounted in Nectoux: *Gabriel Fauré* (Cambridge, 1991), 35–6.

doubt to make sure I'm aware of all this flattering activity'.[46] This commercially motivated dimension to Fauré's salon career should however be juxtaposed with the committed musical and poetic inspiration he received from the salon of Marguerite Baugnies and of Montesquiou's most important introduction: to his cousin, the Comtesse Greffulhe.

Not only composers benefited from the power and influence of the salons. They could also launch a performer's career, which could then develop rapidly through a clearly identifiable network of contacts. This is seen in the sudden emergence of the dancer Isadora Duncan in 1900. Starting at the salon of Marguerite Baugnies (since 1892 Madame de Saint-Marceaux), Duncan's rapid rise to fame shows the salons as sophisticated interconnected institutions with close personal ties and artistic agendas.

In 1900 Duncan was an unknown young American in Paris. She had just arrived from London where she had been befriended by Saint-Marceaux's son, Jacques Baugnies. Through him, she was invited to the salon, 'that room [which] held all who counted in Parisian life'.[47] There she danced to Chopin preludes and waltzes, accompanied by Messager, by then music director of the Opéra-Comique. The audience included the playwright Victorien Sardou, Madeleine Lemaire and Comtesse Greffulhe. The latter was astonished by Duncan's talent, in which she sensed the spirit of Ancient Greek dance; Rodin, whose admiration is described vividly in the dancer's memoirs, proclaimed her to be 'sculpture itself'.[48] This success unleashed invitations to perform in the most important artistic salons of Paris.

One of Isadora Duncan's next performances was at Madeleine Lemaire's studio at 31 rue de Monceau, where she danced to Gluck's *Orpheus et Euridice*. Lemaire, called ironically 'L'Impératrice des Roses' by Robert de Montesquiou for her paintings and the flowers that perfumed her apartment, was not renowned for artistic ability. It is not unduly cruel to claim that it was only when Lemaire was not working on what George Painter calls her 'gracefully repellent brush-drawings' that the studio took on artistic significance, when she hosted the most diversely creative gatherings in Paris. As well as Isadora Duncan, the composer Reynaldo Hahn owed much to the Lemaire salon: in 1894, as a nineteen-year-old pupil of Massenet, his singing of his own song cycle from poems by Verlaine, *Les chansons grises*, helped to establish his reputation; it also resulted in his introduction to Marcel Proust. The socially open character of Lemaire's salon made it especially attractive to unknown musicians without the right connections. This openness is seen in the description of Lemaire's salon by the Italian composer Alfredo Casella while a student at the Paris Conservatoire from 1896 to 1902:

> She was a mediocre, superficial artist, who had made herself a Parisian celebrity by specialising in flowers and still life. However, she was a very intelligent woman, who had maintained for years one of the most interesting Parisian salons. ... It was unbelievably heterogeneous: one met there, besides the most illustrious names of the aristocracy and the wealthy middle class,

---

46 Ibid., 225. Comtesse Nicolas Potochka (née Emmanuella Pignatelli) was the dedicatee of Fauré's Impromptu no. 1, 25 (1881); the Comtesse de Gauville: *Poème d'un jour*, 21 (1880). The first performance of *La Bonne Chanson* took place on 25 Apr. 1894 in the salon of Comtesse de Saussine, also frequented by Proust and another important centre for concerts, with close connections to d'Indy.

47 Isadora Duncan: *My Life* (London, 1996), 55.

48 Huddleston: *Paris Salons*, 193; Duncan: *My Life*, 68–9.

> politicians [*sic*] like Zola and Léon Daudet; writers like Marcel Proust and André Gide; journalists such as Rochefort, Bailby and Cassagnac; painters like Degas and Boldini, sculptors such as Rodin; musicians like Saint-Saëns, Cortot and Reynaldo Hahn; or singers such as Chaliapin, Victor Maurel and Muratore. The Lemaire home was always open on Tuesday evenings, and you could bring anybody: it was enough to be a friend of a friend. The maddest animation reigned on those evenings. There was no set programme, but there was always some great artist … and every Tuesday a youth like myself was certain to learn something. Madame Lemaire received everyone with a vast smile. She was extremely ugly but extremely likeable. One received the impression … that the lady of the house remained strangely extraneous to everything that went on in her studio. At any rate, it was a typical salon and perhaps a historic one, as it was so completely representative of Parisian society in the early twentieth century.[49]

Like Madeleine Lemaire, the Comtesse Greffulhe left the Saint-Marceaux salon with a strong impression of Isadora Duncan and engaged her immediately to perform at her own salon. Described as 'that beautiful and unchallenged sovereign of sophisticated Paris … leader of the smart intelligentsia and unchallenged queen of the upper monde … the most distinguished lady in the whole of Parisian society', the Comtesse was born Elisabeth de Caraman-Chimay in 1860. Her father was a Belgian prince, and her great-grandfather was the Prince de Chimay who had founded the Brussels Conservatoire; her mother, Marie de Montesquiou, had studied piano with Chopin's last pupil, Camille O'Meara, and with Clara Schumann; it was at her grandparents' house that Liszt played in Paris for the first time. In 1878 she married the Viscomte Henri Greffulhe of the wealthy banking family; a mazurka, *Soyez heureuse* for piano by Eliseo Lucat, was commissioned for the celebrations.[50]

At the Greffulhe mansion Isadora Duncan remembered dancing in 'an overcrowded salon full of marvellously dressed and bejewelled women, stifled by the perfume of the thousands of red roses, and stared at by a front row of *jeunesse dorée,* whose noses just reached the end of the stage and were almost brushed by my dancing toes'.[51] Her ambivalence is indicative of the Greffulhe salon's significance: not so much for its performances but for its social position at the centre of so many artistic and political circles, and the base from which the Société des Grandes Auditions Musicales de France would be launched in 1890. The Comtesse's cousin, Robert de Montesquiou, introduced Edmond de Goncourt, José-Maria de Heredia, Henri de Régnier, Dumas fils, Catulle Mendès, Paul Bourget, Anatole France, Octave Mirbeau, Rostand and Maurice Barrès. Another collaborator was the eclectic amateur composer Prince Edmond de Polignac, with whom she performed piano duets.[52] Comte Greffulhe, who was elected in 1888 to the National Assembly as a deputy for Dieppe, brought a large number of politicians. On 24 June 1894 the contralto Maria Delna, who had made her Paris debut as Dido at the Opéra-Comique two years before, was performing when a messenger entered unexpectedly. The

49 Alfredo Casella: *Music in My Time: The Memoirs of Alfredo Casella*, ed. and trans. Spencer Norton (Norman, Okla., 1955), 64–5. Lemaire's salon is also discussed in Scheikévitch: *Time Past*, 64–5, and George D. Painter: *Marcel Proust: A Biography* (London, 1989), 170–71 and 175.

50 Skinner: *Elegant Wits*, 57 and 66; Painter: *Marcel Proust*, 142; Brissac: *La Comtesse Greffulhe*, 14.

51 Duncan: *My Life*, 60.

52 Brissac: *La Comtesse Greffulhe*, 99–102; 65.

President of the Republic, Sadi Carnot, had been assassinated by an anarchist. Among the audience at Greffulhe's was Jean Casimir-Périer, President of the Chamber of Deputies, who became the next head of state three days later.[53]

In 1887, after Greffulhe met Fauré through Montesquiou, she invited the composer to stay at her summer villa, 'La Case', on the cliff-tops overlooking Dieppe; he also organized concerts for her salon at 8 rue d'Astorg. He was soon referring to her in gratitude as his 'King of Bavaria', alluding to Ludwig II's support for Wagner.[54] In return, she received the dedication of the famous *Pavane*: first performed at the Concerts Lamoureux in 1888, Greffulhe arranged for it to be played according to Fauré's wishes by an invisible orchestra at a night-time party she threw on the island in the Bois de Boulogne on 21 July 1891, accompanied by mime, dance and a Verlaine-inspired text written by Montesquiou. Greffulhe's ability to undertake such large-scale events had been enhanced three years previously after her father-in-law's death in 1888; her husband had inherited his title and his fortune. For the next season, Greffulhe organized her first concert: Handel's *Messiah* in June 1889, which complemented the annual charity sale of the venerable Société philanthropique at the Trocadéro.[55] The return was a profit of 25,000 francs. (For comparison, Fauré's salary as choirmaster at the Madeleine was 3000 francs per annum.)

The success of the 1889 *Messiah* encouraged Greffulhe to found an organization for large projects beyond the capabilities, means or artistic aims of pre-existing institutions such as the SN, the Société des concerts du Conservatoire and the commercial Concerts Colonne and Concerts Lamoureux. This was the origin of the Société des grandes auditions musicales. With a committee that included Franck, Chausson, Chabrier, Fauré, d'Indy, Messager, Widor and Camille Chevillard, it launched its first subscriptions in April 1890. Its declared aims were 'to give performances of complete works by composers old and new' and 'to be a centre for French composers, to ensure to our country the first performance of their works'.[56] Supporters included Edmond de Rothschild, who gave 1000 francs, and the ill-fated President Sadi Carnot, who pledged 3000 francs. The Society's first performance was Berlioz's *Béatrice et Bénédict* at the Odéon, conducted by Lamoureux in front of 'une salle extra-select', followed by *Les Troyens* and Handel's *Israel in Egypt* (1892), and Grétry's *Les deux avares* and Monsigny's *Le déserteur*, at the Opéra-Comique (1893).

Until 1891, Greffulhe's knowledge of Wagner was, like many of her contemporaries, limited only to extracts of the music dramas, an interest kindled by Montesquiou and by visiting Bayreuth that summer. Her encouragement now influenced the Opéra's decision to stage *Lohengrin* the same year, and she planned for the Société des grandes auditions to

53 Ibid., 112.

54 Fauré to Marguerite Baugnies, 12 Sept. 1887; Jean-Michel Nectoux (ed.): *Gabriel Fauré: His Life through his Letters* (London, 1984), 129.

55 Brissac: *La Comtesse Greffulhe*, 85.

56 'Un groupe de Français vient faire appel aux sentiments de patriotisme artistique de Paris. Il s'agit de la fondation d'une société qui aurait pour but 1° de donner de grandes auditions d'œuvres musicales complètes d'auteurs anciens ou contemporaines, 2° de constituer un centre pour les compositeurs francaises, afin d'assurer à notre pays la primeur de leurs œuvres, trop souvent résérvée à l'étranger', quoted in Brissac: *La Comtesse Greffulhe*, 87. A summary of the Société's aims was given by Gaston Calmette in 'Les compositeurs français joués en France', *Le Figaro* (10 Apr. 1890), 1–2.

mount *Tristan* in 1893. Budgeting for 75,000 francs, leading subscribers would provide 50,000 francs between them, including 5000 from Greffulhe, with the remaining money from ticket reservations. Whilst a production in 1893 proved impossible, it was achieved six years later at the Nouveau Théâtre in 1899, conducted by Camille Chevillard. The Society continued, in close conjunction with those who attended the Greffulhe salon, to mount ambitious productions up to 1913, although the Princess's musical activities were much reduced after 1910 in favour of painting.[57]

When Isadora Duncan danced at the Greffulhe salon in 1900, a final prize awaited her: an invitation from the Prince and Princesse de Polignac. The Princess invited Duncan to dance at the studio in her rue Cortambert mansion where a public concert was arranged. Its success led the Polignacs to assist the dancer to establish subscription performances in her own studio. These events played an important role in launching Duncan's career to international stardom.[58]

While the patronage of the Princesse de Polignac was of the utmost importance to Isadora Duncan, for the Princess it was only one small act in her career as a salonnière and patron that lasted from the 1880s to the Second World War. It would be hard to overestimate the contribution of the Polignac salon to French music: the Princess was responsible for the commissioning of many of the greatest French compositions written from the 1890 to the 1930s.[59]

Born in New York in 1865 as Winnaretta Singer, the Princess was the daughter of the American sewing-machine inventor Isaac Merritt Singer and Isabelle Eugénie Boyer. Winnaretta's motivation was always more musical than social: her fourteenth birthday present in 1879 was a performance of Beethoven's opus 131 String Quartet, and she grew up with her mother owning an octet of Stradivarius string instruments used in her salon established at 27 avenue Kléber after her second marriage to the Duc de Camposelice in 1878.[60] The salon put on weekly chamber music concerts and inspired Winnaretta's own career. In 1880, aged sixteen, she first met Fauré playing Schumann at her mother's château at Blossville in Normandy, and lavished enthusiasm on the Piano Quartet he had finished in the previous year; during the coming decade, Winnaretta provided Fauré not only with moral but also financial support. Her other most formative musical experience was the Bayreuth Festival, first attended with her mother in 1882, where she saw the first production of *Parsifal*. Summer visits to Germany, especially to hear Wagner's music dramas in Bayreuth and Munich, became annual events; it also increased her contacts

57 Brissac: *La Comtesse Greffulhe*, 170–75.

58 Duncan: *My Life*, 62–3.

59 Works inspired or commissioned by the Princesse de Polignac, or first performed at her salon include Fauré, *Larmes*, op. 51/4, 1888, *Cinq mélodies de Venise*, 1891 and *Pelléas et Mélisande* (1898); Ravel, *Pavane pour une infante défunte*, 1899; Stravinsky, *Renard*, 1917 and Piano Sonata, 1924; Satie, *Socrate* (1918), Weill, Symphony no. 1 (1921), de Falla, *El retablo de maese Pedro*, 1923; Tailleferre, Piano Concerto, 1924; Milhaud, *Les malheurs d'Orphée*, 1925; Markevitch, *Partita*, 1930 and *Hymnes*, 1932; Poulenc, Concerto for Two Pianos, 1932 and Organ Concerto, 1938, and Françaix, *Le diable boîteux*, 1937.

60 8 Jan. 1879: Polignac: op. cit., 'Memoirs', 111. The Duchess inspired Frédéric Bartholdi's sculpture *La Liberté éclairant le monde* exhibited at the 1878 Paris Exhibition, the model for the Statue of Liberty. Michael de Cossart: *The Food of Love: Princesse de Polignac and her Salon* (London, 1978), 11. This study is unfortunately unreferenced and unreliable; the Princesse de Polignac's memoirs are also prone to small errors of detail.

Plate 4.2 The 'grand salon' at the Paris residence of the Princesse Edmond de Polignac (Winnaretta Singer).

among musicians: in 1884 she met d'Indy, who was attending rehearsals for the *Ring*, by chance in the Café Maximilian opposite the Munich Opera House.

Winnaretta's first marriage to Comte Louis de Scey-Montbéliard from 1887 to 1891 was followed in 1893 with a more suitable match with Prince Edmond de Polignac. Arranged by the Comtesse Greffulhe and Robert de Montesquiou, it proved a successful if unconventional partnership until 1901 with the death of the Prince, who was described by Proust as 'gracious, a great wit and a formidable musician'.[61] The first marriage in 1887 gave Winnaretta control over her inheritance and the freedom to pursue her own artistic agenda. Chabrier was an immediate beneficiary: in 1888, Winneretta, now the Comtesse de Scey-Montbéliard, presented a concert performance of *Gwendoline* arranged for chamber orchestra and sung by leading singers from the Opéra, at her house. In the same year, she rented the Schloss Fantasie, former summer residence of the Margraves of Bayreuth, and organized a private festival of music by Fauré, including songs, both piano quartets, the first violin sonata and piano-duet versions of *Shylock* and *Allegro symphonique* played by the composer and Édouard Risler. Fauré's attendance at Bayreuth

61 Marcel Proust: *Chroniques* (Paris, 1927), 39. The Scey-Montbéliard marriage ended in divorce in 1891 and was annulled in 1892 by the Church on grounds of non-consummation. The marriage of Winnaretta and Prince Edmond was described, bluntly, by the mother of painter Jacques-Émile Blanche to the prospective bridegroom as a 'union paradoxale' of 'the lyre and the sewing-machine', referring to the Prince's musical interests and the source of Winnaretta's fortune; the imagery of incompatibility alluded also to the homosexuality of both parties, observing that this would not be a marriage at which Mendelssohn's bridal march from *A Midsummer Night's Dream* would be appropriate. Blanche: *La pêche*, 249.

that summer was already assured by the proceeds of a tombola organized at the salon of Marguerite Baugnies; he returned as a guest of the Polignacs in 1896 to hear the *Ring*.

After Prince Edmond's death in 1901, Winnaretta rebuilt her house on the rue Cortambert. The replacement included a grand salon seating 200, still used for concerts, and a smaller 'atelier' for more intimate recitals which included two pianos and a Cavaillé-Coll organ. Unlike the Saint-Marceaux and Lemaire salons, which were organized informally, performances at the rue Cortambert had printed programmes; attendance was by invitation only except when public concerts were held. The balance between conversation and music was weighted in favour of the latter; more and more events at the Polignac salon became separate performances rather than weekly gatherings on an appointed day.

It would be a mistake to limit the importance of the salon to those genres, most notably chamber music and the French *mélodie*, that most fitted its context of performance, general sociability and scale. Salons also played an important role in the cultivation of early music. Aristide and Louise Farrenc, compilers of the twenty-three-volume *Trésor des pianistes* (1861–74), had given 'séances historiques', including performances of Frescobaldi, Couperin and Scarlatti, during the Second Empire; the Saint-Marceaux and Polignac salons developed this interest in early music during the Third Republic. Bach cantatas could be heard at both salons, and Rameau's *Dardanus* received its only nineteenth-century performance at the Polignacs in 1895.[62] The salon was also the main forum for new works in all genres, often in their early stages of composition. It was the ideal place to cultivate a cadre of supporters who could then become prominent advocates for a work when it faced press and public for the first time.

The reception of Debussy's *Pelléas et Mélisande* shows how the support of the salons worked. The Princesse de Polignac, Marguerite de Saint-Marceaux, the Comtesse Greffulhe and a good number of *le gratin* attended the first performance on the evening of 30 April 1902, which followed its riotous *répétition générale*. These salonnières had the power to confer social legitimacy and fashionable chic on a production by their frequent attendance, and all were favourably disposed towards Debussy. Madame de Saint-Marceaux knew the composer through the poet Pierre Louÿs; she had maintained her support after Debussy compromised himself socially through his broken engagement to the singer Thérèse Roger in 1894. Comtesse Greffulhe was introduced to Debussy through the critic and musicologist Louis Laloy; later she was responsible for Debussy's meeting with Mahler in April 1910 before the first Paris performance of the latter's Second Symphony.[63] Had the salonnières stayed away, one of the functions of the Opéra and Opéra-Comique for at least a proportion of subscribers, namely to see and be seen, would have lost much of its purpose. Fortunately for *Pelléas*, the endorsement of the *Faubourg* persisted beyond the scandalous *répétition générale* and the novelty of the first night: Jules

62 Bea Friedland: 'Farrenc', *The New Grove Dictionary of Music and Musicians*, 2nd edn vol. 8 (London, 2001), 580–82; Jeanice Brooks: 'Nadia Boulanger and the Salon of the Princesse de Polignac', *Journal of the American Musicological Society*, 46/3 (1993), 415–68; Polignac: 'Memoirs', 127.

63 Letter, 22 Mar. 1894: Louÿs to Madame de Saint-Marceaux; Lockspeiser: *Debussy his life and mind*, I (London, 1962), 183–5; Christian Goubault: *La critique musicale* (Geneva and Paris, 1984), 108. The Princesse de Polignac's support for Pelléas is discussed in her 'Memoirs', 128 and de Cossart: *The Food of Love*, 80–81.

Renard recorded dismissively nearly a fortnight later 'a special public of rich ladies' and the hostile Jean Lorrain claimed that most of the opera's supporters sat in the expensive seats.[64] Debussy had reacted with disdain in 1898 to the success of Fauré's incidental music to *Pelléas* commissioned for a performance of Maeterlinck's play in London, claiming that 'I can't see his music lasting beyond this present production' and that 'Fauré is the mouthpiece of a group of snobs and imbeciles who will have nothing whatever to do with the other *Pelléas*'.[65] Four years later, snobbery and fashion mixed closely with artistic appreciation in making Debussy's *Pelléas* a success: René Peter later admitted frankly the importance of 'an insufferable and [yet] indispensable spectator, without which no truly original artistic event would know how to be consecrated: the snob'.[66] From long experience of the theatre, the satirist Georges Courteline knew that, paradoxically, snobbery could serve artistic innovation. 'Why, the snobs are useful to art. What would we do without them? They applaud indiscriminately and they sometimes do harm. But how often they help the author – especially the new author who tries to be original! That is better than the spirit of routine which only applauds what is established or what is conventional.'[67]

Pelléas demonstrated the power of the salons to help launch an individual production, however their role in the history of the Ballets Russes showed an even higher level of sustained support and was perhaps the supreme expression of the salon's power. Diaghilev's first patron in Paris was the Comtesse Greffulhe, who sponsored his exhibition of Russian painting at the Salon d'automne in 1906. The same year, he met the Princesse de Polignac at a dinner party given by Grand Duke Paul of Russia and his wife, the Comtesse Olga de Hohenfelsen.[68]

Like the Comtesse Greffulhe, the Princesse de Polignac and before them Geneviève Halévy, the basis of Misia Sert's crown as unofficial 'Queen of Paris' was developed by a series of marriages. Born Misia Godebska in 1872, she was the daughter of a sculptor and granddaughter of the Belgian cellist and composer Adrien Servais. In 1893 she married Thadée Natanson, co-founder of the avant-garde literary and artistic journal *La Revue blanche*. With contacts that already included Fauré as her former piano teacher and Mallarmé, whose *mardis* she frequented, and her marriage to Natanson led to her taking charge of the daily salon meetings of the *Revue blanche* in the rue Saint Florentin. These were dominated by the journal's contributors who were as diverse as André Gide and Willy. However, there was also time for exploration of the latest music: Stravinsky's *Rite of Spring* was performed in its piano duet version there in 1913 and, during the First World

64 Renard: *Journal*, 11 May 1902, 510. Earlier he describes how the Greffulhes epitomize the Parisian social élite, complaining that 'notre République qui, depuis la Révolution, n'a pas fait un pas vers le bon sens ni vers la liberté. C'est une République qui ne tient qu'à être reçue chez les Greffülhes'; ibid., 3 Jan. 1898, 311. Lorrain: *Pelléastres: Le poison de la littérature* (Paris, 1910), 24–5.

65 Debussy to Georges Hartmann (9 Aug 1898); *Debussy Letters*, ed. and trans. François Lesure and Roger Nichols (London, 1987), 99–100.

66 'Un spectateur insupportable et indispensable, celui sans qui nulle manifestation d'art vraiment originale ne saurait être consacrée: le snob'; René Peter: '*Pelléas* devant le snob', *Le théâtre et la vie sous la troisième république* (Paris, 1947), 159.

67 Huddleston: *Paris Salons*, 62.

68 Polignac: 'Memoirs', 133.

War, she brought together the fascinating combination of Cocteau, Massine and Picasso to collaborate on Satie's surrealist ballet *Parade* in 1917. Looking back, this seems inevitable. In fact, it showed both discernment and prescience.[69]

After Misia divorced Natanson and married Alfred Edwards in 1905, her opportunities for artistic patronage expanded. Edwards had graduated from being a newspaper editor into one of Paris's supreme plutocrats, owning the Théâtre de Paris, its accompanying Casino and the powerful mass-circulation newspaper *Le Matin*. Romain Rolland observed that the paper could 'hold ministers, politicians and artists like dogs on a lead'.[70] She quickly put her new-found influence to good use in publicizing the 'Affaire Ravel', when the composer was excluded from the 1905 Prix de Rome, which *Le Matin* turned from an injustice into a public scandal. Ravel's gratitude to Misia is evident in the dedications of his song *Le cygne* and of his *Introduction and Allegro*.

Ravel dedicated his Piano Sonatina to Misia's half-brother, Cyprien (Cipa) Godebski and to his pianist-wife Ida, and his *Mother Goose Suite* to their children, Marie (Mimi) and Jean. Ravel's description of the Godebskis as 'subtle and spiritual' is a tribute to a close and creative friendship: at their Sunday soirées from the 1900s to the 1920s, Ida frequently performed her guests' works. In 1909, the salon became an important forum for the newly founded Société musicale indépendante.[71] The Godebski salon was 'where all French or foreign artists who really counted gathered on Sundays'.[72] However, like other salons its activities were disrupted severely by the First World War, of which the economic and artistic consequences were deeper than the 1870–71 conflict.

After 1918, with the Comtesse Greffulhe withdrawn from an active role in musical life and the lack of a new generation of salonnières with both the inclination and the means to renew the institution as had happened in the 1870s and 1880s, the Polignac salon began to appear an exception in a picture of decline. By 1928, Sisley Huddleston observed with more than a hint of nostalgia:

> The Third Republic which encouraged the bourgeoisie drove the old nobility into its last trenches. Still, one could mention beautiful and accomplished women who queened it over salons which were frequented by the leading personalities of Europe, including the Prince of Wales, afterwards Edward VII. There still existed what the French called *bon ton*. It is not quite dead but it is dying.[73]

The reference to King Edward VII, who had died in 1910, rather than a contemporary monarch, suggested how many salons rested on pre-war reputations. The affluence on which salon culture was based could not help being further affected by the 1929 Wall

69 Jean Mysinski: 'Rue d'Athènes', *La Revue internationale de musique française*, 22 (Feb. 1987), 82; Brissac: *La Comtesse Greffulhe*, 105–6.

70 [Il] tient les ministres, les hommes politiques, les artistes, comme des chiens en laisse'. Romain Rolland to Sofia Bertolini Guerrieri-Gonzaga (1909); Christian Goubault: *La critique musicale dans la presse française* (Paris and Geneva, 1984), 35. Misia's third husband was the Spanish artist José-Maria Sert, 'the Tiepolo of the Ritz', whom she married in 1920. He designed the set for the Ballets Russes' realization of Fauré's *Pavane as Las Meninas* (1916–17).

71 Casella: *Memoirs*, 108.

72 Suzanne Demarquez: *Manuel de Falla*, trans. Salvator Attanasio (Philadelphia, 1968), 49. Ida Godebski was the dedicatee of Falla's *La Vida Breve*.

73 Huddleston: *Paris Salons*, 22.

Street Crash. Cipa and Ida Godebski were forced to leave 22 rue d'Athènes, moving out of Paris to 'La Grangette', Misia's former summer cottage.[74] New private initiatives tended to be concert-giving societies, such as the Marquise de Casa Fuerte's La Sérénade, founded in 1931, rather than salons in the pre-1914 style. The Polignac salon continued until 1939, with Nadia Boulanger taking an increasingly leading role organizing its concerts after the death in 1929 of Diaghilev, who had been the Princesse's principal music adviser after the First World War. This allowed Boulanger to found her 'Ensemble vocale' in 1934, funded directly by the Princess. Important first performances still took place, including that of Poulenc's Organ Concerto in 1938.[75]

Superficially, pre-war salon culture appeared to continue during the German occupation of Paris between 1940 and 1944. A number of prominent musicians fled the city, including Milhaud who fled to Provence; Ibert sailed into exile on the *Massalia* on 21 June 1940.[76] However, Marie-Louise Bousquet continued to give concerts including a recital by the cellist Pierre Fournier in 1941: her house in the place du Palais-Bourbon was described as a 'sanctuaire' by the francophile German officer and wartime literary censor in Paris, Gerhard Heller.[77] Wartime salons were also maintained by Duchesse Antoinette d'Harcourt and by Comte Étienne de Beaumont, attended by German visitors including Herbert von Karajan. Florence Gould (née Lacaze) maintained regular Thursday lunches whose wartime guests included Pierre Benoit, Bousquet; Jean Cocteau; Marcel Jouhandeau and Heller; these continued seamlessly after the war's end.[78] Cocteau read his *Renaud et Armide* for the first time at Madame Boudot-Lamotte's on the rue de Verneuil; Paul Valéry his *Mon Faust* in July 1944 at Alfred Cortot's just before the Liberation.

However, the creative energy that had distinguished the Princesse de Polignac's salon before 1939 was absent from the wartime salons. Their continued enthusiasm for music lost direction and integrity with many musicians either in prison camps, refugees in the southern Unoccupied Zone or scattered abroad. Moreover, Paris salons, like all music institutions in Occupied Europe, suffered from the Nazis' irrationally proscriptive music aesthetics and anti-semitism. After the war the Princesse de Polignac's niece Marie-Blanche preserved the family connection with Poulenc; Vicomtesse Marie-Laure de Noailles remained in Paris during the Occupation and maintained her salon into the 1950s, described vividly by the young American composer Ned Rorem. He saw how Nadia Boulanger's salon soirées now seemed at odds with the spirit of the age, describing how, 'At her "Wednesdays", she moves like an automaton with still enough oil in its unreal veins to provide transfusions for certain human ladies. ... She *receives*, and in a manner unrivalled for quaintness.'[79]

74 Leung-Wolf: 'Women, Music and the Salon Tradition', 322–3.

75 Brooks: 'Nadia Boulanger', 415–68.

76 Gilles and Jean-Robert Ragache: *La vie quotidienne des écrivains et des artistes sous l'occupation, 1940–1944* (Paris, 1988), 34 and 36; Julian Jackson: *France: The Dark Years, 1940–1944* (Oxford, 2001), 300–316.

77 Ibid., 310; Gerhard Heller: *Un allemand à Paris* (Paris, 1981), 62. He was attached to the Wehrmacht's 'Propaganda-Staffel' from Nov. 1940 to July 1942, then to the German Embassy until Aug. 1944.

78 Ragache: 'Salons privés et vie publique', 130–33.

79 Ned Rorem: *The Paris Diary of Ned Rorem: With a Portrait of the Diarist by Robert Phelps* (New York, 1966), 20.

Not all private patronage of music after the Occupation was so moribund. Boulez first heard Schoenberg's Wind Quintet in 1945 at the house of the conductor René Leibowitz. This initiated the young composer's interest in serialism which was nurtured during the late 1940s and early 1950s by Suzanne Tézenas and her friends. They funded Boulez's performances at the Théâtre Marigny which evolved into the Domaine musical concerts and publications (1954–73). However, private patronage was yielding to state support as the leading source of funding new music. From 1937, the government started commissioning composers directly; after 1945, radio became a state monopoly, and it became an important alternative to the salon. In 1959, the establishment of the Ministry of Culture under André Malraux was partly a response to the decline of private sources of support. With the death of the Princesse de Polignac in 1943, exiled in London, it is not unreasonable to see the end of an era. She and her salon were irreplaceable. It is not only poignant but pertinent that the most important premiere of a French work during the war years – Messiaen's *Quatuor pour la fin du Temps* (1941) – was given in a prison camp. The 'brave new world' of the post-1945 era would make the salon, central to the history of French music through the Third Republic, a historical anachronism.

Suggested Further Reading

General Studies

Myriam Chimènes: *Mécènes et musiciens* (Paris: Fayard, 2004).
Jane Fulcher: *French Cultural Politics and Music* (New York: Oxford University Press, 1999).
Sisley Huddleston: *Paris Salons, Cafés, Studios* (Philadelphia: J. B. Lippincott, 1928).
Julian Jackson, *France: The Dark Years, 1940–1944* (Oxford: Oxford University Press, 2001), 300–16.
Elaine Leung-Wolf: *Women, Music and the Salon Tradition: Its Cultural and Historical Significance in Parisian Musical Society* (DMA thesis: University of Cincinnati, 1996).
Gilles and Jean-Robert Ragache: *La vie quotidienne des écrivains et des artistes sous l'occupation, 1940–1944* (Paris: Hachette, 1988).
Nancy Reich: 'Women as Musicians: A Question of Class', in Ruth Solie (ed.): *Musicology and Difference* (Berkeley and Los Angeles: University of California Press, 1993), 125–46.
Cornelia O. Skinner: 'Some Salons and Their Leaders', *Elegant Wits and Grand Horizontals: A Sparkling Panorama of 'La Belle Epoque': Its Gilded Society, Irrepressible Wits and Splendid Courtesans* (Boston: Houghton Mifflin, 1962).

Specific Studies

Anne de Cossé Brissac: *La Comtesse Greffulhe* (Paris: Perrin, 1991).
Jeanice Brooks: 'Nadia Boulanger and the Salon of the Princesse de Polignac', *Journal of the American Musicological Society*, 46/3 (1993), 415–68.
Marcia Citron: *Cécile Chaminade: A Bio-Bibliography* (New York: Greenwood Press, 1988).
Michael de Cossart: *The Food of Love: Princesse de Polignac and her Salon* (London: Hamish Hamilton, 1978).
Isadora Duncan: *My Life* (New York: Boni and Liveright, 1927).
Jean-Michel Nectoux (ed.): *Gabriel Fauré: His Life through his Letters*, trans. J. Underwood (London: M. Boyars, 1984).
Princesse Edmond de Polignac: 'Memoirs', *Horizon*, 12/68 (Aug. 1945).
Joanna Richardson: *Judith Gautier* (London: Quartet Books, 1986).

——, *Princess Mathilde* (London: Weidenfeld & Nicholson, 1969).
Ned Rorem: *The Paris Diary of Ned Rorem: With a Portrait of the Diarist by Robert Phelps* (London: Barrie & Rockcliff, 1967).
Cécile Tardif: *Portrait de Cécile Chaminade* (Montreal: Courteau, 1993).

Chapter 5

French Operatic Spectacle in the Twentieth Century

Richard Langham Smith

Telling the story of French spectacle is not quite the simple task it might have been only a few years ago. Musicology has spread its wings, expanded its perspectives and poses more questions than it used to. Certainly a list of operas done, with a few comments on their relative merit, is neither the story nor the history. Not only does some kind of historiographical method need to be established – what is the 'history' of opera? – but also the fundamental ontological question of 'what is opera?' has to be posed. Is it a series of scores? A documentation of what was done? A list of pieces that have, more or less, 'entered the repertoire'? All, and none of these alone, it might be said. Furthermore why are we writing about it anyway?

For the writer on music these are fundamental questions which necessarily involve perspectives of time, place and changing values. No writer can entirely escape the view of music history that Dahlhaus put forward: that the history of music is essentially a history of 'works', creations of relative 'worth'. On the other hand, a historical overview must give account of what happened: certainly in both nineteenth- and twentieth-century France there was by no means a correlation between what was performed a lot, and what current standards 'value'. For this reason selective tables of French operas premiered at the two major opera houses in Paris have been provided, giving an indicaion of the volume of performances each work received. This overview shows a significant number of works which were well-loved during the first half of the century but which entirely disappeared during the second. It also shows a considerable drop in the commissioning of new works in the latter part of the century. Amongst forgotten composers are Erlanger, Laparra, Savard, Dupont and Leroux, to name but a handful: more unfamiliar names will crop up. On the other hand, works which have been recently revived or enjoyed the luxury of a recording, for example Chausson's *Le roi Arthus*; Magnard's *Bérénice*; and Alfred Bruneau's collaborations with Zola have received delayed attention though success in their day was limited. Is there here another role for the writer on music: to bring out forgotten works in the hope of luring an opera company into reviving them?

In another sense, the traditional role of the historian has been to perceive patterns 'to build the dams in the ever-flowing stream of history', to paraphrase the German music historian Friedrich Blume. While periodization *per se* is of no relevance in the present study, interrogation of the boundaries of the twentieth century may be. Certainly there are striking patterns revealed by an overview of operatic activity in France, for no account of new French opera can ignore the context of operatic activity in which they were produced.

In the nineteenth century new works were born into an environment in which continuity was provided by revivals of a corpus of operas from the 1830s and 1840s. At the Opéra, for example, Meyerbeer's *Les Huguenots* had twelve revivals up to 1913, by which time it had been given 1120 times; Halévy's *La juive* disappeared from the repertoire by the 1890s but by this time it had clocked up 562 performances; Auber's *La muette de Portici* was another staple as was his *Fra Diavolo* at the Opéra-Comique where Boieldieu's *La dame blanche* continued to be revived up to 1910.

A similar perspective on the twentieth century – for the moment ignoring foreign works – yields rather a different context. The staples of the early nineteenth century quickly fell out of favour, and a handful of works from the latter part replaced them and are still in the repertoire. *Carmen*, of course, crowns them all, but was not given at the Opéra until 1959, although it became widely known in the 'operatic' version (without spoken dialogue) throughout the world. Beside Bizet's masterpiece, Massenet's *Manon* and *Werther* have continuously remained in the repertoire: the former enjoyed its 2000th performance at the Opéra in 1952, the latter had already clocked up 1000 by 1928.

But exactly in the year 1900 another important trend began when an extract from Gluck's *Alceste* was given at the *Palais Garnier* for the first time since 1776. Revivals of Rameau; of Rousseau's *Devin du village*; and of the operas of Lully followed and of course became particularly popular during the latter part of the twentieth century, in the wake of the so-called Early Music revival. Beyond the scope of this overview, this aspect of twentieth-century operatic practice merits a study in itself for here, in part due to its attendant train of musicologists, dance historians and design researchers, earlier traditions of French spectacle were revived, imbued with a new vitality.

In another way the revivals of early spectacle were an important symptom of France's rediscovery of her musical heritage and a reassertion of national identity, and were also influential on newly composed French operas of the twentieth century, both in orchestration and subject matter. Neoclassicism particularly took note of the revival of the French baroque, but so, after the Second World War, did such composers as Maurice Ohana, for whom the harpsichord was important. His opera *La Célestine* (1982–87) is not the only twentieth-century opera to rework the idea of the continuo group. Some early landmarks in the revival of seventeenth- and eighteenth-century French opera have been detailed in Table 5.1 (see p. 153).

There's also the problem of 'Frenchness'. In one sense French opera is different from a history of opera in France. What happens in a country is different from what it produces in music in general and in opera in particular. Nineteenth-century Paris boasted a theatre devoted to the performance of Italian opera, and Italian opera profoundly marked nineteenth-century French opera. Its main opera house, the Opéra, or as it was and is officially titled the 'Académie nationale de musique', by no means devoted itself to the promotion of French music alone: quite the reverse. The Opéra first gave Wagner in France, and Wagner was someone who can in no way be written out of the history of French opera. Reactions for and against his work, discussion of his ideas, and operatic outcomes in some way or another indebted to him (whether by reacting against or furthering his methods) figure constantly in any survey of the repertoire of opera by French composers well into the twentieth century. Messiaen's *Saint François d'Assise*, for example, is a work still shot through with leitmotive techniques which, in his earlier work, were explicitly allied to his admiration for *Tristan*.

Then there are also the buildings themselves. Newly sandblasted and still an impressive and unavoidable fixed point in the tourist map of Paris, the Opéra continues to remind us of the centrality of opera not only in the cultural life of the city, the nation and the empire, but also of its place in the political scene, when the tensions between Germany and *la patrie* were played out in front of it, more than once. With riots, cafés wrecked and deaths incurred – all for the sake of warding off German culture – somehow the 'threat' of the operas of Wagner symbolized a threat to the nation herself. Here, surely, was a moment in the history of French opera more important to music history than the charting of plots and their musical projection in some of the best box-office successes of French opera of the day. And here again were events which were still simmering during the first years of the new century, leading once again to reaffirmations of 'Frenchness' as the 1914–18 war loomed.

Certainly the institutions disseminating opera, their remits and their commissions, are central to an understanding of the elusive subject in hand. And since its charter demanded it to focus on Frenchness – both in its commissioning and its engaging of artists – the Opéra-Comique continued to play an unparalleled role as an institution central in the promotion of French opera as is evident if Table 5.2 is compared to Table 5.3 (see pp. 154–9). But while it continued to lead the way in its fostering of French opera up to the Second World War, its fortunes were less secure afterwards. It had foundered economically in the late 1930s and was to founder again in the 1970s, definitively closing in 1972 when a period where it was allied to the Opéra ensued, with the house open for hire to external promoters. It reopened, once more autonomous, but with a diffierent administrative structure in 1990.

Less national than the German problem, in musical terms suffered by many nations – not least our own 'Land ohne Musik' – was the problem of centralization. Everything happened in Paris, it may be thought, but the fight against this, debated and enacted in the many operatic outlets of provincial France, is not only a part of the history of French opera, but brings minor composers and their works into the arena. Brittany, Alsace and especially Provence, where the langue d'Oc (the various dialects of the *midi*) still prevailed, all attracted opera composers to their literature, history and culture. Debates about what their opera houses should promote surfaced from time to time. Should they import the best products of the capital? Or should they serve their regions? There were several answers to these questions and several outcomes.[1]

Having moved for a moment to the furthest tributaries of provincial practice, a response to the previously posed ontological question, 'what is opera?' might be returned to with a final remark before proceeding to the corpus of operas themselves. This is simply that opera is surely act and not text. 'Opera' whatever it is, does not happen until performance, and performance is a dynamic and evolving art. Here a fundamental difference between operatic practice of the nineteenth and twentieth centuries (to generalize a little) might be put forward. While the nineteenth century disseminated operas, the twentieth century

1 For a full picture of the hierarchy of French opera houses see *The New Grove Dictionary of Opera* under 'France', vol. 2, 276–7. In the first rank is the RTLMF (Réunion des Théâtres Lyriques Municipaux de France); in the second a further 'provincial' group of five more, with seventeen in the third group. Useful entries under the names of the towns where these theatres are found are featured in the same publication.

produced them. Practice in the nineteenth (and earlier twentieth century) was to export operas together with their *mises-en-scène*. Production books, largely from Paris premieres, were mass-produced for sale or hire to foreign and provincial theatres and the idea of the 'production', involving 'directors' and 'producers' was an unknown concept.[2] Such figures, involving a modification of the nature of opera, were twentieth-century innovations and have become an integral part of our operatic culture. So Carmen set as a Car-man in a garage is a part of twentieth-century culture, as are all interventionist interpretations of plays and operas which interfere with the topos of composer intention: the 'armchair' *Pelléas*, set in the Edwardian era, seems to have been particularly in vogue of late. Here, too, is a subject for someone, beyond the scope of the present chapter: how has French opera been reinterpreted during the twentieth century? Certainly nineteenth-century operas have formed a large part of its operatic culture and *Pelléas*, as well as Ravel's delicious little operas, continue to fascinate present-day producers who continually seem to find new slants, often stemming from links with the concepts of relatively new disciplines such as psychology and sociology.

To cite one example, Bizet's *Carmen* in its day was an entirely different spectacle from every *Carmen* we witness now, and these present-day re-enactments of Bizet's 'composition' may differ from each other as much as chalk differs from cheese. The continuing life of these operas, which enjoy reinterpretations as knowledge builds upon knowledge, is surely the essence of opera's greatness as an art and is as much a part of operatic history as is a parade of new works.

In terms of genre many difficulties of categorization need to be confronted, more perhaps than in other types of music. France has particularly delighted in them since the seventeenth century. A major though gradual definition was that of Opéra-Comique (not in the sense of 'comic opera' but of pieces allied to 'the' Opéra-Comique.) Originally required to blend acting and music, this requirement gradually eroded and was gone by the beginning of the new century. Composers were free to through-compose at last and could also dream up all kinds of subtitles for their works to add to the already complex taxonomy. So while d'Indy used 'action musicale' and Milhaud 'opéra-minute', more recent inventions have been 'opéra-jazz' and even an 'opéra-clinique'.

Three operas from the first years of the new century conveniently open up distinct pathways in French opera, all of them premiered at the Opéra-Comique: Massenet's *Cendrillon*, Charpentier's *Louise* and Debussy's *Pelléas et Mélisande*. There are good reasons for stretching the boundary back to May 1899 to include *Cendrillon*, even though studies of French opera from the 1920s to the 1970s would probably have excluded such a work, when interest in Massenet was at a low ebb. All too easily dismissed as saccharine, it might have been claimed that by 1900 he'd had his day: certainly his later operas have lacked the staying power of the earlier pieces. More recently his work has undergone intensive re-evaluation, publications on his operas have mushroomed, and an annual festival in his native town of Saint-Étienne has done much to foster interest in his work.

Cendrillon was a great success, not least because of the lavish staging it received from

2 An important collection of these is the collection of production books (*mises-en-scène*) from the nineteenth and early twentieth centuries made by the Association de la régie théâtrale, held in the Bibliothèque de la ville de Paris. See H. R. Cohen and M-O. Gigou: *Cent ans de mise en scène en France* (New York, 1986).

the incoming director of the Opéra-Comique, Albert Carré, who was to exert an enormous influence on French opera both through his commissions and his productions. *Cendrillon* displayed several of Massenet's talents to their best advantage, among them his complex and questioning portrayal of female characters; his clever use of onstage music (in this case a period band for the ball including a viola d'amore); and his skill at the *féerique* – the use of various stock-in-trade techniques to portray magic. But the reason *Cendrillon* has lasted is surely in part due to its retelling of a fairy story which – like that of *Pelléas* – lends itself to translation into the vocabulary of modern-day concepts of the psychoanalytic. Like many children's tales, Cinderella has many variants but its essence is that it is a tale of the absent mother replaced by a cruel stepmother and of the 'ash-child' who has to resort to fantasy to deal with the impossible tasks she is made to perform: in one version of the story Cinderella is made to retrieve lentils which her horrible stepmother has deliberately thrown into the cinders. While its essence is that of sibling rivalry and of the ugly wielding power over the beautiful, the theme of erotic awakening lies beneath the surface, embedded in the symbolic fitting of the slipper by the would-be life partner. In the make-believe world of childhood which opera was increasingly beginning to explore, the happy ending was easy to achieve. Massenet cleverly keeps the love-interest within the realms of childhood fantasy by allocating the role of Prince Charming to a *soprano falcon*, whom he stipulates must be of the right size ('ayant le physique du costume') although modern revivals have sometimes given this part to a tenor. Cain (the librettist's) and Massenet's slant downplays the element of degradation but takes time to explore Cinderella's feelings in their full complexity, in an extended soliloquy 'Ah! Que mes sœurs sont heureuses' ('Ah! How happy my sisters are!') and ends with her resignation to her fate as she falls asleep ('Résigne-toi, Cendrille') Massenet uses distant voices and a chorus of six solo sopranos to accompany the fairy who might be seen as Cendrillon's fantasy-mother – a necessary antidote to the uncaring stepmother who is no mother at all. The fairy godmother's magic powers are projected through virtuosity and *pianissimo* '*notes Eiffel*' (Example 5.1). The opera was an enormous success and had run to nearly seventy performances by the end of 1900.

Also in a similar vein of the *féerique*, *Titania*, by the now forgotten Georges Hüe, deserves a mention, not least because Debussy in his spell as a critic praised the work, finding echos of Weber and 'the atmosphere of magic essential to all those who know how to remain grown-up children'.[3] This idea of the grown-up's relationship to childhood was to be a recurrent theme in twentieth-century French spectacle.

Massenet's creative powers by no means faded in the first decade of the new century, indeed, he was to lead French opera across the boundary even if his reputation was to fade with the 'new spirit' of the 1920s. Alongside revivals of his earlier works at the major opera houses of the world came new creations for both Paris houses and for Monte Carlo. The next of Massenet's *opéras-comiques*, *Grisélidis*, continued to explore an age-old tale which had resurfaced many times in European literature, in this case that of 'patient Griselda', told by Chaucer among others, and although in a different mould, shares with *Cendrillon* the theme of the resigned, self-sacrificing woman (a shepherdess) who vows

3 Debussy: 'Titania', *Gil Blas*, 26 Jan. 1903. Repr. in Debussy: *Monsieur Croche et autres écrits* (Paris, 1971, rev. 1987), 81, and R. Langham Smith (trans.): *Debussy on Music* (London and New York, 1977), 99 and 102–3.

Example 5.1 Jules Massenet, *Cendrillon* (Cinderella), Act III, 2nd tableau: chez la fée

(Come, glide above the heather, Wing o'er the broom your flights!, Come, glide, slide and glide!)

chastity to her Marquis husband, despite hankerings after her first love, the shepherd Alain. A strongly characterized Devil, at times a comic foil, is strongly drawn. Predictably, heavenly choirs assure a happy ending, a feature repeated in the composer's first Monte Carlo venture: *Le jongleur de Notre-Dame* (The juggler of Notre-Dame), again based on a medieval tale, and again with a comic foil for one of Massenet's favourite singers, Lucien Fugère, in the character of Brother Boniface.

The second Monte Carlo venture, *Chérubin*, is in an entirely different vein and well characterized as a *comédie chantée*. The seventeen-year-old Chérubin is a travesty role and this initially unsuccessful opera deals with his dalliances deftly. The five-act *Ariane* has perhaps been overshadowed by Strauss's, if not Dukas' s, treatment of similar subjects, but it was clearly a work of which the composer himself was particularly proud. It enjoyed a revival in Bordeaux in the 1920s and, more memorably, when it reopened the Opéra in 1937. On the comic side, *Don Quichotte* lasted particularly well up to the 1940s and together with *Panurge* (quaintly subtitled a *haulte farce*, after Rabelais) it has been recently revived. Interlocking with their premieres came two Roman spectacles, *Roma* and *Cléopâtre*, the first of these notable as Massenet's most classically pared-down work while *Bacchus* was undoubtedly the composer's greatest flop. Some of these works have still to be reassessed, but there can be little doubt that the twenty-first century will delight in reinterpreting the spectacles of this great musician, a superb psychological characterizer and man-of-the-stage.

Carré's first production of the new century was *Louise*, the only French naturalist opera to secure a firm place in the repertoire. Charpentier had completed the work in 1896 but Carvalho, Carré's predecessor at the Opéra-Comique, disliked the sordid Montmartre setting and wanted the composer to counterbalance this with more lyricism and provide a happy ending. Carré's championing of the work as it was, which he himself directed, proved successful and the opera remained popular for many years, although its sequel *Julien* (1913) quickly faded. The composer was involved in both a film and a recording of parts of the opera which remain an evocative legacy of this streak of urban realism in early twentieth-century French opera. Reminiscent of Gounod, Charpentier's harmonic language is clearly traditional, but in its word-setting, where the dialect of the streets of Montmartre overrides the conventions of conventionally correct prosody – as well as in its use of motives – *Louise* captured on stage the 'thought of the age', which was the composer's intention.[4] The convention of the crowd scene, inherited from the nineteenth century, gave him a chance to portray the poorer side of Paris, not least because the celebrated stage designer Lucien Jusseaume modelled his sets on real-life Montmartre. *Louise* became France's answer to Puccini's *La Bohème* with which it shared the garret-room setting and the ubiquitous stove. Here, like *Bohème*, was not just an opera set in Paris, but an opera *about* Paris. *Louise* has entered the repertoire as one of the most celebrated operatic products of French naturalism, succeeding where the works of Alfred Bruneau – in many ways a more interesting, if less immediately appealing composer – never quite made it.

The same team responsible for mounting *Louise* – Carré and Jusseaume – were also the creators of Debussy's *Pelléas et Mélisande*, the French opera of the twentieth century which has lasted above all others and which continues to be reinterpreted in all kinds of

4 See Manfred Kelkel: *Naturalisme, vérisme et réalisme dans l'opéra de 1890 à 1930* (Paris, 1984).

Plate 5.1 Montmartre as portrayed in the set for Act II of Charpentier's *Louise*, the first time a poor area of Paris had been realistically depicted on the Paris musical stage.

ways. Its genesis is relatively well known: Debussy had seen the single Paris matinée of the play of the same title by the Belgian playwight Maurice Maeterlinck, given at the Théâtre des Bouffes-Parisiens in May 1893. In common with many productions of Maeterlinck's early plays which enjoyed considerable popularity at this time, the production was dreamy, mysterious and vaguely medieval, its visual aspect influenced by the English Pre-Raphaelites, and the fairy-tale books of Walter Crane. But this was a *féerique* with little in common with the fairy godmother of *Cendrillon*: no happy endings, only death, remorse and the old man Arkël 'pitying the hearts of men', and waiting for the cycle to begin all over again in this world-weary kingdom whose name Allemonde indicates its universality.

The opera has generated a considerable amount of commentary and continues to inspire productions which vary considerably in their emphasis. Suffice here to focus on a few of the contrarieties embedded in the work. It has been dubbed *the* 'symbolist' opera for many reasons, first because it sets a play which itself was considered a landmark in the theatrical wing of the Symbolist movement in poetry centred on France and Belgium in the 1880s–1890s. Its symbolism operates on several levels, bearing in mind that a symbol is different from a sign in that it may have a wide spectrum of associations. To pin down a symbol to one interpretation is to miss the point: perhaps even to try to translate the symbols of the play is to destroy them. In *Pelléas* there is a recurrent framework of darkness and light underpinning the whole play, symbols which are developed as the play progresses, sometimes at the expense of much else. To cite one of many examples of the development of these symbols: in Act I, scene iii, darkness and light are virtually the sole subject of the discussion between Mélisande and Geneviève, the former remarking on the darkness of the castle surrounds. Geneviève confirms that there are places where the 'sun is never seen'. They have come, as has Pelléas, to seek the light of the sea, only to find that the sea is dark. Out to sea are guiding beacons but a mist comes down and they become hard to see. Without destroying this symbolism, which incidentally is written into the dialogue both skilfully and most beautifully, it might be remarked that it appears to have something to do with aspiration for the light, and with being able to see ahead or the reverse.

Second, there are more local symbols, often, but not always, adjuncts to the dark–light axis: a shining crown, rings, lamps and lanterns, windows, caverns and eventually the setting sun are among these. Other symbols may be more conventional and rooted in Maeterlinck's severe Catholic upbringing: the scene where Mélisande loses her doves, and the scene where the sheep are seen going to the slaughter. Elsewhere there are symbolic tableaux, less a local mention in the text than a whole scene dependent on staging and musical continuity. The celebrated love scene where Pelléas 'drowns' in Mélisande' s hair as she remains untouchable in her chamber at the top of the tower is the most memorable of these.

The musical language of the opera has been approached in many ways. While some have followed Debussy's self-confessed disdain for the procedures of Wagner, others have noted that at least the use of leitmotives takes over from where Wagner left off. On the one hand Debussy promised an article in the 1890s entitled 'On the uselessness of Wagnerism', and poured scorn on the idea of the character-motive ('they never appear unless accompanied by their damnable leitmotive ... It's rather like those people who hand you their calling-cards and then recite the information printed on them').[5] On the other, his use of leitmotives in *Pelléas* includes clear character-motives for both Mélisande and Golaud which he wrote out in his own hand for an article on his opera in a major Parisian operatic magazine.[6] In this sense too, *Pelléas* is essentially a 'symbolic' opera because the leitmotive itself is the musical symbol *par excellence*, and while on the one hand Debussy uses character-motives, he extends Wagner's later technique of developing motives to express less tangible ideas. Most notable in *Pelléas* is a motive first heard in connection with Golaud's mention of his father Arkël, and returning to signify the

5 Debussy: *Gil blas*, 1 June 1903.

6 *Le théâtre*: June 1902, 5–11.

Example 5.2 Claude Debussy, *Pelléas et Mélisande*, Act V

(You do not know what the soul is …)

blind old man's perception of higher things rather than the character himself (Example 5.2).

There are of course profound differences in Debussy's harmonic language which had at times been Wagnerian in his earlier work and particularly in his first attempt at an operatic work, *Rodrigue et Chimène*, dating from the early 1890s.[7] Some forward-looking ideas from this earlier opera emerge in a varied form in *Pelléas et Mélisande* (Example 5.3a and 5.3b), but more interestingly he reuses a structure where contrasting keys a tritone apart project the underlying themes of the two operas; in *Rodrigue* the conflict between love and duty, and in *Pelléas*, that between light and dark. The extreme sharp key of F sharp major, though often spelt as G flat in *Pelléas*, represents the love between Rodrigue and Chimène, and also that between Pelléas and Mélisande (their love scene in Act IV, scene iv), suggesting that the search for the light, and the discovery of love, are allied (Examples 5.4 and 5.5).

In terms of production, it could be said that Jusseaume's realistic sets were at odds with the symbolic feel of Maeterlinck's play. Some subsequent productions have used more symbolic settings, sometimes based on the symbolist painting of the period, to great effect. In terms of interpretation, the Covent Garden production of 1969, conducted by Boulez and with sets by the Czech designer Joseph Svoboda, was a landmark. Boulez tightened up the crueller scenes of the opera, projecting the scenes beween Golaud and Yniold with a terrifying immediacy.[8] Subsequent productions have to varying degrees obliterated the fairy-tale aspect bringing out the reality of Golaud's dilemma, his jealousy and his cruelty by treating the characters as flesh-and-blood. Arkël has more than once been seen to derive sexual pleasure in his scene with Mélisande, where he was previously a kindly uncle, and the setting of the opera in a drawing room, with scant reference either to the forest or the sea, has also become fashionable. Graham Vick's 1999 production for Glyndebourne saw

---

7 Debussy: *Rodrigue et Chimène*, 1st edition by Richard Langham Smith (Paris, 2003).

8 See Roger Nichols: 'Pelléas in performance I and II', in Roger Nichols and Richard Langham Smith: *Claude Debussy, 'Pelléas et Mélisande'*, Cambridge Opera Handbook, 1989, 140–83.

Example 5.3 Example of an idea from Claude Debussy, *Rodrigue et Chimène* reworked in *Pelléas et Mélisande*

(a) Debussy, *Rodrigue et Chimène*, Chimène's soliloquy, Act I

(The night is as beautiful as our love is tender …)

continued

Example 5.3 *concluded*

(b) Debussy, *Pélleas*, Act II scene i, Pélleas and Mélisande by the well

(It's almost as if the water is sleeping …Would you like to sit on the edge of the marble around the pool?)

the opera as portraying a 'cycle of abuse' where Mélisande becomes the repeating victim, first of Bluebeard and then of Golaud who also, in the most graphic way, abuses Yniold. *Pélleas*, not only in its potential for exploring themes explored in contemporary psychiatry, will no doubt yield further secrets, and perhaps the old way of producing it, where it was often treated as that of a beautiful but impossible love, unable to thrive in a cruel world, will once more fall into favour.

There can be little doubt that Debussy discussed the Wagner 'problem' with his one-time father-figure Ernest Chausson, whose own opera *Le roi Arthus* (King Arthur) was first given in Brussels in 1903, although it had been composed during the years immediately before Debussy began work on *Pelléas*. Chausson admitted that it was only in the last act that he had managed to find a musical language which was 'clear and de-Wagnerised'.[9] Although the opera has many fine moments – for example the entry of Merlin and the scene where Guinevere strangles herself with her own hair – it was not revived complete until the 1980s when a fine recording was made, although the third act was given at the Opéra in 1916. Where Debussy had found a language that has lasted, Chausson had not really found a way out of the Wagnerian impasse, and despite its striking moments, it remains an opera of the nineteenth century, and evidently had little to say to the twentieth.

9 Quoted in J.-P. Barricelli and L. Weinstein: *Ernest Chausson* (Norman, Okla., 1955), 67.

Example 5.4 Claude Debussy, *Rodrigue*, use of F sharp (G flat) major as the 'love' key, at the key moment, projected through its dominant (Act I)

(The moon sleeps in the azure sky, and we dream beneath the caress of her dappled rays …)

Of the several operas testifying to the considerable popularity and musical potential of Maeterlinck[10] only Paul Dukas's *Ariane et Barbe-bleue* ('Ariane and Bluebeard') has lasted. While it includes a tribute quote from Debussy as the character of Mélisande appears, it is different from *Pelléas* in several respects. First, the play is entirely different in feel from Maeterlinck's plays of the 1890s: less symbolic and less fatalistic. Second, he wrote the work as a libretto not a play, and had set-pieces in mind. Dukas's score is more opulent, especially in the series of variations which accompany the opening of the cupboards which contain different types of jewels. The work is also notable for its use of a folk song sung in chorus by the crowd of villagers. Naturally reception of the piece

10 Other French composers who set his works as operas included Albert Wolff and Henri Février; and Lili Boulanger did not live long enough to complete her operatic setting of *La Princesse Maleine*. See *The New Grove Dictionary of Opera*, revised edition, entry on Maeterlinck.

Example 5.5 Claude Debussy, *Pelléas et Mélisande*, Act I scene iii
This shows a first association between a C major diatonicism with 'darkness' and F sharp (G flat) major, with 'light'

delighted in comparisons with Debussy's opera but most perceived different strengths: 'Where Debussy's qualities are more refined, Dukas's are more solid' wrote the critic of *La grande revue*.[11] Dukas himself was perhaps his own most perceptive interpreter, seeing the character of Ariane as representing someone who prefers 'a familiar slavery to freedom'.[12] His pupil Messiaen wrote a little-known interpretation of the piece based on the ideas of darkness and light already perceived as being at the heart of Debussy's opera, though he conceived this opposition in religious terms: 'The light shines in the darkness but the darkness comprehendeth it not.'[13]

11 Litté, *La grande revue*, 25 May 1907, quoted Catherine Lorent: 'Echos de la presse après la création', in *L'avant-scène*, issue on Dukas's *Ariane et Barbe-bleue* (149–50) (Paris, 1992), 70–73.

12 Paul Dukas, article written in 1910 and given to the critic Robert Brussel, first published in *La Revue musicale* (Dukas issue May–June 1936), 4–7, repr. in *L'avant-scène*, 14–17.

13 Olivier Messiaen: 'La lumière dans les ténèbres', *La Revue musicale*, ibid., repr. in *L'avant-scène*, ibid., 79–86.

One composer less influenced by Wagner, and who has seen little revival of interest, deserves a mention if only because of tremendous success in his time. Camille Erlanger's *Le juif polonais* had enjoyed some success at its premiere in 1900 but his *Aphrodite*, based on a series of gently pornographic prose poems by Debussy's friend Pierre Louÿs, became a lavish and celebrated spectacle, as had his teacher Delibes's *Lakmé* with which it shares at least exoticism. Despite its success, *Aphrodite* seems to have been written out of operatic history relatively early on: Henry Malherbe, in his important survey of the repertoire of the Opéra-Comique, gives it scant attention alongside works which enjoyed considerably less success, although he does give us one picture of an empty set. He attributes its popularity largely to the basis of its libretto, which fantasises upon female goings-on around the temple of Aphrodite.[14] Its author, Henri de Gramont, successfully focussed on a few episodes and wove these into a storyline where the sculptor Demetrios, under the spell of the irresistible courtesan Chrysis, agrees to steal certain objects for her from Aphrodite's temple. This Hellenistic fantasy fills the stage with crowds of beautiful courtesans, lesbians, and eunuchs, and alternates extended seductions and flowing dances with scenes of extreme cruelty, most notably a scene where the young Corinna, who is thought to have stolen from the temple, is crucified on stage, with eight blows of a hammer from the ubiquitous despot, in this case Bacchus, drunk at the end of an orgy. Possibly it was this ugly, sadistic scene, which resulted in the opera almost being unmentionable: it was notably omitted from the illustrated magazine *Le Théâtre* which normally covered all operas at both the Paris houses.

All this gives Erlanger ample scope for sensuous arias, dances and use of wordless choruses, and although he claimed to have used the Greek modes as the basis for the work, it is the chromatic scale which is more evident (Examples 5.6 and 5.7). Gramont delights in fashioning a lengthy seduction scene in Act I where Chrysis promises Demetrios anything he wants in an aria which certainly adds grist to the mill to the theory of patriarchal reinforcement so common in turn-of-the-century opera. As an example of the fashioning of stock-in-trade exotic librettos, this moment of pure tosh is worth quoting:

Si tu ne veux que des tendresses enfantines,	If you only desire the caresses of a child
Je t'aimerai comme une enfant!	I shall love you like a child!
Si c'est d'ardentes voluptés que tu desires,	If it is more ardent, voluptuous love that you want
Je te les donnerai!	That is what you shall have!
Je me tairai, si tu veux le silence,	I will be quiet if it is silence you desire
Et si tu veux que je chante, je chanterai:	Or sing if you want song
Ah! [extended vocalise]	Ah!
Je danserai pour toi tout habilleé ou sans voile ou nue	I will dance for you either clothed or naked
Je sais toutes les danses, même celles qu'on n'ose pas danser,	And I know limitless dances, even those which no one dares to dance,
Et rien ne finira que pour reommencer !	And whatever finishes, will only end to begin again!

If Erlanger tried to keep Hellenistic and oriental traditions alive, the equally forgotten Raoul Laparra specialized in operas on Spanish themes. Much admired by Ravel, Laparra was the author of the most comprehensive study to date on Spanish music: an

14 Henry Malherbe: 'Opéra-Comique', in L. Rohozinski (ed.): *Cinquante ans de musique française (1874–1925)*, I, (Paris, 1925), 197–8.

Example 5.6 Camille Erlanger, *Aphrodite*, Act I

(I will be there waiting for you: dressed to your taste, ready to bow to your whims! If you only want the caresses of a child, then I'll love you like a child …)

Example 5.7 Camille Erlanger, *Aphrodite*
Use of chromaticism to evoke the Hellenistic scene

ACTE II

2e. TABLEAU

LE TEMPLE D'APHRODITE

Un temple d'une beauté et d'une richesse merveilleuses. Ornementation compliquée. – Fleurs. – Encens. – Au fond, portes d'or donnant à l'extérieur sur des jardins. – La statue colossale de la Déesse se dresse sur un piédestal de pierre rose chargé de trésors appendus. – Elle est nue et teintée des couleurs de la femme. – Son cou est orné d'un collier de perles à sept rangs dont la plus grosse s'allonge entre ses seins. – A droite on voit le commencement d'un escalier qui s'enfonce dans le sous-sol du temple. – A gauche, au fond, un autre escalier monte en tournant vers des galleries supérieures. – Il fait nuit. – Au dehors clarté lunaire. – Au lever du rideau la scène est vide.

THE TEMPLE OF APHRODITE

A temple of extraordinary beauty and marvellous richness. Ornate ornamentation. – Flowers. – Incense. – At the back gold doors leading to the gardens. – The huge statue of the Goddess is mounted on a pedestal made of pink stone hung with jewels. – She is naked and made up in womanly colours. – Around her neck is a pearl necklace in seven rings, the longest of which goes down to her breasts. – On the right is a staircase going down to the temple. – On the left, at the back, another staircase spirals up to the upper galleries. – It is night with moonlight outside. – As the curtain rises, the stage is empty.

exhaustive article on the various musical traditions of all the regions of Spain, with copious musical examples taken down from fieldwork.[15] This ethnomusicological work was germane to his composition which, as one commentator noticed, owed nothing either to Wagner or to the pre-existent traditions of French opera. Laparra's style was simple, mainly consisting of a succession of undeveloped Spanish-style dances, melodies and *cante jondo* in the two operas which established his reputation, *La habanera* and *La jota*. In both of these – as their titles suggest – the idea of dance is central to the plot, woven into tales of Latin jealousy set within a framework where Catholicism looms large. *La jota*, for example, ends with two lovers struck dead as a cathedral crumbles around them, standing petrified as if still dancing while the jealous priest who tried to break up the couple appears hanging from the crucifix. Laparra was only twenty-eight years old when *La habanera* was first given.

The young Laparra was noticed by Maurice Ravel in 1903 when the latter had served on the jury for the Prix de Rome which awarded Laparra the prize, although Fauré had vigorously dissented from the overall view. Ravel was impressed enough, especially by his elegant command of Basque, to ask a colleague for his address. It is highly possible that Laparra's exhaustive research into Spanish music was known to Ravel since in Ravel's *L'heure espagnole* there are hints of borrowings from the copious transcriptions Laparra presented in this extraordinarily rich article. *L'heure espagnole* was the first of his two one-act operas, often paired in performance with his other, *L'enfant et les sortilèges*, often regarded as lightweight, much-loved favourites which have certainly retained their place in the repertoire. *L'heure espagnole* was first performed at the Opéra-Comique in May 1911.

Significantly, Ravel categorized it as a 'comédie musicale': in one sense a musical comedy, and in another simply a 'musical play' since the word 'comédie' in French means both a play and a comedy. Both these meanings have some significance since the idea of a play set to music was relatively novel, and of course brings to mind Debussy's *Pelléas*. In fact the work was written in a period when Ravel was quite open about his extraordinary enthusiasm for Debussy's opera: he went to every single performance of *Pelléas* during its first run. Perhaps this very enthusiasm explains why he never produced a full-length opera himself, suffering from a case of 'influence-anxiety'.

In both his mini-operas several characteristics that pushed the boundaries of music theatre forward are evident, not least because of his sense of humour, explicitly expressed with regard to *L'heure*:

> I have written a comic opera which I would like to think will prove to be a fresh source of inspiration. Note that in France, this musical genre doesn't exist. Offenbach wrote parodies of opera; today, Terrasse,[16] with delightful verve, distorts rhythms and amuses with his unexpected orchestration, but it isn't the music which makes one laugh. I wanted the chords, for example, to seem funny, like puns in language. If I may put it this way, I wanted to 'hear the humour' [J'ai 'entendu drôle', si je peux dire.] … You should also understand that I did my utmost to make my

15 Raoul Laparra: 'La musique et la danse populaire en Espagne', *Encyclopédie de la musique et dictionnaire du conservatoire* (Paris, 1920), 2353–400. The article is dated 1914.

16 The French composer Claude Terrasse (1867–1923) was a successful composer of light opera and incidental music, collaborating with central (and often humorous) literary figures of his day. Among his output was incidental music for Alfred Jarry's *Ubu-Roi* (1896) and several operas for which Franc-Nohain was a co-librettist.

> work express Spain, and that the numerous rhythms of the jota, habanera and the malagueña will underpin my musical phrases [caderençont mes phrases musicales].[17]

Elsewhere Ravel claims that Mussorgsky's *The Wedding* had been his 'only inspiration' but it seems evident from his parallel claim that the opera was almost entirely an 'opéra dialogué' that the style was indebted also to Debussy's opera. As with *Pelléas*, its text was virtually a straight transcription of the play, in this case a rather trivial one-acter by Franc-Nohain which was premiered at the Théâtre de l'Odéon in 1904 as a warm-up for a more substantial play, *La déserteuse*, also on the theme of an unfaithful wife. Described by one critic as 'mildly pornographic vaudeville', *L'heure espagnole* would be entirely forgotten were it not for Ravel's setting.

Representing a day in the life of a Spanish clockmaker who goes out to wind up the town clock every day, the play exploits all the stereotypical characteristics of Spanish life, among them the idea of the degeneracy of the male stock and the consequent sexual dissatisfaction of the average Spanish woman. But there's also a sense of the surprises of life, captured in the play because it is ultimately the most unexpected suitor that the clockmaker's wife takes to bed: the muleteer. Muleteers, incidentally, were another stereotypical feature of the French constructions of Spanish life, deemed to be so slow because everything, according to the French view, went everywhere on their backs, a view reinforced in the play because Ramiro is the 'government' muleteer. Ravel himself recognized the French perspective describing the play as 'a Spain seen from the heights of Montmartre'.[18]

While *L'heure* will never overtake *L'enfant et les sortilèges* as Ravel's best opera it is worth reflecting on some of its features which refreshed twentieth-century French opera: first, parody; second, a real absorption of the techniques of Spanish music – far beyond a shallow introduction of 'local colour' – and third its extraordinary use of metronomes to introduce the crucial idea of time: the composer himself described the clocks as 'mischievous' and 'grotesque'. Although this may be related to Ravel's delight in mechanical toys, the counterpoint of the ticking clocks which opens the work, coupled with dark music, as if this is a serious play, is striking. It pre-dates similar mechanistic ploys which would have seemed novel even in the 1960s. Furthermore, the parody element, particularly of the final chorus (see Example 5.8), was an element which would come to fuller fruition in *L'enfant*, where Ravel openly confessed his pastiche of many models.

This final scene, after the wife Concepcion has had her way with Ramiro, is a brilliant double parody, on the one hand of flamenco vocal techniques and Spanish inflections, and on the other of eighteenth- and nineteenth-century operatic traditions. It is explicit that she takes him to bed, after a farce with various suitors hiding in clocks, and this was also something of a step forward for opera. Humour is in the music itself in trills and swoops; cascading semiquavers punctuated by over-the-top harp arpeggios; staccato singing in chords; and *notes Eiffels* for everyone. All this is cleverly supported by the triplet-duplet

17 René Bizet: 'L'heure espagnole', *L'intransigeant*, 17 May 1911, repr. in Arbie, Orenstein (ed.): *A Ravel Reader* (New York and Oxford, 1990), 411.

18 Charles Tenroc, 'Les avant-premières: "Thérèse" et "L'heure espagnole"', *Comœdia*, May 11, 1911, quoted Orenstein: *Ravel Reader*, 413.

Example 5.8 Maurice Ravel, *L'heure espagnole*, final chorus
Note the virtuosity demanded from the soloists in the chorus

rhythm of the Habanera. The relationship of *L'heure* to Ravel's other 'little' opera is clear, but before this is examined, an important interlude must be taken: that of the 1914–18 war.

The 'great war' was an important time for opera not only because of what happened during it, but also because musical spectacle seemed to emerge differently after it. Of course things largely shut down, but opera houses played their part with benefit performances, often of popular highlights. Some efforts to harness the power of opera to the cause were made and one composer who was 'conscripted' was Alfred Bruneau, already celebrated, because of his collaborations with Zola, for exploiting the interface between real life and opera. *Les quatre journées*, premiered at the Opéra-Comique in 1916, was based on Zola but its reflection of current affairs at the front was its predominant appeal. The first act celebrates the onset of spring in the provinces, bringing life; the first glimpse of agricultural profit; love, and the renewing of a sense of the locals' allegiance to their region. (Similar reinforcements of regional identity were used for spectacles in the Second World War.) The second act transforms the scene into a battleground, with all the weaponry of the real war. Amidst cannon-smoke on stage, a dying soldier is portrayed, looking forward to the harvest of autumn in this opera which is structured on the concept of the seasons, but turns them on their side. Its point is that *la vieille France* is being disrupted if not destroyed. Perhaps Paris needed reminding. Given only nine times, it was not a spectacle which lasted, but it was, perhaps, one which showed opera at its most topical and in the service of the state.

The Opéra closed at the end of July 1914 and Jacques Rouché took over as director, mounting various concerts at the Trocadéro. The war seemed to energize the revival of Early Music, no doubt in reinforcement of a national identity: a ballet to a mélange of French baroque music reopened the Palais Garnier in 1915 and the following year another ballet, with the music reconstructed by the musicologist Henri Prunières, reminded the Parisian audiences of the musical tastes of Cardinal Mazarin.[19] In 1917 a gala included *La victoire en chantant*, a spectacle based on patriotic songs. Almost entirely forgotten is César Franck's 'scène biblique' *Rebecca* which was the sole work premiered in 1918. In 1919 the normal level of premieres quickly returned.[20] Antoine Mariotte's opera based on Oscar Wilde's *Salome* – pre-dating that of Strauss – only ran to nine performances and was overshadowed by the latter composer's version which ran to 117, and d'Indy's *Légende de Saint Christophe*, premiered the following year which ran only to nineteen performances. Delayed by the war, 1921 saw the first performance of the opulent oriental opera *Antar* by Gabriel Dupont, a composer now neglected, who enjoyed some success in his time. This has been several times revived.

Meanwhile at the Opéra-Comique the most significant premiere was that of Sylvio Lazzari's *La lépreuse* (The leper woman). Lazzari, who had studied wth Gounod, made his name with this opera based on a Breton legend where the heroine shares a cup with her lover to ensure that he is also tainted with leprosy. In common with several former operas with the theme of disease, his later opera *La tour du feu*, first given at the Opéra in 1928, was one of the first operas to use cinema as an integral part. *La lépreuse* was four times revived, before 1945. Here was a composer with a traditional voice, albeit a forceful one.

19 The music was by Monteverdi, Cavalli and Rossi.

20 Although the issues arising out of the promotion of music in France during the First World War are less complex than of those of the Second, the question of the promotion of the arts between 1914 and 1918 merits closer attention.

Enough of Paris. What of elsewhere? No history of French opera would be complete without a mention of the initiatives at Béziers in the South of France: one of several towns where a Roman arena remained and was used for theatrical and operatic productions. They were important not only because some celebrated composers wrote works especially for them, but also because the mounting of works there contributed to the much debated causes of decentralization and regionalism. Why should Paris have all the glory, and in particular all the opera? And why should the regions not have their own voice, and their own 'regional accent' as far as music was concerned? Béziers had rebuilt its amphitheatre and Saint-Saëns had mounted his *Déjanire* there in 1898, revived together with his *Parysatis* in 1902. Performances at Béziers employed huge forces, including what Saint-Saëns himself referred to as a 'curtain of harps'. New works were commissioned including a work by Charles Levadé, *Les hérétiques*; Rabaud's *Le premier glaive*; André Gailhard's *La fille du soleil*; and *Héliogabale* by the composer most vocal in the ongoing polemics about decentralization, Déodat de Sévérac. This latter work, following an evident tradition of themes related to the region or the history of France, is perhaps the most interesting of the clutch.[21]

For the next significant venture it is time to focus on the Opera in Monte Carlo, for it was for the Opéra there that Ravel's second short opera *L'enfant et les sortilèges* was commissioned by the influential director Raoul Gunsberg who had previously championed Massenet, commissioned Fauré's *Pénélope* and would go on to mount operas by Honegger and Ibert. Translations of the title of Ravel's piece vary: 'The bewitched child' doesn't quite hit the mark: it's more concerned with a child's relationship to objects which magically come to life. Viewed at first as a 'charming' and 'delightful' entertainment this 'little' opera has increasingly attracted both interpretation and attention. It presents challenges to producers, since its cast has to double as many characters, as well as challenging costume designers: how do you dress as an armchair, a pouffe, or a grandfather clock? Sometimes roles have been divided: dancers 'act' the furniture and the singers sing. Whatever the case, Ravel is unremittingly demanding on the vocal prowess of his cast.

In terms of its interpretation and its placing in the context of opera two routes may be followed. The first is the way it relates to Ravel's earlier opera, *L'heure espagnole*; the second to its relationship with previous explorations of the world of the child. In the first context, its allegiance to the old idea of an 'opéra à numéros' (a 'number' opera consisting of set-pieces rather than a continuous whole) is clear. In the second, the many previous pieces dealing with children may form a background – from Bizet's *Scènes d'enfants*; Fauré's *Dolly Suite*; and more recently Debussy's *Childrens' Corner* and *La boîte à joujoux*.

L'enfant et les sortilèges is clearly the most profound exploration of childhood opera has so far ventured. A long-forgotten critique of the piece by the child psychologist Melanie Klein has only recently begun to attract attention, because the concepts it develops are themselves fertile, and ripe for more detailed exploration in terms of later child psychiatrists such as Meltzer and Winnicott.[22] Klein, a follower if not a pupil of

21 See J.-M. Nectoux, 'Notes sur les spectacles musicaux aux arènes de Béziers, 1898–1910', in *150 ans de musique française* (Lyon, 1991), 151–60.

22 Melanie Klein: 'Infantile anxiety-situations as reflected in a work of art and in the creative

Freud, wrote an essay on the piece in 1929. She identifies all kinds of symbolism to support her theory of the child's compulsion repeatedly to attack the objects he most desires. Freudian concepts were, surely, not the model for its librettist Colette, who was seen as a writer who wrote from experience and from the heart: it could be argued that her novel *Chéri* and her libretto for *L'enfant* were her masterpieces. One of her recurrent themes is that of the growth into adolescence – in such delightful works as *Le blé en herbe* – and this libretto, in which there was minimal collaboration with Ravel, also has this theme at its heart.

If Klein's ideas are applied to the work a clear structure emerges. (see Figure 5.1). The child is at first rebellious and sadistic in his tantrum (and it must be a 'he', she claims). His will is to destroy those things he most desires: food and drink. There is also the identification of 'mother' with 'world': something he has to grow away from. Feelings projected on the denying mother are projected onto material objects. But then there is a magical transition, and the child's selfishness begins to turn to altruism, his tantrums to tender care.

The manic sadism is projected by Ravel in the extraordinary instrumental techniques demanded: oboe repeated notes to the limit of endurance; sibillant splashes of percussion combined with trills and fluttertongue, and falsetto from the voices. To the listener the sound is shrill in the extreme. Important events in the child's growing up occur as he realizes his need for love and his sexuality: as the princess woos him he becomes aware of an idealized love, as yet asexual because, as he admits, 'his sword is inadequate' (Si j'avais une épée, une épée – if only I had a sword!). The turning point occurs in a magic garden, portrayed with static chords and a 'flûte à coulisse' (swanee whistle) by a phallic tree trunk. Here his sadism turns to altruism, and eventually he binds the wounds he himself has inflicted on the squirrel.

There are tantalizing features in Ravel's music. What is the opening all about? It sounds oriental, with the parallel fourths, and yet there is nothing oriental to be found in the libretto (except the china cups somewhat later). Or are those fourths *elemental*? Is this Ravel's way of introducing the 'child'? Certainly the extraordinary double-bass melody, sounded in harmonics, which joins the oboe fourths sounds like a warped setting of a nursery rhyme, bitonal against the oboe organum. Ravel himself mischievously delighted in the eclecticism of the piece, claiming it as a 'well-blended mixture of styles from all periods from Bach to … Ravel! … going from opera to the American musical, passing through the Jazz band en route'. But according to Roland-Manuel, Ravel was well aware of the dangers of this catch-all approach, knowing that he would be 'severely criticized'.

Never one to wear his heart on his sleeve, or to reveal kitchen secrets about his work, the musical elements that uncannily chime in with Klein's theories may well be fortuitous. An important element is the childlike way in which instruments are approached, and ideas conceived, for example the treatment of the piano as if a child was thumping the black notes with one hand and the white notes with the other gives rise to a musical idea early

impulse', paper read to the British Psycho-analytical society (23 Mar. 1927), repr. in Klein: *Contributions to Psycho-analysis 1921–1945* (London, 1948), 227–35. See also Debbie Hindle: '*L'enfant et les sortilèges* revisited', *International Journal of Psychoanalysis*, 81 (2000), 1185–96; and Richard Langham Smith: 'Ravel's operatic spectacles' in Deborah Mawer (ed.), *The Cambridge Companion to Ravel* (Cambridge, 2000), 188–210.

INTRODUCTION: The mother and transgression

Misbehaviour
Mother
Punishment: deprivation and solitary confinement. 'Dry bread and sugarless tea'.

FRENZY

Child's frenzy ('frénésie de perversité), pleasure in destruction, acceptance of punishment: 'Je suis libre !' 'Ça m'est égal' 'Je suis très méchant'.

[Expressed musically in sybillant use of percussion, manic repeated notes on wind, bitonal attack on piano, 'warped nursery-rhyme' etc.] Attacks on

Teapot
Cup and saucer
Squirrel
Cat
Kettle
Wallpaper
→ Clock and pendulum
Books and papers

LES SORTILÈGES : series of 'entrées' as inanimate objects come to life

Armchair } Symbols of mother and father. (Child is motionless during this.) ←
Bergère }

→ Grandfather clock
Teapot and cup
Fire
Wallpaper shepherds and shepherdesses

CENTREPIECE: Princess (Awakening of feelings of tenderness, nascent sexuality) ←

Maths master
Copulating cats ←

Growth of child's sexuality

INTERLUDE: Garden of renewal

GROWTH OF ALTRUISM

Binds squirrel's paw. (Klein's theory of reparation)
Recognition of beauty of dragonflies (Waltz)

Reacceptance of Maman and authority

Figure 5.1 Ravel, *L'enfant et les sortilèges*: structure of opera

Example 5.9 Maurice Ravel, *L'enfant et les sortilèges*, black-and-white note device

Derived from childish piano-playing

on (Example 5.9). And even if the work is a parade of pastiches, the choice of pastiche styles signifying the child's relationships with the objects is surely by no means random. For example the child's relationship to the duet between the armchair and the bergère seems to be one where he is powerless against parental authority, signified by a neo-baroque style of music with ornaments over a regular pulse, this 'older' style representing the grown-ups. Later, in his crucial duet with the Princess, representing a growth towards the ability to love, the counterpoint is less ordered, more like an oriental heterophony. Is it fortuitous that in the raunchy cat duet where the child becomes aware of the act of coitus, the same descending fourth that represents the mother is used? Here is a piece which follows Debussy's *Pelléas* in following a symbolist path, though in this case the real-life symbolism explored by Freud.

By comparison with Ravel's minor masterpiece, many of the other operas premiered during the 1920s seem rather old hat. Hardly any other opera of the decade came anywhere near *L'enfant* as far as lasting in the repertoire was concerned. While the forgotten Charles Silver's *Taming of the shrew* (*La megère apprivoisée*), an opera very much in the traditional mould, had made little impression in its short run at the Opéra in 1922, Roussel's exotic *Padmâvatî*, premiered the following year, was certainly more in tune with the adventurous spirit of the 1920s. A hybrid spectacle involving dance, choral singing and a considerable use of synthetic exotic modes, the opera is in many ways static rather than dramatic, as were many stage works of the period. In such works, costume and design assume a more important significance, replacing the forward-drive of narrative. The piece is extreme in its use of incantation and a richly scored and often wordless chorus. Later the same year a reconstructed Alfred Bruneau, no longer concerned with Zolaesque naturalism, achieved one revival with his *Le jardin du paradis*, an entirely fantastic piece based on an Andersen fairy-tale. Charles-Marie Widor, now remembered largely as an organist, mounted several operas with only limited success. His *Nerto* based (like Gounod's successful *Mireille*) on the Provençal writer Frédéric Mistral ran at the Opéra in 1924 although it had been composed some thirty years earlier. Another opera on a realistic Provençal theme, *Les pêcheurs de Saint-Jean* had been given with some success at the Opéra-Comique back in 1905: both were finely orchestrated works, an art in which Widor was particularly skilled. Similarly short-running were other forgotten works: *Miarka* by Alexandre Georges; *Esther, princesse d'Israel*, by Antoine Mariotte, *Le Mas* by the folk-song collector and arranger Joseph Canteloube and *Salamine* by Maurice Emmanuel. More successful, and recently revived, was Henri Rabaud's *Marouf, savetier du Caire* (Marouf, the cobbler of Cairo) based on a tale from the Arabian Nights. Originally premiered just before the war at the Opéra-Comique, it was transferred to the Opéra in 1928 having enjoyed performances in Brussels and Milan. It was revived until the 1950s at the Opéra, where Rabaud also enjoyed a considerable reputation as a conductor. Its style is traditional employing a kind of oriental Wagnerian language. His *L'appel de la mer*, one of several 'maritime' operas, was based on Synge's *Riders to the Sea*, had some success, and again has been recently revived.[23]

The 1920s were an even less interesting decade at the Opéra-Comique where French versions of *Gianni Schicchi* and Albéniz's *Pepita Jimenez* were more successful than the French operas premiered: among them Milhaud's full-length *La brebis égarée* (1923) and his forty-minute mini-opera *Le pauvre matelot* to a libretto by Jean Cocteau, premiered in 1927. While other operas reached the stage with difficulty, this latter opera became the most widely performed of Milhaud's operas, which perhaps suffered because they adhere less to the traditions of the Paris opera houses, and more to the pared-down, static traditions of music theatre which emerged during the 1920s. A work such as Milhaud's Orestes trilogy, composed between 1913 and 1922, was not given complete until 1963, dribbling out in concert versions and extracts during the 1920s. More successful were the tiny pieces entitled 'Opéra-minute' ('Minute' operas) dating from the late 1920s.

Another composer whose success in the operatic field was limited was Jacques Ibert. His *Persée et Andromède*, written in the early 1920s, was premiered at the Opéra in 1929. Its librettist, known as Nino, actually Ibert's brother-in-law, wrote librettos for several composers during the 1920s and 1930s. He also wrote the libretto for Ibert's most successful opera, the one-act farce *Angélique*, which again chimed in with the pared-down, de-romanticized spirit of the 1920s. It makes considerable demands on both the singers and the small orchestra, an aspect of which Ibert was particularly proud. The farcical story, where a husband auctions his wife, is matched by wrong-note harmony and acerbic dissonance. More substantial, but less successful, was the full-length *Le roi d'Yvetot* created at the Opéra-Comique in 1930. This was followed by two operatic collaborations with Honegger, one of which, *L'aiglon* (a nickname for Napoleon's son) was the French opera given at the Opéra during the 1930s which achieved the highest number of performances: a modest thirty-eight.

The 1940s were for obvious reasons also a lean time for the production of new operas, affected by national policies on the promotion of the arts discussed in Chapter 10. Perhaps

23 *Marouf* was given in Marseille in 2001 and *L'appel de la mer* in Nancy in 1998. Lazzari's works have also enjoyed recent revivals.

the most telling reminder of operatic activity in Paris during the war was the memorable recording of *Pelléas* made there under Roger Désormière in 1941 with Irène Joachim as Mélisande and Jacques Jansen as Pelléas, immortalized in a CD transcription and still considered by many as the benchmark interpretation of the piece. Jansen was a seasoned interpreter of the role but remembered the extraordinary circumstances of this recording session made during the occupation. His touching memoir of 1948 evokes the event poignantly:

> A sort of miracle happened there, though nobody realised then what tremendous significance it was to acquire. … Wax was so scarce – it was during the occupation – there was no question of doing the same bit over ten times. We had to be on our marks, ready and prepared. I confess that I don't listen to this recording any more. I carry it with me now, it is part of me, it dwells in me. Today, if I hum something from the opera to myself, unconsciously and instinctively, my mind goes back to it. And I recall the atmosphere, the warmth, of Gramophone's recording studios, Désormière's gestures, and the voice of Irène Joachim, born predestined to interpret Mélisande and to go with me on that long voyage to the fountain-head of Debussy.[24]

Could it be claimed, perhaps, that this recording event was of far more resonance than all the weak attempts of the French opera houses during the 1930s and 1940s to revive French opera? It was certainly in need of refreshment. Was it that there were no composers around with the necessary talents, or that the opera managements persisted in supporting the old guard?

With that left as an unanswered question, the composer who first hit the operatic stage after the war was one who bequeathed to the operatic world a real comic opera and a masterpiece, namely Francis Poulenc. The comic opera was *Les mamelles de Tirésias* ('Tirésias's tits' is really the most accurate translation), to a text he wrote himself based on a play by Guillaume Apollinaire. The play was revised and its theme became the need for repopulation, and the problem this presented for the liberated woman who would rather do something with her life than become a baby-producing machine. It is all highly surreal. Husband and wife kill each other in the Act I finale but reappear later on rollerskates. The title refers to Tirésias's rejection of her femminity: she opens her blouse and her breasts fly away in the form of two balloons.

The original 1947 production at the Opéra-Comique was designed by Erté, and Poulenc's score is an eclectic mix of styles, pastiched as only Poulenc could. No other classical composer could make a café-concert waltz as nostalgic as he: Tirésias sings a delicious parody in this vein as her breasts float away (Example 5.10). As the husband announces, dressed as a nurse, that he has sired forty thousand children in a day, the music-hall band in the pit are also asked to sing falsetto. But like many of the best works of French comedy, the work is ultimately of serious import. The prologue, where the stage manager announces how families are to be reorganized, draws weighty music from Poulenc: like much of the music of his later serious opera *Les dialogues des Carmélites* it is over a relentless ostinato in four time. The director's last lines underline the topicality: 'Écoutez, o français, la leçon de la guerre et faites des enfants, vous qui n'en faisiez guère' (Listen, you French, to the lessons of the war. Bear children, those of you who scarcely have') (Example 5.11).

---

24 Repr. in the CD booklet of the remastered recording, EMI Références CHS 761038 2.

Example 5.10 Francis Poulenc, *Les mamelles de Tirésias*, Act I

Elle entr'ouvre sa blouse dont il en sort ses mamelles, l'une rouge, l'autre bleue, et, comme elle les lâche, elles s'envolent, ballons d'enfants, mais reste retenues par les fils.

(She opens her blouse out of which her breasts fly out, one red, the other blue, and as they come out they become children's balloons, and the boys hold on to them.)

In the post-war era when the angry young Boulez emerged announcing that all composers wanting to remain in musical history must take account of serialism (adding that opera was effete), it may seem somewhat bizarre to claim that it was Poulenc who refreshed French opera by returning to the ethos of Les Six and the 1920s, wheeling out a play for which he had always had an affection, uncaring about whether it reached the stage. Poulenc himself saw the opera as a work to celebrate the end of the war, describing it to the poetess Louise de Vilmorin as a 'spectacle gai pour la paix' (a happy show for when peace is resumed).

Poulenc also fashioned his own libretto, in this case after the playwright Georges Bernanos, for his other opera *Les dialogues des Carmélites* based on a true event during the French Revolution when the Carmelite sisters at Compiègne were accused of counter-revolutionary activities and executed. Documents charting the accusations made and the Mother Superior's responses – the 'dialogues' – were used by the Catholic writer Bernanos and form the basis of Poulenc's opera. Poulenc came across a copy of the play in a

Example 5.11 Francis Poulenc, *Les mamelles de Tirésias*: opening soliloquy of the director

(Listen, you Frenchmen, to the lessons of the war, and have children, you who haven't done that much …)

bookshop in Rome, having already seen it performed in the early 1950s. Suddenly he saw it as his ideal libretto, and began working on the piece at once. The process of its composition, and of Poulenc's concurrent emotional traumas which were intimately connected with it, was charted in a series of letters, mostly to the singer Pierre Bernac, the composer's lifelong performing partner. Poulenc had embarked on a passionate affair with a young salesman Lucien Roubert in 1950; soon afterwards Lucien's health declined and the letters reveal how Poulenc in some way associated the progress of the opera with Lucien's gradual decline. He died an hour after Poulenc's last Carmelite had been executed.[25]

As with *Les mamelles de Tirésias*, Poulenc was particularly concerned with prosody, to ensure that the text would be clearly understood. He constantly sought advice on this matter from Bernac, and was also concerned to make the orchestration light and transparent. Poulenc's religious style had developed from his re-conversion to Catholicism which occurred after a visit to Rocamadour and the death of a composer colleague. The simple style of the *Litanies à la Vierge noire*, for female voices and organ, is reworked in

25 See Poulenc's copious correspondence. The French originals are in Poulenc: *Correspondance 1910–1963*, ed. Myriam Chimènes (Paris, 1994) and a translation with excellent supporting commentary is found in Francis Poulenc: '*Echo and Source*', trans. and ed. by Sidney Buckland (London, 1991).

the *Dialogues* as are the mystical harmonies of such pieces as the organ concerto. A series of memorable chords recurs several times, underlining words of particular significance, and associated with the idea of martyrdom, but otherwise the opera is not particularly dependent on motives. The choral style he developed in countless liturgical motets is also evident in two moments where the nuns sing: perhaps the most beautiful a cappella music Poulenc ever wrote. Besides this, the composer's love of Bachian rhythms is evident and only when the outside world intervenes is there a hint of his former, more extrovert side. There is a moment of bathos as the gaoler sings out the names of the condemned as if in a patter song.

The end of the opera is unforgettable. As the choral sound wells up and the thump of the guillotine is heard, no one can escape without a lump in the throat in this slow procession of doom whose narrative is explicit rather than tantalizing, and whose exploration of the fear of death is perhaps its profoundest aspect. The opera was commissioned by La Scala, Milan, and first given there in 1957. It was followed by one more theatrical work the *tragédie lyrique La voix humaine* in which the single character, a woman, is heard on the end of a telephone as her lover breaks off their relationship. This last major work to a text by Cocteau, premiered at the Opéra-Comique in 1959, seemed to mark the end of an era animated by children of the 1920s and of a composer who at one time apologized that his nuns could only sing tonal music. Nowadays we worry less about that and recognize Poulenc as a composer, above all, with a heart.

The other major figure of twentieth-century French music who refrained from trying his hand at opera until late in life was Messiaen. The subject of Saint Francis preaching to the birds was almost inevitably the subject for the first opera by this passionate ornithologist whose music from the outset had been deeply influenced by birdsong, and indeed by landscape and the natural world in general. In fact this aspect is by no means to the foreground in this reflective work which has been accused of lacking the necessary drama for the opera house. Yet in an age which increasingly brought oratorio into the opera house, particularly in mainland Europe if rarely in France, a static religious narrative heard in a scenic context can be a powerful event, especially in these days of surtitles. It is naturally an opera shot through not only with the Christian symbolism of darkness and light, but also of Messiaen's own longstanding association between colour and sound. In this respect too, the setting of the opera house for a spectacle which is in part ritualistic, could never be matched in concert performance. The composer's indications as to the scenery and costumes are full of precise references to colours, attitudes and props, sometimes with reference to particular paintings – several from the chapels at Assisi – whose details or mood should be imitated in production. There are also references to the traditional religious processions held in the same town.

Saint François is a wordy opera. As with Poulenc's nuns, the dialogue conveys religious ideas at every turn, thus every nuance must be heard, especially as regards the wisdom of the Saint himself. In common with many of his other works – in particular the 'Tristan' trilogy – Messiaen has used an explicitly Wagnerian motivic construction and himself has published a 'motive guide' in his own manuscript. Themes, as they have been in several previous works, are attached to people, events and spiritual ideas. After an introduction where several brothers converse with Saint Francis, and a celebration of Laudes, the principal idea of the first section is that of Saint Francis asking God to show him a leper 'that he might learn to love him'. The third tableau depicts the miraculous cure

Plate 5.2 Denise Duval in Poulenc's *La voix humaine*.

of the leper with the apparition of an angel, but only after a dialogue exploring the problem of a God who permits evil and disease has been explored. The second act continues the exploration of theological ideas, in particular of the afterlife and the issue of predestination. Its fifth tableau is one of the strongest dramatically, portraying an angel musician, announced by a kestrel – the angels in the opera are the only female roles – here announcing how 'we may speak to God in music, and He may respond in music. Know the full joy of the blessed through colour and melody. ... Listen to the music which suspends life at the limits of heaven.'[26] Such ideas are hardly new in Messiaen's musical philosophy, but such apparitions could be immensely powerful in the opera house, not least because the audience (congregation?) have had to wait for them. The angel exits in an orchestral interlude, playing a viol as if in a medieval painting, but shrouded in light and with a 'thème d'accords' which could have come from the *Vingt regards sur l'enfant Jésus* of 1944. Only in the sixth tableau do we witness Saint Francis preaching to the birds. The final tableaux represent the receipt of the stigmata and the passing into a new life.

Messiaen's musical language seems to hark back to many of his previous languages, sometimes especially to his earlier, rich harmonic style. There are strong echoes of *Turangalîla*, especially when the leper is cured and gets up and dances. The orchestra boasts a huge percussion section, and despite deliciously indulgent uses of the composer's old favourite the Ondes Martenot, there is also an element of austerity in the conversations between the saint and the brothers. It has appropriately been described as a 'crown' to the composer's work. Certainly it is a profound and striking work which will be hampered only by the expense of reviving it, and those prejudiced against religious works in the operatic arena.

Since Messiaen's crowning work, and surrounding it, there have been a steady stream of other works, some adventurous and some more traditional. Among more traditional approaches, the works of Henri Tomasi (1901–71) may be cited. He, incidentally, also wrote a *François d'Assise*, one of some ten stage works. His *L'Atlantide* (premiered Marseille, 1954) and *Miguel Mañara* (Munich, 1956) were the most successful. The former music director for the Ministry of Culture, Marcel Landowski (1915–99) has also had some considerable success as an opera composer, and his works have particularly been revived in the provinces. *Montségur*, telling the story of a hopeless love between a Cathar woman and a Christian knight, explores an era in French history of particular interest, and his *Galina* is based on the lives of his friends Mstislav Rostropovitch and Galina Vishnevskaya. Jean-Michel Damase (born 1928) was winner of the Prix de Rome in 1947 and has had several operas performed since the 1950s and also been active as a conductor. His operas have been premiered in Marseille, Nice and Bordeaux and include three settings of works by the playwright Jean Anouilh. His *L'héritière* is based on Henry James's *Washington Square*. Antoine Duhamel (born 1925) is another composer who has produced a steady stream of operas mounted since the 1960s. Son of the writer Georges Duhamel, he achieved some prominence through his work with major film directors such as Godard and Truffaut. Again, his works have been premiered mostly outside Paris, and particularly at Lyon. Several are based on the works of celebrated writers, among them Hugo, Baudelaire, Alfred Jarry and Cendrars.

While Dutilleux has not to date written an opera, Maurice Ohana's *La Célestine*, based

---

26 See Messiaen: 'Saint François d'Assise', *L'avant-scène opéra* (Paris/Salzburg, 1992).

on the often bawdy sixteenth-century Spanish play by Fernando de Rojas, was commissioned by the Paris Opéra. Already mentioned for its prominent use of the harpsichord, it was also unusual in that the main text is spoken, while the sung music is either vocalise or meaningless syllables. For Ohana this allowed the work to be performed in many languages and freed the singers from the constraints of word setting, a genre which held no attraction for the composer.

In a different vein, Philippe Hersant (born 1948) has a communicative tonal language and has written two operas: *Les visites espacées*, which is a chamber work, and the more substantial *Le château des Carpathes* (The chateau of the Carpathians) after Jules Verne. It has lush orchestration and delights in the archetypes of villain, good guy and a manic-depressive baron. Curiously for an opera, the soprano dies at the beginning. It was premiered at Montpellier in 1992.

Amongst more avant-garde composers, especially those more influenced by Messaien and Boulez, the two operas of Philippe Manoury (born 1952 and considered one of France's leading contemporary composers) have employed electronics. His *K...*, based on Kafka, was criticized for its ineffective use of voices, although its effects and spectacle were admired. His earlier *60ᵉ Parallèle*, premiered at the Châtelet in 1997 but which the composer has subsequently withdrawn, is one of several operas set in an airport and is based on the story of a Nazi war criminal who commits two murders during the opera. Pascal Dusapin (born 1955) has written three operas; he has been described by one critic as 'le maître du son et du timbre'. His first opera was a *Romeo and Juliet* (premiered at Montpellier in 1988), followed in 1992 by *Medeamaterial*, commissioned by the Théâtre de la Monnaie in Brussels, and using a baroque orchestra of original instruments. The latest is *To be sung*, described as a 'number' opera in forty-three parts, fashioned after Gertrude Stein's *A lyrical opera made by two*, and first performed at the Pans Autumn festival of 1994. It uses reciters as well as singers, and a chamber ensemble and electronics.

It was Philippe Fénelon who enjoyed the first commission from the newly built Opéra de Bastille. This was *Salammbô*, premiered in 1998 and based on the novel by Flaubert and was his second opera. His first, *Le chevalier imaginaire*, was based on Cervantes's Don Quixote. Gilbert Amy, formerly the director of the Lyon Conservatoire and a co-student with Boulez, has not wavered from the path of serialism and has produced many much-admired works in this vein. His *Le premier cercle*, after Solzhenitsyn, was his first opera, given in Lyon in 1999. Its extended soprano solos and powerful orchestral music were much praised by critics.

This chapter, focusing on the major opera houses, and touching down here and there for more detail, was designed in the hope that it might open up new approaches and suggest further lines of enquiry. It has attempted to discern changing patterns, not only of composition, genre definition and style, but also of production. It has given scant attention to the many lively smaller-scale initiatives which promote spectacles on the borderland of opera, and lean more towards music theatre: such places range from the *Opéra-ateliers* (opera studios), the festival of music theatre at Avignon, and even the Opéra-Péniche (a converted barge, still on the Seine) in Paris. In such venues, in the hands of composers such as Georges Aperghis and Claude Prey, many small-scale operatic ventures have been mounted, as well as 'outreach' projects, sometimes involving children. The revival of baroque opera continues to flourish, and any study of its continuing revival in France would begin with a charting of the initiatives of Les Arts Florissants who, under their founder and director William Christie, have made an inestimable contribution to the operatic scene. When once he was alone in this venture, there are now several groups fostering an approach to opera which is in some way historically informed. It was Marc Minkowski, for example, who was entrusted with a live performance of *Pelléas* to celebrate the centenary of its creation.

Can other major trends be perceived? Internationally it seems to be that alongside the regular parade of new productions of the best-known operas, there is once more an interest in bringing alive the history of opera, not in books but in productions. The old stalwarts of the Opéra and the Opéra-Comique – such pieces as *Les Huguenots*, *La dame blanche* and *La juive* – are beginning to be revived. More recently some of the forgotten works brought out in the current chapter have been revisited and recorded to much acclaim, among them works by Leroux, Lazzari, Magnard and Rabaud. In our constant quest for novelty these will surely play their part. It is a mistake to see the twentieth century as showing opera in decline, for while there has certainly been a downturn in the commissioning of new French opera, or a shortage of composers inspiring sufficient confidence for such commissions, it must be remembered that since the war the opera houses of France have been generous in their commissioning of works from abroad. Operas from the USA, Poland, Russia, Scandinavia and even England have achieved far more popularity among French opera-goers than ever before.

Suggested Further Reading

A primary source for many of the composers and operas discussed in this chapter is the series of issues of *L'avant-scène*, often produced to accompany creations and revivals. Apart from issues devoted to the major operas of the earlier part of the century (there are single issues on many of Massenet's operas, for example), such composers as Messiaen, Landowski, Ohana, Prey and Tomasi are also featured.

The *New Grove Dictionary of Music* and its companion *The New Grove Dictionary of Opera* are well-known sources, but it is often forgotten that the articles on production, France and individual articles on the towns of France and its opera houses also contain useful information and provide extensive further reading. Articles on the Paris Opéra and the Opéra-Comique are particularly detailed.

At the time of going to press I know of no comprehensive websites giving detailed information about past repertoire. Opera-house websites are variable; reliable and detailed sources of information may be found on the composer profiles for contemporary composers on the IRCAM and CDMC (Centre de documentation de la musique contemporaine) websites (www.ircam.fr and www.cdmc.asso.fr). Similarly, the websites of the various publishers active in France are variable in their detail.

Books

Histoire du Théâtre Lyrique en France, vol. 3, 'De l'année 1900 à nos jours' (various authors) (Paris, 1939).

Le théâtre lyrique français 1945–1985, ed. Danièle Pistone (Paris: H. Champion, 1987).

Manfred Kelkel: *Naturalisme, vérisme et réalisme dans l'opéra* (Paris: Librairie philosophique J. Vrin, 1984).

Raphaëlle Legrand and Nicole Wild: *Regards sur l'opéra-comique* (Paris, 2002).

L. Rohozinski (ed.): *Cinquante ans de musique française (1874–1925)* (Paris: Librairie de France, 1925).

Nicole Wild and David Charlton: *Théâtre de L'Opéra-Comique, Paris, Répertoire 1762–1972* (Sprimont: Mardaga, 2005).

Stéphane Wolff: *Un demi-siècle de l'Opéra-Comique 1900–1950* (Paris: A. Bonne, 1953).

——: *L'opéra au Palais Garnier (1875–1962)* (Paris, 1983).

Plate 5.3 The official programme for the premiere of Xavier Leroux's *Le Chemineau* in 1907. By the early twentieth century programmes had taken on much of the format which has lasted until the present day. Advertisements shared an equal amount of space with photos of the cast, the sets and the composer and librettist and there was an extended programme note, often in the form of a critical review combined with a synopsis.

Table 5.1 Select repertoire list of early twentieth-century revivals of French baroque opera

Year	Composer	Libretto	Theatre
1908	Rameau	*Hippolyte et Aricie* edited d'Indy	Opéra. First revival since the 18th century; 10 performances. This was the last at a major Paris house until the Early Music Revival
1912	J-J. Rousseau	*Le devin du village* reconstruction by Julien Tiersot	Opéra-Comique (13 performances)
1918	Rameau	*Castor et Pollux*	Opéra
1925	Rameau	*Les Indes galantes* (3rd entrée) edition by Paul Dukas	Opéra-Comique
1929	Creation of l'Association des Amis de l'Opéra-Comique and a review devoted to the preservation of the eighteenth- and nineteenth-century repertoire of the Opéra-Comique		
1937	Monteverdi	*L'incoronazione di Poppea* edition by G-F. Malipiero, French version by Charles van den Borren	Opéra-Comique
1949	Philidor	*Blaise le savetier* (revival 190 years after its premiere)	Opéra-Comique
1950	Rameau	*Les fêtes d'Hébé*	Opéra. Two performances were given under Désormière. The opera had been given at the Académie Royal de Musique between 1739 and 1765, 228 times
1952	Rameau	*Les Indes galantes* edition by Paul Dukas and Henri Busser	Opéra

Table 5.2 Select repertoire list of French operas given at the Opéra-Comique 1889–1971. Column four gives an indication of the number of performances at the Opéra-Comique itself

Date of premiere	Composer	Librettist(s)	Title of opera and number of performances
May 1899	Jules Massenet	Henri Cain after Perrault	*Cendrillon* (24 before 1950)
February 1900	Gustave Charpentier	Composer's libretto	*Louise* (943 by 1950)
April 1900	Camille Erlanger	Henri Cain and P.-B. Gheuzy	*Le juif polonais* (53 with two revivals, the last in 1933)
April 1901	Alfred Bruneau	Émile Zola	*L'ouragan* (14. Act III was revived at the Opéra in 1916)
November 1901	Jules Massenet	Armand Sylvestre and Eugène Morand	*Grisélidis* (73 with two two revivals up to 1942)
April 1902	Claude Debussy	Maurice Maeterlinck	*Pelléas et Mélisande* (343 at the Opéra-Comique before 1950 but by far the most widely performed opera in this table worldwide)
January 1903	Georges Hüe	Louis Gallet and André Corneau	*Titania* (12)
December 1903	Reynaldo Hahn	Catulle Mendès	*La Carmélite* (27)
December 1903	Xavier Leroux	Catulle Mendès	*La Reine Fiamette* (56 by 1935)
May 1904	Jules Massenet	Maurice Léna	*Le jongleur de Notre-Dame* Premiered Monte-Carlo, February 1902 (356 at the Opéra-Comique in four revivals up to 1939)
March 1905	Alfred Bruneau	Émile Zola	*L'enfant roi* (12)
May 1905	Jules Massenet	François de Croisset and Henri Cain	*Chérubin* (14) (Premiered Monte-Carlo, February 1905)
May 1905	Gabriel Dupont	Henri Cain	*La Cabrera* (17)
December 1905	Charles-Marie Widor	Henri Cain	*Les pêcheurs de Saint-Jean* (Scènes de la vie maritime (13)
March 1906	Camille Erlanger	Pierre Louÿs	*Aphrodite* (182, last revived 1927)

Date of premiere	Composer	Librettist(s)	Title of opera and number of performances
May 1907	Paul Dukas	Maurice Maeterlinck	*Ariane et Barbe-Bleue* (79 up to 1927 revival. It entered the repertoire of the Opéra in 1935)
June 1907	André Messager	Robert de Flers and André de Caillavet	*Fortunio* (77 with five revivals up to 1948)
November 1907	Xavier Leroux	Jean Richepin	*Le chemineau* (106, 7 revivals. Last revived 1945)
February 1908	Raoul Laparra	(Laparra)	*La Habanéra* (120 with 4 revivals up to 1947)
December 1909	Déodat de Sévérac	Maurice Magre	*Le cœur du moulin* (14)
May 1910	Claude Terrasse	Jules Lemaître and Maurice Donnay	*Le mariage de Télémaque* (50, revived three times, the last in 1922)
May 1911	Jules Massenet	Jules Clarétie	*Thérèse* premiered at Monte Carlo in February 1907 (31 at the Opéra-Comique with revivals in 1915 and 1930)
May 1911	Maurice Ravel	Franc-Nohain	*L'Heure espagnole* (58 up to 1950), widely performed worldwide, entered the repertoire of the Opéra in 1921
December 1911	Albéric Magnard	(Magnard)	*Bérénice* (9)
February 1912	Sylvio Lazzari	Henri Bataille	*La lépreuse* (70 with four revivals up to 1945)
June 1913	Gustave Charpentier	(Charpentier)	*Julien* (20)
May 1914	Henri Rabaud	Lucien Népoty after 'A thousand and one nights'	*Marouf savetier de Caïre* (128 with two revivals. The work entered the repertoire of the Opéra in 1928)
January 1919	Gabriel Fauré	René Fauchois	*Pénélope* (63) (premiered Monte-Carlo 1913 and previously given in Paris at the Théâtre des Champs-Élysees in the same year)

continued

Table 5.2 *concluded*

Date of premiere	Composer	Librettist(s)	Title of opera and number of performances
January 1920	Charles Levadé	Georges Docquois after Anatole France	*La rôtisserie de la Reine Pédauque* (39 with two revivals, the last in 1939)
May 1920	Ernest Moret	After Musset	*Lorenzaccio* (46 with two revivals)
December 1920	Alfred Bruneau	Maurice Donnay	*Le roi Candaule* (18)
December 1921	Georges Hüe	Maurice Léna and Henri Ferrare	*Dans l'ombre de la cathédrale* (27 with one revival in 1932)
December 1922	Alfred Bachelet	Hansewick and de Wattyne	*Quand la cloche sonnera* (60 with two revivals, the last in 1936)
December 1922	Jean Cras	Albert Samain	*Polyphème* (16, revived 1924)
March 1923	Marcel Samuel-Rousseau	André Rivoire	*Le Hulla* (Conte-lyrique oriental: 44 with one revival in 1926)
December 1923	Darius Milhaud	Francis James	*La brebis égarée* (5)
October 1924	Jules Massenet	Henri Cain after Jacques le Lorrain	*Don Quichotte* (premiered Monte Carlo in February 1910, 60 up to 1945 at the Opéra-Comique)
December 1925	Raoul Laparra		*Le joueur de viole* (36 with a revival in 1929)
February 1926	Maurice Ravel	Colette	*L'enfant et les sortilèges* (premiered Monte Carlo 21 March 1925)
December 1927	Darius Milhaud	Jean Cocteau	*Le pauvre matelot* (25 with two revivals in 1938 and 1945)
December 1927	Marcel Samuel-Rousseau	André Rivoire	*Le bon roi Dagobert* (72 up to 1943)
December 1928	Georges Hüe	Raoul Gastambide	*Riquet à la houppe* (18 with one revival in 1930)
January 1930	Jacques Ibert	Jean Limousin and André de la Tourrasse	*Le roi d'Yvetot* (15)
June 1930	Jacques Ibert	Nino	*Angélique* (81) (premiered Théâtre Femina, Paris, January 1927)

Date of premiere	Composer	Librettist(s)	Title of opera and number of performances
February 1931	Roger Ducasse	Raymond Escholier	*Cantegril* (18)
March 1937	Albert Roussel	Nino	*Le testament de Tante Caroline* (7)
May 1942	Paul le Flem	Jean Gandrey-Réty	*Le rossignol de Saint-Malo* (22)
June 1947	Francis Poulenc	Apollinaire	*Les mamelles de Tirésias* (27)
June 1948	Henri Busser	After Mérimée	*Le carrosse du Saint Sacrement* (24)
March 1951	Germaine Tailleferre	Henry Jeanson	*Il était un petit navire*
February 1959	Francis Poulenc	Jean Cocteau	*La voix humaine*
March 1964	Francis Poulenc	Georges Bernanos	*Dialogues des Carmélites* (premiered in Milan 1957)
April 1971	Maurice Ohana	(Ohana)	*Syllabaire pour Phèdre*

Table 5.3 Select repertoire list of French operas given at the Opéra 1900–1950

Date of premiere	Composer	Librettist(s)	Title of opera and number of performances
February 1901	Xavier Leroux	Louis de Gramont	*Astarte* (23)
April 1901	Georges Hüe	Henri Bouchut	*Le roi de Paris* (9)
October 1901	Camille Saint-Saëns	Victorien Sardou and P. B. Gheusi	*Les barbares* (32) Act II alone was revived in galas in 1913 and 1914
January 1903	Vincent d'Indy	(d'Indy)	*L'étranger* (premiered Brussels, January 1903, (39 at the Paris Opéra, with revivals in 1916, 1934, 1944 and 1951)
April 1904	Camille Erlanger	Catulle Mendès	*Le fils de l'étoile* (26)
October 1906	Jules Massenet	Catulle Mendès	*Ariane* (75, revived 1907 and 1937)
January 1909	Henri Février	Maurice Maeterlinck	*Monna Vanna* (80 with seven revivals up to 1947)
May 1909	Jules Massenet	Catulle Mendès	*Bacchus* (6)
December 1910	Georges Hüe	P. B. Gheusi and A. Mérane	*Le miracle* (30, one revival in 1927)
April 1912	Jules Massenet	Henri Cain after Alexandre Parodi	*Roma* (premiered Monte-Carlo in February 1912; 20 at the Opéra, with one revival in 1917)
May 1914	Alfred Bachelet	Charles Méré	*Scemo* (interrupted by the closure of the theatre after 6 performances. Revived at the Opéra-Comique in 1926 for 7 performances)
June 1920	Vincent d'Indy	d'Indy after J. de Voragine	*La légende de Saint Christophe* (19)
March 1921	Gabriel Dupont	Chékri-Ganem	*Antar* (40, revived in 1924 and 1946)
January 1922	Charles Silver	Henri Cain and Edouard Adenis after Shakespeare	*La mégère apprivoisée* (*The taming of the shrew*) (13, revived in 1925)
June 1923	Albert Roussel	Louis Laloy	*Padmâvatî* (Opéra-ballet, 39 representations up to 1947)
October 1923	Alfred Bruneau	G. A. de Caillavet after Andersen	*Le jardin de paradis* (27, once revived in 1926)

Date of premiere	Composer	Librettist(s)	Title of opera and number of performances
October 1924	Charles-Marie Widor	Maurice Léna after Mistral	*Nerto* (7)
June 1925	Albert Roussel	Théodore Reinach	*La naissance de la lyre* (9)
January 1928	Sylvio Lazzari	(Lazzari)	*La tour du feu* (36, with three revivals up to 1946)
March 1929	Joseph Canteloube	(Canteloube)	*Le mas* (8)
May 1929	Jacques Ibert	Nino	*Persée et Andromède* (11)
June 1929	Maurice Emmanuel	Théodore Reinach after Aeschylus	*Salamine* (8)
January 1931	Alfred Bruneau	Henri Duvernois	*Virginie* (7)
April 1931	Albéric Magnard	(Magnard)	*Guercœur* (12)
January 1932	Darius Milhaud	After Franz Werfel	*Maximilien* (7)
November 1932	Alfred Bachelet	Franc-Nohain after Maurice Barrès	*Un jardin sur l'oronte* (12)
June 1933	Joseph Canteloube	Étienne Clémental and J. Louwyck	*Vercingétorix* (9)
May 1934	Henri Rabaud	Lucien Népoty	*Rolande et le mauvais garçon* (16, revived once in 1937)
March 1935	Reynaldo Hahn	After Shakespeare	*Le marchand de Venise* (32, one revival in 1949)
June 1937	Max d'Ollone	Edmond Rostand	*La samaritaine* (7)
August 1937	Arthur Honegger and Jacques Ibert	Henri Cain after Edmond Rostand	*L'aiglon* (premiered at Monte Carlo in March 1937, 38, revived in 1952)
March 1939	Henri Sauget	Armand Lunel after Stendhal	*La chartreuse de Parme* (8)
January 1943	Arthur Honegger	Jean Cocteau after Sophocles	*Antigone* (premiered at the at the Théâtre de la Monnaie, Brussels, in 1927; 17, with a revival in 1953)
May 1950	Darius Milhaud	Madeleine Milhaud after Jacques Supervielle	*Bolivar* (22, revived in 1958)

Chapter 6

Church and Organ Music

Nigel Simeone

> We were both young, and on the *grand orgue* and the *orgue de chœur* we would have clever musical dialogues with each other: holy, liturgical and in perfect harmony. Often one of us would play a theme which the other would then develop. And I would also ask my colleague on the choir for his comments on my performances, and their effect over a distance, given the nave [of Saint-Sulpice] which is a hundred metres long.[1]

This charming reminiscence by Widor of his improvised duets with André Messager in the 1870s neatly demonstrates three significant factors in the growth of organ and church music in France from the mid-nineteenth century: the musical requirements of French church architecture, the revival in organ building led by Aristide Cavaillé-Coll, and the importance of improvisation. Churches of any size had two organs: first, the *grand orgue* at the West End, often in a spacious gallery which might even include a modest salon, as at Saint-Sulpice. Second, there would be a smaller *orgue de chœur* on the Sanctuary, at the opposite end of the building, to accompany the choir in the sung parts of the liturgy. The *grand orgue* was used for extended solos at the beginning and end of Mass, for improvisations during services, and for recitals, but seldom with the choir. Apart from high-spirited extemporizations using both instruments, like those described by Widor, there was usually a clear distinction between solo pieces, using the *grand orgue*, and those for choir and organ, usually more intimate in character. This pattern is reflected in sacred music ranging from Franck and Fauré in the 1870s, to Messiaen a century later.

Some Noted *Titulaires*[2]

A survey of organists working in Parisian churches from the second half of the nineteenth century onwards reveals a remarkable historical continuity. Several of the finest organs designed by Cavaillé-Coll were already installed in Parisian churches and the musical

1 Charles-Marie Widor: *Notice sur la vie et les œuvres d'André Messager*, Académie des Beaux-Arts, 30 novembre 1929, quoted in H. Février: *André Messager, mon maître, mon ami* (Paris, 1948), 24; 'Nous étions jeunes alors. Grand orgue et orgue du chœur se répondaient du tac au tac, saintement, liturgiquement, en parfaite harmonie. Souvent l'un proposait un thème que l'autre développait. Plus souvent j'interrogeais mon collègue du chœur, implorant sa critique sur l'interprétation d'une œuvre, son effet à distance, vu l'amplitude d'une nef de cent mètres de long.' Widor was scarcely exaggerating the vast distances between the two organs: the interior of Saint-Sulpice is 113 metres long and 34 metres high.

2 For a fuller account, arranged by churches, see N. Simeone: *Paris: A Musical Gazetteer* (New Haven, 2000), 153–72.

consequence of this revival in organ building was that churches were able to attract significant composers and performers as *titulaires*. In terms of playing styles and technical mastery of the organ, the performances in Paris by the Belgian Jacques-Nicolas Lemmens in the 1850s were also significant influences on French organists of the time.

César Franck served for over thirty years at the church of Sainte-Clotilde. A pupil of François Benoist at the Paris Conservatoire, he inaugurated the organ of this new basilica in December 1859 (sharing the programme with Lefébure-Wély), and worked there for the rest of his life. Franck's successors were two of his pupils: Gabriel Pierné from 1890 until 1898, then Charles Tournemire, who remained in the post until his death in 1939 (his assistants included Maurice Duruflé, Jean Langlais and Daniel-Lesur). Tournemire's most distinguished successor was Langlais.

At the Madeleine, Camille Saint-Saëns – like Franck, a pupil of Benoist – was organist from 1857 until 1877, and Fauré often served as his deputy. Saint-Saëns resigned in 1877 and was replaced by Théodore Dubois, while Fauré was appointed *maître de chapelle* (choirmaster). In 1896, Fauré was promoted to the job of *titulaire* when Dubois left to become director of the Paris Conservatoire (as Fauré was himself to do in 1905).

One of Cavaillé-Coll's greatest instruments was at Saint-Sulpice. The first *titulaire* after the completion of the new organ was Alexandre Guilmant (from 1862). He was replaced in 1870 by Charles-Marie Widor who was to remain there for sixty-four years (and whose assistants included Fauré, André Messager, Louis Vierne and Marcel Dupré). It was only in the early 1930s, when the ageing Widor could no longer climb the long spiral staircase to the organ gallery, that there was any question of retirement. He resigned in 1934, at the age of eighty-nine, to be replaced by his pupil Dupré.

The Église de la Sainte-Trinité was designed by Théodore Ballu and completed in the 1860s. The first organ was installed by Cavaillé-Coll in 1868 but it was damaged during the Commune, and a rebuilt instrument was inaugurated in 1871. The first organist was Charles-Alexis Chauvet who succumbed to consumption in the same year. He was succeeded by Alexandre Guilmant, who held the post until 1901, and whose strong liturgical instincts led him to take a detailed interest in plainchant. The church's greatest – and longest-serving – organist was Olivier Messiaen, appointed in September 1931 and active there for over sixty years.

The appointment of Louis Vierne as organist of Notre-Dame de Paris in 1900 was to end almost four decades later with Vierne's death in 1937 – appropriately enough at the console. Later holders of the post included Pierre Cochereau and Olivier Latry.

In the wider context of church music, Charles Bordes was an interesting figure. He worked from 1890 as choirmaster at Saint-Gervais, formerly the church where generations of Couperins had served as organists. Bordes's interest in Renaissance polyphony led to a systematic revival of this repertoire at the church, and his Chanteurs de Saint-Gervais attracted wide interest from musicians. Bordes's admirers included Debussy (who attended concerts of Palestrina and Vittoria in 1893), and the elderly Gounod who, as a young man, had baffled congregations at the Église des Missions étrangères with his own performances of Palestrina half a century earlier. Bordes's work at Saint-Gervais led directly to the foundation of the Schola Cantorum. This started in 1894 as a society for the promotion of plainchant and of Palestrina and his contemporaries, and to encourage new church music. The three founders were Bordes, Guilmant and d'Indy. From 1895 the society published a magazine and its school opened in October 1896 at premises in the rue

Stanislas. The teachers were Bordes for choral music, d'Indy for harmony and composition, and Guilmant for the organ (he became professor of organ at the Conservatoire in the same month). After a modest start (sixty-five students in 1899), the Schola Cantorum moved in 1900 to larger premises in the rue Saint-Jacques and by 1904 had almost 300 students. With this move, the courses became more broadly based, though still with a focus on church music, including memorable field trips to Solesmes led by Bordes.[3] The pupils who came through the Schola's doors were a remarkable group, including Albéniz, Canteloube, Abel Decaux, Roussel, Satie, Séverac and Varèse.

While almost every Parisian *titulaire* would use plainsong as the basis for improvisations, usually on a weekly basis, two different strands can be seen emerging in the composed – rather than improvised – music of these organists from around 1900 onwards. First, there were those like Tournemire (and, later, Jehan Alain and Duruflé) whose language was profoundly imbued with plainsong and which derives much of its melodic shape and harmonic colouring from modal chant. Second, there were composers like Vierne, and even Messiaen, who were intimately familiar with the *Liber usualis*, who would improvise extensively upon chants, but seldom (if ever) employed direct quotation from plainsong in their published compositions.

Among other *titulaires* in the twentieth century, Joseph Bonnet was succeeded at Saint-Eustache by two brilliant players, both also remarkable improvisers: André Marchal and Jean Guillou. Eugène Gigout played for over half a century – from 1868 until his death in 1925 – at the iron-framed church of Saint-Augustin (designed by Victor Baltard, one of the pioneers of building with iron who was most famous for his massive and beautiful 'pavillons' at Les Halles, controversially demolished in the early 1970s). One of the more enigmatic *titulaires* was Henri Mulet. His father was choirmaster at the Sacré-Cœur and after studies with Widor and Guilmant, Mulet served at Saint-Roch (1912–22) then at Saint-Philippe du Roule, from 1922 until 1937, when he destroyed his manuscripts and left for Provence, working at the cathedral in Draguignan until 1958, then living in penury at a convent there until his death in 1967.

The Organ Repertoire from Franck to Messiaen and Beyond

The art of improvisation was (and remains) an essential pre-requisite for any *titulaire*, and a great deal of inspired music-making thus enjoyed only the shortest and most fleeting of lifespans, since it was extemporized. Such work, much of it by the finest composers of the day, is now almost entirely lost to us, since so few improvisations were ever written down or recorded (rare exceptions include three by Vierne, five by Tournemire and later examples by Pierre Cochereau and Jean Guillou). The importance of the organist as part of the liturgical act needs to be understood too: it is no accident that the consoles of many large French organs are arranged so that the player is facing the high altar; both Tournemire and Messiaen commented that improvisation was something they could only do effectively with the Blessed Sacrament before them, and the extent to which organists

3 For details of the establishment of the Schola Cantorurn, see 'The Schola Cantorum' in O. Ochse: *Organists and Organ Playing in Nineteenth-Century France and Belgium* (Bloomington, Ind.: 1994), 219–23.

are a crucial part of the ritual action of the Mass in a large Parisian church can hardly be overemphasized. Marcel Dupré put it with characteristic pragmatism and lucidity: 'Before presuming to induce others to pray one must first take care not to distract them. Widor taught me this.'[4]

What was it that students were taught in improvisation classes at the Paris Conservatoire and elsewhere by the likes of Franck, Widor, Dupré and Tournemire? Essentially, they were encouraged to work on a series of extemporizations on given themes ranging from plainsong to Wagner and beyond, sometimes in the form of a fugue or an extended sonata-form movement, sometimes in a free style. This teaching presupposed a highly developed understanding of harmony and, especially, counterpoint, as well as great facility at the console: the purpose was not to teach these basic skills so much as to develop the resourcefulness and spontaneity of improvisations within specific structures or formal constraints.

While much of the music heard as part of church services was improvised and has thus disappeared, there remains a vast amount of published organ music from the period. Two issues were of particular importance during the second half of the nineteenth century: the liturgical function of the organist (particularly important with improvisations, but increasingly so with composed works as well) and raising the technical standard of performance. As a player, the Belgian Jacques-Nicolas Lemmens (1823–81) caused something of a sensation when he gave a recital at Saint-Vincent-de-Paul, Paris, on 25 February 1852 – attended by Boëly, Benoist, Franck, Alkan and Lefébure-Wély among others – though his star was to wane markedly over the next twenty years, as French players not only reached but surpassed him in terms of virtuosity. Lemmens was still only in his twenties when, in 1849, he had been appointed professor of organ at the Brussels Conservatoire. He was also an important influence in developing the organist's role in the liturgy: in 1850–51 he edited the *Nouveau journal d'orgue à l'usage des organistes du culte catholique* which sought to reassert the value of plainsong, suggested new solutions for its accompaniment and included pieces (by Lemmens himself) which treated chant melodies as a *cantus firmus* or fugally. In revised and enlarged form, the *Nouveau journal d'orgue* became Lemmens's *École d'orgue basée sur le plain-chant* (Paris, 1862). Lemmens also wrote some more extended compositions for organ, including three sonatas (published in Paris in 1874) with titles: 'Pontificale', 'O filii' and 'Pascale' (based on the chant *Victimae paschali laudes*) which may well have influenced Widor, among others. Lemmens was not an easy man, and this may go some way to explaining why he failed to secure the post of *titulaire* at Saint-Eustache in 1854, though he was specially invited to the church to play at the organ's inauguration.[5] Of those who were present at Lemmens's recital in February 1852, none was to have a more far-reaching impact than another musician of Belgian origin.

César Franck (1822–90) composed his first major works for organ, the *Six pièces*, in 1856–64, derived from improvisations he played at the end of Mass. They were immediately praised by Liszt as worthy of comparison with 'the masterpieces of Bach',

4 Dupré quoted in M. Murray: *French Masters of the Organ* (New Haven, 1998), 169.

5 For a fascinating evaluation of Lemmens see W. Corten: 'Le "premier organiste du monde": virtuose "théorique plus que pratique"? Quelques controverses autour de J.-N. Lemmens', *Revue belge de Musicologie*, 60 (2001), 209–22.

and the second of them, the 'Grande pièce symphonique' shows the extent to which Liszt's own music had influenced Franck, notably through the use of cyclic techniques. 'Prière', the fifth of the set, was considered by both Vierne and Dupré to be the most profound of all Franck's works for organ and certainly the idea of a long, sustained meditation (it lasts well over ten minutes) was to influence not only these two composers (notably some of the pieces in Dupré's *Le chemin de la Croix*), but also those of later generations (several of Messiaen's early works seem to inhabit a similar world in which time stands still for prayer). The *Trois pièces* of 1878 ('Fantaisie', 'Cantabile' and 'Piece héroïque') were written not for Sainte-Clotilde, but for the inauguration of the much larger Cavaillé-Coll instrument in the Trocadéro. Franck's last major compositions were the *Trois chorals* for organ, completed in 1890. Their title deserves some comment, since these are not 'chorales' in any conventional sense. Jacques Chailley has suggested that with Franck the choral was 'not a form at all, but a genre endowed with a particular spirit, drawing on a range of very different forms'.[6] Essentially, they are extended, rhapsodic pieces of considerable harmonic daring and formal freedom, notable, too, for long-breathed melodies.[7] It is perhaps this last characteristic which suggested the title to Franck (one which was taken up with enthusiasm by his pupil Tournemire, sometimes modified as 'Fantaisie-choral', 'Postlude-choral', 'Choral-poème' or even, at its grandest, 'Symphonie-choral'; the second movement of Vierne's Second Organ Symphony is entitled 'Choral'). Among Franck's numerous smaller works, perhaps the most intriguing are those published posthumously as *L'organiste*, a collection of fifty-five short pieces for organ or harmonium which he was working on when he died. The French harmonium of the time was a highly sophisticated and beautifully voiced instrument, often showing much more imagination in its design than American models. The principal makers – firms like Mustel (inventor of the celesta) and Alexandre – aimed to produce a range of timbres which would not merely be an affordable domestic alternative to the great pipe-organs, but would have a particular musical appeal of their own. That they succeeded is demonstrated by the large output of shorter pieces written for their instruments by French composers, of which Franck's are distinguished examples.

The evolution of the organ sonatas of Mendelssohn into the organ symphonies of Widor and others has as much to do with the 'symphonically' conceived instruments being built by Cavaillé-Coll as it does with any specific formal innovations. However, the individual movements of the French organ symphony were generally rather more free in structure, and some noteworthy characteristics emerged, such as brilliant concluding toccatas. During the early 1870s, Charles-Marie Widor (1844–1937) composed the first four of his symphonies for organ, drawing much of his material from separate pieces written for performance during services. These works often exhibit a remarkable eclecticism, ranging from the rigours of strict baroque counterpoint to long cantabile melodies in slow movements which recall the latest operatic styles in France. Another speciality was the spectacular finish, and the most famous example of this – the closing Toccata of Symphony no. 5 – came in his next batch of symphonies (nos. 5–8), almost certainly

6 J. Chailley: *Les chorals pour orgue*, 1re partie: 'Qu'est-ce qu'un choral?' (Paris, 1974), 4.

7 For a detailed examination of Franck's formal procedures in the *Trois chorals* see M. Fischer: 'Les Trois chorals pour orgue: de la modification d'un genre à l'appropriation de l'inattendu', *Revue européenne d'études musicales*, 1 (1991), numéro special: César Franck, 123–48.

written during the 1880s, and first published as a set in 1887. Widor later wrote two more organ symphonies, the *Symphonie gothique* and *Symphonie romane*, during the last years of the nineteenth century. After 1900 he produced only two major organ works: the *Suite latine* and his last composition, the *Trois nouvelles pièces*, written in 1934.

Camille Saint-Saëns (1835–1921) produced a number of organ works, including several which remain unpublished. Few approach the scale of Franck, Widor or Vierne, since at least half are short pieces dating from the 1850s, but among Saint-Saëns's later music the sets of preludes and fugues op. 99 (1894) and op. 109 (1898), the Fantaisie in D flat major op. 101 (1895), the *Sept improvisations* op. 150 (1916–17) and the Fantaisie in C op. 157 (1919) are substantial if not always especially memorable. His pupil and friend Fauré is a curious case: despite many years of service at the Madeleine, he wrote no solo work for the organ.

Alexandre Guilmant (1837–1911) produced eight sonatas for organ between the 1870s and the end of his life. Less musically or technically demanding than the symphonies of Widor or Vierne, they have moments of real charm as well as the more predictable splendour. In one of the later sonatas (no. 7, composed in 1902), Guilmant shows an unstuffy attitude to recent musical trends, embracing a benign Impressionism: it was in a spirit of genuine enthusiasm that he took his pupils to see Debussy's *Pelléas et Mélisande*. Of his other organ music, one volume demonstrates – even in its title – a true understanding of the organist's role: the ten volumes of *L'organiste liturgiste* were published in 1887–99, during the last years of Guilmant's tenure at the Trinité. He was Franck's successor as organ professor at the Conservatoire; in turn his place was taken by Eugène Gigout (1844–1925) whose own works include the impressive *Grand chœur dialogué* (1881) and the Toccata in B minor (1890), a splendid example of the genre. Gigout's shorter pieces include an interesting collection of modal works for organ or harmonium: *100 pièces brèves dans la tonalité du plain-chant*.

Léon Boëllmann (1862–97) was a Gigout protégé and during his short life made an impact as a player (*titulaire* at Saint-Vincent-de-Paul in Paris) and as a composer. His most celebrated work is the *Suite gothique* published in 1895, with its tender 'Prière à Notre Dame', somewhat reminiscent of Franck, and the well-known Toccata, a brilliantly effective conclusion; it was followed by a much less successful *Deuxième suite*. Other works include *Douze pièces*, short pieces for the liturgy, and *Heures mystiques*, written in a sparing and severe style for manuals only.

Louis Vierne (1870–1937) composed six organ symphonies between the late 1890s and 1930. These works develop the genre from the Widor-like Symphony no. 1 of 1898–99, with its splendid and triumphalist 'Final' – described by the composer as 'my Marseillaise' – to the tortured chromaticism of the later symphonies (two themes in Symphony no. 6 use all twelve notes of the chromatic scale). Vierne's other organ music includes an important group of later pieces, the four books of *Pieces de fantaisie* (1926–27), containing twenty-four works in all and including the celebrated 'Carillon de Westminster'. Vierne's musical language, especially his harmony, is entirely his own: the sense of unease, of anguish and of struggle is expressed through writing of extreme chromatic intensity. Whereas other composers of his generation found new directions by exploring the possibilities modal writing, Vierne, in his most advanced pieces, stretched the conventional tonal system to its limits. In his art, as in his life, he seems an enigmatic and troubled soul.

Charles Tournemire (1871–1939), an exact contemporary of Vierne, is best remembered for the largest of all his works for organ: the series of over 250 pieces which make up *L'orgue mystique*, composed in 1927–32. Published in fifty-one books, one for each of the Offices of the liturgical year, each 'office' contains five pieces.[8] According to the composer, this mighty collection was 'inspired by Gregorian chant and freely paraphrased'. Olivier Messiaen, a devoted disciple of Tournemire (though never his pupil), called it: 'a religious and living work like the plainsong from which it is derived, made to illustrate, to comment upon the drama of the liturgical year, coloured with each mystery, each feast of Christ'.[9] The books follow a set pattern: Prelude to the Introit, Offertory, Elevation, Communion and finally the longest and most rhapsodic movement. Messiaen captures the essence of these extraordinary final pieces:

> It is always very long, and sums up the important religious ideas of each feast, paraphrasing the texts of the sequences, hymns or Alleluias for each occasion. An interior stronghold of the feelings and blessings corresponding to each mystery, a stained-glass window in sound where the fortissimo of the organ unfurls its splendour and prolongs time.[10]

Tournemire occupies a remarkable place, perhaps a unique one, in the development of French organ music: a devoted Franck pupil whose own harmonic freedom, highly imaginative integration of plainsong, and profound sense of the organist's role in the liturgy were to have a lasting impact on younger composers. Tournemire's influence on Messiaen was far more in the area of improvisation than in composition, but his use of modal harmonies and plainsong was to make a more enduring impression on the likes of Duruflé, Alain and Langlais.

The composers of Les Six never worked as organists, but three of them produced significant organ works. One of Honegger's earliest pieces was his well-crafted, somewhat Reger-like *Fugue and Chorale*, composed in 1917. Milhaud composed a three-movement Sonata for organ in 1931 (first performed at the Berlin ISCM Festival in 1932), as well as some smaller pieces, including a charming *Petite suite* (1955) for his son's wedding. Poulenc's Concerto for organ, strings and timpani was a commission from the Princesse de Polignac. He took a number of years to complete the piece, working on it with great care until it was eventually finished in August 1938 (with technical advice from Duruflé). The result is arguably the finest concerto ever written for the instrument. It opens with an overt tribute to the organ music of Bach, but this is followed by a profusion of ideas which could only have come from Poulenc. In no other piece, perhaps, can the two complementary sides of his musical nature ('moine et voyou' – monk and vagabond – as Claude Rostand described them) be heard united to such good purpose: the mixture of Bachian rigour, an unmistakably French streak of mysticism (particularly moving in the

---

8 The single exception to this is no. 16 which contains only three movements.

9 O. Messiaen: 'L'Orgue Mystique de Tournemire', *Syrinx*, May 1938, pp. 26–7: 'Œuvre religieuse et vivante comme le plainchant qui est sa source; faite pour illustrer, commenter le drame de l'année liturgique, avec ses teintes à chaque mystère, à chaque fête du Christ.'

10 Ibid., 2–3; 'Elle est toujours très longue, et résume les idées religieuses importantes de chaque fête, en paraphrasant les textes des *séquences*, *hymnes* et *alléluias* propres. Château intérieur des sentiments et grâces correspondant à chaque mystère, vitrail sonore où le fortissimo de l'orgue déploie ses splendeurs et prolonge le temps.'

slow, triple-time music near the close) and pure vaudeville in some of the racier material, is unified into a particularly convincing and impressive whole.

Marcel Dupré (1886–1971) wrote extensively for the organ, but only his best works avoid an occasional lack of rhythmic imagination. What are arguably his two finest pieces both had their origins in improvisations, subsequently written down. The imposing *Symphonie-Passion* (completed in 1924) began as a series of improvisations on plainchant themes given by Dupré during December 1921. These were not performed in a great church but in the Wanamaker department store in Philadelphia, on a six-manual juggernaut of an instrument – the mastodontic Grand Court organ on which many great virtuoso players gave recitals after the store had closed in the evenings.[11] *Le chemin de la Croix* (1931) was originally a series of extemporizations on texts by Paul Claudel. These powerful and highly expressive Stations of the Cross were notated shortly afterwards and constitute a remarkable work of musical contemplation. Dupré's didactic works are particularly important, notably the *Traité d'improvisation* (1926) and *Méthode d'orgue* (1927). Perhaps Dupré's greatest legacy is the roster of pupils who graduated from his notoriously demanding organ class at the Conservatoire, notably Alain, Langlais and Messiaen.

The career of Jehan Alain (1911–40) ended tragically when he was killed in battle on 20 June 1940 as German forces swarmed into France. Despite his death at the age of twenty-nine, he left a wholly original group of organ works. *Le jardin suspendu* (1934) which seems to inhabit an enchanted modal dream-world, while the *Variations sur un thème de Clément Janequin* (1937) reflect Alain's interest in early music (and in old instruments). *Litanies* is a toccata of astonishing energy and harmonic inventiveness. It is based on a theme with obvious roots in plainsong, boldly announced unaccompanied at the start, then repeated and developed over a series of brilliantly-lit modal harmonies driven along by propulsive, lopsided rhythms (Example 6.1). All three of these works were performed on 17 February 1938 by Alain himself, at the Trinité, as part of a recital for *Les Amis de l'Orgue* when he shared the programme with Messiaen and Jean-Jacques Grünewald (playing works by the indisposed Daniel-Lesur). Alain's other achievements include two quietly memorable modal chorales – *Choral dorien* and *Choral phrygien* (both 1934), and *Trois danses*, written in 1937–38: 'Joies', 'Deuils' and 'Luttes'. Along with *Litanies* these dances are outstanding contributions to the organ repertoire, expressed in an original, highly coloured modal language.

Jean Langlais (1907–91) studied at the Conservatoire with Dukas and Dupré, and privately with Tournemire which proved to be a decisive encounter with the man he considered the true poet of the organ. Langlais's output of solo organ music was prolific – about ninety opus numbers – and there is no denying occasional unevenness. But the best is very good indeed: of his earlier style, characterized by its use of relatively straightforward modal harmonies and lucid, transparent textures, the *Trois paraphrases grégoriennes* (1934) and *Suite mediévale* (1947) are fine. Of the later pieces, which are often more rhythmically elaborate and harmonically daring, two of the finest are *Offrande à une âme* (1979, dedicated to the memory of his first wife[12], and *Mort et résurrection*, a searing tribute to Jehan Alain on the fiftieth anniversary of his death.

---

11 I am most grateful to Ms Ciarraíne Fitzgerald of Philadelphia for information about this instrument. The store was subsequently renamed Lord & Taylor.

12 In an interview given in June 1982, Langlais spoke movingly about Messiaen's immediate

Example 6.1 Jehan Alain, *Litanies*: opening bars

'Quand l'âme chrétienne ne trouve plus de mots nouveaux dans la détresse pour implorer la miséricorde de Dieu, elle répète sans cesse la même invocation avec une foi véhémente. La raison atteint sa limite. Seule la foi poursuit son ascension.'

JEHAN ALAIN

(When the Christian soul cannot find words to plead for God's mercy, it repeats the same invocation vehemently and increasingly. Reason has reached its limits. Only faith can result in its ascension.)

Maurice Duruflé (1902–86) was a pupil of Tournemire and later Vierne. But like Messiaen, Alain and Langlais, he also studied composition with Dukas, whose influence on the music of the 1930s and beyond was to be highly significant. Dukas's avowed aim when appointed to teach composition at the Conservatoire was to 'de-industrialize' it (as he put it) – to spend much less time preparing students for the annual Prix de Rome competition and a lot more on developing their individuality. The situation Dukas inherited from the ageing Widor was one which worried him, since 'if there is ambition, it's along the lines of M. Citroën rather than père Franck! I shall very gently try to de-industrialize music.'[13] While each of his most talented pupils developed distinctive voices of their own, the brilliant resourcefulness of Dukas's own technique, and his acute sense of musical colouring had an impact on all of them. It can be heard most obviously in a piece like the

enthusiasm for this work. This interview was later issued on Édition Lade ELCD 02 and includes fascinating reminiscences of Vierne, Widor, Dupré and Tournemire as well as Messiaen.

13 Letter to Guy Ropartz, 13 Nov. 1927, quoted in R. Nichols: *The Harlequin Years* (London, 2002), 184.

third movement of the orchestral version of Messiaen's *L'Ascension* ('Alléluia sur la trompette, Alléluia sur la cymbale'), but it is apparent in many other works, and in a more general sensitivity to the most subtle of nuances in music. This is certainly the case with Duruflé. His music for organ follows the same pattern of ruthless self-criticism which characterized his whole output: there is outstanding work but in small quantities (incidentally, another parallel with Dukas). The eventual tally of Duruflé's published works is sparse indeed – barely a dozen pieces – including four major works for solo organ: the Scherzo op. 2 (1928, written for a Conservatoire examination), the *Prélude, adagio et choral varié* op. 4 (1930, on the theme of the *Veni Creator*), the Suite op. 5 (1933, dedicated to Dukas), and the *Prélude et fugue sur le nom d'Alain* op. 7 (1942). Of these, the finest of all is Duruflé's heartfelt tribute to Jehan Alain. Based on a theme derived from a musical cypher for Alain's name, there is also a direct quotation from Alain's *Litanies*. A fine example of Duruflé's individual brand of modal harmony, this is a powerful and ebullient memorial which seeks perhaps to capture the essence of Alain's personality rather than to mourn him. There are two smaller pieces: *Prélude à l'Introït* for manuals only, composed for an anthology in 1961, and the jig-like *Fugue sur le thème du carillon des heures de la cathédrale de Soissons* (1962).

Messiaen's works for organ stand as the most outstanding and original contribution to the instrument's repertoire by any twentieth-century composer. Shorter pieces include the early meditation *Le banquet céleste* (1928) and the curiously unsatisfying *Diptyque* (1930), with a first part which is reminiscent of Dupré (and even Vierne), and a much more characterful vision-of-paradise second part which was reworked a decade later as the final movement of the *Quatuor pour la fin du temps*. Another early piece, *Offrande au Saint-Sacrement*, composed in about 1930, was rediscovered by Yvonne Loriod-Messiaen in 1997 (and published in 2001); similar in some respects to *Le banquet céleste*, it is more successful than the *Diptyque*, not least because of its greater stylistic coherence. The granite-like *Apparition de Église éternelle* (1932) – an imposing crescendo and decrescendo which the composer called 'very simple in its monolithic effect'[14] – was the last of these smaller pieces until 1960. But most striking are the series of great cycles and more extended works. The earliest of these is *L'Ascension*, which began as a piece for orchestra in 1932–33 and was transcribed for organ in 1933–34, with the third movement of the orchestral version replaced by the earliest of Messiaen's brilliant pieces in the French toccata tradition: 'Transports de joie'. But the real stylistic breakthrough, and a moment which Messiaen described as an attempt to bring about a 'renewal of organ writing',[15] came with *La Nativité du Seigneur* (1935). Here was organ writing on an epic scale. However, these vast musical frescos were not merely gigantic (in the manner of some earlier organ symphonies) but articulated an explicit religious vision through music of breathtaking inventiveness. Messiaen's preface to the score makes particular reference to the use of Hindu rhythms (transformed here into Messiaen's own characteristic additive rhythms) and the modes of limited transposition, already apparent in his earlier music but here made explicit and later to form such an important keystone of his theoretical writings as well as his compositions. But this preface also includes a theological explanation of the work and each of its nine movements, giving substance to the 'emotion and sincerity'

---

14 C. Samuel: *Conversations with Oliver Messiaen*, trans. F. Aprahamian (London, 1976), 77.
15 Ibid.

Plate 6.1 Messiaen at the organ of the Trinité c. 1938.

Messiaen was seeking to express and providing a demonstrable Christian inspiration and purpose for the music. The issue of just how a performer or listener might respond to Messiaen's explanatory texts is one which has been explored most perceptively by John Milsom with specific reference to the organ works.[16] But the music itself speaks with blazing conviction, drawing on an astounding kaleidoscope of musical colour, harmonic inventiveness and asymmetical rhythmic energy, whether in the slower more reflective movements like 'Desseins éternels', the powerful rigours of 'Le Verbe' or the exultant abandon of the final movement, 'Dieu parmi nous', a blazing musical response to Christ's Incarnation: 'And the Word was made flesh and dwelt among us.'

Messiaen's next organ work was *Les Corps glorieux*, written during the summer of 1939, just before the outbreak of the Second World War. In terms of its overall structure and the relationships between movements it is a more sophisticated work than *La Nativité*, and Messiaen's harmonic language and, especially, his exploration of timbre is still richer and bolder. At the heart of this seven-movement work is 'Combat de la mort et de la vie', a vast piece in two parts: in the first, the Passion and suffering of Christ are depicted as a violent struggle between life and death. The second part is a complete contrast: marked 'extremely slow, tender, serene, in the sun-drenched peace of Divine love', and in the radiant key of F sharp major, Messiaen represents the serenity of eternal life after the Resurrection, where Christ lives and reigns for ever, with His Father (Example 6.2). *Les*

16 In Peter Hill (ed.): *The Messiaen Companion* (London, 1995), 51–71.

Example 6.2 Olivier Messiaen, 'Combat de la mort et de la vie' ('Struggle between death and life'), second section, from *Les Corps glorieux* (1939)
Note the typical use of F sharp major for the vision of serenity depicted here

Corps glorieux was first performed in public on 15 November 1943 – in a freezing cold Trinité – as part of a series of three recitals in which Messiaen performed virtually all his organ works to date.

The *Messe de la Pentecôte* (1950) is of particular interest as the composer described it as an anthology of his most daring extemporizations at the Trinité: 'a resume of all my collected improvisations' and 'the result of more than twenty years improvising'.[17] This may explain why some of the more elderly parishioners occasionally detected 'the devil in the organ pipes': it's an uncompromising work, but one which succeeds in its stated purpose of providing 'a commentary on different aspects of the mystery of Pentecost, the feast of the Holy Spirit'.[18] The *Livre d'orgue*, written the following year, is perhaps Messiaen's most intractable organ work, though from a compositional point of view it is certainly a *tour de force*. The first, fourth and last of the seven movements – 'Reprises par interversion', 'Chants d'oiseaux' and 'Soixante-quatre durées' – are the only pieces among Messiaen's organ works to have no explicit religious inspiration. The work thus begins and ends with brilliantly conceived explorations of 'rhythmic personalities' and 'chromatic durations', while the fourth movement was written among the birds of the forest at Saint-

17 Samuel: *Conversations with Olivier Messiaen*, 6 and 78.
18 Programme note by Messiaen in *Hommage à Olivier Messiaen* (Paris, 1978), 58.

Germain-en-Laye, where Messiaen would go for moments of respite. After this, there was no new organ music in the 1950s, but in 1960 Messiaen wrote his short *Verset pour la fête de la dédicace* for the annual *concours* at the Paris Conservatoire, based on ideas derived from plainchant and birdsong. Three years later, the *Monodie*, an angular single-line melody, was written for an organ method by Jean Bonfils, Messiaen's assistant at the Trinité. The next major work for the instrument came in 1969: *Méditations sur le Mystère de la Sainte-Trinité*. The theoretical basis of this cycle is particularly intriguing, notably the introduction of 'communicable language', a complex system of musical cyphers. Gillian Weir has described this as follows:

> Messiaen invented (and used here for the first time) a 'communicable language', for which he gave to each letter of the alphabet a fixed musical note – fixed in pitch and duration as well as musical name. Furthermore, he devised a musical motif for important verbs such as *to be* and *to have*, and another used in different forms for each member of the Trinity – Father, Son and Holy Spirit.'[19]

Messiaen treated this as an elaborate and fascinating musical game, but one with a serious purpose: to express ideas and emotions which were beyond words.

Finally, in 1984, Messiaen produced the *Livre du Saint-Sacrement*, the longest of all his organ works: an eighteen-movement reflection on the Sacrament of the Eucharist lasting two hours. The work falls into three vast sections: the first four movements are acts of adoration before Christ, an 'invisible but a real presence in the Blessed Sacrament'; the next seven are scenes from the life of Christ, from Nativity to Resurrection, and the last seven are meditations on the transforming power of the Eucharist, particularly transubstantiation, ending with an 'Offrande et Alléluia final' which is 'an offering to God of all the prayers of all the Saints' followed by their exultation: 'JOIE' is spelt out in communicable (and, indeed, unmistakable) language as the work comes to its blazing conclusion.

Among Messiaen's pupils, several have written interesting works for organ. Gilbert Amy (b. 1936) is best known as Boulez's successor at the Domaine musical, but at the Conservatoire he was an organ pupil of Rolande Falcinelli as well as studying with Milhaud, Messiaen and Loriod. Two organ works stand out: *Sept bagatelles* (1975) and *Quasi una toccata* (1981), a substantial piece in which Amy deliberately sought to explore the concept of dazzling virtuosity allied to an uncompromisingly contemporary idiom. Jacques Charpentier (b. 1933) made a formidable debut as an organ composer with his brilliant *L'ange à la trompette*, written in 1954 while he was still a Conservatoire student. Indebted to Messiaen and to the Alain of *Litanies*, it is an exciting rethinking of the French virtuoso toccata, with a dazzlingly effective coda. Charpentier followed this with several more important pieces, notably *Messe pour tous les temps* (1964), an imposing organ mass modelled on Messiaen's *Messe de la Pentecôte*, and the *Livre d'orgue* (1973) in honour of Saint Thomas Aquinas on the 700th anniversary of his death. In three sections, entitled 'La Création', 'La Créature' and 'La Rédemption', it lasts over an hour. Charpentier draws on Indian raga as well as on a visionary grandeur and theological symbolism which owe something to Messiaen's *Méditations sur la Mystère de la Sainte-Trinité*. Xavier Darasse (1934–92) was a brilliantly gifted organist – and a passionate advocate of new music for

19 G. Weir: 'Organ Music II', in Hill: *The Messiaen Companion*, 374.

the instrument – before a serious accident ended his playing career. His first organ piece, commissioned by the Royan festival in 1971, was *Organum I* and Darasse's subsequent works (*Organum II–VIII*), written in 1972–89, continued in a similarly innovative vein. *Organum I* requires two assistants (a total of six hands and six feet are needed in places) and Darasse draws some extraordinary sounds from the instrument, at times creating almost percussive timbres. Of the later works, *Organum IV* calls for three percussionists, *Organum VII* for a soprano voice, and *Organum VIII* for a brass quintet. This last piece was written in memory of Jean-Pierre Guézec, who died in his thirties. Guézec (1934–71) composed just one work for organ, with the unprepossessing title of *Piece no. 1* (1964). Dedicated to Darasse, it shows Messiaen's influence in terms of its carefully planned structure and its brilliant use of timbre. Jean-Louis Florentz (1947–2004) produced two large-scale organ works: *Laudes* op. 5 (1985), and *Debout sur le soleil: Chant de Résurrection* op. 8 (1991). The first of these was inspired by the ancient liturgy of the Ethiopian Christians, specifically the prayers for the morning Office. The last of its seven movements, 'Seigneur des lumières', has a title which inevitably calls Messiaen to mind, as does some of the music itself. *Debout sur le soleil* also draws on the Ethiopian tradition, and the most central of all Christian beliefs, the Resurrection. Jean Guillou (b. 1930) has had a long and successful career as an organist (notably as *titulaire* at Saint-Eustache), and he also has a considerable output of organ compositions to his name, including an exciting Toccata (1963) which is his most frequently played work, a *Symphonie initiatique* for three organs (1969; rearranged for two organs in 1989), the cycle of seven pieces called *Sagas* (1970–83), the disarmingly titled *Scènes d'enfant* (1973, based on Henry James's *The Turn of the Screw*), and *Hypérion ou la rhétorique du feu* (1988), a four-movement work which ends with the exultant and elemental 'Agni-Ignis'. The only organ work by Iannis Xenakis (1922–2001) is *Gmeeorh*. Composed in 1974, it is a stunningly original piece, extraordinarily difficult to play, with an ending described by Darasse (who gave the European premiere) as 'a monumental paroxysm in sound which only the organ can achieve.'[20]

Vocal Music

The École Niedermeyer was an important nursery for the formation of church musicians. The study of plainchant was a central concern of its curriculum and it nurtured some outstanding young talents, including Fauré in the 1860s and Messager a decade later. The resolutely agnostic Gabriel Fauré (1845–1924) was certainly one of its greatest alumni. As a pupil he was taken under the benevolent wing of Saint-Saëns, ten years his senior. For much of his professional life, Fauré worked as an organist. He was Widor's assistant at Saint-Sulpice (1871–74), and held various posts at the Madeleine from 1874 until 1905: first as Saint-Saëns's deputy, then choirrnaster in April 1877, and *titulaire* from June 1896 until 1905. He also played the *grand orgue* during his time as choirmaster, including at the funerals of Gounod (27 September 1894 when he improvised on themes from Gounod's *Rédemption*) and Verlaine (10 January 1896). Fauré's output of liturgical music consists mainly of small-scale motets; these have sometimes had rather a bad press, even from

20 G. Cantagrel (ed.): *La musique d'orgue* (Paris, 1991), 796.

Fauré's admirers, but their simple melodic charm and very individual modal inflections raise the best of them well above the routine.

Dating from 1865, the *Cantique de Jean Racine* – not sacred in the strict sense, but certainly appropriate for use in religious services – was originally written for the composition competition at the École Niedermeyer (it won the first prize), and was dedicated to César Franck. Over the next forty years, Fauré produced a substantial body of sacred music including an utterly charming Mass in collaboration with his friend André Messager, the Requiem – which took well over a decade to evolve – and motets, mostly written for performance at the Madeleine.

In August 1871 he wrote an *Ave Maria* for male choir and organ, and the following year a short and robustly triumphalist *Tu es Petrus*, for baritone, mixed choir and organ. The year 1877 saw the composition of an *Ave Maria* for two sopranos and organ and the *Libera me* for baritone and organ, later recycled to memorable effect in the Requiem. The 1880s were Fauré's most productive decade as a composer of religious music. In 1881, with his friend and former pupil Messager, he composed the *Messe des pêcheurs de Villerville* for women's voices with harmonium and violin accompaniment. The two composers revised the piece the following year for accompaniment by a small orchestra and much later, in December 1906, Fauré completed a thorough reworking of it, replacing the movements by Messager with his own settings, and providing an accompaniment for organ alone. This was published the following year as the *Messe basse*. Fauré's *O Salutaris* (op. 47 no. 1) was first performed at the Madeleine on 21 November 1887 by his near-namesake, the singer Jean-Baptiste Faure.

Less than two months later, on 16 January 1888, the funeral at the Madeleine of a parishioner (the architect Joseph Le Soufaché) saw the first performance of the 'Kyrie', 'Sanctus', 'Pie Jesu', 'Agnus Dei' and 'In Paradisum' of Fauré's Requiem.'[21] This work evolved into its definitive form over the next decade: by the mid-1890s all the movements had been composed, and in 1900 a version using full orchestra intended for larger concert halls (almost certainly orchestrated by Roger-Ducasse, with Fauré's blessing) was given for the first time.

Thanks to the dedicated archaeological and editorial efforts of Jean-Michel Nectoux, two distinct versions can now be performed, either using the more modest instrumentation of performances from the 1890s, or the larger setting of 1900. Certain aspects of the earlier version in Nectoux's edition are so magical – such as the solo violin descant in the 'Sanctus', the aptness and simplicity of the 'Pie Jesu' without woodwind, and the exquisite instrumentation of the 'In paradisum' – that the more 'public' full orchestral version can seem rather too grandiose for the essentially intimate musical language of the work. Despite its initial success in France, the Requiem took almost half a century to become

21 The subsequent composition and performance history of Fauré's Requiem has been meticulously documented by Jean-Michel Nectoux in the preface to his edition of the 1893 version (Paris, 1994). It may be summarized briefly as follows: a second performance took place at the Madeleine on 4 May 1888 (with trumpet and horn parts added). The 'Libera me' was given its premiere in Saint-Gervais at a Société nationale concert on 28 Jan. 1892, and the complete work, with the 'Hostias' (original version of the 'Offertoire') and the 'Libera' me took place on 17 May 1894 at the Théâtre de la Bodinière. The first performances of the full orchestral version were on 6 Apr. 1900 at Lille and on 12 July 1900 in Paris – the occasion when the 'Pie Jesu', sung by Mlle. Torrès, was encored.

known in Britain: a performance conducted by Charles Münch at the Fauré centenary celebrations in London in 1945 and Nadia Boulanger's recording for Pathé (made at the Salle Gaveau in October 1948 with Gisèle Peyron and Doda Conrad as the soloists, and with Duruflé at the organ) did much to encourage interest, and in the half-century since then it has become one of the most widely known works in the repertoire. What are the reasons for the remarkable appeal of this rather atypical Requiem? As well as the inspired stream of melodic invention which characterizes the piece, perhaps its other main attraction is the originality of Fauré's conception of what a Requiem should be. The mood, sustained almost throughout, and maintained by subtle deviations from the standard text of the Requiem Mass, is one of blissful meditation – a serene evocation of paradise. This was very different from the more wrathful settings of Mozart, Berlioz or Verdi. Fauré's vision – and his choice of texts (strictly speaking the 'In paradisum' is not part of the Requiem Mass) – was highly original, and it can now be seen as the first of a particularly French 'school' of Requiem-writing, with settings by Ropartz, Duruflé and Desenclos as its most obvious successors.

On 23 December 1888, just in time for a performance on Christmas Day, Fauré made a charming arrangement of the carol *Il est né le divin enfant* for unison children's choir, organ, harp, oboe, cellos and double basses. In about 1890, he composed a wonderfully operatic *Tantum ergo* (op. 55) for solo tenor, mixed choir, organ and harp, first performed at Saint-Gervais, as part of a Société nationale concert on 22 January 1891. During the mid-1890s Fauré wrote several more small-scale motets, including the well-known *Ave verum* for two-part female choir, and the *Tantum ergo* for three-part female voices, both with organ, published as op. 65 nos. 1 and 2. The *Salve Regina* op. 67 no. 1, for solo

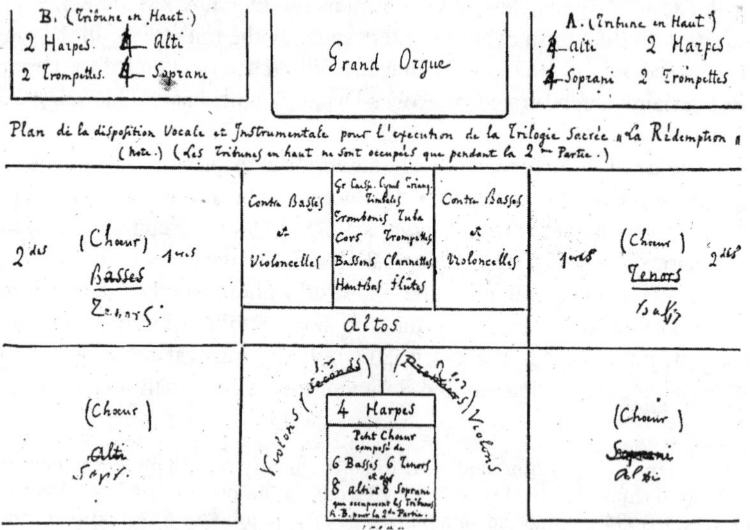

Plate 6.2 Gounod's own plan for the layout of the choral and orchestral forces of his oratorio *Rédemption*, showing three layers of activity, with a celestial choir of harps and female voices, and also two trumpets, in the organ loft at the highest level. A 'petit chœur' in front of the main orchestra is backed by four harps.

soprano and organ, is a little-known gem among Fauré's sacred works. Completed on 25 March 1895, it was dedicated to Emma Bardac and first published as a supplement to *L'Illustration* on 4 May 1895 (Example 6.3). The Nuptial Mass of Mademoiselle Greffuhle on 14 November 1904 was an occasion Fauré celebrated with another *Tantum ergo*, this time for solo soprano, mixed choir and organ.

Example 6.3 Gabriel Fauré, *Salve Regina* op. 67 (1895)
Note the simple style which renders it suitable for parish use

Franck's sacred music ranges from a simple Mass intended for parish use at Sainte Clotilde (1860, to which he later added the famous 'Panis Angelicus' – particularly effective in its original scoring for tenor, cello, harp and organ), to the monumental scale of his large choral-orchestral works, of which perhaps the most successful is *Rédemption*. This was completed in September 1872 and extensively revised the following year after an unsuccessful premiere. In terms of genre it is unique. Franck described it as a 'Poème-Symphonie', and its unusual features, including passages of spoken text and extended music for orchestra alone, take it far away from conventional oratorios; perhaps that is why it never enjoyed much success during the composer's lifetime. However, the profusion of memorable musical ideas, the radiant, mystical quality of much of the writing, the magnificent chorus of affirmation which closes Part I ('Devant la loi nouvelle'), the ecstatic union of the Angels with those on earth at the conclusion of the work, and the glorious assurance of Franck's chromaticism all contribute to the truly impressive impact of *Rédemption*. Franck's other religious works include some inspired moments, especially *Les Béatitudes* (1869–79), based on the famous passage in St Matthew's Gospel.

A decade after Franck's *Rédemption*, Charles Gounod (1818–93) composed his oratorio of the same title – a lucrative commission from the Birmingham Festival, backed by the publisher Novello. It was in Protestant England that Gounod's work enjoyed the most spectacular success and *Rédemption* (1882) was performed on numerous occasions during the last two decades of the nineteenth century. The musical language has a directness and appeal which it is all too easy to dismiss. Eduard Hanslick did just that, declaring that *Rédemption* and its successor *Mors et vita* (1885) were 'the work of a man who is pious, but, on account of so much piety, feeble as music'. Despite Hanslick's lofty view, Gounod's straightforward use of motifs in both works is extremely effective, and the composer's devout faith is allied to a sure sense of dramatic timing; if these oratorios occasionally seem to be seeking to articulate a rather grander vision than they can actually express, they still deserve revival.

Written at the same time as Franck's *Rédemption*, Massenet's *Marie-Magdeleine* is subtitled a 'drame sacré' and was first performed in 1873. His other large-scale works included the 'légende sacrée' *La Vierge* (1878) and the 'oratorio biblique' *La terre promise* (1900). Massenet also wrote a handful of smaller works for church use.

Ernest Chausson (1855–99) was among Franck's greatest disciples. He wrote no large-scale religious music but several motets including *Deus Abraham* and *Ave verum* op. 6 (both 1883) for voice, violin and organ, *Trois motets* op. 12 (1886) for mixed voices, cello, harp and organ, and *Trois motets* op. 16 (1888–91) for solo soprano and organ.

Among opera and ballet composers of the time, one of the most resourceful was Léo Delibes (1836–91). He began his professional career as organist of Saint-Pierre de Chaillot and he left a charming *Messe brève* for two-part children's or women's voices and organ. Another name which is hardly the first to come to mind in connection with church music is Erik Satie. However, his *Messe des pauvres* (1893–95), written for Satie's homegrown 'Église Métropolitaine d'Art de Jésus Conducteur' is a partial Mass setting (originally including a Gloria, now lost), with some additional fragments of psalms. While the choral writing is in a rarefied pseudo-medieval style, the organ is given music of extraordinary harmonic inventiveness and the work is extremely effective in performance.

André Caplet (1878–1925) never worked as an organist, but he was one of the most original composers of religious music in the first quarter of the twentieth century. Winner of the Prix de Rome in 1901 (beating Ravel into second place), his settings of traditional religious texts include a set of three songs entitled *Les prières* (1914–17). The first of these ('Oraison dominicale') sets the Lord's Prayer, the second ('Salutation angélique') the Hail Mary, and the third ('Symbole des apôtres'), the Creed. Written for voice and piano or organ, Caplet later made an arrangement for voice with string quartet and harp. Caplet was gassed during the Great War and never fully recovered his health. But while he was obliged to give up most of his conducting appointments, the last six years of his life saw a remarkable output of sacred music. His *Pie Jesu* (1919), in 5/4 time, scored for voice and organ, has a ravishing air of gentle mystery which approaches the heights of inspiration achieved by Lili Boulanger with the same text. The same year he also wrote a *Panis angelicus*, in versions for voice and organ or piano, and for solo voice, chorus, harp, violin or flute and organ. The most remarkable of Caplet's strictly liturgical works is his *Messe à trois voix* (otherwise known as the *Messe dite des Petits de Saint-Eustache-la-Forêt*), scored for three-part female choir. Written for the church near Caplet's Normandy retreat, it is one of his finest achievements. The melismatic writing in the Kyrie owes much to his study of plainchant (he visited Solesmes on several occasions), and the Gloria includes a striking refrain in parallel fourths and fifths which suggests a twentieth-century reworking of organum techniques; there is no Credo. The harmonic language of the Sanctus is more radiantly diatonic, from the wonderfully rapt opening, with its gradually expanding intervals, to the fanfare-like hosannas with their bright parallel triads. In the conciliatory Agnus Dei Caplet uses unusually wide spacing, the texture often comprising intervals of tenths, elevenths and twelfths as well as thirds and sixths. The Mass concludes with the Communion motet 'O salutaris hostia', set with a devotional simplicity which evokes, but never imitates, early polyphony. Caplet's Mass is a work of compelling individuality and deeply felt spirituality, which also exploits the forces of a three-part female choir to brilliant effect: seldom has such a range of musical colour and texture been achieved with unaccompanied women's voices (Example 6.4). The first performance was on 13 June 1922 in the impossibly beautiful surroundings of the Sainte-Chapelle.

Caplet's religious masterpiece was not composed for performance in church: *Le miroir de Jésus* (subtitled 'mystères du Rosaire') sets poems by Henri Ghéon which are meditations on the fifteen decades of the Rosary, divided – as is the liturgical devotion which inspired it – into three sets of five mysteries: joyful, sorrowful and glorious. Scored for solo mezzo-soprano, female chorus, strings and harp, *Le miroir de Jésus* was composed in April–September 1923 and first performed at the Concerts Witkowski in Lyon on 22 February 1924, conducted by the composer, with Claire Croiza as the soloist. Caplet and Croiza gave the first Paris performance at the Théâtre du Vieux-Colombier on 1 May. The musical language of this work is, again, a brilliant fusion of old and new: the female chorus announces the title of each 'mystery' – musical parallels of the illuminated initials in medieval manuscripts – though most of the narrative is given to the solo voice. The core of the work is the sequence of sorrowful mysteries, with an extraordinary depiction of Christ's Agony in the garden and the Crown of Thorns: music which is as remarkable for its restraint as for its dissonance (Example 6.5). In this work Caplet produces a miraculous summation of his art described by Felix Aprahamian as:

> a synthesis of his religious aspirations with the two musical streams which nourished him: the late works of Debussy and the music of the early middle ages. ... In *Le miroir de Jésus* it is not by the use of plainchant themes, but by applying to his own themes processes similar to those used by the early medieval French composers that Caplet creates a unique atmosphere, modern, yet at the same time Catholic and ancient. These subtle mirrors reflect at once the polychrome tones and timbres of Debussy's art and the fourths, fifths, discant and parallel motion of the *ars antiqua*.[22]

To set devotional texts in a work for the concert hall was unusual, and not until Messiaen's *Trois petites liturgies* was such overtly liturgical music created for so secular an environment. Caplet went to Solesmes for the last time in 1924 and wrote to Yvonne Gouverné about the direction in which his music would move next: 'I dream of a song, a beautiful song in unison, an unaccompanied song with no barlines, where the rhythm would be determined by that of the text.'[23] Caplet died on 22 April 1925 and his vision remained unrealized, but his achievement with *Le miroir de Jésus* was already a

22 F. Aprahamian: 'André Caplet', *The Listener*, 23 Mar. 1950, 536.

23 Letter quoted in *André Caplet. Exposition*, Bibliothèque nationale de France, Département de la Musique, 1 Jan.–15 Apr. 2000 [handlist], 20; 'Je rêve d'un chant, d'un beau chant à la

Example 6.4 André Caplet, Mass for Three Voices (1922), Gloria

Example 6.5 André Caplet, *Le miroir de Jésus* (1923), Christ's agony

remarkable one: a concert piece with a structure which perfectly reflects one of the Church's great cycles of prayer.

The religious music of Lili Boulanger (1893–1918) was mostly for concert use. The three Psalms from 1916–17 are among her greatest achievements. Psalm 24 ('La terre appartient a l'Éternel') is a short, celebratory setting for chorus, brass, timpani, harp and organ, notable not only for its driving energy but also for its use of blazing fanfares piling up intervals of fourths and fifths which give to the work an austere splendour, a rugged grandeur which is certainly mirrored if not consciously imitated by Arthur Honegger in *Le roi David*, composed a couple of years after Boulanger's death (Example 6.6). Psalm 129 ('Ils m'ont assez opprimé') is a more extended work, with an important part for baritone. But the most extraordinary is *De profundis* ('Du fond de l'abîme'). The dates given in the

---

l'unisson, d'un chant sans accompagnement ni barre de mesure, dont le rythme serait déterminé par celui du texte.'

Example 6.6 Lili Boulanger, Psalm 24 (1916–17), opening
Note the diatonic musical language and use of quartal harmony

published score indicate that Boulanger worked on this large-scale choral work over four years, from 1914 until 1917. From the very start, with its stark evocation of the abyss, the orchestral writing is stunningly imaginative. The vocal setting – with an important solo contralto part, and the chorus often divided into subgroups – is equally resourceful and the result is a work which is among Boulanger's most inspired and grandest conceptions. Her last sacred work is the *Pie Jesu* – some of it sketched a few years earlier – scored for soprano, string quartet, organ and harp, and it was dictated from the composer's sickbed

Example 6.7 Lili Boulanger, extract from *Pie Jesu* (1918)
A work dictated from her sickbed to her sister Nadia

to her sister Nadia. This is music of understated eloquence and, at the close, true serenity: the earlier chromaticism giving way to a gently diatonic radiance which movingly suggests a young composer at peace with herself in the face of mortal illness (Example 6.7). It was completed in January 1918 and Boulanger died less than two months later. She was twenty-four.

While Caplet and Boulanger took liturgical music into the concert hall, Arthur Honegger (1892–1955) took it into the theatre. During childhood he had drawn on the Bible for his lost *Oratorio du Calvaire* (Calvary Oratorio), a miniature Passion composed in 1907 (and performed by family and friends). His first mature work of a religious nature is the *Cantique de Pâques* (1918), the only music to be completed for an Easter Mystery project for the Théâtre du Vieux-Colombier in Paris. Though a short piece, it shows Honegger's distinctive voice beginning to emerge, and its origins as a sacred work for theatrical performance are a significant indicator of the direction in which he was to move next. In 1921 he completed the first version of *Le roi David*, a 'biblical drama' first performed at the Théâtre du Jorat, Mézières, on 11 June 1921. Concert performances as a 'symphonic psalm' during 1923 – in two versions, one for chamber forces, the other for large orchestra – led to an immediate and enduring success. The librettist René Morax took his texts for *Le roi David* from the Bible and the Huguenot psalter. He collaborated with Honegger on another 'biblical drama' for the Théâtre du Jorat in 1925: *Judith*, first performed in Mézières on 13 June 1925. It was later recast as a 'serious opera' in autumn 1925, and as an 'action musicale' in 1927. The largest and most magnificent of all Honegger's works with religious themes is *Jeanne d'Arc au bûcher* (1935; Prologue added in 1944), a 'dramatic oratorio' on a text by Paul Claudel, a brilliant libretto in which time runs backwards 'until the crucial moment when the earthly present and the spiritual come together in the devouring flames'.[24] The moving Prologue quotes from Genesis and draws a poignant and striking parallel between the Chaos before the Creation and the ruins of a French nation reeling from five years of Occupation and division. Honegger's last religious work is *Une cantate de Noël*, finished in 1953. By now the composer was gravely ill, but his Christmas cantata, introducing numerous traditional carol melodies, exudes a sense of radiance and hope.

Honegger's only settings of traditional liturgical texts are little-known delights. In May 1943 he composed a *Panis angelicus* for voice and piano, in glowing B major and owing much to Fauré, whom Honegger admired immensely. His slightly earlier *O Salutaris* exists in versions for voice and piano (or harp) and for voice, organ and piano (or harp) and it was first performed at Saint-Séverin, Paris, on 9 October 1943. It is a delicious Fauré pastiche which had started life in 1939 as part of the film score which Honegger co-wrote with Milhaud for *Cavalcade d'amour*. The film also included a Kyrie for soprano and unaccompanied chorus which has not been published.

Francis Poulenc (1899–1963) was to be a much more prolific composer of church music. It was the gruesome death of the composer Pierre-Octave Ferroud in a car accident in Hungary which rekindled Poulenc's long-dormant faith. Poulenc was on holiday at Uzerche when he heard the tragic news, and he immediately set out on a pilgrimage to the nearby shrine of the Black Madonna at Rocamadour. On the evening of this visit (22 August 1936) Poulenc began his first religious work, *Litanies à la Vierge noire*, and he completed it a week later. Scored for female chorus and organ, it is a setting of the devotional text printed on a little card which Poulenc bought at Rocamadour. In terms of Poulenc's creative development, this work perhaps revealed the spiritual depth of his music for the first time, expressed in a very particular language, 'the simple fervour, the mingled sweetness and humility that are to emanate from all Poulenc's religious works'.[25] The short but intensely moving *Litanies* was soon followed by more sacred music. The Mass in G major for unaccompanied chorus was written in August 1937 and dedicated to the memory of Poulenc's father. It was first performed by the Chanteurs de Lyon at the Chapelle des Dominicans in Paris on 3 April 1938, and the same choir made a recording for Columbia a few weeks later. Poulenc described his style in the Mass to Claude Rostand, then spoke endearingly about what he hoped to have achieved in the work:

> I tried to write, in a direct and severe style, this act of faith which is my Mass. This severity is particularly striking in the initial Kyrie, but don't forget that in the early Church the unbaptized

24 H. Halbreich: *Arthur Honegger*, trans. R. Nichols (Portland, Ore., 1999), 423.

25 H. Hell: *Francis Poulenc*, trans. E. Lockspeiser (London, 1959), 46.

> were permitted to sing this hymn along with the priests. It is that which explains the almost savage side of my Kyrie. For the Sanctus I had in mind the clustered heads of angels ... It's a carillon for voices. In the Agnus Dei, a solo soprano sings in the upper register as a symbol of the Christian soul, confident in the prospect of heavenly bliss. ... Forgive my immodesty, but this Agnus Dei is certainly one of the pieces where I have best realized what I want to express.[26]

The *Quatre motets pour un temps de pénitence* were started in July 1938 and completed in January 1939. With this work, Poulenc established himself as the outstanding exponent of the unaccompanied motet in France during the middle years of the century: these short pieces for Holy Week have real devotional power as well as being by turns dramatic and ravishingly beautiful (Example 6.8). Less complex than the Mass, Poulenc freely admitted the influence of Vittoria here. They were written with a particular choir in mind, the Petits Chanteurs à la Croix de Bois, who performed them for the first time in several Parisian churches during Lent in 1939. In May 1941 Poulenc wrote two more motets: a joyous *Exultate Deo* and a setting of the *Salve Regina* which is all the more moving for its gentle simplicity. In 1948 came a work for male voices, *Quatre petites prières de Saint François d'Assise*, dedicated to the monks at Champfleury, one of whom was his nephew Jérôme. Poulenc described the inspiration of the work to Rostand:

> One of my nephews, a young Franciscan, sent me four little prayers, asking me to set them to music for the choir of his monastery. I accepted with enthusiasm since the Franciscan spirit has always moved me deeply. If I had ever taken Holy Orders, a vocation which sadly I never had, it would certainly have been as a Franciscan. ... I venerate Saint Francis, but he intimidates me a little too. By setting these marvellously touching prayers to music, I wanted to make an act of humility. That's why in the fourth one, for example, a solo tenor starts very simply, like a monk leading his brothers in prayer.[27]

At the end of 1948, Poulenc composed his *Hymne traduit du bréviaire romain*, for voice and piano, which moves from 'Dark night, blind shadow' to 'eternal light' and ends with a song of praise to the Trinity. His next religious work took another sacred text into the concert hall, but on an altogether grander scale. The *Stabat Mater*, composed in 1950–51, was the first of three major sacred choral-orchestral works; first performed at the Strasbourg Festival on 13 June 1951, it is dedicated to the memory of Christian Bérard, the

26 F. Poulenc: *Entretiens avec Claude Rostand* (Paris, 1954), 155–6; 'J'ai donc tenté d'écrire, dans ce style rude et direct, cet acte de foi qu'est une messe. Cette rudesse est frappante surtout dans le *Kyrie* initial, mais n'oubliez pas qu'aux origines de l'Église, les non baptisés pouvaient aussi chanter cet hymne avec les prêtres. C'est ce qui explique le côté presque sauvage de mon *Kyrie*. Pour le *Sanctus*, j'ai pensé aux têtes d'anges entremêlées ... C'est un carillon de voix. Quant à *l'Agnus* final, qu'un soprano solo chante dans un registre aigu, c'est la symbole de l'âme chrétienne, confiante dans la vie céleste ... Pardon de mon immodestie, mais c'est sûrement une des pages où j'ai le mieux réalisé ce que je voulais.'

27 Ibid., 158–9; 'Un de mes petits neveux, jeune franciscain, m'a envoyé ces quatre petites prières en me demandant de les mettre en musique pour la chorale de son couvent. J'acceptai avec enthousiasme car l'esprit franciscain m'a toujours profondément ému. Si j'étais entré dans les ordres, vocation qu'hélas! je n'ai jamais eue, c'eût été sûrement chez les Franciscains ... Je vénère saint François, mais il m'intimide un peu. En tout cas, en mettant en musique ses petites prières, j'ai voulu faire acte d'humilité. C'est ainsi que dans la quatrième, par exemple, un ténor solo commence, simplement, comme un moine qui entraîne ses frères à la prière.'

Example 6.8 Francis Poulenc, 'Vinea mea electa', from *Quatre motets pour un temps de pénitence* (1938–39), opening

artist and set-designer. The explicitly 'spiritual' strain of Poulenc's language is deployed to magnificent effect here, uniting the Vittoria-like writing of the motets with the orchestral colours so memorably deployed in the wartime ballet *Les animaux modèles*.[28] In 1951–52 Poulenc returned to the motet with a serene and radiant set of *Quatre motets pour le temps de Noël*. Shortly afterwards he completed a short *Ave verum* commissioned for a women's choir in Pittsburgh: 'I've just written, in two days, an *Ave verum* which is very simple, very pure and, I think, a success.'[29]

For most of the mid-1950s, Poulenc was preoccupied with his opera *Dialogues des Carmélites*, a work which is deeply religious in its subject matter, and which also places liturgical ritual on the stage: among the moments of collective prayer (setting Latin texts), the last Mass said by the Priest for the sisters of the doomed convent is one of the most sublime passages; and the inexorable *Salve Regina* which brings the opera to its close is one of Poulenc's most powerful inspirations. In 1959 work started on the most joyful of Poulenc's large-scale religious works: the *Gloria*, commissioned by the Serge Koussevitzky Music Foundation and completed in June 1960; the first performance was conducted by Charles Munch with the Boston Symphony Orchestra on 20 January 1961. At the time, Poulenc described it as 'without doubt the best thing I have done … I must confess that I have surprised myself. It has given me a confidence *that I badly needed*'.[30]

Poulenc's last religious work returns to the liturgy for Holy Week (the Tenebrae responses for Maundy Thursday, Good Friday and Holy Saturday) and it is one of the composer's most unaccountably neglected pieces. *Sept répons des ténèbres* was composed in 1961–62, though the commission, and Poulenc's first thoughts about the work came a year earlier. From Rocamadour in the summer of 1960 he wrote to Bernac: 'I am beginning, not without fear, to think of the *Office des Ténèbres*. May the Holy Virgin grant that I carry out this task successfully.'[31] As usual, Poulenc was soon having doubts about the precise mood he wanted to capture, but by Autumn 1960 he was writing in more detail:

> I think I have found my first *répons*. … Either it is *superb* or too theatrical. At any rate, it is definitely something. From 'Una hora' to 'Vel': darkness. From 'Judam' to 'Judaeis': an armed crowd. From 'Quia dormitis' to the end: calmness and forgiveness. 'Judas mercator pessimus' will also be tragic.[32]

But by May 1961, Poulenc more or less started from scratch, writing to Milhaud that he was 'working on my *Répons de la Semaine Sainte* for Bernstein. It is not going badly as I have scrapped all that I did last autumn and begun again.'[33] Finally, on 26 March 1962 an exhausted composer reported to Bernac that 'I have finished *Les Ténèbres*. I think it is

28 *Les animaux modèles* contains a poignant self-quotation of a passage in the *Litanies à la Vierge noire*: 'Dieu le père créateur, ayez pitié de nous'.

29 Poulenc writing to Pierre Bernac on 20 Aug. 1952, quoted in C. Schmidt: *The Music of Francis Poulenc: A Catalogue* (Oxford, 1995), 425; 'Heureusement je viens de faire en deux jours un *Ave verum* très simple, très pur et je crois réussi.'

30 Poulenc writing to Bernac, in S. Buckland (ed. and trans.): *Francis Poulenc 'Echo and Source': Selected Correspondence 1915–1963* (London, 1991), 281.

31 Ibid., 273.

32 Ibid., 275–6.

33 Ibid., 285.

beautiful and I do not regret having taken all this time over it as it is very well done. With the *Gloria* and the *Stabat* I think I have three good religious works. May they spare me a few days of purgatory, if I do narrowly avoid going to hell.'[34]

Poulenc died ten months later, on 30 January 1963, and the premiere of *Sept répons des Ténèbres* took place in New York on 11 April 1963. The work has only rarely been performed since, and it is hard to determine why. Certainly the writing is more austere than in the *Stabat Mater* (let alone the *Gloria*), and the musical lines are more angular and perhaps more short-winded. But Poulenc did not set out to write an earlier piece all over again: there is a harmonic boldness here which is strikingly effective in evoking the sense of fear and loss in the texts. Among the most obviously 'modern' aspects of the work is the opening of the third movement, 'Jesum tradidit', which begins with a twelve-tone row, though the first phrase is still unmistakably Poulenc (and provides the basis of the treble solo which follows). Equally striking are the strange sonorities at the start of the fifth movement 'Tenebrae factae sunt', providing an aptly anguished and uncertain context for the text which describes the darkness falling across the earth at the moment of the Crucifixion. Keith W. Daniel has made a good case for the *Sept répons des Ténèbres*: 'there is as much beauty, as much characteristic Poulenc writing, and perhaps more profundity and revelation of Poulenc's religious fervour and views of life and death in the *Sept répons* than in the vastly more popular *Stabat* and *Gloria*.'[35]

Darius Milhaud wrote a good deal of religious music. The *Service sacré* is a heartfelt affirmation of Milhaud's Jewish faith, composed in the aftermath of the Holocaust and of years in enforced exile. Commissioned in 1947 by the Temple Emanuel in San Francisco, it sets the text used in the Saturday morning service. As Henri Barraud has noted, the work was a brave departure, not least in writing a work specifically for the Jewish liturgy with an important part for organ or orchestra:

> Milhaud was Jewish, but his religious sentiment was far more than mere compliance with tradition. He was a profoundly religious man and deeply immersed in his people's communal faith. ... What he attempted, and superbly succeeded in accomplishing, was to uphold traditional stylistic purity, while using the broadly expanded resources of his own vocabulary, which is itself a composite of a long spiritual heritage and the dynamic, innovative influences of our present century. Only he could have met the challenge so well.[36]

Milhaud was anything but doctrinaire: Pope John XXIII's *Pacem in terris* (Peace on Earth) was a visionary document which prescribed an all-embracing ecumenism. The Pope's death in June 1963 and his reforming spirit inspired Milhaud to compose a simple but heartfelt choral symphony (surely the only symphonic work to be named after a Papal Encyclical Letter) for the inauguration of the new concert hall at Radio France. Smaller religious works appeared throughout his career. His songs for voice and piano include the *Poèmes juifs*, composed in 1916 and described by Collaer as a work which 'springs from the deep recesses of Milhaud's soul and is a true profession of faith'.[37] Later songs include

34 Ibid., 288.

35 K.W. Daniel: 'Poulenc's Choral Works with Orchestra', in S. Buckland and M. Chimènes (ed.): *Francis Poulenc: Music, Art and Literature* (Aldershot, Ashgate, 1999), 84.

36 Barraud quoted in P. Collaer: *Darius Milhaud*, ed. and trans. J. H. Galante (San Francisco, 1988), 180.

37 Ibid., 170.

Deux hymnes op. 88 ('Hymne de Sion', dedicated to Chaim Weizmann, and 'Israël est vivant') from 1925; *Prières journalières à l'usage des juifs du Comtat Venaissin* on liturgical texts (1927), and *Liturgie comtadine* (*Cinq chants de Rosch Haschana*), for voice and orchestra (1933).

Psalm 129 for voice and orchestra, written in New York in 1919, is among the earliest of many Psalm settings. Two years later he composed *Psalm 126* for the male voices of the Harvard Glee Club, and in 1928 produced the *Cantate pour louer le Seigneur* for mixed chorus, children's voices and small orchestra, taking words from Psalms 117, 121, 123 and 150. Milhaud drew freely from Old Testament texts for several choral works. For his parents' golden wedding anniversary in 1937, Milhaud wrote a *Cantate nuptiale* based, appropriately enough, on the Song of Songs. In January 1945 he composed a short *Kaddish* for cantor, mixed chorus and organ; this setting of the famous Hebrew prayer for the dead is inscribed 'to the memory of my parents'. It was first performed at the Synagogue in Temple Park Avenue, New York, for which Milhaud had written two other short liturgical pieces the previous year, *Borechu* and *Schema Israël*. Milhaud's wartime works included a new version of the incidental music for Claudel's *L'annonce faite à Marie*, performed as the Christmas Play at Mills College in 1942. From this he extracted *Cinq prières* op. 231c, for solo voice and organ, on Latin liturgical texts selected by Claudel including some of the most famous prayers and canticles of the Catholic church: 'Salve Regina', 'O magnum mysterium' and 'Verbum caro factum est', set to music of touching directness and simplicity. The use of the Bible is a persistent feature of Milhaud's output, and in 1951 he completed a *Cantata from Proverbs* for women's chorus, oboe, cello and harp, on verses from the Book of Proverbs. Further Psalms included *Trois psaumes de David* for unaccompanied chorus (1954), and the short liturgical *Service pour la veille du Sabbat* for children's voices (1955). In 1960 the state of Israel commissioned the *Cantate de L'initiation* (*Bar mitzvah Israël 1948–1961*), using readings from the Torah and first performed in Jerusalem in 1962. A commission from the synagogue in Buffalo for the consecration of the Beth Zion Temple in 1967 resulted in the *Cantata from Job*, for baritone, chorus and organ, and among Milhaud's last works *Promesse de Dieu* op. 438, for unaccompanied choir (1971–72), draws from Isaiah and Ezekiel. One of the great sacred texts of the Christian church, the *Te Deum*, forms the finale of Milhaud's Third Symphony, for chorus and large orchestra (1946): it's a magnificent piece – a marvellous example of Milhaud at his most celebratory.

> I've imposed the truths of the [Catholic] Faith on the concert hall, but in a liturgical sense – so much so that my two main religious works played in concert are *Trois petites Liturgies de la Présence Divine* and *La Transfiguration de Notre-Seigneur Jésus-Christ*. I didn't choose these titles idly; I intended to accomplish a liturgical act, that is to say, to bring a kind of Office, a kind of organized act of praise, into the concert room.[38]

Thus Messiaen stated his position on the place of religious music and theology beyond the walls of a church, para-liturgical music for secular performance (Example 6.9). All but one of the works specifically composed for use in church are for organ (discussed above); the only exception is the simple and lovely communion motet *O sacrum convivium*, written in

38 O. Messiaen: *Music and Color: Conversations with Claude Samuel*, trans. T. E. Glasow (Portland, Ore., 1994), 22.

Example 6.9 Olivier Messiaen, *Trois petites liturgies de la Présence Divine* (1943–44), II

Note the triangular conductor's marking over the 3/16 bars, indicating that each semiquaver should be beaten

Célesta.
Vibr.
Ped.
Marac.
Cymb. Ch.
Tam-Tam
Choeur
mé, C'est pour nous!
(8)
Piano
Ped.
Onde
1ers
Vons
2es
Altos
Velles
C.B.

1937. However, it is not only the *Trois petites liturgies* and *La Transfiguration* which have an explicitly theological content: the early orchestral pieces – *Les offrandes oubliées* (1930), *Le tombeau resplendissant* (1931), *Hymne au Saint-Sacrement* (1932; reconstructed in 1946), and *L'Ascension* (1932–33) are all works with a clearly articulated basis in faith. The song cycles of the later 1930s (*Poèmes pour Mi* and *Chants de terre et de ciel*) combine reflections on the bliss of married love and God's grace; Messiaen's wartime works, too, are almost all rooted in scripture or in contemplation of the Divine: the *Quatuor pour la fin du Temps* (dedicated 'to the Angel of the Apocalypse', and famously first performed in Stalag VIII-A at Görlitz, on 15 January 1941), *Visions de l'Amen* for two pianos (1943), the *Trois petites liturgies* (1943–44) and *Vingt regards sur l'Enfant-Jésus* (1944). The 'Tristan' works of the late 1940s show an apparent move away from explicitly religious inspiration, but by the mid-1960s, with *Couleurs de la Cité Céleste* (1963) and *Et exspecto resurrectionem mortuorum* (1964), Messiaen was once again writing concert works of unambiguously sacred substance. After *La Transfiguration* (1965–69), the later works combine religious thinking with a dazzling vision of nature, brilliantly combined in *Des canyons aux étoiles* (1971–74), and triumphantly brought to the operatic stage, after an exhausting decade of composition and orchestration, in *Saint François d'Assise* (1975–83). The last great orchestral work, *Éclairs sur l'Au-Delà* (1987–91), is a visionary apotheosis of Messiaen's sacred music for the concert hall. Its eleven movements begin with the 'Apparition Christ glorieux' and end with 'Le Christ, lumière du Paradis', a shimmering, valedictory glimpse of Eternity.

The other composers of La Jeune France also produced some religious music. André Jolivet's fascination with magic and the esoteric did not prevent him from writing an unusual setting of the Mass, the *Messe pour le jour de la paix* for soprano, organ and drum, first performed by Messiaen's favourite soprano Marcelle Bunlet in 1942 (with Messiaen himself at the organ). A slightly later work, *Hymne à Saint-André*, composed in 1947, is also for soprano and organ. In 1962 Jolivet's son was married and for the occasion he wrote the *Messe 'Uxor tua'* for five voices and five instruments or organ. As well as setting the Ordinary, the work also includes a Gradual and Alleluia, Offertory and 'dédicace' which are specific to the Nuptial Mass. The diffident Yves Baudrier composed an *Agnus Dei* for voice and organ in 1939, and in 1953 he completed a *Credo* for chorus and orchestra. Daniel-Lesur's religious music includes one major concert work: *Cantique des cantiques*, written for the Chorale Marcel Couraud in 1953. Setting texts in Latin and French drawn from the Song of Songs and elsewhere, this is a strikingly inventive work for twelve-part voices. The final section, 'Épithalame', uses the resources at Daniel-Lesur's disposal to particularly splendid effect: over an ostinato ('Veni, sponsa Christi'), the texture becomes fuller (and harmonically richer) as the upper voices enter with the French text ('Pose moi comme un sceau sur ton cœur') (Example 6.10), and the movement ends with a magnificently harmonized 'Alleluia'. A later *Messe de jubilé* (1960) is more conventional.

Twentieth-century French Requiems have often attempted to emulate the essential serenity of Fauré's famous setting, some with conspicuous success. Most notable is Duruflé's Requiem (1947), integrating plainchant melodies to marvellous effect, fitting them seamlessly into a modal harmonic framework to produce a work which is consistently moving, and the conclusion of which is absolutely magical: Duruflé's 'In paradisum' places the plainsong melody into the context of a kaleidoscope of quietly

Example 6.10 Daniel-Lesur, *Cantique des cantiques* (1953), final section

Example 6.11 Maurice Duruflé, Requiem (1947), 'In paradisum'
Note the plainsong-based melodic lines accompanied by rich added-note harmony, a typical feature of Durufle's style

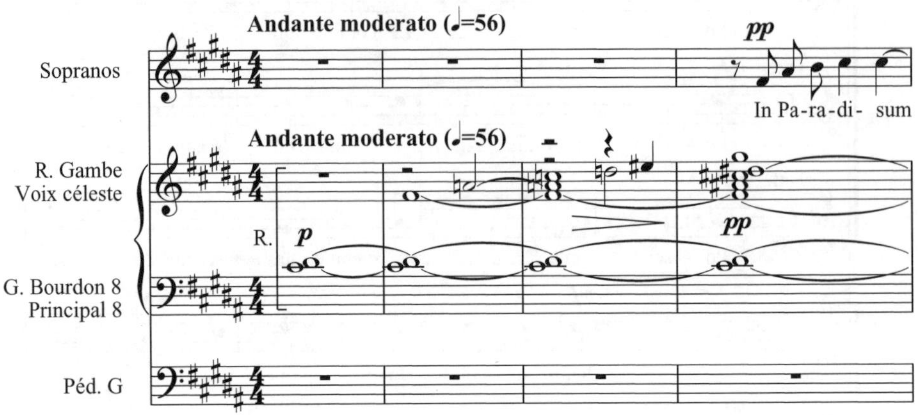

changing chords – a halo of sound where harmonies seem to move with infinite slowness (Example 6.11). Duruflé's Requiem exists in three versions: the first with large orchestra, the second with organ, and the third a smaller (and flexible) instrumental formation with organ. All three versions are identical except in terms of instrumental sonority. Other settings of the Requiem include an interesting example by Guy Ropartz (1864–1955) written in 1937–38, it ends with a charming and rather sunny 'In paradisum', dominated by a gently dancing dotted rhythm in the accompaniment. A touching and very successful later example is the Requiem by Alfred Desenclos (1912–71),[39] who worked as choirmaster at Notre-Dame de Lorette. He wrote this conciliatory work in 1963, firmly in the Fauré tradition but with some imaginative modal colourings which give it a very particular harmonic character.[40] Henri Tomasi (1901–71) dedicated his *Requiem pour la*

39 Desenclos won the Prix de Rome in 1942.

40 According to an extraordinary American newspaper report, this serene and unduly neglected work has had the rather bizarre privilege of being plagiarized in its entirety. See Philip

paix (1945) 'à tous les Martyres de la Résistance et à tous ceux qui sont morts pour la France'. A streak of defiance is apparent from the outset: Henry Malherbe reviewing the the first performance wrote that 'each section of the *Messe des Morts* is illustrated by music of vibrant devotion, almost theatrical'.[41] Among settings of psalms for concert use, there are two outstanding examples. Florent Schmitt (1870–1958) completed *Psalm 47* in 1904 as an *envoi* from Rome and it was first performed in 1906. Ravel called it 'an important and highly distinguished work':[42] Schmitt's brilliantly coloured orchestration, his response to the inherent drama of the text, and his highly effective handling of vast forces have a tremendous impact – and gave the composer a success of a kind which he was only to enjoy intermittently during his long career. Albert Roussel (1869–1937) was a great admirer of Schmitt's *Psalm 47* and may have been inspired by it when he wrote his own, more austere, *Psalm 80*, composed in 1928 as a commission from the Boston music publisher C. C. Birchard. In the first edition, the text is printed in English only, as Roussel originally set it, he added a French translation in time for the premiere, on 25 April 1929 at the Paris Opéra.

The Mass in honour of Joan of Arc – canonized as Saint Joan of Arc in 1920 – is inevitably a uniquely French speciality. Paul Paray's *Messe du cinquième centenaire de la mort de Jeanne d'Arc* dates from 1931 and drew warm praise from Florent Schmitt in his review for *Le Temps*: 'A beautiful work – the soul of a true and sensitive musician'. Henri Busser's *Messe de Domrémy: A la gloire de Sainte Jeanne d'Arc*, conceived, according to the composer's preface, for outdoor performance, was written in 1948. Scored for mixed chorus, four trumpets (which may be doubled or even trebled) and an optional organ part (in the event of an indoor church performance), it is festive and heroic in character.

Another work originally written as a *pièce d'occasion* deserves a special mention. Jean Langlais's *Missa 'Salve Regina'* was composed in November 1954 for Midnight Mass on 24 December 1954 in Notre-Dame. Scored for three-part male choir, unison voices (the entire congregation), two organs and brass, it brilliantly exploits the building.[43] Written in Langlais's most effective neo-medieval style, with bold arching phrases in parallel fourths and fifths, it places groups of brass with the organs at opposite ends of the cathedral. The *Salve Regina* chant is woven into this monumental tapestry to great effect.

France took a leading role in the composition of a new kind of liturgical music, both before and after the Second Vatican Council in the early 1960s, with the intention of involving the congregation more fully in liturgical singing. Two figures were particularly prominent. During the 1950s, Joseph Gelineau (b. 1920) wrote a vast number of short responsorial psalm settings, using the vernacular texts of *La Bible de Jérusalem*. Gelineau trained as a musician at the École César Franck in Paris, before becoming an ordained member of the Jesuits. The international impact of his psalms has been a lasting one, especially in the Roman Catholic church. Jacques Berthier (1923–94) was inspired by Gelineau to produce antiphons, canticles and psalms for parish use. For over thirty years

Kennicott: 'A Composer's Too-Familiar Refrain: Detecting Plagiarism in the Music World Takes a Sharp Ear, and Chance', *Washington Post*, 7 June 2001.

41 Quoted in CD booklet notes by Frédéric Malmazet Ducros for the recording of the work issued on French Naxos 8.554223.

42 A. Orenstein: *A Ravel Reader* (New York, 1990), 346.

43 A spectacular recording of the work made in Notre-Dame (in the presence of the composer) on 10–11 Dec. 1979 has been issued on Solstice SOCD 14.

he was organist at the Jesuit church of Saint-Ignace in Paris, but as early as 1955 he supplied chants for the ecumenical community at Taizé, near Cluny, with which Gelineau had been associated since 1948. In 1975 Berthier was asked to write many more such chants for Taizé, almost all setting Latin texts (to ensure universality) and often characterized by repeated ostinatos, varied with vocal and instrumental solos and descants, or by simple canons. Anthologies of Berthier's music for Taizé have been published internationally, and his undemanding, carefully crafted music has become well known throughout the Christian world. Among the most successful of his Taizé pieces are *Laudate Dominum* (on a chord sequence derived from *La follia*) and the jubilant compound-time *Gloria IV*, with Christmastide versicles ('Hodie Christus natus est, Salvator apparuit, Alleluia'). At the end of the twentieth century, these unpretentious pieces have had an enduring impact on the repertoire of parish churches around the world.

Suggested Further Reading

Sidney Buckland and Myriam Chimènes (eds): *Francis Poulenc: Music, Art and Literature* (Aldershot: Ashgate, 1999).
Gilles Cantagrel (ed.): *La musique d'orgue* (Paris: Fayard, 1991).
Paul Collaer: *Darius Milhaud*, ed. and trans. J. H. Galante (San Francisco: San Francisco Press, 1988).
Harry Halbreich: *Arthur Honegger*, trans. Roger Nichols (Portland, Ore.: Amadeus, 1999).
Peter Hill (ed.): *The Messiaen Companion* (London: Faber, 1995).
Olivier Messiaen: *Music and Color: Conversations with Claude Samuel*, trans. E. Thomas Glasow (Portland, Ore.: Amadeus, 1994).
Michael Murray: *French Masters of the Organ* (New Haven: Yale University Press, 1998).
Roger Nichols: *The Harlequin Years* (London: Thames & Hudson, 2002).
Orpha Ochse: *Organists and Organ Playing in Nineteenth-Century France and Belgium* (Bloomington: Indiana University Press, 1994).
François Porcile: *La belle époque de la musique française: Le temps de Maurice Ravel 1871–1940* (Paris: Fayard, 1999).
François Porcile: *Les conflits de la musique française 1940–1965* (Paris: Fayard, 2001).
Francis Poulenc: *Entretiens avec Claude Rostand* (Paris: Julliard, 1954).
Nigel Simeone: *Paris: A Musical Gazetteer* (New Haven: Yale University Press, 2000).
— and Peter Hill: *Messiaen* (New Haven: Yale University Press, 2005).
WEBSITE: *Musica et memoria*, http://musicaetmemoria.ovh.org/

Chapter 7

Modernization: From Chabrier and Fauré to Debussy and Ravel

Roy Howat

Few musical eras can equal the excitement of the Parisian transition into the twentieth century, with its interaction across the arts and between science and art, often in ways that are still being discovered. If only a handful of composers have changed our perception of music as radically as Claude Debussy (1862–1918) did, the appearance of Maurice Ravel (1875–1937) at almost the same time is just as astonishing. Add the word 'impressionism' and history leaves us with what the composer Betsy Jolas has amusingly called (in conversation and lectures) the 'Debussyravel', a mythical amalgam of floating impressionistic daubs of colour supposedly far removed from the philosophical depths of German music. Closer observation reveals Debussy and Ravel – besides the various facets of their musical philosophy and poetic interests – as two very contrasted temperaments, but linked by a quest for concision, exactitude and emotional cohesion in the way their music communicates.

Even before Debussy and Ravel were active, a velvet revolution was under way, mostly in the hands of Gabriel Fauré (1845–1924) and Emmanuel Chabrier (1841–94). Bizet, had he lived longer, would undoubtedly have played a larger part; as it is, *Carmen* transformed the emotional climate of French music. Non-Conservatoire-trained (unlike Debussy and Ravel), both Fauré and Chabrier entered the field with visions of their own, and Chabrier's small but concentrated œuvre, as much as Debussy's larger one, can quite radically change our perception of music. This is especially remarkable considering that Chabrier, until 1880, worked as a civil servant, composing in his spare time. If Fauré is less often viewed as a revolutionary, many in his time saw him differently, including Ambroise Thomas, director of the Paris Conservatoire in the early 1890s, who considered him too dangerous to be allowed to teach there. A decade later Fauré, already in his sixties, became director of the same institution where his sweeping reforms earned him the nickname Robespierre.

His aims as Conservatoire director had effectively been mapped out by his compositional output; even while Debussy was still a student, Fauré's early works established a lasting French repertoire in the fields of song, piano and chamber music by the 1880s. (In the field of song, honours have to be shared with Henri Duparc's (1848–1933) astonishing contribution; he composed all of his seventeen surviving songs between 1868 and 1884.) The breadth of Fauré's vision can be grasped if we consider that his first major piece of chamber music, the A major Violin Sonata op. 13 of 1875–76, antedates all but one of the sonatas of his teacher Saint-Saëns. (It precedes César Franck's A major Violin Sonata by a decade.) This work and Fauré's First Piano Quartet, op. 15, along with Franck's Piano Quintet, are virtually the first French large-scale chamber works

Plate 7.1 Marguerite Long was one of the major pianists to record her experiences of lessons with Debussy, Ravel and Fauré. This uncredited cover for *Au piano avec Gabriel Fauré*, probably printed left to right, shows Long and Fauré playing piano duets.

which are now established in the top league of today's concert repertoire.[1] Fauré was also the first French composer whose piano Nocturnes, Barcarolles, Impromptus and Waltzes (*Valse-caprices*) can confidently stand alongside Chopin's. While the earliest of these genre pieces ante-date Debussy's adulthood, the last of them post-date not only Debussy's death but also Ravel's last solo piano works. (As many pianists have observed, the ostinato figure from Fauré's Thirteenth Nocturne of 1921 echoes the second theme of the 'Toccata' from Ravel's *Le tombeau de Couperin*, premiered not long before.) As for Chabrier, Ravel repeatedly claimed that no other composer had influenced him so much, and – as we shall see – several of Debussy's most characteristic inventions and footprints can be traced to Chabrier.

In part, the quietness of the Fauré–Chabrier revolution relates to the French way of thinking visually – even today Parisian concerts are habitually advertised under the heading '*spectacles*' – a climate in which opera dominated the musical field. Fauré, not primarily a man of the opera, was never to achieve quick or wide fame in such circumstances. Many have also lamented how much of his mature career Chabrier spent pursuing operatic success at the expense of chamber music (he left only a few unfinished sketches) or a larger body of songs and piano or orchestral music. While the Parisian public was still coming to terms with Bizet's *Carmen* in 1875, the less highly visible success of Fauré's A major Violin Sonata in 1877 (premiered at the Société nationale de musique) failed to draw any French

1 Franck's Quintet and Fauré's First Piano Quartet were composed almost contemporaneously in 1879 and first performed early in 1880; Fauré then rewrote the finale of his Quartet in 1883 before the work's publication in 1884.

publisher into the ring, and the sonata had to be published in Germany.[2] A few years later, however, Fauré's First Piano Quartet (op. 15) was accepted by the Parisian Hamelle, an event that can be seen in retrospect as launching a new tradition, together with Franck's Piano Quintet, and followed in that decade by works like Franck's remaining chamber music masterpieces and Fauré's Second Piano Quartet.

At the same time, Emmanuel Chabrier was producing piano and orchestral music of equal boldness, concentration and quality. Again musical commerce was so unprepared that Chabrier, throughout his life and after, was poorly marketed. His bemused publisher, Enoch & Costallat, left some of his best piano pieces and songs unpublished, and in general his piano music and songs (the latter equal in quantity and quality to those of his friend Duparc, if very different in character) are still establishing their place in the repertoire. Debussy, Ravel, Albéniz, Poulenc and many others were in no doubt about Chabrier's stature. Towards the end of his life Poulenc felt impelled to redress matters by writing a book about Chabrier, in which he unhesitatingly declared Chabrier's *Pièces pittoresques* for piano (1880) to be 'as important for French music as Debussy's Preludes'.[3]

In itself the durational scale of Fauré's and Chabrier's works would say little new, were it not for the music's emotional directness and concentration, reflecting for the first time in French music where French poetry had gone via and since Baudelaire. Wagner was an obvious influence, but Fauré and Chabrier found their own way to combine comparable intensity with concision, intimacy and clarity, free from Wagnerian grandiloquence. Chabrier's relationship to Wagner in many ways foreshadows Debussy's: if Chabrier was reduced to helpless sobs on hearing the opening of *Tristan und Isolde* in Munich in 1879, it did not inhibit him a few months later from mercilessly sending up the same themes as quadrilles in his *Souvenirs de Munich* for piano duet, each Leitmotiv in turn chopped off by slap-happy cadences.[4]

Cadences are of the essence here, for their function was being quietly redefined in the process. 'Paysage', the first of Chabrier's *Pièces pittoresques*, opens the cycle with a straight perfect cadence to the tonic D flat, blithely downgrading what textbooks would tell us should be reserved for a more conclusive moment. Ravel later made this device something of a signature, as in the 'Rigaudon' and 'Menuet' of *Le tombeau de Couperin* or the finale of his Piano Concerto in G. Innocent though Chabrier's 'Paysage' may appear on the printed page, it is riddled with rhythmic and harmonic games, not least the absence throughout this five-minute piece of a single clear four-bar phrase. This must have been deliberate, for the piece's opening section, all in three-bar phrases, makes two teasing feints at four-bar phrases, both thwarted – once by a new phrase that starts with the *ritardando* that would otherwise be expected to finish the previous phrase (bar 16), and then a page later by contrapuntal imitation across the hands that sows ambiguous trails of phrase articulation and bar groupings. As in French usage of the word, *la cadence* in this music involves rhythm as much as harmony.

---

2 The resulting edition, by Breitkopf & Härtel, incidentally never earned Fauré a centime.

3 Francis Poulenc: *Emmanuel Chabrier* (Paris/Geneva, 1961), 57.

4 Fauré, along with André Messager, followed suit a few years later in *Souvenirs de Bayreuth*, duet quadrilles on *Der Ring* that Fauré and Messager originally improvised for amusement at parties. Debussy's later 'Golliwogg's cake walk', with its repeated caricatures of *Tristan*, comes of the same stock.

Example 7.1(a) Emmanuel Chabrier, *Pièces pittoresques*, no. 1 'Paysage', bars 55–7

Example 7.1(b) Gabriel Fauré, Piano Quartet no. 1, first movement, bars 226–8

Other moments of 'Paysage' equally reveal Chabrier's rethinking of standard gestures, notably the piece's second theme with its chromatic quasi-slide up to a 'blue' minor seventh, soon underpinned by a blur of major and minor (Example 7.1a). Within a decade Debussy had made that chromatic run his own – in major and minor modalities, and *in rovescio* – in the songs 'Chevaux de bois' and 'Green' from the *Ariettes oubliées* (1885–88). As for the major-minor blur in Example 7.1a, echoes of it are clear over the next fifty years, from the end of Ravel's Sonatine (1904), via the start of Debussy's 'Poissons d'or' (1907) or the central part of 'Golliwogg's cake walk' (1908), to Ravel's Piano Concerto for the Left Hand, where a similarly blue combination of major-minor blur with minor seventh still sounds modern for a piece composed in 1930. An equal affinity between Example 7.1a and Manuel de Falla's Ritual Fire Dance (from *El amor brujo*) not only speaks for Falla's known enthusiasm for Chabrier, but also suggests an endemic Moorish tint to Chabrier's idiom, reflecting the expatriate Spaniards who taught him music as a child. These explorations are not just Chabrier's, however, as Fauré's First Piano Quartet shows a remarkable melodic match to Example 7.1a (Example 7.1b). Who wrote what first is sometimes uncertain: if it was probably Fauré in this case (given the Piano Quartet's premiere in 1879), Chabrier's major-minor blur may be seen as the point where Chabrier goes his own way, rather as Ravel was later to do relative to Debussy.[5]

One of the most remarkable historical bridges here – especially coming from one who was not then a professional musician – emerges from Chabrier's piano *Impromptu* of the 1860s, whose central part is effectively a study in redirection of the major seventh. Instead of letting the leading note G resolve upwards in traditional fashion, Chabrier draws it down to the fifth (Example 7.2a) and derives a whole episode from the result, returning to it *fortissimo* in the piece's coda. As often, Chopin provides the foundation (Example 7.2b).[6] Chabrier's decisive difference, though, lies in turning Chopin's closing gambit (a prolongation of the final cadence of the *Fantaisie*) into an opening one. In *España* of 1883, Chabrier makes even more of a meal of this device, combining it this time with Chopin's second-inversion cadence (Example 7.2c) but without Chopin's looming resolution to root position. Ravel and Debussy doubtless loved this 7–6–5 motive, which returns as a fanfare to end not only Ravel's *Pavane pour une Infante défunte* but also Debussy's 'Jardins sous la pluie', 'Les collines d'Anacapri' and 'Hommage à S. Pickwick Esq.' (It also permeates Debussy's 'La soirée dans Grenade' and the coda of *L'isle joyeuse*. Even Debussy's early Piano Trio of 1880 makes a feature of it, letting us wonder if the teenage Debussy had intuitively happened on the same motive, or had already come by Chabrier's piece in 1873, seven years after its publication.) More echoes of Chabrier's *Impromptu* emerge from Debussy's prelude of almost fifty years later, 'La terrasse des audiences du clair de lune', whose ending, like that of the *Impromptu*, similarly teeters until the last moment on a chromatically decorated tonic second inversion.

Fauré's role in similarly prising away the leading note from the tonic emerges towards the end of his piano *Ballade* (op. 19) of 1879 (Example 7.3). While Fauré equally echoes Chopin (in this case the latter's Barcarolle op. 60), he turns the gesture into a more radical conundrum by thwarting the harmonic resolution each time the E sharp resolves to F sharp, quietly keeping the listener on tenterhooks. Again Chabrier has a part in this, for the

5 See Arbie Orenstein (ed.): *A Ravel Reader* (New York, 1990), 385, for Ravel's observations on the musical relationship and mutual influences between Chabrier and Fauré.

6 As a teenager Chabrier was taught piano by Chopin's friend Édouard Wolff.

Example 7.2(a) Emmanuel Chabrier, *Impromptu*, bars 84–9

Example 7.2(b) Fryderyk Chopin, *Fantaisie*, op. 49, coda (bars 320–22)

Example 7.2(c) Emmanuel Chabrier, *España*, bars 94–7

central part and coda of his *Impromptu* play repeatedly on the device of resolving a discord in one voice just as another voice sounds a new discord. Ravel's later enjoyment of all this can be seen and heard in the unresolved sevenths that start and end *Jeux d'eau*, and in the chains of dissonances passing across voices in pieces like 'Le gibet' from *Gaspard de la Nuit* (of which more below).

The cadence *per se* also took on new colour from a variety of modal approaches, again well illustrated in Chabrier's *Pièces pittoresques*, from the penultimate bar of 'Mélancolie' (where VII^7 in third inversion resolves to I in second inversion) to 'Idylle' with its kaleidoscope of supertonic, mediant and other modal cadences. Another cadential mask that Fauré and Chabrier introduced almost simultaneously is a full close in the bass masked by a plagal progression above – arguably an elaboration of the opening gesture of Bizet's *Carmen*. Although this can occasionally be heard in Schumann (the C major

Example 7.3 Gabriel Fauré, *Ballade*, op. 19, coda

Fantasy and *Dichterliebe*), Faure's *Berceuse* takes it to a new ostinato level (Example 7.4), possibly just antedating Chabrier's repeated use of the same cadence in the central part of 'Scherzo-valse' (the last of the *Pièces pittoresques*) – though such dating says little of what these good friends may have improvised around the piano at meetings, salons or parties. (Fauré and Chabrier's youthful friendship is reflected in Chabrier's being one of the few people addressed as 'tu' in Fauré's letters.) The freshness of this hybrid cadence remains undimmed thirty years later, as can be heard from Debussy's prelude of 1910 'La fille aux cheveux de lin' (bars 9–10) and throughout the 'Rigaudon' of Ravel's *Le tombeau de Couperin* – a remarkable concurrence in two such different pieces. On a larger scale this cadence forms an important structural element from the start of Debussy's piano *Image*, 'Reflets dans l'eau' (1905).

Late in life, Poulenc recalled first hearing Chabrier's 'Idylle' in his teens, an experience that still made him shiver with emotion as the 'premier baiser d'amour' for his own music.[7] Uppermost in his mind was probably a passage that echoes throughout his own music and well sums up Chabrier's magical touch: viewed separately, the melody, accompaniment and bass of Example 7.5 appear uselessly unpromising – until they are combined. Echoes of this – oscillating melodic fourths above repeated notes in one voice and a chromatic pendulum in the other – emerge in Ravel's 'Noctuelles' (the first of his *Miroirs*; bars 47–50 and 57–60) and the 'Pavane' of *Ma mère l'Oye* (1908–10; bars 5–8). An equally appealing variant of this appears towards the end of Fauré's *Pavane* (1887), a repeated melodic alternation of F sharp and G sharp whose monotony is foiled by the varied harmonies

Example 7.4 Gabriel Fauré, *Berceuse*, op. 16, bars 1–4

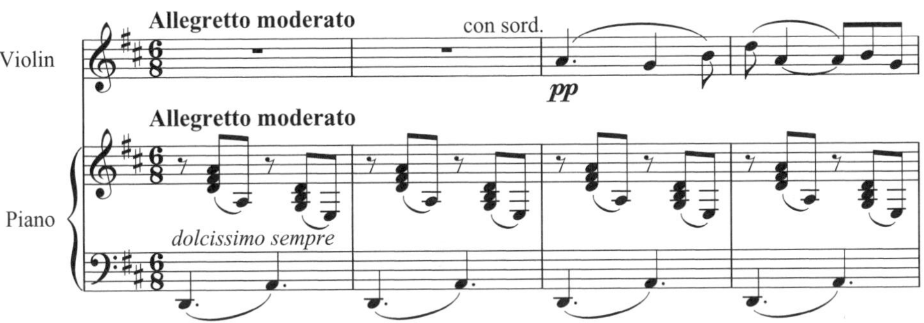

7 Poulenc: *Emmanuel Chabrier*, 62.

Example 7.5 Emmanuel Chabrier, *Pièces pittoresques*, no. 6 'Idylle', bars 20–22

underneath (F♯ minor, G♯^{7}, F♯ minor^{7} and B^{7}). This provides a major parallel to the series-paintings of Impressionism, where an object (cathedral, haystack, whatever) was repeatedly depicted by painters under different light conditions, just as Fauré's fixed melodic fragment is lit from below in varied harmonic colours. Debussy was to make this technique his own, as in the opening bars of 'La cathédrale engloutie' (where the stepwise descending bass forms the equivalent of the moving light source), or with the opening flute melody in *Prélude à l'Après-midi d'un faune* (1892–94), presented first on its own, then relaunched at the same pitch over a D major chord, and then again over an E major chord, with different implications and colours each time for the melody and its opening C sharp.

Another Chabrier favourite is the unresolved chord of the ninth. One decorated example of this (Example 7.6), from the third of the *Valses romantiques* (1883) – a lifelong favourite of Debussy's – soon found a home with Debussy, first in the 'Menuet' of the *Petite suite* of 1888 (in the interim, in 1886, Debussy and Paul Vidal had played the *Valses romantiques* to Liszt in Rome), and then in the fountain scene of *Pelléas et Mélisande*, as well as in various later piano pieces. In his opera *Le roi malgré lui*, Chabrier makes a

Example 7.6 Emmanuel Chabrier, *Valses romantiques*, no. 3, bar 71

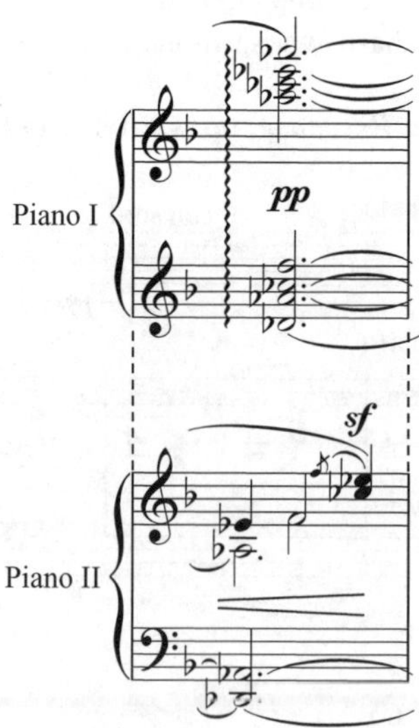

novelty of exploring both diatonic and chromatic chains of consecutive ninths (Example 7.7, from the wild 'Fête polonaise' that opens Act II). Similar progressions can be heard in *Pelléas* and in the finale of Debussy's Violin Sonata (1916–17) (see Example 7.12 below), or diatonically in Ravel's *Pavane pour une Infante défunte*. The underlying harmonic logic of these chains is shown in Example 7.8 in terms of the implied intermediate chords. In addition to all that, the left-hand ostinato that follows Chabrier's chain of ninths in Example 7.7 reappears note for note in the final build-up of 'Scarbo' from Ravel's *Gaspard de la nuit*; and the passage's final resolution to D major closely foreshadows a prominent repeated passage in Ravel's *La valse*, while its hemiola cross-rhythms echo several Ravelian moments including the fourth of the *Valses nobles et sentimentales*. Example 7.9, from *La valse*, is just one of many passages supporting Ravel's claim that *Le roi malgré lui* – an opera he knew in its entirety from memory – 'changed the orientation of French harmony';[8] the rising chromatic scale in Example 7.9 is equally a Chabrier footprint, in works like the piano *Ronde champêtre* and 'Improvisation', and *España* (cf. Example 7.2 above).

On a larger scale, Chabrier's use of form foreshadows Debussy and Ravel's, ranging from simple or modified ternary forms to some works so densely and intricately packed (*Joyeuse Marche* or *España*) that their forms are impossible to categorize. (*España* in particular carves out a kind of free varied binary form that Ravel later took up in similarly tight-packed movements like the finale of his Piano Concerto in G.) Also, even to codify the formal outlines of a piece like 'Mélancolie' (from the *Pièces pittoresques*) would miss the point of what happens inside – a sophisticated blend of textural inversion, canon and rhythmic compression that essentially determines the piece's outer envelope. With typical irony Chabrier's 'Improvisation' from the *Pièces pittoresques* reveals itself under close study as one of the tightest-knit sonata forms in French music, yet still manages to sound improvisatory.

As for Fauré, his first Violin Sonata and Piano Quartet show a mastery of classical forms that match the technical expertise of his teacher Saint-Saëns while moving into new emotional regions, without any stiffness of outline. This goes with a more explicit interest in formal innovation visible in works like the piano *Ballade* op. 19, where each of the opening sections generates a second theme which then returns to start the following section. This technique returns on a smaller scale in Ravel's 'Alborada del gracioso' (1905), and can be related to *pantun* poetry, a technique imported from Malay literature. Baudelaire's poem 'Harmonie du soir' is an example, where lines 2 and 4 of each stanza (that is, the consequent line of each couplet) become the first and third lines (the antecedents) of the next stanza. In 1975 Brian Newbould showed how Ravel incorporated this structure in the 'Pantoum' of his 1915 Piano Trio; in fact it underlies much of Ravel's mature writing, notably in *Le tombeau de Couperin* (a suite contemporary with the Piano Trio).[9]

Aside from considerations of such 'isms' as impressionism and symbolism, a major strand of Debussy's musical revolution lies in his treatment of key. From his youth onwards he appears little interested in diatonic modulation (a major difference from Fauré, a lifelong virtuoso at modulation); even Debussy's early works often hold a single key for

---

8 See ibid., 96; and Orenstein: *Ravel Reader*, 303.

9 See Brian Newbould: 'Ravel's "Pantoum"', *Musical Times*, 116 (Mar. 1975), 228–31; and Roy Howat: 'Ravel, rhythm and form', *Musicology Australia*, 16 (1993), 57–65.

Example 7.7 Emmanuel Chabrier, *Le roi malgré lui*, 'Fête polonaise' (Chabrier's piano reduction, vocal lines omitted)

ff

sf

[21 bars later:]

Più stretto.

ff *sf* *sf* *sf* *sf* *sf*

ff

8va

sf

ff

Example 7.8 Emmanuel Chabrier, *Le roi malgré lui*, and Maurice Ravel, *Pavane pour une Infante défunte*, functional logic of chains of ninth chords (omitted but implied chords bracketed)

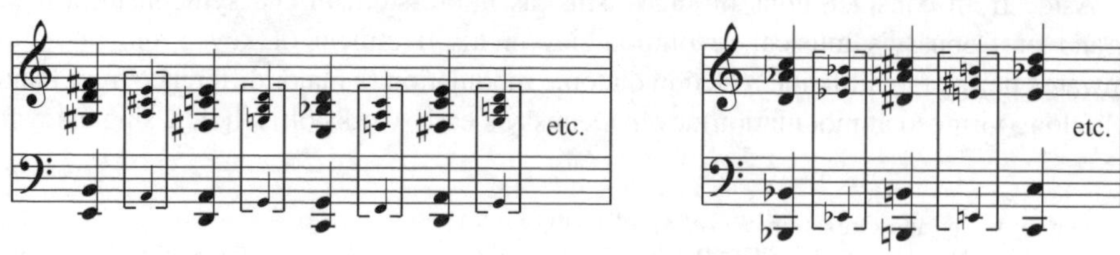

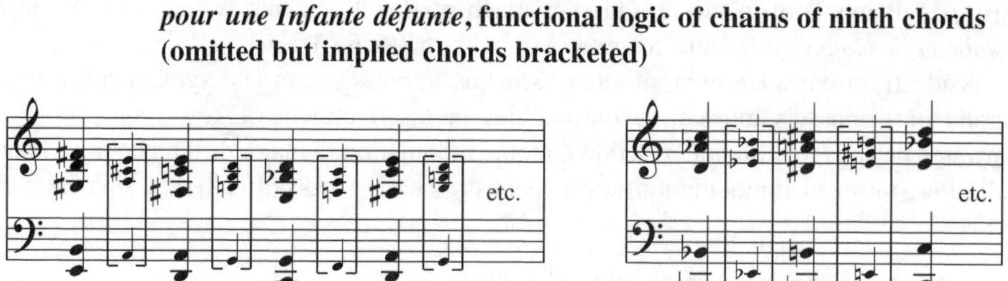

Example 7.9 Maurice Ravel, *La valse*, Ravel's piano reduction, top of p. 23 of printed score

a long span, modulating only at section changes.[10] Even then, a few of these modulations make it by the skin of their teeth (an example can be heard in the coda of the second *Arabesque* for piano, as Debussy determinedly elbows the music out of an attractive F major detour and back to the tonic G). As his idiom and skill developed, he found two ways of avoiding both stasis and forced modulations.

One technique was to anticipate a piece's tonic from the start, but then spend most of the piece delaying its resolution. An example is 'Spleen' from the *Ariettes oubliées*, which delays its tonic chord (F minor) until the song's last bar, while implying it repeatedly through the song by alternating Neapolitan and dominant harmonies. This technique continues through to pieces like the piano prelude 'La terrasse des audiences du clair de lune' (1912) and the Étude 'Pour les sonorités opposées' (1915). However, others are in the field by then, for the tonal structure of 'Pour les sonorités opposées' in some ways echoes Ravel's piano piece 'La vallée des cloches' (the last of his *Miroirs*), which likewise opens with a bell-like G♯ whose eventual function as a dominant emerges only very late in the piece. Each piece also uses F♯ major as a diversionary move (though at a different stage of each piece) from G♯ to the tonic C♯. How much Ravel's piece in turn owes to the likes of 'Spleen' risks turning into a chicken-and-egg debate, because of the originalities in its own structure, including some chromatic contrary motion that effects the unusual modulation across bars 6–12 (E–E♯–F♯ above G♯–G–F♯).

Debussy's other alternative to modulation is the long tonic pedal point, with the texture above it progressively coloured in ways that can be related to Indian rāga, a topic of known

10 According to Edward Lockspeiser (*Debussy, his life and mind*, London, 1962, vol. 1, 33), in Franck's organ class the young Debussy would resist the teacher's exhortations to modulate: 'Mais pourquoi voulez-vous que je module puisque je me trouve très bien dans ce ton-là.'

interest to Debussy.[11] 'Pagodes', the second of his piano *Estampes* (1903), is a vivid example, avoiding modulation throughout by being primarily based on a pentatonic scale that can serve as either B major or G♯ minor, depending on the bass pedal note at any given point. While the most obvious evocations in this piece are of Chinese pentatonicism and the textures and rhythms of Indonesian gamelan, the way Debussy progressively colours in the piece's basic pentatonic scale with added notes (respectively E, D♯, A♯, G♮/F𝄪 and E♯) relates more closely to Indian rāga. A later piano piece that similarly avoids any key modulation, while systematically exploring all twelve semitones of the octave, is the piano prelude 'Des pas sur la neige' (1909).[12] These examples start to suggest how Debussy made the most radical break of all with existing Western tradition, by letting modes themselves set the tonal agenda for a piece.

The most strategic advantage of this technique is that it lets Debussy operate on two levels of tonality at once – direct key relationships on the one hand against contrasts between tonal stability and instability on the other, or between diatonicism and chromaticism. In the piano *Image* 'Reflets dans l'eau', the actual keys enunciated form a surprisingly classical sequence of D♭–D♭–E♭–A♭^{7}–D♭. However, the brevity with which some of them are defined draws attention to the bars where tonality is discernible (mostly bars 1–8, 15–16, 35–42, 56–8 and finally 69 onwards), setting the intervening chromaticism off in dramatic contrast. The piece's climax manages to combine the best of both worlds, starting with a surprise modulation to E♭ before making a further crescendo into some of the piece's most intense dissonances. This was doubtless in Debussy's mind when he wrote to his publisher in 1905 that the piece was to incorporate his 'most recent discoveries of harmonic chemistry'.[13]

Part of Debussy's strategy here is that his chromaticism allows many possible tonal exit routes, letting him hold us in suspense until he decides which one to take and when. Chromaticism can thus be a tonal end in itself rather than just a sort of modulating highway. The resulting contrasted areas of tonal stability and instability often have a large hand in driving the music's overall form – in the case of 'Reflets dans l'eau' an unusual type of rondo with two recurring main motives. One main advantage of this tonal polarity is its instinctive effect on the listener: even the untrained ear easily picks up the qualitative contrasts involved, with no need to understand the techniques any more than the viewer of an Impressionist canvas needs a training in colour theory or brush technique.[14]

---

11 Edmond Bailly, owner of the bookshop *l'Art Indépendant* which Debussy frequented in the late 1880s, is reported to have taught Debussy about Indian music, just at the time this music was heard at the 1889 Exposition Universelle. Many years later Debussy became friendly with the Sufi musician Inayat Khan: see Elisabeth de Jong-Keesing: *Inayat Khan, a biography* (The Hague, 1974), 120–21, and other sources quoted in Roy Howat: 'Debussy and the Orient', in Andrew Gerstle and Anthony Milner (eds): *Recovering the Orient* (Chur, 1994), 66–7.

12 For more detailed modal analysis of these two pieces see Howat: 'Debussy and the Orient', 61–3; and Roy Howat: 'Modes and semitones in Debussy's *Préludes* and elsewhere', *Studies in music*, 12 (1988), 83–4 and 97–8.

13 Letter dated 19 Aug. 1905; in François Lesure and Roger Nichols (eds): *Debussy Letters* (London, 1987), 155.

14 Edgar Allen Poe, one of Debussy's artistic heroes, enjoyed pointing out the difference between what he was actually doing in a poem and what he was making readers think he was doing. Ravel insisted that Poe's major essay on that topic, 'The Philosophy of Composition', was a precise description of how he (Ravel) composed (see Orenstein, *Ravel Reader*, 394 and 433).

Other piano pieces by Debussy that highlight – and to varying extents are driven by – contrasts of modes include the prelude 'Voiles' (1909) (outer whole-tone sections around a climactic pentatonic passage that makes veiled cadences to E flat minor), 'Hommage à Rameau' (the second of his piano *Images*), notably its central section, and *L'isle joyeuse*, where Debussy builds a large symphonic structure by exploiting the relationships of various scales built on A: A major, the whole-tone scale on A, plus a sort of halfway house between the two that includes D♯ as a lydian fourth and G♮ as a mixolydian seventh. Unclassified in Western modal theory, this last scale figures in South Indian karnatic tradition under the name *Vachaspati*, and was also used by Fauré, Ravel and Bartók.[15] It plays an equally important role in the first movement of Debussy's *La mer* (the 6/8 section following the slow introduction), where it grows out of D♭ major pentatonicism by the strategic addition of the tritonally opposed dyad G♮/C♭.

More than any of Debussy's other orchestral works, *La mer* is effectively his symphony, subtitled 'three symphonic sketches' by a composer who wished to avoid the title 'symphony', a genre he felt had been polluted by being over-theorized. Although the forms of each of the three movements appear at first to be largely self-generating, closer study reveals something not unlike sonata form across the finale, plus the fact that on a larger scale the finale recapitulates much of the first movement's material, suggesting a sonata element across the entire work. One can infer a link here (one of several) to Schumann, whose Fourth Symphony also omits a recapitulation in the first movement, jumping straight from the development section to the coda and delaying a recapitulation proper until the finale. While the outlines of *La mer* are less symphonically explicit than those of Franck's D minor Symphony, echoes of the latter can nonetheless be heard in *La mer*, notably in the finale. (More literal allusions to Franck's Symphony can be heard in Debussy's String Quartet of 1893, near the end of the first movement and again in the slow movement's main theme – the latter case suggesting a shared ancestry from the finale of Fauré's A major Violin Sonata.)

Probably no composer reveals such visual thinking in music as Debussy does. If visual or even tactile shapes are apparent throughout *La mer*, the pictorial titles of many other pieces can be seen to drive details or larger aspects of their forms. According to Marguerite Long, Debussy specifically linked the opening texture of 'Reflets dans l'eau' (and its return at bar 35) to pebbles dropping into water, with resultant ripples spreading outwards.[16] Under the pianist's hands (pebbles from the left hand, ripples from the right) this takes on another hue, as it were, in suggesting the pen-and-brush technique of Chinese ink drawing (one of Debussy's many enthusiasms in oriental art), where the pen first etches a line that is then gently washed over by the damp brush, just as the right hand does over the left in the opening of 'Reflets dans l'eau'. Other examples of vividly visual thinking in Debussy's music are the rising layers of arabesque that open 'Pagodes' by tracing the layered shape of a pagoda roof (Example 7.10), or bars 2–4 of 'Feuilles mortes' (which suggest a breath of wind followed by leaves fluttering to earth).

15 See Françoise Gervais: *Étude comparée des langues harmoniques de Fauré et de Debussy*, *La Revue musicale*, special nos 272–3 (1971), vol. 1, 41. This mode is sometimes called the overtone or acoustic mode because of its relationship to the harmonic series with its first two dissonant overtones; in the key of C these come nearest to the lydian F♯ and mixolydian B♭.

16 Marguerite Long: *At the piano with Debussy* (London, 1972), 25.

Example 7.10 Claude Debussy, *Estampes*, no. 2,'Pagodes', bar 4

On a larger scale, if the tonal and dynamic outlines of Debussy's piano prelude 'Danseuses de Delphes' are traced, in their steady rise from the quiet B♭ opening through the dominant F to the piece's climactic C major – and thence back to the closing quiet B♭ – a sort of corresponding energy graph can be drawn that corresponds closely to the frontage of a Greek temple like that at Delphi. This is quite exact, for not only does the piece's climax straddle its exact centre, but also the shorter paragraphs, at least in the first half, measure out a symmetrical sequence of beats within that, somewhat in the manner of a temple's pillars. Read that as one may, such tendencies are widespread in this music (a more specific aspect of proportion remains to be touched on later). Vladimir Jankélévitch's and Edward Lockspeiser's discussion of geotropism in Debussy's melodic shapes (a tendency for lines and melodies to curl or tail downwards) relates to all this preoccupation with shape and gesture,[17] and if these often do not immediately concern conventional key procedures, it reminds us that conventional tonal analysis tends to reveal only a small part of Debussy's musical thinking.

That said, I would insist (in the teeth of much existing literature) that Debussy's harmonic thinking – like Fauré's – remains functional in the most elementary sense, in that each harmonic step sets up implications that he answers, even if not in the way or at the place we expect. What often makes his procedures impervious to fixed analytic systems is his (and likewise Fauré's) free range of modality, which opens up varied cadential possibilities different from Germanic norms. This French modal tradition is undoubtedly a main reason why tonality remained endemic to French music up to the 1940s and in some cases beyond. (It might thus be regarded as ironic that only after the German defeat in the Second World War was much French music swamped by a German-based system of atonality. Given that French music's greatest upsurge since the era of the *clavecinistes* followed the catastrophic French defeat of 1870, Mark Twain's *bon mot* comes to mind that history doesn't really repeat itself, but it certainly often rhymes.)

While claims have occasionally been made of atonality in some of Debussy's tonally most adventurous pieces, closer study makes such arguments hard to sustain. Even those pieces that end on something of a musical question mark – like the Étude 'Pour les quartes' – have too many tonal reference points to ignore. However, it is clear that Debussy was sometimes happy to end a piece on a tonal question mark, once tonality has been defined

17 Vladimir Jankélévitch: *Debussy et le mystère de l'instant* (Neuchâtel, 1949), 89–100, summarized in Lockspeiser: *Debussy, his life and mind*, vol. 2, 237–9.

and centred, as it were. This is the case in 'Voiles', and can even be found as far back as the 1880s in 'L'ombre des arbres' from the *Ariettes oubliées*, whose basic key can be argued as either C♯ (from its ending) or F♯ (from its climax and the Neapolitan implications of its C♯^{7}/G^7 opening). This can be seen as a variant of the technique where he delays a clear tonal resolution until the end of a piece or a song. 'Et la lune descend sur le temple qui fut' (from his 1907 set of *Images* for piano) takes another tack again, masking its essential E tonality with added fourths that sound throughout the organum-like opening phrase. Remove these fourths and the tonality becomes clear (a worthwhile point to note when voicing the passage). The piece's minor modality, incidentally, is defined by its melodic line, not its harmonies, as the opening chords contain no modally defining thirds.

Some years later Debussy's second book of Preludes uses a different sort of tonal masking, sensuously driven this time by visual or even tactile factors at the keyboard, the white keys versus the black keys. (This anticipates *En blanc et noir*, the suite for two pianos he was to write shortly afterwards.) The first of these preludes, 'Brouillards' (composed late in 1911), starts with clear tonality in the left hand, literally fogged by the right hand's chromatic overlay. This turns out to be a larger motive running through the collection, for that tactile opening pattern – left hand on white keys overlaid by right hand mostly on black keys – recurs at the start of the fourth prelude, 'Les fées sont d'exquises danseuses'. Here, however, the tonal sense is reversed, because the right-hand pentatonic black notes now provide the tonality (albeit starting on what later turns out to be the dominant), spiced by short appoggiaturas from the left hand.

The last prelude of the series, 'Feux d'artifice', opens with the same hand layout (left hand on white keys, right hand on black keys) but with the tonality deliberately ambiguous (the haze of cordite, perhaps, as we approach the firework display); only on the piece's last page is it resolved, in a way that inversely mirrors the opening of 'Brouillards', with right-hand fragments of *La Marseillaise* in C major merely forming modal colour over the bass D♭. In fact the fourth prelude of the set, 'La Puerta del vino', has already established a similar tonal inversion: its main theme features sustained melodic notes decorated by rapid Moorish ornaments; in normal harmonic practice the former would be consonant and the latter dissonant, but Debussy does exactly the opposite. Debussy's procedure in these pieces also has to be seen against Stravinsky's *Petrushka*, premiered just as Debussy was embarking on the pieces. Two simultaneous echoes of *Petrushka* emerge from the very opening of 'Brouillards': the left hand taken alone (an alternation of C major and B diminished triads) echoes the closing lines of *Petrushka*, while the two hands taken together in the first beat cover what now tends to be known as the 'Petrushka' chord of superimposed C and F♯ major triads.

The whole-tone mode has long been associated primarily with Debussy, not with total accuracy. Not only can the mode be heard in music by Liszt and various Russian composers, but also the single French work with the most sustained use of it is probably Dukas's symphonic scherzo *L'apprenti sorcier*. In Debussy, it appears mostly in short passing bursts, except for the outer parts of the prelude 'Voiles' (composed a decade after *L'apprenti sorcier*), where Debussy defies the mode's intrinsically atonal nature by using it to mark out a repeated emphasis of the notes B♭, D and A♭ as a dominant to the piece's central E♭ minor climax. Elsewhere, as in the dungeon scene of *Pelléas et Mélisande* (Act III, scene II), Debussy's use of whole-tone colour alternates with other modes to produce a range of shifting colours. In many contexts Debussy uses the whole-tone mode more as a sort of tonal eraser, letting him move in and out of clear tonality as he wishes. In 'Reflets dans l'eau' he uses for this purpose a mixture of the half-diminished chord (often known as the 'Tristan' chord), as at bars 17–20 and 43, and the whole-tone scale as at bar 44. His technique here is essentially the equivalent of Liszt's use of the diminished seventh.

Ravel, by contrast, largely avoids whole-tone colour, using instead the more piquant octatonic mode (of alternating semitones and tones) as a sort of tonal solvent. This scale relates both to the diminished seventh – as two diminished seventh chords a semitone apart – and to the whole-tone scale – as a symmetrical mode of limited transposition that in itself can define no tonality. Even in his student days, and especially from his String Quartet (1902–03) onwards, Ravel used this scale as a source of harmonic piquancy and tonal undermining, exploiting its ability to provide both major and minor thirds in a chord, or to contain two triads separated by the tritone. Well before Stravinsky made a showcase of it in *Firebird* and *Petrushka*, this followed not only Rimsky-Korsakov but also some octatonic works by the French prince Edmond de Polignac.[18] Otherwise any methodical use of the scale had concentrated on the scale's harmonic basis as a diminished seventh chord with passing notes, as can be heard in various parts of Debussy's 'Jardins sous la pluie' (1903) or 'Reflets dans l'eau'. (In the latter case, Debussy's combination of octatonic scale and 'Tristan' chords echoes the first movement of Ravel's String Quartet of two years earlier (Examples 7.11a and b)).

Only in the wake of Ravel and Stravinsky's more colouristic explorations did Debussy move to a more piquant exploration of the octatonic scale's dissonant possibilities, mostly in the ballets *Khamma* and *Jeux* and the second book of Preludes. (The opening beat of the prelude 'Brouillards' is wholly octatonic, as is the *Petrushka* chord which it echoes.) It can be added that even Chopin had started to explore the modal clashes inherent in the octatonic scale, notably in the coda of his Fourth Ballade.[19] Debussy's last works move on again, leaving octatonicism largely to the finale of *En blanc et noir* of summer 1915. The transparent-sounding tonality of the Violin Sonata (1916–17, his last completed work) does not, however, mark any regression, but rather a stripping back to essentials – a transparency that increasingly reveals Debussy's lifelong debts to Chabrier and Chopin (Example 7.12). While one can easily list the key sequences of works like this, tying the music down to established forms is less easy. If Debussy's earlier piano *Image* 'Et la lune descend sur le temple qui fut' is viewed without the added fourths of its opening (as discussed above), its relationship to the last works like the Violin Sonata becomes clearer, and Debussy's lifelong essential classicality increasingly emerges.

Debussy's early works come into clearer focus in this light, relating more visibly to his mature works through their evocative links to the poetry of Verlaine, with its semi-mythical romantic *Fête galante* links to seventeenth century French painting and the world of the *commedia dell'arte*. At present these early works are arguably underestimated, partly because of his own modesty about them in later years. However, played with the

18 See Sylvia Kahan, *Music's modern muse: a life of Winnaretta Singer, Princesse de Polignac* (Rochester, 2003), 70–71.

19 For more illustration of this see Roy Howat: 'Chopin's influence on the *fin-de-siècle* and beyond', in Jim Samson (ed.),: *The Cambridge Companion to Chopin* (Cambridge, 1992), 275–8.

Example 7.11(a) Claude Debussy, *Images, 1er série*, 1, 'Reflets dans l'eau', bars 20–21

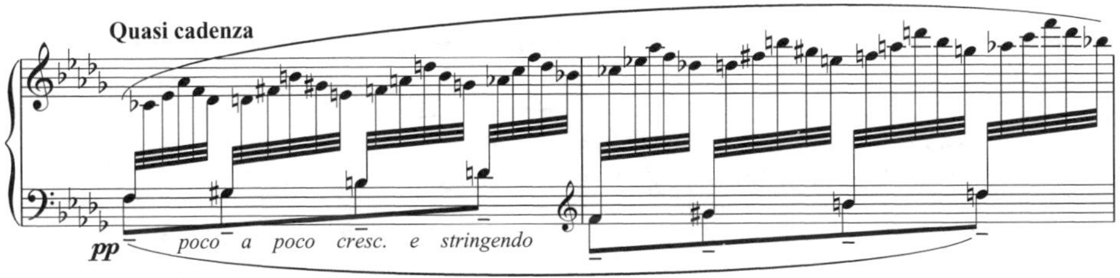

Example 7.11(b) Maurice Ravel, String Quartet, I, before figure 3

rhythmic alertness and vigour endemic to other music of the time, they reveal young Debussy already reinventing the tradition of the French baroque keyboard suite, most notably in the *Petite suite* (piano duet) and *Suite bergamasque* of 1888 and 1890 (the latter revised before its first publication in 1905).[20] Even Debussy's Piano Trio of 1880, since its rediscovery and publication in 1986, has shown itself strong enough to establish a place in the repertoire, as may now happen with the early piano duet works recently given their first publication in the *Œuvres complètes* (series 1 vol. 7). The dynamic and rhythmic robustness of these works suggests that the anaemic haze often imposed on Debussy's later music is far from the composer's character (it was never encouraged by him).

From those early suites, a logical line leads through Debussy's *Pour le piano* (1901) (which makes more reference to J. S. Bach, both in its 'Prélude' and more cheekily in the main theme of its closing 'Toccata') to Ravel's *Le tombeau de Couperin* which, like his Piano Trio of the same time, virtually clears the field of anything more to say. In his commentary to the *Œuvres complètes de Claude Debussy*, series 1 vol. 7 (early piano

20 In this respect the 'Andantino' indication of 'En bateau', opening the *Petite suite*, can well be read against the opening melody rather than the accompanying arpeggios; this allows the piece to move into its central section without an undignified kick. The same applies to the *allegretto* 'Berceuse' that opens Fauré's *Dolly* suite (see the Peters Edition of the latter, EP7430).

Example 7.12 Claude Debussy, Violin Sonata, III

(a) bars 51–6 (cf. Example 7.7 above)

(b) bars 106–7 (cf. coda of Chopin's *Barcarolle* at bar 110)

duets), Noël Lee draws attention to Debussy's use of archaic rhythmic augmentation and diminution in the finale of the *Divertissement* (1884), and this can be related to rhythmic augmentations on the last page of the *Suite bergamasque* (in the left hand), the end of the suite *Pour le piano*, and in the closing pages of *En blanc et noir* (1915).

Those somewhat formal augmentations, however, are just part of a more pervasive penchant for rhythmic counterpoint that finds its most inventive outlet in the *Images* for orchestra 'Gigues' (1903–12) and 'Rondes de printemps' (1903–9), where augmentation and diminution make themselves clearly heard as melodies or fragments playing in counterpoint against themselves at different superimposed tempos or metres. Those *Images* were incidentally Debussy's first orchestral works whose orchestration he felt no need to revise after publication – unlike notably *Pelléas*, the *Nocturnes* and *La mer*, with whose scoring he continued to tinker throughout his life. Not only the rhythmic play in the orchestral *Images*, but also the vertical stratification of sound textures, suggest how thoroughly Debussy had digested the texture of the gamelan music he heard at the Paris Expositions of 1889 and 1900.

That twofold revelation of gamelan was also probably what gave him the confidence eventually to embark on his fully characteristic mature piano works, from the *Estampes* of 1903 onwards. Besides the many bell- and gong-like sonorities of this music, and its exploitation of the piano's natural resonance, the music's top line is increasingly given over to arabesque figurations, with slower-moving melodic lines lower in the texture. Not only is this important for performers to recognize, but for Debussy it solved problems of piano texture and balance, moving the lines that most need sustaining away from the instrument's shortest strings, and letting the layers of musical texture support one another, often in rhythmic polyphony. However, this sort of texture becomes endemic to Debussy's mature works generally, and long sustained melodies in his music are more often found in the middle of his musical textures. This is one major difference from Ravel, whose more exposed sustained melodies reflect his apparent habit of sketching with melody and figured bass. (Try imagining Debussy's *Jeux* or orchestral *Images* sketched in such a form.)

Obviously a major structural influence for this era is poetry. For Debussy up to the early 1890s, the structural canvas of a poem allowed his songs more fluidity and tonal adventure than his instrumental works of those years. In *Prélude à l'après-midi d'un faune* Debussy first carried this over to a purely instrumental piece, essentially by stretching its canvas over Mallarmé's poem (as Arthur Wenk observed, Debussy's score comprises the same number of bars as Mallarmé's poem has lines).[21] As with many composers, the vocal inflections of the composer's language have a natural bearing on the natural phrasing of his lines. This, with all its links to the era of Rameau and Lully, was by its nature one of Debussy's main antidotes against being swamped by Wagner. In Ravel's case an added element is Spanish, the language in which his Basque mother sang to him as a child, something that arguably explains much of his idiomatic and temperamental difference from Debussy. (As further refinements here, one may imagine the southern French and Auvergnat accents native to Fauré and Chabrier which, by all accounts, they never lost.)

21 Arthur Wenk: *Claude Debussy and the poets* (Berkeley, 1976), 152. See also David Code: 'Hearing Debussy and the poets read Mallarmé: Music *après* Wagner in the *Prélude à l'Après-midi d'un faune*', *Journal of the American Musicological Society*, 54/3 (2001), 493–554.

If *La mer* was effectively Debussy's symphony, Ravel arguably produced several of them in disguise, the largest being the ballet *Daphnis et Chloé*.[22] Ravel himself described this score as a '*symphonie chorégraphique* … symphonically constructed on a very strict tonal scheme'.[23] Most obviously, the work starts and ends in A major, but what lends it much of its robust geometry is the network of modal relationships that stem from there. The ballet's very opening aptly suggests the country of the Greek philosophers by showing us acoustically how scales and a harmonic series are formed. (This is just one of the ways in which Ravel, like Chabrier, can make us hear music anew.) Ravel does this simply by piling up open fifths, forming first a pentatonic cluster, then adding a leading note (G♯); finally, with the biting tritone in place (D♯), the music moves off melodically.

Picturesquely this also serves Ravel's ends, simultaneously alluding to ancient Greece and suggesting a rising curtain. Comparison with the first movement of Debussy's *La mer* is revealing, since the latter also opens with a pentatonic combination of fifths, and its 6/8 section (from bar 31) brings in a very similar melody (Example 7.13a–b). The main difference is in the modal placing of the melody relative to the mode: Debussy's first blue note is his flattened seventh (C♭ in Example 7.13b), whereas Ravel homes in directly on the tritonal D♯ to launch the ballet's immensely long melodic line. The ballet's very first harmonic move is equally telling, spelling the 'love' motive (bar 11) with the same half-diminished chord as Wagner used for the same purpose in *Tristan und Isolde*. The expressive and evocative use of this particular chord throughout *Daphnis* and several other Ravel works of the 1900s – notably as a 'sigh' motive in 'Le gibet'– would make an interesting study in itself.

As examples of Ravel's geometric, almost visual use of tonal form, we can take the ballet's first formal key change, to a somewhat mixolydian D♭ major for the *danse générale* of shepherds and nymphs – a sounding major third from the opening key. As the rivalry for Chloé's affections grows between Daphnis and Dorcon, the latter's clumsily earthbound dance returns to the earth key of A, before Daphnis's graceful dance flies off weightlessly to F major, the same distance in the other direction. This is just one of many balances and symmetries that bear out Ravel's comment, not just that the structure is carefully planned but in terms of *why* it is so strictly organized, conveying the drama and expression as cogently and symphonically as possible.

Another typically Ravelian footprint is his use, for the ballet's opening melody (Example 7.13a below), of an oboe virtually in the oxygen-mask range, leaving the impression of an exotic flute-like instrument never quite heard before. In his later operetta *L'enfant et les sortilèges* Ravel took this further, opening with two oboes mixed with what sounds again like a strangely exotic flute. Without reference to the score it is virtually impossible to guess that the third instrument is in fact a double bass playing high harmonics.

Ravel's orchestral virtuosity, at times deliberately ironic, reflects not just his paternal background of a French-Swiss inventor and precision engineer, but also the brilliant originality of Chabrier's orchestration, the more astonishing in that Chabrier learnt the craft himself – ostensibly by copying out Wagner scores that use the orchestra in very

22 Yan Pascal Tortelier's skilfully idiomatic orchestration of Ravel's Trio has recently revealed another hidden symphony in Ravel's œuvre.

23 Ravel's Autobiographical Sketch, quoted in Orenstein: *Ravel Reader*, 31.

Example 7.13(a) Maurice Ravel, *Daphnis et Chloé*, bars 5–7

Example 7.13(b) Claude Debussy, *La mer*, I, bars 35–7 (Debussy's piano duet reduction)

different-sounding ways. (Chabrier might thus be seen as giving French music the orchestral complement of what Chopin gave via the piano.) Much of the brilliance of French orchestration from the *fin de siècle* can also be traced to Russia – ironically, since the brilliance of Russian orchestration up to Rimsky-Korsakov resulted in large part from the orchestration treatise of Berlioz, then a standard textbook in Russian translation (and virtually ignored in France). The Russian influence is particularly audible in the orchestral virtuosity of Dukas's *L'apprenti sorcier* and his later ballet *La Péri* (1912) – a ravishing score which is still surprisingly little known.

Debussy's orchestration arguably relates to Ravel's much as his textures relate to Ravel's melody and figured bass sketches. Manuel Rosenthal has related how Ravel praised Debussy's orchestration but warned severely against imitating it since it effectively flew by the seat of its pants, broke all rules and worked only for the particular piece for which it had been devised.[24] (One might say the same of Debussy's forms.) Debussy's orchestral originality shows particularly in his elemental use of textures in movements like 'Jeux de vagues' from *La mer*, where light divided strings, wind arabesques and delicate percussion blend so well as to become almost interchangeable, while each provides its own colour. In this context Fauré's orchestration deserves some support. If, from the late 1890s onwards, he often left orchestration to colleagues, the cause was more often lack of time

24 *Ravel, souvenirs de Manuel Rosenthal*, recueillis par Marcel Marnat (Paris, 1995), 74–5.

than lack of interest, possibly compounded by a loss of orchestral confidence after his hearing deteriorated in the 1900s. His skill, however, can be judged from the exquisite orchestration of works like the *Pavane* op. 50 (especially if the piece is played properly up to tempo), and perhaps even more in the marvellous delicacy of his incidental music for *Caligula* (op. 52) and *Shylock* (op. 57), not least the 'Air de danse' from the former. Had it started life with a more memorable title, this ravishing short piece might now enjoy equal fame to his *Pavane* if not Ravel's *Boléro*.

Ravel's contribution to piano literature, slimmer in quantity than Debussy's, is more precisely focused in terms of his determination to set and achieve a different goal with each work. (Hence we have nothing like '*Gaspard de la nuit*, book 2', although Ravel did start sketching a work along similar evocative lines, *Les farfadets* [*'Sprites'/'Elves'*], abandoned in all probability because it was too near what he had already done.) Experience has taught many pianists to be cautious of programming Debussy and Ravel together, for the dramatic impact of something like *Gaspard de la nuit* easily swamps the intimate expression of much Debussy ('conversations between the piano and oneself', as he called his early *Images* of 1894). The effect is not just of size, though, for *Le tombeau de Couperin*, played with finesse and delicacy, can be one of the most emotionally intense experiences in this repertoire, all the more so for Ravel's determination not to wear his heart on his sleeve. When the underlying emotional force does explode, in the Musette of the 'Menuet', and again at the end of the 'Toccata', the result can be the more overwhelming for its careful placing.

Like Debussy, Ravel uses the piano orchestrally but tends to notate more pianistically or prescriptively: compare for example his indication *un peu en dehors mais sans expression* (for the most intense moment of 'Le gibet', at bar 28) with the detailed evocative description Debussy provides at the evocatively similar start of his prelude 'Des pas sur la neige'. The point in Ravel's case is (typically) that the intended expression is built exactly into the writing, complete with the absolute stillness of dynamics at that point. By visual contrast at least, Debussy's complex notation of voicing, literally unrealizable if not self-contradictory at the piano, is obviously a descriptively notated appeal to think beyond the piano in vocal and orchestral terms.

Ravel also makes much of sustained or carried-over dissonance. 'Le gibet' relates interestingly in this respect to Debussy's 'Voiles' of a year later, since both pieces hold our attention by playing hide-and-seek with E♭ minor. At first sight 'Le gibet' appears to give the game away from bar 3 onwards, but in one respect the piece is less explicit than 'Voiles', for while 'Voiles' climaxes with a series of distinct cadences to an E♭ minor triad, 'Le gibet' consistently avoids any such triadic resolution. Thus at bar 3 our impression of E♭ minor is gleaned by superimposed fifths (E♭, B♭ and F) that suggest an appoggiatura F waiting to resolve to G♭. No sooner, however, does G♭ appear than the rest of the chord moves away, thwarting the desired harmonic resolution, and Ravel carries this process through the whole piece, holding our attention at the slowest sounding tempo of any piece of French music before Messiaen.[25] In fact the basis of this technique – a sort of pass-the-parcel game of appoggiaturas or dissonance – appears in Fauré and Chabrier's piano works of 1880 or earlier, as already noted above (Example 7.3). Ravel was well aware

25 For more detailed analysis of *Gaspard de la nuit* see Roy Howat: 'Ravel and the piano', in Deborah Mawer (ed.): *The Cambridge companion to Ravel* (Cambridge, 2000), 81–7.

of this technique, for he later analysed his *Valses nobles et sentimentales* in related terms.[26]

In the field of song Ravel shows the closest affinity with Chabrier, essentially using song to tell a story, often as if speaking to children. In choice of poetry his mature songs similarly opt for unhackneyed topics, often humorous, sometimes to a Rabelaisian degree as in *Sur l'herbe*, a Verlaine burlesque of a tipsy priest (one of only two Verlaine settings by Ravel). Ravel's *Histoires naturelles* (like Poulenc's later *Le bestiaire*) also owes a clear debt to Chabrier's four barnyard songs of 1890. Ravel's temperamental difference from Debussy in those respects is well summarized by his provocative use of colloquial French in the *Histoires naturelles*, along with mute 'e's (in defiance of declamatory and singing convention of the time). This shocked Debussy, who always maintained classical norms of declamation in his songs (a point arguably relevant to a debate now current among French singers, of whether to adopt the spoken guttural Parisian 'r' when singing Debussy songs).

As in his piano music, Debussy's songs move from single items in his early years (apart from the Vasnier songbook, more an album than a cycle) towards short cycles or sets. Fauré made this transition more slowly: apart from *Poème d'un jour* op. 21 of 1878, only from the 1890s did he seriously assemble songs in sets, leading to the final cycles *Mirages* (1917) and *L'horizon chimérique* (1921). In many ways posterity still has to catch up with the astonishing quiet modernity of these final two cycles, composed after Debussy's death, in which Fauré somehow can make the musical equivalent of a dropping leaf rock the ground under us (as at 'Si je glisse ...' from 'Reflets dans l'eau'). Fauré's lifelong contrast with Debussy's relationship to poetry is well seen from the Verlaine poems which both he and Debussy set, notably in Fauré's *Cinq mélodies* op. 58, mostly composed in Venice in 1891. If these show Fauré at the absolute height of his powers (along with the Sixth Nocturne and Fifth Barcarolle for piano that followed soon after), it is fair to say that they do not eclipse Debussy's very different settings of some of the same poems in the *Ariettes oubliées* and first set of *Fêtes galantes* (plus the one-off *Mandoline*), all written at a much earlier stage of Debussy's career.

Vocal tessitura is also telling in this repertoire. After his early virtuoso soprano songs (written specifically for the light high soprano of Marie-Blanche Vasnier), Debussy moved the voice considerably lower (revising in this manner some of the songs originally written for Marie-Blanche Vasnier when they came up for publication). This was doubtless in order to maximize clarity of diction, a priority inherent in all his word-setting techniques. Fauré's songs avoid extremes of compass for the same reason, and he sometimes similarly eschews melodic beauty *per se* in favour of accommodating the natural rhythm and expression of the poetic lines (though arguably less than Debussy, who wrote for the voice in sheer terms of natural diction). According to Claire Croiza and others, Fauré was adamant that expression is obtained by variation of colour without fluctuations of musical tempo – above all without unmarked rallentandi.[27] As in his piano and chamber music, Fauré's bass lines are immensely important. This may relate to the melody and figured-bass sketching habits of Fauré's pupil Ravel, in that Fauré's piano textures in particular

26 Ravel's analysis is quoted in Orenstein: *Ravel Reader*, 519–20.

27 Quoted in Hélène Abraham: *Un art de l'interprétation, Claire Croiza – les cahiers d'une auditrice, 1924–1939* (Paris, 1954), 212.

need very careful voicing to avoid thickness, usually by letting the melody and bass stand out and keeping other lines very discreet except at strategic moments.

One of the hardest questions to answer in this entire repertoire is whether it counts as classical or romantic. While the emotions explored, and the allusions of many titles, point distinctly towards the latter, the form can be argued as distinctly classical in that clarity and balance of form (and thus of expression) are an integral part of the music's expression. (Debussy is on record as linking form and expression in this way, observing that when the architecture is not clearly understood the expression becomes distorted.)[28] Ravel's pleas to performers just to 'play, not interpret my music' are on record, and Debussy was apparently as adamant as either Ravel or Fauré about his music being played in time (as can be heard on the audio recordings he made in 1904, accompanying Mary Garden in three of the *Ariettes oubliées* and the tower song from *Pelléas et Mélisande* – a more reliable record of his playing than the later piano rolls he made for the Welte reproducing system). This is clearly reflected in his scores by the wide and subtle variety of rhythm notated on the music's surface (including all the tied-over beats), a careful architecture that is shredded by any rhythmically sloppy performance.

How exactly Debussy measured his musical structures in the course of construction can only be debated, since his remaining sketches leave few explicit signs of construction. Whatever the case, in many of his scores from the late 1880s onwards, most notably *La mer*, *L'isle joyeuse* and the piano *Images*, the precisely focused tonal, thematic and other formal turning points in the music can be shown to form sophisticated proportional structures based on exact symmetry and golden section. These often follow the numbers of the related Fibonacci series, as measured by notated bars or beats, usually focusing the structure geometrically to the music's climactic points.

By its nature this topic is bound to remain contentious (unless some unambiguous comment from Debussy should be discovered one day); its main interest lies in linking different aspects of the structure into a naturally balanced dramatic flow. This structuring also appears very precisely in the climactic Act IV, scene iv of *Pelléas et Mélisande*, and the dramatic shaping of this scene can be related to the whole opera, and beyond to other symphonic movements including 'Jeux de vagues', 'Gigues', 'Rondes de printemps' and *Jeux*.[29] The benefits of such a technique (if it can be called that) include the way it draws attention away from itself towards the musical events that it geometrically links, and the way it can embrace such contrasted structures as *L'isle joyeuse* (with its triumphant ending) and the piano *Images* with their variously arched forms and quiet endings (never mind the three movements of *La mer* and various songs from the *Ariettes oubliées* onwards). However these structures occurred, they visibly relate to structures like the symmetrical arch shape already discussed in the Prelude 'Danseuses de Delphes', in forming part of the music's sensuously or pictorially driven elements and providing an integral part of the musical expression in terms of its harmonious balance. Such structures can also be seen as a larger-scale deployment of the smaller-scale kind of rhythmic play that can be found in much of Chabrier's and Ravel's music. Study of Fauré's phrase structures and bar groupings is equally revealing, and provides an essential tool for

28 Letter of 1908 to Georges Jean-Aubry, quoted in Margaret G. Cobb: 'Debussy in Texas', *Cahiers Debussy*, nouvelle série, 1 (1977), 46.

29 The topic is explored in Roy Howat. *Debussy in proportion* (Cambridge, 1983).

performers for articulating textures in his later works. Although these large-scale exactitudes of proportion appear mostly in Debussy, some cases occur in Ravel (who appeared to favour exact symmetries across some binary forms, as in the finale of his Piano Concerto in G) and in Fauré (for example in the song 'Reflets dans l'eau' from the late cycle *Mirages*).[30]

As the twenty-first century takes stock and artistically reassesses the twentieth century, the music of this French renaissance is still receiving increasing attention from performers and listeners. If Debussy and Ravel are now well established (after Debussy took decades to be fully appreciated in his own land), new editions and research show Chabrier's and Fauré's music to be rising strongly in public appreciation. Any view of them that discourages sloppy, understated or condescending performance helps, and it is encouraging to note how performing trends of the last decade or two are now recovering some of the strongest aspects of performing tradition that can be linked directly to the playing of these composers, far from the sentimental habits or over-indulgence that have long disfigured this repertoire.[31]

Suggested Further Reading

James Briscoe (ed.): *Debussy in performance* (New Haven: Yale University Press, 1999)
Jessica Duchen: *Gabriel Fauré* (London: Phaidon, 2000).
Roy Howat: *Debussy in proportion* (Cambridge: Cambridge University Press, 1983).
François Lesure and Roger Nichols (eds.): *Debussy Letters* (London: Faber, 1987).
Edward Lockspeiser: *Debussy, his life and mind*, 2 vols (London: Cassel, 1962).
Deborah Mawer (ed.): *The Cambridge Companion to Ravel* (Cambridge: Cambridge University Press, 2000).
Jean-Michel Nectoux: *Gabriel Fauré, a musical life*, trans. Roger Nichols (Cambridge: Cambridge University Press, 1991).
Roger Nichols: *Ravel Remembered* (London: Faber, 1987).
— *Debussy Remembered* (Portland, Ore.: Amadeus, 1992)
— *The Harlequin Years* (London: Thames & Hudson, 2002).
Arbie Orenstein (ed.): *A Ravel Reader* (New York: Columbia University Press, 1990).
Robert Orledge: *Gabriel Fauré* (London: Eulenberg, 2/1983).
Francis Poulenc: *Emmanuel Chabrier* (Paris/Geneva: La Palatine, 1961); also in English, trans. Cynthia Jolly (London: Dennis Dobson, 1981).
Richard Langham Smith (ed. and trans.): *Debussy on Music* (translation of *Monsieur Croche et autres écrits*) (London: Secker & Warburg, 1977).
Charles Timbrell: *French Pianism: A Historical Perspective* (Portland, Ore.: Amadeus, 2/1997).
Simon Trezise (ed.): *The Cambridge Companion to Debussy* (Cambridge: Cambridge University Press, 2003).

30 For more detail see Roy Howat, 'Ravel and the piano', 96 and *Debussy in proportion*, 189–93.
31 See James Briscoe (ed.): *Debussy in perfomance* (New Haven, 1999).

Chapter 8

Satie & Les Six

Robert Orledge

Satie's Achievements

Erik Satie (1866–1925) remains an iconoclast who forged his own path with feline independence and cunning, overturning nineteenth-century artistic traditions left, right and centre (though his own politics were distinctly to the left). He was perhaps Debussy's closest friend over a quarter of a century, yet he took virtually nothing from him in artistic terms and rather claimed that he had suggested the application of Impressionistic techniques to music and the rejection of Wagnerism when they first met in 1891. Ravel acknowledged the influence of Satie's early songs and *Gymnopédies* too, though Satie fell out with Ravel (and even Debussy for a while) over their derogatory views of his ballet *Parade* (1917). For despite regarding music critics as the lowest of the low, Satie still remained sensitive to the opinions of those he respected, even if their number were few.

Few, too, were the identifiable influences on his own music: perhaps a little Chabrier in the early *Sarabandes*, and certainly the spirit of Gregorian chant in his Rose†Croix period.

Plate 8.1 Jean Cocteau introduces Les Six [sic] to Erik Satie.

Debussy christened him the 'precursor' and one can find numerous twentieth-century innovations in his sparse little scores, from the first piece of organized total chromaticism in *Vexations* (1893), through neoclassicism and minimalism to something close to 'muzak' in his wartime *musique d'ameublement* (furniture music). Above all, he rejected the concept that music should develop, or be directional, or romantically expressive, and it is small wonder that John Cage declared him 'indispensable'[1] when he rediscovered his anti-art concepts after the Second World War.

If Satie's ideas can seem more impressive than his music, and if he perhaps bypassed Impressionism and the beguiling sonorities of Debussy and Ravel because his technique was simply not up to these, then his cross-referential art derived more from painters and sculptors than any other composer of his period. His knowledge of Cubism was second to none, and his equivalent of the flattened surfaces and geometric abstractions of Analytical Cubism can be seen in the juxtaposed blocks of orchestral sound and mirror structures that characterize *Parade*. Similarly, he wrote of his masterpiece *Socrate* that it represented 'a return to classical simplicity with a modern sensibility. I owe this – very useful – return to my "Cubist" friends.'[2] But, most importantly, Satie's apparently limited art formed the basis of a living tradition after his death, providing a source of inspiration for composers like Cage and Reich; for Surrealist artists like Magritte, Man Ray and Miró; and for sculptors like Brancusi and Calder. In short, his own constant renewal stimulated a similar approach in others, and the rather high-handed dismissal of him by Boulez in his article 'Chien flasque'[3] stems from a different approach to what music can and should achieve. As Glenn Watkins observes: 'Critics and historians have debated Adorno's admonition that "difficulty" in some measure was a prerequisite for membership, and surely for canonization, in the avant-garde.'[4] Satie's case, in particular, proves how vital this debate has been for, while there is no parallel in his music to the rhythmic innovations or technical complexities of Stravinsky, Apollinaire's preface to *Parade* was still able to establish Satie as the musical catalyst in the wartime *esprit nouveau* in France. And he maintained his position at the forefront of the post-war avant-garde through his association with Cocteau's Art of the Everyday, his collaborations with Picasso and others, and through his position as artistic mentor to Les Six. If the question of Satie's 'canonization' has been challenged in some quarters by posterity, then there was no doubt about it in the minds of the most influential of his contemporaries.

Satie's Rose†Croix Period (to 1895)

To revert to the start of Satie's career, his poet friend Contamine de Latour summed up what was both Satie's problem and his salvation as follows:

1 In John Cage: *Silence* (London, Calder and Boyars, 1968), 82.

2 From a letter to Henry Prunières of 3 Apr. 1918, cited from a copy in the Archives de la Fondation Erik Satie, Paris: 'C'est un retour vers la simplicité classique, avec sensibilité moderne. Je dois ce retour – aux bons usages – à mes amis "cubistes".'

3 In *La Revue musicale*, 214 (June 1952), 153–4.

4 Glenn Watkins: *Pyramids at the Louvre: Music, Culture, and Collage from Stravinsky to the Postmodernists* (Cambridge, Mass., 1994), 222.

> His musical education was extremely incomplete. But he put together the things he had and manufactured from them a formula of his own, maintaining that all other techniques were non-existent and even a barrier to true musical expression. He was in the position of a man who knows only thirteen letters of the alphabet and decides to create a new literature using only these, rather than admit his own insufficiency. For sheer bravado, it was unparalleled at the time.[5]

The idea of 'a new literature' was extremely perceptive, for one can see literary techniques as well as Satie's limited musical alphabet in constructive action in Rose†Croix compositions like the enigmatic *Préludes du Nazaréen* of 1892. Example 8.1 shows the final (recapitulation) section of the first *Prélude*. Here, the solo statement (A) derives from

Example 8.1 Erik Satie, first *Prélude du Nazaréen*, final section

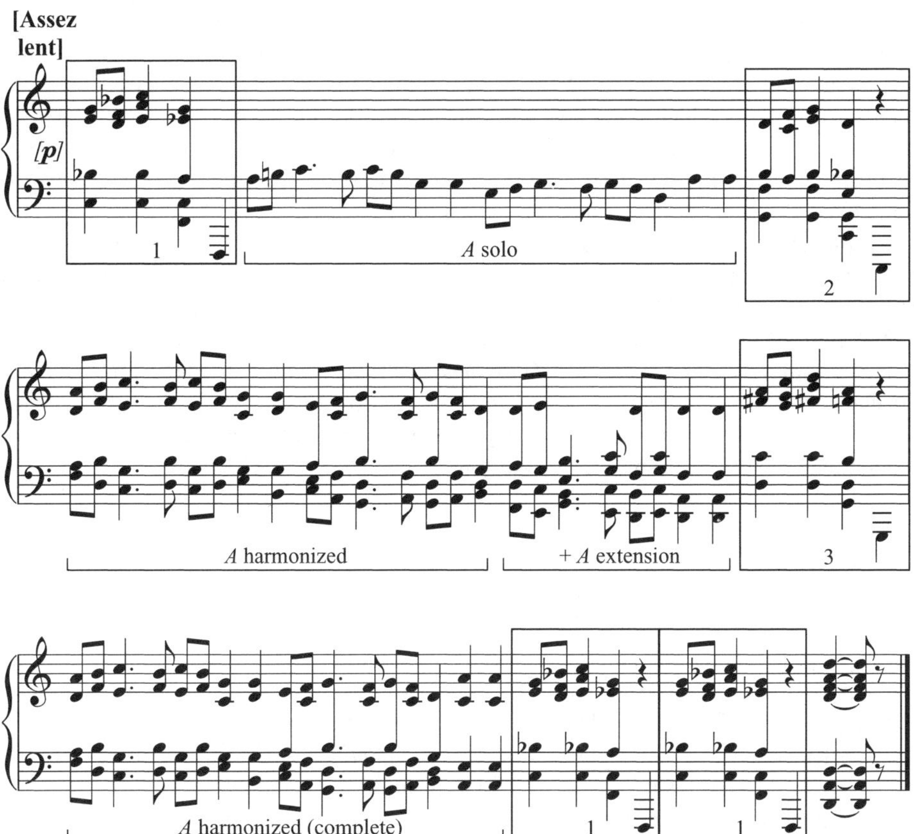

5 From P. Contamine de Latour: 'Erik Satie intime: souvenirs de jeunesse', *Comœdia* (3 Aug. 1925), 2: 'Son éducation musicale était très incomplète. Il rassembla les éléments qu'il possédait et s'en fit une formule particulière, décrétant tout le reste inexistant et même nuisible à une bonne expression de la musique. Il était dans la situation d'un homme qui ne connaîtrait que treize lettres de l'alphabet et déciderait de créer une littérature nouvelle avec ces seuls moyens, plutôt que d'avouer sa pauvreté. Comme audace on n'avait pas encore trouvé mieux.'

plainchant and its harmonized recurrences (the first incomplete and extended) are punctuated by short cadential cells (numbered 1–3), rather like commas in the musical prose. Whereas the harmonizations of A consist of simple first inversion or root position triads in contrary motion, those of the punctuation points are sensuous sevenths, thirteenths and ninths (which Satie may have taken from Chabrier's parallel ninths in *Le roi malgré lui*). Moreover, the punctuation points are transpositions of each other, with two statements at the end forming a full stop. This minimalist approach is mirrored in the musical prose, whose barlessness and irregularity is more striking than its harmonic content. Thus Satie was making something new from the limited resources at his disposal, carefully segregating the traditional and modern harmonic elements he knew about, which were each given a different, but complementary literary function. And although the piece was never performed, it was intended to accompany a voluptuous, esoteric play by the Symbolist author Henri Mazel (1864–1947), from which it is timelessly and utterly detached, like a 'scenic backcloth'.

Although the prelude appears to be mostly a formless chain of slow, quiet, directionless chords, analysis reveals this to be far from the truth. In fact, its four musical ideas are juxtaposed as cells which transpose and extend, but do not develop, punctuated by the sensuous modern cadences in strict rotation. All Satie had to do once his plan had been established was to find a suitable chord to end his novel modal creation, and (typically) this proved almost as difficult as the rest of the piece put together.

All of Satie's Rosicrucian music from the 1891–95 period is equally fascinating, and the superficial similarity of these largely private experiments in making a lot out of a little grew out of the four *Ogives* (c.1888), whose inspiration came as much from Gothic architecture as from music. They have, of course, been eclipsed in popularity by the haunting *Gymnopédies* (1888) and *Gnossiennes* (1890), whose timeless antiquity and detachment have made them ideal accompaniments to films and TV adverts. And even Satie must have realized that his early works were a rhythmic cul-de-sac, for he experimented with greater metrical fluidity in the six *Pièces froides* of 1897.

1897–1912

After this came many years of directional uncertainty, during which composing for and accompanying cabaret singers like Vincent Hyspa and Paulette Darty came to the fore, although this means of keeping body and soul together was to provide him with experience that he put to good use in his later ballets (see *Mercure* and *Relâche* below). After the 'absolutely astounding'[6] revelations of Debussy's *Pelléas et Mélisande* in 1902, Satie thought he had found his own new way forward in the *Trois morceaux en forme de poire* (1903), though this combination of pieces from the early 1890s with more recent cabaret songs arranged for piano duet proved too retrospective to offer a lasting solution. Gradually, Satie came to the wise conclusion that he needed to know all twenty-six letters of the musical alphabet if he was to make real headway as a composer and, despite Debussy's advice to the contrary, he enrolled for a counterpoint course under Albert Roussel at the recently founded Schola Cantorum in 1905, which he passed with flying

6 From a letter to Conrad Satie on 27 June 1902: 'absolument époilant'.

colours three years later. In fact, he remained there till 1912, studying orchestration, analysis and sonata composition with Vincent d'Indy, putting his knowledge to constructive use in whimsically titled works like the *Aperçus désagréables* of 1908 and the new 'modern fugue' used in *En habit de cheval* (1911).

But the main legacy of the Schola Cantorum was to make Satie's later music more linear and sparse in conception, and a far more important event for him (in practical if not aesthetic terms) was the rediscovery of his early works by Ravel in a concert at the prestigious new Société Musicale Indépendante in January 1911. Although Satie was dismayed to find the 'fruit of his great ignorance'[7] (which had led him to enrol at the Schola) now suddenly being acclaimed as precursive, the ensuing publicity put him on the musical map at last. This encouraged him to give up practical cabaret work for good and also led to publications by Rouart-Lerolle in 1911–12: first of earlier works like the *Sarabandes* of 1887 and then of his most recent works like *En habit de cheval*. But the most important breakthrough came when Eugène Demets accepted his *Véritables préludes flasques (pour un chien)* for publication in December 1912. When these proved popular, Demets asked for more and so stimulated the most productive period in Satie's life – that of the humoristic piano pieces of 1912–15.

The Humoristic Piano Pieces (1912–1915)

In over sixty such pieces, Satie focused his ironical gaze on just about everything from his musical past that he thought merited deflation or reinterpretation. He cocked a snook at the nineteenth-century operettas of Aimé Maillart and Robert Planquette in the *Chapitres tournées en tous sens*, and even at Gounod's *Faust* in the *Vieux séquins et vieilles cuirasses* in 1913. He produced a hilarious version of the repetitive ending of Beethoven's Eighth Symphony and reduced the romantic trio of Chopin's Funeral March to a matter-of-fact, monochrome statement in the *Embryons desséchés,* as well as providing his own complete reinterpretation of sonata form in its first movement ('d'Holothurie'). In his *Croquis et agaceries d'un gros bonhomme en bois* he focused on Mozart's 'Rondo alla Turca' and Chabrier's *España*, and he even ventured some references to his friend Debussy in 'Regrets des enfermés' (the last of the *Chapitres tournés*), though these were in no way parodies.

In the best of the humoristic pieces, the *Sports et divertissements* of 1914, Satie produced a miniature *Gesamtkunstwerk* by combining beautifully calligraphed musical cameos with illustrations by Charles Martin, and expanding the humorous directions that he had habitually provided for pianists since his *Gnossiennes* of 1890 into tiny prose poems. 'Le Pique-nique' (Example 8.2) shows how far Satie's style had developed since the 1890s, even if it is still constructed from juxtaposed cells. It begins with an adapted folk song, in which the sudden harmonic activity at the end of the second phrase was a cadential feature he was to develop in his later works. Then follows a veiled reference to Debussy's cake walk *The Little Nigar* (at 'Ils ont tous apporté'), a brief lyrical passage, a repetitive Stravinskian ostinato, and a brief recapitulation and coda in which a passing

7 From a letter to Conrad Satie of 17 Jan. 1911, cited in Pierre-Daniel Templier: *Erik Satie* (Paris, 1932), 32: 'œuvres jadis considérées comme fruit d'une grande ignorance'.

Example 8.2 Erik Satie, *Sports et divertissements*, 15 ('Le pique-nique')

aeroplane turns out to be a quasi-operatic storm in a teacup. As the moods mercurially change, we can see how the lessons of the Schola had borne fruit in the careful voice-leading, linear approach, brief imitative counterpoint, and precautionary accidentals. At the same time, everything has been stripped to its bare essentials in this ultra-concise, yet ultra-precise, cross-referential epitome of the 'cult of restraint', whose true source is the Japanese haiku.

Satie's piano pieces were to become more surrealistic in the *Heures séculaires et instantanées* later that summer and we can tell that this productive vein was almost exhausted when he began producing titles and commentaries for new sets without completing (or in some cases even starting) the music for them towards the end of 1914. In short, he was ready for a new phase in his career. This was stimulated by his second rediscovery by Jean Cocteau in 1915 and led to his adoption as the musical figurehead of the new avant-garde as proclaimed by Cocteau in *Le coq et l'arlequin* in 1918, with its emphasis on simplicity, accessibility and the popular roots of French art.

Parade, *Socrate* and the Later Ballets (1917–1924)

Satie's further elevation came about largely through *Parade*, as we have seen, which caused a scandal when it was first produced (in collaboration with Picasso, Cocteau and Massine) by Diaghilev's Ballets Russes at the Théâtre du Châtelet on 18 May 1917. Everything about it was new and provocative, from Picasso's unwieldy Cubist costumes for the Managers (which upset Debussy), to the typewriters, sirens and other extraneous noises in Satie's score (which were imposed on him by Cocteau). Satie's main concern, as in all his later ballets, was to construct a perfectly balanced score which could stand up independently amid all the theatrical paraphernalia surrounding it. To this end, he invented an elaborate series of interlocking mirror structures which embraced the three separate parts ('Chinese Conjurer', 'Little American Girl' and 'Acrobats') and the introductory and closing material. At the heart of all these formal reflections was the 'Ragtime du paquebot' which used Irving Berlin's 1911 hit 'That Mysterious Rag' as a rhythmic model.[8]

Apart from the unusually graphic portrayal of the sinking of the *Titanic* which follows this, Satie's orchestration was a model of transparency as he brought the oscillating ostinatos (which are its true thematic material) to life. Just as his chord progressions 'lack harmonic perspective in much the same way that a cubist painting lacks spatial perspective',[9] so his transparent orchestration matches the colouristic restraint of early Cubism, and the self-sufficiency of his score can be likened to the 'assassinated' objects in the paintings of Picasso or Braque. Although much has been written about the extraneous noises in *Parade* resembling the collage techniques of Synthetic Cubism – not least by Cocteau, who became jealous when Satie found Picasso's ideas more inspiring than his own – it was the reordering of objective reality in new structures and forms through the subjective reality of the artist which most interested Satie. This perhaps explains why *Parade* was described as a 'ballet réaliste', and why Apollinaire praised its 'sur-réalisme' in his preface. Even if Satie's music was put together as a collage of cells and did frequently involve aspects of the other arts, his main allegiance was with the pure period of Analytical Cubism, as Gertrude Stein was the first to observe.[10]

As we have seen, the Cubist connections continued with his 'symphonic drama' *Socrate*, which Satie composed in 1917–18 to his own selection of extracts from Plato's *Dialogues* in the French translation by Victor Cousin. This was Satie's most obvious return to the world of Greek antiquity since his early *Gymnopédies*, with which it shares the same qualities of timeless simplicity and restraint. At the same time, Satie saw its conception as 'modern', perhaps as a combination of the linear, monochrome flatness of early Cubism with Picasso's attraction to the classical style of Ingres after 1915. The main differences from *Parade* are that the orchestration is string-based and there is more concern for continuity between phrases as the motivic score pursues its slow, inexorable course towards the death of Socrates beneath an almost psalmodic soprano vocal line. As Poulenc observed in 1920, we can see in *Socrate* 'the beginning of horizontal music which will succeed perpendicular music. It is to this self-same criterion that *Socrate* owes its

8 The details of this can be found in Robert Orledge: *Satie the Composer* (Cambridge, 1990), 172–5, and can be seen to apply both to the 1917 version and the extra outer sections added at Diaghilev's request in 1919.

9 Constant Lambert: *Music Ho!* (London, 1934), 119.

10 Cited in Martin Howe: 'Erik Satie and his Ballets', *Ballet*, 6/1 (Oct. 1948), 25: 'the pure period of cubism, that is to say the cubism of cubes, found its final expression in *Parade*.'

Example 8.3 Erik Satie, *Socrate*, I ('Portrait de Socrate'), vocal score, pp. 9–10

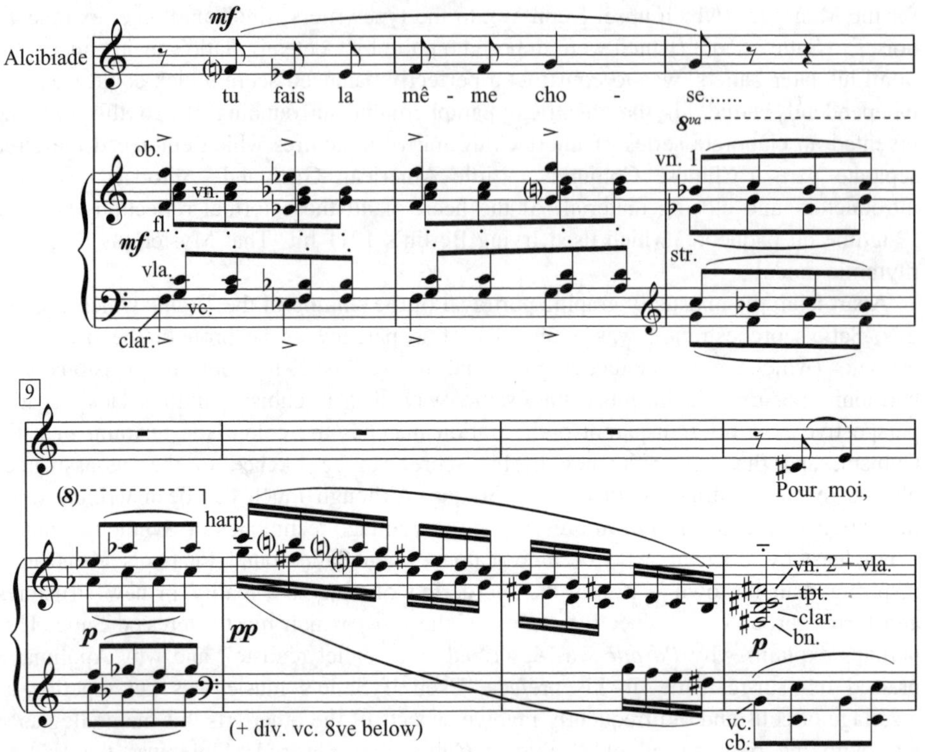

limpidity, which is like running water.'[11] A good illustration of this can be found in the initial 'Portrait de Socrate' (Example 8.3). Here the oboe leads into the first violins in bars 2–3; the strings into the descending scale for harp and divided cellos at figure 9; and the scale into the chord in the final bar, all with commendable smoothness and logic. Scales in perfect fourths recur frequently in Satie's later works and act as a force for continuity and unity within this remarkable work where dignity and self-denial are the *sine qua non*.

During the early 1920s Satie, as the foremost musical exponent of the *esprit nouveau*, worked mainly to commission with the great names in the avant-garde and strove to keep ahead of the throng and make his music chic, Parisian and striking. His collaborations with Picasso continued with the divertissement *La statue retrouvée* in 1923 and, more importantly, with the ballet *Mercure* in 1924, both of which were written for the wealthy Comte Étienne de Beaumont. Again, Satie structured his score extremely carefully, but kept repeated music to a minimum because he wanted to match Picasso's series of 'poses plastiques' with different music. As he explained, *Mercure* was

11 From a letter to Paul Collaer of 15 May 1920, cited in Collaer: 'La fin des Six et de Satie', *La revue générale: perspectives européennes des sciences humaines*, 6–7 (June–July 1974), 2: 'C'est là le commencement de la musique horizontale qui succédera à la musique perpendiculaire. C'est à cette essence même que *Socrate* doit sa limpidité d'eau courante.'

> a purely decorative spectacle and you can imagine the marvellous contribution of Picasso which I have attempted to translate musically. My aim has been to make my music an integral part, so to speak, with the action and gestures of the people who move about in this simple exercise. You can see poses like them in any fairground. The spectacle is related quite simply to the music hall, without stylization, or any connection with things artistic.[12]

So the aesthetic of *Le coq et l'arlequin* was still very much a reality for Satie, even if he had by now parted company with Cocteau, whom he had come to see increasingly as an interfering reactionary.

Satie's delight in provocation reached its zenith in his final ballet *Relâche*, the only musical product of the Dada movement, via its offshoot of 'Instantanéisme' as propagated by Satie's collaborator, Francis Picabia. Despite constructing his music-hall score in two exactly proportioned, mirrored parts even more carefully than *Parade*, the deliberately offensive production by the Ballets Suédois resulted in chaos and left Satie's reputation in tatters at the time of his death. In Act II 370 car headlights blinded the onlookers and lurid onstage posters told the society audience that 'Those who aren't satisfied are authorized to f*** off'. The only redeeming feature most critics found was the surrealist film *Entr'acte*, which came between the two acts of *Relâche*, and which established the reputation of the young film-maker René Clair. Satie's minimalist score for *Entr'acte* was, however, revolutionary in its non-realistic musical equivalent of a film cutting from image to image: the successful transference of 'furniture music' to the cinema in the first synchronized sound film (see Plate 8.2).

Les Nouveaux Jeunes (1917–1918)

Satie, whose music remained youthful as he grew older, also delighted in championing the cause of young musicians. After *Parade*, this sponsorship was repaid when Georges Auric, Louis Durey and Arthur Honegger were so impressed by Satie's score that they organized a concert of their own works around a duet performance of *Parade* (by Juliette Méerovitch and Satie) at the Salle Huyghens in Montparnasse on 6 June 1917. This homage to Satie marked the beginnings of the group which progressed through the larger enterprise of Les Nouveaux Jeunes to become Les Six in 1920, though its genesis was far from straightforward and has been subject to many misinterpretations since. Germaine Tailleferre joined the initial trio of young composers in a concert which accompanied an art exhibition at the same venue on 1 December 1917 and Francis Poulenc's name appeared when his *Rapsodie nègre* closed a programme on 11 December at the Théâtre du Vieux-Colombier which included works by Auric, Durey, Tailleferre and Satie as well as others by Jean Huré, Roger-Ducasse, Robert de Fontenoy and Stravinsky. Milhaud, who

---

12 From an interview with Pierre de Massot in *Paris-Journal* (30 May 1924), 2: 'Il est purement décoratif, et vous devinez le merveilleux apport de Picasso que j'ai essayé de traduire musicalement. J'ai voulu que la musique fasse corps, pour ainsi dire, avec les faits et gestes des gens qui se meuvent dans ce simple problème. Ces poses sont exactement semblables à celles que l'on peut voir dans toutes les foires; le spectacle s'apparente au music-hall tout bêtement, sans stylisation, et par aucun côte n'a pas de rapport avec les choses de l'art.'

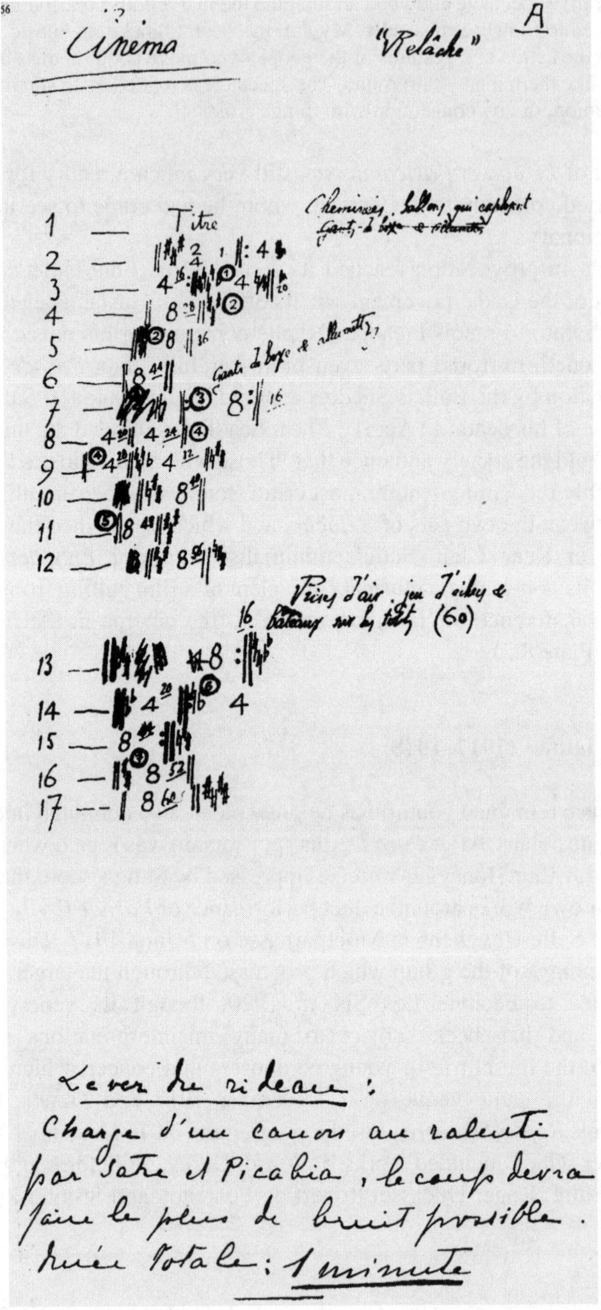

Plate 8.2 Satie's plan for the layout of the orchestral score for the first 17 pages of *Entr'acte* indicating the way the music must be fitted to the silent film.

was in Rio de Janeiro as secretary to Paul Claudel between February 1917 and early 1919, did not appear with the other five in a concert until 5 April 1919,[13] but in this 'Concert Huyghens' there was no work by Satie, though three piano pieces by Roland-Manuel (sometimes known as the seventh member of Les Six) were performed.

Satie's title Les Nouveaux Jeunes referred back to the pre-war support he had received from the Jeunes Ravêlites who, as Ornella Volta says, 'he preferred to call simply "Jeunes" – the Young Ones'.[14] For various reasons (not least his admiration for Debussy), Satie had by now distanced himself from Ravel, so it was quite logical that he now wanted to distinguish his own followers from Ravel's: calling them the 'Nouveaux' Jeunes also gave them a more up-to-date image. Although he may have used the title on a familiar basis during 1917, its first datable use comes from the 'Ier Essai de Musique d'Ameublement ... Divertissement mobilier organisé par le groupe des musiciens "Nouveaux Jeunes"' in conjunction with an exhibition organized by Germaine Bongard and Amédée Ozenfant at the Jove fashion house in March 1918.[15] Unfortunately, this never materialized and in fact no concert specifically advertising Les Nouveaux Jeunes as a group on its programme is known to have taken place. Satie's (undated) draft for an introduction to a concert by Milhaud, Honegger, Taillefer [*sic*], Durey and himself, would seem to refer to the Vieux-Colombier concert on 5 February 1918 because the performers in Honegger's *Rapsodie* ('MM. Manouvrier, Le Roy, Duqués and Mlle Vaurabourg') are specifically listed.[16] But Auric (whose *Poèmes de Jean Cocteau* were also performed) is not mentioned and the concert was introduced on the afternoon itself by Satie's famous 'Éloge des Critiques'.[17]

Curiously, the only dated, if negative statement about Les Nouveaux Jeunes comes in Satie's letter of 28 September 1918 inviting the fifty-one-year-old Charles Koechlin to join the group, which was to have 'No subscription; No rules; No Committee: Just – *Us*.'[18] A similar invitation was also sent to Roussel (according to Koechlin) and it seems that the

13 Though his works were performed in Paris during his absence. For instance, his Second Violin Sonata (composed in Rio in May 1917) was played at the concert at the Théâtre du Vieux-Colombier on 5 Feb. 1918, when only Poulenc (of the future Six) was not represented. I am indebted to Ornella Volta for providing me with copies of the programmes for the 1917–21 concerts involving Les Six, and for much other helpful information during the writing of this chapter.

14 Ornella Volta: *Satie Seen Through His Letters*, trans. Michael Bullock (London, Marion Boyars, 1989), 89.

15 A facsimile of Satie's manuscript advertisement for this concert can be found in Ornella Volta: *Erik Satie et la tradition populaire* (Exhibition Catalogue) (Paris, Fondation Erik Satie, 1988), 28.

16 The draft appears in full in Erik Satie: *Écrits*, ed. Ornella Volta (Paris, Editions Champ Libre, 1977, 3/1990), 80–81. The title 'Les Nouveaux Jeunes' was added editorially. Jean Roy in *Le Groupe des Six* (Paris, Seuil, 1994), 23, mistakenly takes this to refer to the Vieux-Colombier concert on 15 Jan. 1918 which contained songs by Honegger, but no works by Satie or Milhaud. The programme he describes in detail is that of the concert on 5 Feb. 1918.

17 Satie compared critics to animals. His attack was published in *Action*, 2/8 (Aug. 1921), 8–11, and reprinted in Satie: *Écrits*, 77–80.

18 Volta: *Satie Letters*, 95: 'Pas de cotisations; pas de statuts; pas de Comité: *Nous*, – simplement.' The undated draft referred to in note 16 also says that there will be 'ni Président, ni Trésorier, ni Archiviste, ni Econome' and its reference to Satie having been 'a quinquagenerian for two years now' may mean that it was written in the summer of 1918 as his fifty-second birthday fell on 17 May 1918.

short-lived 'New Youth' was conceived as a loose assemblage of young or young-at-heart composers. Satie clearly saw performing artists like Marcelle Meyer, Juliette Méerovitch, Pierre Bertin and Jane Bathori as an integral part of the group, which had no numerical limitations and embraced the other arts as well. Milhaud was kept in touch with its activities in South America, and Cocteau, as ever, was quick to muscle in on the act, though the failure of his ill-organized *Séance Music-Hall* in the autumn of 1918 probably hastened its demise. In this, each contributor was deliberately kept in the dark about the activities of the others so that the whole affair would be a surprise, and Satie may have felt that a noble idea was being turned into a publicity stunt in the process. Moreover, the surviving programme (which again featured 'musique d'ameublement' during its interval), listed as its finale a piece (or pieces) he surely had no intention of writing, entitled 'Gais lurons (polka) Caprice brillant' for violin and piano.

In any event, Satie handed in a curt letter of resignation from the Nouveaux Jeunes to its secretary, Durey, on 1 November 1918. If he offered no explanation at the time, his reasons lay in Durey's growing friendship with (and admiration for) Ravel, to the extent of wanting to include him in the group's concerts. Poulenc, who was by now a fully fledged nouveau jeune, tried to keep Satie on board by organizing a concert in homage to him, but Satie would have nothing to do with these 'comico-idiotic manoeuvres' and rejoiced in the fact that the cancellation of Cocteau's *Séance Music-Hall* had left him in his favourite position of being a free agent.[19]

Henri Collet and the Official Baptism of Les Six in 1920

During 1919 Les Six crystallized as a group, giving joint concerts both with and without Satie, in which the added presence of Milhaud as an organizing and as a conciliatory force should not be underestimated. The 'Samedistes', as they called themselves in 1919, began and ended their informal Saturday evening gatherings at Milhaud's apartment in Pigalle, enjoying a meal at a nearby bistro, or visits to the music hall, the Cirque Médrano, or the Montmartre Fair in between. Their joyous group, like the Nouveaux Jeunes, was invariably augmented by performers, as well as by painters and writers, but under the presidency of Cocteau rather than Satie. Between March and August 1919, Cocteau's 'Carte Blanche' column in *Paris-Midi* aimed to create a new public for what he saw as his group, and the dedication of a copy of *Le coq et l'arlequin* to the musicologist Henri Collet in January 1919[20] strongly suggests that his famous article 'Les Cinq Russes, Les Six Français et Erik Satie' in *Comœdia* on 16 January 1920 was the result of a carefully organized plan masterminded by Cocteau.[21] So, too, does the fact that what turned out to be their only complete collaborative publication (the *Album des 6*) was actually composed

19 See his letter to Pierre Bertin of Nov. 1918 in Volta: *Satie Letters*, 97. By 1919 Satie was utterly opposed to 'the deplorable and outmoded aesthetic' of Ravel, whose 'art' left him 'cold' (ibid., 89).

20 Reproduced in Volta: *Le Groupe des Six et ses amis – 70ᵉ anniversaire* (Exhibition Catalogue) (Paris, 1990), 11, together with an organized joint letter of thanks from Les Six to Collet for his articles, dated 'Janvier 1920'.

21 It was followed by Collet's article specifically titled 'Les "Six" Français: Darius Milhaud, Louis Durey, Georges Auric, Arthur Honegger, Francis Poulenc et Germaine Tailleferre' in *Comœdia*

during the second half of 1919. And Milhaud's assertion that Collet had chosen their six names 'quite arbitrarily'[22] because they had appeared together in a concert which included his Fourth String Quartet and Durey's *Images à Crusoë* is surely suspect, as that concert occurred on 5 April 1919, over nine months before Collet's article which officially launched the group. And if the inspiration for Les Six had come spontaneously from this concert, how did the additional name of Roland-Manuel happen to be omitted? Was it because Satie had disapproved of his former protégé's decision to take lessons from Ravel, and because he knew Roland-Manuel disliked his recent symphonic drama *Socrate*, as did Durey and Ravel?

In reality, the choice of the six names must have been made by arrangement with Collet, based on the way that they had come to be associated together in the public eye on concert programmes since 1917. For, as Poulenc later admitted: 'We had never had any common aesthetic and our musical styles have always been dissimilar. Our likes and dislikes were opposed [which calls into question their other description of themselves as a 'Mutual Admiration Society']. Thus, Honegger has never liked Satie's music [and vice versa], and [Florent] Schmitt, whom he then admired, was a pet aversion for Milhaud and me.'[23] Milhaud, of course, was the most tactful in public (and the only one to remain friends with Satie), but the recently published correspondence of Paul Collaer shows that Milhaud disliked most of Honegger's music too and could, at times, be equally critical of the other members of the group, and even Satie. As early as October 1921 he considered *Le roi David* to be 'like a Prix de Rome cantata ... made up of clichés, scholastic fugal exercises, developed themes, chorales and ready-made formulae'.[24] After he had heard it with orchestra in 1924 he was even more derogatory, declaring that 'the music is horrible. It's real shit.'[25] In the same year, Auric and Poulenc are accused of being over-pushy and desirous of immediate success; Auric is accused of cribbing most of his ballet *Les matelots* from Milhaud's opera *Le pauvre matelot*; and he speaks of Satie's '1000 follies, his gossips outside the musical domain and his often false slanders' which are best overlooked.[26]

So, despite their later anniversary reunions and partial collaborations (like *L'éventail de Jeanne* (Milhaud/Poulenc/Auric and others, 1927) and *La guirlande de Campra* (Honegger/Poulenc/Auric/Tailleferre and others, 1952)), the real value of Les Six was as a launching pad for individual careers, which Cocteau (in his own interests) did his best to promote and prolong. Honegger, the Swiss composer with strong Germanic musical

---

on 23 Jan. 1920. It was the identification of Les Six that was all-important, as Albert Roussel had already published an article on them (and Roland-Manuel) as a group, titled 'Young French Composers', in *The Chesterian* in Oct. 1919 (vol. 1 no. 2, 33–7).

22 See Milhaud: *My Happy Life: An Autobiography* (London, 1995), 84.

23 Poulenc (trans. James Harding): *My Friends and Myself* (London, 1963), 42: 'Jamais nous n'avons eu d'esthétique commune et nos musiques ont toujours été dissemblables. Goûts et dégoûts étaient chez nous contraires. Ainsi, Honegger n'a jamais aimé la musique de Satie, et Schmitt qu'il admirait était alors la bête noire de Milhaud et de moi-même.'

24 Paul Collaer: *Correspondance avec des amis musiciens*, ed. Robert Wangermée (Liège, 1996), 90–91 (letter of 24 Oct. 1921): 'comme une cantate de Concours de Rome ... étant faite de clichés et d'exercices de classe de fugue et de thèmes développés et de chorals et de formules toutes faites'.

25 Ibid., 182 (letter to Collaer of 5 May 1924): 'La musique est horrible. C'est vraiment du KaKa.'

26 Ibid., 178 (letter to Collaer of 4 Apr. 1924): 'ses 1.000 folies, ses potins hors du domaine de la musique et ses calomnies souvent mensongères.'

affinities, was the real odd man out, even if Durey was the first to quit in February 1921 at the time of *Les mariés de la Tour Eiffel* – their final 'manifestation' as a group, in which Tailleferre was brought in at the last moment to replace Durey.[27] In fact, the advertisement for a 'Soirée consacrée au groupe des "Six"' on 19 December 1921 adds the rider 'qui ne sont plus que "Cinq"', and in April that year, Satie had already divided them into two groups in a lecture he gave in Brussels. Auric, Poulenc and Milhaud were, for him, the true exponents of the 'modern sensibility', of the 'spontaneity, fantasy and audacity' inherent in Apollinaire's *esprit nouveau*; whereas Durey, Honegger and Tailleferre were 'pure "*impressionnistes*"'.[28]

By October 1923 Satie had publicly dissociated himself from Les Six, and was promoting another group of young composers, L'École d'Arcueil (Henri Cliquet-Pleyel, Roger Désormière, Maxime Jacob and Henri Sauguet). Although he had proclaimed in 1920 that 'There is no Satie school. Satieism could never exist',[29] this group (named after the Parisian suburb where he had lived since 1898) was the nearest thing to the former. All four composers were pupils of his friend and intended 'nouveau jeune', Charles Koechlin (as were Poulenc and Tailleferre), and Sauguet had already formed his own group, Les Trois, in his native Bordeaux in 1920 in imitation of Les Six. This brings us back to the power of organized publicity and the corporate identity, of which Satie and Cocteau were early masters.

The Music of Les Six to 1930

It is by no means easy to give an overall assessment of the musical achievements of a group of composers as diverse as Les Six, as any superficial unity they had sprang mostly from Cocteau's organizational dexterity. But the new aesthetic of *Le coq et l'arlequin* was essentially framed around Satie's example, so it was against all reasonable odds that it should have been expected to provide a neat blueprint for his followers. Indeed, Satie's swift withdrawal from each group that formed around him must have been galling for Cocteau, and the extent to which this became like a manipulative game for Satie seems somewhat negative until we remember that Cocteau's motives were as much personal as artistic: he wanted to establish himself as the figurehead of the post-war avant-garde in succession to Apollinaire, and if he chose composers as his main means of achieving this, it has to be said that music was the weakest area in his artistic armoury.

But this also gave Les Six a greater freedom to exercise their own various talents. Except for Honegger (and initially Milhaud, with his strong South American influences), preserving Cocteau's aesthetic of essential Frenchness was naturally no problem, even if

27 This avant-garde, surrealist spectacle to a scenario by Cocteau, with scenery by Irène Lagut and costumes by Jean Hugo, was first performed by the Ballets Suédois at the Théâtre des Champs-Elysées on 18 June 1921. Its ten movements focus on a wedding lunch, and a photographer whose camera has a life of its own, spawning all sorts of animals, and even the couple's future child, before devouring the whole party. Its original title was *La noce massacrée*, and as a mixture of unpretentious farce with the poetic that was neither ballet, play nor revue, it had a considerable influence on Jean Anouilh and the Theatre of the Absurd.

28 Cited in Satie: *Écrits*, 90.

29 In *Le Coq*, no. 2 (June 1920), 8 (see Satie: *Écrits*, 45 and 253): 'Il n'y a pas d'école Satie. Le satisme ne saurait exister.'

this meant Parisian chic rather than anything specifically regional – though here we run up against the robust Mediterraneanism inspired by Milhaud's native Provence, and his stoutly defended Frenchness proves a confusing issue when Jewish elements also enter the equation. Again, apart from Honegger, eschewing the lofty edifices of nineteenth-century German music and symphonic development suited what was essentially a group of inexperienced young composers, and if Satie's brevity, simplicity and clarity was by no means always the norm, then they all set Cocteau's poems (apart from Tailleferre) and even the idealistic Durey contributed to the popular spirit of the times with his *Scènes de cirque* (1917), as did Honegger with his *Skating Rink* written for the Ballets Suédois in 1921.

Cocteau's anti-Impressionist stance was, however, far harder to maintain, as both Durey and Tailleferre were deeply attracted to the magical sonorities of Ravel. So Satie's division of Les Six into two groups on this basis had some justification, as works like Durey's *Neige* for piano duet (1918) or Tailleferre's *Ballade* for piano and orchestra (1920–22) demonstrate, although classing Honegger as a 'pure Impressionist' was simply a measure of his disapproval. To see both the closeness of subject matter and the diversity of approach in operation in the early years of Les Six, Example 8.4a and b shows the start of 'Le serpent' from Apollinaire's *Le bestiare* as set by Poulenc in 1918 and by Durey in 1919. Although Poulenc denied that he used jazz in his compositions, the spirit of ragtime at least is evident from the outset of his tiny, unpublished song, which is very much of the 'modern sensibility'; whereas the soft modal textures and interweaving lines of Durey are closer to the spirit of Ravel. Both settings pause at the crux of Apollinaire's poem as 'Ève, Eurydice, Cléopâtre' are cited as 'victims' of the serpent's cruelty, but it is hard to say whether Durey's undulating guile or Poulenc's contemporary brashness and more venomous opening lines provide the apter setting. And both are classic examples of brevity and clarity. In Poulenc's case, 'Le serpent' and 'La colombe' were among the twelve settings from *Le bestiare* he completed in May 1919, all of which can be found amongst the twenty-six poems Durey set simultaneously and (it seems) quite independently. If the six songs Poulenc chose to publish (on Auric's advice) appeared first, the spirit of friendship that prevailed amongst Les Six can be seen in Poulenc's dedication of his cycle to Durey.

Louis Durey (1888–1979)

Although Durey was the oldest member of the group, he came to music late and was essentially on a technical par with the others by 1917. But unlike them, he showed no interest in the theatre, and very little in the orchestra, composing mostly chamber music and songs. Like Satie he was a Communist, and like Roussel or Koechlin, he was a true independent who disliked compositional systems whilst still remaining aware of them. His acknowledged influences were Stravinsky, Schoenberg, Satie, Ravel and Debussy,[30] and the discovery of Schoenberg's *Das Buch der hängenden Gärten* when he began composing in 1914 made a profound impression on him. This led to a dichotomy in his music, in which certain pieces are of extreme textural complexity with a good deal of dissonant chromaticism and counterpoint (like the *Trois préludes* for piano of 1920), while his songs

30 According to f. 2v of his 'Notice biographique' in the Bibliothèque Nationale de France, Paris (Rés. Vmb. MS 48, 3 ff.).

Example 8.4(a) Francis Poulenc, 'Le serpent', bars 1–6

Example 8.4(b) Louis Durey, 'Le serpent', bars 1–7

tend to be gentle, modal and Ravelian, avoiding dramatic climax and tending towards sparse accompaniments.

Like so many French composers of the time, Durey's greatest gift was harmonic rather than melodic, and in some works which bridge the gap between the two categories, he experimented with bitonality. His First String Quartet (1917) is a case in point, with a first movement which begins with a repetitive C sharp minor idea on first violin accompanied by a C major chord, but has a sensuous, undulating, Ravelian second subject in B flat at bar 22. The same sort of conscious experimentation can be found in the superposed whole-tone modes which begin *Carillons* (1916), a latter-day version of Debussy's *Cloches à travers les feuilles*. And so can the same tendency to over-repeat accompaniment textures and melodic ideas, from which even tiny songs like 'La colombe' or 'Le dauphin' (from *Le bestiare*) are not exempt. The Saint-Léger Léger song-cycle *Images à Crusoë* (1918) often reverts to Ravel, though its seven songs are carefully linked by recurring ideas, even if the approach is sectional and the style suggests that Durey was grafting his modernity onto a more congenial modal idiom. He comes closest to Satie in the sparse *Trois poèmes de Pétrone* of the same year, which also show a Satiean predilection for exposed parallel fourths and fifths. The loose fugue which begins the Second String Quartet (1919–22) suggests that Durey was unlikely to rival Honegger as a contrapuntist, and he made a rare venture into neoclassicism in its second movement, which sounds like Haydn with a few wrong notes. But it is clearly not meant to be a parody, for Durey and humour never really went together.

Germaine Tailleferre (1892–1983)

For Tailleferre, however, neoclassicism was a godsend. Her highly successful ballet *Le marchand d'oiseaux* (1923) so impressed the discriminating Princesse de Polignac that she commissioned a Piano Concerto from her, which is one of the finest examples from its period, and shows her natural affinities with the eighteenth-century *clavecinistes*. Stravinsky admired its honesty. The problem with Satie's 'fille musicale' (as he called her after hearing her *Jeux de plein air* for two pianos in 1917) was that she did not have the confidence to promote her own music in the way that Auric and Poulenc did. Although she remained prolific and tried to obtain teaching posts in America in 1925–26 after the initial impetus generated by her membership of Les Six began to fade, two unhappy marriages seriously hampered her professional career. Continual financial problems led her to compose mainly to commission, resulting in some uneven and swiftly written works (for her technical facility was on a par with that of Auric, and even Milhaud). But she wanted no allowances made for her sex and to dismiss her music as gracious and feminine is to do her a serious injustice. Her First Violin Sonata (1920–21) showed that she could compose expansive and challenging music, and in her *Six chansons françaises* (1929) she produced some of the most attractive and sensitive settings of fifteenth- to eighteenth-century French poetry to be found during the 1920s. She was also a mistress of the *perpetuum mobile* and the subtle modulation, and the vitality and sheer sense of enjoyment in her best music certainly merit its revival.

Georges Auric (1899–1983)

Stravinskian neoclassicism also provided the ideal métier for the equally precocious (and equally uneven) Auric. In many ways he was the musical embodiment of the public perception of Les Six, the ideal provider of energetic, superficial ballets for Diaghilev like *Les matelots* (1925) and *La pastorale* (1926). His conversations with Cocteau influenced *Le coq et l'arlequin*, which is dedicated to him, and his declaration 'Bonjour, Paris!' begins the first numbered issue of the short-lived broadsheet *Le Coq* in May 1920 with its bold denunciation of Debussy, whose aesthetic has now been supplanted by 'the music-hall, the fairground parade and American orchestras'. As Martin Cooper says, he and the equally youthful Poulenc were 'soon dubbed ... *les sportifs de la musique*. Certainly there is an atmosphere of physical bustle, a display of muscularity and an absence of all fine sentiments in much of their music, which often seems to be envisaged more as a game than as an emotional communication.'[31] But this is also true of a ballet like Milhaud's *Le train bleu* (1924), and when he was inspired by a character such as Orphise in *Les fâcheux* (1923), Auric could compose lyrical dances of greater depth and complexity, albeit under the close influence of Stravinsky.

Of greater musical interest are Auric's compositions at either end of the 1920s: the songs – which are superbly crafted and show him to be a tonal rather than a modal composer – and the Piano Sonata in F major (1930–31), which sounds as if it is tonal, but only reaches a clear tonic in its final chord after a turbulent and deliberate experiment in modernity which is sustained across its three contrapuntal and intricately developed movements. Here the at times Bergian atonality is integral to the bold conception, in strong contrast to the artificial bitonality of a song like 'L'Ange a perdu son auréole', the second of the *Quatre poèmes de Georges Gabory* (1928). In Example 8.5 a folklike melody in B major is accompanied by the piano right hand in the same key, with the left hand transposed a semitone down into B flat. The artificiality is shown by the way the left hand has joined the right in the same key by bar 5. It may be a sign of his strong tonal affiliations that Auric never takes the Bartókian plunge of notating his bitonality with two different key signatures, even when the parts are more genuinely independent, as at the start of the middle section of Orphise's second dance in *Les fâcheux*.[32] Here the parts are a more manageable third apart (B and A flat major) and the same is true of the opening song from the Radiguet cycle *Les joues en feu* (1921, in E flat and B major), where we might see an aggressive forerunner of the genuinely atonal approach of the 1930–31 Sonata were it not for the fact that the vocal part modulates quite conventionally from E flat to A flat and back again. But, as always in Auric, melody is the controlling factor, supported by essentially tonal harmony, and enlivened by rhythm and imaginative textures.

To my mind, Auric's best music of the period comes in his early songs, and as far as evolution is concerned, they were remarkably assured and accomplished from the start. In the *Trois interludes* (1914), René Chalupt's poems receive varied and succinct treatment in settings that show equal sensitivity to the piano and voice. To be sure, there are some rather obvious musical illustrations in 'Le pouf', but in 'Le gloxinia' we find a text-led arch structure (ABCDBA) of balance and conviction, as well as a prototype for Milhaud's *Catalogue des fleurs* (1920), and the lightness and metrical flexibility of 'Le tilbury' make

31 Martin Cooper: *French Music: From the death of Berlioz to the death of Fauré* (London, 1951/repr. 1961), 197.

32 This comes on p. 39 of the piano reduction published by Rouart-Lerolle in 1923 (R.L. 11471, 58pp.). Its start is cited in Cooper: *French Music*, 198 as Ex. 56, though both staves are notated in four flats in the score.

Example 8.5 Georges Auric, *Quatre poèmes de Georges Gabory*, 2, 'L'ange a perdu son auréole', bars 1–8

it equally impressive. By 1918, in his *Huit poèmes de Jean Cocteau*, Auric was producing more melismatic songs of greater length, but if the musical references are subtler (it being extremely hard to spot the Satie allusions in the opening 'Hommage' to his mentor), then some of the fantasy of the 1914 *Interludes* has disappeared. The final 'Portrait d'Henri Rousseau' shows the beginnings of Auric's neoclassicism and was clearly designed to leave its audience with an impression of what the young virtuoso with his agile pianism could achieve. But it is still witty, and its expansive, lyrical and wide-ranging vocal lines could not be further from the recitative-like settings of Debussy if they tried – which, of course, is precisely what they did.

In the seven Radiguet settings of *Alphabet* (1920), Auric's ready wit rises even more obviously to the fore with his delightful parody of Grieg in 'Filet à papillons' (no. 4) and its second song ('Bateau') which is half tango and half mazurka (with a passing reference to a Chopin waltz). The start of 'Hirondelle' (shown in Example 8.6) shows that Auric had taken Poulenc's first *Mouvement perpétuel* (cf. Example 8.7 below) to heart, making it superficially his own through acciaccaturas, rhythm and pianistic range. Similarly, the start of 'Escarpin' (no. 7) suggests that he was a neo-romantic as much as a neoclassicist. Indeed, such is Auric's chameleon-like skill at synthesis and subtle transformation that it is not easy to say what his original contribution was. Which made him the ideal composer for film music in the 1930s, but is sad when one considers that his genuine effort to

Example 8.6 Georges Auric, *Alphabet*, 6, 'Hirondelle', bars 1–5

find a new path forward with his 1930–31 Sonata met with no success and was not followed up.

Francis Poulenc (1899–1963)

Poulenc, on the other hand, had an immediately identifiable harmonic style and was blessed with the greatest gift for memorable melody among Les Six. If much of his music derives from Mozart and especially Stravinsky, he was somehow able to transform it into something original. We can see this happening with Mozart in the closing bars of the first *Mouvement perpétuel* (Example 8.7), chiefly through the ironical little aside that leaves the music piquantly in mid-air at the end (a typical feature), but also through the mildly dissonant major sevenths and ninths that crop up quite naturally in the undulating tenor part, and the sparse, genuinely *neo*classical textures elsewhere. Even if it is not true, we get the impression that more genuine musical thought went into this than the contrived passage by Auric cited in Example 8.6.

Stravinsky makes his impression from the very start in the ostinati and 'wrong-note' harmonies of Poulenc's *Rapsodie nègre,* which was both his first performed piece and his deliberately provocative *entrée* to the exciting world of the Nouveaux Jeunes in December 1917. Here, at a stroke, Poulenc also shows his awareness of Schoenberg's *Pierrot lunaire* by his scoring, his awareness of Satie in his monotonous repetitions, and his awareness of polytonality in the second movement. He also shows that he had humour rather than wit

Example 8.7 Francis Poulenc, *Mouvements perpétuels*, I, closing bars

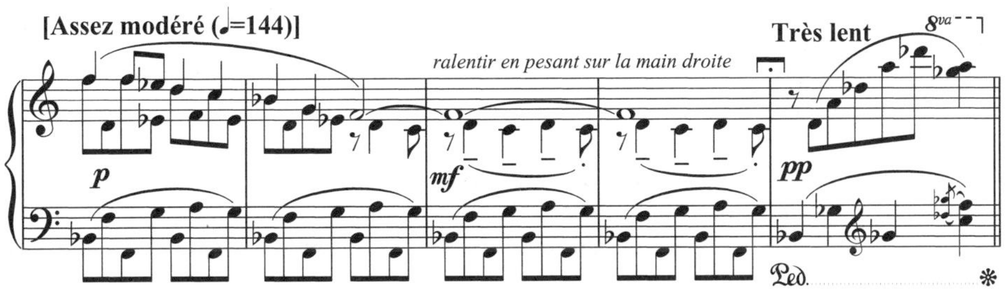

through his treatment of the nonsense texts by 'Makoko Kangourou' (actually his friend, Marcel Ormoy) and through his impertinent codas.

In the first half of 1919 Poulenc composed his first song cycles, *Le bestiare* and *Cocardes*, the latter being a set of three 'chansons populaires' to poems by Cocteau, again with a striking accompaniment from violin, cornet, trombone and percussion which took Cocteau's popular roots theme to heart in its recreation of a typical ad hoc café-concert 'orchestra'. Poulenc's preference for the more objective and less romantically expressive wind instruments can be seen in his numerous chamber works of the 1920s, like the Sonata for Horn, Trumpet and Trombone (1922), and is another Stravinskian feature. In the early 1920s he experimented with more extreme dissonance in works like the *Promenades* for piano (1921), almost as if he had to get complexity out of his system, and this heaviness and contrived dissonance persists into his *Poèmes de Ronsard* (1924), and is perhaps tied up with his period of study with Charles Koechlin between 1921 and 1925.

But during this, Poulenc also achieved his first real success with his exquisite neoclassical 'ballet avec chant' *Les biches*, composed for Diaghilev's Ballets Russes in 1923. The gem of this carefree score is the languid and sensuously beautiful 'Adagietto', with its veiled eroticism. Like the rest of the ballet, it was meant to suggest diverting affairs rather than eternal love, and audiences adored it. He then achieved mastery over the art song in his *Chansons galliardes* in 1925–26, and as a climax to his neoclassical works of the 1920s, composed two concertos: the *Concert champêtre* for the harpsichordist Wanda Landowska (1927–28) and *Aubade* (1929), a 'choreographic concerto for piano and eighteen instruments' to his own scenario about the goddess Diana and the themes of chastity and repressed sexual desire. Although he was homosexual, the concerto has clear parallels with a period of great anguish in Poulenc's own life, and the deeply felt conflict between seriousness and gaiety can be seen in the opening scene for Diana and her companions. Poulenc had come a long way from the musical 'gamin' of 1917 whose main aims were to shock or amuse Parisian high society, and even if *Aubade* was not a success, its autobiographical element can help us achieve a fuller understanding of the profound sensitivity and developing spirituality which form the true heart of this Janus-like composer, and which were to be developed in the religious choral works which followed the renewal of his Catholic faith in 1936.

Darius Milhaud (1892–1974)

Milhaud was both the most prolific of Les Six and the least self-critical. Like Charles Koechlin, to whose polytonal experiments in his songs of 1905–09 Milhaud owed a great deal, he hardly ever rejected or revised his compositions, and when not incapacitated by poor health, was a workaholic. Like Koechlin too, he was a pupil of André Gedalge at the Paris Conservatoire, who taught the primacy of melody in musical composition and the necessity of strengthening counterpoint. Although not a distinguished melodist like Poulenc, Milhaud only abandoned it when making experiments in pure rhythm, like those in his innovative 1918 ballet *L'homme et son désir*. He could change styles at will, and within a single work. Thus, also in 1918, we find a lively pastorale with a folklike melody beginning his Fourth String Quartet, but polytonal combinations in its third movement. In 1920, the year of Les Six, the jazzy 'shimmy' *Caramel mou* and the aleatoric *Cocktail* (for a singing barman accompanied by four clarinets playing freely in different keys: see Example 8.8) rub shoulders with the extreme polytonality of the Fifth Quartet and the alluring tangos of the *Saudades do Brazil*.

During his years in Rio with Paul Claudel (1917–18), Milhaud found himself as a composer and his first 'big hit' after his return to Paris came with *Le bœuf sur le toit* (1919), a 'cinéma-fantaisie' intended to accompany a Charlie Chaplin film, whose rondo theme is similar to the Brazilian popular song 'O boi no telhado'. If its score had nothing to do with Paris, it still took it by storm in conjunction with Cocteau's slow-motion pantomime production for masked acrobats and clowns of February 1920. 'Le bœuf sur le toit' was also adopted as the name for the bar near the place de la Concorde to which Les Six decamped for their Saturday meetings in December 1921 (from the nearby La Gaya bar). In the rue Boissy d'Anglas they were again entertained by the piano duo of Jean Wiéner and Clément Doucet, who played the latest American jazz; Milhaud had developed his interest in this new medium when *Le bœuf* went to London on tour in the summer of 1920, where he heard Billy Arnold and his band perform. During a concert and lecture tour of the States in 1922 Milhaud had his first encounter with authentic 'Black' jazz in Harlem, and this experience inspired him to write the ballet *La création du monde* with Blaise Cendrars in 1923. If this alternately reflective and jubilant score does not sound particularly 'jazzy' today, then much has happened to the medium in the interim. But, at the time, this 'ballet nègre' captured the spirit of jazz perfectly and also deepened it through a serious and balanced composition which can still be extremely moving, even in concert form. Although Milhaud preferred to be known for his symphonic and operatic works, his 'popular' works of the early 1920s are still widely regarded as his best compositions, not least for their accessibility.

Besides composing five symphonies between 1917 and 1922 and reaching his Seventh String Quartet by 1925, Milhaud's main interest lay in opera. After completing his monumental Claudel trilogy based on Aeschylus's *Oresteia* in 1922 (*Agamemnon, Les choëphores* and *Les euménides*), he turned to his friend, Armand Lunel, for *Les malheurs d'Orphée* in 1924, still preoccupied by the myths of Greek antiquity. But now his aim was compression (the opera lasts only thirty-five minutes) and its action was transported to his native Provence with Orpheus as an itinerant vet and Eurydice as a gypsy. For the second of his three-act chamber operas based on the theme of fate, *Le pauvre matelot* (1927), his collaborator was Cocteau. Finally he reached the ultimate in brevity with his trilogy of Greek 'opéras-minute' in 1927–28 with Henri Hoppenot (*L'enlèvement d'Europe, L'abandon d'Ariane* and *La déliverance de Thésée*) which together last only about twenty-five minutes. But to confound all expectations, Milhaud then reverted to Claudel for the massive *Christophe Colomb* (1930), which remains the most impressive monument to

Example 8.8 Darius Milhaud, *Cocktail aux clarinettes*, from the *Almanach de Cocagne*, 1920. Facsimile of the original manuscript

Note sur l'exécution de ce cocktail

Le Barman doit chanter cette recette très librement, comme un récitatif. Pendant toute la durée de cette mélodie, les clarinettes devront recommencer leur danse sans souci de mesure. A la fin, les clarinettes attendront sur le point d'orgue placé au bout de leur cadence que chacune d'elles y parvienne.

(Translation of instructions: Performance note for this cocktail: The Barman should sing this recipe very freely, in the style of a recitative. Throughout this melody, the clarinets should repeat their dance without concerning themselves about synchronization. At the end, the clarinets should wait on the pause indicated at the end of their line until they have all finished.)

their many collaborations, which were so influential to the development of Milhaud's career as an innovative dramatic composer from 1913 onwards.

Arthur Honegger (1892–1955)

Honegger, while almost as prolific as Milhaud and possessing the same receptivity to other useful influences, was far less of an idealist. In fact, his allegiances were German rather than French, even if he spent most of his time in Paris. Alone among Les Six he admired Beethoven and Wagner, and the influence of the former is strongly evident in his First String Quartet of 1916–17. Similarly, Bach chorales turn up in several of his works, not least in the final movement of *Le roi David*, which was converted into an oratorio in 1923 from the incidental music to a 'drame biblique' by René Morax of 1921 and remains his most popular work. If he was disparaging about what he saw as Satie's poverty of technique, it was because, like Tailleferre, he saw himself primarily as an artisan. His aim, as he put it in his preface to *Antigone* (Cocteau's 1922 adaptation of Sophocles' tragedy) was 'to produce an honest piece of work as an honest craftsman'.[33] Indeed, his utilitarian aims can be compared to those of Hindemith, for we find in his far from elitist book, *I am a Composer*, such statements as 'My inclination and my effort have always been to write music which would be comprehensible to the multitude of listeners and yet sufficiently free of banality to interest true music lovers'.[34] If *Antigone*, with its deliberately awkward declamation, is generally regarded as one of Honegger's finest scores, all this should not be taken as false modesty, because Honegger, for all his contrapuntal strength and developmental expertise, was slower to find an individual voice than most of Les Six, and was as much of a musical jackdaw as Poulenc.

Honegger's other main claims to fame in the 1920s are the 'mimed symphony' *Horace victorieux* (1920–21) and the 'symphonic movements' *Pacific 231* (1923) and *Rugby* (1928). As Martin Cooper says, *Horace victorieux* is 'powerful and concentrated in manner, in the direct line of Honegger's earlier chamber music, and quite untouched ... by the anti-emotional bias of the Six'.[35] However realistic the evocation of a railway engine in *Pacific 231* may be, Honegger's intention was that it should be heard as absolute music, or at most as a glorification of power and speed through rhythm and orchestral virtuosity. But the piece evoked comparisons with Richard Strauss as well as with Marinetti and the Italian Futurist movement, and he wisely left his third *Mouvement symphonique* without a descriptive subtitle in 1933. Deep down he remained a traditionalist, to whom nothing was taboo except atonality and the deliberate (Satiean) rejection of expressiveness. Like Durey, he was not afraid to embrace Debussy when it suited his purpose (as in his *Pastorale d'été* for orchestra of 1920), and his obvious awareness of what the rest of Les Six were up to can be seen in his Clarinet Sonatina of 1921–22 and his jazz-based Piano Concertino of 1924. If his diversity of styles and runaway success with *Le Roi David* were disapproved

33 Paris, Senart, 1927: 'faire l'honnête ouvrage d'un honnête ouvrier'.

34 Honegger: *Je suis compositeur*, ed. B. Gavoty (Paris, Éditions du Conquistador, 1951), 129: 'Mon goût et mon effort ont toujours été d'écrire une musique qui soit perceptible pour la grande masse des auditeurs et suffisamment exempte de banalité pour intéresser cependant les mélomanes.'

35 Cooper: *French Music*, op. cit., 194.

of by many of his illustrious contemporaries, it should be remembered that Honegger was really no more eclectic than Milhaud, Auric or Durey, and that three of his settings from Apollinaire's *Alcools* were performed at the concert in the Salle Huyghens which started the whole movement off in June 1917.

Conclusions

Although Les Six were a group united only by friendship, their works still came to represent the exuberant spirit of French music in the decade after the Great War. By selecting the composers he thought most likely to succeed, shock or amuse from Satie's loose assemblage of Nouveaux Jeunes in 1919, Cocteau seized the opportunity to provide both a springboard for promising young careers as well as to consolidate his own position as the head of the new avant-garde in Paris. All they needed was a corporate identity, which Henri Collet gave them in 1920. If Cocteau's attempts to provide his chosen few with a common aesthetic met with varying degrees of resistance from the individual careers he sought to manipulate, the beauty of his stratagem was that there were no losers and that a chic post-war society eager for diversion after a period of austerity was delighted by the antics involved in the diverse expressions of the 'new spirit'.

Satie remained an ever-present but unpredictable godfather, first supporting, then dissociating himself from the various groups, and breaking off relations with all but Milhaud by February 1924. And it is surely no coincidence that by then the heyday of Les Six was past: the relative lack of success (or the lesser talents – Sauguet excepted) of the École d'Arcueil proved that a winning formula could not be repeated endlessly. That it succeeded once is surely a tribute to the quality of the work produced by Les Six, of whom Poulenc, Milhaud and Honegger at least went on to substantiate Satie's 1923 claim that 'several members have irretrievably entered into the realms of Glory'.[36]

Suggestions for Further Reading

Sidney Buckland and Myriam Chimènes: *Poulenc: Music, Art and Literature* (Aldershot: Ashgate, 1999).

Jean Cocteau: *Le Coq et l'arlequin: Notes autour de la musique* (Paris: Éditions de La Sirène, 1918); repr. in *Œuvres complètes*, vol. 9 (Lausanne: Marguerat, 1950); trans. Rollo Myers in *A Call to Order* (London: Faber & Gwyer, 1926), 3–77.

Keith Daniel: *Francis Poulenc: His Artistic Development and Musical Style* (Ann Arbor: UMI Research Press, 1982).

Jeremy Drake: *The Operas of Darius Milhaud* (New York: Garland, 1992).

Alan Gillmor: *Erik Satie* (Boston: Twayne Publishers, 1988).

Harry Halbreich: *Arthur Honegger*, trans. Roger Nichols (Portland, Ore.: Amadeus, 1999).

James Harding: *The Ox on the Roof: Scenes from Musical Life in Paris in the Twenties* (London: Macdonald, 1972).

Éveline Hurard-Viltard: *Le Groupe des Six ou le matin d'un jour de fête* (Paris: Méridiens Klincksieck, 1987).

36 In an open letter from Arcueil on 12 Oct. 1923, published in *L'Écho des Champs-Élysées*, 1/8 (included with the Oct. 1923 issue of *La danse*): 'quelques-uns des membres sont irrémédiablement entrés dans la Gloire'.

Darius Milhaud: *My Happy Life: An Autobiography* (London: Marion Boyars, 1995).

Roger Nichols: *Conversations with Madeleine Milhaud* (London: Faber, 1996).

Robert Orledge: *Satie the Composer* (Cambridge: Cambridge University Press, 1990).

Robert Orledge: *Satie Remembered*, trans. Roger Nichols (London: Faber, 1995).

Nancy Perloff: *Art and the Everyday: Popular Entertainment and the Circle of Erik Satie* (Oxford: Clarendon Press, 1991).

Caroline Potter: 'Germaine Tailleferre: A Centenary Appraisal', *Muziek & Wetenschap*, 2/2 (1992), 109–28.

Francis Poulenc: *Echo and Source: Selected Correspondence 1915–1963*, trans. and ed. Sidney Buckland (London: Gollancz, 1991).

Jean Roy: *Le Groupe des Six* (Paris: Seuil, 1994).

Ornella Volta: *Satie Seen Through His Letters*, trans. Michael Bullock (London: Marion Boyars, 1989).

Steven Moore Whiting: *Satie the Bohemian* (Oxford: Clarendon Press, 1999).

Chapter 9

'Dancing on the Edge of the Volcano': French Music in the 1930s

Deborah Mawer

> A prophetic warning about matters that then had no name ... quality of life, the environment, pollution, enlistment, mass culture ... in short, everything that contributes to the destruction of the soul and the death of the individual. In 1931 the warning from this all-too-prophetic Cassandra came too early not to upset a civilization that was unwittingly dancing on the edge of the volcano due to destroy it a few years hence.[1]

Thus Harry Halbreich sums up and contextualizes Honegger's significant choral/orchestral landmark of 1931, the *Cris du monde* (Cries of the World). In so doing, he also provides a useful way into the study of French music of the 1930s and at least a partial response to the initial question which might be asked: how are these problematic years most appropriately characterized? The problem is that time, along with a perceived lack of a clear musical identity, has sifted the contents so well that musicians today may be left with a parenthetical, even empty, view of a period that existed merely to connect the 'années folles' with the years of post-war radicalism.

At this point, it is helpful to summarize the events and personnel of this decade, launched in 1929 with the Wall Street Crash in New York and the ensuing economic depression of global proportions. The resulting unemployment and poverty ('the bitter cry of the workless was in every ear')[2] meant that the European populus became vulnerable to the fascist propaganda and racial hatred peddled by Mussolini and Hitler. Hitler became Chancellor in 1933 and removed Germany from the League of Nations, following which, in spring 1935, he reinstated conscription in breach of the Treaty of Versailles.

By contrast, France, as noted by the contemporary historian Herbert Fisher, was politically weak: 'In France the executive is too weak, the legislature too strong. The average duration of a French ministry between 1918 and 1934 has been eight months and twenty-five days ... Lesser men may not succeed where the venerable and respected Doumergue [President, 1924–31] ... was miserably frustrated.'[3] The period 1936–37 saw the rise of France's short-lived Popular Front (a coalition between the Socialists of Léon Blum and the Communist Party) as a response to weak government and the increasing pro-fascist threat. By 1938, however, this opposition itself had been seen to fail (with premier Édouard Daladier's ill-fated signing, together with Neville Chamberlain, of the Munich accords) and the next event of appalling consequence was the outbreak of the Second World War on 3 September 1939.

1 Harry Halbreich: *Arthur Honegger*, trans. Roger Nichols (Portland, Ore., 1999), 417.

2 Herbert A. L. Fisher: *A History of Europe*, 2 vols (Glasgow, 1984; first pub. 1935), vol. 2, 1304.

3 Ibid., vol. 2, 1309.

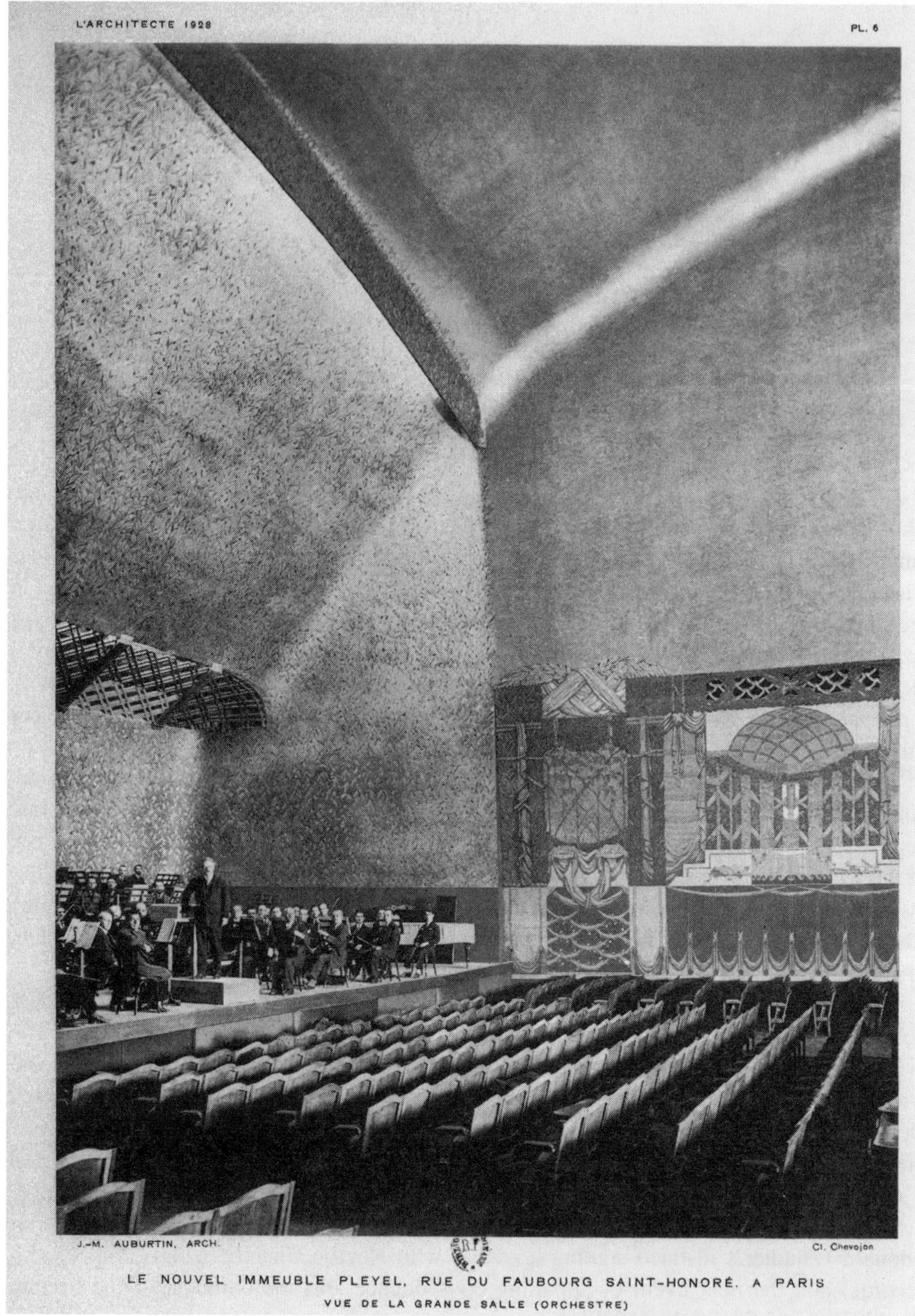

L'ARCHITECTE 1928
PL. 6
J.-M. AUBURTIN, ARCH.
Cl. Chevojon
LE NOUVEL IMMEUBLE PLEYEL, RUE DU FAUBOURG SAINT-HONORÉ. A PARIS
VUE DE LA GRANDE SALLE (ORCHESTRE)

Plate 9.1 The new Salle Pleyel, which opened in 1927, was not only a striking example of 1920s architecture but hosted numerous important premieres.

From an artistic stance, 1929 also marked the death of Diaghilev and the hugely influential Ballets Russes; 1930 itself witnessed the premieres of Milhaud's *Christophe Colomb* (in Berlin) Stravinsky's *Symphony of Psalms* (Brussels) and Prokofiev's Fourth Symphony (Boston and Paris) – music by Russian émigrés in France was of continuing importance with a resulting stylistic *mélange*. (Russian influence had long been a catalyst for developments in French music, from the impact of modality, innovative ballet, and particular skill in orchestration in the pre-war years, through to the neoclassical landmarks of Stravinsky and Prokofiev in 1918 and beyond). The following year saw the death of Vincent d'Indy, old-guard of the Schola Cantorum (and a known anti-Semite), together with first performances of Honegger's *Cris du monde*, Messiaen's orchestral *Offrandes oubliées* and chamber vocal work *La mort du nombre*, Roussel's ballet *Bacchus et Ariane* and Third Symphony (French premiere). Meanwhile, 1932 revealed Ravel's piano concertos (premiered in Vienna and Paris respectively), and saw the composition of Milhaud's *L'annonce faite à Marie* and the staging of *Maximilien* at the Opéra. In 1933 two further pieces by Messiaen appeared: *Le tombeau resplendissant* and the *Hymne au Saint Sacrement*, as well as Honegger's Third Symphonic Movement. 'This *Mouvement* has a fondness for grey; but it certainly isn't the grey of mist, it's the grey of steel!' was the comment in *La Revue musicale*.[4] In 1934, Paris first heard Ibert's Flute Concerto, Stravinsky's *Perséphone* (Ballets Ida Rubinstein), Roussel's Sinfonietta and what was to be Ravel's swansong, the set of songs entitled *Don Quichotte à Dulcinée*.

The mid-point of 1935 was notable for the death of the man dubbed by the critic Henry Prunières as 'the lofty figure of Paul Dukas, this Degas of music',[5] and for the premieres of Honegger's *Radio-Panoramique*, Roussel's Fourth Symphony and Messiaen's *La nativité du Seigneur*, while the following year saw Poulenc's *Litanies à la vierge noire* and the first concert of the movement known as La Jeune France, including Jolivet's *Danse incantatoire*.[6] With 1937 came serious losses: the deaths of Ravel, Roussel, Widor and Gabriel Pierné. More optimistically, it also saw the Paris Exposition and performance of Georges Migot's *Le sermon sur la montagne*. In 1938, Roussel's ballet *Aeneas* received its Opéra premiere and Honegger composed his sacred cantata, *La danse des morts*. This year also marked the death of Maurice Emmanuel and the 500th Concert of the Orchestre National de la Radiodiffusion. The year 1939 saw the composition of Jolivet's *Danses rituelles* and the staging of Honegger's *Jeanne d'Arc au bûcher* (Joan of Arc at the stake), to a text by the Catholic writer Paul Claudel. The Breton composer Guy Ropartz also had his *Requiem* premiered in this year. Once war was declared, there was an increasing exodus of musicians to the United States, among them Stravinsky. Finally, 1940 was marked by Milhaud's bitterly topical *Cantate de la guerre* op. 213 and Jolivet's imploring *Messe pour le jour de la paix*, together with the American emigration of many Jewish

---

4 The work was first performed on 21 Oct. 1933 at the Concerts Pasdeloup and reviewed in *La Revue musicale* (*RM*), 140 (Nov. 1933), 315–6: 315 ('Ce *Mouvement* affectionne le gris; mais ce n'est point le gris du brouillard, c'est le gris de l'acier!'); note the embedded anti-impressionist jibe. All translations are my own unless otherwise indicated.

5 Henry Prunières: 'Adieu à Paul Dukas', *RM*, 157 (June 1935), 1–3: 3 ('la haute figure de Paul Dukas, ce Degas de la musique').

6 This group comprised Olivier Messiaen, André Jolivet, Daniel-Lesur and Yves Baudrier. Its aesthetic stance and main products are discussed in detail below.

artists including Milhaud, as well as that of Nadia Boulanger and the harpsichordist Wanda Landowska.

This fairly bald outline of diverse events and products nevertheless supports the case for a strengthening spiritual dimension suggested – even symbolized – by *Cris du monde*. Representative of this 'period of musical humanism'[7] and not unrelated to wider disquieting events (whether in support of the political left or right), the idea of spiritual 'otherness' constitutes the main focus of the present chapter. The trajectory which leads there embraces *en route* a continuing 'temporal otherness', in terms of neoclassicism beyond Les Six, and 'cultural otherness', as a lingering fascination with things oriental and 'exotic'. These 'othernesses' (the 'erstwhile' and 'elsewhere') are to some extent countered and superseded by a spirituality headed by La Jeune France which draws deeply on both Christian and non-Western inspiration. Messiaen and Jolivet, reacting against the supposed shallowness of Les Six, were particularly important in this respect. Before embarking on this trajectory, with a subsidiary theme of endings and beginnings, French concert life and its new-found competition must be explored.

Various ports of call on the way are characterized partly by reference to the criticism of Martin Cooper, René Dumesnil and the journal *La Revue musicale*.[8] Officially, the 1930s is the first decade not covered by Cooper; however, in his 'Epilogue', he does mention 'Tradition and innovation in French music', including late d'Indy, Ravel and Roussel. Meanwhile, Dumesnil and *La Revue musicale* provide a particular window on, or barometer for, the decade. Despite Cooper's assertion that 'A generation must elapse before it is possible to see any work of art in a true historical perspective',[9] it is illuminating to see how far contemporary assessments and predictions have withstood the passage of time, and how reception may have changed. Dumesnil clearly had his finger on the pulse regarding *Cris du monde*: 'the isolation of man in the midst of men',[10] and hence the need for spiritual solace and communion beyond. On the other hand, the extent of documented enthusiasm for Léon Thérémin's 'sensational device' threatened to overplay its likely role in future music, a point noted by Lionel Landry who aptly favoured a broader agenda directed by timbre, acuity and modes of sound production.[11] Additionally, Henry

7 Rollo Myers: *Modern French Music: Its Evolution and Cultural Background from 1900 to the Present Day* (Oxford, 1971), 134. For a complementary reading here, with more detail on connections between music (including spirituality) and politics but less discussion of actual music, see Jane F. Fulcher: 'Musical style, meaning and politics in France on the eve of the Second World War', *Journal of Musicology*, 13/4 (Fall 1995), 425–53. Such connections are complex, encompassing a matrix of often conflicting or ambiguously related elements, with factions that include left/right-wing, Popular Front/pro-fascist press, Conservatoire/Schola Cantorum, polarized supporters of secular/sacred music.

8 Martin Cooper: *French Music from the Death of Berlioz to the Death of Fauré* (London, 1951); René Dumesnil: *La Musique en France entre les deux guerres*: *1919–1939* (Paris, 1946); *RM*, founder-editor: Henry Prunières.

9 Cooper: *French Music*, 202.

10 Dumesnil: *La Musique*, 168 ('l'isolement de l'homme au milieu des hommes').

11 Lionel Landry: 'La Musique de l'avenir', *RM*, 81 (Feb. 1928), 17–20: 17. The theremin is an electric instrument which first came to prominence in the early 1920s. It is played without being touched: a vertical antenna controls pitch whilst a horizontal antenna controls volume. Movements of the hand towards and away from the antennae create gradations of pitch and dynamic. For more information, consult www.thereminworld.com.

Prunières offered perceptive assessments, as in 1931 when he stated emphatically: 'Messiaen certainly has gifts which should be left to ripen.'[12]

On French concert life and its music, Dumesnil enables us to expand our horizons beyond our too neatly time-sifted view. Although his treatment of Messiaen (and Jolivet) in a final chapter entitled 'L'avènement de la génération nouvelle' (The advent of the new generation) was, with hindsight, far too brief, he usefully reminds us of other composers who have been edited out of histories directed primarily by technical change: Georges Migot, Henri Tomasi, P.-O. Ferroud (who founded the new music group Triton), Henri Barraud, Manuel Rosenthal and Jean Rivier.[13] Apart from Roussel's symphonies and Ravel's piano concertos, we are reacquainted with Florent Schmitt's works; Joseph Canteloube's *Chants d'Auvergne*, the fourth series of which was completed in 1930; Maurice Emmanuel's *Salamine* staged at the Opéra in 1929; and G.-M. Witkowski's four-act opera after Edmond Rostand, *La princesse lointaine*, staged in 1934.

In a special section on 'Le public', Dumesnil discussed the decline of the 'théâtre lyrique' and concert life more generally, with reduced public support caused not so much by economic depression as by conservatism in the face of new music ('j'ai horreur de la musique moderne') and simple distraction due to increasing leisure activities: the automobile, sports, cinema, popular music and radio.[14] This is slightly ironic given the strong interest in mechanisms, film and popular music, especially jazz, of many composers of the 1920s (and 1930s). Despite considerable growth in chamber and orchestral activity around 1930, an alarming overall numerical descent was nonetheless demonstrated by a statistical tabulation extracted from the *Guide musical* (in conjunction with its companion publication the *Guide du concert*), which compared the amount of Parisian concerts in the mid-1920s with that in the early and late 1930s (see Table 9.1).

Table 9.1 Parisian concert activity (1924–39)

Year	1924–25	1929–30	1938–39
Orchestral music	451	537	321
Chamber music	142	260	125
Piano recitals	296	223	121
Total	1810	1517	1025

It is unclear exactly what constituted the other concerts within the annual totals, but significant components must have been stage productions and song recitals. Although various societies and orchestras still operated during the 1930s, almost all became less active, some series merged, others folded. Casualties included the Société musicale indépendante (SMI) which folded in 1935, the new music societies Triton and Sérénade

12 Henry Prunières: 'Les tendances de la jeune école française', *RM*, 117/18 (July–Aug. 1931), 97–104: 103 ('Messiaen a certainement des dons qu'il faut laisser mûrir').

13 Dumesnil: *La Musique*, 163–216.

14 Ibid., 77, 67, 76.

and even the Société nationale (SN), all of which ceased in 1939. Outfits still surviving in 1938–39 included the Concerts Colonne, Siohan and Poulet (merged from 1937), Pasdeloup, Lamoureux, the Société des concerts, the Opéra and (floundering) Opéra-Comique, the Orchestre Symphonique de Paris and Orchestre National de la Radiodiffusion. Some concerts were also promoted under the auspices of the Communist publisher, Le Chant du Monde: notably the performance of Shostakovich's Fifth Symphony in June 1938. There were still festivals to promote the music of twentieth-century composers such as Koechlin, Schmitt, Prokofiev, Ravel, Milhaud and Fauré, though several were modest in scale, and more occurred in the early than late 1930s, with the exception of the 1937 Exposition. Overall, the extent of the reduction in concert activity constituted a serious threat: 'The crisis is putting French music in danger, and the newspapers and specialist reviews are full of woe. People are looking for the causes of the trouble.'[15]

Aside from obvious economic issues (though in part because of them), radio was regarded as a prime suspect: Cooper himself was slightly suspicious of the new and the popular, although there was truth in his assertion that radio, cinema and ballet had 'created a large demand for heteronomous music; music for use, in which the quality of the composer's material is less important than his technical assurance'.[16] Dumesnil, too, reproached radio for encouraging people to stay at home, though he supported rehearing works through broadcasts (and appreciated that negative or positive arguments could be constructed 'according to the mood of the moment'); he also considered the need to educate the listener (and not to 'dumb down') claiming that 'Among the thousands of letters addressed to the Radio, there are few which claim to prefer an orchestral concert to a programme of comic songs or accordion music'.[17] And despite his frustrations that artistic excellence could be compromised by poor administration and technical back-up, he applauded the setting up of the Orchestre National de la Radiodiffusion in 1934, with its subsequent achievements including performance of the original version of *Boris Godunov* (under Inghelbrecht, 1935) and the premiere of Ropartz's *Requiem* (under Rhené-Baton, 1939).

The topic of French Radio has been introduced by way of the views of Cooper and Dumesnil, so a factual resumé may now provide a useful balance.[18] In 1915 the first radio telephonic transmission was received from the United States by the pioneering General Ferrié, followed in 1921 by the inauguration of regular transmissions from the Eiffel Tower. The radio microphone was welcomed at the Opéra from 1923 and, some nine years later, in response to public demand, a stronger broadcasting agreement was brokered between the Opéra and State Radio, commencing with Henri Rabaud's *Mârouf* in summer 1932.[19] April 1935 marked the first public television broadcast, and the following March

15 Ibid., 75 ('La crise met en danger la musique française, et les journaux et revues spéciales sont pleins de doléances. On cherche les causes du mal').

16 Cooper: *French Music*, 210.

17 Dumesnil: *La Musique*, 79, 78 ('Parmi les milliers de lettres adressés à la Radio, il en est peu qui déclarent préférer un concert symphonique à une émission de chansonnettes ou d'accordéon').

18 The main reference source here is Jean-Noël Jeanneney: *L'Echo du siècle: Dictionnaire historique de la radio et de la télévision en France* (Paris, 1999), which has an authoritative chronology and usefully specialized case studies.

19 Christian Brochand: *Histoire générale de la radio et de la télévision en France*, 2 vols (Paris,

saw French broadcasts in German to respond to Hitler's propaganda. With Le Front Populaire (1936–37) came a paradox: 'The Popular Front carries a formidable cultural dynamism on the subject of the arts ... and yet Léon Blum's government neither knows how nor wants to make the airwaves an instrument of leisure and popular education.'[20] Even so, the Popular Front did effect a turning point in French radio and 1935–40 marked the start of 'la radio moderne'.

Radio also figured significantly at the 1937 Exposition (supported by the Popular Front), as Arno Huth discussed in *La Revue musicale*: 'Imagine an international exhibition twenty years ago ... no one would have dreamt of making a place there for Radio.'[21] Huth reported on the impressive Palais de la Radio, designed for state broadcasting and reception, with symphonic and chamber studios, interview cubicles, and site space reserved for the Laboratoire National de Radio-Électricité and a research laboratory honouring the name of Édouard Branly.[22] Moreover, he continued, 'It is through radio that the various aspects of the Exposition were presented to the world'.[23]

Although some traditional activities were diminishing, radio and music technology were opening up new avenues. In 1938, an engineer and key pioneer of electronic music, Pierre Schaeffer (1910–95), wrote a visionary article which posed the central question, looking forward to 'musique concrète' and electronic possibilities: 'What are the real resources of radio broadcasting? Does it offer the opportunity for an original art to be born?'[24] Such radical enquiries were made within a wider context of 'music and electricity' (connecting with 'la musique mécanique', recording, the phonograph and music for cinema) and alongside continuing explorations into quarter-tones and microtones;[25] Schaeffer's significant position, however, was confirmed by French Radio's decision in 1942 to set up a Studio d'Essai under his directorship.

The other figure crucial to experimentation with percussion, timbre, sound-masses, urban noise (from Futurism) and then electronics, was Edgard Varèse (1883–1965), surely amongst the most influential catalysts of this period. Despite his French birth, his training with Roussel and Widor, and his early interest in Bertrand's electric 'dynaphone', he was

---

1994), vol. 1 *1921–1944*, 397–8. Brochand provides a comprehensive general history covering private and state stations, development plans, legislation, broadcasting frequencies and programming.

20 Jeanneney: 'Le Front populaire', *L'Echo du siècle*, 30 ('Le Front populaire porte un formidable élan culturel en matière de beaux-arts ... et pourtant, le gouvernement de Léon Blum ne sait ni ne veut faire des ondes un instrument de loisir et d'éducation populaire').

21 Arno Huth: 'La Radio à l'Exposition', *RM*, 175 (June–July 1937), 61–4: 61 ('Imaginez une exposition internationale il y a vingt ans ... personne n'aurait songé y faire une place à la *Radio*').

22 Branly (1844–1940) was a long-lived French physicist closely involved in the invention of wireless telegraphy.

23 Huth, 'La Radio', 63 ('C'est par radio qu'on a présenté au monde les divers aspects de l'Exposition').

24 Pierre Schaeffer: 'Problème central de la radiodiffusion', *RM*, 183 (Apr.–May 1938), 317–22: 317 ('Quelle sont les ressources réelles de la radiodiffusion? Offre-t-elle à un art original l'occasion de naître?').

25 See, for instance, Eric Sarnette: 'Musique et électricité', *RM*, 151 (Dec. 1934), 80–87; and Alois Hába: 'Quelques réflexions sur l'interprétation de la musique à quarts et à sixièmes de ton', *RM*, 175 (June–July 1937), 92–5. Maurice Ohana (1913–92), co-founder of the group *Zodiaque*, would later pursue thirds of a tone.

by the 1930s regarded more as an American than a French composer. Nonetheless, he returned to France from 1928 to 1933 where he quickly re-established himself, taught André Jolivet and doubtless heard Messiaen's music.

Products of this sojourn included the extraordinary *Ionisation* (1930–31), for forty percussion instruments, including anvils and sirens, the premiere of which was given in New York in 1933. Meanwhile, the French premiere of *Amériques* (1918–21; revised 1927) had been presented in May 1929 at the Concerts Poulet (an event which much inspired Jolivet), when the recently invented Ondes Martenot substituted for the siren. In his *Ecuatorial* (1932–34), which sets a translated prayer from the *Popol Vuh* of the Maya Quiché (an indigenous Indian people of Central America) for bass or unison chorus and ensemble, Varèse initially selected Thérémin's instrument though he later substituted two of Martenot's devices to obtain the highest pitches. Again, the work was first heard in America in 1934.[26] Nevertheless, French connections continued and in 1954 Schaeffer invited Varèse to the studios of Radio-Télévision Française to complete the two-channel magnetic tape elements of *Déserts*, premiered later that year in the first live, stereo broadcast.[27]

In August 1934, Jacques Ibert gave his views in *L'opinion* on the crisis of the Opéra-Comique (salvaged across 1936–39 by Jacques Rouché, joint director of the Opéra and Opéra-Comique):

> They are completely taken over by sport and the cinema. One can imagine just how much a young man knows, and in what detail, about the life and work of a Garbo, a Maurice Chevalier, and how little idea he has about a Mme Lubin – a magnificent, celebrated singer – or a Mlle Germaine Hoerner, whose voice is a wonderful miracle.[28]

Ibert's observations signal changing priorities in favour of popular music – French chanson, film and cabaret. Its most prominent exponents are usefully summarized in Sevran's *Dictionnaire*: 'From the crazy years to the Popular Front ... It's the time of Josephine Baker, Maurice Chevalier and Mistinguett ... The sky lights up; to the mingled voices of Léon Blum [Prime Minister] and Maurice Thorez, that of Trenet echoes back: *Y'a d'la joie partout y'a d'la joie*.'[29]

Josephine Baker (1906–75), 'the Parisian queen of the inter-war years', set up the cabaret *Paris qui remue* (1930) at the Casino de Paris. From *La Revue nègre* onwards, her

---

26 This interest in non-Western – specifically Central American Indian – incantation and so-called 'primitivism', inspired by Cubism and figures such as Fernand Léger, is picked up later in the chapter.

27 The most detailed exploration of Varèse's work is still that by Jonathan Bernard: *The Music of Edgard Varèse* (New Haven, 1987); among an increasing collection of articles note Boulez's tribute: 'Hommage à Varèse', *RM*, 265/6 (1969), 30.

28 Ibert quoted in Dumesnil: *La musique*, 76 ('Ils sont accaparés par le sport, le cinéma. Qu'on songe seulement à l'abondance et à la précision des notions qu'un jeune homme possède à présent sur la biographie et le travail d'une Garbo, d'un Maurice Chevalier, et qu'on pense à l'ignorance où il est quant à une Mme Lubin – illustre et magnifique cantatrice – ou une Mlle Germaine Hoerner, dont la voix est un prodige merveilleux').

29 Pascal Sevran: *Le dictionnaire de la chanson française* (Paris, 1988), 9 ('Des années folles au Front Populaire ... C'est l'heure de Joséphine Baker, de Maurice Chevalier et de Mistinguett ... Le ciel s'éclaircit, aux voix mêlées de Léon Blum et de Maurice Thorez, celle de Trenet répond en écho: *Y'a d'la joie partout y'a d'la joie*').

phenomenal art helped to create, played on and to some extent was exploited by the preoccupation with jazz, a racially stereotyped *art nègre* and *art primitif*, which in turn provided part of the context for Jolivet's later spiritual quests of a primitivist nature. Meanwhile, the immensely popular Chevalier (1888–1971), 'the poor boy of Ménilmontant'[30] returned to France from Hollywood with *Prosper* (1935), the superficially lighthearted *Y'a d'la joie* (1937) and *Ça fait d'excellents Français* (1939). 'Le cas Chevalier' was contradictory: he sang for the Popular Front, yet during the Occupation he supported the pro-Nazi Pétain, while trying to protect his wife, who was Jewish, and suffering inevitable turmoil.[31] In Mistinguett – Colette's 'national property' – Cocteau heard the voice of the Parisienne, revealing 'This tragic actress who sums up our city because her poignant voice contains the cries of the newspaper vendors and the all-season barrow-girl'.[32]

Finally, the multi-talented and complex Charles Trenet, known as 'the singing Fool', was deeply influential; his duo with Johnny Hess ran until 1936. As a result of a deliberate poetic aesthetic to suppress sombre emotion, he famously composed *Y'a d'la joie*, recommended to Chevalier by Cocteau and Max Jacob; conversely, he also produced serious criticism, including a commentary on Gershwin's Concerto in F.[33] In 1938 Trenet won the 'prix du disque' with *Boum* (also the period of *Je chante*) and was instrumental in establishing the modern French chanson.

As a committed fan of Chevalier (especially *Si fatigué*), as well as the work of Henri Christiné (1867–1941; songwriter of *Valentine*) and Vincent Scotto (1876–1952; songwriter of *Prosper* and *J'ai deux amours*), Francis Poulenc well illustrates the impact of such popular music – particularly melody – upon his own art. In his dedicated broadcast on Chevalier of 1947, Poulenc remarked: 'Of course, what touches us Parisians most deeply is that Ménilmontant voice of his, but by what faultless artistry is it refined, so as to grip audiences, thousands of miles from Paris, who have never even seen a postcard of the Faubourg Saint-Martin.'[34]

Another aspect of popular music, which engaged composers with left-wing sympathies, was the Fédération Musicale Populaire, headed in 1937 by the philanthropic Roussel who, in the words of Marc Pincherle, 'saw there a means of lifting souls, at the very least to offer them a diversion from the fatigue and monotony of daily chores'.[35] A broad group

---

30 Chevalier had a frugal childhood in the old Parisian district of Ménilmontant, earning his own living from about the age of eleven after his father left home.

31 Lucien Rioux: *50 ans de chanson française: De Trenet à Bruel* (Paris, 1992), 23. See also Maurice Chevalier: *Ma route et mes chansons* (Paris, 1948).

32 Cocteau quoted in Chantal Brunschwig, Louis-Jean Calvet and Jean-Claude Klein: *100 ans de chanson française* (Paris, 1972), 250 ('Cette tragédienne qui résume notre ville parce que sa voix poignante tient des cris des marchands de journaux et de la marchande de quatre-saisons'). Mistinguett was the stage-name of Jeanne Bourgeois (1873–1956).

33 Lucienne Cantaloube-Ferrieu: *Chanson et poésie des années 30 aux années 60: Trenet, Brassens, Ferré ... ou Les 'Enfants naturels' du surréalisme* (Paris, 1981), 83, 70.

34 Poulenc quoted by Lucie Kayas: 'Francis Poulenc – disc jockey', in Sidney Buckland and Myriam Chimènes (eds), *Francis Poulenc: Music, Art and Literature* (Aldershot, 1999), 363–82: 367. See also Francis Poulenc: *Entretiens avec Claude Rostand* (Paris, 1954), 135.

35 Marc Pincherle: *Albert Roussel* (Geneva, 1957), 131 ('il y voyait un moyen d'élever les âmes, à tout le moins, de leur offrir une diversion à la fatigue et à la monotonie des besognes quotidiennes'). This classic text is useful especially for its quotations of Roussel.

including Milhaud, Honegger, Auric, Ibert, Koechlin, Tailleferre, Roland-Manuel, Marcel Delannoy, Manuel Rosenthal, Daniel Lazarus and the young Marcel Landowski collaborated in projects allied to the Popular Front. Whilst these works were not necessarily great music, they were important symbolically for their cooperative espousal of socialist principles. *Le quatorze juillet* (Bastille Day) was Romain Rolland's initiative, premiered in July 1936 under the auspices of the Maison de la Culture and favourably reviewed by Léon Kochnitzky in *La Revue musicale* of July–August 1936. *Liberté* ..., a collective show on a text by Maurice Rostand, was performed for the opening of the Exposition, by 'May 36', the Popular Movement of Art and Culture. Finally, *La construction d'une cité*, a staged spectacle using popular song, was produced by the Communist writer Jean-Richard Bloch with sets by Fernand Léger and premiered at the Vélodrome d'Hiver in October 1937.

Honegger was particularly committed to such causes, producing the Popular Front's aural symbol, the song *Jeunesse* (Youth, 1937) which featured in his score to *Visages de la France* – a short film that summarized French history through Marxist eyes, in commemoration of the October Revolution. It is worth noting this more unusual, left-wing 'nationalism' on the part of one whose music was banned in Germany after 1935; and, according to Halbreich, beyond specific creeds: 'as the political dangers forced themselves into the public consciousness during the winter of 1937–1938, Honegger began to make the denunciation of war his absolute and lasting priority'.[36]

There is in the 1930s still some adherence to a neoclassicizing tendency. The notion of temporal 'otherness' here (i.e. use of the 'erstwhile') does not imply that this music exists in a time-warp, although some may regard neoclassicism of the 1930s as at least a decade out of date given that its heyday was indisputably within the 1920s. Rather, the notion suggests that composers continued to revisit the past (often a French past) as a means of acquiring inspiration for (re)composing the present. Although the continued recourse to neoclassicism in the 1930s might indicate a lack of awareness of the growing 'volcano' (i.e. Halbreich's 'unwitting dancing'), the idea has nevertheless undergone some development in that its admittedly diverse products do generally have an increased expressive, emotional dimension. This is true even of original protagonists such as Les Six, whose designs of the 1930s – especially those of Honegger and Milhaud – can exhibit a distinct grandeur.

Such neoclassicism may be associated with a French identity (and traditional right-wing politics), in the quest for an idealized national heritage, as in Milhaud's *Suite d'après Corrette* (1937) after the eighteenth-century composer Michel Corrette or Ibert's ballet *Diane de Poitiers*, produced in 1934 by the Ballets Ida Rubinstein, where 'Dances from the sixteenth century, the *Chant des oiseaux* by Janequin, Passereau's *Il est bel et bon*, and old popular airs have been very skilfully blended by Jacques Ibert with his original score'.[37] In keeping with the French *tombeau* or tribute, Ibert honoured Roussel with a *Toccata sur le nom d'Albert Roussel* (for piano, 1929) and Schmitt orchestrated his *In*

36 Halbreich: *Arthur Honegger*, 539, 583. Fulcher provides evidence that Honegger's overall position was in fact more equivocal, with some involvement in activities associated with the political right ('Musical style, meaning and politics', 435, 448–50).

37 Dumesnil: *La Musique*, 191 ('Des danceries du XVIe siècle, le *Chant des Oiseaux* de Janequin, *Il est bel et bon*, de Passerau, des airs populaires anciens, ont été fort habilement mêlés par Jacques Ibert à sa partition originale').

Memoriam (*Cippus feralis*; *Scherzo sur le nom de Gabriel Fauré*) for the tenth anniversary of Fauré's death, given at the Concerts Colonne in November 1935.[38] These compositional quests for Frenchness were balanced by writings (and *tombeaux*) in *La Revue musicale* – our yardstick journal – especially in the late 1930s.[39] Robert Bernard bemoaned the fact that 'There is a certain condescending admiration for our composers which is unjust to the point of sacrilege. The idea that it was foreign parts which developed many French musicians, from Costeley to Couperin, from Rameau to Ravel, an idea which – alas – has only too many followers among ourselves, is profoundly prejudicial to the renown of France.'[40]

Apart from the eighteenth century of Couperin, a broader interest in the past was shown by the production of special issues of *La Revue musicale*, such as that of December 1932 devoted to Bach, and by the new Société d'Études Mozartiennes, which held its inaugural concert in 1930. Mozartian connections were also made, for instance, apropos of Ravel's piano concerto writing, described by one critic as a combination of classical and romantic traits: 'selon Mozart, selon Liszt'.[41] With regard to Italian and English heritages, Roland-Manuel wrote a ballet, *Élvire*, on themes of Scarlatti presented at the Opéra in 1937; Reynaldo Hahn (1874–1947) composed *Le marchand de Venise*, after Shakespeare, again produced at the Opéra in 1935 and Ibert created his wartime orchestral *Suite élisabéthaine* (1942), with four of the nine movements modelled on the music of Blow, Bull, Gibbons and Purcell.

Essentially, there was still some mileage in extended tonality and absolute music – even if this domain was typically regarded as non-French: 'As a general rule, absolute music ... is hardly favourable to French musicians as soon as it becomes a matter of a large-scale score', with Bernard finding an exception in Albert Roussel who appeared as 'the locus where specifically French thought becomes mistress of a form which is not authentically national'.[42] Beyond the highlights of Roussel's Third and Fourth Symphonies and Honegger's First Symphony, absolute music also included Paul Paray's *Symphonie en ut* performed in 1935: 'a triumph', claimed Dumesnil, 'the tonality itself – C major –

38 See Robert Bernard: 'A propos de *In Memoriam* de Florent Schmitt, *RM*, 163 (Feb. 1936), 122–4 (relevant also to discussion of the concert crisis).

39 See, for example, the musical supplement: 'Le tombeau de Paul Dukas', *RM*, 166 (May–June 1936). Relevant articles include Charles Koechlin's historicized survey, with discussion of (poly)tonality, modality and the melodic line: 'Sur l'évolution de la musique française avant et après Debussy', *RM*, 155 (Apr. 1935), 264–80; Robert Bernard: 'Défense et illustration de la musique française: Versailles sera-t-elle le pendant de Bayreuth ou de Salzburg?', *RM*, 174 (May 1937), 275–8; and André Boll: 'Pour un réveil de la musique française', *RM*, 193 (Apr.–Nov. 1939), 86–8.

40 Robert Bernard: 'Les caracteristiques de la musique française', *RM*, 180 (Jan. 1938), 120–31: 131 ('Il y a une certaine admiration condescendante pour nos musiciens qui est injuste jusqu'au sacrilège. L'idée que l'étranger se fait de maints musiciens français, de Costeley à Couperin, de Rameau à Ravel, idée qui – hélas – n'a que trop d'adeptes parmi nous, est profondément préjudiciable au renom de la France').

41 Frederik Goldbeck: 'Sur Ravel et ses concertos', *RM*, 134 (Mar. 1933), 193–200: 196.

42 Robert Bernard: review of Roussel's Fourth Symphony, *RM*, 160 (Nov. 1935), 273–5: 273 ('D'une façon générale, la musique pure ... n'est guère favorable aux musiciens français dès qu'il s'agit d'une partition de grande envergure'; 'le lieu géométrique où la pensée spécifiquement française s'est rendue maîtresse d'une forme qui n'est pas authentiquement nationale').

affirmed the contempt for complications, the good taste of clarity'. Interestingly, in terms of the decade's leanings towards spirituality, he also saw the work as 'a profession of faith, a *credo*'.[43]

Diminutive forms were especially attractive, as witnessed by Inghelbrecht's *Sinfonia breve*, given in 1930, and Roussel's Sinfonietta (1934),[44] with eighteenth-century stylistic notions also inspiring Markevitch's *Concerto grosso* (1930), *Concerti da camera* by Henriette Roget and Henri Barraud – performed in 1934 and 1936, respectively – and Schmitt's *Symphonie concertante* op. 82, premiered by Pierre Monteux and the Orchestre Symphonique de Paris in 1933. Time has however largely endorsed Cooper's view that Schmitt's later, impersonal music lacked his former 'characteristic profuseness and violence'.[45]

A first brief case study is the Third Symphony in G minor op. 42 (1929–30) of Albert Roussel (1869–1937), whose individual neoclassicism was defined by Arthur Hoérée as 'back to a balance between depth and form, proscribing any aestheticizing tendency, and any fad for pastiche'; meanwhile, Cooper concluded that it was Roussel's music which at this time most successfully preserved the traditions of French art.[46] In his own lifetime, though less so today, Roussel's status was assured: he was elected to membership of the Academy of Saint Cecilia, Rome (1931), awarded the Brahms Centenary Medal (the only Frenchman to receive this award, and one whose symphonies were much admired in Germany),[47] and elected President of Music for the Exposition and head of the French committee of the ISCM. Roussel's contemporary importance was attested to by a dedicated issue of *La Revue musicale* in April 1929 ('Hommage à Roussel', together with a 'Semaine Roussel'). A further issue devoted to his music appeared after his death in 1937.

The Third Symphony, rated amongst Roussel's finest scores, was one of several French works, together with Honegger's First Symphony and Stravinsky's *Symphony of Psalms*, commissioned to celebrate the fiftieth anniversary of the Boston Symphony Orchestra in 1930. It was dedicated to Serge Koussevitsky, and its premiere duly took place in Boston on 24 October, with the French premiere given at the Concerts Lamoureux on 28 November 1931. While the orchestral forces required are standard – 3.3.3.3; 4.4.3.1; timp., perc. (3), celesta, hp. (2); strings – the work lasts a mere twenty-three minutes, and is thus suggestive of a neoclassical scaling and tautness of treatment. Of course the very act of designating keys and assigning opus numbers also indicates a certain traditionalism.

Dumesnil, for one, felt that this was neoclassicism with emotional intensity: 'Roussel depicts himself fully in the adagio with an intense poetry, and in the scherzo with a charming lightness and spirit'; Cooper also commended Roussel in his Third and Fourth

43 Dumesnil: *La Musique*, 159 ('un triomphe: sa tonalité elle-même – l'ut majeur – affirmait le mépris des complications, le goût de la clarté'; 'un profession de foi, un *credo*').

44 Premiered by the Orchestre Féminin Jane Évrard and reviewed by Arthur Hoérée in *RM*, 152 (Jan. 1935), 44–5, the opening of Roussel's accessible and tautly structured Sinfonietta was regarded as 'direct music. The rhythm here is continuous, in the classical style' ('musique directe. Le rythme en est continu, à la manière classique').

45 Cooper: *French Music*, 208.

46 Arthur Hoérée, review of Roussel's Trio, *RM*, 100 (Jan. 1930), 70 ('le retour à l'équilibre entre fond et forme et d'en proscrire toute velléité esthétisante, toute manie du pastiche'); Cooper: *French Music*, 216.

47 See André François-Poncet: 'Roussel et les Allemands', *RM*, 178 (Nov. 1937), 353–4; Marius Schneider: 'Albert Roussel', *Anbruch*, 12 (1930), 158–60.

Symphonies for having the confidence to position his main emotional peaks within the slow movements and noted that his apparent harmonic harshness was often a consequence of contrapuntal working rather than of a particular harmonic theory.[48] Certainly the linear ('voice-leading') perspective of his music is crucial.

Roussel's four movements use explicit key signatures: G minor, E♭ major (C minor); balanced by D major, G major, and employ cadential gestures that are intensified by moderate dissonance, including added notes and chromatic appoggiaturas. (Both Third and Fourth Symphonies open with a minor ninth, Neapolitan inflection, over the tonic.) The opening tutti, highlighting horns, *divisi* second violins and violas over a heavy bass line, establishes a gritty G minor, with strongly accented, incisive rhythms in triple metre (Example 9.1a). This characterful tonality has itself an illustrious Austro-German lineage which extends back through Schubert's Fifth Symphony and Mozart's Fortieth; conversely, though, Roussel's darkly tritonal and dotted rhythmic writing, especially in the first subject (D–A♭), may also be seen to anticipate that of Shostakovich. Neoclassical features such as sequences and appoggiaturas are mixed with more expansive gestures that have a rich, impressionistic grandeur; the second subject, *dolce*, enjoys notable quartal elements (and another tritone). Much symphonic development ensues, both here and later in the work – a certain Franckian cyclicity, particularly with elements of the first subject.

Example 9.1 Albert Roussel, Third Symphony, I and II (reduced scores)

(a) I (bars 1–2)

(b) II (bars 1–3)

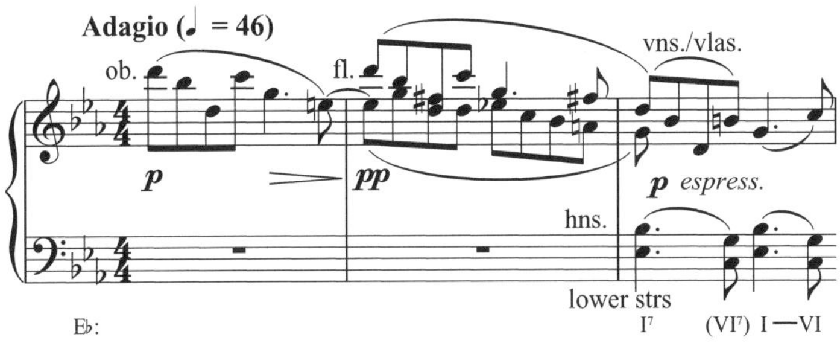

48 Dumesnil: *La Musique*, 99 ('Roussel se peint tout entier dans l'adagio d'une poésie intense et dans le scherzo, d'une légèreté, d'un esprit charmants.'); Cooper: *French Music*, 215–16.

By contrast, the tonality of the expressively dissonant Adagio is just a little more ambiguous (hints of bitonality), with meandering imitative lines, transferred from oboe to flute thence to violins/violas, utilizing scalic 'mixture': both E/E♭, B/B♭ (Example 9.1b). Its central Andante leads to an extended 'Più mosso' episode in neo-baroque fugal style complete with subjects, answers and countersubjects, distinguished by dotted rhythms and *Fortspinnung*.

The latter two movements, whilst of lesser gravitas – as in the classical symphony, exhibit suitably bucolic characteristics and complement the other two. As with Roussel's *Petite suite* (1929), Cooper found the lighthearted Vivace to be 'comparable in robust vigour with the scherzos of Beethoven and Bruckner, in whom the peasant origins of the dance were still strong'.[49] In fact, part of its character is achieved by an initial dotted motive (D–B: tonic–submediant) in 3/8 metre, attractively suggestive of a minor-third cuckoo call. Inevitable Beethovenian association is set up by the finale's move to the tonic major; its initial theme on woodwind (featuring flute, thence to strings) again utilizes dotted rhythms, with 3/4 metre from the first movement interpolated within 4/4. Two subsequent thematic ideas also derive from the opening movement and are combined in Franck-like fashion. Such allusive observations should not be seen to downplay the structural strength and impressive concision of this music.[50]

The popular Flute Concerto (1932–33) of Jacques Ibert (1890–1962) also merits attention. This composer's contribution to music is difficult to pinpoint because of his eclectic nature and his seemingly flippant assertion that 'All systems are valid provided that one derives music from them.'[51] Where Ibert's rigorous self-discipline is concerned, David Cox makes a comparison with Stravinsky; similarly, and in common with several Frenchmen, Ibert wanted to exist independently of fashions and schools (though his influential status was recognized with his directorship from 1937 onwards of the Académie de France in Rome). Essentially, Ibert did subscribe to a neoclassical approach, favouring closed forms which exert balance, control and some lightheartedness, combined with less predictable fantastical and romantic elements.

As Cox acknowledges, the Flute Concerto's status is as 'a masterpiece of the genre, effectively exploring the full technical range of the solo instrument without ever lowering the expressive quality of the music'.[52] Indeed, after its premiere at the Société des concerts du conservatoire in 1934, Suzanne Demarquez commented that 'Philippe Gaubert directed as an artist enamoured by the rare lines of this Concerto of which Marcel Moyse [the dedicatee] is the ideal performer: delicious sonority, unrivalled virtuosity, he united all this within the most supple understanding that a composer could wish for'.[53]

---

49 Cooper: *French Music*, 216.

50 The Third Symphony is analysed by Philippe Allenbach as representative of Roussel's third stylistic period ('Albert Roussel (1869–1937): Symphonie no. 3 en sol mineur (1930)', *L'Éducation musical*, 237 (1977), 19–22; 238 (1977), 12–13). Alain Pâris also regards Roussel's last two symphonies as the most important early–mid-twentieth-century French works of their genre ('La Symphonie française de 1918 à nos jours', *Le courrier musical de France*, 67 (1979), 91–3).

51 Ibert quoted in David Cox: 'Jacques Ibert', *The New Grove Dictionary of Music and Musicians* (London, 1980), vol. 9, 1–3: 1.

52 Ibid., 2.

53 Suzanne Demarquez: review of Ibert Flute Concerto, *RM*, 144 (Mar. 1934), 224–5: 225 ('Philippe Gaubert a dirigé en artiste épris de lignes rares ce *Concerto* dont Marcel Moyse est

From the outset, Ibert's exuberant neoclassicism is evident in his use of economical orchestral forces (double woodwind, two horns, trumpet, timpani and strings), regular 2/4 metre, a slightly chromaticized F minor, with a fanfare-like cadential gesture before the entry of the solo flute (bar 5), whose arpeggiated figurations are again reminiscent of baroque *Fortspinnung* (Example 9.2).

Example 9.2 Jacques Ibert, Flute Concerto, I (bars 1–6, reduced score)

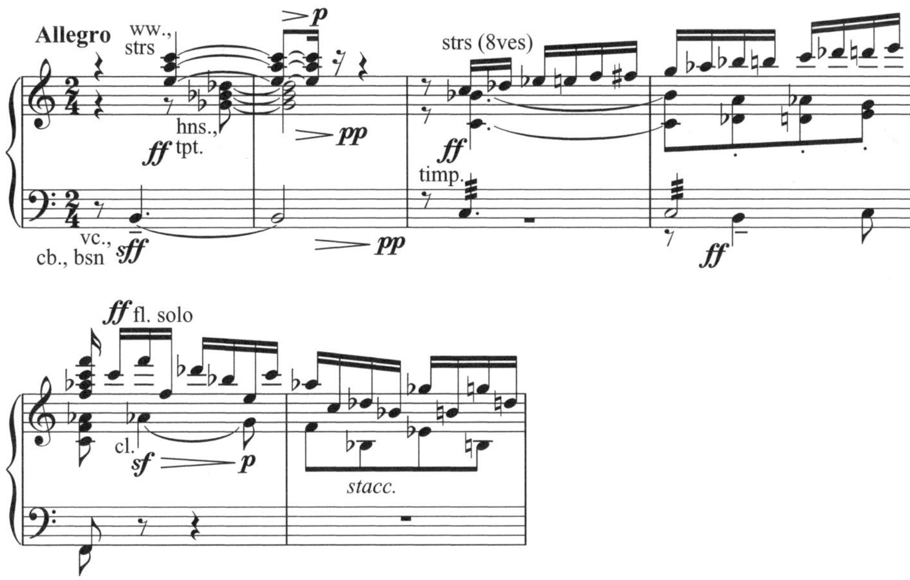

The ensuing Andante is in the submediant D flat major, but not without its bitonal twists: against a cadential oscillation of chords of tonic (in second inversion) and dominant ninth (again favouring fourths: B♭, E♭, A♭) played by violins and violas, the flute commences with a poignantly expressive white-note melody, focused on B (bars 3–5), which is then pulled into (the flattened) line at bar 6 (Example 9.3). Predictably, given its classical modelling, the finale marked 'Allegro scherzando' is a lighthearted affair in the tonic major; interest and impetus are created by alternating metre – predominantly 4/4 plus 3/4 – with syncopated chords followed by vivacious, scalic triplets in 'saltarello' style. Within and between movements, Ibert enjoys keys related by thirds, including some quite dramatic switches: F minor–A minor; F minor–D♭ major; D♭ major–B♭ minor (relative); F major–A major. Although such neoclassical music is highly attractive, it was nonetheless limited in terms of further potential for growth.

The continued pursuit of cultural, or geographical, 'otherness' (i.e. the 'elsewhere') through the orientalizing of Western music and the conscious use of exoticism is a second (overlapping) concern; as with neoclassicism, this may involve pastiche or *mélange* – whether new/old, or French/foreign – and fantasy. This exoticism was the last flowering

l'interprète idéal: sonorité délicieuse, virtuosité hors de pair, il unit tout cela dans la plus souple compréhension qu'un auteur puisse souhaiter').

Example 9.3 Jacques Ibert, Flute Concerto, II (bars 1–7, reduced score)

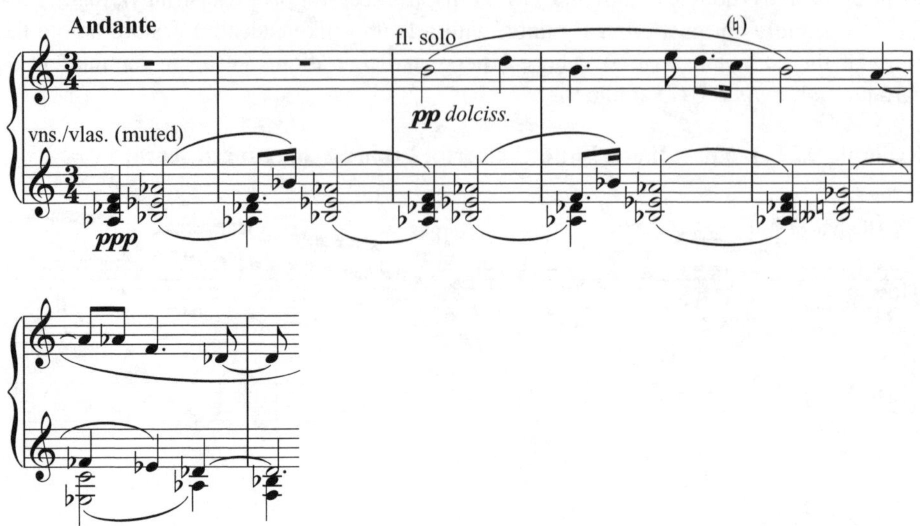

of a notion which, however stereotyped, had had a place in French music since the colonially influenced later nineteenth century of Saint-Saëns's *Samson et Dalila* (1877) and which was then nourished and substantiated by the 1889 Paris Exposition. Following the establishment of the Institut d'Ethnologie in 1925, the Mission Dakar-Djibouti of the early 1930s, while supposedly embracing a new anthropological seriousness, still espoused a collector mentality (typical of earlier 'primitivist' enquiries) in furnishing the Musée d'Ethnographie, Bibliothèque nationale and private collectors with abstracted exhibits.[54] To return to the initial quotation, the impending 'volcano' does not really seem relevant here (i.e. 'unwitting dancing').

Products of this ongoing fascination included Respighi's *Marie l'Egyptienne* with its French premiere at the Opéra-Comique in 1934; Tomasi's symphonic poem, *Tam-tam*: 'a colonial drama written for Radio' on a text of Julien Maigret, also given in 1934; and Henri Martelli's symphonic suite, *Bas-reliefs assyriens*: 'a massive tableau, a faithful translation into sound, of Ninevite art' performed at the Concerts Pasdeloup in 1935.[55] Roussel's music also features here: unusually, he had actually travelled to India, Ceylon, Singapore and Saigon – a trip which resulted in *Évocations* first performed in 1912; his exploration of Hindu legend then famously led to the opera-ballet *Padmâvatî*, premiered in 1923. He had also set several Chinese poems (opp. 12, 35 and 47).

An increasing academic interest in orientalism is also evident from the Exposition Coloniale of 1931 (where Messiaen heard Balinese music) and the pages of *La Revue musicale*, which typically in one issue of 1932 carried an article on Arabic music and a

54 See *Minotaure*, 2 (special issue): 'Mission Dakar-Djibouti, 1931–33' (Paris, 1933); and James Clifford: *The Predicament of Culture: Twentieth-Century Ethnography, Culture and Art* (Cambridge, Mass., 1988), 137. I am grateful to my former research student, Andy Fry, for his enthusiastic explorations into the cultural background of primitivism.

55 Dumesnil: *La Musique*, 194, 210 ('une image massive, transposition sonore fidèle, de l'art ninivite').

review of Hindu music and dance. Two years later, a 'Récital de musique vocale et instrumentale hindoue, cinghalaise et tibétaine', where music was exquisitely fused with movement, seemed to have proved something of a revelation for Parisians.[56]

Orientalism in the 1930s is nicely illustrated by selected songs of Roussel; Basil Deane commended Roussel's 'evocative qualities ... apparent in the later songs, especially the later *Poèmes chinois* (opp. 35 and 47)'.[57] This latter opus was Roussel's final set of Chinese Poems, composed in 1932 and first performed at the Concerts Triton in May 1934. The composer's starting point is two Chinese texts by Li-I and Huang-Fu-Ian, albeit reached at two removes, translated into English by Herbert Allen Giles and then into French by Henri-Pierre Roché: 'Favorite abandonnée' and 'Vois, de belles filles'.

A nocturnal impression is created in the opening six-line poem of the 'Forsaken favourite' languishing near a moonlit palace; this image, together with musical allusion ('the sounds of lutes and songs'), suggestion and ambiguity, sets up resonances with Debussy's 'Et la lune descend sur le temple qui fut' (1907) from the composer's first set of *Images*. A metaphorical mention of the sea ('the clepsydra [water-clock] of the entire sea'), of which Roussel himself was so fond, offers a further point of connection. The setting is as a melancholic, fifteen-bar miniature, featuring a modal centricity on E♭ which involves ambiguous 'mixture' at the third and sixth degrees (G/G♭; C/C♭); the main pitches form an aeolian-type collection, but with a raised fourth: E♭, F♭, G♭, A, B♭, C♭, D♭, E♭ (Example 9.4: bars 1–5). An exquisite richness is afforded by the choice of pianistic harmonies, utilizing mainly secondary chords such as II and III, with added sevenths, ninths and thirteenths, while from a linear perspective the prominent tritones (treble: E♭–A, bass: C♭–F; marked '*a*' in Example 9.4, have their own poignancy. Roussel's chromaticized impressionistic writing is intimate, intricate and nicely balanced, with small details such as a 'voice' exchange in the piano part of bar 2 (treble: G♭–F, bass: F–G♭; denoted by arrows). A special moment occurs at bar 10 with the phrase 'de la mer entière' (fourth line) concluding on a pure F major, supertonic (quasi-dominant) chord.

By contrast, the second, frivolous song is faster and lighter in touch (staccatos, anacruses, syncopations), in a nonchalant 2/4 metre, with a mischievous melodic line in the piano introduction that enjoys its ascending major sevenths. Its five-line text, presented from the opposite perspective to the first, exclaims: 'Look! beautiful girls run in groups'. This song operates within an extended C major that exhibits a Neapolitan inflection of the second and sixth degrees (D♭, A♭: see Example 9.5), and consequent augmented seconds (E–D♭, B–A♭; marked '*b*'), with their touch of 'exoticism'. A slower concluding section (Moderato, bar 33), exaggerates through its rhythmic augmentation angular leaps (a minor ninth and seventh intervals) in piano and voice in mock expressive, imitative fashion, with seemingly flippant references back to the 'music', the 'night' and perhaps the girl of the opening song.

56 Baron Rodolphe d'Erlanger: 'La musique arabe', *RM*, 128 (July–Aug. 1932), 118–23; Alexandre Stefanesco: review of 'Danse et musique hindoues au Théâtre des Champs-Elysées', ibid., 126–7; and Alexandrine Troussevitch: review of 'Récital de musique vocale', *RM*, 146 (May 1934), 395.

57 Basil Deane: 'Albert Roussel', *The New Grove Dictionary of Music and Musicians* (London, 1980), vol. 16, 273–6: 275. See also Raymond Pouilliart: 'Poésie et musique: Les *Poèmes chinois* d'Albert Roussel', *Les Lettres romanes*, Université Catholique de Louvain, 38/3 (1984), 241–5.

Example 9.4 Albert Roussel, *Deux poèmes chinois* op. 47, I, 'Favorite abandonée' (bars 1–5)

Whilst Roussel's writing in these songs is hardly cutting-edge, favouring respectively romanticized and more neoclassical, extended tonal language, his text setting largely avoids the problems of clichéd oriental pastiche and marks the conclusion of his long-term interest in Chinese poetry and *chinoiserie*.

'Three songs which had to be a farewell to music':[58] Ravel's *Don Quichotte à Dulcinée* (1932–34) marks specifically the end of a well-developed theme of Spanish exoticism in his music. These songs involve not only a geographical 'otherness', but also a fondness of fantasy, story and reinterpretation of the past – temporal otherness – in respect of Cervantes's early seventeenth-century novel. Performed in their orchestral version at the Concerts Colonne in 1934, the songs were reviewed with enthusiasm and understanding by the respected contemporary musicologist, Fred Goldbeck: 'This new Ravelian Spain, under the invocation of Don Quixote, is a new magical landscape of Ravel's.'[59] It is

58 Dumesnil: *La Musique*, 119–20 ('Trois chansons qui devaient être un adieu à la musique'). Tragically, from this work onwards, Ravel was increasingly crippled by the brain disease which was to claim his life in 1937.

59 Frederik Goldbeck: review of *Don Quichotte*, *RM*, 152 (Jan. 1935), 42–3: 42 ('Cette nouvelle Espagne ravélienne, sous l'invocation de Don Quichotte, est un nouveau paysage féerique de Ravel').

Example 9.5 Albert Roussel, *Deux poèmes chinois* op. 47, II, 'Vois, de belles filles' (bars 14–17)

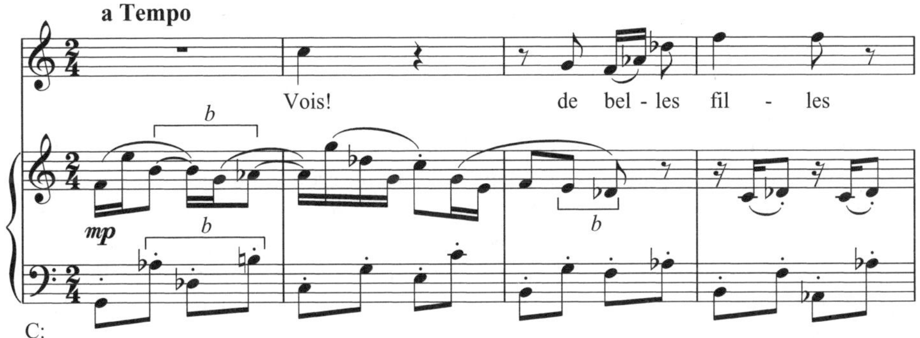

appropriate to stress the fantasy aspect; Ravel is typically much more interested in creating the imaginary and fake than in any strict representation: 'A magical cook'!

The work comprises three strophic settings of poetry by Paul Morand, commencing with a chivalric, slightly melancholic, 'Chanson romanesque' (B♭ aeolian–major), presented in an alternating 6/8, 3/4 metre as stylized Spanish *quajira*. A hymn-like 'Chanson épique' (D dorian–F major) follows with suitably antique parallel-chord movement and modal inflection – especially phrygian-type pitch flattening, its quintuple metre suggestive of inspiration from Basque *zortzico*. Finally a jocular and operatic 'Chanson à boire', in fast triple metre derived from the Spanish *jota*, is presented nominally in C minor–major. In fact, it enjoys a brief bitonal introduction and postlude, with 'white' against 'black' notes, and in common with the first song puts much emphasis on the dominant. In its use of Moorish vocal arabesque, this song also bears affinity with *Boléro*. Goldbeck, while noting its 'full Spanish rhythm', added perceptively that 'it could yet be heard very much after the famous bacchic song of *The Abduction from the Seraglio*, with which it connects by means of its urbane physicality'.[60]

In his recent discussion of Ravel's songs, Peter Kaminsky comments on how the composer's own personality comes through in these folksong-like settings, with 'shifting phrase lengths subtly distorting the metric symmetry of Morand's poetry in the first song, the musical merging of the Madonna and Dulcinea in the second and – the crowning touch – the musical representation of the hiccup in "Chanson à boire"!'[61] From our stance, the most interesting observation is this synthesis of fiction and faith in the second (looking to our spiritual focal point), with the textual invocation of St Michael and St George, and the final reaching out 'A Vous, Madone au bleu mantel! Amen'.[62]

60 Goldbeck: review of *Don Quichotte*, 43 ('elle s'écouterait cependant fort bien après la fameuse chanson bacchique de *l'Enlèvement au Sérail*, à laquelle elle s'apparente par son svelte matérialisme').

61 Peter Kaminsky: 'Vocal music and the lures of exoticism and irony', in Deborah Mawer (ed.), *The Cambridge Companion to Ravel* (Cambridge, 2000), 162–87: 185.

62 For more on Ravel's Spanishness, see chs. 2, 4, 6 and 9, in Mawer (ed.): *The Cambridge Companion to Ravel*. Ibert too was inspired by Cervantes's novel and extracted some *Chansons*

Although there was little further potential in simple ('exterior') evocation, this facet, together with the earlier primitivist celebrations of Picasso, Léger, Apollinaire, Cendrars, Stravinsky, Milhaud and so on, nonetheless paved the way for non-Western enquiries of a more sophisticated anthropological and artistic ('interior') nature, as tended to be embedded in the later music of Messiaen and Jolivet.

After the neoclassicism and orientalism discussed above, the main developing characteristic of music through the 1930s is that of spiritual 'otherness', an aspect which increasingly acknowledges the existence of Halbreich's smouldering volcano. (On the larger scale, this trend is part of what Glenn Watkins describes as a 'postwar psychology' following the First World War, with a limited presence even in the 1920s).[63] Such 'otherness' implies a need to find sanctuary both within and beyond the individual – an other-worldliness which rarely constitutes a form of escapism, but rather involves a positive recognition and expression of humanity, including man's relation with God or the forces of the cosmos ('the revived sense of awe').[64] As Roussel put it: 'The worship of spiritual values is at the foundation of all society which claims to be civilized'.[65] Although this facet of otherness is the most dynamic, there is again potential overlap with the neoclassical and oriental/exotic facets – the latter may offer a partial foundation for some of the non-Western spiritual enquiries, and particular works may exhibit characteristics of more than one facet. Such spirituality embraces a broad spectrum of music ranging from the overtly Christian (including liturgical and theological works), to the more loosely biblical; and from the non-Western – often pantheistic, mystical and magical – through to that which affirms matters of individual conscience and morality. In fact, much of this music upholds a paradox, being at once intensely personal yet also universal.

In the *tour de force* of *Christophe Colomb* (1928), Claudel and Milhaud were considered to have made Columbus into a mythical hero, reuniting the two halves of humanity through Christianity. (The 1930 Berlin premiere itself, for which honour two German companies competed, might have seemed to mark a new warmth and cooperation between nations, but one which, alas, was not set to last.) Their collaboration continued in *L'annonce faite à Marie*: 'Paul Claudel's mystical lyricism suited his [Milhaud's] fundamentally religious temperament ... A subtle and profound impression of compassion, faith, love and sorrow.'[66] At the same time, Stravinsky's *Symphony of Psalms* (1930) was explicitly inscribed to the glory of God, while his later melodrama after Gide, *Perséphone* (1933–34), was viewed as 'this *Mystery*, where the action, as if static, conserves a religious

---

de Don Quichotte from his film score of 1932 which led to his ballet, *Le Chevalier errant* ('épopée chorégraphique', 1935–36).

63 Glenn Watkins: *Pyramids at the Louvre* (Cambridge, Mass., 1994), 355. Watkins offers a most useful discussion of twentieth-century music within its cultural context. For more detail on spirituality in the 1930s, see Fulcher who argues that 'French fascism promoted the sacred and subjective' ('Musical style, meaning and politics', 443), though this should not lead one to a false deduction that spiritual music, whether symphonic or not, was therefore necessarily tainted by right-wing associations.

64 Stephen Walsh: *The Music of Stravinsky* (Oxford, 1988, pb. 1993), 135.

65 Roussel quoted in Myers: *Modern French Music* ('Le culte des valeurs spirituelles est à la basse de toute société qui se prétend civilisée').

66 Henry Prunières: review of *L'annonce faite à Marie*, *RM*, 143 (Feb. 1934), 165–6: 165 ('Le lyricisme de Paul Claudel convient à son tempérament foncièrement religieux ... Impression subtile et profonde de pitié, de foi, d'amour, de douleur').

and ritual character'. In the words of Stephen Walsh, such works reflect 'the permeation of his essentially devout nature by the atmosphere of intellectual and spiritual renewal which was gaining intensity in France at that time.'[67] Meanwhile, the lesser-known Jewish composer Daniel Lazarus composed his biblically inspired *Symphonie avec hymne*, given in 1934: a large-scale set of five tableaux following the history and sufferings of the Jewish people; and from a Catholic perspective, Migot's *Psaume XIX* (composed in 1925) and Roget's *Prière* were presented together in a concert at the Oratoire du Louvre in December 1936. Migot's *Le sermon sur la montagne* composed in 1936, for five solo voices, chorus, string orchestra and organ, also exemplifies this trend.

Death and requiem were topical – in music and reality, as in the Honegger/Claudel, *La danse des morts* on the biblical prophecies of Ezekiel, and Ropartz's *Requiem*. This theme found a particular expression with the quincentenary of the death of Joan of Arc: her inner voice of conscience and saintly sacrifice inspired Paray's *Messe de Jeanne d'Arc*, given in Rouen in 1931, together with two works performed by the Orchestre Symphonique de Paris: Rosenthal's suite in five tableaux, *Jeanne d'Arc*, performed in 1936, and Rivier's *Paysage pour une Jeanne d'Arc à Domrémy*, given in 1937. The best-known and arguably finest representation is the Honegger/Claudel dramatic oratorio, *Jeanne d'Arc au bûcher*, which received its French premiere at Orléans in May 1939. *Jeanne* was discussed in detail by Dumesnil who summarized it as 'at once profound, simple, humane and grandiose'.[68]

La Jeune France, with its motto of 'sincerity, generosity, artistic conscience' (and a partial former existence as La Spirale), may be viewed as a figurehead for French spirituality in the 1930s. Essentially, within a nationalist context and supported by the right-wing press, La Jeune France – Olivier Messiaen (1908–92), André Jolivet (1905–74), Daniel-Lesur (1908–2002) and Yves Baudrier (1906–88) – constituted a reaction to Les Six, as well as to over-rigorous Second Viennese serialism. In fact, the groups loosely complement each other, encompassing elements of opposition (expressive versus unemotional; serious versus witty) and similarity (both were somewhat contrived short-term groupings, but have enjoyed longer-term, symbolic significance as embodiments of musical 'Frenchness'). But whilst men of letters such as Paul Valéry, François Mauriac and Georges Duhamel supported La Jeune France, they would never have sanctioned the perceived frivolity of Les Six. Nonetheless, it pays to avoid over-simplification: after all, Honegger supported La Jeune France and Tailleferre's *Ballade* was included in its first concert on 3 June 1936.

The main programme included Messiaen's *Hymne au Saint Sacrement* and *Les offrandes oubliées*, together with the premiere of Jolivet's percussive *Danse incantatoire* which revealed '[rhythmic] tendencies which find in the orchestra their maximum range and intensity'. The reviewer, Demarquez, also noted common ground with Varèse and Villa-Lobos in Jolivet's emphases on nuance, attack and extra-musical means.[69]

67 Henry Prunières: review of '*Perséphone* d'Igor Stravinsky aux Ballets de Mme Ida Rubinstein', *RM*, 146 (May 1934), 380–82: 380 ('ce *Mystère* où l'action, comme immobile, conserve un caractère religieux et rituel'); Stephen Walsh: *The Music of Stravinsky*, 135.

68 Dumesnil: *La Musique*, 169–71: 169 ('à la fois profonde, simple, humaine et grandiose'). Although *Jeanne d'Arc au bûcher* was declared a masterpiece by representatives of the far right-wing press (amongst others), this should not implicitly compromise the work's stature; see Fulcher: 'Musical style, meaning and politics', 450.

69 Suzanne Demarquez: 'Premier concert de "Jeune France"', *RM*, 167 (July–Aug. 1936), 49–50:

Meanwhile, the works of Baudrier, a late starter then plagued by illness, showed 'beaucoup de jeunesse' and those of the Schola Cantorum teacher Daniel-Lesur were rather conventional; unlike their more successful counterparts, they felt ideologically that any use of theoretical systems would compromise a rehumanizing of music with the cosmos.[70] A subsequent review by Demarquez commented on the group's achievements of the first two years, including the founding of a society of friends. Although her praise was still tempered, she observed particularly that her prediction for 'The future, *chez* André Jolivet, has in large part been realized and the composer resolutely follows the path that he originally marked out for himself';[71] Messiaen's *Poèmes pour Mi* were also performed at this concert.

Messiaen was undoubtedly the musician with the greatest potential to emerge in the 1930s, his early music constituting a celebration of Catholicism and including a detailed exploration of theological symbolism. Beyond his contemplation of the sacraments, his approach has also been seen as embracing a broader mysticism – somewhat as for Jolivet – in the dictionary sense of 'a system of contemplative prayer and spirituality aimed at achieving direct intuitive experience of the divine'.[72] In 1931, Messiaen's stature and spiritual commitment were demonstrated in his appointment as organist at La Trinité – a post he would hold for an extraordinary sixty years. As early as 1946, Dumesnil was slightly troubled by the composer's adherence to musical systems and by what he regarded as his undiscriminating use of his own texts, but his discussion of 'le cas Messiaen' already acknowledged that Messiaen's qualities had put him in a league of his own.[73]

Les offrandes oubliées (The Forgotten Offerings, 1930) is a short orchestral piece of less than twelve minutes' duration, first performed in February 1931 by the Orchestre Straram (3.3.3.3; 4.3.3.1; timpani, percussion and strings). It makes an apt initial focus since it already exhibits Messiaenic hallmarks: 'the savage, disjunct, surrealistic contrasts typical of Messiaen's later and larger works are unleashed in *Les offrandes oubliées* for the first time at full force' and contribute to a poetic 'utterance of startling spiritual density'.[74] Such spirituality was well illuminated by Dumesnil who perceived that 'Messiaen ... is endowed with a deep sense of the inner life; he is thirsty for the divine', and thus

50 ('Tendances qui trouvent dans l'orchestre leur maximum d'épanouissement et d'intensité'), with reference to Fred Goldbeck's discerning discussion of Jolivet's rhythmic tendencies: *RM*, 162 (Jan. 1936). We may also relate Jolivet's and Varèse's use of sound-masses.

70 See Myers: *Modern French Music*, 137; apart from entries in *The New Grove*, the most comprehensive text is Serge Gut: *Le Groupe Jeune France* (Paris, 1977, repr. 1984), though even this says little about the group's identity after its inaugural concert. Recently, this gap within the literature has been bridged by Nigel Simeone. See, for instance, 'Group identities: La Spirale and La Jeune France', *Musical Times* (Autumn 2002), 10–36.

71 Suzanne Demarquez: 'Jeune France 1938', *RM*, 184 (June 1938), 382–3: 383 ('L'avenir, chez André Jolivet, est en grande partie réalisé et le compositeur suit résolument la voie qu'il s'est originairement tracée'); Demarquez went on to write a classic biography: *André Jolivet* (Paris, 1958).

72 Patrick Hanks (ed.): *Collins Dictionary of the English Language* (London, 1985): 'mysticism', 974.

73 Dumesnil: *La Musique*, 206–7.

74 Malcolm Hayes: 'Instrumental and choral works to 1948', in Peter Hill (ed.): *The Messiaen Companion* (London, 1995), 157–200: 159.

his meditative score is characterized by 'a sorrowful gravity on the mystery of the Eucharist'.[75]

The first stanza of Messiaen's prefatory religious text focuses on the sorrowful scene of the Cross, concluding: 'You love us, sweet Jesus, we had forgotten that'; the second deals with the pain of sin as purgatory; and the third on the redemptive power of Communion, with the invocation of Love, Pity and charity – a trinity of divine images personified. This tripartite nature is mirrored in the three-part structure of Messiaen's musical commentary – a *transposition*, though beyond this, a 'symphonic meditation' suggests freedom for rhapsodic exploration of musical spirituality. Bars 1–13, extremely slow and sad, present the image of the Cross with constantly changing quaver metre (grouped in twos and threes), troubled and sinuous melodic lines. By stark contrast, the substantial core of the ternary design is 'fast, ferocious, desperate, breathless' (bars 14–106); a brief 'Modéré' (bars 107–10) then links to a transformed 'return' (bars 111–37), now compassionate and tender, presented in 4/4 metre with predominantly homophonic texture.

Messiaen's irregular phrases operate within a surprisingly focused modality – the main melodic collection is octatonic: B, C, D, D♯, F, F♯, G♯, A (Messiaen's second mode),[76] heard over a tonic pedal on E (Example 9.6); a subsidiary collection then utilizes a pattern of two semitones plus a tone (his third mode). Melodically, the arching contour on muted strings features semitonal movement and anguished augmented seconds, stylized by small-scale symmetries: B–C–B, F–G♯–F (see brackets in Example 9.6), and contrary motion. Harmonically, the centre on E – essentially 'minor' – is reinforced by triads built on the flattened seventh, D major: a quasi-dominant, but with less tonal 'pull' – a common characteristic of modal writing. While the sonorities are only mildly dissonant, profound sorrow is conveyed by the unbearably slow tempo. Texturally, the intervallic openness of unisons and octaves, which is spiritually fitting rather like the monody of plainsong, looks ahead to the *Quatuor pour la fin du Temps*. The melodically derived 'chorus' of bars 10–13 ('You love us ...) then links to the 'Vif', though the second musical occurrence (bars 107–10) precedes, proportionally speaking, the final textual repetition.

'Vif' (bars 14–106) commences with a shocking 'fanfare' which is almost a physical body-blow. It is overtly dissonant, though still on a quasi-dominant chord: B, F, A, D♯, E. Textual 'breathlessness' receives literal representation in the form of reiterated dotted rhythms, glissandos and fevered semiquaver/triplet diminutions. Relentless rhythm proceeds within fluctuating metre (reminiscent of Stravinsky's *The Rite of Spring*); chromaticism and harmonic movement are heightened. A remote E flat section is reached, while the tempo exhibits its own instability, occasionally pulling back to exaggerate a large-scale, inexorable *accelerando*. Registrally, the music is expanded from deep bass-notes through to upper descant voices: literally stretched and tortured on a rack. Its climactic peak (bars 93–106) suggests imminent explosion: frenetic movement continues at increasingly violent dynamic, but such momentum is undirected, with obsessive motivic

75 Dumesnil: *La Musique*, 206 ('il est doué de sens profond de la vie intérieure; il est assoiffé du divin'; 'une gravité douloureuse sur le mystère de l'Eucharistie').

76 Messiaen described his modes of limited transposition and principles of additive rhythm in the preface to *La nativité du Seigneur* (Paris, 1936). It was also about this time that he was influenced by the Indian rhythmic *deçî-talas* tabulated in Sharngaveda's treatise *Samgîta-ratnâkara*: see the appendix listing in Robert Sherlaw-Johnson: *Messiaen* (London, 2/1989).

Example 9.6 Olivier Messiaen, *Les offrandes oubliées* (bars 1–5, piano reduction)

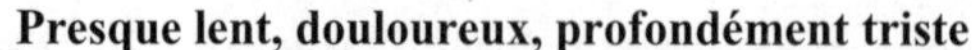

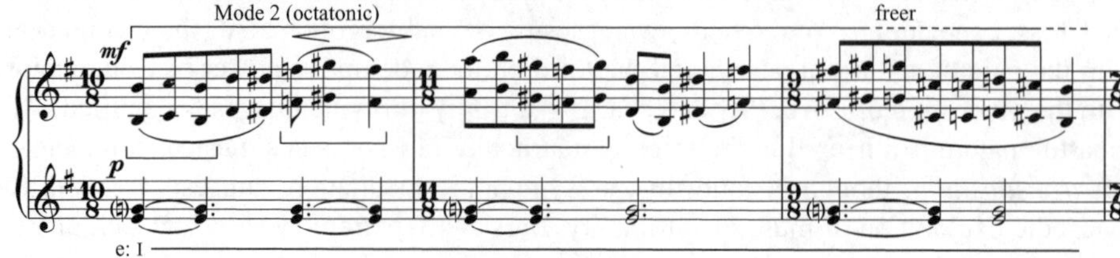

repetitions – some against the grain of the metre – which result in stasis and impotence. Messiaen makes impressive use of his instrumentation, with forceful whoopings, surges, cymbal clashes and triangle tremolos, in what is after all his first published orchestral score.

As a merciful act, the chorus-like link (with hints of additive rhythm) brings deliverance. This phrase on melancholic basses is slightly reminiscent of the connective material in the finale of Beethoven's Ninth Symphony; spiritually, too, such associations are not inappropriate. The linear material of the ensuing, peaceful and spacious 'Lent' is intervallically derived, though now controlled within the metrical/chordal framework of a hymn in the tonic major: 'the traditionally "heavenly" key of E major'.[77] Its octatonic-type colouring and strong melodic emphasis on C♯ in muted first violins nonetheless creates a distinct ambiguity with the relative minor. Despite the metrical framework, melodic repetitions against such a slow pulse do suggest a hypnotic, ritualistic meditation: time is endless, or eternal. Pitch reorderings and reversions hint at the future importance of symmetry in Messiaen's writing, together with more flexible motivic expansion and contraction. A certain serenity has been achieved through a process of purging: the heavy bass has disappeared; ethereal connotations accompany musical word-painting which extends heavenwards, before the image fades exquisitely to ***ppp***.

A second portrait, '"true" in sentiment, and typical of my manner',[78] is the ritualistic celebration, *Poèmes pour Mi* (1936), dedicated to Messiaen's first wife, Claire Delbos.

---

77 Wilfrid Mellers: 'Mysticism and theology', in Hill (ed.): *The Messiaen Companion*, 220–33: 225.

78 Olivier Messiaen: *Technique de mon langage musical*, 2 vols (Paris, 1944), trans. John Satterfield, *The Technique of my Musical Language* (Paris, 1956), vol. 1, 71.

This song cycle, 'a work primarily concerned with the sacramental and spiritual aspects of marriage',[79] comprises nine poems for soprano and piano, or orchestra, and was first performed by Marcelle Bunlet and Messiaen in April 1937. It is often associated with *Chants de terre et de ciel* (1938): a song cycle on parenthood following the birth of Messiaen's son Pascal.

The opening 'Action de grâces' (Thanksgiving) contrasts its materials as a kind of dialogue (Example 9.7). A 'chromatic' chordal introduction, with pitch symmetry and additive rhythm demarcated by barlines, contrasts with the rhythmically free, yet melodically restricted, vocal recitative extolling nature. Such musical means mirror spiritual dualities concerning heaven/earth and the two loved ones, now united in marriage. (The idea of recitation also links to Jolivet's music.) We might perceive the bell-like chords as chromatic bitonality on initial triads of D♭ and A; in fact Messiaen has reached these sonorities via his modes of limited transposition. The upper stave (bars 1–2) employs mode 3, the lower stave mode 2 (octatonic), while the latter part of bar 2 uses one of his fourth modes, later renamed mode 6: C, D, E, F, F♯, G♯, A♯, B. As before, it is hard not to associate these upper-register descending triads, played by silvery strings and woodwind, with the image of the 'sky' (heavens). For its part, the voice intones quasi-ecclesiatically on F♯ with occasional supporting neighbour-notes, E and F (still mode 6). In further literal word-painting, the pitches are transformed melismatically with the word 'transforms', instigated by the 'light' (bars 4–5).

Further dialogues ensue: some quite extensive, others bringing percussive interjection or overlap between voice and accompaniment. Melismatic writing emphasizes special text such as the moment of conjoinment: 'unie' (bars 13–15), the beautiful portrayal of 'lumière' (bars 28–9), so extended immediately after the short articulations of 'Truth',

Example 9.7 Olivier Messiaen, *Poèmes pour Mi*, I, 'Action de grâces' (bars 1–4)

Très modéré
CHANT
PIANO
Mode 3
Mode 2
Mode 6
Mode 6
Le ciel, Et l'eau qui suit les va - ria - tions des nu - a - ges, Et la ter - re,

79 Johnson: *Messiaen*, 10.

'Spirit' and 'grace'. Sequences of instrumental 'chromatic' contrary motion alternate with three marked solo phrases (bars 33–9). Responsorial in style, these lead to the most elaborate melisma on 'étoiles' (bars 41–5), fully supported by the accompaniment and heightened by additive rhythm. This sumptuous climax which descends, in an ecstatic surge, from the soprano's powerful upper register (top B♭) to a low C♯ has a distinctly Wagnerian air, especially reminiscent of *Tristan und Isolde*.[80]

By contrast, the intimate simplicity of the intoning of 'Mon Dieu' on A♯ leads to a concluding section, in the octatonic mode on F sharp, which presents a continuous, mechanical background of semiquavers for the ultimate, repeated melismas on 'Alleluia' – a Christian mantra (Example 9.8). The score indicates that these are to be presented 'with a serene joy': they are heightened, trance-like reflections on the mystic power of the divine, and their sonorous treatment bears some affinity with early Schoenberg. In the losing of the self – here a female 'self' – to 'jouissance', as a state of bliss and ecstasy not divorced from physical pleasure, we may also make more controversial association with feminist musical aesthetics.[81] Essentially, both Messiaen (Jolivet, Boulez) and certain feminist writers emphasize the virtues of circularity, non-progression and stasis – in short, alternative, non-teleological modes of thinking and being in time and space. As at the end

Example 9.8 Olivier Messiaen, *Poèmes pour Mi*, I, 'Action de grâces' (bars 48–9)

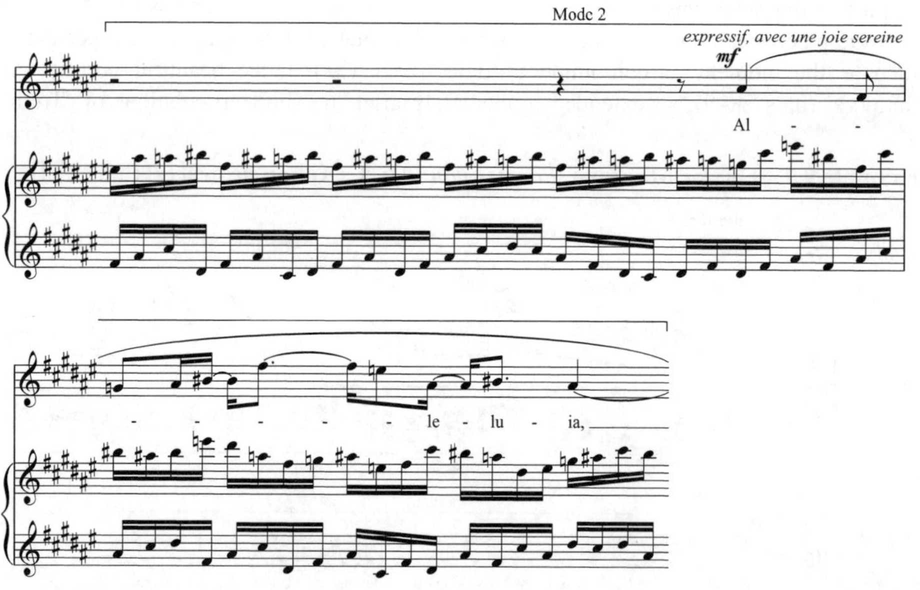

80 For more on Wagner and Tristan in Messiaen, see Paul Griffiths: 'The Tristan trilogy', in *Messiaen and the Music of Time* (London, 1985), 124–42.

81 See Renée Cox: 'Recovering *Jouissance*: an introduction to feminist musical aesthetics', in Karin Pendle (ed.): *Women and Music: A History* (Bloomington, Ind., 1991), 331–40; the idea is also at least implicitly related to Messiaen by Mellers, who prefaces his 'Mysticism and theology' with a quotation from Thomas Aquinas's *Summa Theologiae*: 'the divine essence is simply bliss itself'. Mellers also acknowledges the importance to Messiaen of matrimony, matriarchy, Mother Earth (nature) and other mythical goddesses.

of *Les offrandes oubliées*, earthly moorings are relinquished as the music reaches celestial heights, with the voice held intensely on an upper A♯.

Jolivet's music complements Messiaen's by revealing a rather different approach to spirituality; typically, he pursues a more elusive (less Christian) mysticism, catalysed by magical incantation and ritual. Music is a vehicle for intuitive communion with – or experiencing of – cosmic forces and a supreme being, rather than primarily an art for the concert hall. The musician may also act as an interpreter of fundamental magical impulses. As increasingly became the case for Messiaen, Jolivet's inspiration emanated broadly from non-Western cultures, in particular Polynesia, the Far East, India and Africa, and from a connected belief in the power of nature and the 'primitive'. Beyond any specific or personal impetus, 'he has tried', claimed Rollo Myers, 'to create a universal language [through cultural cross-fertilization.]'.[82] Similarly, although the 'primitive' and primordial might suggest the 'ancient', Jolivet's idealized conception conflates past and present.

Early success came in 1935 with *Mana*: a work acknowledged in the 'barometer journal', *La Revue musicale*, and for which Messiaen enthusiastically provided the preface.[83] These piano pieces explore metaphysically man's association with the primitive power, or 'life-force', of fetish objects (within Polynesian/Melanesian culture) and were stimulated by presents from Varèse, including 'L'oiseau' with its obvious Messiaenic links 'La Princesse de Bali' and 'La vache', sacred to Hinduism and other religions.[84]

Cinq incantations, for solo flute (1936; premiered 1938) fuses the universal and the autobiographical (as did *Poèmes pour Mi* discussed earlier). The fifth piece relates to the death of Jolivet's mother and the second to the recent birth of his child.[85] Also as with Messiaen, music and text are specially related, with extended titles providing a spiritual agenda: 'To welcome the intermediaries – and that the meeting should be peaceful'; 'That the child which will be born should be a son'; 'That it should be a rich harvest which will spring from the furrows that the labourer marks out'; 'For a serene communion of the being with the world'; and 'At the funeral rites of the chief – to obtain protection for his soul'. Christian allusion is at least implicit in the second and fourth pieces; 'serene communion' also suggests common ground with Messiaen just as the celebration of the earth's fecundity suggests a spiritual kinship with Stravinsky's *The Rite of Spring*. 'Incantation' denotes a ritualized recitation of magical text, as in the creation of a spell, but on another level the work exists within a rich French tradition of solo flute-writing stretching from Debussy's *Syrinx* (1910), to Honegger's *Danse de la chèvre* (1921) and Varèse's *Densité 21.5* of the same year, 1936.

Beautifully intricate writing features reiterated pitches (as in *Poèmes pour Mi*) decorated by multiple grace-notes, quintuplet/sextuplet groupings and registral transfer.

82 Myers: *Modern French Music*, 141. As already mentioned, such primitivist enquiry is part of a wider cult, see for instance, Marianna Torgovnick: *Gone Primitive: Savage Intellects, Modern Lives* (Chicago, 1990).

83 Frederik Goldbeck: 'André Jolivet: *Mana* (Spirale)', *RM*, 162 (Jan. 1936), 54–5.

84 Hilda Jolivet: *Avec ... André Jolivet* (Paris, 1978), 125–6.

85 Ibid., 132. For an extended reading of *Cinq incantations* (notwithstanding some superficial errors), see Katherine Kemler: 'Is there magic in Jolivet's music?', *Music Review*, 44/2 (May 1983), 121–35: 125–34. For a more recent, detailed treatment of this work and others within their context, see Bridget Conrad: 'The Sources of Jolivet's musical language and his relationships with Varèse and Messiaen' (Ph.D. diss., City University of New York, 1994).

The fifth piece, especially, has a hypnotic preoccupation with G♯ which borders on the obsessive. The flute speaks eloquently and skilfully, utilizing flutter-tonguing, trills, portamentos and occasional non-vibrato. Ironically, to create an illusion of improvisation, score markings are meticulous: expressive directions, phrasing, tempos, dynamic gradations, accentuations and articulatory commas. Nonetheless, some matters are left to the performer's interpretation, for instance in the third piece where the player is instructed to 'Repeat this extended bar 4 times in succession, varying the nuance each time'. Jolivet employs a profusion of rhythmic cells (but with restricted pitch components – once more, as in Messiaen's *Poèmes*) often dispensing with barlines: a notation which contributes to the air of spontaneity. Mysticism and introspection are implicit in directions such as the 'très intérieur' at the head of the fourth piece.

Jolivet's skill lies in incorporating his extra-musical inspiration within the musical fabric: thus the first piece is constructed as a dialogue between mortal and immortal forces, marked ceremonially 'Pompeux', with 'voices' differentiated across parameters of pitch, register, metre, rhythm and timbre (Example 9.9).

After an initial high call to invoke and welcome the 'intermediaries' (between man and nature?), voice 1 (earthly) occupies the flute's lower register in 3/4 metre. Its pitch identity is essentially diatonic: D, C, supported by balancing semitonal neighbour-notes, E♭ and B – all played *legato*. The upper voice 2 (supernatural) enters in bar 5 with a less stable chromatic identity: C♯, G, G♯, A, A♭, G, B♭, A, A♭, presented in 9/8 as mysterious flutter-tonguing: 'sifflant' – 'whistling'. This second voice powerfully supplies the central, missing ingredient from the pitch-span of the first: C♯. In fact, the pitches of the voices are mutually exclusive: the earthly and god-like exist on different planes and communicate in different tongues.

As the encounter continues, the lower voice maintains its four-pitch cell, interpolating tentative comment between the extended arching contours of the upper voice which accrues the remaining chromatic pitches: F♯ (bar 7), F and E (bar 8). The process of complementation is now complete and a state of total chromaticism results. Interestingly,

Example 9.9 André Jolivet, *Cinq incantations*, I, 'Pour accueillir les négociateurs – et que l'entrevue soit pacifique' (bars 1–6)

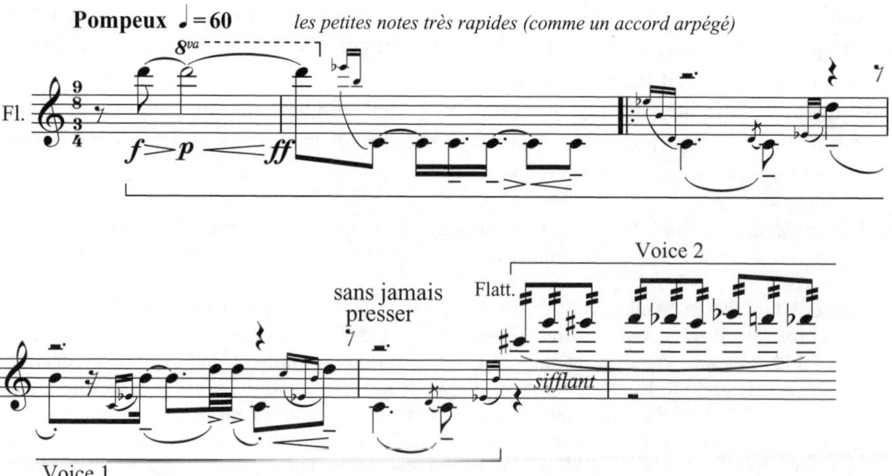

following the meeting, some understanding has been gained: in its balancing postlude the earthly voice acquires new confidence with its own arching phrase (bars 13–17). Its forceful peak (high D) is achieved via previously 'foreign' chromatic pitches and the final repose (low D) is approached via a prominent F♯, 'sans vibrer' (bar 16). So the exchange with the intermediaries seems to have been successful.

Also meriting close attention is Jolivet's highly successful *Cinq danses rituelles* of 1939, originally for piano.[86] Its titles again convey a spiritual programme: 'Initiation dance', 'Hero's dance', 'Nuptial', 'Abduction' and 'Funerary' dances. Jolivet once more favours sets of five (and cycle): *Cinq incantations*, *Cinq poèmes intimes*, a five-note cell in the 'Danse initiatique' – with symbolic resonances of the Indian god Shiva or indeed Pythagoras (via Varèse) – rather than sets of three, with its Christian, trinitarian associations. Through the primordial dance metaphor, Jolivet spans human/mythical experience from birth to death (and resurrection). Although his music is often nonspecifically primitivist, Jolivet noted a fortuitous affinity between his 'Hero's dance' and a Peruvian rhythm.[87] Closer to home, we may compare his 'Nuptial dance' with Messiaen's *Poèmes pour Mi*; equally, regarding dances of initiation, abduction and death (sacrifice), association with Stravinsky's *The Rite of Spring* is unavoidable. The important notion is that of suggestion – ambiguity, imagination and mystery.

Regarding Jolivet's *musical* language here, Arthur Hoérée, with reference to the composer's essay in *Contrepoints*, explained how 'the tonal system is enlarged through the incorporation of distant harmonics and putative subharmonics ... In order to intensify his music he made use of "doubled basses", on which complementary harmonic edifices were built.'[88] Having been trained in Schoenbergian compositional techniques via Varèse (and Paul Le Flem), Jolivet employed fully chromatic writing and serial principles to manipulate motivic cells. He tended not, however, to employ both notions together, and his processes still create pitch emphases and tonal/modal association. As with Messiaen, Jolivet's compositional theories may usefully be compared with analytical approaches to his music to see how well the two mesh, or indeed what tensions result.

His final 'Danse funéraire' proceeds slowly in 5/4 metre within an overall modality on B♭, intensified by chromatic appoggiaturas: F♯–F; B–B♭ (Example 9.10). In terms of compositional theory, we might argue a case for 'doubled basses' on B♭ and B: Jolivet directs half of the cellos to tune the C-string down to B♭ and half of the basses (five-string) to tune down to B♮. The important pitch of G – also an incantatory tone in the 'Danse nuptiale' and a bass feature of the 'Danse du rapt' – is however still present, in association with minor and major third: B♭/B, thus creating a tonal ambiguity between two centres a third apart. Over this anguished background is heard a mournful, sighing monody played by the prominent flute in G, in unison with bassoons and violas. Further doubling by cor anglais, clarinet, bassoons, horns and lower strings occurs in its final ritual statement (bars 63–7), marked 'à peine plus fort, mais très intense d'expression'. (This musico-emotional

86 As with the Messiaen works selected (and Jolivet's own *Cosmogonie*, 1938), *Cinq danses rituelles* exists in both piano and orchestral versions, thus aiding analytical study. The work had its first public performance in 1942, while the orchestral premiere was given in 1944.

87 Jolivet: Avec ... *André Jolivet*, 142.

88 André Hoérée: 'Andre Jolivet', *The New Grove*, vol. 9, 686–9: 687; the source is André Jolivet: 'Réponse à une enquête: André Jolivet, ou la magie expérimentale', *Contrepoints*, 1 (Jan. 1946), 33–7.

intensification through timbral diversity and literal amplification represents another meeting point with Messiaen.) As elsewhere, the central core of this movement is the most complex, fantastical portion, here alluding to and developing the principal melodic material. Towards the close of Jolivet's dance of death, tonal ambiguity reduces in favour of B♭ (tonic pedal: bars 63–76), though fittingly, beneath the final open-fifth sonority (B♭/F), Jolivet places a rogue bass G♭ – the melodic F♯ in disguise.

Example 9.10 André Jolivet, *Cinq danses rituelles* (piano version), V, 'Danse funéraire' (bars 1–4)

Although this 'Danse funéraire' might be seen as denoting the death of a young girl as in *The Rite of Spring*,[89] it could also be viewed on a larger scale, marking the end of Jolivet's early audacious period and indeed that of La Jeune France (with the conscription of its members). In the company of various other funerary monuments of the late 1930s it is also somehow symbolic of the death of the decade itself and of the Third Republic.

In conclusion, this survey of French music in the 1930s has sought to convey, after Martin Cooper, the sense on the one hand of 'tradition': neoclassicism and orientalism, and on the other, of relative 'innovation': spirituality and humanism. This latter development suggests a gradual awareness of the impingement of dark, external forces that fuelled Halbreich's volcano and a parallel strengthening of principles of artistic and human freedom. With the exceptions of the overtly political Fédération Musicale Populaire and the inevitable economic factors embedded at some level in the concert crisis, the precise extent of correlation between politics and music in the 1930s was much dependent on the varying political, moral and religious beliefs of individual composers. Politics aside, it is hopefully also apparent that this diverse decade, albeit to some extent transitional, was more than merely 'a kind of interregnum, an uneasy lull'.[90] In short, it housed some very powerful music.

In respect of La Jeune France, while 'le cas Messiaen' has been well made in a wealth of scholarly literature, 'le cas Jolivet' undoubtedly merits further analytical, critical and aesthetic investigation: he was after all regarded as 'one of France's most distinguished

89 With reference to *Danses rituelles*, Jolivet wrote of his attraction to so-called 'primitive' societies, 'where the human soul has kept its virginity intact'. Hilda Jolivet: *Avec … André Jolivet*, 142 ('chez lesquels l'âme humaine a gardé toute sa virginité').

90 Myers: *Modern French Music*, 147.

Plate 9.2 The first orchestra of Ondes Martenots, 1937.

composers'.[91] Jolivet's extra-musical concern with a universal spirituality, anti-materialism, primitivism, magic and the occult (these latter aspects acquiring a certain popular currency today) may yet fulfil a need within our unsustainably materialistic twenty-first century which could afford his music a higher profile, especially outside France. With regard to contemporary sources, although Dumesnil rather downplays Messiaen's significance and overplays others, his account is nonetheless refreshing and enlightening – especially on the concert crisis. Meanwhile, the coverage of *La Revue musicale* constitutes a well-balanced and accurate indicator of activity.

The violent volcanic eruption of the Second World War left French music in a temporary state of hiatus,[92] and tragically deprived it of many more of its key players who had not already emigrated: Romain Rolland, Louis Laloy, Pierre Lalo, Paul Landormy and Henry Prunières (terminal illness). If the continuing high stature of Messiaen after the war is taken for granted, the greatest original scope arguably lay in those areas which served primarily to contextualize the agenda for the 1930s: first, the popular domain including the chanson and, second, the radical, emerging domain of 'musique et électricité', to be dominated for many years by the overarching figure of Pierre Boulez.

91 Ibid., 137.

92 This is not to underestimate the impressive wartime achievements of Ibert's String Quartet (1937–42) and Messiaen's profoundly spiritual, apocalyptic *Quatuor pour la fin du Temps* (1940) for violin, clarinet, cello and piano, first performed in January 1941 at the prisoner-of-war camp Stalag VIIIA, Görlitz, Silesia.

Suggested Further Reading

Jonathan Bellman (ed.): *The Exotic in Western Music* (Boston, Mass.: Northeastern University Press, 1998).

Ian Darbyshire: 'Messiaen and the representation of the theological illusion of time', in Siglind Bruhn (ed.), *Messiaen's Language of Mystical Love* (New York: Garland, 1998) 33–51.

Robert Follet: *Albert Roussel: A Bio-Bibliography* (New York: Greenwood Press, 1988).

Jane F. Fulcher: 'The composer as intellectual: ideological inscriptions in French interwar neoclassicism', *Journal of Musicology*, 17/2 (Spring 1999), 197–231.

Joscelyn Godwin: *Music, Mysticism and Magic: A Sourcebook* (New York: Arkana, 1987).

— *Music and the Occult: French Musical Philosophies, 1750–1950* (Rochester, NY: University of Rochester Press, 1995).

Paul Griffiths: 'Olivier Messiaen', in Stanley Sadie (ed.), *The New Grove Dictionary of Music and Musicians*, 29 vols (London: Macmillan, 2/2001), vol. 16, 491–504.

Peter Hawkins: *Chanson: The French Singer-Songwriter from Aristide Bruant to the Present Day* (Aldershot: Ashgate, 2000).

Julian T. Jackson: *Politics of Depression in France, 1932–36* (Cambridge: Cambridge University Press, 1985).

— *The Popular Front in France: Defending Democracy 1934–38* (Cambridge: Cambridge University Press, 1988).

Odile Jaubourg and Anne-Hélène Rigogne: *André Jolivet (1905–1974): Un musicien humaniste* (Amiens, Bibliothèque municipale, 1995).

Christine Jolivet-Erlih (ed.): *Edgard Varèse, André Jolivet, Correspondance 1931–1965* (Geneva: Éditions Contrechamps, 2002).

Lucie Kayas and Laetitia Chassain-Dolliou (eds): *André Jolivet: Portraits* (Arles: Actes sud, 1994).

Barbara Kelly: 'André Jolivet', *The New Grove Dictionary of Music and Musicians*, 29 vols (London: Macmillan, 2/2001), vol. 13, 174–7.

Nicole Labelle: 'Albert Roussel', *The New Grove Dictionary of Music and Musicians*, 29 vols (London: Macmillan, 2/2001), vol. 21, 806–10.

Alexandra Laederich: 'Jacques Ibert', *The New Grove Dictionary of Music and Musicians*, 29 vols (London: Macmillan, 2/2001), vol. 12, 42–4.

Cécile Meadel: *Histoire de la radio des années trente* (Paris: Anthropos, 1994).

Gérard Moindrot: *Approches symboliques de la musique d'André Jolivet: Musique et expression du sacré* (Paris: L'Harmattan, 1999).

Pascal Ory: *La Belle Illusion: Culture et politique sous le signe du Front populaire* (Paris: Plon, 1994).

Anthony Pople: 'Messiaen's musical language: an introduction', in Peter Hill (ed.), *The Messiaen Companion* (London: Faber, 1995), 15–50.

— *Messiaen: Quatuor pour la fin du Temps* (Cambridge: Cambridge University Press, 1998).

Charles Rearick: *The French in Love and War: Popular Culture in the Era of the World Wars* (New Haven: Yale University Press, 1997).

Nigel Simeone: 'Music at the 1937 Paris Exposition: the science of enchantment', *Musical Times* (Spring 2002), 9–17.

— 'Group identities: La Spirale and La Jeune France', *Musical Times* (Autumn 2002), 10–36.

— and Peter Hill: *Messiaen* (New Haven: Yale University Press, 2005).

Chapter 10

French Music and the Second World War

Caroline Potter

'A country at war should always be mindful of the image it presents to other countries ... Evidently, no intellectual achievement is the equal of a battle won. But nevertheless, it is good and indeed necessary that Europe should be aware that French culture has lost none of its quality.'[1] These words, from the editorial of the weekly newspaper *Candide*, dated 17 January 1940, summarize the aims of the Parisian musical establishment during the Second World War. Whatever the circumstances, appearances must be kept up and *la gloire française* projected to the outside world.

However, the editor of *Candide* is insinuating that one might assume that French culture was going through a difficult period because of wartime pressures. It surely goes without saying that every aspect of French life was affected by the outbreak of war and by the division of the country into occupied and non-occupied territories from August 1940. When assessing the musical life of the period, it is important to recognize stresses created by the daily struggle to survive; it was hard to retain quality in the face of material deprivation. Newspapers and journals were affected, too, not least with the inevitable lowering in quality of debate in their pages because one issue obsessed everyone. Many newspapers appeared irregularly and in reduced sizes because of paper shortages, and the pre-eminent music journal *La Revue musicale* did not appear from April 1940 until March 1946. Its editor, Robert Bernard, explained in the first edition to appear after the war: 'Our traditions of political independence, complete freedom of expression and of support for the most daring of new artistic movements could not have been compromised without betraying us. The laws in force during the Occupation would not have permitted us freely to continue to serve the cause of composers such as Dukas, Milhaud, Hindemith, Schoenberg, Tansman and others who the journal would defend in all situations.'[2] While

1 'Le pays en guerre ne néglige rien de ce qui peut accroître au dehors de l'idée qu'on a de lui ... Évidemment, il n'y a pas de prestige intellectuel qui vaille une bataille gagnée. Mais enfin, il est bon, il est nécessaire que l'Europe sache que la culture française n'a rien perdu de ses qualités séculaires.'

2 Robert Bernard: editorial, *La Revue musicale*, 198 (Feb./Mar. 1946), 3–4; 'La tradition d'indépendance relative aux questions politiques, de totale liberté d'expression, de soutien vis-à-vis des mouvements artistiques les plus audacieusement novateurs ne pouvait être bridée sans la trahir. Les lois en vigueur durant l'occupation ne nous auraient pas matériellement pas permis de continuer à servir librement la cause de certains musiciens tels que Dukas, Milhaud, Hindemith, Schoenberg, Tansman et d'autres encore que la *Revue musicale* a défendus en toutes circonstances.'

Plate 10.1 The Paris Opéra during the occupation.

Frenchmen were on active service, Bernard's wife founded an organization which gave practical help to mobilized musicians, aiming to ensure, for instance, that mail reached them.

Concerts and Orchestras

It was impossible for orchestral life to continue unaffected during the war years. Most obviously, the general mobilization of young men at the outbreak of war on 3 September 1939 removed a large percentage of the workforce from their jobs. The effect of mobilization on the musical world is amply illustrated by statistics relating to the French Radio Orchestra: of eighty musicians employed in September 1939, forty-two were called up.[3] This orchestra moved out of Paris during the Occupation, initially to Rennes.

The focus of French musical life in the war years on the capital city, and the resulting lack of Parisian interest in regional musical life, has been criticized by many (though this was hardly an unusual state of affairs). While Paris was, of course, the principal showcase for French music during the war years, there is evidence that this concentration of musical resources on the capital city was even more marked in this period than in other times. All four of the main Paris orchestras (Pasdeloup, Colonne – renamed Pierné during the war because Colonne was a Jew – Lamoureux, and the Société des concerts du Conservatoire) were dependent on state subsidy, and this financial support actually increased during the four years of the Occupation. According to a report in *Comœdia* published on 29 August 1942, the orchestras received 2.8 million francs subsidy for the year, 459 per cent more than they had received before, though in the same period, provincial orchestral subsidies were reduced to the tune of 40–50 per cent, and funding for provincial radio stations also dried up.[4] The pre-eminence of Paris was, as has been suggested, nothing unusual; it was no doubt assumed that nobody would notice the erosion of musical funding to the regions. Several writers, including Robert Bernard, bemoaned this situation, suggesting that the Paris orchestras should perhaps undertake regional tours. However, only the Société des concerts du Conservatoire, with their principal conductor Charles Münch, did so, visiting Bordeaux, Nantes, Rennes and Le Mans in May 1942 despite the extreme difficulties of travel during the war years.

Concert life in Paris under the Occupation was, perhaps surprisingly, active, and newspapers of the period show that the number of performances at established venues is similar to the number given there today. There was clearly a desire (felt both by the Vichy regime and the Nazi Occupiers) to prove that French musical culture did not suffer deterioration in quality because of the war. Gilles and Jean-Robert Ragache, authors of a study on artistic life during the Occupation, wrote: ‘Despite the absence of heating in concert halls, financial and material difficulties, concert halls had never before been so full.’[5] But one music critic believed that if this popularity ‘may be partly due to the efforts of the national broadcasting company and Radio-Paris to interest the masses in great music and the excellent virtuosi who appear in their programmes, it is also significantly due to the fact that the public cannot amuse themselves as they wish, and want to get away from the obsessions of the present time’.[6]

Concert promoters and music journalists worked under censorship, and it is fair to say that concert programmes are notable as much for the absence of certain composers as for the music that was actually heard. Jewish composers were, of course, proscribed by the Nazis, removing Milhaud, Schoenberg, Dukas and even Mendelssohn from

3 Germaine Inghelbrecht: *Désiré-Émile Inghelbrecht et son temps* (Neuchâtel, 1978), 139.

4 Report by Francis Bousquet: *Comœdia* (29 Aug. 1942), 5.

5 Gilles and Jean-Robert Ragache: *La vie quotidienne des écrivains et des artistes sous l'Occupation* (Paris, 1989), 152.

6 Jacques Sorbets: untitled article in *L'illustration* (29 Jan.–5 Feb. 1944), 43; ‘S'il est dû en partie aux efforts de la Radiodiffusion nationale et de Radio-Paris tendant à intéresser la multitude aux belles œuvres et à l'excellence des virtuoses qui se produisent, il est dû aussi pour beaucoup à l'impossibilité dans laquelle se trouve le public de s'amuser à sa guise et à son désir de se dégager des obsessions actuelles.’

programmes, and anything the Occupiers considered to be 'degenerate music' (including Bartók) was also banned. As will be seen, some brave concert promoters defied this ban although in general, concert promoters shied away from risk or novelty, and many critics, of whom Arthur Honegger (writing in *Comœdia*) was the most prominent, condemned the lack of adventure of concert programmes and the consequent lack of opportunities offered to young French composers. Several cycles of Beethoven symphonies were given between 1940 and 1944, and 'bleeding chunks' of Wagner operas were equally popular. The lack of variety in the programmes of the four main orchestras was compounded by their tendency to perform at the same time, as the tradition of giving concerts on Sundays at five in the afternoon was continued during the war. The Paris orchestras were funded on condition they each played three to four hours of new music per year – a situation judged problematic by the composer Francis Bousquet, who also worked as a *Comœdia* journalist, and who doubted whether enough music worthy of performance was being composed to justify this subsidy.[7] Moreover, in spite of the increased financial support given to Paris orchestras, Honegger noted on 19 December 1942 that orchestral rehearsal time had not increased.[8]

Jewish musicians were progressively forced out of their jobs, leaving a huge gap in concert life, and all musicians – performers, critics and radio employees as well as composers – were affected by censorship. The name of Milhaud, who lived in exile in the United States from 1940 to 1946, is absent from newspaper discussions on contemporary French music. His fellow Jew, the composer and pianist Jean Wiéner, was suspended from membership of SACEM (the French society for composers' rights) and therefore could not receive royalty payments. He could only continue to make a living as a writer of film music because the celebrated conductor Roger Désormière offered to sign his scores for him and forward payment to Wiéner. Désormière also paid Milhaud's rent from June 1940 until his return to Paris in 1946.[9]

But it would seem that Nazi censorship of musical works was often lax. Honegger's oratorio *Judith*, in which the chorus sing the words 'Israël revivra', was performed at the Opéra during the war years, and Poulenc's ballet *Les animaux modèles* (1940–41) features the popular song 'Non, vous n'aurez pas l'Alsace-Lorraine' as an inner part towards the end of the score. Also, music by banned composers occasionally appeared on programmes despite official opposition. The pianist Geneviève Joy recalls playing in a performance of Bartók's *Music for Strings, Percussion and Celesta* with the Radio Orchestra conducted by Charles Münch. The conductor insisted on the inclusion of the Bartók work on the programme in the face of opposition from the Occupiers, and, because of frequent power shortages, the concert hall was lit by candles.

Arthur Honegger was far and away the contemporary composer who featured most frequently on concert programmes and, perhaps not coincidentally, he was also one of the most prolific music journalists of the time; almost every weekly issue of *Comœdia* featured an article by Honegger. These articles often have a strangely contemporary feel: he regularly berates concert promoters for not including more new French music in orchestral programmes, and frequently expresses regret that the anniversaries of

7 Bousquet: report in *Comœdia*, 5.
8 Article in *Comœdia*.
9 D. Mayer and P. Souvtchinsky (eds): *Roger Désormière et son temps* (Monaco, 1966), 28.

composers' births or deaths play such an important role in concert programming. For instance, the 150th anniversary of Mozart's death in 1941 was widely commemorated, and several French musicians (including Jacques Rouché, the director of the Opéra, and the composer Marcel Delannoy) were invited on a cultural visit to Austria to commemorate this occasion. Honegger himself went on two trips to Vienna, and the musicians who went on these trips were criticized after the war. Artists such as the pianist Alfred Cortot, the first French performer invited to Berlin since the start of the Occupation, reinforced connections with the German-speaking world. Cortot first performed in this city in 1941, and Amouroux states that 'however noble the motive, a trip to Germany was viewed as a political statement because the collaborationist press interpreted it as such'.[10] Few musicians, however, were as vocal in their support for German culture as the pianist Lucienne Delforge. She declared in April 1942: 'Franco-German collaboration seems absolutely essential to me; we have too many thoughts, tastes, feelings and interests in common for an open, loyal and strong collaboration not to take place between us.'[11] Such sentiments would have seemed harmless outside the highly charged atmosphere of Occupied Paris.

Nevertheless, it would be unjust to conclude that every musician who benefited from Austro-German hospitality was necessarily a collaborator. Honegger, for one, knew that the truth was a good deal more complex, not least because after the premiere of his *Danse des morts* at the Conservatoire in 1941, he was accused of being a Jew. The composer responded in the editorial column of *Comœdia*: 'Will this filthy mess continue for much longer? When will people stop denying or denigrating the talents of those who are currently sculpting the eternal face of the thought of our country?'[12] Was Honegger's intention to praise the Jewish contribution to French artistic life, or simply to respond to a slur against him? No doubt he intended both interpretations to be possible.

Writing in exile in the United States in 1942, Germaine Tailleferre eloquently described the difficulties facing musicians in the war years. In the 1930s, Tailleferre started a prolific career as a film composer, and thus had first-hand knowledge of the difficulties of the film industry during the war. She writes that her work in this industry was made impossible by 'censorship, racial discrimination, refusal of technical means from the chemical industries for the developing of films', and, on an even more basic level, by the lack of manuscript paper.[13] Tailleferre also highlights the scarcity of transportation and food shortages, practical problems which took up a great deal of energy. Like many other commentators, she stresses her sympathy for the plight of Jewish musicians, for example in her account of the conductor Paul Paray's attempts to conduct concerts in Marseille (where Tailleferre was based before leaving for the USA). Paray, conductor of the Concerts Colonne, was

10 Henri Amouroux: *Les beaux jours des collabos* (Paris, 1978), 503; 'quelle que soit la noblesse de son but, un voyage en Allemagne représente une contribution à la politique allemande puisque la presse collaborationniste l'interprète ainsi'.

11 Cited in ibid., 496; 'La collaboration franco-allemande m'apparaît comme une indispensable nécessité, nous avons trop de pensées, de gouts, de sentiments et d'interêts communs pour que la collaboration franche, loyale et forte ne s'établisse pas entre nous.'

12 *Comœdia,* 19 July 1941; 'Est-ce que toute cette sale besogne va continuer longtemps? Quand s'arrêtera-t-on de nier ou de dénigrer les talents de ceux qui sculptent aujourd'hui le visage eternal de la pensée de notre pays?'

13 Germaine Tailleferre: 'From the South of France' in *Modern Music* (Nov.–Dec. 1942), 15–16.

instructed to cancel the performance of a work by Paul Dukas; when he refused to comply with this demand, he was ordered to discharge all his Jewish instrumentalists. Again refusing to bow to the authorities, he resigned, and took a job as the conductor of the (independent) Monte Carlo symphony orchestra.[14]

At the outbreak of the war, Désiré-Émile Inghelbrecht conducted the Orchestre National de France. The Director of the Radio decided to move broadcasts of orchestral concerts to Rennes at this time, and the ensemble performed these concerts in the Théâtre Municipal de Rennes. Inghelbrecht started a newsletter which kept mobilized players in touch with the orchestra's activities.[15] At the beginning of the Occupation, the orchestra returned to Paris, but refused to broadcast from the city. In 1941, they moved to Marseille via Angoulême. Alfred Cortot, then working for the Service de la Musique in Vichy, sent a note to Inghelbrecht informing him that the musicians would have to reaudition for the orchestra; Cortot would, henceforth, be the director. By 1943, they had returned to Paris, where an important incident happened on 17 July: the Occupiers insisted the orchestra performed a programme ending with Henri Busser's *Hymne à la France*, the members being threatened with forced labour in Germany if they did not cooperate. For the same concert, Inghelbrecht refused to conduct *La Marseillaise*; the following day, President Laval suspended him from his post.[16]

If the French were determined to demonstrate that Parisian cultural life could flourish under wartime conditions, the Germans were also eager to parade their major musical institutions and performers before the French. The Berlin Philharmonic Orchestra visited Paris during the Occupation, as did the Berlin and Vienna Opera companies. Visiting conductors included Eugen Jochum, Clemens Krauss, Wilhelm Kempf and Wilhelm Mengelberg; the latter conducted a Beethoven symphony cycle in 1943. As Henri Michel puts it, 'the Germans often achieved their objective to convince Parisians that German culture survived, even flourished, under the Nazi regime.'[17] Although book and newspaper publication suffered from a shortage of paper, *Comœdia* announced in 1943 that two volumes of Wagner's correspondence were to be published by the *Nouvelle Revue Française*, and also that Gustave Samazeuilh was to edit the memoirs of Wagner's last mistress, Judith Gautier.[18]

Under the Nazi occupation of Paris, the Occupiers effectively dictated programmes at the Opéra; the French premiere of Milhaud's *Médée* on 6 May 1940, shortly before the fall of Paris, was of course to be the last work by this composer performed at the Opéra until after the war. As Henri Amouroux succinctly states, 'it was not by chance that the great successes at the Opéra were invariably Germanic works.'[19] In 1941, the Berlin Opera were in residence at the Paris Opéra, programming three Mozart operas, two by Wagner, *Fidelio* and Pfitzner's *Palestrina* – a work by a composer with links to the National Socialist

14 Ibid., 15.

15 Inghelbrecht: *Inghelbrecht et son temps*, 161–2.

16 Ibid., 166.

17 Henri Michel: *Paris allemand* (Paris, 1981), 340; 'l'objectif recherché est souvent atteint: convaincre les Parisiens que la culture allemand survit, s'épanouit même, dans le national-socialisme.'

18 *Comœdia*, 5 and 26 May 1943.

19 Amouroux: *Les beaux jours*, 503; 'ce n'est pas par hasard que les grands succès de l'Opéra sont systématiquement d'essence germanique.'

Party.[20] The composer Henri Dutilleux was employed as *chef de chant* (choir accompanist) at this time, a post he disliked because of the difficulties of the Occupation and because he did not enjoy Pfitzner's work. At the end of the 1941 season, seven performances of Johann Strauss's *Die Fledermaus* were given. This production, starring Elisabeth Schwarzkopf, was organized by the Occupiers for an exclusively German audience. In May 1943, the fiftieth anniversary of the Paris premiere of Wagner's *Die Walküre* was celebrated at the Opéra – an event which neatly combined the contemporary vogue for Wagner and anniversary mania. Nevertheless, it would be wrong to suggest that Opéra programmes featured only German works: in the 1941–42 season, contemporary French composers were well represented in ballet programming, as works by Claude Delvincourt, Francis Poulenc, Joseph-Guy Ropartz and André Jolivet were all premiered.

Some concert organizations reacted against the conservative programmes of the time: the *raison d'être* of both the Triton and the Pléiade concert series was to promote contemporary music and little-known music of the past. Le Triton had been founded in 1932 by Pierre-Octave Ferroud, who was tragically killed in a car accident in 1936. Their twice-monthly concerts continued under the Occupation, and featured composers such as Bartók, Dallapiccola, Hindemith and Milhaud. The Pléiade series was conceived late in 1942 by Gaston Gallimard (the publisher of the *Nouvelle Revue Française*, who baptized the concerts with the same name as his prestigious complete editions of works by France's most respected literary figures) and the film producer Denise Tual, who organized the concerts, along with Jean-François Méhu and the music critic André Schaeffner. In Tual's words, each programme was to consist of 'a period work, little played or even unknown, one or more first performances of works by young composers, and a work by a forbidden composer such as Stravinsky, or one of the composers in the Free [unoccupied] Zone, such as Poulenc or Auric'.[21] Their concerts were held either in the Conservatoire or, more often, in art galleries; the first concert took place in the Galerie Charpentier on 8 February 1943. Fashionable Paris eagerly supported the Pléiade series, as the concerts were seen as social events as much as opportunities to hear new music; the opportunity to rub shoulders with artists and writers including Jean Cocteau, Marie Laurencin and Georges Braque was a major source of appeal for some. Even Poulenc described the audience members as 'snobs' and bemoaned 'the mediocre level of the public' in a letter to Jolivet written in October 1943.[22] However, thanks to a German edict prohibiting gatherings of more than forty people without special permission,[23] the concerts had to be private affairs, accessible only to invited guests.

The concert series featured several important premieres. At the fourth Pléiade concert, on 10 May 1943, Messiaen's *Visions de l'Amen* was premiered by the composer and his pupil, Yvonne Loriod, in the Galerie Charpentier, incongruously surrounded by paintings by Morisot, Renoir and Braque. This two-piano work had been commissioned by Denise Tual. Arthur Honegger welcomed the work, describing it as 'remarkable, rich, musical, a

20 Pascal Ory: *Les collaborateurs* (Paris, 1976), 61.

21 Tual: 'Itinéraire des Concerts de la Pléiade', unpublished typescript; cited by Nigel Simeone: 'Messiaen and the Concerts de la Pléiade: A Kind of Clandestine Revenge against the Occupation', *Music and Letters*, 81/4 (Nov. 2000), 553.

22 Myriam Chimènes (ed.): *Francis Poulenc: Correspondance 1910–1963* (Paris, 1994), 543; 'la médiocrité actuelle du public'.

23 Simeone: 'Messiaen and the Concerts de la Pléiade', 553.

truly grand conception'.[24] He ended his review expressing the hope that it would be selected for performance by the Jeunesses Musicales movement, which had been founded by René Nicoly in May 1942 with the aim of bringing music to a younger public. Concerts in traditional halls and schools were arranged by this organization, which distributed free or cut-price tickets to young people under the age of twenty-five. By the beginning of 1944, it had 150,000 members, 50,000 in Paris alone.[25] *Visions de l'Amen*, introduced by the composer, was indeed played in the Salle Gaveau, under the auspices of the Jeunesses Musicales, on 22 June 1943. The Salle du Conservatoire was the venue for the controversial first performance of Messiaen's *Trois petites liturgies de la Présence Divine*, also commissioned by Tual, on 21 April 1945 (for which Pierre Boulez was the page-turner for the vibraphone player). Other items on this programme included Poulenc's *Un soir de neige*.

Another benefactor, Marguerite Roesgen-Champion, founded a concert series entitled Suites Françaises in 1940. Each concert showcased a young singer who had received a distinction at the Paris Conservatoire.[26] She also supported an all-female chamber orchestra, the Orchestre Jane Évrard, which programmed some contemporary works including the premiere of Guy Ropartz's *Petite Suite* and arrangements by Roesgen-Champion herself. Reviews of the ensemble reveal more about contemporary views of femininity than about the music or the standard of performance; an assessment of the concert featuring the above works stated that the orchestra 'sounds very pretty, which is not surprising'.[27]

Performances of *Pelléas et Mélisande* at the Opéra-Comique were central musical experiences for many critics and composers in Paris. Auric vividly described the emotions unleashed by a performance in September 1940: 'I could not precisely describe our feelings while listening to it. Indeed, not only us but the whole auditorium was listening with a degree of attention and enthusiasm which one would have liked to have analysed, which burst forth at the end of the opera with a sort of shiver of fervent gratitude.'[28] Performances of Debussy's opera, often considered an ideal marriage of music and the French language, were morale boosters for French music lovers in the capital. Its first complete recording was made, in very difficult conditions from 24 April to 25 May 1941, conducted by Désormière and featuring the era's most celebrated interpreters of the leading roles: Jacques Jansen (Pelléas), Irène Joachim (Mélisande) and Henri Etcheverry (Golaud). In September that year, the same performers were obliged to perform the opera before Maréchal Pétain in Vichy.[29]

24 *Comœdia* (15 May 1943); 'remarquable, d'une grande richesse, musicale, d'une vraie grandeur dans la conception'.

25 Ragache: *La vie quotidienne*, 155.

26 *Revue musicale*, 197 (Apr. 1940), ii.

27 Ibid., 241; 'qui sonne très joliment, ce qui n'est pas pour surprendre'. The orchestra also gave a concert in the Triptyque series in October 1943; the programme included premieres by Daniel-Lesur and Florent Schmitt.

28 Review published in the *Nouvelle Revue Française* and quoted in Ragache: *La vie quotidienne*, 154–5; 'Nous l'écoutions avec une emotion que je ne saurais exactement définir. Et, en même temps que nous, toute une salle, avec une attention, une ferveur qu'on voudrait décomposer et qui se manifestait à la fin par une sorte de grand frémissement, de reconnaissant enthousiasme.'

29 Inghelbrecht: *Inghelbrecht et son temps*, 139.

Other Institutions and Organizations

The Paris Conservatoire remained open during the war years, initially directed by Henri Rabaud. On 3 October 1940, Rabaud wrote to the Occupiers on the subject of 'la question raciale au Conservatoire', a euphemism for the Jewish question.[30] Jean Gribenski suggests that Rabaud may have heard rumours that the Occupiers were concerned about the Conservatoire, but nevertheless, he encouraged them to keep an eye on the institution by writing to them. The director drew up lists of the numbers of Jewish staff and students in the Conservatoire, distinguishing Jewish students with four Jewish grandparents from those who were half-Jewish. His investigation revealed that only two of the seventy-five staff were Jewish (Lazare Lévy and André Bloch); the former was sacked and the latter encouraged to retire. Also, of the 580 enrolled students, 540 were not Jewish, of which about twenty or twenty-four were and another fifteen came under his half-Jewish category.[31] Unwilling to take any steps to remove these students without the prior authorization of the Occupiers, Rabaud did nothing.

Claude Delvincourt replaced Rabaud as director on 15 April 1941, and instituted a rule that Jews could constitute only 3 per cent of the student body. Delvincourt tried to support students from all backgrounds as best he could – he suggested the following year that Jewish students could be examined in private and not have their names on the official roll – but the Education Minister, Abel Bonnard, categorically wrote to him on 21 September 1942: 'Il convient de ne maintenir ou de n'admettre au Conservatoire aucun élève juif.'[32]

Towards the end of 1943, Delvincourt founded two ensembles: a choir for inexperienced singers, and the Orchestre des Cadets du Conservatoire. The latter group was conceived as a training orchestra, and – importantly – as a means of ensuring its members would be able to stay in France. At this time, all students who began their studies in 1941 or 1942 received a letter from the Service du Travail Obligatoire (Forced Labour) asking them to prepare to leave for Germany. After many difficult meetings, Delvincourt managed to convince the Occupiers that these young people were needed to form an orchestra and choir. The two ensembles toured extensively early in 1944 and often gave charity concerts. But the Occupiers interrupted their activities shortly before the Liberation, and planned to transport the young musicians to Germany. At this point many members of the ensemble became involved in Resistance activity. Delvincourt tried to procure false identity cards and safe houses for his players, and he found out when they were to leave Paris. All orchestra members received an order from him to escape by night; the young people were freed, and the orchestra continued to give concerts after the war.[33]

Delvincourt's support for the most gifted contemporary composers of his time is clear. Two days after his appointment, he took the radical step of naming Messiaen as professor of harmony, and Messiaen's class quickly gained a reputation as a sympathetic home for the most adventurous student composers. The director of the Conservatoire also supported

30 Jean Gribenski, in Myriam Chimènes (ed.): *La vie musicale sous Vichy* (Paris, 2001), 146.

31 Ibid., 147.

32 Ibid., 155.

33 Anne Bongrain and Yves Gérard (eds): *Le Conservatoire de Paris, 1795–1995* (Paris, 1996), 261.

young composers by commissioning test pieces for end-of-year exams from them: Dutilleux's *Sonatine* for flute (1943) was composed for this purpose.

The greatest achievement for Conservatoire composition students was to win the Prix de Rome at the end of their studies, but while the competition took place as normal in the early 1940s, the Villa Medici in Rome, where the winner of the first prize spent four years, was closed. Jacques Ibert, director of the Villa, was absent from the declaration of hostilities to 1946. Although Ibert was obliged to leave his post and was called up to serve with the Marines, the Vichy authorities considered that he had abandoned the job without permission. He was sacked on 17 October 1939, and forced to leave the Marines. Obliged to live in the South of France and then Switzerland, he was reinstated as director of the Villa Medici only in October 1944.[34] He began his only String Quartet in 1937 and restarted it two years later in Antibes, where he had taken refuge. Its often austere mood (particularly in the long Andante second movement) and complex contrapuntal writing is unusual in his output, and many commentators view it as a musical metaphor for the struggles he experienced during the war years.

In Paris, a musicians' branch of the *Front national* was created in September 1941; similar groups existed for film-makers, actors, writers and other artists. The organization had no connection whatsoever with today's political party. Henri Dutilleux, a member, has stated that it was a mutual support group rather than an active political force, and indeed its members embraced a broad spectrum of political views: Claude Delvincourt, a right-wing sympathizer, rubbed shoulders with Roger Désormière, a Communist. Dutilleux's sympathy with the predicament of Jewish musicians led him to help shelter Manuel Rosenthal. He also remembers being invited by the composer Max d'Ollone to join a group of composers sympathetic to the Nazi Occupation.[35] D'Ollone's support for this regime was made clear when he was named director of the Opéra-Comique in 1941. Some organizations, notably the group 'Collaboration', promoted friendly Franco-German artistic relations by fostering concerts featuring composers from both countries; for instance, in 1942, Jean Françaix and Tony Aubin were involved in a concert promoted by the Institut allemand and 'Collaboration'.[36]

'Will there be wartime music?'

In December 1939, an article in the *Revue musicale* posed the question 'y aura-t-il une musique de guerre?' Most composers responded in a similar manner to Poulenc, who stated: 'I don't know whether there will be a wartime musical genre … I hope [the war] will be so short that a musical style would not have time to establish itself.'[37] Nevertheless, Poulenc was one of a small number of composers who wrote pieces in response to contemporary events. The most obvious way for a composer to do this was to set a text which referred to the difficulties of the war; poems based on military archetypes, prayers

34 Alexandra Laederich: *Catalogue de l'œuvre de Jacques Ibert* (Hildesheim, 1996), xi.

35 Conversation with the author, 3 Aug. 1994.

36 Ory: *Les collaborateurs*, 60–61.

37 Interview in the *Revue musicale*, 194 (Dec. 1939), 150; 'Je ne sais s'il y aura une musique de guerre … j'espère que celle-ci sera si courte que ce nouveau genre n'aura pas le temps de s'instituer.'

for peace or evocations of an idealized France were all popular with composers of the period, not least Poulenc. His setting of Apollinaire's *Bleuet* (1939), which reflects on the poet's time as a soldier in the First World War, was naturally viewed as an anti-war statement. The year before, he had set Charles d'Orléans' *Priez pour paix* for a four-part choir, having read excerpts of the poem in the newspaper *Le Figaro*, and his song cycle *Chansons villageoises* (1942), to poems by Maurice Fombeure, suggested an affinity with the rural *France profonde*.

Contemporary poets who took sensitive contemporary issues as their subjects risked their work being banned; many poems were printed clandestinely and distributed only to trusted friends. Poulenc received regular hand-printed copies of poems by Paul Éluard during the war, and settings of Louis Aragon – François le Colère, to use his Resistance pseudonym – were made by Georges Auric (*Quatre chants de la France malheureuse*, 1943) and Poulenc (*C*, 1942) amongst others. The final bars of the final song of Auric's group, 'La rose et le réséda' (Example 10.1), hint at 'La Marseillaise', the composer thus ensuring that the audience would carry away a patriotic image. By this stage in his career, Auric was better known as a film composer than as a composer of concert works; his choice of texts underlines his desire to be taken seriously as a creative artist during this period in history.

Example 10.1 Georges Auric, 'La rose et le réséda', bars 150–56

Poulenc's predilection for the poetry of Paul Éluard was again shown in his cantata for double choir, *Figure humaine*. The eighth and final movement of this work is a setting of the long poem *Liberté*, a poem which was first published in Algiers in 1942, and was known thanks to the RAF dropping clandestinely produced copies into occupied areas. The composition of *Figure humaine* was suggested to Poulenc by Henri Screpel, the director of the record company La Compagnie des Discophiles, and it was also Screpel's idea that he should incorporate a setting of *Liberté*.[38] But, speaking in 1954, Poulenc said: 'The idea of a secret work which could be published, clandestinely prepared for a performance on the long-awaited day of the Liberation, came to me after a votive pilgrimage to Rocamadour ... I enthusiastically started working on *Figure humaine* and finished it at the end of the summer.'[39] While this plan did not come to fruition, on the day US soldiers entered Paris, Poulenc proudly placed the score of *Figure humaine* on a music stand in a window beneath a French flag. Its triumphant closing bars, declaiming the word 'Liberté', are shown in Example 10.2. All eight Éluard poems set in this cantata were selected from the collection *Poésie et vérité 42* (1942). The BBC Singers premiered the work in spring 1945, though in London rather than Paris.

Later, Poulenc set three other poems from this collection as the second, third and fourth movements of a cantata for six-part a cappella choir, *Un soir de neige* (the first of the four movements is a setting of 'Des grandes cuillères de neige' from Éluard's 1944 volume, *Digne de vivre*). This cantata was written between 24 and 26 December 1944 – therefore, during an unusually cold winter towards the end of the war. Poulenc's choice of poetry is interesting, not least because he opted not to set any poems from another wartime collection by Éluard, *Au rendez-vous allemand*. No doubt, Poulenc considered that these poems, such as *Chant nazi* and *Les armes de la douleur*, were too explicitly linked to the time and place of their composition and too political in character. Many of the Éluard poems that Poulenc selected feature animal imagery, for instance the second poem of *Un soir de neige* (featuring the words 'Honte à la bête pourchassé' at the climax; see Example 10.3), or the sixth poem of *Figure humaine* ('Un animal sur la neige a posé / Ses pattes sur le sable ou dans la boue'). Here, Éluard surely aimed to distance the human feelings involved by ascribing them to animals.

Poulenc's substantial contribution to the genre of musical works inspired by wartime events suggests that he would have liked to be remembered as a hero of the period, but his musical achievements conceal the more ambiguous face he, and many others, showed during the war. Benjamin Ivry, for one, believes that 'Poulenc's reaction to the war and German Occupation was self-centred' because he missed his exiled Jewish friends Milhaud and Wanda Landowska at least partly because he greatly valued their critical input. Poulenc also told Milhaud, untruthfully, in a letter that his country home in Noizay had been pillaged, perhaps wishing to show that he, too, had suffered during the war.[40]

Some of Dutilleux's vocal compositions of the war years overtly reflect current events. In 1943, he set a poem by his friend, the poet Jean Cassou (the third poem in his book of

38 Chimènes (ed.): *Francis Poulenc: Correspondence*, 537.

39 Francis Poulenc: *Entretiens avec Claude Rostand* (Paris, 1954), 104; 'L'idée d'une œuvre secrète qu'on pourrait éditer, préparer clandestinement pour la donner le jour, tant attendu, de la Libération, m'était venue à la suite d'une pèlerinage votive à Rocamadour. ... Je commençai dans l'enthousiasme *Figure humaine*, que j'achevai à la fin de l'été.'

40 Benjamin Ivry: *Francis Poulenc* (London, 1996), 117.

Example 10.2 Francis Poulenc, *Figure humaine*, final bars

Example 10.3 Francis Poulenc, *Un soir de neige*, II, 'La bonne neige ...', bars 6–9

Trente-trois sonnets composés au secret published clandestinely under his Resistance pseudonym, Jean Noir)[41] for baritone and piano, which the composer entitled *La geôle* and dedicated to his brother, Paul, who spent five years in a prisoner-of-war camp. This song is one of the few works written before 1947 which Dutilleux has not repudiated, and one of the few which he released for publication, and the first commercial recording was issued in 2005. It may be presumed that the personal circumstances of the song's dedication to his brother lie behind his refusal to authorize a recording, as the setting is of very high quality as well as being deeply touching. The opening bars (Example 10.4) reflect the hopeless reverie of the poet, who is imprisoned and dreaming of life outside his cell: a meandering chromatic line which constantly turns back on itself. After the first verse, a very Messiaen-like piano phrase gives the voice a breathing space: these added value rhythms are a feature of many of Dutilleux's wartime songs.

In 1994, Dutilleux himself accompanied the baritone Gilles Cachemaille in two other Cassou settings, *Il n'y avait que les troncs déchirés* and *J'ai rêvé que je vous portais entre mes bras*, for a CD recording. Dutilleux's music mirrors the emotional world of Cassou's poems: the vocal line of the latter song opens with all twelve notes of the chromatic scale, though the song is not strictly serial and the accompaniment does not use this 'row' at all. Besides being, as Dutilleux put it, an 'amusing' experiment, this heightens the emotionally contained mood of the poem. For the final lines of *Il n'y avait que les troncs déchirés*, a wild and aggressive dance is abruptly introduced in the piano part, underlining the ironic surprise of the poetry: 'La scène était prête pour des acteurs / fous et cruels à force de bonheur' (The stage was set for actors who were wild and cruel in the intensity of their happiness). Another sonnet from Cassou's collection set around the same time,[42] *Éloignez-vous*, remains unrecorded and unpublished.

41 Manuel Rosenthal set two sonnets from this collection, *Eloignez-vous* and *Le couple*; Darius Milhaud also made vocal settings of Cassou's poetry.

42 It is by no means easy to date these songs; Dutilleux, characteristically, revised them several

Example 10.4 Henri Dutilleux, *La geôle*, bars 1–11

times. The manuscripts, now housed in the Bibliothèque Nationale de France, Paris, and the Paul Sacher Stiftung, Basel, show dates ranging from 1944 to 1954.

Similarly, Dutilleux's *Chanson de la déportée*, a 1945 setting of a poem by Jean Gandrey-Réty, is accessible to enthusiasts only via a manuscript copy now owned by the Paul Sacher Stiftung in Basel. This simple but moving poem concerns a mother's feelings at being separated from her child; though the poem specifies no time or place, it is clear that contemporary listeners would have identified the mother with Jewish women deported to concentration camps, forever separated from their families. The song was performed by Dutilleux's friend Irène Joachim, who frequently broadcast it in the aftermath of the Liberation of Paris, but there is no record of subsequent hearings. The concluding bars of this song again reflect the influence of Messiaen on Dutilleux's music, as upper resonances colour the piano part.

If works explicitly connected with wartime events are rare, it is equally true that commentators did not hesitate to use criteria relevant to the mood of the times when reviewing some musical works. This attempt to be 'politically correct' affected most writers on music in the period. On 6 March 1940, Émile Vuillermoz reviewed the premiere of Florent Schmitt's choral and orchestral work *L'arbre entre tous* (1939), performed as part of the Concerts Pasdeloup season. He explains that the tree mentioned in the title is 'the tree of freedom, nourished by the powerful sap of French soil' and describes the piece as 'this great cry of independence which sprung from the heart of the great French composer, whose strong and uncompromising voice ought to be heard by the whole universe, because it exalts the dignity of man which is under threat'.[43] During this performance, the work's theme of freedom spoke to the public more powerfully than Schmitt could perhaps have imagined. On the other hand, Honegger considered that light and entertaining works such as Marcel Delannoy's comic opera *Ginevra* (1942), the first performance of which he reviewed on 25 July 1942, did not reflect the contemporary mood sufficiently. He wrote: 'Musical theatre is devoted to a constant return to ideas of the past, to looking back on little love stories and amusing tales of adultery, which makes us smile for a while, but which truly has very little interest for us in the 1940s.'[44] Like Vuillermoz when reviewing Schmitt's choral work, Honegger focuses on the composer's choice of subject matter rather than the music.

The background to Messiaen's *Quatuor pour la fin du temps* is one of the most touching musical stories of the war years. Unfit for active service because of his poor eyesight, the composer was called up as a medical auxiliary, and was captured in Nancy in May 1940. He was transported as a prisoner of war to Stalag VIIIA in Görlitz, Silesia and, according to the cellist Étienne Pasquier, a first draft of the *Quatuor*'s third movement, 'Abîme des oiseaux', must have been composed on this journey.[45] Messiaen was provided with manuscript paper by a guard, and met up with Pasquier, the violinist Jean Le Boulaire, and clarinettist Henri Akoka; Le Boulaire and Akoka had managed to keep their instruments, and Pasquier was given a cello with one string missing. Messiaen initially wrote a light-hearted 'Intermède' for his three companions, a piece which became the fourth movement

43 *Candide*, 6 Mar. 1940; 'l'arbre de la liberté, nourri du suc puissant de la terre de France. … 'ce grand cri d'indépendance jailli du cœur du grand musicien français dont la voix forte et rude doit être entendue de tout l'univers, parce qu'elle exalte la dignité humaine menacée'.

44 *Comœdia*, 25 July 1942; 'Le théâtre musical est voué au retour constant vers les inventions du passé, la retrospective de tout un théâtre d'amourettes et de cocuages qui nous font sourire un instant mais qui n'ont vraiment guère d'intérêt pour un esprit de 1940.'

45 Cited in Anthony Pople: *Quatuor pour la fin du temps* (Cambridge, 1998), 8.

of the *Quatuor*. To this ad hoc chamber group he added a piano part (which he could play); the ensemble of the *Quatuor*, one he would surely never have considered outside the camp, was born.

Malcolm Hayes has described the work as 'perhaps the single most significant work that Messiaen was ever to compose, in that the *Quatuor* is the technical source from which all of his subsequent output was directly to spring'.[46] The title is taken from the Book of Revelation – the angel's proclamation 'There shall be Time no more' – and, in addition to the religious dimension of the quotation, the title may well have technical and personal significance. Firstly, Messiaen's extensive use of non-retrogradable (palindromic) rhythmic patterns, and added-value rhythms which negate any sense of regular pulse, suggests that the piece embodies an end of metrical time. The fifth and eighth movements – both transcriptions by memory of earlier works – are respectively homages to the eternity and immortality of Jesus, the first for cello and piano, the second for violin and piano. Both are extremely slow, and both feature an ostinato rhythm in the piano accompaniment; again, these are technical devices which aim, as far as possible, to suspend the sense of time – or, at least, forward momentum – in music (Example 10.5 illustrates the opening of the eighth movement, 'Louange à l'immortalité de Jésus'). Secondly, Messiaen was unaware, when composing the work, when he would leave the camp, or indeed if he would survive. The first performance was given at the camp on 15 January 1941; despite the less than ideal performance conditions (the piano keys constantly stuck because of the very cold weather), the premiere was attended by around 5000 fellow prisoners. Messiaen was repatriated in spring 1941 and returned to Paris, where he was named professor of harmony at the Conservatoire.

Late in 1942, Honegger wrote a short article on the *Quatuor pour la fin du temps*, interviewing Messiaen about his recently published treatise on his musical language (*Technique de mon langage musical*). Messiaen stated that he wished, in writing the treatise, to 'take the reader by the hand, search with him, and gently guide him through the shadows of my hope towards a subtle light, which prepares him for the improvement which he could discover later'.[47] Surely, Messiaen is referring not only to the progressive enlightenment of the teaching process, but also to his hopes for a future after the war and his obsessive religious symbolism.

The musical ideals of the group Jeune France (comprising Olivier Messiaen, André Jolivet, Daniel-Lesur and Yves Baudrier), which was founded in 1936 and ceased existence from the outbreak of hostilities, were surely more important than ever to the members of the group during the war years. The response of the audience to the first performance of the *Quatuor pour la fin du temps* must have been, for Messiaen, proof that they could respond to a work which eschewed the frivolity and lack of spiritual dimension that the members of Jeune France disliked in so much French music of the 1920s and 1930s. One of Messiaen's fellow group members, André Jolivet, also responded to contemporary events with a characteristic seriousness of musical purpose. In 1940, he wrote a *Messe pour le jour de la paix* for the unusual combination of voice, organ and

46 Peter Hill (ed.): *The Messiaen Companion* (London, 1995), 180.

47 Interview in *Comœdia*, 5 Dec. 1942; 'je rédige mon traité en prenant le lecteur par la main, en cherchant avec lui, en le guidant doucement dans les ténèbres où j'ai espéré, vers une lumière restreinte et préparatoire à ce "mieux" qu'il pourra trouver ensuite.'

Example 10.5 Olivier Messiaen, *Quatuor pour la fin du temps*, VIII, 'Louange à l'immortalité de Jésus', bars 1–6

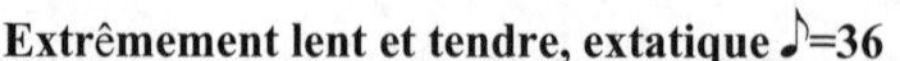

tambourine, and the same year composed a song cycle, *Les trois complaintes du soldat*, on his own texts, based on his experiences as a soldier.

On 5 September 1942, *Comœdia* launched a composition competition for two categories of work: a march, and a song for choir. A first prize of 2000 francs was offered, with two runner-up prizes of 1000 francs and additional prizes for song texts, and prisoners of war were specifically encouraged to enter. It appears that ideals of human solidarity, or working together with a common purpose, lay behind the choice of the two genres: the march, according to *Comœdia*, 'donne un rythme à l'être humain tout entier, puis à des masses d'hommes', and they hoped that the choral works would encourage the young to sing. However, this competition was more or less hijacked by the Secrétariat d'État à la

Jeunesse. On 17 October 1942, *Comœdia* announced the Secretariat's proposal for a new composition prize of 3000 francs, with two runners-up prizes of 1500 francs, for a hymn to Maréchal Pétain. The journal mentioned that the topic was 'not so much imposed as affectionately proposed' and that the work should be 'a hymn of praise to him, his work and his example'.[48] In July 1942, *Comœdia* had announced two competitions for collaborative works to be broadcast on the radio; the first question on the application form for these competitions asked whether the candidates were Jewish.

The Radio

Radio programmes were immediately affected by the outbreak of the war, not least because the Radio orchestra and administrators moved to the relative exile of Toulouse. André Boll, writing in *La Revue musicale* in January 1940, said, 'The current chaos of music radio, which is obvious to the listener but not due to technical difficulties, has surfaced because of the absolute necessity to improvise on the spot.' For instance, he mentions a broadcast of *Pelléas et Mélisande* in which the third act was cut short, and the broadcast was replaced by 'un disque de mélodies anodines'. He also quotes Auric, who wrote that planned broadcasts of *Benvenuto Cellini* and Mussorgsky's *Boris Godunov* were both replaced at the last minute by Franco-British gala musical events, which were no doubt well-intentioned attempts to reinforce the ties between the two allied countries. Auric also criticized the half-hour time limit placed on the first half of any music broadcast.[49]

Pierre Schaeffer founded Jeune France, a movement which aimed to foster collaboration between practitioners of different art forms, in 1941. It was a short-lived organization (it was dissolved later that year) but, while it existed, it was subsidized by the Ministry for Youth. When asked whether he was, therefore, a supporter of the Vichy regime, Schaeffer frankly replied: 'Well, yes ... Pretty well forty million of us were ... Many people – directors, musicians, painters – almost every well-known artist or literary figure of my generation was involved with Jeune France.'[50] Schaeffer reminds us that we should be wary of viewing the war years as a time when there were easy choices to be made for or against Vichy France and the Resistance.

From 1 January 1943, Schaeffer was the director of an experimental radio studio (the Studio d'Essai). The studio was rebaptized Club d'Essai after the Liberation, and was the venue for the first experiments in *musique concrète*. The Studio d'Essai acted as a forum for experiments in sound, and its members also devised novel radio programmes. Their first programme, broadcast on 3 July 1943, was the five-hour-long 'Laboratoire d'étude',

48 'moins imposé qu'affectueusement proposé'; 'un hymne à sa personne, à son œuvre et à son exemple'.

49 André Boll: article in *La Revue musicale* (Jan. 1940), 49–52; 'Le désordre actuel de la radio musicale, plus apparent qu'organique, est dû beaucoup plus à l'impérieuse nécessité d'improviser tout de suite, n'importe quoi.'

50 Pierre Schaeffer: *Entretiens avec Marc Pierret* (Paris, 1969), 132; 'Eh oui ... Nous étions presque quarante millions ... Beaucoup de gens, metteurs en scène, musiciens, peintres, tous ceux ou presque qui ont un nom dans les Arts et les lettres de ma génération, sont plus ou moins passés à la Jeune France.'

which was 'a large-scale experiment and not … a programme constructed according to traditional grammatical rules'.[51] The broadcast included a section entitled 'L'humeur en musique', featuring works by Satie, Poulenc and Stravinsky, and a 'fable radiophonique' entitled *La vie privée d'Adam et Eve*, written by Claude Roy and with music by Auric. The following year, the Studio, advised by Désormière, launched a series of programmes entitled 'Concerts de minuit', which promoted music banned under the Occupation. The series was conceived as a pendant to Éditions de Minuit, which had identical aims in the literary sphere.

After the War

The first number of the *Revue musicale* to appear after the war included an obituary section devoted to the small number of musicians who were killed on active service. The composers Maurice Jaubert (shot in the Moselle region on 19 June 1940) and Jehan Alain (killed at the age of twenty-nine while on a reconnaissance mission near Saumur) are remembered here, as is Jean Vuillermoz, who was killed on 21 June 1940, the day the Armistice was signed. The column also pays tribute to Jean-Claude Touche, an eighteen-year-old organ pupil of Marcel Dupré and active member of the Resistance, who was killed on 28 August 1944.[52]

The first concert given by the orchestra of the Société des concerts du Conservatoire, conducted by Charles Münch, after the Liberation of Paris took place on 22 October 1944. The programme naturally reflected the celebratory mood of the times, and included Ibert's *Ouverture de fête* (1940–41) and Honegger's *Chant de libération* (composed, oddly, in 1942). The Ibert overture had been commissioned in celebration of the 2600th anniversary of the Japanese empire, and was first performed in Tokyo in 1941, but its significance would clearly have been different for a post-Liberation audience. The Pierné orchestra rebaptized itself the Concerts Colonne on 30 August 1944, and the Lamoureux orchestra gave a concert featuring music by the previously banned composers Mendelssohn and Dukas.[53]

For Messiaen, the combined stimuli of Yvonne Loriod's virtuosity and his Catholic faith resulted in *Vingt regards sur l'Enfant-Jésus*, a mammoth solo piano work lasting over two hours in performance which, astonishingly, was composed from 23 March to 8 September 1944. The title should be understood as 'contemplations' or even 'meditations' on the infant Jesus, and Messiaen was inspired by various theological writings, particularly Maurice Toesca's *Les douze regards* and Dom Columba Marmion's *Christ and his mysteries*. Messiaen unifies the work by using a number of cyclic themes, most notably a theme of God which is most prominent in the fifth, tenth, fifteenth and twentieth movements. But perhaps the most memorable aspect of the *Vingt regards* is the overwhelming feeling of joy; though Messiaen may not endorse such an interpretation, surely the atmosphere of liberated Paris must have been an additional important stimulus for him.

51 Report in *Comœdia*, 3 July 1943; 'une expérience livrée en masse et non … un programme établi selon les règles de la ponctuation'.

52 *RM*, 198 (Feb./Mar. 1946), 50–56.

53 Alexandra Laederich: 'Les associations symphoniques parisiennes', in Chimènes (ed.): *La vie musicale*, 232.

In the aftermath of the war, composers were eager to discover contemporary works (by composers such as Schoenberg and Webern) which had been unavailable to them. Pierre Boulez recalls the frequently mediocre standards of performance of these works, referring specifically to a 'boring' performance of *Pierrot lunaire* under the direction of René Leibowitz.[54] The French Radio Orchestra was also in a very poor state after the war. Manuel Rosenthal was charged with bringing it back up to scratch, and he conducted an important concert in November 1945 featuring works by composers from Allied countries (including William Walton's *Portsmouth Point*) and an orchestration by Dutilleux of the organist Jehan Alain's *Prière pour nous autres charnels*, originally composed for tenor, baritone and organ.

From 1945, Schaeffer's experiments with *musique concrète* brought new sounds and ideas to French music, and Boulez – no enthusiast of *musique concrète* – established himself as the 'angry young man' of the Parisian music scene. He did not share the general public's nostalgia for pre-war musical life and musical languages; not surprisingly, as he came to Paris from the provinces in 1943, when he was eighteen. The nationalist concerns of many composers during the war years held no interest for Boulez in the late 1940s and early 1950s, other than, perhaps, as something to react against. Ironically perhaps, both the French composer Boulez and his German colleague Stockhausen were to become the joint leading European figures of the immediate post-war period.

Suggested Further Reading

Sidney Buckland (ed. and trans.): *Echo and Source: Francis Poulenc, Selected Correspondence 1915–63* (London: Weidenfeld & Nicolson, 1991).
Myriam Chimènes (ed.): *La vie musicale sous Vichy* (Paris: Éditions Complexe, 2001).
Peter Hill (ed.): *The Messiaen Companion* (London: Faber, 1995).
Benjamin Ivry: *Francis Poulenc* (London: Phaidon, 1996).
Olivier Messiaen: *Music and Color, conversations with Claude Samuel*, trans. E. Thomas Glasow (Portland. Ore.: Amadeus, 1994).
Anthony Pople: *Olivier Messiaen: Quatuor pour la fin du temps* (Cambridge: Cambridge University Press, 1998).
Caroline Potter: *Henri Dutilleux* (Aldershot: Ashgate, 1997).
Gilles and Jean-Robert Ragache: *La vie quotidienne des écrivains et des artistes sous l'Occupation* (Paris: Hachette, 1989).
Nigel Simeone: 'Messiaen and the Concerts de la Pléiade: A Kind of Clandestine Revenge against the Occupation', *Music and Letters*, 81–4 (Nov. 2000).
— and Peter Hill: *Messiaen* (New Haven: Yale University Press, 2005).

54 Interview with Roger Nichols for Radio 3 programme *France in the 1940s*, broadcast on 7 Mar. 1995.

Chapter 11

Pierre Boulez and the Foundation of IRCAM

Peter O'Hagan

'Maybe I could have composed more if I had been less busy with orchestras ... but I don't regret it, because I think a life is a complete thing, closed on itself, and these activities are complementary.'[1] There are few who would dissent from the notion that the work of a creative artist must be considered in its overall context, a view affirmed by Boulez during the course of a gracious speech at the Royal College of Music in London following the conferment of an honorary doctorate. More remarkable is his evident need to justify the range of his musical activities over the course of a public career spanning almost sixty years. After all, his position as one of the major influences on the music of the last half-century is incontestable. As a conductor, especially in the decade preceding the opening of IRCAM in 1976, during his years as principal conductor of both the BBC Symphony Orchestra and the New York Philharmonic, he was responsible for redefining the orchestral repertoire of the twentieth century.

Prior to this, during the immediate post-war period, he had exercised a decisive influence on an emerging generation of composers by developing an innovative musical language based on serial principles. As the rigour of these years began to disintegrate under the impact of John Cage's compositional philosophy, so Boulez's own creative drive seemed to lose its certainty of purpose, at least temporarily. The series of works designated 'in progress' continued to grow, and it was perhaps a consciousness of the apparently provisional nature of so much of his creative work over the last forty years that prompted this defence of his range of musical activities.

When the eighteen-year-old Pierre Boulez arrived in Paris in the autumn of 1943, there was little prior evidence to suggest that by the end of the decade, he would have produced a series of works of startling daring and originality. His two years of study with Andrée Vaurabourg-Honegger, commencing in April 1944, were a decisive influence, only surpassed by that of Olivier Messiaen, whose classes he joined in the autumn of the same year. The resulting series of piano compositions included two triptychs:, *Prélude, Toccata et Scherzo* (*c*.1945) and the slightly later *Trois Psalmodies* (*c*.1945). Stylistically, these pieces are the most direct acknowledgement in all Boulez's music of the enormous influence exercised by the dominating musical personality of Messiaen, and they help to explain the subsequent need for the young composer to react against it in order to find his individual voice. All three of the 'Psalmodies' alternate homophonic sections in strict rhythm with more rhapsodic passages, these contrasts being at their most extreme in the

1 Pierre Boulez,: lecture given at Royal College of Music, London, 12 Feb. 1997.

first piece (Example 11.1). On a directly musical level, the melodic line of 'Psalmodie 1', *comme une improvisation,* recalls the birdsong figurations of Messiaen.

Example 11.1 Pierre Boulez, *Trois Psalmodies*, no. 1, bars 1–7

Boulez's harmony is based on the chord of fourths, perfect and augmented, derived from Messiaen's fifth mode of limited transposition, and continues with chords derived from mode two (the octatonic scale). The most stylistically advanced piece is the third, which is prefaced by the inscription 'phrase mélodique longue accompagnée – Honegger. Hindemith – étude p/piano'. Boulez's reference to Hindemith is as puzzling as it is unexpected in the light of his subsequent development, but may well refer to a Toccata for mechanical piano dating from the 1920s. The Honegger model can be identified with more confidence: the opening of 'Lamento' from the cantata *La danse des morts* (1938). There is an added significance in the choice of quotation, especially given Boulez's frequently expressed reverence for Bach's music, since he would doubtless have been aware that the Honegger piece is itself a homage to Bach, being modelled on the aria 'For love my Saviour now is dying' from the St Matthew Passion. Despite these references, it is the pervasive influence of Messiaen which imposes a stylistic unity on *Trois Psalmodies*, sealed in the final chord of the third piece, a transposed form of the chord of fourths which had opened the first 'Psalmodie'. If this cohesion is achieved at the cost of an absence of any strong individuality, it must be said that Boulez has demonstrated a remarkable grasp of the components of Messiaen's technique. However, there are already glimpses of a world of violent emotional extremes, the articulation of which will shortly lead to a repudiation of the harmonic and melodic style of these student works.

In the spring of 1945, shortly before the Liberation of Paris, Boulez was able to attend a private concert at which a landmark performance of Schoenberg's Wind Quintet (op. 26) was conducted by René Leibowitz. It was the first occasion he was able to hear a piece of Schoenberg's twelve-note music, and in the autumn of that year, Boulez was to organize a group of fellow students to work with Leibowitz each Saturday afternoon, sessions in which he was introduced to the music of Webern. In the meantime, the encounter with Schoenberg was the catalyst for *Thème et variations pour la main gauche,* his boldest and most ambitious work to date, completed in June 1945. The piece consists of a twelve-note theme and thirteen variations. An interesting feature of Boulez's pencil draft is that his first thought was evidently to open the work with the unadorned melodic statement of the theme, which, in the pen manuscript, forms the final variation. This theme, the thirteenth variation in the pen manuscript, consists of four overlapping statements of the prime series, P0, P5, P10, and P4, and recalls Schoenberg's technique both in melodic shape and in its comparatively conservative rhythmic structure (Example 11.2). It is worth noting in passing that Boulez's first twelve-note row is dominated by the minor seconds and tritones which become so characteristic of his later methods. The last four notes form a cell of adjacent semitones: permutation of this cell yields the BACH cipher, which, in carefully disguised form is a background presence in much of his later music, as in the final page of the Second Sonata and 'Sigle' from the Third Sonata. Coincidentally, the opening notes of the row have a remarkably similar shape to the opening of 'Psalmodie 1', an indication that, despite his adoption of Schoenberg's technique, the young composer's melodic and harmonic thinking is still very much influenced by Messiaen. The accompanying left-hand chords are based on a four-note cell, D♮ – G♮ – C♯ – F♯, which, together with its two transpositions, has the potential to form an independent twelve-note

Example 11.2 Pierre Boulez, *Thème et variations pour la main gauche*, variation 13

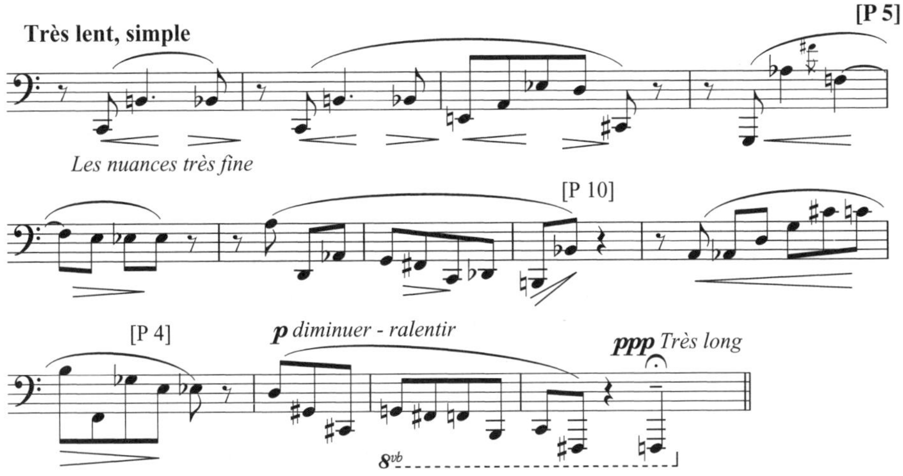

series.[2] The two rows are used independently and in combination to generate the entire piece. Virtually throughout, Boulez confines his use of transpositions to those contained in the theme, and the series is used only in its prime form, apart from the motivic use of inversion. Despite the restrictions imposed by Boulez's still rudimentary knowledge of twelve-note technique, the work as a whole is a remarkable achievement, and it is a pity that it has remained unpublished.

If *Thème et variations pour la main gauche* can be seen as a first response to the twelve-note music of Schoenberg, the next work for piano is the direct result of an influence that was to be even more far-reaching in its consequences. *Notations* was completed in the late autumn of 1945, and Boulez must have worked almost simultaneously on an orchestral version of eleven of the pieces (no. 6 was not orchestrated), the pencil draft of which is dated 'Décembre 1945–Janvier 1946'. Little of Webern's later music was published at this time, and Boulez's hand copies of the Symphony opus 21 and other works date from the time of his study with Leibowitz. The profound effect of this encounter may be judged by the stylistic gulf which separates *Notations* from the preceding works: the music is much more terse and concise, the pianistic textures mirroring the musical discourse in their more fragmentary character. The device of using the same twelve-note row for each piece imparts a certain unity, as does the concept of a cyclical structure generated by the series. Each piece commences with that note in the series which corresponds to its order in the cycle (the only exceptions to this sequence occur in pieces four and five, where the order is reversed, no. 4 beginning with A natural, the fifth note of the series). Unity of pitch structure is paralleled by one of proportions, each piece consisting of twelve bars.

Despite these features, *Notations,* more than any previous work, reveals the range of stylistic influences on Boulez during the latter part of 1945, some of which were soon to be violently repudiated, others absorbed into the astonishingly individual style which characterized the first published works. The continuing influence of Schoenberg can be observed in the textures of nos. 3, 5, 7 and 9, consisting of twelve-note melodic line and complementary harmony. A more angular, cell-like treatment characterizes nos. 1 and 10, where the fragmented textures suggest the impact of Webern. Elsewhere, as in nos. 4 and 8, despite intervallic links to the original series, the creative impulse owes more to the exploration of rhythmic patterns than to twelve-note technique. If the influence of Messiaen can be seen clearly in the structure of no. 4, with its constant lengthening and foreshortening of rhythmic patterns, and in the harmonic style of nos. 3 and 7, then the ethnic style of no. 8 (entitled 'Afrique' in the pencil draft) may well have its origins in the quasi-oriental world evoked in 'La princesse de Bali' from Jolivet's suite *Mana*. Taken as whole, *Notations* stands at the crossroads of Boulez's development. We observe him experimenting in various ways with a pitch structure affording possibilities for rigorous organization much greater than that found in the music of Messiaen, and yet at the same time struggling to reconcile serial technique with the liberating approach to rhythm derived from his teacher. This conflict, with the first hints of a realization that serial technique could be used in the linking of larger structures, was to dominate Boulez's thinking over the remainder of the decade.

---

2 Gerald Bennett: 'The early works', in William Glock (ed.): *Pierre Boulez: a Symposium* (London, 1986), 45; Example 5 quotes the theme and accompaniment.

It was not until 1985 that the solo piano version of *Notations* was finally released for publication. Until that time, the earliest works, chronologically speaking, to enter the public arena were the Flute Sonatina and the First Piano Sonata, the composition of which occupied Boulez between November 1945 and February 1946. Neither these pieces nor the four subsequent works – the two Char cantatas *Le visage nuptial* (1946) and *Le soleil des eaux* (1948), the Second Piano Sonata (1946–48), and *Livre pour quatuor* (1948–49) – have been published in their original form. A development which appears in retrospect to proceed surely, with a succession of radical works, was, in fact, a painful period of trial and error in which the old was only gradually stripped away from the new. Thus both the Flute Sonatina and the First Piano Sonata were extensively revised before their eventual release for publication in 1954 and 1951 respectively.[3] The original opening of the First Sonata (Example 11.3) shows numerous stylistic links with his earlier unpublished works, and implicitly with Messiaen and Jolivet. The drum-like clusters, so reminiscent of 'La princesse de Bali', were an important unifying feature in the 1946 version, whilst the opposition of pairs of adjacent semitones in bar 4 is identical in layout and intervallic content to bars 4–5 of 'Psalmodie 1', that most Messiaenic of all Boulez's early works. Most remarkable of all however are the numerous passages in two-part writing, of an essentially melodic nature, which lay bare their serial origins in a way which Boulez was to reject so comprehensively by the end of the decade.

Example 11.3 Pierre Boulez, Piano Sonata no. 1, bars 1–11

3 For a discussion of the genesis of the Flute Sonatina, see Susanne Gärtner: 'Pierre Boulez's Sonatine für Flöte und Klavier und ihre neu aufgetachte Frühfassung', *Die Musikforschung* 55 (2002), 51–9.

The suppression of such traditional features in the published edition helps to explain the apparent paradox that the First Sonata in its final version is in some respects a more radical work than the Second Sonata. The publication of the latter work in 1950 (effectively Boulez's 'opus 1') was surely one of the most remarkable debuts in twentieth-century music. Yet even this work, with its avowed intention of annihilating classical forms, had a prolonged gestation over two years, starting life as an independent *Variations-Rondeau* completed as early as May 1946, and dedicated to Andrée Vaurabourg-Honegger. It was eventually to become, in revised form, the third movement of the Second Sonata. Its overall shape is essentially fixed at this stage, with three modified returns of the brief opening Scherzo section, marked *Modéré, presque vif* in the published version, separated by somewhat more extended episodes. The first draft of *Variations-Rondeau* provides labels for this sectional structure: the three episodes were conceived as 'Variations' but interestingly, the first return of the opening section is marked, 'Deuxième Répons Rondeau Rétrograde contraire'. This confirms the conscious nature of Boulez's serial thinking with regard to structure as early as 1946.

The arresting beginning of the Second Sonata shares a similarity of gesture with the opening of the final movement of the *Quatuor pour Ondes Martenot,* completed in March 1946 (Exx. 11.4a and b). This unpublished quartet, the composition of which was spread out over some nine months, sums up in its uneasy mix of styles the variety of influences with which the young Boulez was wrestling: two movements which look back to the pre-1945 style of the *Psalmodies* and other Messiaen-inspired works are followed by a finale written under the influence of his encounter with serial procedures. Boulez thought sufficiently well of the piece to rework the second and third movements in the Sonata for two pianos. This work reached its final form in February 1948, but has also remained unpublished. One reason for this may be that material from the first movement was incorporated in the cantata, *Le soleil des eaux*, which started life as music for a radio play by René Char before its subsequent revision.

Two years earlier, Boulez's response to his first encounter with the poetry of René Char was in the form of the cantata *Le visage nuptial,* scored for soprano, two ondes martenot, piano and percussion. Originally dedicated to Messiaen, the piece was subsequently revised for soprano, alto, female chorus and orchestra in 1951–53. Quarter-tone tuning, first found in the *Quatuor pour Ondes Martenot,* is used extensively in both the 1946 and 1951–53 versions of *Le visage nuptial,* a feature which accounts in part for its relatively infrequent performance. During the 1980s, Boulez embarked on a further revision of both Char cantatas. The (presumably) final version of *Le visage nuptial*, published in 1994, eliminates both quarter-tones and the passages in *Sprechstimme,* but retains the structure and proportions of the 1946 version, even down to details of textual underlay. There is a great gain in both clarity of texture and exquisite detail of orchestral writing in the 1994 revision, but arguably some dilution of the starkness of emotional loss, expressed with almost unbearable poignancy in the final movement of the 1951–53 version. Rarely was Boulez to express himself with such directness in his later music, and *Le visage nuptial* remains one of his finest achievements.

One view of Boulez's subsequent development seeks to identify a period of experimentation, leading to a brief flirtation with integral serialism followed by a progressive relaxation of the compositional rigours of the two-piano piece, *Structures 1a* (1951), and the withdrawn *Polyphonie X* (1951) for an ensemble of eighteen instruments.

Example 11.4(a) Pierre Boulez, *Quatuor pour quatre ondes martenot*, finale, opening

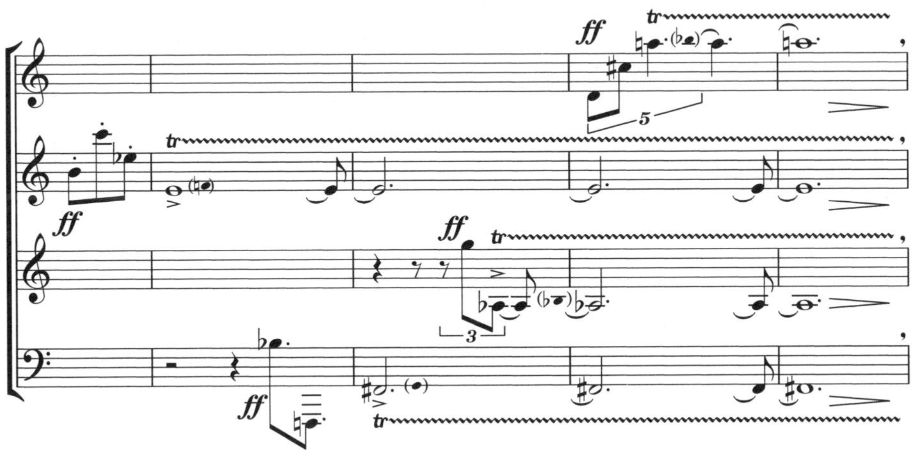

Example 11.4(b) Pierre Boulez, Piano Sonata no. 2, I, bars 1–9

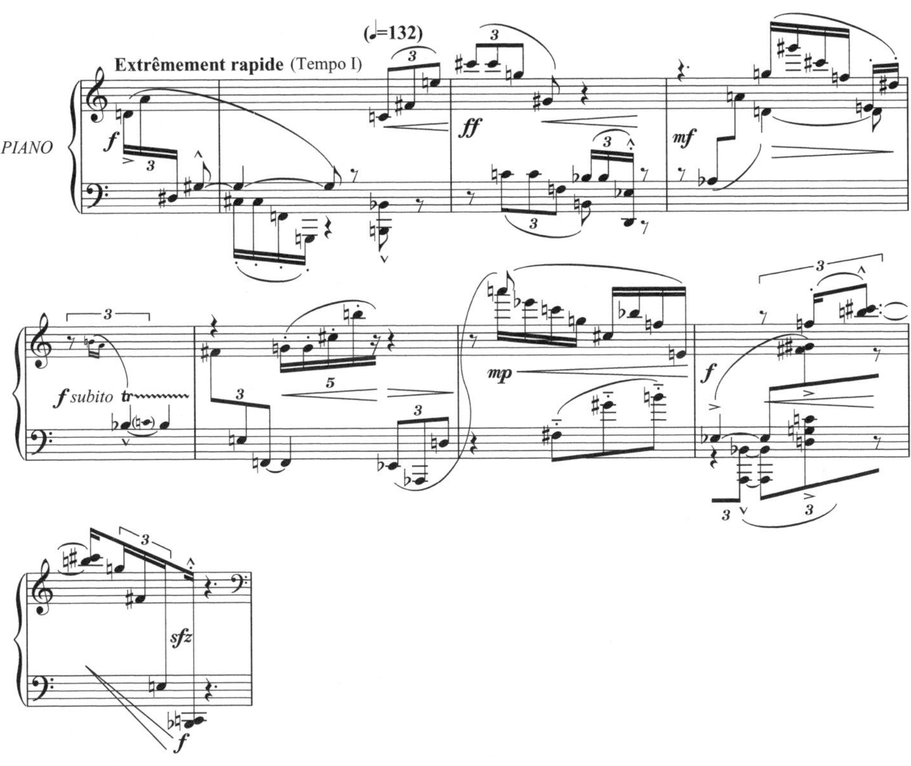

There is a double irony in the fact that, for many years, György Ligeti's analysis of *Structures 1a*[4] remained the most detailed available examination of Boulez's compositional methods. One of the most distinguished composers of Boulez's generation has produced, as his most extended piece of criticism, an analysis of a compositional method which has had virtually no influence on his own compositional procedures. Furthermore, in its concentration on the serial mechanics, Ligeti's approach is in the tradition of Leibowitz's studies of twelve-note technique, pioneering in its day, but violently repudiated by the young Boulez. Ligeti's exposition of the method whereby Boulez employed for the first time a serial (as opposed to chromatic) ordering of the twelve transpositions of the row (see Example 11.5) as a means of deriving rhythmic durations, has distracted attention from the music itself. This has led in turn to a series of misconceptions regarding the character of the works that followed. *Structures 1a* is indeed an extreme piece in Boulez's output, but as the piece unfolds, the austerity of the opening is counterbalanced by considerable textural variety. Tritonal relationships serve as poles in the musical discourse, belying the notion that the serial procedures strip the music of any potential for hierarchies of pitch and rhythm.

In 1952, the year following *Structures 1a,* Boulez produced two pieces for twelve-part unaccompanied chorus, *Oubli signal lapidé,* to poems by Armand Gatti, and withdrawn after a single performance in October 1952. Meanwhile, a setting for soprano and alto flute of the René Char poem, *L'artisanat furieux*, had been completed during the month prior to the premiere of the choral pieces. This was to become the third movement of *Le marteau sans maître,* the composition of which was spread over a period of some three years. Boulez broke his silence about the work in a letter to John Cage, written in July 1954: 'With the two *a cappella* choral pieces I wrote last year [*sic*], it is one of the works that has given me the most trouble. I am trying to rid myself of my fingerprints and taboos; I am trying to have an ever more complex vision – less visible and more worked out in depth – I am trying to expand the series and expand the serial principle to the maximum of its possibilities.'[5] Central to this vision are new principles of serial proliferation, first developed in *Oubli signal lapidé*, and partly described by Boulez in the article, 'Éventuellement ...'.[6] Here, using material drawn from the sketches for *Oubli signal lapidé,* he demonstrates the method by which the prime form of the row is segmented into five unequal groups, arranged vertically. They are then subject to a process of chord multiplication, whereby more complex aggregates result, whilst retaining the intervallic characteristics of the original series.

The two sets of chords thus derived, for the prime form of the row and its inversion, and originally sketched for *Oubli signal lapidé,* are crucial to an understanding of the serial mechanics of Boulez's subsequent works. Not only do they form the building blocks for *Le marteau sans maître,* but they have an important function in the outer movements of *Pli selon pli* (1957–62). Even more remarkable is the extent to which the choral parts of

4 György Ligeti: 'Pierre Boulez: Entscheidung und Automatik in der Structure 1A', *Die Reihe*, 4 (1960), 36–62.

5 Jean-Jacques Nattiez (ed.): *Pierre Boulez/John Cage: Correspondance et documents* (Winterthur, 1990), trans. Robert Samuels as *The Boulez–Cage Correspondence* (Cambridge, 1993), 149.

6 Pierre Boulez: *Relevés d'apprenti* (Paris, 1966), trans. Stephen Walsh as *Stocktakings from an Apprenticeship* (Oxford, 1991), 128–9.

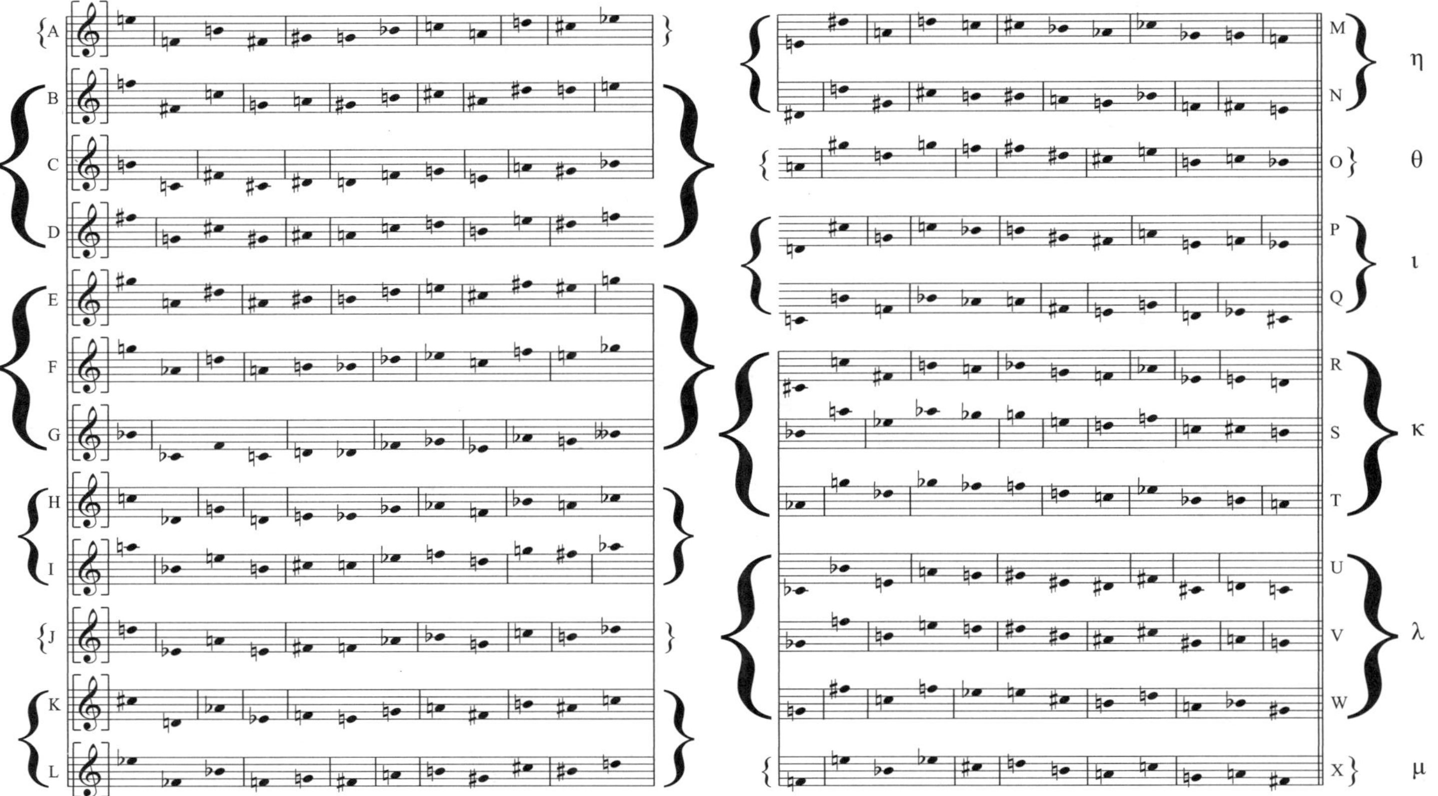

Example 11.5 Pierre Boulez, *Constellation*, row structure

e. e. cummings ist der Dichter (1968) are modelled on material which forms the basis for the second part of *Oubli signal lapidé*. That the same material can become a starting point for works of strikingly different musical character is a testimony both to Boulez's imaginative power, and his success in expanding principles inherent in the series. His settings of the three poets with whom he is most associated – Char, Mallarmé and cummings – share fundamental musical characteristics, whose origin in *Oubli signal lapidé* helps to explain the remarkable stylistic cohesion and sense of unity which is a feature of his mature music. Hardly, then, a loosening of serial rigour, but more a breakthrough into a universe of vastly expanded possibilities.

The development of a new serial language is one of Boulez's greatest achievements during these years, yet to fail to acknowledge the extent to which it is rooted in those of his predecessors would be to underestimate its nature. The intervallic cohesion which he valued so much in the music of Webern is achieved to a greater extent in Boulez's works after 1950, directly as a consequence of the extension of serial parameters. Furthermore, the appropriation of one of Messiaen's modes as the series for *Structures 1a* is hardly an isolated gesture of homage to the composer of *Modes de valeurs et d'intensités* (1949). When the chordal structures of *Oubli signal lapidé* and related works are examined, the extent to which the morphology (to use a Boulezian term) relates to that of Messiaen becomes clear. Thus many of the chords can be categorized in terms of Messiaen's modes 2 and 3, with their division of the octave into cells of minor and major thirds respectively. This is not to imply a diminution in the strikingly original features of Boulez's style, but an acknowledgement of the extent to which his innovations sit within the framework of a musical tradition.

Reference has been made to the gradual emergence of *Le marteau sans maître* towards its final form, and it is now possible to trace in more detail the chronology of the work as a whole.[7] An early, undated sketch was for a cycle containing settings of four Char poems, including *L'artisanat furieux,* the only one of the original choices to survive in the final version of *Le marteau sans maître*. These four vocal movements were to alternate with instrumental commentaries for alto flute, vibraphone and guitar. The three movements of 'L'artisanat furieux' were evidently composed prior to spring 1954, at which point Boulez departed with the Barrault Company for a tour of South America. A letter to Alfred Schlee of Universal Edition, received on 18 May 1954, provides information concerning the progress of the composition.[8] Boulez lists an order of movements:

1 Avant 'L'artisanat furieux'
2 'L'artisanat furieux'
3 Après 'L'artisanat furieux'
5 Commentaire I de 'Bourreaux de solitude'
6 Commentaire II de 'Bourreaux de solitude'
7 'Bourreaux de solitude'
8 Commentaire III de 'Bourreaux de solitude'

7 See R. Piencikowski: 'Au fil des esquisses du "Marteau"', in *Mitteilungen der Paul Sacker Stiflung*, 16 (March 2003), 12–17.

8 © With kind permission from Universal Edition AG.

The erased fourth movement is 'Bourreaux de solitude', now to be interpolated between 'Commentaire II' and 'Commentaire III'. Boulez promises to send scores of these two movements, suggesting that 'Bourreaux de Solitude' and 'Commentaire I' had already been completed. By the middle of July, the tour had moved on to Chile, and a further letter from Boulez, written in Santiago, confirms that 'Commentaire II' has been dispatched to Universal Edition. 'Bel édifice et les pressentiments' is identified as the third poem in the cycle, with its *double* forming the final movement of *Le marteau sans maître*. Given the available information as to the final form of the work, the decision by Universal to issue an unauthorized six-movement version of the piece in the autumn of 1954 must be viewed as an unfortunate episode in its relations with the composer. A performance planned for the Donaueschingen Festival in October 1954 was cancelled, and it was only in the following year that, after further revision, *Le marteau sans maître* received a triumphant premiere under the direction of Hans Rosbaud. This took place at Baden-Baden in June 1955, although the work was still not entirely complete, the coda of the ninth movement being added the following month.

As Lev Koblyakov has demonstrated,[9] chord multiplication was not the only new method of serial proliferation introduced by Boulez in *Le marteau sans maître*. An equally important development was the generation of new series by a principle of intervallic displacement of the pitches of the prime form of the row. The technique will be discussed in more detail below in relation to the Third Sonata, but it was first developed in the sketches for *Oubli signal lapidé* which, in turn, formed the basis for the 'Bourreaux de solitude' cycle.

Immediately prior to the first performance of *Le marteau sans maître*, the long-awaited first performance of another Boulez piece was scheduled to take place in Munich on 22 April: the *Symphonie concertante,* for piano and orchestra, written in 1947. Unfortunately, the score was lost in mysterious circumstances in the months prior to the scheduled premiere. Boulez intended to replace it with a new work for the same forces, but was eventually forced to acknowledge that the time-scale was too short to complete such an ambitious undertaking. The project split into two, with plans for an orchestral piece and a new work for solo piano. Meanwhile, in October that same year, Heinrich Strobel celebrated ten years of activity at South-West German Radio, Baden-Baden. He remained one of Boulez's most important musical champions, having been instrumental in securing the premiere of *Le marteau sans maître*. Among other tributes to mark the anniversary was a contribution by Boulez, consisting of a fragmentary piano piece, prefaced by a dedication, described as 'a work in progress', and dated 9 October. The piece dedicated to Strobel became the subsequently withdrawn final formant, 'Séquence', of the Third Sonata, whilst the numerous unused sketches for 'Séquence' were used as the basis for the first version of a new orchestral piece. Although the sonata was given its premiere by Boulez at Darmstadt on 25 September 1957, and *Doubles*, the preliminary version of *Figures Doubles Prismes,* was first heard in Paris the following year, neither work has reached a final form.[10]

9 Lev Koblyakov: *Pierre Boulez: A World of Harmony* (Chur, 1990), 36.

10 See Allen Edwards: 'Boulez's '*Doubles*' and '*Figures Doubles Prismes*': a Preliminary Study', *Tempo*, 185 (June 1993), 6–17, for a discussion of the sketch material for this work.

The Third Sonata, which occupied Boulez intermittently over an eight-year period, stands at the crossroads of his career. He worked on the piece at a time when the always fragile unity of the Darmstadt group began to disintegrate under the beguiling influence of Cage's advocacy of chance procedures as a solution to problems of musical form. The appearance, in 1956, of Stockhausen's *Klavierstück XI,* with its random ordering of the nineteen sections, any of which can be played (or omitted), was a watershed in the acceptance of Cage's philosophy. Boulez's riposte was the article *Alea* (1957), with its savage attack on the operation of chance, and a refinement of ideas already postulated in the correspondence with Cage concerning the admission of performer choice. As performed by the composer, on several occasions over the two years following its premiere, the Third Sonata consisted of five movements, albeit with three of them in a still fragmentary state.

Boulez elaborated on this structural plan in the article *Sonate, que me veux-tu*.[11] Since it is the only published indication of the work's projected overall shape it is of obvious importance in relation to the two movements that have so far been released for publication. He lists five 'formants', the titles of which 'underline their individual characteristics':

1 Antiphonie
2 Trope
3 Constellation, and its mirror image, Constellation-Miroir
4 Strophe
5 Séquence[12]

Boulez, echoing Joyce, describes it as 'a work in progress', and suggests that the work is open-ended on the most fundamental structural level: 'The five formants clearly permit the genesis of other distinct entities, complete in themselves but structurally connected with the original formants: these entities I call "developments". Such a "book" would thus constitute a maze, a spiral in time.'[13] This gives rise to the thought that the piece has an incompleteness integral to its conception, in the manner of a spiral-bound volume, open to additional insertions, and remaining in a state of perpetual evolution. Of particular interest in a general context is his description of the overall design of the work, in which the third movement occupies a fixed position but the other movements revolve around it in a variety of possible orders. His concluding remarks include the following: 'You will now realise the wealth of possibilities in the interaction of these formants – just imagine parenthesis pages, mobile cahiers, constellations of formants! The imaginative possibilities are, in fact, endless, provided the craftsmanship is there …'[14]

11 Pierre Boulez: 'Sonate, que me veux-tu' first published in German in *Darmstädter Beiträge zur neuen Musik*, vol. 3 (1960). Available in French in P. Boulez: *Points de repère* (Paris, 1981); English trans. Martin Cooper in *Orientations* (London, 1986), 143–54.

12 Ibid., 148–9.

13 Ibid., 148; 'Aussi bien les cinq formants me laissent-ils sans doute le loisir d'engendrer d'autres 'développants', s'imposant comme des touts distincts, se rattachant, toutefois par leur structure aux formants initiaux. Ce livre constituerait un labyrinthe, une spirale dans le temps.'

14 Ibid., 154; 'On aperçoit, dès maintenant, la richesse des possibilités incluse dans la rencontre de ces formants: supposez des pages-parenthèses, des cahiers mobiles, des constellations de formants. Bref, l'imagination n'est point en peine si le métier y pourvoit. …'

Preliminary sketches indicate the arch-like proportions of the overall structure, a long central movement being flanked by two movements of medium duration, each in turn framed by a brief opening and concluding movement. In the event, the two movements which had been completed in time for the 1957 premiere, formant 2, 'Trope', and formant 3, 'Constellation', were published by Universal Edition in 1961 and 1963 respectively, although 'Constellation' was printed in its alternative version, 'Constellation-Miroir', in which the order of the six sections is reversed. The remaining formants were all withdrawn for revision, since when only one short section, 'Sigle', itself an excerpt from 'Antiphonie', has appeared in print as part of an anthology.[15] Both published movements of the Sonata allow the performer a limited degree of freedom in articulating the details of the musical structure, with variable routes through the six sections of 'Constellation' and optional parenthetical insertions in two of the four sections of 'Trope'. One of the many paradoxical features of the work is that, notwithstanding this partial relinquishing of control on one level, the musical parameters are organized with a serial rigour remarkable even by Boulez's standards. From the profile of each individual note to the generation of the overall structure, there is an inexorable unity, with the sectional structure of both formants derived from Boulez's segmentation of the series into four ('Trope') and six ('Constellation').

Boulez has openly acknowledged his increasing indebtedness to the poetry of Mallarmé during these years, and an abortive project from the early 1950s was a setting of Mallarmé's final completed poem, *Un coup de dés*. It is interesting to note that the first explicit mention of this project, in a letter to Cage, dated 30 December 1950,[16] occurs just prior to a reference to the subsequently withdrawn *Polyphonie X*, during the course of which Boulez speculates on the possible employment of open forms. This challenges the conventional view of Boulez as an increasingly conservative figure in the later years of the 1950s, responding only reluctantly to Stockhausen's adoption of chance procedures in *Klavierstück XI* (1956). Indeed, one of the many paradoxes in any consideration of Boulez's compositional aesthetic during the 1950s is his engagement with the work of a poet whose richness of imagery is complemented by an ambiguity of expression seemingly at odds with the certainties of integral serialism. No sketches for *Un coup de dés* appear to have survived, but Boulez was soon to pay formal homage to Mallarmé in a large-scale work, *Pli selon pli*. In the meantime, the poet's imagery is a strong underlying influence on the Third Sonata, extending far beyond the obvious links in typographical layout which exist between 'Constellation' and *Un coup de dés*. The recurrent symbol of the constellation Ursa Major in Mallarmé's poetry, and specifically the symbolism of the cross formed by the four brightest stars intersecting at the Pole Star has a parallel in the design of the Sonata, with its four formants revolving around 'Constellation'.

In this context, it is relevant to mention another influence on the Third Sonata. Whilst Boulez's acknowledgement of his indebtedness to Paul Klee is documented, less well known is the extent to which the designs in his sketches at times trace patterns found in Klee's theoretical writings. Thus the spiral shape of 'Trope' is found in Klee's *Notebooks*, and number sequences similar to those found in the sketches for 'Constellation' formed an important part of Klee's teaching at the Bauhaus as an illustration of the transformation of

15 Universal Edition, no. 12050 (1968).

16 *The Boulez–Cage Correspondence*, 80.

forms by displacement. The relevant passage in *Notebooks*, volume 2 cites examples, including the patterns of bricks in masonry, in the context of specific reference to stars and constellations.[17] Boulez's compositional grid for the overall structure of 'Constellation' has parallels with those found in the 'Notebooks', and a startling coincidence is Klee's derivation patterns including the form of a cross to demonstrate the structure of the painting 'Harmony from Rectangles'.[18] The symbolism is obvious both in relation to the revolving formants of the Third Sonata and to the technique of chord multiplication in 'Constellation'. Indeed, in its masterly balance of overall design and musical detail, 'Constellation' arguably attains a richness of imagery and an absorption of serial principles unsurpassed in any of Boulez's later works.

The overall plan of the Third Sonata, with formants revolving around 'Constellation', has never been realized. There is a reference in *Conversations with Célestin Deliège* to a third formant being 'in an advanced state'[19] and examination of the sketches confirms that this refers to 'Antiphonie'. In Boulez's performances of 1957–58, this section of the Sonata was almost as fragmentary as the other unfinished formants. However, it continued to occupy him intermittently over the next six years. The reasons for this are at the heart of Boulez's aesthetic philosophy, and the technical procedures he developed during the 1950s to serve his expressive needs. Unlike the other formants of the Third Sonata, 'Antiphonie' employs a type of serial expansion to which reference has already been made in the context of the 'Bourreaux de solitude' cycle in *Le marteau sans maître,* and with the potential for generating a vastly increased network of serial relationships. The technique of obtaining these is simple in principle, and is succinctly described in *Penser la musique aujourd'hui*: 'If the pitches are accorded durations directly (or inversely) proportional to the intervals which separate them, another form of generation will result from the order of the size of interval being brought to bear on the order of succession.'[20]

That is to say, in order to generate a second series derived from the first, each note moves forward the number of steps which correspond to the number of semitones between it and the adjacent note in the series. It was this technique to which Boulez returned in 'Antiphonie', and his example in *Penser la musique aujourd'hui* is drawn from the sketches for that formant. Unfortunately, as with the illustration of chord multiplication in the same book, this example is incomplete. The complete sketch (Example 11.6a) shows the logic of the process, which can be followed more readily on the accompanying numerical grid (Example 11.6b) (C natural = 1, C sharp = 2 etc). Within two years of the first performance of the Sonata, Boulez had to all intents and purposes completed 'Antiphonie' in the form as described in *Sonate que me veux-tu*, and indeed plans were at an advanced stage to print the formant along with 'Trope' and 'Constellation'. However, an expanded serial technique clearly had possibilities only hinted at in the 1960 version of

17 Paul Klee: *Unendliche Naturgeschichte* (Basel, 1970), trans. Heinz Norden as *Notebooks* vol. 2, *The Nature of Nature* (London, 1973), 245.

18 Ibid., 183.

19 Pierre Boulez: *Par volonté et par hasard: Entretiens avec Célestin Deliège* (Paris, 1975), trans. as *Conversations with Célestin Deliège* (London, 1976), 83.

20 *Penser la musique aujourd'hui*, 40; 'si j'affecte les hauteurs de durées directement – ou inversement – proportionelles aux intervalles qui les lient, j'obtiendrai une autre forme d'engendrement sériel en reportant l'ordre de grandeur de l'intervalle sur l'ordre de succession.'

'Antiphonie'. By 1963, he embarked on a plan for a vast expansion of the first formant, with four 'Traits' into which were to be interleaved the existing 'Antiphonie' and the miniature 'Sigle'. One section, 'Trait Initial' was completed, but the project appears to have been abandoned indefinitely, with a second 'Trait' having reached only the preliminary sketching stage.

Boulez's other Mallarméan project, *Pli selon pli,* has been realized with greater sureness of purpose than the Third Sonata, and is unquestionably one of his greatest achievements. Even so, although complete performances of this work have been given since 1962, its genesis was in many ways as problematic as that of the Sonata. This 'Portrait de Mallarmé', as it is subtitled, originated in material composed for Jean-Louis Barrault's theatrical production of *Orestie* in 1955. Two settings of sonnets for voice and chamber ensemble were completed in the autumn of 1957. By 1959, these two 'Improvisations' were complemented by a third setting, and an additional movement, 'Tombeau', was added. In November of that year, Boulez was able to write to Alfred Schlee confirming his intention of adding an introductory movement, 'Don', adding the explanation 'pièce symétrique à Tombeau' (a pendant to Tombeau).[21] In the event, 'Tombeau' was revised and expanded after its premiere at Donaueschingen in 1959, prior to the first performance of the work in its five-movement form in 1960, under the composer's direction. At this point, 'Don' consisted of a piano piece introduced by the first line of Mallarmé's poem, interrupted by the single spoken interjection, "Palmes", the opening word of the verse. Boulez completed an expanded, orchestral version of 'Don' in time for the first performance of the revised version of *Pli selon pli* in October 1962. Here, the concept of vocal interjections within the framework of an essentially orchestral movement is developed further, with anticipatory references to the three central 'Improvisations'.

The symmetrical design of the work is obvious on one level. The central triptych is framed by outer movements, which are primarily orchestral interpretations of the poems. 'Don' sets only the opening line of *Don du poème,* while it is not until the concluding pages of 'Tombeau' that the final line of *Tombeau de Verlaine* emerges in a vocal setting, bringing the entire cycle to a close on the same chord which had opened it. Reference has already been made to the use of material originally sketched for *Oubli signal lapidé* and *Le marteau sans maître,* and it can be readily observed that the vocal phrase which opens the entire cycle derives from this source (Example 11.7b being a horizontal ordering of the pitches of the first two chords of Example 11.7a). The same series is used as the basis for the piano chords in the opening section of 'Tombeau' (Example 11.7c), before being quoted in its melodic form at the entrance of the guitar. At the climax of this final movement, immediately before the setting of the final line of Mallarmé's poem, the entire chordal sequence is heard ***ffff*** in the piano (Example 11.7d): the creative cycle has run its course and is about to be extinguished. There is surely a conscious irony in Boulez's use of this material, especially in the context of *Don du poème,* which was itself a direct precursor of Mallarmé's unfinished *Hérodiade*.

The structure of the central triptych of 'Improvisations' is similarly weighted towards the concluding 'A la nue accablante tu', the longest movement in the work (it is longer than the first two 'Improvisations' combined). Reference has already been made to the

---

21 © With kind permission by Universal Edition AG.

Example 11.6(a) Pierre Boulez, sketch for 'Antiphonie' row table

Example 11.6(b) Pierre Boulez, sketch for 'Antiphonie', numerical grid

5	4	10	3	1	2	11	9	12	7	8	6
	3	2	12	11	1		4–10	8		9–7 –6	5
4–2		3–1		12	5–10 9		11–8	7	6		
1		11– 12	2–6			10–9 –8	7			5–4	3
8	12		10–1 –11	9		7		5–6	3	2	4
3–12 –7	10–11		9		8	6		4	5	1	2
11		9	8	10	7	5–4 –12	3–6		2		1
			7	5–8 –6				3–2 –9	4–1		10–11 –12
10	9–8	6		4–7	11	3	5–2	1	12		
	7–2	5			3–4 –6		1			10–11 –12	8–9
9–6	1	8	5–4	3		2	12	11	10		7
	5–6	4–7		2	12	1		10	11–9 –8	3	

extensive use of music originally composed for *Orestie*, and the pieces draw freely on existing additional material from various sources. The interlude in the first 'Improvisation' contains references to nos. 5 and 9 of the then unpublished *Notations,* whilst the opening of 'Une dentelle s'abolit' uses material already sketched for 'Séquence', the final formant of the Third Sonata. Again, the fact that these derivations do not detract from the stylistic unity of *Pli selon pli* as a whole emphasizes the unprecedented degree of consistency in Boulez's expansion of serialism. Such is its flexibility that references to the BACH cipher, which introduces the voice in the second 'Improvisation' and reappears in the closing bars, can pass by almost unnoticed (Example 11.8). 'A la nue accablante tu' takes this gesture as its point of departure, but the motive is refracted through the quarter-tone tuning of the harps (Example 11.9). Of all the poems chosen by Boulez, this sonnet is perhaps closest to the imagery of *Un coup de dés*, its ambiguities of syntax belying its traditional structure. In the 1959 version, all but the three opening lines of text were submerged, and the piece commenced with a statement from each of the four principal musical protagonists in turn:

Example 11.7(a) Pierre Boulez, chord sketch for *Oubli signal lapidé*

Example 11.7(b) Pierre Boulez, *Pli selon pli*, I ('Don'), soprano solo, p. 1

Example 11.7(c) Pierre Boulez, *Pli selon pli*, V ('Tombeau'), piano solo, p. 1

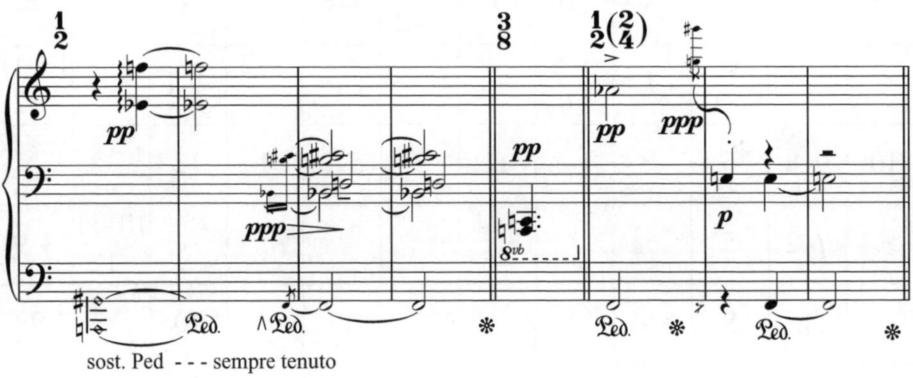

Example 11.7(d) Pierre Boulez, *Pli selon pli*, V ('Tombeau'), piano solo, bar 529

Example 11.8 Pierre Boulez, *Pli selon pli*, III, 'Improvisation sur Mallarmé II', closing bars

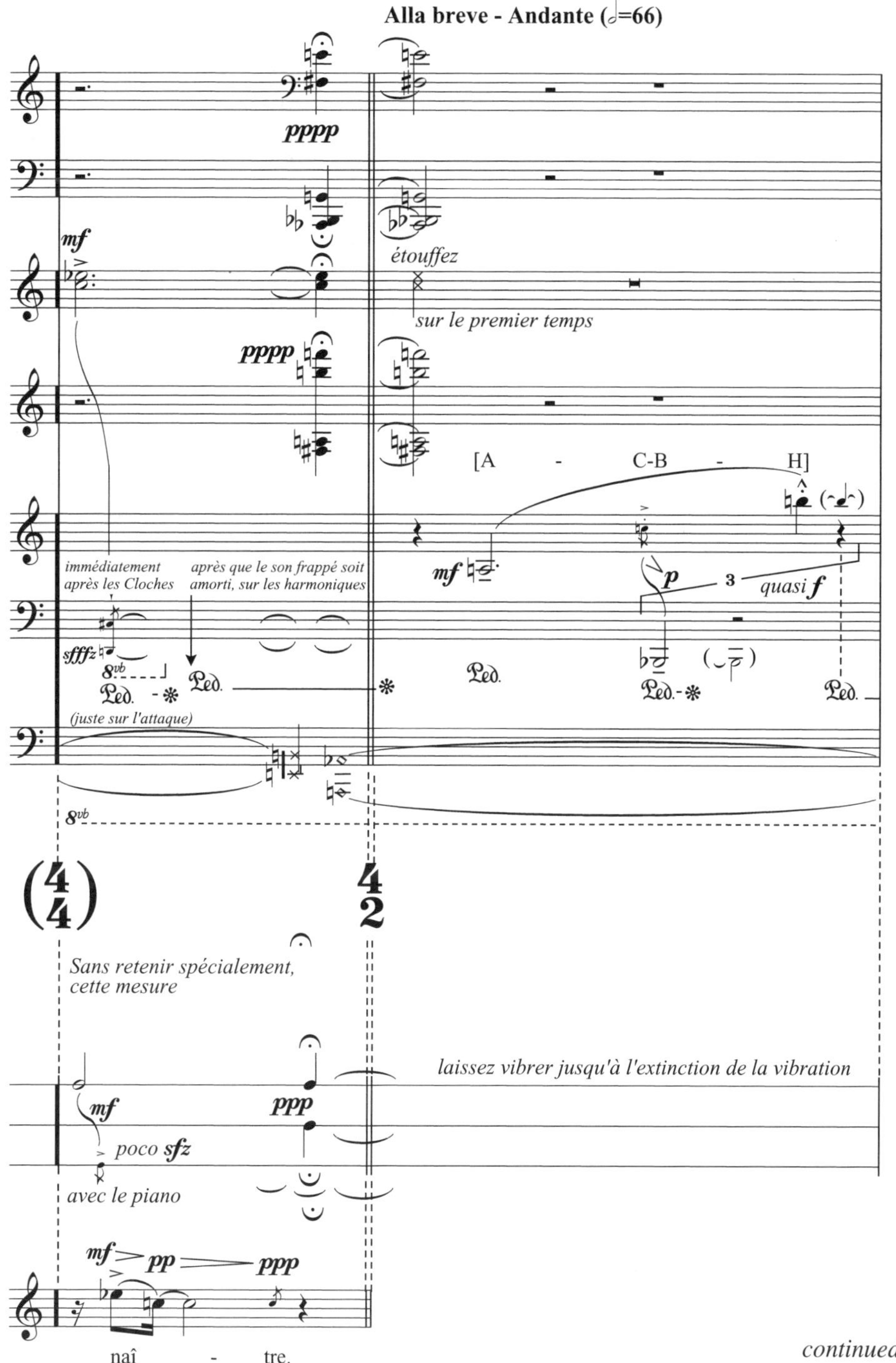

continued

Example 11.8 *concluded*

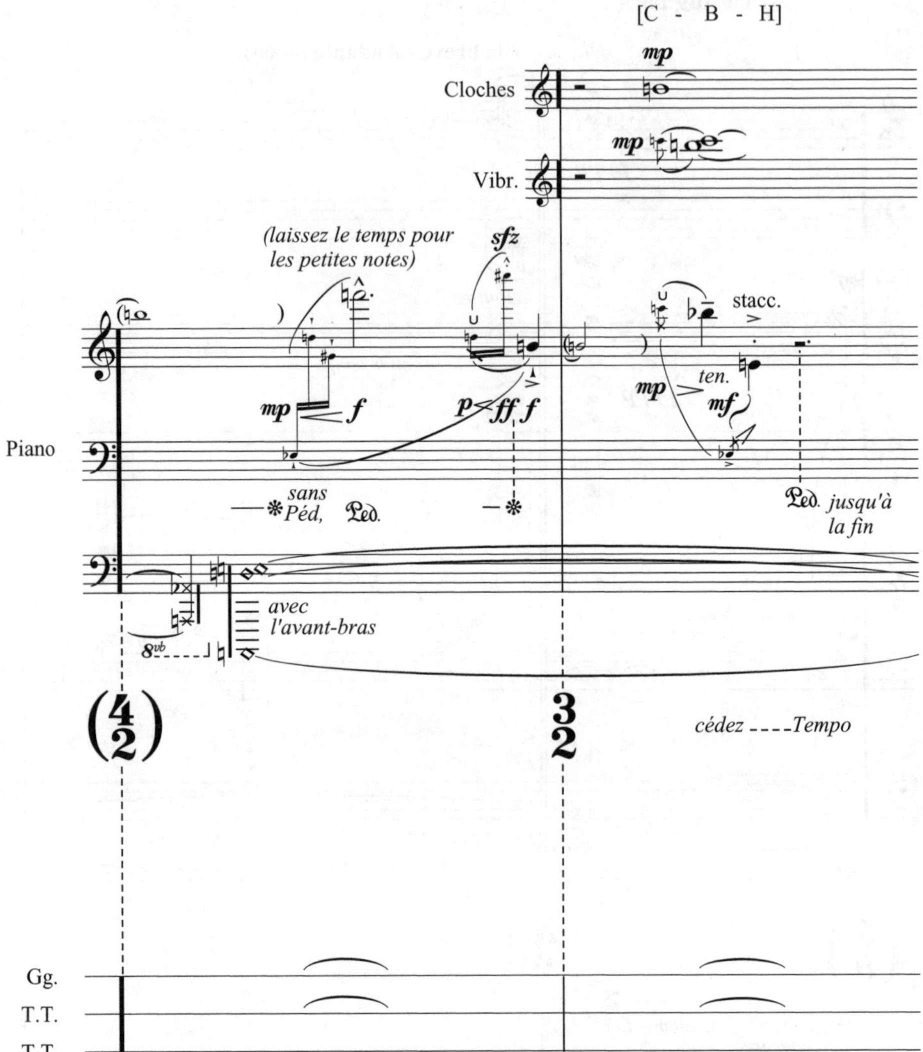

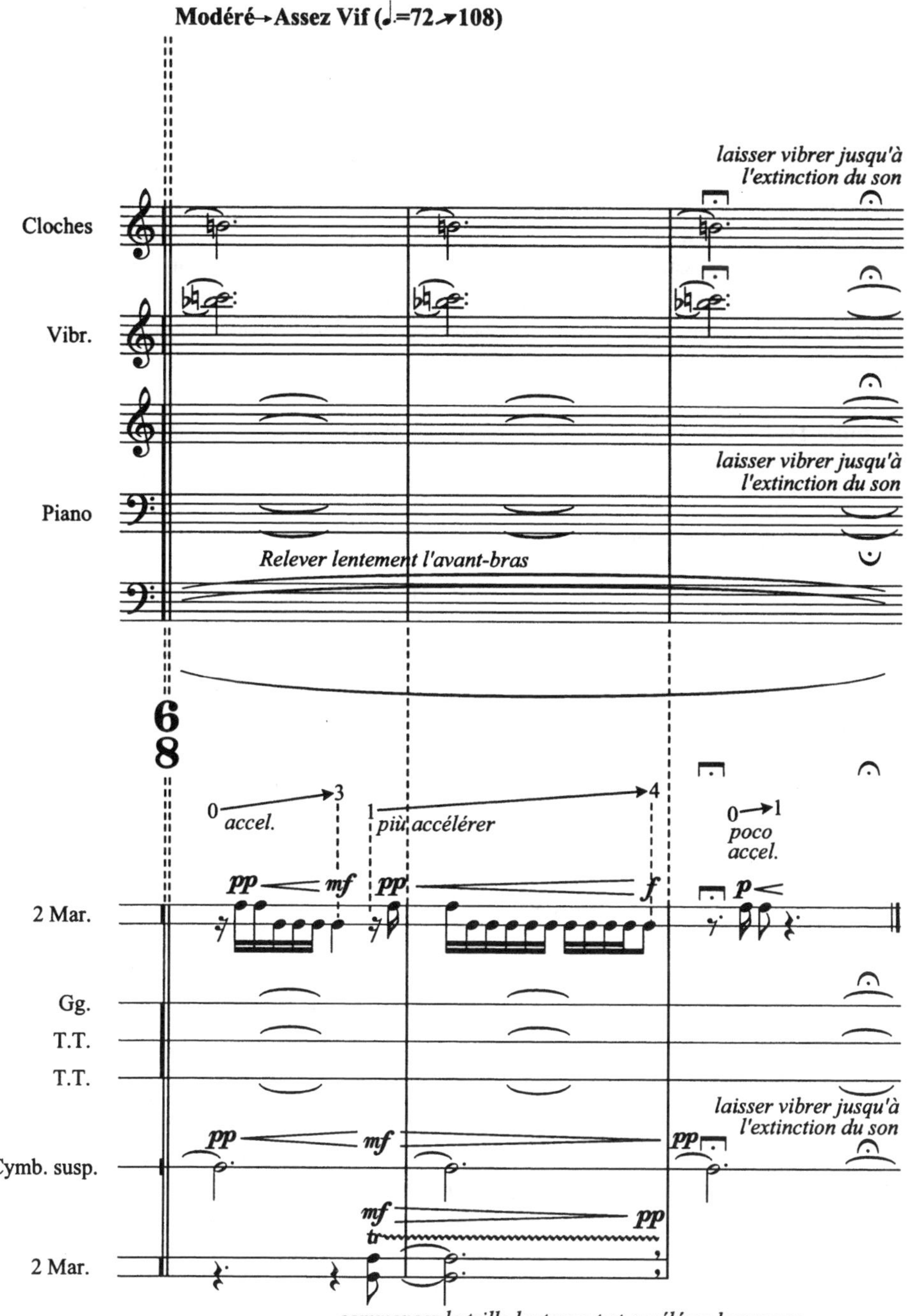
Modéré→Assez Vif (♩.=72→108)
laisser vibrer jusqu'à l'extinction du son
Cloches
Vibr.
laisser vibrer jusqu'à l'extinction du son
Piano
Relever lentement l'avant-bras
6
8
0→3
accel.
1→4
più accélérer
0→1
poco accel.
pp
mf
pp
f
p
2 Mar.
Gg.
T.T.
T.T.
laisser vibrer jusqu'à l'extinction du son
pp
mf
pp
Cymb. susp.
mf
pp
tr
2 Mar.
commencer le trille lentement et accélérer beaucoup

harps, vocalise, plucked strings and tuned percussion. In seeking to find a musical parallel to this enigmatic poem, Boulez employed open structures, which, whilst precisely notated, allowed some freedom on a local level – means not dissimilar to those employed in 'Constellation'. The setting in this form remained unpublished, although two commercial recordings directed by Boulez have been issued. Eventually, a revised version was issued in 1982, in which, as in the first two 'Improvisations', the previously suppressed text of the entire sonnet is set. Here, 'une trompe sans vertu', in the guise of a solitary tenor trombone, is a less shadowy presence than in the original version, as it provides a quietly menacing background from the first vocal entry. Revelation of its true character is saved for the final pages of 'Tombeau', where the horn emerges from the climactic piano chords as a summons to the final dénouement: 'Un peu profond ruisseau calomnié la mort'.

Example 11.9 Pierre Boulez, *Pli selon pli*, IV, 'Improvisation sur Mallarmé III', opening, harp I

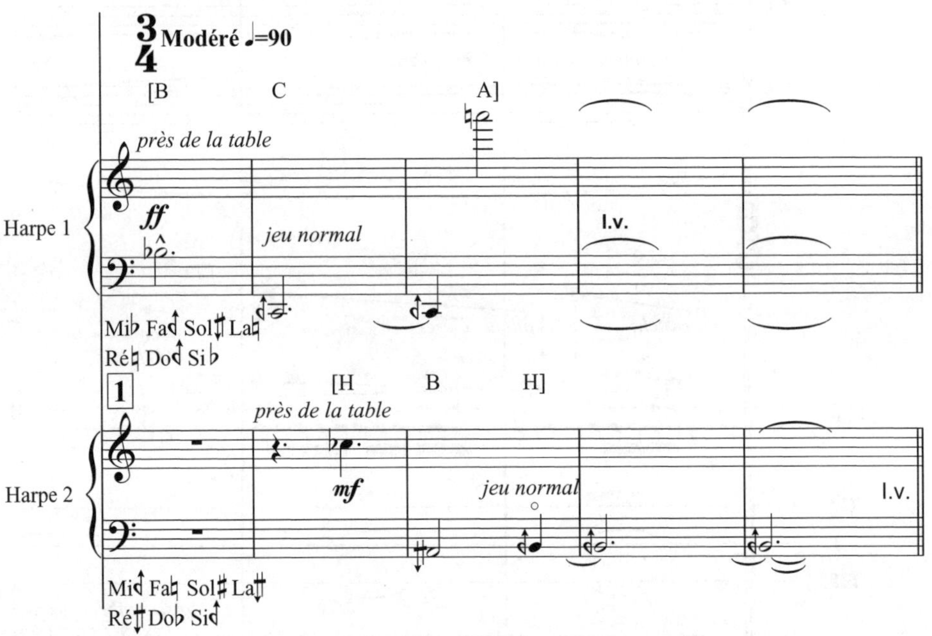

Notwithstanding later revisions, the completion of *Pli selon pli* and of *Structures*, livre 2 in 1962 effectively marks the end of a chapter in Boulez's compositional career. The next decade is characterized by a comparative dearth of new works, and a rapid expansion of his conducting activities. Despite continuing work on *Figures Doubles Prismes* (1964/68) and a revision of two movements from the *Livre pour quatuor* for string orchestra, as *Livre pour cordes* (1968), there are few major new projects. Reference has already been made to the cantata *e.e. cummings ist der Dichter* (1968) in the context of the works of the mid-1950s. *Éclat* (1965), for fifteen instruments, likewise has its origins in unpublished material, in this case passages originally drafted for

Orestie.[22] Both *Éclat* and *Domaines* (1961–68) for solo clarinet have each been subsequently expanded: a version of *Domaines* for clarinet and six instrumental groups dates from 1969, whilst *Éclat/Multiples* (1966–70) for vastly expanded orchestral forces remains a 'work in progress'. Inevitably there is an increasing ring of irony in this phrase, first used by Boulez in relation to the Third Sonata. While it is certainly the case that the concept of open forms imparts a provisional character to any musical structure, Boulez's forays into this area have proved increasingly problematic, with works 'withdrawn for revision' having seemingly been abandoned. There is a growing sense that the tensions between serial organization and open forms are fundamentally irreconcilable – an impression strengthened by the various revisions to *Pli selon pli,* including the recent reworking (2000) of the final section of 'Don'.[23]

In the light of this, it is paradoxical that Boulez's most extreme example of open form ... *explosante-fixe* ... should point the direction for much of his creative work over the next two decades. Following the death of Stravinsky in 1971, he was commissioned by the magazine *Tempo* to write a short memorial piece. Boulez's response consisted of a compositional matrix occupying a single sheet, and supplemented by five pages of instructions for possible realizations.[24] The matrix consists of an 'Originel' containing seven pitches, and six related 'Transitoires'. 'Originel' is played either at the beginning or the end, and arrows provide possible routes through the other six sections. Whilst the piece could be played solo, or by any combination of instruments, Boulez suggests an ensemble of seven instruments consisting of harp, with two each of violins, flutes and clarinets. According to Susan Bradshaw, Boulez made a realization of the piece in this form shortly afterwards, but it was withdrawn after a single performance.[25] A new version for flute, clarinet, trumpet, violin, viola, cello and vibraphone/harp was produced in 1972–73, and first performed in New York on 5 January 1973. This, while retaining the principle of indeterminacy inherent in the work's conception, introduced an electronic dimension in the form of the halaphone, named after its inventor, Hans-Peter Haller. Boulez described the role of electronics at this stage in the piece's evolution as follows: 'This transformation of sound is produced by an electro-acoustical process that is totally independent of all the rest: the sound of the instrument passes through a channel that transforms it, and it is not necessary that it should be transformed out of all recognition. On the contrary, in everything related to the original – references to the original itself – the sound is barely transformed at all, or if it is, its origin can be quite clearly identified.'[26]

The reintroduction of electronics into Boulez's work for the first time since the 1950s is of the utmost significance in relation to his later work. In fact, he had long viewed technology with a mixture of excitement at its potential and frustration at the limitations of the available resources. If his earlier work in the field has received comparatively little attention, this is primarily because all four works involving tape – the two *Études*

22 See Robert Piencikowski: '"Assez lent, suspendu, comme imprévisible." Quelques aperçus sur les travaux d'approche d'*Eclat*', *Genesis* 4 (1993), 51–67 for a detailed examination of the manuscript sources.

23 As performed at the Royal Festival Hall, London, on 26 Mar. 2000.

24 *Tempo*, 98 (Jan. 1972).

25 Susan Bradshaw: 'The instrumental and vocal music' in Glock (ed.): *Pierre Boulez*, 209. Bradshaw's chapter is indispensable reading in any consideration of Boulez's musical style.

26 *Conversations with Célestin Deliège*, 105.

de musique concrète (1952), *Symphonie mécanique* (1955) and *Poésie pour pouvoir* (1958) – have been withdrawn. The clues to Boulez's dissatisfaction with the results of the comparatively primitive technology of the 1950s may be found in its imprecision as compared to the developed musical syntax he had achieved in his instrumental works.

Poésie pour pouvoir, performed at Donaueschingen in October 1958, was his most ambitious attempt to date at integrating the two worlds. The massive forces employed in this eighteen-minute work consisted of three orchestral groups, one of which comprised solo instruments. A five-track tape was assembled using instrumental sound as its basis, with the superimposition of fragments drawn from the eponymous poem by Henri Michaux. The component elements thus combine those of Stockhausen's recent electronic piece, *Gesang der Jünglinge* (1956) and his work for three orchestras *Gruppen*, at the premiere of which (in March 1958) Boulez had been one of the three conductors. In *Poésie pour pouvoir,* the two sound worlds are to a large extent kept separate, with only brief sections of overlap between orchestral and electronic sound. Dissatisfied with these results, and specifically with the inflexibility of tape as a medium, Boulez abandoned the exploration of electronics during the 1960s.

In 1968, during a public lecture, 'Où en est-on?' ('Where are we?') given at Saint-Étienne in May, Boulez addressed the inadequacy of achievements in the field of electronic music up to that time, and offered a vision for the future: 'I think that all today's discoveries, whether in the instrumental of the electro-acoustic field, demand a much wider basis, and to achieve this we need a kind of general school, or laboratory, where researchers in different disciplines can study these problems with a view to finding solutions applicable to music.'[27] So, when he was invited the following year by President Pompidou to direct musical activities in a planned arts complex at the Beaubourg in Paris, Boulez put forward counter-proposals for a research centre along the lines he had advocated. Indeed its very title, 'Institut de Recherche et Coordination Acoustique/Musique' (IRCAM) (Institute for Research and Coordination of Acoustics/Music) is anticipated in an earlier part of the Saint-Étienne lecture: 'Why have almost all electronic music studios failed hitherto? Simply because there has been no coordination between the experts, the inventors and the musicians.' IRCAM, a subterranean building with access in Place Igor-Stravinsky, immediately adjacent to the Pompidou Centre, was finally completed in 1978.

Under Boulez's direction, priority was given to the development of a more flexible means of sound synthesis involving computer technology. Effectively, the opening of IRCAM marked the beginning of a new chapter in Boulez's artistic development, and a planned revision of *Poésie pour pouvoir* was laid aside in favour of a new project, *Répons*. Henceforth, the integration of technology and instrumental forces could be pursued on a more equal basis, as Boulez sought to realize successfully a vision he had first expounded over twenty years previously: 'I thus refuse to believe in the idea of "progress" from instrumental to electronic music; there is only a shift in the field of action. What then is the most enticing prospect? To bring, I repeat for the last time, the two sound universes face to face within multi-dimensional constructions, an experiment which would doubtless lead us, nay drag us (to borrow the title of one of Paul Klee's pictures) to "the edge of fertile land ...".'[28]

---

27 *Orientations*, 455.

28 *Stocktakings from an Apprenticeship*, 172; 'Ainsi nous refusons-nous à croire en un 'progrès'

Répons was written in response to a commission from the Donaueschingen Music Festival, and first performed in 1981. Formal work on the piece had begun the previous year, but prior to that, Boulez had spent a period absorbed in the technical developments at IRCAM, in particular the rapid progress of computer technology with its potential for 'real-time' transformation of instrumental sound. *Répons* is scored for a small orchestral group, and six soloists – two pianos, harp, vibraphone, glockenspiel/xylophone and cimbalom – which are subject to live transformation of various kinds. The choice of solo instruments was dictated by the capability of the 4X computer to exploit their resonating characteristics to the limits of the technology available at the time. Whilst Boulez had apparently already conceived a vast formal plan for a work lasting an entire concert, the premiere consisted of about twenty minutes' music. An expanded version was heard at the BBC Proms the following year, and a further section was composed in time for a performance in Turin in 1984, resulting in a total duration of some forty minutes.

Boulez's use in *Répons* of a generating motive based on the name of his friend and patron Paul Sacher is anticipated in the short *Messagesquisses*, written in 1976 to mark Sacher's seventieth birthday, and scored for the unusual combination of solo cello and six cellos. Also notable in this piece is a return to pulsed rhythmic gestures, a characteristic which was to play an increasingly important role in Boulez's music from *Répons* onwards. In terms of musical structure, the nearest antecedent to *Répons* is the seemingly abandoned *Éclat/Multiples* with its chamber group of soloists from the original *Éclat* augmented by vast orchestral forces. In *Répons*, an opening tutti for the orchestral group serves as a prelude to the overwhelming first entry of the soloists, an impact made all the greater by the immediate electronic transformation of the component elements. Andrew Gerszo has demonstrated that this massive arpeggiated chord is in essence derived from a single seven-note chord played on the vibraphone.[29] This, together with the related SACHER cipher, will generate the pitch material for the ensuing sections. These are clearly audible in performance, and Dominique Jameux, in an analysis of the piece in its 1982 version, characterizes them successively as 'Balinese', 'Funeral March', 'Rain Music', 'Finale' and 'Coda'.[30] By the time of the 1984 Turin performance, Boulez had inserted two additional episodes between 'Finale' and 'Coda'. Thematic elements come increasingly to the fore in these new sections, but the continuing overall unity of the piece can readily be demonstrated in the prominent appearance of material derived from the SACHER cipher at the beginning of the section immediately prior to the coda (Example 11.10). The contrast between rhythmically strict material confined to the orchestra and cadenza-like embellishments for the soloists remains a principal textural characteristic of this latest

de la musique instrumentale à la musique électronique; il y a seulement déplacement des champs d'action. Ce qui serait pour nous séduire? Confronter, nous le répétons encore pour conclure, les deux univers sonores en des constructions multidimensionelles; investigation qui, sans doute, nous mènerait, nous forcerait, selon le titre que Paul Klee avait choisi pour un de ses tableaux, *à la limite du pays fertile* ...'.

29 Andrew Gerzso, 'Reflections on *Répons*', *Contemporary Music Review* (1984, vol. 1), 23–34. This short article, written by Boulez's assistant, provides an excellent introduction to the technology employed in the work.

30 Dominique Jameux: *Boulez* (Paris, 1984), 440–43. (Jameux's categorization of sections is identical to that used in the banding of the commercially issued CD [457 605-2] under Boulez's direction.

Example 11.10 Pierre Boulez, *Répons*, SACHER motif

version of *Répons*. However, the transition to the coda is more gradual, as the orchestra recalls the sustained trills which had featured in the opening section of the work, before the massive chordal resonances of the six soloists again take centre stage in bringing the work to a conclusion. Despite its many innovations, *Répons* is in some respects a work of consolidation. That this should be so is unsurprising given Boulez's essential consistency of style throughout his composing career. Thus the SACHER cipher itself, when reduced to scalic form, has strong affinities with Messiaen's mode 2, and the treatment of the solo instruments has parallels with Messiaen's theory of harmony derived from natural resonances, albeit raised to a new level of sophistication and technological ingenuity.

Immediately after the completion of the third version of *Répons*, the sudden death of the Ensemble Intercontemporain flautist Lawrence Beauregard prompted Boulez to return to the material for … *explosante-fixe* …, and the result was a six-minute piece for solo flute, two horns, and a sextet of strings (three violins, two violas, and cello) entitled *Mémoriale* (1985). The subtitle, … *explosante-fixe … Originel,* explains the origins of the piece, which is essentially a flute solo with accompaniment, based on one section of the single-page score produced in 1972. Flexible, almost improvisatory sections, marked *Rapide, irrégulier, vacillant*, are framed by *Lent* cadences, set apart by their distinctive

Example 11.11 Pierre Boulez, *Mémoriale*, fixed register of pitches

sonority of flutter-tonguing on the flute supported by horns marked ***pp**, bouché*. The cadential figures are gradually expanded from two notes, until at the end, their source is fully revealed as the seven-note cell of 'Originel'. Elsewhere, the rhapsodic character of the flute arabesques masks a rigid disposition of registers, each of the twelve chromatic notes appearing throughout at the same transposition (Example 11.11). Only lower strings and horns are allowed occasionally to depart from this scheme, and the result is a beguilingly translucent texture, ranging in dynamics from ***ppp*** to ***mf***. Reflecting Boulez's new confidence of purpose in the 1980s, the open forms of the 1972 matrix and the 1973 version are here abandoned in favour of a through-composed structure.

As so often in Boulez's earlier career, a compositional project is allowed to take wing as he sees new possibilities in the material. In the case of … *explosante-fixe* …, a vast expansion of the original concept was prompted by developments in digital technology during the late 1980s. A new version of 'Originel' for MIDI flute and ensemble (1991–93) was produced alongside realizations of 'Transitoires' V and VII, as the first stage in a revised plan to produce a substantial seven movement work. Perhaps it would be more accurate to describe the 1991–93 version of 'Originel' as an arrangement of *Mémoriale* rather than a new version: the instrumental forces of *Mémoriale* are retained, and indeed their parts are identical to those of the 1985 version. However, a richer texture is achieved by the addition of a full complement of woodwind and brass instruments, together with a double bass, an instrumentation consistent throughout the three completed movements of … *explosante-fixe* … Gone is the indeterminacy implicit in the 1972 matrix, and the instrumental texture, far from being an equal interplay of seven instruments as in the first realization of … *explosante-fixe* …, is now dominated by the presence of the MIDI flute, the keys of which trigger the various modes of electronic transformation. These three movements are linked by brief interludes consisting entirely of electronic sounds, and throughout there is a homogeneity of texture which is in direct contrast to that of *Répons*.

Both … *explosante-fixe* … and *Répons* remain 'works in progress', as does another project from this period. In 1980, Boulez produced the first four of a planned recomposition for full orchestra of the solo piano *Notations* (1945). These virtuoso pieces were eventually followed by a new version of 'Notation VII' in 1997, in which the orchestral dimensions are increased even further. A comparison of this piece with the 1946 orchestration of *Notations* is revealing. There, Boulez had opted for a chamber ensemble of only eleven players for this piece, making it among the most delicately scored of the *Notations*. Traces of the instrumental timbres of the 1946 version remain in the 1997 recomposition: the alternating two-part chords which underpin the entire piece were originally scored for oboe and cor anglais. A similar orchestral colouring is heard at the beginning of the 1997 version, with the chords sustained on two cor anglais, whilst the reiterated C sharp – G natural motive is characterized by the trumpet in both versions. In 1946, Boulez orchestrated the melodic motive (bars 6–8 of the piano score) with a solo viola, the only string instrument used in this scoring of no. VII. By contrast, the 1997 version employs a full complement of strings, divided with the utmost textural finesse into as many as forty-five parts. Despite the recurrences of the ***ff*** trumpet motive, the overall effect is one of diaphanous delicacy of an almost impressionistic character, the starkness of the bare fifths of the original version being softened by shimmering clusters in the strings.

If *Notations* in its various stages exemplifies the consistency of Boulez's approach over a fifty-year period, two more recent works of the 1990s reveal a continuing preoccupation with the material of those defining works of the two preceding decades, … *explosante-fixe* … and *Répons*. *Anthèmes* (1991) began as a short piece for solo violin developed from material originally composed for the 1973 realization of … *explosante-fixe* …. Boulez has subsequently expanded the piece, and *Anthèmes 2* (1997), whilst retaining the sectional structure of the original, has added electronic amplification and transformation of the material to produce a piece of some twenty minutes' duration.

The genesis of *Incises* been more protracted. Written in response to a commission to produce a competition piece for the 1994 Umberto Micheli piano competition in Milan, the original version of *Incises* consisted of a slow introduction followed by a *Prestissimo* toccata. The first indication of Boulez's revised plans for the piece came two years later when *sur Incises* was premiered in Basel at a concert to mark the ninetieth birthday of Paul Sacher. Here, the solo *Prestissimo,* in somewhat expanded form, was framed by an ensemble version of the slow introduction, and a brief coda. The nine instruments of the ensemble – three each of pianos, harps and vibraphones – affirmed Boulez's continuing absorption in the possibilities of resonating instruments, exploited in such masterly fashion in *Répons*. Within two years, this ten-minute version of *sur Incises* had been expanded to massive proportions, with the *Prestissimo* of the original piano solo piece now the starting point for a series of developments scored for full ensemble. As an unexpected postlude to the expansion of *sur Incises*, Boulez has recently returned to the piano solo *Incises*, and a new version has recently (2002) been published in which returns of material from the slow introduction are separated by rapid sections in constant pulse and mainly two-part texture.

The shape of this piece is characteristic in the context of Boulez's career as a whole: the explicit references to the SACHER cipher are a final tribute to the great patron and conductor following his death in 1999, while the alternation of rhapsodic passages with those in strict metre addresses compositional issues first articulated in works dating from the 1940s. His development is characterized by an extraordinary consistency of vision, which stands in stark contrast to the plurality of styles which characterizes the current musical scene – a development which, with the benefit of hindsight, seems inevitable following the rejection, in the second half of the 1950s, of Boulez's vision of a universal serial language. Now, evidence increasingly suggests that he has entered a new phase in which the sureness of purpose of the 1950s has been recaptured with greatly enriched resources. A series of projects have harnessed the evolving technology developed as IRCAM in a masterly way, and with *sur Incises*, his first completed large-scale ensemble piece since *Rituel*, Boulez has reaffirmed his commitment to purely instrumental composition. Whatever the shape of his future creative endeavours, his is an achievement of fundamental importance in any consideration of the course of music during the second half of the twentieth century.

Suggested Further Reading

Pierre Boulez: *Boulez on Music Today*, ed. and trans. Susan Bradshaw and Richard Rodney Bennett (London: Faber, 1971).

—— *Conversations with Célestin Deliège* (London,: Eulenberg, 1976).

——*Stocktakings from an Apprenticeship*, ed. and trans. Stephen Walsh (Oxford: Clarendon Press, 1991).

—— *Orientations*, ed. and trans. Martin Cooper (London: Faber, 1986).

Mary Breatnach: *Boulez and Mallarmé: A Study in Poetic Influence* (Aldershot: Ashgate, 1996).

Allen Edwards: 'Boulez's "Doubles" and "Figures Doubles Prismes": a Preliminary Study', *Tempo*, 185 (June 1993), 6–17.

Andrew Gerzso: 'Reflections on *Répons*', *Contemporary Music Review*, vol. 1 (1984), 23–34.

William Glock (ed.): *Pierre Boulez: a Symposium* (London: Eulenberg, 1986).

Dominique Jameux: *Boulez*, trans. Susan Bradshaw (London: Faber, 1991).

Lev Koblyakov: *Pierre Boulez: a World of Harmony* (Chur: Harwood, 1990).

Jean-Jacques Nattiez (ed.): *The Boulez–Cage Correspondence*, trans. Robert Samuels (Cambridge: Cambridge University Press, 1993).

Peter F. Stacey: *Boulez and the Modern Concept* (Aldershot: Ashgate, 1987).

Chapter 12

French Musical Style and the Post-War Generation

Caroline Potter

Boulez, Stockhausen and other composers who attended the summer courses at Darmstadt who brought serialism to its most extreme form are generally viewed as the most important European composers of the early 1950s. However, many French (and other) composers of this period and the following decades were uninterested in these developments or considered they were irrelevant to their style. Moreover, integral serialism – where the duration of notes, dynamics and even mode of attack and number of notes in a chord could be subjected to serial principles – was a very short-lived technique; even composers who once adhered to it had abandoned it by the mid-1950s.

There are dangers in considering music history purely in terms of 'developments'. This viewpoint sees novelty as the prime focus of interest, neglecting many fine composers who seem, on the surface at least, to be less radical in their approach to musical language. It is also unwise to categorize those French composers who did not embrace the most avant-garde developments of their day as 'independent' or 'unclassifiable', as tends to happen when writers discuss the music of Messiaen, Dutilleux, Ohana and other composers active after the Second World War – not to mention Poulenc. Certainly, these composers have a good deal in common, and one of the aims in this chapter is to demonstrate this.

Naturally, there are dangers in attaching a national label to composers where there are simplistic, and potentially misleading, perceptions of what this label stands for. In particular, it is important to dismiss the clichéd view of French music as being, in the words of Henri Dutilleux, full of 'charm, elegance and *esprit*';[1] his near-contemporary Pierre Boulez has more irreverently dubbed the standard description of 'French musical style' as 'a cross between Descartes and *haute couture*'.[2] There is certainly a grain of truth in the notion that these clichés stem from a perception that French music should be opposed to German music, which (according to an equally clichéd view) tends to be associated with seriousness and the use of standardized forms. Though this perceived divide between French and German music had no meaning in the short-lived period in which the international movement of integral serialism held sway, for many French composers, there was naturally an enhanced socio-political dimension to the traditional Franco-German artistic rivalry in the years immediately following the Second World War.

1 Henri Dutilleux: interview in John Beckwith and Udo Kasanets (eds): *The Modern Composer and his World* (Toronto, 1962), 80.

2 Cited in Peter Heyworth, 'The first fifty years', in William Glock (ed.): *Pierre Boulez: a symposium* (London, 1986), 7.

In an interview with Roger Nichols in 1991, Henri Dutilleux declared: 'At heart, I am not a serial composer.'[3] His near-contemporary, Maurice Ohana (1913–92), described post-Webern serialism as 'mere academic sterility, but as intimidating and terrifying as the propaganda systems of the Nazis ... These systems in music destroy more than they create – they remove all the art of risk.'[4] Ohana's uncompromising personality (and, no doubt, his wartime service in the British Army and part-Jewish origins) led him to use extreme language. Moreover, Ohana admired very few composers, reserving a particular dislike for the Austro-German symphonic tradition. Dutilleux spoke of the twelve-note system in characteristically more moderate terms, though in 1991 he did refer to the 'dogmatic and authoritarian' attitudes of certain integral serialist composers active in the 1950s.[5] It is likely, however, that he found the principles of integral serialism 'dogmatic and authoritarian', because he had a problem with the notion that all twelve members of the chromatic scale should be equally prominent. As he put it: 'As far as this system [serialism] is concerned, I have honestly never been able to accept *the abolition of every form of hierarchy* (in the ordering of the degrees of the chromatic scale) which is its fundamental principle.'[6]

Perhaps the only conviction shared by French composers active just after the Second World War was the belief that Debussy and Ravel are the pre-eminent French composers of the early years of the twentieth century, and that all subsequent French composers have to come to terms with their impact. In particular, Debussy's approaches to form, instrumental sonority, word setting and rhymic flexibility have had an immense impact on his musical descendants. The impact of his only completed opera, *Pelléas et Mélisande*, seems, with hindsight, to have been a negative one. Dutilleux hit the nail on the head when he said: 'I know that we composers all fear coming up against the problem of pleonasm where prosody is concerned, the problem of a simplistic word-for-word translation, and we should also beware of anything resembling *Pelléas*-type declamation, especially where theatrical works are concerned.'[7] Not that Dutilleux dislikes Debussy's opera; on the contrary, in response to a 1965 questionnaire from the Société Philharmonique de Bruxelles, he voted it the most significant musical work of the twentieth century by any composer and in any genre.[8] I am sure this is partly because he views Debussy's setting of the French language, and in particular his approach to sung conversation, to be an ideal and therefore unsurpassable treatment of an opera libretto.

Like many of his contemporaries, Dutilleux has not written an opera, and no French opera composed since *Pelléas* is even remotely as important or influential as Debussy's

3 Cited in Caroline Potter: *Henri Dutilleux: his life and works* (Aldershot, 1997), 96; 'Je ne suis pas foncièrement un musicien atonal.'

4 Interview with Pierre Ancelin in 1964, cited in Caroline Rae: 'Maurice Ohana: iconoclast or individualist?', *Musical Times* (Feb. 1991), 70.

5 Interview with Roger Nichols on 19 Apr. 1991; this interview was partially published in the *Musical Times* (Jan. 1994). I am grateful to Roger Nichols for giving me a copy of his complete interview with Dutilleux.

6 Pierrette Mari: *Henri Dutilleux* (Paris, 1998), 100.

7 Henri Dutilleux: *Mystère et mémoire des sons, Entretiens avec Claude Glayman* (Paris, 1997), 199; 'Je sais bien qu'il faut redouter l'écueil de pléonasme dans la prosodie, celui d'une servile traduction du mot à mot, et l'on doit se défier également de ce qui se rapprocherait de la déclamation à la *Pelléas*, surtout en matière de théâtre lyrique.'

8 Questionnaire cited in Mari: *Henri Dutilleux*, 192.

work. Of recent French operas which have been staged more than once (a small category), Messiaen's *Saint François d'Assise* (1975–83) is the most substantial, in scale as well as in terms of its international renown. However, this huge work – four hours long and written for an enormous orchestra including three ondes martenot – is hardly a conventional opera, being a series of eight non-developing tableaux with almost no traditional dramatic situations. The life of the saint who preached to the birds is a subject with obvious appeal for this most ornithologically minded composer, and Messiaen's music is a treasure trove of the musical techniques we associate with this composer, including birdsong transcription and irregular rhythms.

If Debussy's only complete opera has had few musical descendants, other aspects of his style have proved more influential on later French composers. His move away from goal-directed tonality (without rejecting tonal chords), his absorption of modal inflections and colouristic approach to harmony and orchestration were a legacy with which later composers had to come to terms.

Pivot Notes

Dutilleux's desire to retain hierarchy in his musical language, though not necessarily a tonal hierarchy, was shared by many of his contemporaries. An obvious way of demonstrating this hierarchy is to ensure that one pitch predominates in a piece or section of a piece. This use of a focal or pivot note is common in the works of many French composers, including Jolivet, Dutilleux and Ohana. The device ensures that the music has an easily identifiable focal point, which acts almost as a magnetic source of attraction to which the music is constantly drawn: one note or chord is continually repeated over a period of time, ensuring the listener is aware of its primary importance. However chromatic the rest of the musical passage may be, the pivot note or chord provides stability and acts as the most obviously important feature in the passage. This emphasis on one note or chord is diametrically opposed to the serialists' view that no member of the chromatic scale should predominate. It could also be argued that pivot notes perform a quasi-tonal function; tonality is a musical language based on the concept of hierarchy, as some notes and chords (principally the tonic and dominant) are perceived as being more important than others.

Frequently, composers use a pivot note as the focus of an ornamental melodic line which could be compared to a Debussian arabesque in its shape and its rhythmic plasticity. The influence of Stravinsky (especially the opening bars of *The Rite of Spring*) is also crucial in this context, as is the music of Edgard Varèse. Varese's melodic lines tend to feature a pivot note with the quasi-magnetic force described above. Though Varèse, like Ohana, was not of exclusively French origin – his mother was French and his father Italian, and the composer later became an American citizen – his formative musical years were spent in Paris, where he was educated at the Schola Cantorum and later came under Debussy's influence. Much of Varèse's music – the opening of *Amériques*, which highlights the alto flute, is typical – is monodic or virtually monodic, as a result of his liking for percussion-based textures whose rhythmic function is far more important than any harmonic background they may provide.

Plate 12.1 Maurice Ohana: *Le bain au clair de lune* (1986).

This obsessive quality of Varèse's melodic lines can also be perceived in the music of his pupil Jolivet. Jolivet used pivot notes and chords for two linked reasons. Firstly, like Dutilleux, he was concerned with providing a reference point in an otherwise tonally ambiguous passage. The technical function of the pivot note is indivisible from its incantatory effect in passages which feature this device. This ritualistic ambience, which is characteristic of Jolivet's musical style, is most obvious in his *Cinq incantations* for solo flute, where the 'incantation' of the title is largely created by the constant reiteration of pivot notes (see Example 9.9). Another of Jolivet's musical fingerprints is the immediate repetition of a bar, a fingerprint he shares with Debussy and with some of Ravel's early works (notably the piano piece *Jeux d'eau* (1901). In *Chant de Linos* for flute and piano (1943) and many other works, he uses the repetition of an irregular rhythm to evoke an imaginary ritual dance (Example 12.1).

Boulez's *Mémoriale* for flute and eight instruments (1985), in which perhaps 90 per cent of the musical material consists of twelve fixed pitches (each note of the chromatic scale is generally employed in one particular register), is therefore also obsessively repetitive. The accompanying ensemble – two horns and six stringed instruments – generally either echoes or anticipates the flute's material, only rarely playing a more

Example 12.1 André Jolivet, *Chant de Linos*, opening

independent role. The flute line typifies Boulez's mature melodic style, combining sustained notes with decorations in the arabesque manner. The plasticity of the arabesque type of melodic line is peculiarly suited to the flute, and Boulez, like other French composers, often exploits this particular expressive power of the instrument.

Ohana's frequent use of pivot notes as the focus of an arabesque-like melodic line shows that his melodic vocabulary has links with that of other French composers of his time. These melodies tend to be improvisatory in character, and they tend to be either unaccompanied, or with a sparse accompaniment which illustrates that harmony is, for him, of secondary importance compared to the melodic line. Even if his background and sources of inspiration are distinctly his own, he, like so many other composers, often uses this type of melodic line in pieces inspired by traditional or invented myths. His *Signes* (1963), for the typically Ohanian combination of flute, percussion, piano and two zithers (one tuned in thirds of a tone) is centred on a flute part which recalls the Pans or Syrinxes of earlier French composers. The flute's rhapsodic, improvisatory melodic lines tend to return constantly to a pivot note. The titles of the six movements of *Signes* show that nature was the central source of inspiration for the composer:

1 L'arbre dans la nuit (The tree at night)
2 L'arbre animé d'oiseaux (The tree enlivened by birds)
3 L'arbre noyé de pluie (The tree drowned in rain)
4 L'arbre prisonnier des fils de la vierge (The tree imprisoned in maidenthread)
5 L'arbre battu par le vent (The tree battered by the wind)
6 L'arbre brûlé par le soleil (The tree burned by the sun)

Ohana is here seemingly following Debussy's imprecation to composers to be inspired by the sounds of nature.

It is also possible to trace an oblique line of descent from Varèse to the Greek-born composer Iannis Xenakis (1922–2001) who arrived in France as an illegal immigrant in 1947, fleeing a death sentence imposed in Greece for his political activities. The two composers were both fascinated by mathematics and the sciences as well as music, and their music has a similarly uncompromising quality. Dynamic levels tend to be high for both composers, and their use of blocks of sound gives their works a static, monumental feel. Xenakis shared Dutilleux's reservations about serial music, criticizing its lack of continuity in his essay 'La crise de la musique sérielle' (1955). Although there is little in Xenakis's music that may be termed a 'melodic line', he shared with Varèse the essentially modal nature of his musical language. These modal elements came more to the surface in his later works, such as *Tetora* for string quartet (1990) and his incidental music for *The Bacchae* (1991).

It is surely also relevant that Xenakis, too, recognized the crucial impact of Debussy on his style; in the last months of the Second World War, Xenakis was searching for his own musical voice and 'felt that [Debussy's] music was closest to what I was searching for.' He preferred the modally-based language of Debussy and Ravel to what he described as 'the tonic/dominant thinking' of German and Central European music.[9] Most significantly, both composers drew inspiration from natural phenomena. In an article on music composed for the open air, Debussy wrote: 'It [music] could renew itself by absorbing the great lesson of freedom illustrated by the growth of trees; what she may lose in subtle charm, she would surely gain in grandeur.'[10] This could well have struck a chord with Xenakis, and it is also

9 Iannis Xenakis: *Conversations with Bálint András Varga* (London, 1996), 52–3.

10 Claude Debussy: 'La musique du plein air' (article written for the *Revue blanche* on 1 June 1901) in *Monsieur Croche*, ed. François Lesure (Paris, 1987), 46; '[La musique] pourrait s'y renouveler et y prendre la belle leçon de liberté contenue dans l'épanouissement des arbres, ce qu'elle perdrait en charme minutieux ne le regagnerait-elle pas en grandeur?'

likely that Xenakis felt an affinity with Debussy's (conscious or unconscious) use of Golden Section structuring,[11] not least because the form of his orchestral work *Metastaseis* (1953) is governed by Golden Section proportions. But unlike Debussy, Xenakis was not reluctant to explain the technical base of his musical language, and he was candid about the use of mathematical structuring in his music. In particular, he applied probability theory to some of his works, a theory which can also explain such natural phenomena as bird migration or cloud formations. While Xenakis's use of mathematical procedures is very much his own, he shared with Debussy a common interest in the organization of natural structures and their application to music. Moreover, Xenakis's early music is indivisible from his work as an architect (he once worked in Le Corbusier's practice), another branch of the arts which has drawn inspiration from the structures of nature.

Mythical and Religious Influences

Jolivet's recourse to Greek myth in *Chant de Linos* and other works inscribes him within a French tradition of flute pieces inspired by Ancient Greece. Perhaps his interest was also awakened by the general interest in myth (both Greek and non-European) evidenced by several French plays and films of the 1940s by authors including Cocteau, Sartre and Anouilh. Ancient Greek artworks – depictions on vases and mosaics of shepherds, fauns and the like – and French poetry inspired by these models, provided the initial stimulus for French composers; they were either not interested in imitating real Greek musical models, or could not access this material. Many figures on these vases and mosaics are shown playing woodwind instruments, which explains the French predilection for important flute parts in pieces inspired by Ancient Greek art. Most important, however, was the hedonism and sensuality portrayed in Greek art, an erotically-charged atmosphere which had its musical counterpart. This idealized, sensual Ancient Greek setting was an important stimulus for Debussy, notably in his *Prélude à l'après midi d'un faune* (1892–94).

This spiritual dimension of music was another prime concern of composers in the post-Second World War period. The group Jeune France had already emphasized the importance of this aspect of music in the mid-1930s, primarily in reaction against the frivolity of much French music of the 1920s. After the war, another short-lived grouping of composers, *Zodiaque*, had similar concerns, but this time the reaction was also partly against total serialism. Maurice Ohana was to become the best-known member of this group; the other members were Stanislaw Skrowaczewski (who was to become renowned as a conductor), the painter Sergio de Castro (then torn between a career in music or art), and the little-known composers Alain Bermat and Pierre La Forest-Divonne. All of the members wanted to emphasize the expressive dimension of music, partly as a reaction against the dehumanizing forces of the war years, an aim which could conveniently encompass a very wide variety of musical styles.

Born in Casablanca in 1913, to Spanish and Gibraltarian parents, Ohana was a British citizen who was given a French education and lived in France from his teenage years,

---

11 See Roy Howat: *Debussy in Proportion* (Cambridge, 1983), a fascinating study of Debussy's music which convincingly demonstrates that many pieces are structured according to Golden Section proportions.

though he did not acquire French citizenship until 1976. Although perfectly trilingual and at home in Spanish, British and French culture, he considered himself to be a French composer and spent the whole of his composing career in Paris.

For Ohana, as for many of his contemporaries, spirituality in music was not necessarily synonymous with writing music for worship. Rather, he believed strongly in the evocative power of rhythm and melody; his works often have a ritualistic and timeless feel. Rhythms inspired by his North African upbringing permeate his music, and the two instruments which are common to all cultures – the voice and percussion – were also the most important to Ohana. His last work, *Avoaha* (1991), features ritual dances of his own invention; these dances are driven by propulsive percussion lines. This type of rhythmic writing is equally characteristic of pieces of his with abstract titles, such as the *Études* nos. 11 and 12 for piano and percussion. Ohana followed Chopin and Debussy in writing a series of studies for piano, but for the last two in his series of twelve studies, he expanded the range of timbres available by adding percussion instruments to the solo piano. His other studies also tend to move the genre forward from Chopin and Debussy; only four of them are based on a specific interval, and he avoids those intervals chosen by Debussy. Instead, he uses intervals considered dissonant in earlier periods, such as the seventh (no. 7, dedicated to Bartók) and second (no. 8).

Flamenco *cante jondo* singing ('deep song') has a strong Arabic flavour in its modal inflections and use of microtones, and Ohana's use of thirds of a tone was inspired by this source. Ohana often drew inspiration from the past (whether historical or mythical), partly because of his distaste for the modern world. In his opinion, Spanish civilization declined from the Catholic Reconquest onwards (the reverse of the traditional European view, as Caroline Rae rightly remarks). Ohana said: 'It was a wonderful time when the Arabs invaded Spain; the result was a synthesis of refined and productive civilizations. We owe the Arabs a lot: gardens and fruits, architecture and trigonometry, algebra, thirds of a tone and quarter-tones, poetry, courtly music and philosophy. This period of civilization demonstrated an exemplary tolerance, which the Catholic Kings destroyed.'[12]

From the technical point of view, Ohana considered the mode of thirds of a tone to be a division of the whole-tone mode, which he associated with the music of Debussy, one of the few composers he admired. Ohana designed a zither tuned in thirds of a tone, and liked this instrument because it 'is much sharper and has a crystalline quality lacking in the zither tuned in quarter-tones … The use of these intervals seems to me to be a natural step towards the conquest of one more of the harmonics, coming after Debussy's ninths and Ravel's elevenths and thirteenths. The only new thing is that they are deliberately played and thus enlarge the possibilities of melody to an immense extent.'[13] Ohana was therefore determined to place himself, a cosmopolitan composer, within the French musical tradition. He rarely uses thirds of a tone systematically, in the manner of composers such

12 Maurice Ohana: 'Sud-Nord', in *XXe siècle: Images de la musique française* (Paris, 1986), 164; 'Ce fut un moment prodigieux que celui où les Arabes ayant envahi l'Espagne, il s'est créé une synthèse de civilisations raffinées et fécondes. Nous leur devons beaucoup: les jardins et les fruits, l'architecture et la trigonométrie, l'algèbre, le tiers et le quart de ton, la poésie, la musique de cour, et la philosophie. Moment civilisateur d'une tolérance exemplaire, qui fut détruit par les rois catholiques.'

13 Maurice Ohana: 'Micro-intervals', in Rollo Myers: *Twentieth-Century Music* (London, 1968), 149–50.

as the Czech Alois Hába, who introduced quarter-tones to his many string quartets and viewed them as the theoretical and practical complement of the chromatic scale. Rather, Ohana uses thirds of a tone for expressive effect, either to 'bend' the pitch of a note, or to provide an astringent clash with a chord featuring only notes from the traditional chromatic scale, both techniques which are illustrated in *Signes*. One of the zithers in this piece is tuned chromatically and one in thirds of a tone (and Ohana used these two zithers in several other works). The zither in thirds of a tone often clashes with the piano, playing adjacent tones either successively or simultaneously with the conventionally tuned instrument.

Gregorian Chant

The absorption of Gregorian chant into French music could be seen as a symbol of the spiritual dimension of many French composers' works, as well as a demonstration of the ease with which French music can absorb modality. In the late nineteenth century, organist-composers including Fauré were already incorporating modal inflections into their music. Fauré's musical education at the École Niedermeyer, whose primary function was the training of church musicians, introduced him to this rich musical resource, and students at the Schola Cantorum (including Franck's pupils) were also introduced to this repertoire. By the mid-twentieth century, Maurice Duruflé had developed a musical language which fused Gregorian chant with Debussian parallel sevenths and ninths, a combination of modality, supple rhythms and a sensuous harmonic language which sounds quintessentially French. Example 6.11, the opening of 'In Paradisum', the final movement of his *Requiem*, is typical of his style, and this vocabulary is common to many French composers of religious music, or music with an avowedly spiritual dimension. Modal inflections are also an essential element of Jolivet's musical style, a feature which can be viewed as characteristically French and perhaps as an indication of the central role of spirituality in his music.

Poulenc's *Gloria* (1962) demonstrates the assimilation of Gregorian chant into the French musical language; Example 12.2 illustrates bars 16–22 of the second movement, 'Laudamus te'. The limited pitch range of chant, its modal inflections and rhythmic simplicity are all apparent in Example 12.2, and Poulenc's use of parallel fourths and fifths in bars 18–19 is clearly also a deliberately archaizing device. Ohana's musical style, which is both timeless and contemporary, also easily absorbed this style, and the unbarred opening of the fourth of his *Cantigas*, 'Cantiga del azahar' (Example 12.3), is rather closer in spirit to medieval music than the Poulenc example.

More unusually, Messiaen used melodic material derived from real Gregorian chant melodies in his orchestral work *Couleurs de la cité céleste* (1963). Messiaen's Catholic faith is of course always at the heart of his music, and for this work he used four Alleluia melodies as source material. Two of these (Corpus Christi and the Alleluia for the Feast of the Dedication of a Church) are used in their original form, but Messiaen deformed the intervals of the other two Alleluias to ensure that the melodies fit in with his musical language, which is far more radical than Poulenc's or Duruflé's. Typically, he precisely indicates on the score which Alleluia melodies are used, and this source is but one of many in the melting pot of his musical style.

Example 12.2 Francis Poulenc, *Gloria*, II ('Laudamus te'), bars 16–22

The harmonic context and instrumentation of these melodies are very much Messiaen's own; they appear alongside birdsong transcriptions, Hindu and Greek rhythms and 'colour chords', whose colour is also noted on the score. *Couleurs de la cité céleste* was inspired by five citations from the Apocalypse which Messiaen quotes in the preface to the score. The last of these quotations most obviously inspired his colour chords: 'The foundations of the city walls were adorned with all kinds of precious stones: jasper, sapphire, chalcedony, emerald, sardonyx, sardius, chrysolite, beryl, topaz, chrysoprase, jacinth and amethyst.'[14] The kaleidoscope of colours evoked parallels the variety of sources of Messiaen's musical language, a variety which some find excessive. As a synaesthete, Messiaen always associated particular colours with music, and his indications of the colours of various chords in *Couleurs de la cité céleste* show him attempting to

14 Olivier Messiaen: 'Deuxième Note de l'Auteur', preface to *Couleurs de la cité céleste* (Paris, 1963); 'Les fondements du mur de la ville sont ornés de toute pierre précieuse: jaspe, saphir, chalcédoine, émeraude, sardonyx, cornaline, chrysolithe, béryl, topaze, chrysoprase, hyacinthe, améthyste …'.

Example 12.3 Maurice Ohana, *Cantigas*, IV ('Cantiga del azahar'), opening

communicate this to an audience; as he writes in the preface, 'the form of the work depends entirely on colours. The melodic or rhythmic themes, the combinations of sounds and of timbres, change in the manner of colours.'[15] Messiaen here gives us a fascinating insight into his most original compositional mind, even if surely no audience member can completely identify with his compositional process.

Modality is also central to Messiaen's musical language. The composer acknowledged the importance of the music history lectures he attended at the Conservatoire, particularly those on modal music given by Maurice Emmanuel. Emmanuel's *Traité de la musique grecque antique* catalogues the modes, tunings and metrics of ancient Greek music, and Messiaen's use of his own 'modes of limited transposition' was constant throughout his composing life. This systematic use of given modes by Emmanuel and Messiaen in their music can be contrasted with the more typically French enrichment of a musical language with modal elements (for example, the use of the flattened seventh in a melodic line) seen in the music of Debussy, Ravel and many subsequent composers.

Dutilleux's mature musical language is also suffused vith modal melodic lines, though his harmonic language is more complex and less obviously tonally based than Poulenc's. His string quartet *Ainsi la nuit* (1973–76), particularly the two movements entitled 'Litanies', shows the continuing importance of modal inflections in Dutilleux's music; perhaps not surprisingly, a movement with an identical title in his *Mystère de l'instant* for twenty-four strings, cimbalom and percussion (1985–89) has a strikingly similar character.

The third movement of his orchestral work *The Shadows of Time* (1995–97) is dedicated 'to Anne Frank and all children of the world, the innocents' and features either one child's voice, or three voices in unison, singing 'Pourquoi nous? Pourquoi l'étoile?' ('Why us? Why the star?'). This allusion to the yellow star which Jews were forced to wear during the Second World War is the most obvious indicator of the wartime theme of the

15 Messiaen: score of *Couleurs de la cité céleste* (Paris: 1963), Première note de l'Auteur; 'La forme de cette œuvre dépend entièrement des couleurs. Les thèmes mélodiques ou rythmiques, les complexes de sons et de timbres, évoluent à la façon des couleurs.'

work. The melodic lines given to the voices (and the woodwind instruments with which they dialogue) are marked 'dans l'esprit du chant grégorien', and it seems that the composer uses the Gregorian-style material to suggest not only a spiritual atmosphere, but also the innocence of childhood. Maxime Joos has written: 'Henri Dutilleux says that he started this work with the third movement, and specifically by starting from a melisma, a melodic contour reminiscent of Gregorian chant. This litany is the kernel of the score.'[16] From bar 31 in the movement, this type of musical material is interrupted by aggressive, rapid and loud woodwind gestures; these gestures eventually overwhelm the children's voices, as their lines become gradually shorter, and disappear altogether after bar 62. Example 12.4 shows the child's vocal line at bars 23–5, an example which also illustrates Dutilleux's fondness for palindromic musical material. Though not usually in a catalogued mode, the melodic lines sometimes resemble either the octatonic mode, or a mode alternating semitones and augmented seconds – indeed, this employment of 'impure' modes (modes with foreign pitches) was also characteristic of Debussy's melodic language.

Example 12.4 Henri Dutilleux, *The Shadows of Time*, III ('Mémoire des ombres'), bars 23–5

East–West Dialogue

With hindsight, we can see that Boulez's integral serialist phase in the early 1950s is not typical of his musical language. The vocal lines of Boulez's 'Le vierge, le vivace et le bel aujourd'hui' ('Improvisation sur Mallarmé II' from *Pli selon pli* (1957–62)), where the voice is treated in an instrumental manner, rotate around a few limited pitches. This is only one example of the influence of non-Western musics (particularly those of East Asian origin) in Boulez's music; what Boulez and many other European composers drew from East Asian music was a certain contemplative, timeless quality, usually expressed in music which is slow in tempo and repetitive. Boulez's preference for an orchestra or chamber ensemble featuring several metal percussion instruments also connects him with what might be called the 'Oriental French' style, the importance of which has been demonstrated many times in this book.

However, Boulez, living as he now does in a post-colonial world, has rejected the view that the influence of non-Western musics on his works can be compared to the importation of 'spices from the colonies'.[17] It is not surprising that Boulez and his

16 Maxime Joos: *La perception du temps musical chez Henri Dutilleux* (Paris, 2000), 214; 'Henri Dutilleux déclare avoir commencé l'œuvre par le troisième mouvement et précisément en partant d'[un] mélisme, d'[un] contour mélodique qui évoque le chant grégorien. Cette litanie constitue la genèse de la partition.'

17 Interview with Edwin Roxburgh: Royal College of Music, 27 Mar. 2000.

contemporaries reject the patronizing, splash-of-colour exoticism of the nineteenth century; pieces such as Bizet's song *Adieux de l'hôtesse arabe* (1866) invite the audience to contemplate something foreign. It is also true that Bizet's musical orientalism – essentially the use of gapped scales and ostinato figures – can have no counterpart in the post-war musical universe, not least because these musical devices were absorbed into the musical language of French composers in the late nineteenth and early twentieth centuries. What was initially considered 'exotic' therefore very quickly became commonplace.

Although many French composers have been inspired by the contrapuntal complexity of Balinese music and by the sonorities of various East Asian instruments, the imagined East is, in the French musical mind, often as Utopian as the idealized Ancient Greece that inspired Debussy, Jolivet and others. Messiaen's orchestral work *Sept haïkaï* (1962), composed after a tour of Japan, features transcriptions of Japanese birds, and, in the fourth movement ('Gagaku'), an imitation of the thin, acidulous timbre of the *sho*. While the imitation of birds and Messiaen's concept of musical time may be considered Asiatic rather than European traits, the instrumental ensembles, tunings and harmonies he uses are unequivocally Western European. There is nothing remotely Balinese about Boulez's musical language, nor could Messiaen's music be classed as other than music by a European composer of the twentieth century.

However, it is particularly interesting to note that several contemporary East Asian composers of concert music have been inspired by French musical models. It is as if they are reappropriating the Asian musical elements which were borrowed by French musicians of earlier generations, and using this as the basis for musical languages of their own which synthesize European and Asian influences. Many Asian composers, from former French colonies and from countries with no links with France, have studied in Paris, and many others, most notably the Japanese Toru Takemitsu (1933–96), acknowledged a debt to Debussy, Ravel and Messiaen.

Unlike Takemitsu, his fellow Japanese Yoshihisa Taïra (born 1937) studied in France (with Xenakis, Messiaen and Dutilleux) and currently lives in Paris, as does the Vietnamese composer Ton-That Tiêt (born 1933). Both Taïra and Ton-That Tiêt have developed musical styles which draw both on French influences and on the musical traditions of their countries of origin. Taïra shows a preference for the flute and harp, both instruments whose sonorities are closely related to Japanese traditional instruments. He even transcribed his *Synchrony* (1986), originally written for two flutes, for flute and shakuhachi, and has described this new version as 'a kind of dialogue between Japan and the West'.[18]

The opening page of Taïra's early *Sonomorphie I* for piano (1971; Example 12.5) is already characteristic of his style. His music tends to have a calm background which is spare in texture, but which is frequently interrupted by violent outbursts. While *Sonomorphie I* may therefore sound East Asian (at least to Western ears), its title betrays the impact of contemporary European music on his thought, and the piano texture and subtitle 'Résonances' shows that he, too, is a musical descendant of Debussy. A series of four works entitled *Pénombres* (1981–90), which are all related musically but each written

18 Yoshihisa Taïra: programme note for Auvidis CD D8302 (1989); 'une sorte de dialogue entre le Japon et l'Occident'.

Example 12.5 Yoshihisa Taïra, *Sonomorphie*, opening

for a different instrumental combination,[19] also illustrate Taïra's love of spacious textures, refinement of timbre, and superb sense of timing. Like Ohana, he deserves to be far better known in the UK.

Ton-That Tiêt moved to Paris in 1958 and studied with Jean Rivier and André Jolivet. He is influenced by Vietnamese traditional music (particularly the sacred and court genres) though like Taïra, he generally writes for Western ensembles which occasionally incorporate traditional East Asian instruments. Nature is an important source of inspiration for him and many other Asian composers, just as it was for Debussy and many other French musicians. In the words of Ton-That Tiêt: 'Music speaks where words cease, and when music stops we must let nature speak.'[20] The first of his two *Légendes de la Terre du Sud*, 'Les rois Hung', is written for a reciter (telling a Vietnamese fairy story-like tale), soprano and orchestra, with the flute playing a prominent role. But his fusion of Asian inspiration and Western musical techniques is perhaps best shown in his *Dialogue avec la nature* (1995), a concerto for two guitars and orchestra. The note G is the focus of the introduction and much of the rest of the piece, and temple bells evoke a ritualistic atmosphere. The concerto is inspired by a poem by the eighth-century Chinese writer Li Po on the subject of Nature. The composer said that the guitarists must imagine they are 'playing on the summit of a mountain and, from there, dialoguing with nature surrounding them: the trees, the fog, the sky, the air, but also with the town which can be seen down below, humans, animals and even with stones and rocks ... with nature.'[21]

Form: Progressive Growth/Mosaic Form

Dutilleux said in 1991: 'It must be said that French composers are perhaps more concerned with harmony than counterpoint; perhaps this is a tradition. They like beautiful chords, there is something sensuous about this preference.'[22] His personal concern was not only to ensure his music had harmonic beauty, but also that it was underpinned by what he considered to be a less French concern for contrapuntal logic and large-scale continuity. His use of *croissance progressive* (progressive growth), where a melodic line grows and is gradually transformed throughout a movement or work, grew out of his concern for unity and formal continuity, and out of his fondness for variation form. Dutilleux denies this procedure is identical to Franckian cyclic form, as he believes his progressive growth of a theme is subtler than this, and that his themes appear in different harmonic contexts; but in practice, it is hard to discern major differences between the two procedures. His denial

19 Contemporary French composers are fond of writing cycles of works under one title: Jolas's *Episodes* for solo instruments (which are akin to Berio's *Sequenzas*), Ton-That Tiêt's *Chu-Ky* cycle and Francis Bayer's eight *Propositions* also illustrate this trend.

20 Ton-That Tiêt: programme note for Calliope CD CAL 9268 (1999), 'La musique parle ou les mots s'arrêtent et à la limite où la musique s'arrête il faut laisser la nature parler.'

21 Ibid: 'jouer du sommet d'un montagne et, de là, dialoguer avec la nature environnante: les arbres, la brume, le ciel, l'air mais aussi la ville que l'on voit en bas, les humains, les animaux et même avec les pierres, les rochers ... avec la nature'.

22 Interview with Roger Nichols, 19 Apr. 1991; 'Il faut dire que les musiciens français, peut-être par tradition, sont peut-être plus harmonistes que contrapuntistes: ils aiment le goût du bel accord, c'est un côté un peu sensuel.'

of a connection with Franck should be interpreted primarily as a denial that his musical aesthetic is linked to the academic, formalist group of composers trained by Franck at the Schola Cantorum. Dutilleux prefers to draw comparisons between Debussy's use of cyclic themes in his String Quartet (1893) and his own *croissance progressive* technique; he also acknowledges the crucial influence of Proust's theories of time and memory on this technique. He first uses progressive growth in the third and fourth movements of his First Symphony (1950–51); the first theme of the third movement recurs in many similar but non-identical guises, and there is a direct link between this movement and the finale, as the variation theme of the finale is, yet again, a modification of the third movement idea.

Dutilleux's criticism of French music as concerned with the beauty of the moment rather than formal coherence is a criticism which has often been applied to Messiaen's music. Messiaen's use of cyclic themes, for instance in his *Tristan* trilogy (*Harawi*, 1945; *Turangalîla-symphonie*, 1946–48; *Cinq rechants*, 1949), was an attempt to impose an external formal solution onto music which was essentially highly sectionalized. In truth, unity in Messiaen's large-scale works is more often suggested by his programme notes (which typically explain the theological character of each movement), rather than perceived by the listener, however attentive. But it would be unfair to ascribe too much importance to an issue which is simply not central to this composer's musical style: Messiaen's music is far more noteworthy for its abundant rhythmic invention and vivid colours.

Messiaen's extraordinarily accurate ear enabled him to transcribe birdsong – usually notated in the field – with unprecedented precision, though he acknowledged that many alterations had to be made to render these transcriptions playable by human instrumentalists. Moreover, the composer admitted: 'Of course, I am the one who is listening [to the bird], and involuntarily I introduce something of my manner, of my way of hearing and reproducing the songs.'[23] He admitted that intervals within the birdsong sometimes had to be widened (though he took care to retain the proportions of the intervals in a song), the song was inevitably transposed down one or more octaves, and the tempo had to be reduced. Most crucially, instruments cannot perfectly reproduce the timbre of birdsong; Messiaen aimed to mimic the bird as closely as possible in his instrumental transcriptions, and he did this by fusing the notions of timbre and harmony. A slight change in the 'harmonization' of a birdsong is therefore equivalent to a slight timbral shift in its call. Messiaen also aimed to depict the bird in its natural habitat, and surrounded the birds' calls with musical images of rivers, mountains and the like. This fusion of extreme technical sophistication (the complex notation of the birdsong) and extreme naivety (the representation of natural phenomena with simple musical gestures) is utterly typical of Messiaen, who embraced whatever procedure was appropriate to a musical work. The central inspiration of (God-created) Nature on his music can be paralleled with Debussy, though unlike Debussy, Messiaen is open about the techniques he uses in his works.

As early as 1944, Messiaen raised the possibility that durations, dynamics and other parameters of the musical language besides pitch, could be subjected to serial procedures; Messiaen was always eager to stress that rhythm, in particular, should be as important as

23 Claude Samuel: *Entretiens avec Olivier Messiaen* (Paris, 1967), 100; 'Évidemment, c'est moi qui entends et, involontairement, j'introduis quelque chose de ma manière, de ma façon d'écouter et de reproduire les chants'.

pitch to a composer. But his piano study *Mode de valeurs et d'intensités* (1949), which inspired the total serialist movement, is wholly uncharacteristic of his style, and his piano works of these years proved isolated experiments. In *Mode de valeurs et d'intensités* (the second of his four *Études de rythme*) the pitch, dynamic, duration and mode of attack of a note is fixed, though the ordering of the notes is free (a significant difference between Messiaen's modal language and the serialists' employment of a tone row). A short passage in his longer piano work *Cantéyodjayâ* (1948) employs a similar technique, but Messiaen chose not to follow up these ideas in a systematic way. Another section of *Cantéyodjayâ* features a rhythmic figure which is repetitive in the right hand and features 'interversions' of these values (i.e. the same number of semiquavers but in a different order) in the left hand (as demonstrated in Example 12.6; bars 253–61); and the contrasting sections of the piece are juxtaposed in mosaic fashion. Typically for Messiaen, this piano work features a cornucopia of ideas, some of which (such as Example 12.6) appear only once, though others are repeated several times. Although the piece does reach a dynamic and textural climax shortly before its close, its overall form is less apparent to the listener than the strong contrasts between adjacent sections.

In general, French composers have been suspicious of introducing improvisatory elements into their music. Perhaps significantly, a composer of mixed French and American origin was one of the first to introduce limited performer choice. Betsy Jolas (born 1925), who studied in the United States but was born in Paris and has been a French resident for most of her life, said that Charles Ives's *The Unanswered Question* (1908) was a crucial influence on her style. In particular, she adapted his occasional use of free rhythm; as Ives noted on the score of *The Unanswered Question*: 'It is not necessary in these parts strictly to respect the indicated note values. They could be played in the spirit of an improvisation.'[24] Jolas invariably indicates the required pitch, instrumentation and (sometimes) tempo, but often uses a time–space notation which allows performers some rhythmic flexibility. An extract of *J.D.E.*[25] (1964) shows how this works in practice (Example 12.7; p. 2). Jolas has noted that performances of this work tend to sound very alike, despite the apparent rhythmic freedom she introduces. (This would also be the case for Example 12.5 above, which features a short section where pitches but not precise rhythms are indicated; Taïra also stipulates the duration of the section in question, ensuring that different performances are likely to be almost identical.) Jolas suggests that her space–time notation is, in fact, designed primarily for the performers' benefit; she wrote: 'I don't think that the eye is capable of precisely assimilating proportional rhythmic notations. It is preferable to indicate duration in terms of elapsed time.'[26] Therefore, this notational device should partly be viewed as a reaction against some of the excesses of integral serialism, which often had recourse to complex irrational rhythms. Jolas adds that Christian Lardé, the first performer of her *Episode 1er* for solo flute (1964; the first of a

24 Betsy Jolas: 'Sur "The Unanswered Question"' in *Musique en jeu*, I (1970), 15. Jolas cited Ives's words in the following French translation: 'Il n'est pas nécessaire dans ces parties de respecter strictement les valeurs indiquées. On pourra les jouer dans l'esprit d'une improvisation.'

25 Jolas has not divulged the significance of these initials.

26 Marie-José Chauvin: 'Entretien avec Betsy Jolas' in *Le courrier musical de France*, 27 (1969); 'Je ne pense pas que l'œil soit capable d'apprécier rigoureusement des notations proportionnelles. Il est préférable de donner des indications de minutage.'

Example 12.6 Olivier Messiaen, *Cantéyodjayâ*, bars 253–61

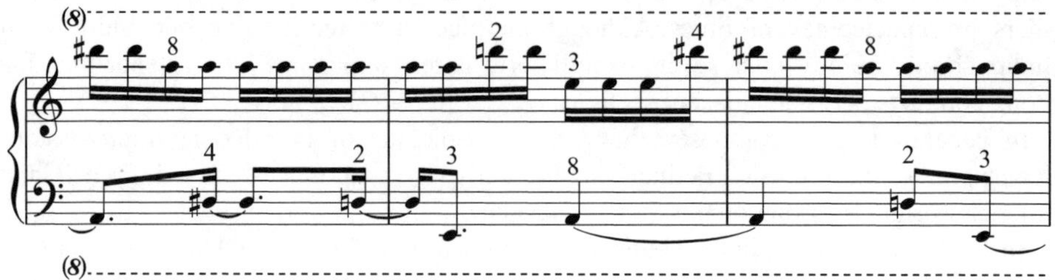

series of virtuoso solo instrumental works in the same vein as Luciano Berio's *Sequenza* series), understood the notational requirements without having to consult her. Messiaen, in his last works including the orchestral *Éclairs sur l'au-delà* (1987–92) does not indicate precise rhythm for birdsongs; he merely indicates the pitches of the song, and instructs the performer to play the material as fast as possible within a given duration, indicated in seconds. This space–time notation is far easier for the performer to read, but there is no appreciable audible difference between birdsong notated this way and birdsongs notated in the complex manner of his earlier works.

Vocal Music: The End of the *Mélodie*?

Dutilleux's small (but very high-quality) output features very little vocal music, and he composed almost all of his songs during the war years (see Chapter 10). He has rightly

Example 12.7 Betsy Jolas, *J.D.E.*, page 2

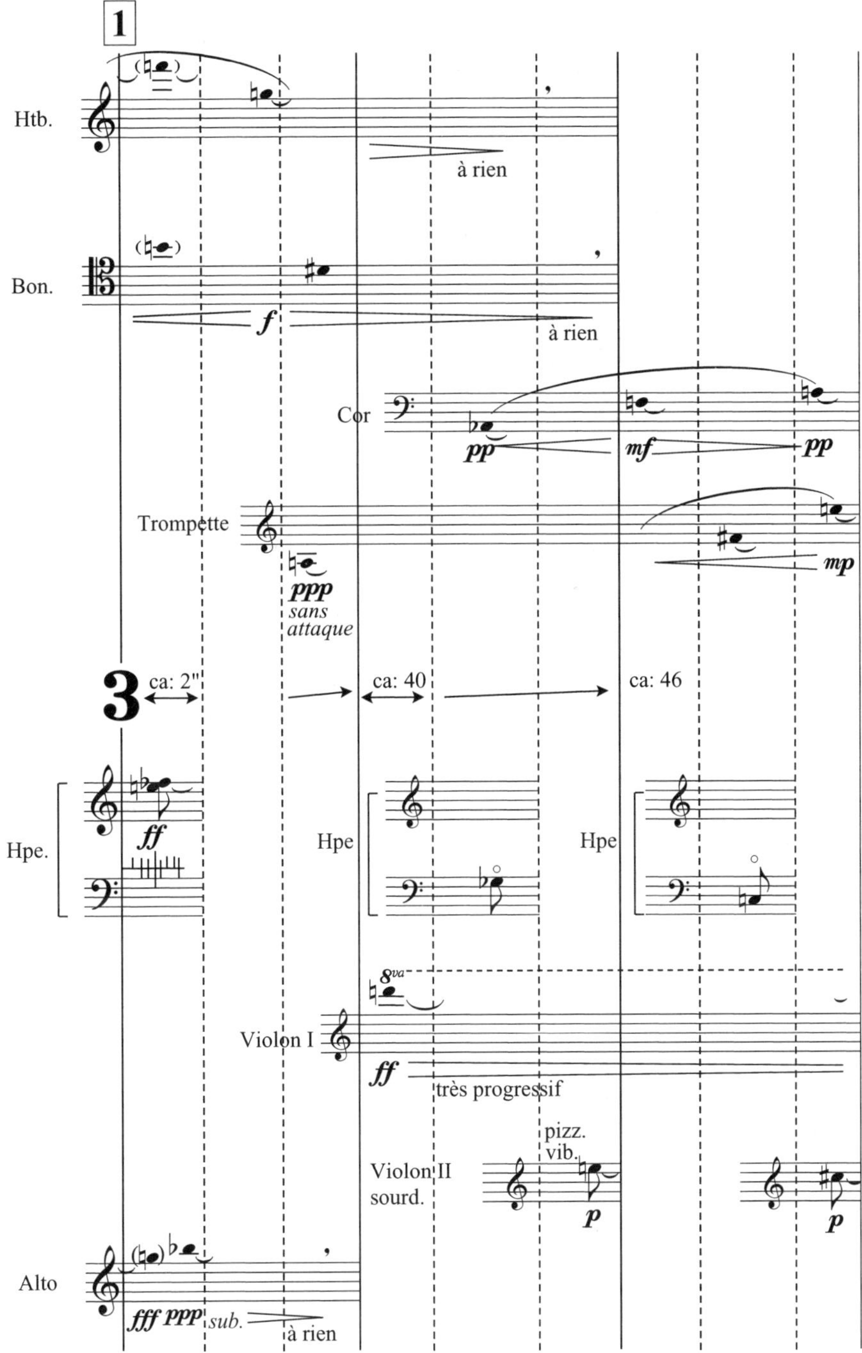

claimed that 'the *mélodie* with piano, especially in France after Poulenc, seems to have been abandoned',[27] adding elsewhere that 'for a long time, publishers have been discouraging composers from cultivating this genre'.[28] It seems clear that the *mélodie* and song cycle were considered to be outmoded after the 1950s, which Dutilleux, for one, regrets. This parallels the decline in operatic composition, and no doubt for the same reason; composers active in the first decades of the twentieth century, most particularly Debussy, brought the genre to such a high point that later composers were dissuaded from attempting to emulate them. Since 1945, composers have preferred to write for the voice plus orchestral or chamber instrumental ensemble, and the unaccompanied vocal ensemble (generally comprising either three or four sopranos, altos, tenors and basses) has been particularly favoured in France. The high standards of performance of ensembles such as the Chœur Yvonne Gouverné (who premiered Messiaen's *Cinq rechants*), the Groupe Vocal de France, and Musicatreize (founded by Roland Hayrabedian in 1987 and particularly associated with the music of Ohana) have inspired composers to write for this formation.

The *mélodie* has also become outmoded because many French composers have reconsidered the traditional relationship between text and music, and reacted against the continuous setting of a poem which is the essence of the song form. Dutilleux's *The Shadows of Time* is the first work he has written including a vocal part for three decades, though there is nothing particularly new about his approach to vocal writing in this work. On the other hand, many of his near-contemporaries have explored one or more of the following: the fragmentation of texts, by breaking words down into phonemes; the use of invented languages; multilingualism; and other new approaches to text, often following the innovations of other European composers, principally Berio and Ligeti. Messiaen's pioneering *Cinq rechants* features all of the above techniques. Ohana, in the fourth movement of his *Cantigas* ('Cantiga del azahar'; see Example 12.3 above), directs the singer to breathe in the middle of a word (aza-har), a technique also used in medieval music. This emphasis on the musical line rather than on communication of the meaning of the text is also characteristic of Boulez's vocal music, especially 'Improvisation sur Mallarmé III' from *Pli selon pli*.[29]

The text of Betsy Jolas's *Caprice à deux voix* (1978) consists of extracts of love poems in both English and French, selected by the composer. At the beginning of the work, the two singers are asked to approach each other gradually on the stage; this limited theatrical element (which is really more an introduction of a specific spatial dimension to the music) is characteristic of her style, and epitomizes the reluctance of French composers to introduce more outrageous theatrical elements into their music.

Interestingly, many French-based composers have set their own texts, most notably Messiaen, the son of a poet and academic, and Jolas, the daughter of two translators. And it is surely not surprising that Xenakis and Ohana, both of whom were multilingual and neither native French speakers, often used several languages in a single work, or used

27 Henri Dutilleux: *Henri Dutilleux* (1997), 50; 'la mélodie avec piano, après Poulenc en France, semble abandonnée.'

28 Ibid.: 'Il faut dire que les éditeurs pendant très longtemps ont découragé les compositeurs de cultiver ce genre.'

29 Many of Boulez's own recordings of his vocal works feature non-native French speakers whose French is far from perfect; Boulez's priority would therefore appear to be the music rather than the text.

invented 'languages' based on phonemes. There is a fascinating parallel between Xenakis's *Nuits* (1969) and Ohana's *Cris* of the same year; both works are composed for unaccompanied vocal ensemble; both feature phonetic texts for at least part of the verbal material; and both are inspired by political events (Xenakis's by Greek protesters towards the end of the Second World War, and Ohana's partly by the war, partly by the events of May 1968).

Musique Concrète

Pierre Schaeffer, the founder of the Studio d'Essai of French Radio, was also the originator of *musique concrète*, with studies written in 1948 including the *Étude violette*. However, Schaeffer always considered himself a technician rather than a composer (he could not even read music), and his first substantial *musique concrète* work was the *Symphonie pour un homme seul*, written in collaboration with the composer Pierre Henry in 1950. *Musique concrète* is based on recorded sounds of various origins; these 'sound objects' could be taken from the environment, and were therefore not traditionally considered 'musical' sounds. For this reason, the music of Schaeffer and composers who worked in his studio, including Pierre Henry, is often opposed to the 'pure' electronic music created in Cologne by composers of whom Stockhausen was the most prominent.

Although many composers visited the Studio d'Essai, few managed to produce a work of art they deemed to be of value (Messiaen almost immediately withdrew his study *Timbres-durées*, realized in 1952 by Pierre Henry, though a recording has recently resurfaced), and most creative and innovative work in the recording studio was carried out elsewhere. The Studio d'Essai was rebaptized the Groupe de Recherches Musicales in 1958; the principal aim of the GRM was research into the perception of sound objects (whether produced by instruments or not). Creative artists involved with the GRM in its early days included Luc Ferrari, François-Bernard Mâche, Varèse and Xenakis. Later, Xenakis founded EMAMu, which became CEMAMu in 1972 (the Centre d'Etudes de Mathématique et Automatique Musicales), and in this laboratory he developed the UPIC (Unité Polyagogique Informatique de CEMAMu) as a means of 'translating' visual ideas directly into music.

Even though most composers did not use the recording studio to create works, the techniques of *musique concrète* proved stimulating. Messiaen used his own transcriptions of birdsong as an important musical resource from the 1950s, and he himself compared these songs to 'sound objects', as he put it, 'I chose the birds – others, the synthesiser'.[30] The 'cut and paste' technique of the studio has obvious links with the sectional nature of Messiaen's music, showing that his studio experiment was stylistically consistent with the rest of his output.

'Spectral' Music

The term 'spectral music' is associated with a group of composers who became prominent in the early 1970s, particularly the French composers who formed the ensemble

30 Cited in Malcolm Troup: 'Orchestral music of the 1950s and 1960s', in Peter Hill (ed.): *The Messiaen Companion* (London, 1995), 394.

L'Itinéraire: Tristan Murail (born 1947), Gérard Grisey (1946–98), Roger Tessier (born 1939) and Michaël Levinas (born 1949). However, it was Hugues Dufourt (born 1943), who became involved with the ensemble from 1975, who coined the term 'spectral music', in an article he wrote in 1979. The style has had a significant impact on many later French composers, including Murail's pupil Marc-André Dalbavie (born 1961).

As Julian Anderson has succinctly noted, spectral music 'uses the acoustic properties of sound itself (or sound spectra) as the basis of its compositional material'.[31] Essentially, a fundamental pitch and its upper partials – its harmonic series – are the starting point for a spectral composition. Clearly, the tonic and dominant notes are the most prominent in the harmonic series, so this compositional method does not exclude tonal harmony, and the opening of Dalbavie's orchestral work *Color* (2001) provides a simple example of this. While the title of this work is derived from the medieval compositional technique, the opening emphasizes the tonic and dominant notes of D minor, though this use of tonal vocabulary does not appear in a tonal context. Equally, a composer may wish to emphasize the higher-numbered harmonics of a pitch, which would not necessarily be pitches belonging to the Western tempered scale.

Spectral music is another manifestation of the French concern for sonority and timbre. Messiaen, in his *Couleurs de la cité céleste* (1963), had already experimented with modifying the timbre of an instrument; at figure 36 of the score, a trombone fundamental note should blend with a clarinet which reinforces one of the upper partials of the fundamental at a much lower dynamic level, and spectral music is often concerned with blendings of this type. Frequently, composers may employ two spectra and, having analysed their differences, combine them; spectra which are closely related (whose harmonic frequencies have a simple numerical relationship) will produce a consonant result, whereas strongly contrasting frequencies will give a more complex, dissonant result (which spectral composers call 'inharmonic'). Grisey's *Partiels* for eighteen musicians (1975, from the cycle *Les espaces acoustiques*, a group of six works all based on the spectrum of the note E) is an excellent illustration of this. The listener to *Partiels* is the witness to a slow-moving, ever-changing process which gives the impression that one is listening inside a sound, and while the end of the work is a progressive decrescendo, absolute silence – and indeed short pauses – is not a feature of music of this type. In a programme note which usefully summarizes many of the principal aims of spectral music, Grisey wrote that his aims in *Les espaces acoustiques* were:

- to compose not with notes, but with sounds;
- to compose not only sounds, but also the difference which separates them (the degree of preaudibility); act on these differences, that is control the evolution (or non-evolution) of the sound and of the speed of its evolution;
- to take account of the relativity of our auditory perception;
- to apply to instrumental music phenomena with which we have experimented for many years in the electronic music studio. [...]
- to search for a synthetic form of writing in which the different parameters all participate in the elaboration of a single sound. For example: the construction of non-tempered [i.e. microtonal] pitches creates new sounds; this construction gives

31 Julian Anderson: 'Spectral music' in www.grovemusic.com (2000).

> rise to particular durations, etc. The synthesis [in the work] aims at the elaboration of the sound (the material) and also at the different relations existing between sounds (form).[32]

Murail's *Mémoire-érosion* for horn and nine instruments (1976) is another example of this process-based music: the members of the ensemble imitate the horn's material after a time-lapse, distorting and therefore transforming its material and building up an ever more complex texture. One may not expect humour to be an element of a work of this type, but Murail's aim was to imitate the sounds of the recording process; tape-hiss appears in the form of breathy instrumental sounds, and at the end, a loud pizzicato signifies the tape-recorder being switched off. However, this emphasis on process, and on the essential unity of the sonic and formal elements of a work, is characteristic of spectral music of the 1970s in particular; Grisey's later works and Murail's music from the 1980s moved away from this.

It may have been expected that, after the Second World War, triumphalist rhetoric could have overwhelmed French composers, but this was not the case. Many composers opted for continuity, while some of the younger generation briefly adopted a musical language which both radically broke with traditional rhetoric and eliminated all traces of personal style and expression. The term 'French style', if it has any significance for composers active from 1945, has nothing to do with self-conscious nationalism, nor indeed (for the most part) self-conscious modernity. French composers have largely rejected traditional genres such as the opera and melodie, and rejected or reinvented the symphony and string quartet. However, they remain preoccupied with timbre, and the expansion of vocal techniques, whether for the solo voice or in a choral context, also typifies French composers' constant search for new sonorities.

The typically French concern for timbre is also one of the factors behind the successful absorption of many foreign elements into French music. Of course, no composer exists in a historical or cultural vacuum; the towering legacy of Debussy is something with which contemporary French composers are still obliged to come to terms, and non-Western musics, however loosely interpreted, have also made their mark on composers active in the second half of the twentieth century. Henri Dutilleux likes to quote André Gide's maxim that 'the transforming influence of foreign cultures'[33] is essential if a national art is to renew itself, and the arrival of composers from overseas, as well as the impact of non-Western musics, plays an essential role in contemporary French musical culture.

---

32 Gérard Grisey: programme note for a recording of *Les espaces acoustiques* (Accord 206532, 1999); 'ne plus composer avec des notes, mais avec des sons; ne plus composer seulement les sons, mais la différence qui les sépare (le degré de pré-audibilité); agir sur ces différences, c'est-à-dire contrôler l'evolution (ou la non-évolution) du son et de la vitesse de son évolution; tenir compte de la relativité de notre perception auditive; appliquer au domaine instrumental les phénomènes expérimentés depuis longtemps dans les studios de musique électronique; [...] rechercher une écriture synthétique dans laquelle les différents paramètres participent à l'élaboration d'un son unique. Exemple: l'agencement des hauteurs non-tempérées crée de nouveaux timbres, de cet agencement naissent des durées, etc. La synthèse vise d'une part l'élaboration du son (matériau), d'autre part les différentes relations existant entre les sons (formes).'

33 Henri Dutilleux: 'Le levain de l'étranger' in *Figures* (14 Nov. 1987), 163.

Suggested Further Reading

Julian Anderson: 'Spectral music', *The New Grove Dictionary of Music Online*, ed. Laura Macy, www.grovemusic.com (2000).

Jérôme Baillet: *Gérard Grisey: fondements d'une écriture* (Paris: L'Harmattan, 2000).

Danielle Cohen-Levinas: *Causeries sur la musique: entretiens avec des compositeurs* [including Murail, Grisey, Levinas and Xenakis] (Paris: L'Harmattan, 1999).

Henri Dutilleux: *Mystère et mémoire des sons. Entretiens avec Claude Glayman* (Paris: Actes Sud, 1997); trans. Roger Nichols as *Henri Dutilleux: Music – Mystery and Memory* (Aldershot, Ashgate, 2003).

Gérard Grisey: '*Tempus ex Machina*: A composer's reflections on musical time', in *Contemporary Music Review*, 2 (1987), 239–75.

Maxime Joos: *La perception du temps musical chez Henri Dutilleux* (Paris: L'Harmattan, 1999).

François-Bernard Mâche (ed.): *Music, Society and Imagination in Contemporary France* (*Contemporary Music Review*, 8/1, 1993).

Olivier Messiaen: *Music and Color: Conversations with Claude Samuel*, trans. E. Thomas Glasow (Portland, Ore.: Amadeus, 1994).

Caroline Potter: *Henri Dutilleux* (Aldershot: Ashgate, 1997).

Caroline Rae: *The Music of Maurice Ohana* (Aldershot: Ashgate, 2000).

Bálint András Varga: *Conversations with Iannis Xenakis* (London: Faber, 1996).

Index